Munakara

Munakara
Planets in Contention

Joy Usher

Revelore Press
Olympia WA, 2025

Munakara: Planets in Contention
Copyright © 2025 Joy Usher

All rights reserved. No part of this publication may be reproduced or transmitted in any form or by any means, electronic or mechanical, including photocopy, without permission in writing from the Publisher. Reviewers may quote brief passages, as may scholars writing astrological journal articles.

Book & cover design by Jenn Zahrt.
Linocut chart on cover by Bear Ryver.
Interior illustrations and charts by Joy Usher.

Publisher's Cataloging-in-Publication
(Provided by Cassidy Cataloguing Services, Inc.).
Names: Usher, Joy, author.
Title: Munakara : planets in contention / Joy Usher.
Description: Olympia WA : Revelore Press, 2025. | Includes bibliographical references.
Identifiers: ISBN: 9781947544536
Subjects: LCSH: Astrology. | Planets. | Horoscopes. | Astronomy--Charts, diagrams, etc. | Moon.
Classification: LCC: BF1724 .U84 2025 | DDC: 133.53--dc23

ISBN: 9781947544536

Printed worldwide through Ingram.

Revelore Press
1910 4th AVE E PMB141
Olympia WA 98506
United States
www.revelore.press

CONTENTS

Acknowledgments ix

Introduction: Munakara ("moon-kai"): al-Biruni's Hidden Gem 1

PART ONE: Munakara in Theory ... 7

Chapter One: Understanding Munakara ("moon-kai") 9
    Blank Worksheet for Determining Munakara 21

Chapter Two: Technical Points to Munakara 23
    Al-Biruni's Table of Friendships and Enmity of Planets 25
    The Three Rules of Sect 26

Chapter Three: Moon in Munakara 31
    The Moon's Sequence: Friends, Associates, and Enemies 34
    Munakara Moon Chart Example: Elvis Presley 42

Chapter Four: Mercury in Munakara 53
    Diurnal Mercury in Munakara 54
    Diurnal Mercury's Sequence: Friends, Associates, and Enemies 56
    Diurnal Mercury in Munakara: Penelope Cruz 63
    Nocturnal Mercury in Munakara 65
    Nocturnal Mercury's Sequence: Friends, Associates, and Enemies....... 68
    Nocturnal Mercury in Munakara: King Henry VIII 74

Chapter Five: Venus in Munakara 87
   Morning Venus and Evening Venus 89
   Munakara Venus and Sect Dignity 91
   Venus' Sequence: Friends and Enemies 93
   Chart Example: Albert, Prince Consort to Queen Victoria 105

Chapter Six: Sun in Munakara 113
   The Sun's Sequence: Friends, Associates, and Enemies 116
   Munakara Sun Chart Example 1: Katy Perry 131
   Munakara Sun Chart Example 2: Kelly Osbourne 140

Chapter Seven: Mars in Munakara 150
   Mars's Sequence: Friends, Associates, and Enemies 158
   Munakara Mars Chart Example: Janis Joplin 168

Chapter Eight: Jupiter in Munakara 181
   Jupiter's Sequence: Friends, Associates, and Enemies 185
   Munakara Jupiter Chart Example 1: Elon Musk 192
   Munakara Jupiter Chart Example 2: Julian Assange 210

Chapter Nine: Saturn in Munakara 218
   Saturn's Sequence: Friends, Associates, and Enemies 222
   Munakara Saturn Chart Example 1: Harry, Duke of Sussex 234
   Munakara Saturn Chart Example 2: Meghan, Duchess of Sussex 244

Chapter Ten: Multiple Munakara Planets 253
   Munakara Sequences where all Three Planets are in Contention 255
   Munakara Multiples: Three Planets in Contention
      1. Queen Elizabeth 258
      2. Billy Connolly 264
      3. Cher 268
      4. Caitlyn Jenner 273
      5. Princess Diana 278
   Munakara Multiples: Four Planets in Contention
      1. Catherine the Great 284
      2. Edgar Degas 292
      3. Neil Diamond 298
      4. Robin Williams 304
      5. Amy Winehouse 309

Munakara Multiples: Five Planets in Contention
   1. Christopher McCandless 316
   2. Prince George 323
Munakara Multiples: Six Planets in Contention
   1. John Dee 327
   2. Helen Keller 333

Chapter Eleven: Al-Biruni's Chronocrators:
Munakara and the Time Lords 344
   Planetary Sect, Firdaria, and Munakara 349
   1. LeBron James: Munakara Venus Firdaria 352
   2. Frida Kahlo: Munakara Mercury Firdaria 358
   3. Harry, Duke of Sussex: Munakara Saturn Firdaria 372
   4. Julian Assange: Munakara Jupiter and Mars Firdaria 381

PART TWO: Munakara in Practice ... 397

Chapter Twelve: Munakara Moon Delineations 399
   1. Queen Victoria 399
   2. Albrecht Dürer 409
   3. Diane Arbus 422
   4. Evel Knievel 433
   5. Christopher Reeve 444
   6. Michael Moore 452

Chapter Thirteen: Munakara Mercury Delineations 463
   Diurnal Mercury in Munakara 463
   1. John Glenn 464
   2. Mark Ruffalo 475
   Nocturnal Mercury in Munakara 485
   1. Kurt Cobain 486
   2. Dave Grohl 500

Chapter Fourteen: Munakara Venus Delineations 513
   1. Lord Alfred Tennyson 513
   2. Tee Corinne 524
   3. Malala Yousafzai 535

Chapter Fifteen: Munakara Sun Delineations 546
    1. *Friedrich Nietzsche* 546
    2. *Vincent van Gogh* 565

Chapter Sixteen: Munakara Mars Delineations 587
    1. *Dennis Rodman* 587
    2. *Michael J. Fox* 599

Chapter Seventeen: Munakara Jupiter Delineations 613
    1. *Wolfgang Amadeus Mozart* 613
    2. *Cindy Sherman* 628
    3. *Oprah Winfrey* 642

Chapter Eighteen: Munakara Saturn Delineations 662
    1. *Paul Watson* 664
    2. *Gordon Brown* 677
    3. *LeBron James* 686

A Final Word on Munakara 703

Notes 707
About the Author 741

ACKNOWLEDGEMENTS

I want to give special thanks to...

Ian, my love, for holding my hand and kicking the pumpkin down the road with me.

Jessica and Michelle, my two brilliant editors, for guiding my hand in describing the pumpkin with such clarity and perception.

Jenn, my publisher, for believing in the pumpkin's existence.

"The stubborn critic would say: 'What is the benefit of these sciences?' He does not know the virtue that distinguishes mankind from all the animals: it is knowledge, in general, which is pursued solely by man, and which is pursued for the sake of knowledge itself, because its acquisition is truly delightful.

For the good cannot be brought forth, and evil cannot be avoided, except by knowledge. What benefit then is more vivid? What use is more abundant?"

– *Abu Rayhan al-Biruni*

INTRODUCTION
Munakara ("moon-kai"): *al-Biruni's Hidden Gem*

Abu al-Rayhan Muhammad ibn Ahmad al-Biruni (aka al-Biruni) has been described as one of the greatest scholars in the Islamic Golden Age.[1] Far ahead of his time, he is now renowned as a great many things – an astronomer, historian, botanist, pharmacologist, geologist, geographer, poet, philosopher, mathematician, and humanist.[2]

Modern scholars agree that al-Biruni was born in Khiva, now Kara Kalpakskava in Uzbekistan. There is some debate over the date of his birth. Some claim it is the 4th September 973, whilst other scholars believe his birth took place days later on the 15th September.[3] Al-Biruni wrote mainly in Arabic, but was fluent in Persian, Syriac, Greek, and Sanskrit. An avid pursuer of knowledge, he once disguised himself as a Hindu in order to learn from religious scholars, proclaiming his love of languages with the phrase, "I would rather be reviled in Arabic than praised in Persian."[4]

While other great scientists from his region were already well known and given Latinized names such as Avicenna, Alhazen, and Averroes, al-Biruni was largely ignored due to translators being "…afraid of the difficulty of his language and [nervous of] treatment of the subjects of his works."[5] He remained relatively unknown in the Western world until the 19th century, when several of his works were translated into German, and his brilliance was acknowledged throughout Europe.

We know from an index al-Biruni himself produced when he was around 60 years of age that he composed at least 155 works. Sadly, approximately five sixths of his works have been lost over time, with a large number of his original texts believed to have been destroyed by Genghis Khan in the 13th century.[6]

Therefore, it seems, incredibly fortunate that one of his works on astrology is amongst the tiny portion of his texts that survived. *The Book of Instruction in the Elements of the Art of Astrology*[7] showcases al-Biruni's fascination with the planets, their relationships, their movements and their abilities. It was translated into English in 1934 by R. Ramsay Wright, Emeritus Professor of Biology. *Elements in the Art of Astrology* is divided into two parts. Part One deals with arithmetical operations, decimal notations, spheres, stars, planets, the ecliptic, mansions of the moon, the galaxy, apogee of the sun, orbits of the planets and moon, daily movement of the planets, and the correct time for prayer.[8] Part Two introduces the signs, planets and houses, the Lots, the planets' relationship to the Sun, the rules of planetary sect, and many of the principles of judicial astrology. In the book, al-Biruni perfected the astrolabe and relied on it for his heavenly calculations, noting that one could pursue mathematical astronomy from either a geocentric or heliocentric perspective.[9]

Contained within this comprehensive guide to the principles and practices of astrology is the description and two examples of munakara. To my knowledge, it has been largely overlooked by astrology, but it is my belief that munakara is a treasure gifted to us by al-Biruni, if only to add depth to the principles of planetary sect and add weight to the division between day and night.

Starting from the division of time and space into two halves (diurnal and nocturnal), al-Biruni explains the concept of *hayz*, where planets sit in ease and comfort within the chart and protected by the rules of accidental dignity. A planet in *hayz* sits in its 'natural place'. Immediately after, al-Biruni introduces the term *'munakara'* and explains that it is in contrast to *hayz*. Bracketed by the English term 'contention', munakara refers to the state of a planet compromised by its location according to its sign and the rules of the planets' sect preferences.

For much of his adult life, al-Biruni travelled throughout India and spent much of his time in the Punjab region, so it should be no surprise that the word *'munakara'* has origins in both the Persian and the Punjabi languages. By definition munakara has links to harsh and accusatory labels such as 'apostate', 'atheist', 'disbeliever', 'repudiator' and 'traitor'; all indicators of someone who is alienated from loved ones, cast out by their clan, and at

Introduction • Munakara ("moon kai"): al-Biruni's Hidden Gem

odds with society's religious order. Al-Biruni advises on how to determine if a planet is in munakara, and a mysterious footnote gives two examples, one diurnal and one nocturnal, of how a planet might display discomfort or insecurity due to its contentious state.

However, while certainly not easy, contention is not necessarily a bad thing. Contention can push us out of our comfort zone and force us to learn, grow and ultimately make better choices. The deepest levels of personal growth are not achieved through easy times, but rather through adversity and discomfort. Seventeenth-century French playwright Jean-Baptiste Poquelin (aka Moliere) once wrote, "The greater the obstacle, the more glory in overcoming it", and this is certainly the case where munakara is concerned.

When I began researching the consistency and validity of munakara, I was nervous to (re)introduce a technique that may support a belief that traditional astrological practices are too fatalistic, too rigid in principle, and too bleak to introduce to clients. I was afraid that munakara would add more weight to these opinions, so I was hesitant at first to integrate contention into my own consulting practice. However, when I did include munakara, I found that clients who had planets in contention knew exactly what I was explaining to them. My words resonated deeply with them, touching on difficulties and challenges that my previous range of astrological tools and techniques had been unable to understand. It is with deep gratitude that I have utilised much of their language throughout this book to describe planets in a state of contention. Though their astrological knowledge may be limited, they are the experts in living with a planet in munakara.

With her kind permission, the words of an astrologer friend, who also recently introduced munakara into her practice, have been reproduced for the purposes of this introduction:

> It struck me that a client with a troubled family background might be a quintessential example of Munakara. I retrieved her chart, and indeed, it was astonishing! Her moon is in Munakara. Suddenly, everything made sense. The chart had always displayed a wealth of information; I just didn't catch the clues. Munakara was a glaring clue. My previous application of Munakara was superficial, but now I am delving deeper.
>
> Finding Munakara has been a joy. It's as if fate were a tangled ball of wool, and while I knew astrology could be the tool to unravel it, I had no idea how.

Munakara has been the key to untangling this complex situation, and it has been immensely satisfying.

Munakara is incredibly practical and powerful, enabling me to focus on details that I previously overlooked. I am truly enamoured with its potential.

I will close with Al-Biruni's parable on knowledge, which I feel is an excellent conclusion to the introduction on munakara. It tells the story of a teacher and his four pupils, each of which uses varying methods to answer the master's question of 'What is this obstacle in our way?'

Al-Biruni's Lesson from Indica, a Compendium of Indian Religion and Philosophy[10]

A teacher was travelling with four of his students on an unfamiliar road towards the end of a dark night. On turning a corner they saw something appear on the road that seemed to stand erect but it was impossible to identify in the darkness. The teacher turned to his pupils and asked them 'What is it?'

Pupil One replies: "I do not know what it is."

Pupil Two says: "I do not know, and I have no means of learning what it is."

Pupil Three confidently responds: "It is useless to examine what it is, for the raising of the day will reveal it."

The teacher pauses to examine the three answers and disappointed, he tells them that none of the three has attained knowledge. The first because of his ignorance, the second because he is incapable of increasing his knowledge through the power of learning, and the third pupil because he is lazy and submits passively to his ignorance.

The fourth pupil gave no immediate answer. Instead, he stood still for a short time and then walked towards the object on the road. On coming nearer, he recognised the shape as pumpkins and a vine on which something was entangled. In his logic he had considered that no living man endowed with free will could stand still in this situation, and therefore it was likely to be a lifeless object. To be sure of his assumption, he went quite close to it and struck it with his foot until it fell to the ground. Having removed all doubt, Pupil Four returned to his master and gave him the exact account of his scientific process.

Introduction • *Munakara ("moon kai")*: al-Biruni's Hidden Gem

Knowledge requires courage and conviction, and at times taking an unknown path towards a new destination. Munakara has sat quietly unnoticed in the middle of astrology's road for a very long time. But its strange shape does not mean it is without merit, or that it has no place in modern astrology's techniques.

With this book I hope that you will take a moment to advance with caution towards munakara, to give it a few gentle foot nudges to gauge if it has merit within your astrological practice. I hope an open mind and inquisitive spirit will help you to find benefits from al-Biruni's shining gem, a gem quietly gifted to us by one of history's truly great minds from centuries ago.

PART ONE

MUNAKARA IN THEORY

The Planets
Multiple Munakara Sequences
Firdaria and Munakara

Fig 1.1: The planets' sign rulerships

Sect Preferences	
Diurnal	**Nocturnal**
Sun	Moon
Jupiter	Venus
Saturn	Mars
Mercury *	Mercury **

* Mercury rising <u>before</u> the Sun is diurnal.
** Mercury rising <u>after</u> the Sun is nocturnal.

Table 1.1: The planets' sect preferences

CHAPTER ONE
Understanding Munakara ("moon-kai")

Al-Biruni's Definition of Munakara

Al-Biruni's Notation #497 reads:

*Munakara (contention) is nearly the reverse of hayyiz and occurs when a diurnal planet is in the domicile [**sign**] of a nocturnal one, and the latter [**the nocturnal planet**] is in the domicile of a diurnal planet; or when a nocturnal planet is in the domicile of a diurnal one, and the latter [**the diurnal planet**] is in the domicile of a nocturnal planet.*[1]

In effect, munakara is determined by the relationship between two critical factors in traditional astrology: Essential Dignities (sign rulership, *Fig 1.1*) and Accidental Dignity (planetary sect preferences, *Table 1.1*). The act of combining these two factors is the cornerstone of determining if there is a planet in munakara.

How Does the State of Munakara Affect a Planet?

"Contention is inseparable from creating knowledge. It is not contention we should try to avoid, but discourses that attempt to suppress contention."
– Joyce Appleby (1929–2016), American historian

In *Elements of Astrology* al-Biruni's translator uses the English word 'contention' as well as providing two separate examples for munakara in footnotes below the text.[2] According to the online English Punjabi Dictionary *Shabdkosh* munakara means atheist, disbeliever, or repudiator.[3] It is a word meant to insult and wound, an accusation of godlessness and disloyalty. The word 'contentious' fares no better, meaning disruptive, troublesome, provocative, or litigious. It calls to mind hostility, friction and agitation.

As such, we can assume that planet in munakara (aka contention) is experiencing some level of inner turmoil. That the planet in question has *to contend with something*. This implies that the chart's owner will not often be presented with the easy option, they will more often be caught between a rock and a hard place. The munakara planet's house placement, aspects, and house rulerships will likely all form part of the chart owner's experience of contention.

However, also worthy of note is that contention's negative implications are very much in the eye of the beholder. While the dictionary may label a contentious person as quarrelsome, opinionated or assertive, this label may not resonate with the person, and it is really only part of the picture. Contentious people can also be outspoken, focused, impassioned, and fierce in defending a cause close to their heart. Taking the hard road to overcome adversity can build resilience, strength and depth of character. In the same way, the owner of a munakara planet may not have negative feelings towards their challenges; adversity has helped to shape who they are today.

When I originally flagged munakara in 2018 as a point of interest in my book *A Tiny Universe's Companion*, I included a table that suggested how a planet might experience contention. Since then, I have broadened my approach to include thoughts on a munakara planet's impact on society, and the interaction between someone in possession of a contentious planet and the world around them.

Part Two of this book includes a wide variety of famous individuals' natal charts intended to demonstrate the workings of munakara, including how it has enriched their lives through influencing character, reputation, ethics or lifestyle. However, while the charts provided are of well-known people, there is no doubt that people with lesser-known lives are also powerful actors for social change. Munakara planets and their chart owners tend to leave legacies, both large and small. Within their spheres of influence, they are fearless in their questioning and challenging of the status quo.

Chapter One • *Understanding Munakara*

In times of tension or dissent, or if a problem is just too overwhelming, others may choose to look the other way. This is exactly the time when a munakara planet rolls up its metaphorical sleeves and goes to work. A munakara planet truly walks the talk of *'when the going gets tough, the tough get going'*. But like all hard work, owning a munakara planet is not easy. It is often messy, exhausting, and requires constant self-reflection. The person with a munakara planet can feel as though they are constantly defending themselves to family, friends, workmates, and to the world in general.

How to Spot a Planet in Munakara

The range of expressions for munakara is wide and varied depending on the planet itself and what I call the 'outcome' planet (the third in the process). But once you know what you are looking for, they are easy to spot in a person's life history. Even the process of finding a munakara planet becomes faster and effortless as you become accustomed to looking for dispositors and recognising the two divisions in sect. *Table 1.2* on the next page is an overarching summary table for quick reference on the possible challenges for each of the seven planets in munakara.

Part One contains a chapter dedicated to each planet's expression of munakara and one or two chart delineations as an example of the planet's expression of munakara. Part One also includes a chapter on multiple munakara sequences and a final chapter on the relationship between Firdaria and munakara. Part Two extends the delineations with a variety of chart examples dedicated to each planet.

Summaries of each Planet's expression of Munakara

Planet	Some Possible Expressions of Munakara
The Moon	- Complex relationship with mother, or history of mother being under attack
- Poor health through illness, emotional stress or accident
- Challenges in maintaining physical strength or mobility
- Highly sensitive or self-protective individual
- Fears of separation, alienation or betrayal by loved ones
- A need for family to provide an emotional 'buffer' against the outside world
- A strong need for privacy or personal space
- Shyness or withdrawal in public arenas
Mercury	- Contending with rumours or gossip
- Cyber-bullying, misunderstandings or arguments
- Poor communication, reading or writing skills
- Shyness or speech impediments
- Financial difficulties or business failings
- Challenges in fine motor skills or movement
- Unresolved issues or conflict with siblings
Venus	- Fear of unpopularity or public rejection
- Unwitting catalyst for hostile environments
- Perceived or genuine attacks or personal criticism from others
- Possible scandals
- Unwelcome advances of a sexual nature
- Concerns about attractiveness
- Difficulty in forming or maintaining friendships or relationships
- Quest for pleasure but self-denial at the same time
The Sun	- Perceived or genuine attacks on opinions, integrity or reputation
- Constant need to defend father's actions or feeling the compulsion to justify one's own actions
- Weakened energy levels or enthusiasm
- Difficulties in setting goals and maintaining focus, or achieving final successful outcomes
- Fear of criticism, public ridicule or humiliation
- Self-doubt concerning one's value to society
- Strong need to be praised or respected
- Issues with organised religion and/or questing for spirituality

Chapter One • *Understanding Munakara*

Mars	• Suspicion about others' motives • Defensive behaviour in the face of threats, whether real or perceived • Experiences of bullying, confrontational or frightening behaviours • Extremes of confrontation – either seeing challenges as full scale battles or avoiding confrontation at all costs • Questioning one's bravery or courage • Struggles over control or power • Long-term battles, possibly involving chronic health issues
Jupiter	• Physical, social or financial risk taking • Excessive behaviour or indulgences which have potentially harmful or addictive consequences • Tendency to exaggeration or resentment when challenged by others • Obstacles or constant set-backs in achieving success, recognition or ambitions • Difficulty with children or money • A feeling of being unprotected or unlucky • Quick rise to fame, but quick fall to oblivion too • Seeks to impress but mannerisms can be exaggerated or fanatical in nature • Zealous opinions alienate people or create larger rifts between divided sides
Saturn	• The feeling of being under constant attack from authority figures • Having one's authority, expertise or integrity challenged by others • A fearful, disparaging or negative attitude towards father, authority or responsibility • A fascination with secret dealings, or a belief in conspiracy theories • A strong desire for autonomy, rebels at having to comply with, or be controlled by, rules or a system they don't respect • High expectations for authority figures in terms of integrity, honesty, transparency, accountability, honourable behaviour etc. Deep disappointment when they consider that standards are not met.

Table 1.2: A brief summary of possible challenges faced by the seven planets in munakara

Munakara in Theory

How does Munakara (*"moon-kai"*) occur?

The steps to determine if a planet is in munakara can take a little time to get your head around but it does become easier with practice. To help with the process I have developed a worksheet and flowchart (*see below*) to guide you through the three steps so that you might practise with any charts in your own circle of familiarity.

Rulership of planets: what is a Dispositor?

Determining munakara starts with understanding the rulership of signs by the original seven planets. When a planet is situated in a sign *other than its own*, the owner of the sign is called its 'dispositor'. This is more commonly known as 'the ruler', but for the purpose of explaining the munakara sequence I have chosen to use dispositor rather than ruler.

For example: the Sun in Scorpio. The Sun is sitting in a sign belonging to Mars, therefore Mars is the Sun's dispositor (*aka Mars is the ruler of Scorpio*).

At the start of this chapter, *Figure 1.1* (*page 8*) shows which planets own which signs. Refer to this diagram to find the dispositor of each of the twelve zodiac signs.

The division between diurnal planets and nocturnal planets is shown in the Sect Preferences Table (*Table 1.1, also on page 8*). Refer to this Table to determine the sect of the planet in question.

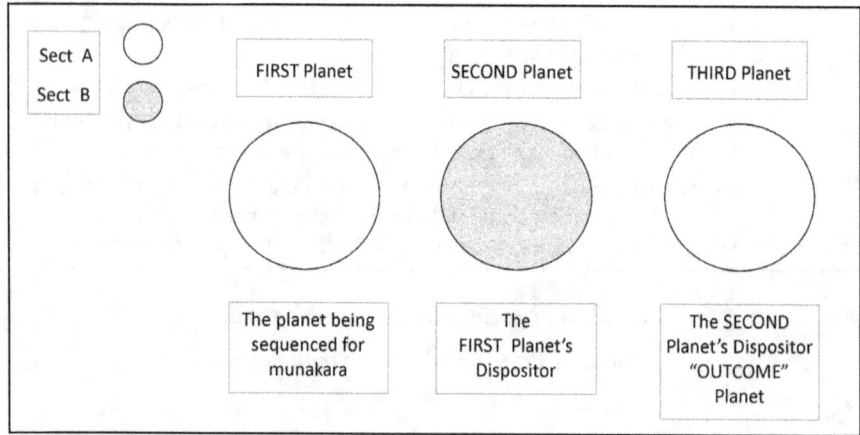

Fig. 1.2: Diagram of a Planet's Sect Preference

Chapter One • *Understanding Munakara*

Overview of the Munakara Sequence

Three planets must be involved to complete the munakara sequence, but it is *always the first planet* which is called munakara. The first and the third planet *must belong to the same sect*. The second planet *must belong to the opposite sect*. To determine if there is a state of munakara, there are several steps to be taken, to consider the rulership of *the first two planets*, and to check their sect preference. The first two planets in the sequence must be assessed for their sign's dispositor, and all three planets checked for their sect preference, whether that is nocturnal or diurnal.

A first example of munakara: Sun in Scorpio

Figure. 1.3 (*next page*) shows the chart for Scorpio Sun in munakara, which will be used below to illustrate the munakara sequence delineating steps.

Step One: When looking for munakara, the first step is to determine the sect of the planet in question. In most sect classifications the Sun, Jupiter, Saturn, and Mercury rising *before* the Sun are diurnal planets. The Moon, Venus, Mars, and Mercury rising *after* the Sun are nocturnal planets. Once you have established the sect classification, note what sign the planet is in. Finally, determine the planet that rules that sign.

Step One: Determine the sect of the FIRST planet:	
	Example Exercise
Is the planet diurnal or nocturnal?	The Sun is a diurnal planet
What sign is the planet in?	It is in the sign of Scorpio
Which planet is the sign's dispositor?	Mars is the dispositor of Scorpio

Step Two: If the sign's dispositor belongs to the same sect, there is no munakara. Or if the dispositor is in a sign of its rulership, there is no munakara. However, if the sign's dispositor belongs to the *opposite* sect, then munakara is still possible and a second step is required. Therefore, step two is to determine the sect of the sign's dispositor.

Munakara in Theory

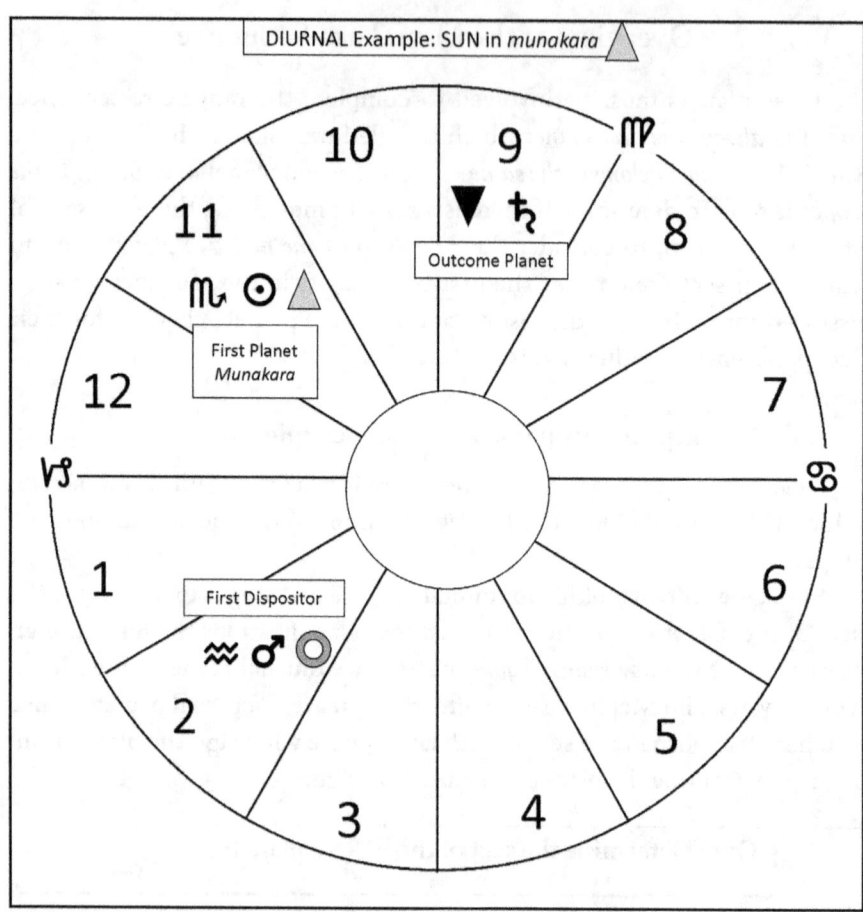

Fig. 1.3: Scorpio Sun in munakara

Sect Nature	STEP ONE △	STEP TWO First Dispositor ◉	STEP THREE Second Dispositor ▼	*MUNAKARA* FIRST PLANET IN CONTENTION △
	First Planet's Sign SECT STATUS Diurnal/Nocturnal	Dispositor's Sign SECT STATUS Diurnal/Nocturnal	Outcome Planet SECT STATUS Diurnal/Nocturnal	
☼	☉ (D) in ♏	♂ (N) in ♒	♄ (D)	♏ ☉ △

Table 1.3: Scorpio Sun in munakara

Chapter One • *Understanding Munakara*

Step Two: Determine the sect of the SECOND planet:

	Example Exercise
Is the planet diurnal or nocturnal?	Mars is a nocturnal planet
What sign is the planet in?	It is in the sign of Aquarius
Which planet is the sign's dispositor?	Saturn is the dispositor of Aquarius

Step Three: If the THIRD planet in the sequence (*i.e.*, Saturn in the example chart) belongs to a *same* sect as the FIRST planet (*i.e.*, the Sun in the example chart) – *the first planet is in a state of munakara.* (*i.e.*, the Sun is in munakara).

If they were the same planet (*e.g.*, they were both the Sun), then the relationship between the FIRST and SECOND planet is called 'mutual reception' if there is an aspect or 'generosity' if there is no aspect – there is no munakara.

The sign the third planet is in, is not relevant to contention, as the process has finished here.

Step Three: Determine the sect of the THIRD planet:

	Example Exercise
Is the planet diurnal or nocturnal?	Saturn is a diurnal planet
Is it a different planet from the first (diurnal) planet?	Yes, Saturn is a different planet from the Sun.
	Saturn is the outcome planet for the Sun's munakara sequence.

Munakara in Theory

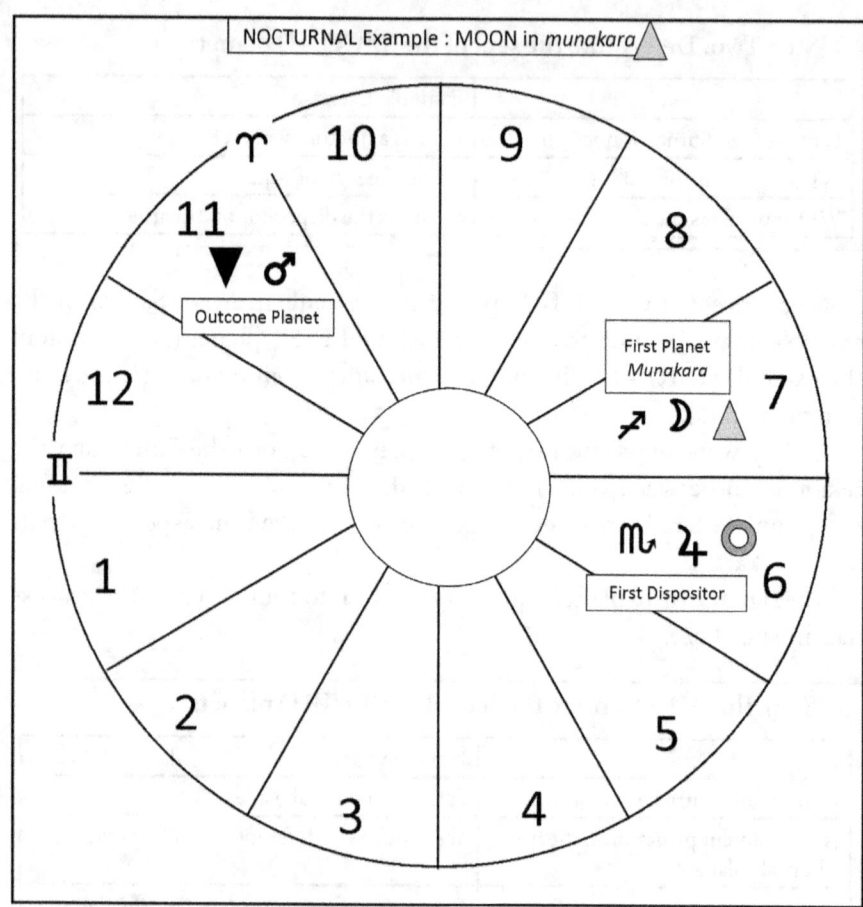

Fig.1.4: Sagittarius Moon in munakara

Sect Nature	STEP ONE ▲ First Planet's Sign SECT STATUS Diurnal/Nocturnal	STEP TWO First Dispositor ◉ Dispositor's Sign SECT STATUS Diurnal/Nocturnal	STEP THREE Second Dispositor ▼ Outcome Planet SECT STATUS Diurnal/Nocturnal	*MUNAKARA* FIRST PLANET IN CONTENTION ▲
☀/☾				
☾	☽ (N) in ♐	♃ (D) in ♏	♂ (N)	♐ ☽ ▲

Table 1.4: Sagittarius Moon in munakara

Chapter One • *Understanding Munakara*

A second example of munakara: Moon in Sagittarius

Figure. 1.4 shows the chart for Sagittarius Moon in munakara, which is also shown in the Table below.

Step One: Determine the sect of the FIRST planet:	
	Example Exercise
Is the planet diurnal or nocturnal?	The Moon is a nocturnal planet
What sign is the planet in?	It is in the sign of Sagittarius
Which planet is the sign's dispositor?	Jupiter is the dispositor of Sagittarius

Step Two: Determine the sect of the SECOND planet:	
	Example Exercise
Is the planet diurnal or nocturnal?	Jupiter is a diurnal planet
What sign is the planet in?	It is in the sign of Scorpio
Which planet is the sign's dispositor?	Mars is the dispositor of Scorpio

Step Three: Determine the sect of the THIRD planet:	
	Example Exercise
Is the planet diurnal or nocturnal?	Mars is a nocturnal planet
Is it a different planet from the first (diurnal) planet?	Yes, Mars is a different planet from the Moon.
	Mars is the outcome planet for the Moon's munakara sequence.

Table 1.5: Steps One, Two, Three: Sagittarius Moon in munakara

Flowchart for determining munakara:

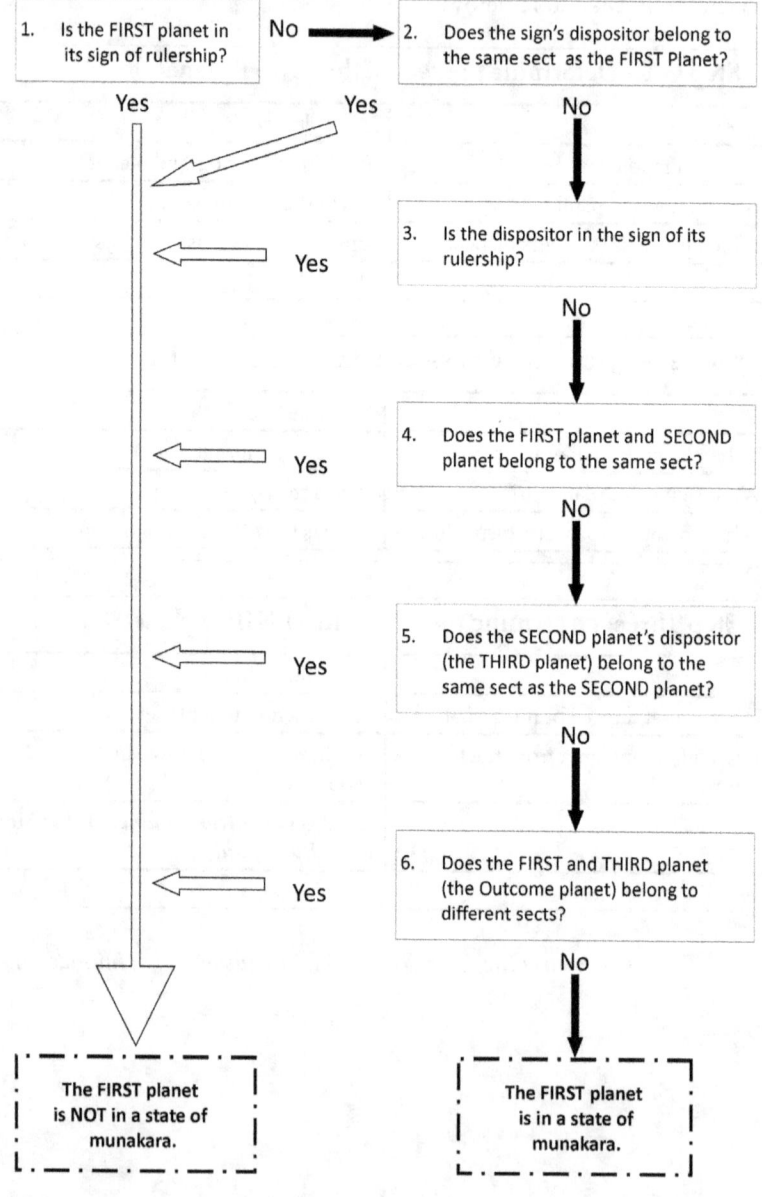

Fig. 1.5: Flowchart for determining munakara

Chapter One • *Understanding Munakara*

Blank Worksheet for Determining Munakara

Step One: Determine the sect of the FIRST planet:

	Answers
Is the planet diurnal or nocturnal?	_____ is a nocturnal / diurnal planet
What sign is the planet in?	It is in the sign of _____
Which planet is the sign's dispositor?	_____ is the dispositor of _____

Step Two: Determine the sect of the SECOND planet:

	Answers
Is the planet diurnal or nocturnal?	_____ is a nocturnal / diurnal planet
What sign is the planet in?	It is in the sign of _____
Which planet is the sign's dispositor?	_____ is the dispositor of _____

Step Three: Determine the sect of the THIRD planet:

	Answers
Is the planet diurnal or nocturnal?	_____ is a nocturnal / diurnal planet
Is it a different planet from the first (diurnal or nocturnal) planet?	Yes/No, _____ is a different planet from _____.
	_____ is the outcome planet for _____ munakara sequence.

A Few Final Points for Determining Munakara

There are three further things to note when delineating a munakara planet in a natal chart:

1. It is *always the initial planet* in the sequence that experiences the effects of munakara.

2. Munakara happens *regardless of the planet's house position in the chart*. Sect dignity may alter the planet's level of comfort, but it will not negate its state of munakara. It may not even be necessary to find the correct birth time, so long as movement from one sign to the next does not occur during the day. Even if a planet does change sign, check to see the connection the new sign's dispositor has to either the diurnal or nocturnal sect.

3. All planets – according to their own nature – *will have a different reaction to being munakara*, and this will very much depend on the planets involved in the three-step process.

CHAPTER TWO
Technical Points to Munakara

Al-Biruni's Table of Friendships and Enmity of Planets

As Chapter One explores, the munakara sequence is created by the involvement of three planets. Two from the same sect (the first and third planets) and one from the opposite sect (the second planet – the first planet's dispositor). The second planet (the first planet's dispositor) should be directing the first planet, but there are a few basic problems here. The dispositor belongs to the opposite sect and does not relate well to the first planet's basic principles. In addition, the second planet (the first planet's dispositor) has its own stress to deal with, as it is also dealing with a dispositor in a sect opposite to its own (the third or 'outcome' planet). This impacts on its willingness or ability to provide its normal level of support and direction. This lack of support can lead to a sense of chaos, instability, or panic for the first planet, which is in a state of munakara.

However, there is another factor to consider that can make munakara easier or more difficult for the munakara planet – which is identified in al-Biruni's *Table of Friendships and Enmities*.[1] Planets share different relationships with one another and this is dependent on their domicile and exaltation signs. A planet finding itself in a sign opposite to its signs of dignity can intensify the discomfort, particularly when detriment or fall occurs and the planet is in the hands of its 'enemy'. The state of munakara is already difficult for the planet, but it becomes even more challenging

Munakara in Theory

Planet	Mutually Hurtful With	Injurious To	Offering Friendship To	Asking Friendship From
♄	Sun: Moon	Jupiter	Mars	Venus
♃	Mars: Mercury	Mercury	Venus	Moon
♂	Jupiter: Venus	Moon	Sun	Saturn
☉	Saturn	Venus	—	Mars
♀	Mars: Mercury	—	Saturn	Jupiter
☿	Jupiter: Venus	Venus	Neither Offers Friendship	Nor Asks for Friendship
☽	Saturn	Mars	Jupiter	Venus

Table 2.1: Al-Biruni's Table of Friendships and Enmities (Notation #447)

when the planets in the munakara sequence have a strained relationship. Al-Biruni's *Table (Table 2.1)* demonstrates the importance of acknowledging these different relationships. The Table focuses on the relationship of the planets based on their rulership (domicile) or exaltation signs. The left-hand column marked 'Mutually Hurtful With' refers to the oppositions between planets in dignity. 'Injurious To' refers to the planet which is dispositor for a planet's fall sign, *e.g.*, Saturn injures Jupiter because Saturn owns Capricorn. Mars, the owner of Scorpio, injures the Moon. The Moon injures Mars through its ownership of Cancer. Interestingly, even though they own each other's fall sign, the Moon and Mars are not considered to be 'mutually hurtful' as neither planet opposes the other in the first rule of dignity, *i.e.*, rulership. Venus should injure the Sun, given that it is the ruler of Libra, the Sun's fall sign, but this is not shown in the Table.

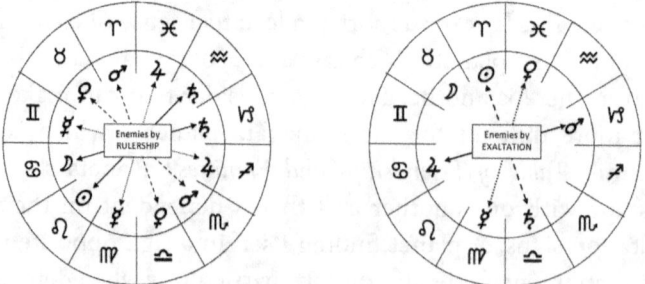

Fig. 2.1: The twelve signs in relationships that are in Rulership, e.g., 'mutually hurtful with' and in Exaltation, e.g., 'injurious to'.

Chapter Two • *Technical Points to Munakara*

Al-Biruni's Table of Enemies

Al-Biruni's Table begins to complicate the munakara sequence the moment we start to include the planets' sect preferences, particularly when we focus on swapping between sects.

For instance, munakara Saturn may be quite comfortable with its state if Mars or Venus is its sign's dispositor, as friendship exists between the diurnal planet and these two nocturnal planets. After all, Saturn lends its sign of Capricorn to Mars, and borrows Venus' sign of Libra for its own exaltation. Even a nocturnal Mercury holds no grudge against Saturn. On the other hand, if Saturn finds itself in the hands of the Moon, Saturn's sequence gets bumpier thanks to its antagonistic relationship with this nocturnal luminary.

For instance in Example #1 from the previous chapter (See *Table 1.3*, p. 16), munakara Sun in Scorpio has good rapport with its dispositor Mars, because the Sun borrows Aries for its exaltation. However, Mars in the sign of Aquarius is disposited by Saturn and there is friction between the two diurnal planets, the Sun and its outcome planet Saturn. The antagonistic relationship between Sun and Saturn creates problems for munakara Sun, which may be sensitive to perceived failures, issues with authority, and blockages in all manners under Saturn's jurisdiction.

In Example #2 (See *Table 1.4*, p. 18), munakara Moon in Sagittarius is disposited by a diurnal friend in Jupiter, as Jupiter borrows Cancer for its exaltation. However, Jupiter in Scorpio is disposited by nocturnal Mars. The Moon is in fall in Scorpio (Mars' sign) and Mars is in fall in Cancer (the Moon's sign). The two planets may belong to the same sect division but they are harmful to one another and therefore munakara Moon is distressed. While the Moon looks for harmony, love, support, nurturance, Mars looks for conquest, conflict, and competition. Therefore, the expression of this munakara sequence is likely to be a restless and unsettled Moon, easily disturbed by emotional drama. The Moon's dispositor, Jupiter, is a friend but it is inclined to exaggerate the Moon's responses, making it difficult for munakara Moon to feel safe and secure in loving relationships.

The Three Rules of Sect

As explained in Chapter One, munakara is determined by a combination of the Essential Dignity of sign rulership and the Accidental Dignity of planetary sect. This means that the rules of sect dignity are a critical factor to understanding munakara. Without the planets' classification into diurnal or nocturnal, there would be no boundaries for a planet to cross. Accidental dignity provides the planet with suitable environments to soothe and pacify the planet when it is in contention, but the opposite is also true when unsuitable environments agitate and aggrieve the munakara planet.

For instance, a suitable environment for a toddler is a playground. Even if they are tired and unruly (a planet in contention), there is a chance their temper and behaviour will improve under the influence of wide open spaces that allow movement, release, and an avenue for freedom of expression. That same contentious toddler, trapped in the unsuitable environment of a crowded airport lounge after a gruelling ten-hour flight, is unlikely to be soothed or pacified.

Similarly, it is vital to know the sect condition of a planet in munakara, as it can give an indication as to how this planet will react in stressful circumstances. Good sect condition equates to a sympathetic environment where contention is not just to be tolerated, but maybe even be celebrated by those who benefit from its efforts. On the other hand, lack of sect dignity can exacerbate a munakara planet's natural sensitivity and add to the planet's feelings of displacement, alienation, misinterpretation or anxiety.

Rule One of Sect: Day or Night Birth

Rule One is the oldest and the most important rule of sect dignity. It provides for a harmonious environment which complements the nature of a planet: *i.e.*, that diurnal planets will prefer a daytime chart, and nocturnal planets will prefer a night-time chart. Therefore, a diurnal munakara planet is likely to be happier and more at ease in a diurnal chart. Likewise, a nocturnal munakara planet is likely to be happier and more at ease in a nocturnal chart.

Rule Two of Sect: Correct Hemisphere – *'halb'*

The second sect rule divides the hemispheres at the Ascendant/Descendant horizon and classifies the division according to the presence of

Chapter Two • *Technical Points to Munakara*

the Sun. A planet travelling with the Sun, that is, in the same hemisphere, is called 'diurnally-placed' regardless of whether the chart itself is diurnal or nocturnal. A planet travelling without the Sun, in the opposite hemisphere, is called 'nocturnally-placed'. As one might expect, diurnal planets prefer to be 'diurnally-placed'. Nocturnal planets prefer to be 'nocturnally-placed'.

Al-Biruni defines 'halb' which is the second rule of sect: (The highlights in bold are mine)

> ... [w]hen a diurnal planet is above the ground by day and beneath it at night, and when a nocturnal planet is above ground at night and beneath it by day, it is said to be in its halb, and a planet is described as **in** or **not in its halb**.

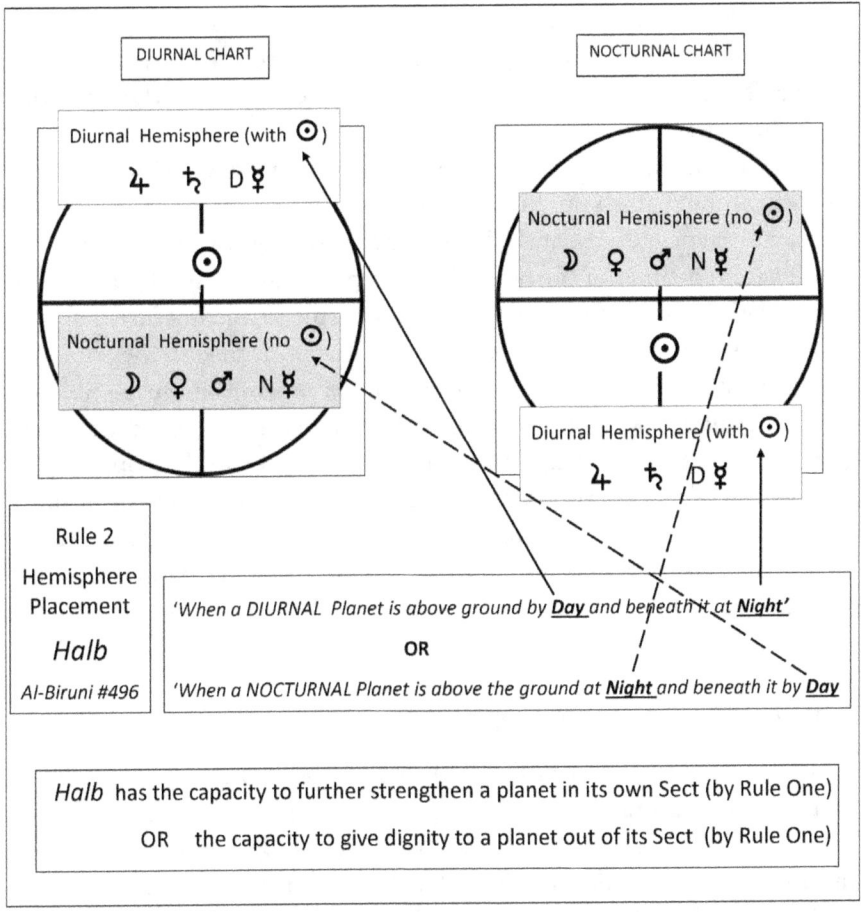

Fig. 2.2: *Rule Two of Sect: Correct Hemisphere (halb)*

The second rule of sect, (*halb*) can be advantageous to a planet for two reasons. For the planet which has already achieved Rule One (that is, a diurnal planet in a day chart or a nocturnal planet in a night chart), *halb* adds to the feeling of a suitable environment which supports the planet's actions and helps to fulfil its potential. This means the planet gains greater sect dignity and fortification of the planet's inner strength. The planet is compatible with, and comfortable in, its external surroundings.

The second benefit to *halb* – i.e., compatibility in hemisphere – is the ability for a planet belonging to the opposite sect to gain almost equal sect dignity as the planets who qualified in the first rule of sect. Gaining environment advantage through either or both the first two rules of sect can be of huge benefit to a planet in munakara. For this reason, sect should never be overlooked in the overall assessment of a munakara planet.

It should be noted that *every planet travelling beneath the horizon will have sect dignity*. Diurnal planets have sect dignity regardless of their position when the Sun is above the horizon as the chart is diurnal (Rule 1). Diurnal planets have sect dignity under the horizon as they are travelling with the Sun, even though it is a nocturnal chart.

Nocturnal planets under the horizon have sect dignity in a diurnal chart as they are travelling in the hemisphere opposite to the Sun (Rule 2). The Sun under the horizon is a nocturnal chart (Rule 1) and nocturnal planets do not lose their dignity by travelling under the horizon with the Sun.

On the other hand, *planets travelling in the upper hemisphere need to be carefully evaluated for poor sect dignity*. Diurnal planets in a nocturnal chart gain no benefit from Rules 1 and 2 as the chart is from the opposite sect and they are removed from the Sun, which is travelling below the horizon. Nocturnal planets travelling above the horizon are in sync with a nocturnal chart, but if the chart becomes diurnal – i.e., Sun above horizon – then they are travelling with the Sun and gain no sect advantage from the Rules 1 and 2.

Rule Three of Sect: The Planet's Sign and Gender

The third rule of sect (*Table 2.2*) divides the planets into gender and preferred sign allotment. The Chaldean Order of the Planets has much to do with the difference between masculine planets and feminine planets. For instance, the four planets on the outermost reach of the spheres – Saturn, Jupiter, Mars and the Sun – are considered to be masculine planets. These four masculine planets prefer to be in one of the six masculine signs which fall into either the fire or the air element. Closer to the Earth in the Order are Venus and the Moon, both of which are feminine planets, and these are planets that prefer the six feminine signs of water or earth element.

In the same vein as Mercury can be either a diurnal or nocturnal planet according to its position in relation to the Sun, it too can fall into either gender classification. Diurnal Mercury is masculine and prefers the fire or air element signs, and nocturnal Mercury is feminine and is in sect dignity when in the water or earth signs of the zodiac.

PLANET	Position Relative to the SUN	GENDER	SECT	ELEMENT
☉	—	Masculine	Diurnal	Fire / Air
♃	Not Applicable	Masculine	Diurnal	Fire / Air
♄	Not Applicable	Masculine	Diurnal	Fire / Air
☿	Oriental Ahead of the SUN	Masculine	Diurnal	Fire / Air
☿	Occidental Behind the SUN	Feminine	Nocturnal	Water / Earth
♂	Not Applicable	Masculine	Nocturnal	Fire / Air
♀	Not Applicable	Feminine	Nocturnal	Water / Earth
☽	Not Applicable	Feminine	Nocturnal	Water / Earth

Table 2.2: Rule Three of Sect: Matching a Planet's Gender with the Gender of the Signs

Where all 3 Rules are met – there is *'hayyiz'* (*'hayz'*)

The term *'hayyiz'* (or *'hayz'* in the latinised version) is the term used to describe a planet which conforms to all three rules of sect:

1. chart orientation
2. hemisphere and
3. sign

Al-Biruni sums this classification at the end of Notation #496:

When in addition to this (halb) a planet is male and in a male sign or female and in a female sign, the condition is called hayyiz, and a planet is said to be in or not in its hayyz. Moreover it is obvious that hayyiz is more comprehensive than halb, because every hayyiz is a halb but not every halb is a hayyiz.[2]

In other words, *halb* is only Rule Two whilst *hayz* is the benefit of the Three Rules trio: the correct alignment of chart (day/night), hemisphere (with/without the Sun), and correct sign according to the planet's gender (*Table 2.2, previous page*).

Hayz is the perfect environment for a munakara planet to express its true nature. Hayz may partially, if not totally, offset the challenges the planet faces through its state of contention.

CHAPTER THREE
Moon in Munakara

What Does it Mean when the Moon is in Munakara?

This chapter (and the subsequent chapters dedicated to a planet each) seeks to walk through some of the possible expressions of a Moon in the state of munakara in an individual's chart. This is followed by a sample delineation, with references to a handful of others who have Moon in munakara. This is intended to support you to understand both the theoretical manifestations as well as provide some practical examples. Part Two of this book contains more examples of delineated charts with planets in munakara to strengthen your practical understanding. Chapter Ten covers charts that have three or more planets in munakara, and Chapter Eleven explores the predictive technique of firdaria and munakara planets. As was shared in the previous chapter, some possible expressions of a munakara Moon might include

- Complex relationship with mother, or history of mother being under attack
- Poor health through illness, emotional stress or accident
- Challenges in maintaining physical strength or mobility
- Highly sensitive or self-protective individual
- Fears of separation, alienation or betrayal by loved ones
- A need for family to provide an emotional 'buffer' against the outside world
- A strong need for privacy or personal space
- Shyness or withdrawal in public arenas

Table 3.1: Some possible expressions of Moon in munakara

However, depending on the sequence and planets involved therein, expressions can vary greatly.

Munakara Moon and Personal Challenges

When delineating a munakara Moon, it is overly simplistic to assume that it will always manifest as a toxic relationship with the mother (or nurturing parent). Munakara Moon may also manifest as an intensely loving relationship with the mother/nurturing parent, but that intensity may mean that both parent and child need to develop their own emotional independence. Otherwise, they risk the healthy separation which must occur in order to give them space to develop as separate entities, and to achieve emotional equality rather than remain in the parent to child dynamic. The planets involved in the Moon's sequence are often clues as to how this healthy separation might occur, but contention will arise if one party is unwilling or incapable of releasing the bonds. A Moon in munakara may also manifest as a mother who has faced many contentious situations. Depending on how the child feels their mother has dealt with those situations, they may unconsciously choose to model and embrace her methods, or to outright reject them.

As the Moon rules the physical body, a munakara Moon can also manifest in health issues or physical restraints due to illness or accident. Munakara, and the contention it brings, does not however mean the issues cannot be overcome or that the condition is without hope. As much as the issues are likely to be challenging, a munakara planet is a feisty fighting planet, determined to succeed and to overcome the barriers that frustrate it.

For a munakara Moon the path to personal growth may be strewn with obstacles, and it may struggle to be resilient in the face of hardship. Certain practices can help with this struggle, such as taking a moment to step away from emotional turmoil and instead, to identify the situation which is creating the emotion. This may help the individual to be more fluent in talking about an issue and to decide if any action is necessary to clear the anxiety surrounding the emotion. Furthermore, as the Moon rules both the body and emotions, it may be beneficial to try to distinguish between the physical feeling and the emotional feeling. The body's reaction to hunger, tiredness, stress or pain is an automatic response so it may confuse these strong triggers with a heightened emotional response.

Chapter Three • *Moon in Munakara*

As with judgements on any planet's condition, several other factors need to be considered. Factors like the planet's **house placement** are important. In the case of a munakara Moon, the house where the Moon resides will show where the individual is looking to get emotional fulfilment. Given that it is a munakara planet, this may be a place where the individual feels triggered or frustrated by a lack of support or the inability to achieve emotional satisfaction.

The Moon is also highly responsive to any **aspects** it shares with other planets, particularly if it is in aspect with either of the planets involved in its sequence. The Moon's relationship with the house it rules (that is, the house with Cancer on the cusp) and the area of life ruled by the Moon will often be key factors that give a deeper understanding of its experience and expression of munakara.

The Moon's sect condition is another important factor in delineating munakara Moon in a chart as the greater support a Moon receives in its environment – by chart, placement and sign – the more capable it is to withstand and recover from setbacks associated with its contentious state.

Munakara Moon and Societal Challenges

Society, have mercy on me
I hope you're not angry if I disagree
Society, crazy and deep
I hope you're not lonely without me
– Eddie Vedder, lyrics from *Society* featured in Into the Wild[1]

The Moon's nature fosters the development of social skills, firstly through the family unit, and then through peer groups as the child grows into adulthood. For this reason, the Moon is a good place to start when considering the social impact for any planet in munakara. Social interaction can provoke a wide range of reactions for a munakara planet, ranging from being glorified for fighting to bring about social change to being ridiculed or cast out for being too radical. The various chart examples for munakara Moon explored in this book are individuals who have experienced both sides of the munakara coin: some suffered in contention and others thrived through the experience. But each one affected public opinion and contributed to society in their own way.

Munakara in Theory

There are a variety of ways in which an individual with munakara Moon can feel society does not support or understand them and their emotional reactions. The Moon may provoke a response simply by challenging or disrupting a norm and the person may not even be aware that their behaviour is provoking a reaction. Society may sense on a deeper, unconscious level that the person with munakara Moon is someone who will upset harmony, and may single them out as a trouble-maker who does not conform to societal standards, opinions, or beliefs. The feeling of being an outcast can result in increasingly extreme behaviour. The person may crave the feeling of being included and do everything in their power to be accepted. Or they may do the reverse and reject societal norms entirely, rebelling against what they feel is dangerous or limiting herd mentality.

Any of these situations will be distressing for the individual with Moon in munakara, creating emotional anxiety and triggering instincts that something is wrong, even when no-one has confronted them or confirmed their suspicions. The Moon represents the body, and a munakara Moon may be highly sensitive to bodily reactions when the individual feels uncomfortable in a social situation. Visceral feelings such as shivers, butterflies in the stomach, sweating, or a flash of nausea can be among the Moon's physical reactions.

The Moon's Sequence: Friends, Associates, and Enemies

The Moon's Table *(Table 3.1)* is an extract from al-Biruni's *Table of Friendship and Enmities* and shows the Moon's relationship with the other six planets. Friends – planets that benefit each other through lending their signs. Associates – planets that have no beneficial or harmful relationship with one another. Enemies – planets that are in debility, either in detriment or fall, in another planet's sign.

D Diurnal / N Nocturnal	Essential Dignity Rulership / Exaltation (Mutual Damage)	Second Essential Dignity (Fall opposes Exaltation)	Second Essential Dignity — Borrowing Signs for Exaltation	
Munakara Planet △	Mutually Hurtful With (☽ 's Two-Way Damage)	Injurious To (☽ Disposits Fall Sign)	Offering Friendship To (☽ Owns Exaltation Sign)	Asking Friendship From (Exalted ☽ 's Dispositor)	Indifferent To ☽ - No relationship
N ☽ △	D Saturn ○ First Dispositor	N Mars (♂) ▼ Outcome Planet	D Jupiter (♃) ○ First Dispositor	N Venus (♀) ▼ Outcome Planet	D Sun : Mercury D / N ○ First Dispositor : D ○ First Dispositor N ▼ Outcome Planet

Table 3.2: Moon's Friends and Enemies

Chapter Three • *Moon in Munakara*

Friends or Associates of a munakara Moon: Jupiter, Venus, Sun and Mercury

A munakara Moon disposited by one of the diurnal planets is still in contention but will likely find itself less aggravated than when disposited by an 'enemy' planet. Generally speaking, the Moon has a good relationship with Jupiter, as Jupiter borrows Cancer for its exaltation. The Moon has no specific relationship with the Sun or Mercury (*Table 3.1*). Therefore, the Moon is less aggravated when any one of these planets is its first dispositor, or in the case of nocturnal Mercury, its outcome planet. Their involvement in the sequence, however, will still bring their own elements to the expression of the munakara Moon's state of contention.

If Jupiter is involved in the sequence (as the first dispositor)

For example, while Jupiter is not inherently antagonistic towards the Moon, a munakara Moon in Sagittarius or Pisces may lead the Moon towards excessive behaviour simply because Jupiter is a planet of excess. As the Moon's dispositor, Jupiter may create either emotional or physical extremes, and can weaken the Moon's ability to cope with upheaval or illness. The Moon is a planet of subtle rhythms, like the Ocean's tides or its monthly cycle of increase and decrease, so it works best with patterns that are gentle, flowing, and consistent in their movement. This gives the Moon a sense of security and provides it with a harmonious relationship with nature. In contrast, Jupiter adds a rollercoaster feeling with frighteningly high peaks and stomach-churning lows. Therefore, Jupiter dispositing the Moon can change the Moon's gentle ebb and flow and turn it into more of a tsunami, sometimes with little provocation. If munakara Moon is in physical distress and illness is a result of its state of contention, then Jupiter is its dispositor may go into overdrive trying any avenue to alleviate its illness or symptoms. Jupiter can even exaggerate physical indicators of a disease and this can be problematic for any physician trying to identify and treat an illness.

Example Charts:
- Helen Keller (outcome planet, Mars)
- Elvis Presley (outcome planet, Mars)
- Robin Williams (outcome planet, Mars)
- Christopher Reeve (outcome planet, Venus)
- Oprah Winfrey (outcome planet, nocturnal Mercury)
- Dave Grohl (outcome planet, Venus)

If the Sun is involved in the sequence (as the first dispositor)

For the Sun to be the first dispositor, the Moon will be in the sign of Leo. The Sun at the centre of the sequence is likely to reinforce this munakara Moon's belief that the individual must be emotionally independent to protect itself from hurt or rejection by loved ones. The Sun has no intention to harm munakara Moon but the person is likely to be giving out emotional mixed messages of hot (Sun) and cold (Moon). Leo Moon is inclined towards shows of affection in its close relationships, but will expect and demand the reward of loyalty for that affection. When Leo Moon is in munakara there are likely to be misunderstandings that trouble the Moon, especially where the Moon's sequence has a second nocturnal planet as the outcome planet. Nocturnal Mercury (Sun in Gemini or Virgo) will seek to resolve problems using Mercury's skills in communication and problem-solving/negotiation. A Sun in Taurus or Libra will place Venus as the Moon's outcome planet, in which case compromise will likely be a key factor in resolving situations which are awkward for the Leo Moon. The Sun in Aries or Scorpio may prove a little confrontational for the Moon and heightened emotions may inflame situations that begin as small irritations. The Moon rules the body so pride in one's physical accomplishments can be part of its munakara sequence. The person may go to extremes to gain and hold attention and this can harm the body if caution is not a part of the person's psyche. It may be that the person is instantly identifiable and this means privacy is something they can no longer achieve once they become famous or easily recognisable. The outcome planet can show whether you love the attention (Venus), hate the attention (Mars), or feel the fame gives you the opportunity to voice your opinions (Mercury).

Example Charts:
- Evel Knievel (outcome planet, Venus)
- Queen Elizabeth II (outcome planet, Venus)
- Prince Philip (outcome planet, nocturnal Mercury)
- Prince Louis of Wales (outcome planet, Venus)

If diurnal Mercury is involved in the sequence (as the first dispositor)

If munakara Moon is in Gemini or Virgo, and Mercury rises before the Sun, then diurnal Mercury will be the first dispositor in its sequence. The Moon's nature is to experience emotion and then react, but its reaction is often in a manner devoid of clear reason or logic. The distressed Moon just wants the pain to end and is not following an analytic process to seek a solution, which causes frustration for logical Mercury. But Mercury's tendency to assist by over-analysing emotional situations or looking for hidden messages is exhausting and distressing for munakara Moon. Mercury's methods work in practical solutions but overwhelming munakara Moon with a list of options only undermines the emotional process and circumvents the Moon's need to *feel* the emotions rather than describe them analytically.

Diurnal Mercury is an agent of the Sun and much of its time is engaged in the working schedule of the day, so it may try to distract the Moon from its anxiety by increasing the workload, thereby believing it is solving two problems at the same time. Mercury reasons that the Moon will be happy if productivity increases but diurnal Mercury's 'solution' only burdens the Moon further by adding exhaustion, neglect and sleeplessness.

Example Charts:
- Albrecht Dürer (outcome planet, Venus)
- Billy Connolly (outcome planet, Mars)
- Prince Archie of Sussex (outcome planet, Mars)

If nocturnal Mercury is involved in the sequence (as the outcome planet)

The Moon is the nocturnal planets' chief luminary. Therefore, nocturnal Mercury can be more perceptive to shifts in emotion, subtle nuances, and more aware of the Moon's need for rest and quiet reflection than its diurnal counterpart. If nocturnal Mercury is the Moon's outcome planet there may be ways in which Mercury can find creative outlets for the Moon. Healthy practices such as increased sleep, meditation, listening to soothing music or engaging in physical activities such as writing or cooking can bring respite to an agitated munakara Moon. However, if nocturnal Mercury becomes intolerant of the Moon's emotional outbursts, then it may start internal monologues criticising the behaviour as unreasonable. Mercury's critical tone is little help to the munakara Moon as the Moon already feels that the world is against it, and Mercury's stings are unhelpful and counter-productive.

Whether nocturnal Mercury is soothing or harmful to the munakara Moon will depend on the nature of the middle planet in the sequence (*i.e.*, the first dispositor). If Jupiter is the middle planet, it adds heightened drama and nocturnal Mercury must find an avenue to dissipate the Moon's distress. If it is Saturn, there are issues over separation and abandonment and nocturnal Mercury is called in to find a solution. If it is the Sun, there can be a sense of arrogance or pridefulness that Mercury then has to deal with when munakara Moon feels it is ignored or treated disrespectfully.

Example Charts:
- Prince Philip
- Oprah Winfrey

If Venus is involved in the sequence (as the outcome planet)

Given that the Moon borrows Taurus for its exaltation, the Moon and Venus share a friendly relationship. As nocturnal planets, both the Moon and Venus seek to feed the cravings of a person's appetites through a variety of pleasures, which may or may not be good for the body. Venus is usually about pleasing the Moon's physical and emotional cravings, but when it is the outcome planet in a munakara sequence, it's as if something either gets in the way (Saturn) or gives permission to pull out all the stops and go for it (Jupiter). The nature of this interruption will vary depending on which diurnal planet is in the middle of these two nocturnal planets (*i.e.*, the first dispositor planet).

For instance, if the middle planet is Jupiter, there are likely to be challenges controlling the emotional state. The combination of Moon, Jupiter, and Venus can create habits that can become addictive and excessive. This may be over-eating, over-drinking, prioritising having a good time over the need for rest, etc. Pleasures may consume the individual and become the patterns of munakara Moon. Jupiter tends to provide the opportunity and neither munakara Moon or Venus are able to say 'No' to vices provided by an accommodating Jupiter. Moon ruled by Jupiter can be a love of wide spaces, independence and adventure, and if contention robs the person of these opportunities then munakara Moon and Venus must find other expressions for enjoyment and pleasure.

If Saturn is the middle planet in the Moon / Venus sequence then Saturn throws up obstacles saying 'no, you can't have it' and the Moon and Venus, with their big appetites, become resentful. The munakara Moon on one side wants it, and Venus wants to give it to the Moon, but Saturn is there in the middle placing blockages, consequences, boundaries, and/or guilt. Alternatively, Saturn may spoil pleasure or throw doubt and fear of missing out into the mix, suggesting that there is a better time to be had elsewhere that it is being deprived of by being a physical body in the wrong place. Saturn is the Lord of Time and it is a constant reminder to the Moon (on one side) that it is ageing and failing in some way, and a nagging fear for Venus (on the other side) that it is becoming increasingly unattractive and invisible to its admirers.

Diurnal Mercury in the middle is easier to manipulate as it will facilitate the Venus giving to the Moon, simply because Mercury can justify anything to both planets. As the planet of mischievous behaviour, Mercury likes to stir things up and observe the fun from the sidelines, so it doesn't place barriers like Saturn or facilitate in the same way as Jupiter.

The Sun in the middle of the Moon / Venus sequence is likely to encourage munakara Moon's appetites too, as the Sun in Venus' signs (possibly Sun in fall in Libra) is pleasure-bound and its monologue is persuasive. The Sun says "it's part of who you are, it's in your nature, you deserve this, don't fight who you are". Once Venus receives permission from the Sun it finds plenty of variety to 'feed' munakara Moon and trying to limit or control the appetites becomes a contentious issue if Leo Moon refuses to cooperate with any enforced restrictions.

Example Charts:
- Albrecht Dürer
- Edgar Degas
- John Dee
- Evel Knievel
- Diane Arbus
- Christopher Reeve
- Neil Diamond
- Dave Grohl
- Queen Elizabeth II
- Prince Louis of Wales

Enemies of a munakara Moon: Saturn & Mars

The two malefic planets (Saturn and Mars) are enemies of the Moon.

If Saturn is involved in the sequence (as the first dispositor)

The Moon in Capricorn or Aquarius shows the presence of an 'enemy' dispositor but there is a difference. The Moon in Capricorn is in detriment

(Cancer opposes Capricorn), whereas the Moon in Aquarius is a sign which is not in direct conflict with Cancer. The detriment between Cancer (Moon's sign) and Capricorn (Saturn's sign) is an archetypal battle between life and death. The Moon gives life and describes everything dense, lush, rampant and fertile whereas Saturn is the inevitability of time passing and the disintegration of living things into decay, loss, separation, and death. Saturn represents death, as time robs all things of life according to their natural cycle; it clears the space for the Moon to start again, but its version of space-clearing is a cold, dry process. Connecting these two planets through munakara is akin to connecting opposing forces of nature.

The Moon is always going to feel this pull when it is in Saturn's signs, but adding munakara takes this to a new level by trying to find an acceptable outcome for the process of growth and decline. Perhaps the contentious Moon tries to hold on too hard or ignores Saturn's signals that it is time to let go, but either way, the Moon's distress becomes heightened when an outcome planet is applying its own level of pressure and munakara Moon feels it is losing control of a situation. Venus or nocturnal Mercury as the outcome planet may show an artistic outlet for munakara Moon's distress and either planet may initiate a creative response that is identifiable to anyone going through a similar process, given that munakara Moon in Saturn's signs manifests as obligations to society. Mars as the outcome planet may choose to go into battle and fight, but with both malefic planets (Saturn and Mars) involved in munakara Moon's sequence there is going to be a separation (cold or hot) that munakara Moon cannot control. Rather than the question being 'Will I hold on to this thing/person that brings me security?' it becomes 'How will I survive the loss of this thing/person?' and this tends to make Mars even more desperate to win the battle if the Moon has no answer to this question.

Example Charts:
- John Dee (outcome planet, Venus)
- Edgar Degas (outcome planet, Venus)
- Diane Arbus (outcome planet, Venus)
- Neil Diamond (outcome planet, Venus)
- Michael Moore (outcome planet, Mars)
- Amy Winehouse (outcome planet, Mars)
- Prince George of Wales (outcome planet, Mars)

Chapter Three • *Moon in Munakara*

If Mars is involved in the sequence (as the outcome planet)

The Moon's nocturnal enemy is Mars. Mars and the Moon are not friends because Mars owns Scorpio, the Moon's fall sign. Similarly, Cancer belongs to the Moon, which is Mars' fall sign. Even though Mars is a nocturnal planet, it is an attacking force focused on defence and protection. If it is munakara Moon's outcome planet, Mars can put the Moon into physical danger and bring extremes of emotional stress because Mars is geared to fight or flight and these are really distressing survival techniques for the Moon.

The amygdala is a part of the limbic system in the brain and its duty is to regulate the body's emotional and behavioural responses. An 'amygdala hijack' is a modern term used to describe a fight-or-flight response to stress, anger or aggression. If munakara Moon is constantly experiencing these hijacks through Mars (as its outcome planet) then the Moon feels constantly in danger but does not understand the nature or source of the danger. The Moon wants to feel safe, secure and comforted and it wants to know it is safe in its environment. Mars is inclined to panic the Moon and provoke it into actions that are more complicated or dramatic under Mars' influence. If amygdala hijacking is becoming munakara Moon 's automatic response to stress then is wearing out its emotional and physical resources, and no matter how hard Mars tries to protect it, the Moon risks being too depleted to cope with any situation it finds stressful.

Munakara Moon needs time to take control of its emotions and to work out if the threat is real and imminent, or just a perceived future threat that Mars is preparing for. In these situations, it may help to use meditation or controlled breathing to focus the body's energy and restore peace and equanimity when a hijack occurs.

Example Charts:
- Elvis Presley
- Billy Connolly
- Robin Williams
- Amy Winehouse
- Helen Keller
- Michael Moore
- Prince George of Wales
- Prince Archie of Sussex

Example of Munakara Moon in a Nocturnal Chart – Elvis Presley

Brief Biography of Elvis Presley

The "King of Rock n Roll", Elvis Presley, was born to Gladys and Vernon on January 8, 1935. A twin brother, Jesse, was delivered stillborn 35 minutes prior, a loss that Gladys was still mourning during Elvis's birth, and that would remain a lifelong burden for Elvis. It was said that he lived a life for both sons.

Elvis's early years were lived in Tupelo, Mississippi which shaped his love of gospel music. He began singing at 10 years of age and received his first guitar on his 11th birthday.

Vernon, Elvis's father, often struggled to hold down work and in 1938 the family lost their home after he was found guilty of altering a check and jailed for eight months. His mother tragically died at age 46 in 1958, when Elvis was just 18.

Elvis's career took off in Memphis, Tennessee in 1954 and he signed with a recording manager, Colonel Tom Parker in the following year. Elvis began touring and performed around the United States and his first single "Heartbreak Hotel" was released in 1956. Elvis became famous for his gyrating hip movements, eccentric dress style and stunning vocal range.

By the early 1970s, years of binge eating and prescription medication had taken a toll on Elvis's body. Elvis's divorce from Priscilla took place in 1973 and twice during that year Elvis overdosed on barbiturates, spending three days in a coma after the first incident. In 1973 Elvis performed in 168 concerts, his busiest schedule ever.

Sadly, Elvis died of a heart attack in 1977 at age 42, just four years younger than his mother at the time of her death.

Elvis's legacy lives on through his music, with sales estimated around 500 million records worldwide. In 2018, Elvis was posthumously awarded the Presidential Medal of Freedom, the highest civilian award of the United States.

- **Key Questions:**
- What does Elvis Presley's Moon contend with?
- What is its driving force?
- What is its trigger? What is its outcome?

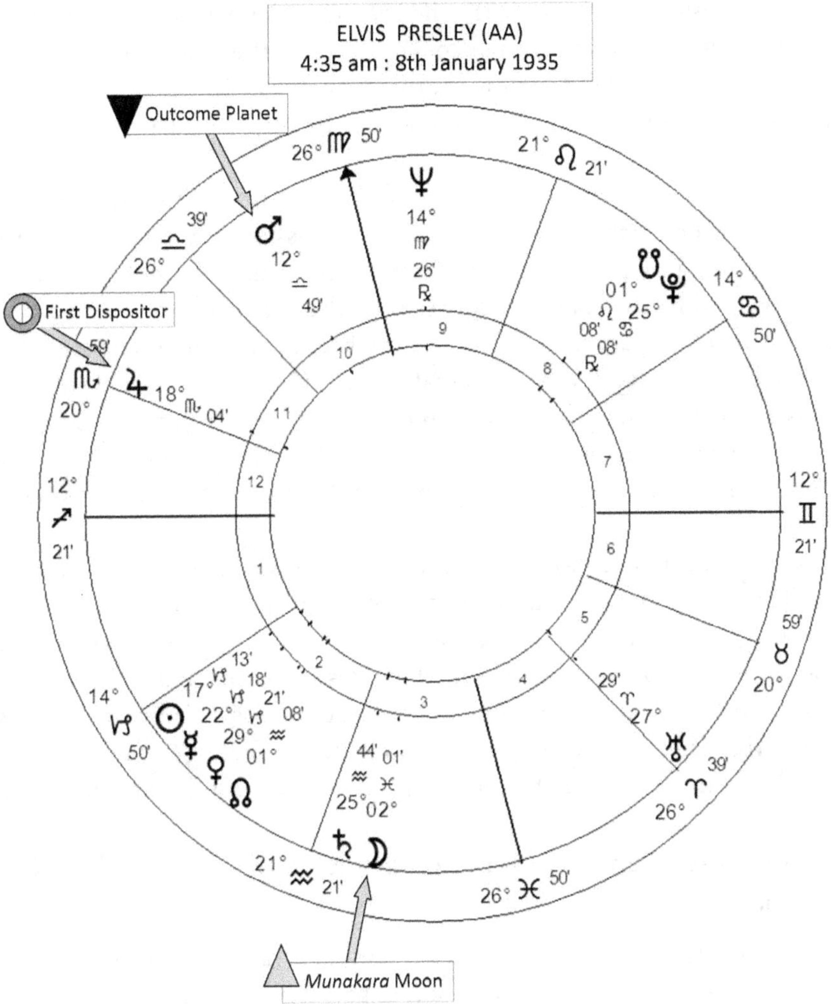

Fig. 3.1: Elvis Presley Natal Chart: Moon in Munakara

Elvis Presley's *Munakara* ☽ 's Sequence				
♓ ☽	⟶	♏ ♃	⟶	♂
N		D		N

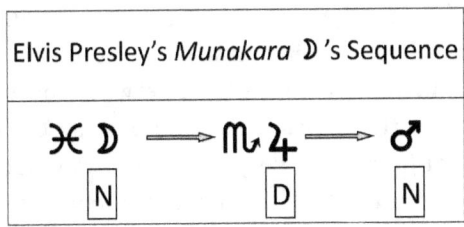

Table 3.3: Elvis Presley: Munakara Moon's Sequence

Elvis Presley's chart shows that he has a munakara Moon in Pisces with diurnal Jupiter as the first dispositor, and Mars as the outcome planet. This means in order to delineate his chart, we must consider how a munakara Moon in Pisces is activated and influenced by the presence of Jupiter and Mars in the sequence.

Elvis Presley's munakara Moon manifests through his extraordinary talent and a desire to grow with the music he passionately loved, beginning with gospel and culminating with the title "King of Rock and Roll". However, with fame came exploitation by the people he trusted the most and his fear and paranoia (Moon) grew with the ever-increasing demands of his manager (Jupiter) and his zealous fans (Mars). The Moon rules the body and Elvis's exaggerated body movements (Moon in Jupiter's sign) and his sexually explicit hip gyrations (outcome planet Mars) caused his female fans to go wild, much to the disapproval of their parents and the public in general.

Elvis's emotional innocence (Pisces Moon) was fodder for greedy agents, publicists, and clever management pushing to model him to their own advantage (Mars). His eventual loss of innocence led to disenchantment and drug use to ease his pain but which destroyed his body. His physical beauty (Pisces Moon) made him a target for both sexes and ultimately he lost the battle to heal himself physically and mentally, feeling trapped within a world he was ill-equipped to understand or control (outcome planet, Mars)

Munakara Planet and Sect Condition – how comfortable is the Moon?

As a nocturnal chart, Elvis Presley's munakara Moon in the feminine sign of Pisces had two benefits according to the rules of sect dignity. Pisces Moon trines its dispositor Jupiter in Scorpio, and whilst the degrees between the two planets are wide, there is still a good connection between Moon and Jupiter. Jupiter is a friend of the Moon (Jupiter borrows Cancer for exaltation) and Jupiter also rules Elvis's Ascendant so there should be potential for good health, strength and vitality with the trine between the Moon – signifying the body – and Jupiter, the planet ruling the house describing the body.

However, diurnal Jupiter in Scorpio is completely out of sect in Elvis's chart (*Fig. 3.1*), and it finds itself in a nocturnal chart, separated from the Sun, in a feminine sign. Scorpio Jupiter cannot see its sign, Sagittarius, and Jupiter's discomfort as the blind ruler of Elvis's Ascendant became more obvious as Elvis aged with ailing health, struggles with weight gain, and an addiction to prescription drugs fuelling his growing paranoia.

Tom Parker (known as Colonel Parker) was Elvis's manager. The honorary title of 'Colonel' was bestowed by Jimmie Davis, the governor of Louisiana for Tom's help in his election campaign, but the Colonel wore it with the same honour as someone returning from the war. Elvis's relationship with his manager began as friendship but Colonel Parker's role took on a more sinister 12th-house flavour (out-of-sect Jupiter) when he began to limit Elvis's movements and control his artistic choices. Under Colonel Parker's influence Elvis's artistic freedom and growth was stymied, prevented from exploring new horizons by Colonel Parker's concern with visa re-entry complications into the US should Elvis pursue his dream to tour internationally.

Mars (ruler of 12th house) is the third planet involved in the Moon's munakara sequence. Despite its good sect condition, this outcome planet is an enemy, therefore it is not friendly towards Elvis's munakara Moon. Mars provided Elvis's Moon with his magnetism, but Elvis was also troubled by the violent adoration displayed by his fans when he performed live shows. Colonel Parker fed Elvis's crippling fear of crazed fans and used it to increase his control over Elvis, removing the star from reality and making him almost completely dependent on Colonel Parker.

Elvis Presley— ☽'s Sect Dignity			
Planet	Sect 1 Status	Sect 2 Hemisphere	Sect 3 Sign
♓ ☽	Night	With the Sun	Water
N	N	D	N

Table 3.4: Elvis Presley: Munakara Moon Sect Dignity

Pisces Moon in Munakara – Elvis Presley

"I've come too far, and I don't know how to get back." – Elvis Presley

Munakara Moon in Pisces in 3rd House (Placidus)

The Moon is in its joy in the 3rd house and physical movements are easy, fluid and part of the individual's personality. Elvis Presley's famous gyrating hips are an expression of his Moon in contention. Biographer Peter Guralnick believes Elvis's strong response to rhythm and nervousness led him to shake his legs as he performed.[2] Guitarist Scotty Moore, who was part of a trio in the early days, recalls "During the instrumental parts, he (Elvis) would back off from the mike and be playing and shaking, and the crowd would just go wild.[3] His movement was a natural thing, but he was also very conscious of what got a reaction. He'd do something one time and then he would expand on it real quick."[4] Elvis's movements were exaggerated, and viewed as sexually explicit. Jupiter is the Moon's dispositor and freedom of expression through the body is natural for this Moon. However, the movement from Jupiter to Mars, the second nocturnal planet, shows there is rage as well sexual invitation.

Elvis challenged societal norms with his singing and the masculinity of his strong physical presence that was a hallmark of his performances. He incited moral panic in the older generations who saw his music as evil and obscene, designed to corrupt the youth of the day with lyrics and deep primal rhythms.

"Presley transformed not only the sound but the emotion of the song, turning what had been written as a lament for a lost love into a satisfied declaration of independence."[5] This statement is a perfect description for Pisces Moon disposited by Jupiter, but by adding a third planet, Mars, and completing the munakara sequence, the style of Elvis's music becomes raw, contentious, and provocative.

Planets in munakara often show a link between deep social divide and the individual's journey through life, and Elvis Presley is no exception. "The iconic image of Elvis and B.B. King, arm in arm at the peak of each man's youthful fame, would become the stuff of legend."[6] American blues guitarist, singer and song-writer, B.B. King, remembers in the early 1950s that other performers in that era, such as Jerry Lee Lewis, Carl Perkins and Johnny Cash, were chilly and silent towards him and he was never sure if it was rivalry or racism that caused the awkwardness. But B.B. remembers Elvis in this way when he met him in 1956 as a 21-year-old: "Elvis was different. He was friendly. I remember Elvis distinctly because he was handsome and quiet and polite to a fault. Spoke with this thick molasses Southern accent and always called me 'sir'. I liked that. In the early days, I heard him strictly as a country singer. I liked his voice, though I had no idea he was getting ready to conquer the world."[7]

Elvis's munakara Moon is situated in his 3rd house in the Placidus system, and Elvis's twin brother, Jesse Presley, arrived 35 minutes before Elvis. Sadly, Jesse was stillborn and Gladys Presley gave birth to Elvis whilst she was mourning the death of her firstborn son. Although Jesse's chart

Chapter Three • *Moon in Munakara*

is not included here, there is little change between the twin boys. Jesse's Ascendant degree is 4 Sagittarius, whilst Elvis's is 12 Sagittarius (*Fig.3.1*) and Jesse's Ascendant degree would be a tight square to the Moon he would have shared with Elvis. Munakara Moon set the stage for Elvis through his mother's grief, as Gladys would impress on Elvis that he was living his life for both her boys. Some child psychologists have hypothesised that Elvis's drive to succeed was partly due to the survivor's guilt he carried throughout his lifetime. "Elvis's twin's death at birth was a tragedy that triggered a process that made his dead sibling the bedrock, the singular driving force in his life" asserts clinical psychologist and researcher, Peter Whitmer, in his book *The Inner Elvis*. Whitmer claims Jesse was "a restless spirit who eventually haunted all of Presley's relationships."[8]

There is little doubt that Elvis felt the loss of Jesse as his Moon occupies the 3rd house (Placidus) and also relates to the 4th house (Whole Sign). Elvis's munakara Moon shifts to the 4th house in the Whole Sign system, the house of father, home and family history. In 1938, when Elvis was three years old, the family lost their home after Vernon Presley, Elvis's father, was found guilty of altering a cheque and jailed for eight months.[9] Even before this event, Vernon moved from one odd job to the next and the family often relied on the goodwill of neighbours or government food assistance.[10] The loss of stability and physical or emotional security is shown by Elvis's munakara Moon moving to the 4th house, and its dispositor, Jupiter, being the ruling planet of the 4th house.

Elvis's purchase of Graceland for his parents in March 1957 is his munakara Moon providing himself and his family with a secure home, even though his mother, Gladys, did not live long to enjoy it. Just eighteen months later her untimely death occurred from a heart attack, at age 46 on August 14, 1958. Elvis's death occurred on August 16, 1977. He passed on at age 42, a lifespan four years shorter than his mother's life and he was buried at Graceland next to his parents. His daughter Lisa Marie and her son Benjamin are also buried at Graceland. Elvis built a memorial for Jesse at Graceland to honour his dead twin. At the time of the boys' birth the Presley family was impoverished and couldn't afford a coffin, so Jesse was buried in a shoebox and laid to rest at Priceville Memorial Gardens in Tupelo. Baby Jesse's grave is marked and the headstone contains no name, but together Gladys and Elvis visited his grave regularly when Elvis was a boy.

First Dispositor: Jupiter in Scorpio in 12th House

The Moon's dispositor, Jupiter, is on the cusp of the 12th house and slips into the same house in Whole Sign as Scorpio is twelve signs from the Ascendant. Jupiter rules the 1st house but is in aversion to its house, meaning that it is blind to the effect it has on the world at large. Elvis was in his own world when he sang. His Moon was instinctive and so receptive to sound that it too was vaguely unaware that his body movements were inappropriate and out of sync with the morals of the day.

Jupiter is the stuff of superheroes, and Elvis, who became one in his lifetime, is believed to have modelled his look on his teenage comic book hero, Captain Marvel Jr. The sideburns, the long-haired quiff, and half-cape jumpsuits he wore in the '70s were inspired by his admiration for the teenage superhero.[11]

Elvis was emotionally reliant on three people in his lifetime: his mother (Gladys), his wife (Priscilla), and his manager, Colonel Parker. Elvis depended on this trio to protect, nurture and nourish him but each one contributed to the stress endured by his munakara Moon. Elvis was 22 in August 1958 and was months into his two-year military service in Texas when he received news that Gladys had hepatitis and was unlikely to survive the disease as she had liver failure after years of alcohol abuse. Elvis arrived home two days before her death. On arrival Elvis maintained a constant bedside vigil until her death on August 14. He was inconsolable when she passed away and his friends believed her death changed his personality.[12] At Gladys' funeral Elvis collapsed on her coffin crying: "Please don't take my baby away! She's not dead. She's just sleeping."[13] The relationship between mother and son had always been close and even into his adulthood Gladys and he would use baby talk as part of their communication.[14]

Elvis was buried next to his mother in Forest Hill cemetery but after an attempt to steal his body in the weeks following his death, their remains were exhumed and both mother and son were reburied in Graceland's Meditation Garden. Jupiter rules both Elvis's 1st house and his 4th where the Moon resides in Whole Sign, so it seems natural that Graceland should be the resting place for Elvis and his beloved family.

Elvis was sent to Germany weeks after his mother's death. He rallied a little when he met 14-year-old Priscilla Beaulieu almost a year later, but close friends say Elvis changed radically after his mother's death and never fully recovered from the loss. Priscilla became his wife seven years after meeting, but she too left him. Although other partners followed, she was larger than life for him and was always his one true love. Originally Elvis's manager Tom 'Colonel' Parker was a mentor to him, a giant in the entertainment business and the one who was going to take Elvis on the road to glory. But Colonel Parker was much more than a manager for Elvis. Colonel Parker's status, his mannerisms and his business acumen earned Elvis's admiration and respect. Elvis loved the older man, even though Colonel Parker eventually crippled Elvis's career and steered him towards the safety of Las Vegas residency. It may have been a lucrative deal for both men, but the city's culture was toxic for Elvis and trapped him in the place that would eventually destroy him.

Twelfth-house Jupiter shows Elvis's emotional and physical undoing. His trust in people who betrayed him (Priscilla and Colonel Parker), and his own hand in destroying his mental and emotional health through addiction to prescription drugs, as well as the deterioration of his body due to his binge-eating habits.

The outcome planet: Mars in detriment

Claims that Elvis was destroying the very fabric of society[15] (Jupiter in 12th house, Mars in 11th by Whole Sign) would have been deeply upsetting for the conservative, shy man that Elvis was when he was off-stage. He saw himself as a law-abiding citizen who willingly performed his military service without avoiding or complaining about it. He stated "the Army can do anything it wants with me."[16]

Elvis's addiction to drugs contributed to his death in August 1977, but his death was not caused by party drugs, unlike many of his rock-and-roll peers. Rather, it was a concoction of legal drugs had been prescribed by a registered doctor whom he had trusted as one of society's health care professionals (Jupiter dispositing his Moon). As a young man with strong ties to the church, Elvis was nervous of recreational drugs so easily available in the entertainment business, and he chose other more traditional methods to comfort his munakara Moon through music, spiritual song and family connections. With Mars as his Moon's outcome planet, drugs became a solution with poor long-term effects to compensate for his body's need for energy and strength. Mars has the ability to attack the body so highs like addictions can easily become patterns that are difficulty for munakara Moon to avoid or abandon.

Elvis's Mars in the 11th house had an impact on his life, whether it described the young women who screamed from the audience, or the young men hung around in the back alleys behind the stage armed with clubs to give Elvis a good beating if he showed his face. Disc jockey / promoter Bob Neal signed a management deal with Presley in 1955, and he recalls "It was almost frightening, the reaction that came to Elvis from the teenaged boys. So many of them, through some sort of jealousy, would practically hate him. There were occasions in some towns in Texas when we'd have to be sure to have a police guard because somebody'd always try to take a crack at him."[17] Mars is represented by the bodyguards who needed to be employed to protect him from both women *and* men.

Mars was also represented by the older generation of fellow artists who should have encouraged Elvis, but instead who tried to tear him down with their comments. Fifteen years after he was causing teenage girls to scream and swoon, Frank Sinatra called rock and roll a "rancid-smelling aphrodisiac" and wrote in a magazine article that it was "brutal, degenerate, vicious...It fosters almost totally negative and destructive reactions in young people. It smells phoney and false and is sung, played and written, for most part, by cretinous goons."[18]

The third planet in a munakara sequence can show both ends of the spectrum for the planet in contention. It can show the outcome and the end product of the planet's challenges, or it can be a trigger that has an impact on the individual's life story. Elvis's increasing isolation and paranoia at the end of his life meant that he surrounded himself with friends from his youth and family members who became known as the "Memphis Mafia". They drove bumper cars in Las Vegas Valley, rode horses in California and hung out at Graceland. "For the first time in his life, he had a group of male friends to pal around with, and he relished being leader of the pack" writes one biographer, Earl Greenwood, author of *The Boy Who Would Be King*.[19] This wall of protective friends indulged him as much as they shielded him from the public, mainly because he made their lives easy and allowed them to party with the King at same time keeping him isolated from the world. Presley faced repeated threats of physical violence from outraged moral extremists and death threats from fanatics[20] so he needed men who he felt were loyal and trustworthy to act as bodyguards. (Mars in detriment rules 5th and 12th house). Mars is the Moon's outcome planet, but it is also in detriment, and Elvis's reputation for generosity was not necessarily extended to Elvis's Mob. The benefits were not fiscal as none of them were paid more than $500 a week. "They all had jobs to do so that Elvis could do his and as far as being there for the money, that's laughable because there really wasn't much in that area to be there for."[21]

Chapter Three • *Moon in Munakara*

Munakara Moon: The Legacy

We might look back and laugh now about Elvis instigating fears of 'moral corruption', particularly in comparison with modern day controversial musicians. But in his day, Elvis was a symbol for intense cultural, social, and musical revolution.

If Elvis was anyone's King, surely it was the generation that embraced rebellion and accelerated human rights by challenging and changing lawful segregation in America.

Little Richard said in tribute to Elvis "He was an integrator. Elvis was a blessing. They wouldn't let black music through. He opened the door for black music."[22]

Further Examples of Munakara Moon

Part Two of this book contains five additional chart delineations. The three diurnal examples are 15th-century artist Albrecht Dürer, daredevil Evel Knievel, and documentary producer, Michael Moore. The two nocturnal examples are Diane Arbus and Christopher Reeve. The following Tables (*Tables 3.4 and 3.5*) feature Moons in munakara in day-time and night-time charts.

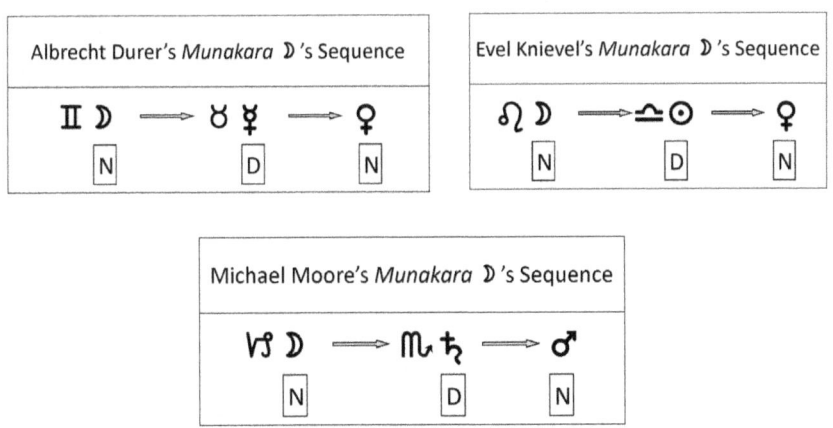

Table 3.5: Munakara Tables for Diurnal Charts: Moon's Sect and Sequences

Munakara in Theory

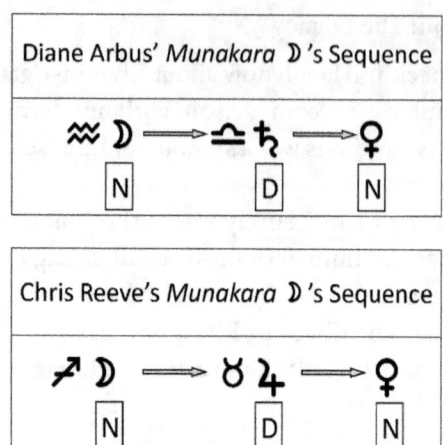

Table 3.6: *Munakara Tables for Nocturnal charts: Moon's Sect and Sequence*

CHAPTER FOUR
Mercury in Munakara

*"For the aimless wandering of the thoughtless will kill them
and the smug overconfidence of fools will destroy them
but those who pay attention to me will live securely,
untroubled by fear of misfortune."*
– Proverbs 1:32, 34

Mercury is a planet of duality and by potentially belonging to both sect categories, it has the capacity to serve both the Sun and the Moon in their separate endeavours. Oriental is ahead of the Sun making Mercury diurnal and a servant of the Sun. Occidental Mercury rises after the Sun, making it nocturnal and a servant of the Moon. In this chapter diurnal Mercury and nocturnal Mercury are split into two sections because they have different expressions, and their sequences will differ according to whether Mercury rose ahead of the Sun (oriental/diurnal) or after the Sun (occidental/nocturnal). However, there are some possible expressions for munakara Mercury which are shared regardless of sect, and these are listed below (*Table 4.1*), along with some expressions unique to Mercury's sect status.

Diurnal Mercury gathers and retains information for the Sun's purpose to achieve success and privilege within society's bounds. This Mercury is geared to communicate, broadcast and network in order to reinforce the Sun's need to promote an individual's value, purpose and placement in the world. Diurnal Mercury will demonstrate solar qualities such as an interest in marketing, gathering qualifications and business acumen, self-promotion and fulfilling timelines so that the Sun knows it is progressing towards its goals. These are all qualities designed to advance the Sun in its journey towards success, respectability, and valuable contributions to society. The last three points in *Table 4.1* refer directly to diurnal Mercury in munakara as these are relevant to munakara when Mercury is the Sun's agent.

In contrast, nocturnal Mercury absorbs and retains information to nourish the individual's inner landscape. This lunar Mercury expresses and communicates ideas to encourage the imagination and intuition, and to hone gut feelings when something does not 'feel' right. This Mercury is a servant of the Moon, and as such it is sensitive to non-verbal cues. It uses memory palaces triggered by emotions and memories, and it has an attraction to rhythm, movement and language, all skills which are based on providing information to nourish and support the lunar luminary by keeping the physical body safe and free from danger.

This is not to say that diurnal Mercury cannot be artistic, or that nocturnal Mercury does not find value or a place in the business world, but the dual nature of Mercury means the two models use different skills, and focus on different objectives, depending on their sect luminary – *i.e.*, Sun for diurnal Mercury, Moon for nocturnal Mercury.

What does it mean when diurnal Mercury is in a state of munakara?

- Contending with rumours or gossip
- Cyber-bullying, misunderstandings or arguments
- Obstacles to clear communication, barriers in reading or writing skills
- Social shyness or restrictions in speech or self-expression
- Effort needed to stay focused, on task, or hold concentration
- Financial anxiety or frustrations in business undertakings
- Challenges in fine motor skills or co-ordination
- Distractions interfere with information transmitted from brain to body
- Unresolved issues or conflict with siblings
- Fear of being misrepresented or dishonoured in society
- Gaining fame or infamous notoriety through one's actions
- Being ignored or feeling aimless or directionless in one's goals

Table 4.1: Some possible expressions of diurnal Mercury in munakara

Chapter Four • *Mercury in Munakara*

Diurnal Mercury in Munakara and Personal Challenges

Mercury is a fickle character at the best of times, but when placed in munakara it can accentuate the 'trickster' element of its nature. Mercury's unpredictability increases with contention, and often this Mercury is inflammatory when discussion arises on sensitive subjects. The individual may not be trying to be provocative in their views and may even dislike the attention they gain when expressing their opinion. Rather, they may struggle to understand their own relentless need to communicate contentious thoughts or strong opinions.

Munakara Mercury wonders how others seem to ignore a problem and look the other way, but cannot comprehend why is it hard for them to adopt the same behaviour and walk away from the issue at hand. A classic Mercury in munakara moment is the necessity to talk about 'the elephant in the room', regardless of the ensuing quarrel that is bound to follow. However, remaining tight-lipped to avoid confrontation can also irritate others, as silence may be seen as a betrayal or lack of support for a mutual view privately shared. Even without being munakara, Mercury is inclined towards being a planet of a contentious nature. Keeping silent or holding differing opinions at bay is only going to last so long before Mercury's dam bursts and words flow forth like water.

The Mercury which rises before the Sun will have one of three choices for its first dispositor: Moon, Venus, or Mars, and Mercury's relationship with each of these three planets will lead to an outcome that varies according to Mercury's dispositor.

Diurnal Mercury in Munakara and Society's Challenges

Diurnal Mercury tends to take its cues from social interaction. This Mercury is finely tuned to reputation, branding, and public display. The person with munakara Mercury risks becoming a scapegoat for a statement or action which gains society's attention, moving quickly from adoration to disapproval. Mercury was the nimblest of all the Greek gods but even he would be astounded at the speed at which information zooms across global social media sites.

Munakara Mercury shuns mediocrity and often uses outlandish behaviour to stand out in the crowd. It rebels against, and is largely unimpressed by, those who prefer to take the path of least resistance, purely

Munakara in Theory

because it requires less effort and there are fewer risks involved. Blending in with the group is not an option for diurnal Mercury in contention, as silence is too big a price to pay for invisibility, security or comfort. Rather, diurnal Mercury in munakara will eventually become desperate to speak out when others fall silent. It will stare down the enemy when everyone else looks the other way and will be convinced it has the solution to the problem, when others deny the problem even exists. Others may roll their eyes when munakara Mercury voices its concerns or refuses to back down from confrontation, but recognition and awareness are essential to bring about change that has been a long time coming.

Diurnal Mercury's Sequence: Friends, Associates, and Enemies

Diurnal Mercury's Table (*Table 4.2*) is an extract from al-Biruni's *Table of Friendship and Enmities* and shows Mercury's relationship with the other six planets. Mercury does not share its two signs with the other planets and nor does it ask to borrow from its divine peers. This removes the need for friendship and four planets are listed in *Table 4.2* as 'indifferent' to Mercury.

D Diurnal / N Nocturnal	Essential Dignity Rulership / Exaltation (Mutual Damage)	Second Essential Dignity (Fall opposes Exaltation)	Second Essential Dignity — Borrowing Signs for Exaltation	
Munakara Planet △	Mutually Hurtful With (☿'s Two-Way Damage)	Injurious To (☿ Deposits Fall Sign)	Offering Friendship To (☿ Owns Exaltation Sign)	Asking Friendship From (Exalted ☿'s Dispositor)	Indifferent To ☿ - No relationship
△ D ☿	D Jupiter : Venus N ▼ Outcome Planet ○ First Dispositor	N Venus (♍) ○ First Dispositor	Neither Offers nor Asks For Friendship (☿ exalted in ♍)	Neither Offers nor Asks For Friendship (☿ exalted in ♍)	D Sun : Moon N ▼ ○ Outcome Planet : First Dispositor D Saturn : Mars N ▼ ○ Outcome Planet : First Dispositor

Table 4.2: Diurnal Mercury's Friends and Enemies (adapted from al-Biruni's Table of Friendship and Enmities

Associates of a diurnal munakara Mercury: Moon, Mars, Sun & Saturn

A diurnal munakara Mercury disposited by one of the nocturnal planets can lead to contention but it will likely find itself less aggravated than when

Chapter Four • *Mercury in Munakara*

disposited by an 'enemy' planet. Mercury has no affiliations with the other planets through friendship as it keeps its own sign for exaltation and does not lend its signs to other planets for their exaltation. Mercury's hesitancy to lend its signs or borrow from another planet gives it a certain level of freedom and makes its relationships more about indifference than obligation.

The relationship that Mercury has with the four planets listed below is concerned more with the individual nature of the planets rather than the two Essential Dignities, rulership and exaltation, which bind or divide the planets through their zodiac signs.

If the Moon is involved in the sequence (as the first dispositor)

Diurnal Mercury in Cancer speaks with feeling but when placed in munakara discussions risk becoming emotionally charged. The other party may be wounded by disclosures that while honest, still sting. Cancer Mercury is disposited by the Moon, and whilst there is no natural conflict between Mercury and the Moon, the person with munakara Mercury may earn the title of 'troublemaker' without much effort on their part. If they do not actively rebel against the family and take the role of the black sheep, they may be an inadvertent reminder of a family scandal. Their name, behaviour or physical appearance could be linked with the unspoken past and they end up an unwitting catalyst for others' discomfort. Family secrets are never comfortable and it may be that the Moon's dispositor – Sun, Jupiter, or Saturn – will be the outcome planet that shows how the family deals with it.

Example Charts:
- John Dee (outcome planet, Saturn)
- John Glenn (outcome planet, Saturn)
- Princess Diana (outcome planet, Saturn)
- Prince George of Wales (outcome planet, Saturn)

If Mars is involved in the sequence (as the first dispositor)

Mars and Mercury are not enemies through their respective rulerships but there is little doubt that Mars' energy can agitate Mercury. If there is contention, then diurnal Mercury disposited by Mars is likely to be volatile, defensive and sometimes high-handed when challenged. If Mars is the first dispositor, it means that diurnal Mercury is situated in either Aries or Scorpio, and contention can create a certain mindset in the individual. Munakara Mercury in fiery Aries may have a tendency to burn bridges by speaking impulsively in a heated moment, or to genuinely forget parts of a conversation in which they have been inappropriate or careless of others' feelings.

Scorpio is a water sign, so this diurnal Mercury may internalise its thoughts, needing time to process the emotions which accompany disturbing thoughts. The individual may find themselves in a state of anguish, especially if they do not release munakara Mercury from any anger or regret. Misunderstandings can abound when Mercury is in the sensitive condition of munakara, and having Mars as its dispositor can inflame a situation that quickly escalates into hurtful and damaging accusations. Mentally revisiting contentious situations won't bring peace or forgiveness, and if the issue is never openly discussed it risks festering quietly under the surface, poisoning attempts at resolution or closure. Mercury's outcome planet – the dispositor of Mars – will give an indication as to where relief may be sought and may even show the event which triggers the situation.

Example Charts:
- Mark Ruffalo (outcome planet, Saturn)
- Michael Moore (outcome planet, Saturn)
- Queen Elizabeth II (outcome planet, Saturn)
- King Charles III (outcome planet, Jupiter)
- Prince Louis of Wales (outcome planet, Saturn)

If the Sun is involved in the sequence (as the outcome planet)

Diurnal Mercury's role is to serve its luminary, the Sun, by promoting the individual and keeping a clear head for decision-making. But if diurnal Mercury is in munakara then visions of failure or missed opportunities can plague the individual. The Sun as its outcome planet can manifest in a fear that the individual will lose face or suffer humiliation, especially if any financial difficulties are on the horizon. The fear of being exposed as a fraud or an individual whose success is based on good luck or privilege is very real for diurnal Mercury in contention, so there is an extra drive from Mercury to prove this is not the case.

Diurnal Mercury in munakara may indicate a mind that is in a constant process of mental agitation as the individual searches for a solution that will restore their dignity. Insecurity, worry, or stress can become munakara Mercury's daily companions but, with the Sun as its outcome planet, pride may force the person to hide their problems rather than seek help. The fear of having no back-up plan is very real for munakara Mercury, particularly

Chapter Four • *Mercury in Munakara*

financially, and the Sun's sign may give clues as to how the Sun tries to resolve Mercury's dilemma.

If Saturn is involved in the sequence (as the outcome planet)

When diurnal Mercury has Saturn as its outcome planet there are signs of restriction, hardship, or control issues. Feelings of guilt or regret may flavour this Mercury sequence, with past incidents or indiscretions buried within the mind. Constantly revisiting the issue and re-inventing different outcomes is mentally tiring and brings little comfort. Munakara Mercury needs to move on, but Saturn can be relentless in pointing out flaws and mistakes, even if they happened years ago.

Mercury is the significator for siblings and it may be that separation or alienation from a member of the family is part of Saturn's expression in the sequence. Saturn is the planet of 'cold separations' and timing or the wrong circumstances can end in estrangement. This could happen to any family, but for munakara Mercury it can be a constant reminder that the person has fallen short of their own expectations to hold the family together. Responsibility for a parent or family member can weigh heavily on munakara Mercury with Saturn as its outcome planet. Diurnal Mercury's first dispositor, whether it is the Moon, Mars or Venus, will be an important player in how the individual deals with this situation. They may be the one taking on the responsibility, or the one avoiding any active involvement.

Example Charts:
- John Dee
- John Glenn
- Mark Ruffalo
- Michael Moore
- Queen Elizabeth II
- Princess Diana
- Prince George of Wales
- Prince Louis of Wales

Enemies of a diurnal munakara Mercury: Venus, Jupiter

Jupiter and Venus are diurnal Mercury's 'enemy' planets. Jupiter's rulership signs oppose Mercury's signs and as a diurnal planet, Jupiter can play the role of outcome planet to diurnal Mercury's munakara sequence. While Jupiter is a benefic planet, it does have the tendency to amplify and dramatise a situation and these types of outcome can jeopardise diurnal Mercury's ability to assist the Sun's agenda as is its duty.

If Venus is involved in the sequence (as the first dispositor)

Venus is the nocturnal planet which becomes the first dispositor if diurnal Mercury is in Libra or Taurus. However, the astronomical distance between Mercury and Venus is a limiting factor as to whether diurnal Mercury in Venus' signs will complete a munakara sequence.

Mercury and Venus are the two planets closest to the Sun in the solar system. Mercury has 28° of maximum elongation from the Sun, and Venus has 48° of maximum elongation from the Sun. The maximum distance between Mercury and Venus is 76° and this distance only occurs on those rare times when both planets are at their maximum elongations on opposite sides of the Sun (east to west, or west to east).

Seventy-five degrees of separation reduces the potential for diurnal Mercury in Libra or Taurus to be munakara when it comes to Venus as the second planet. Mercury must be in front of the Sun in order to be classified as diurnal, whilst at the same time, no further than 28° from the Sun.

Diurnal Mercury in Libra

Diurnal Mercury in Libra can result in contention if Venus is *following two signs behind* in the sign of Sagittarius, in which case Jupiter will be Venus' diurnal dispositor, and will be the outcome planet for diurnal Mercury in Libra (*Table 4.3*). The Sun can be in the sign of Libra (so long as Mercury in Libra is ahead of the Sun), or Scorpio, but with no greater distance than 28° from Libran Mercury.

Media personality and former Olympian athlete, Caitlyn Jenner, is just one example of diurnal Mercury in Libra dispositing to Venus in Sagittarius, and the implications of Caitlyn's Libran Mercury in munakara are examined in Part Two of Mercury's delineations.

In the signs that precede diurnal Mercury in Libra, Venus can be two signs ahead in the masculine sign of Leo, which belongs to the Sun, and the result will be diurnal Mercury in munakara. However, the Sun must be in the degrees later than Mercury in Libra, if Mercury is to be classified as a

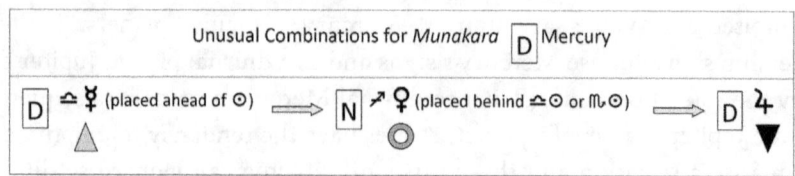

Table 4.3: *Diurnal Mercury in Libra disposited by Venus in Sagittarius*

diurnal. The greatest distance between Leo Venus, and its dispositor, the Sun, is 46°, so conditions must be just right to create contention for this Mercury. Mercury must be travelling in the early degrees of Libra, Venus must be in the last ten degrees of Leo (20–29°) and the Sun no more than halfway through Libra to make it possible for the munakara sequence to follow through to the Sun (*Table 4.4*).

It would seem therefore that Venus in Leo dispositing diurnal Mercury in Libra is a highly unlikely, though not impossible, munakara sequence.

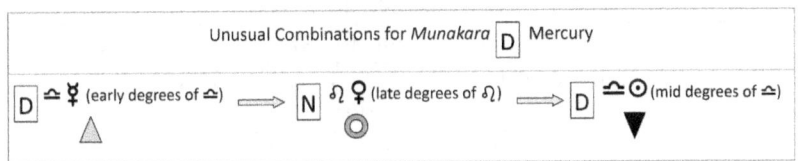

Table 4.4: Diurnal Mercury in Libra disposited by Venus in Leo

Diurnal Mercury in Taurus

The possibility for diurnal Mercury in Taurus to be munakara is rare, given that Venus is most likely to be in the same sign as Mercury and therefore in rulership. Venus in the sign preceding Taurus (Aries) is disposited by Mars, another nocturnal planet, so there is no munakara. Venus is in the sign following Taurus (Gemini) is disposited by Mercury, the two planets are in each other's signs and again, and there is no munakara.

Two signs behind Taurus is Cancer, and if Venus is in the Moon's sign there is no possibility of munakara as both Venus and the Moon are nocturnal planets. The only possibility for diurnal Mercury in Taurus to be munakara is Mercury is in early degrees of Taurus travelling ahead of the Sun with Venus is in late degrees of Pisces (*Table 4.5*). Any other scenario will exclude diurnal Mercury in Taurus from being in munakara.

The rarity of this situation is demonstrated by *Table 4.6* which covers the number of times diurnal Mercury in Taurus has been munakara over a period of 130 years.

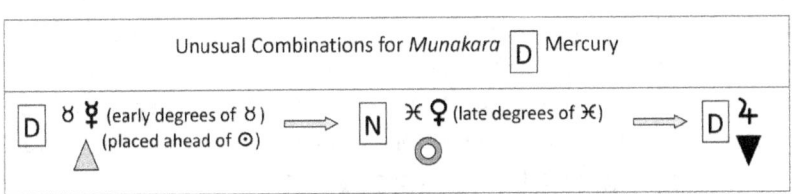

Table 4.5: Diurnal Mercury in Taurus disposited by Venus in Pisces

Munakara in Theory

Number	Commencement Date	End Date	Time Period
1	26th April 1902	7th May 1902	12 days
2	26th April 1915 10:00 pm	27th April 1915 Midnight	2 hours
3	28th April 1918	6th May 1918	9 days
4	3rd May 1934	6th May 1934	4 days
5	22nd April 1955 3:00 am	23rd April 1955 4:00 am	25 hours
6	28th April 1974	4th May 1974	7 days
7	4th May 1990 Midnight	4th May 1990 4:00 am	4 hours
8	23rd April 2030	28th April 2030	6 days

Table 4.6: *Table of Diurnal Mercury in Taurus in Munakara, 1900–2030 (130 years); Taurus Mercury ahead of the Sun; Venus in Pisces.*

If Venus is involved in the sequence (as the first dispositor)

Diurnal Mercury in Libra, or Taurus dispositing to Venus, may be desperate to avoid confrontation, but as munakara is by its very nature contentious, any moves to be the 'peacekeeper' are likely to be seen as a sign of weakness or worse, an act of manipulation. Diurnal Mercury in munakara in Venus' signs can be sensitive to rumours about the person's romantic liaisons and this can lead to social awkwardness or the feeling of having to watch one's words in case they are misinterpreted. Munakara Mercury disposited by Venus may indicate social awkwardness, whether that is uncomfortable conversations with friends about personal topics or small talk in a large room with strangers.

Munakara Mercury's hindrance to clear communication may also be speaking in a second language, as complex nuances, phrases and humour rarely translate well. The chart below (*Fig. 4.1*) belongs to the Spanish actor Penelope Cruz, who has diurnal Mercury in munakara. The adjustment of her career from Spain to the United States brought with it the challenge that her language and mannerisms effectively stalled her career advancement. Luckily the very nature of contention is to keep getting up when knocked down and fighting for a better outcome, regardless of the obstacles and personal cost.

Chapter Four • *Mercury in Munakara*

Diurnal Taurus Mercury in Munakara – Penelope Cruz

Spanish actor Penelope Cruz was born on 28th April 1974. Cruz was born during the seven-day period in 1974 when diurnal Mercury in Taurus was in munakara, only the sixth time this occurred since 1900 (*Table 4.6*).

Cruz's munakara Mercury is 2° away from her Aries Ascendant in late degrees, and Mercury is a highly visible planet placed so close to the chart's rising degree. In a Whole Sign chart munakara Mercury moves to the 2nd house, the house of finances. For the Spanish-born-and-raised actor, the language barrier hindered her career choices and stretched her finances as she tried to move from a series of successful Spanish films to the highly competitive US film industry.

Munakara Mercury's rulership of the 2nd house in the Placidus chart would confirm her financial struggles in finding enough work to support herself whilst trying to establish her career as an actor in a foreign land. The Whole Sign 3rd house with Gemini on the cusp further confirms Cruz's efforts and dedication towards gaining acceptance within the American film industry and her efforts to become a household name in the US.

Cruz' charm and beauty are shown by the strong position of Mercury's first dispositor Venus, in exaltation in Pisces. Her outcome planet diurnal Jupiter is in its sign of rulership. Cruz is the first and only Spanish female actor to win an Academy Award (for Woody Allen's *Vicky Cristina Barcelona*), as well as being the first Spanish female actor to receive a star on the Hollywood Walk of Fame. But fame was a long time coming, and many of her early roles were savaged by the film critics who criticised her heavy accent, her distinctive acting style and the unfamiliar nature of her onscreen presence, so different from her American counterparts. Both munakara Mercury's first dispositor, Venus, and its outcome planet, Jupiter, move into Cruz's Whole Sign 12th house, speaking of a difficulty to join mainstream Hollywood, which at the time was dominated by stereotypical blonde, blue-eyed actresses in leading female roles.

Cruz's Taurus Sun is also munakara and follows the same sequence as diurnal Mercury, making the two planets a duet in the state of contention. The addition of munakara Sun's conjunction to Mercury tightens the sextile to Jupiter, their outcome planet, and the ruler of the 9th house. The Sun also brings in rulership of the 5th house, the house of creativity and entertainment. With the Sun's trine to the Mid-heaven, Cruz's struggle for fame was assisted by the combination of Sun and Mercury.

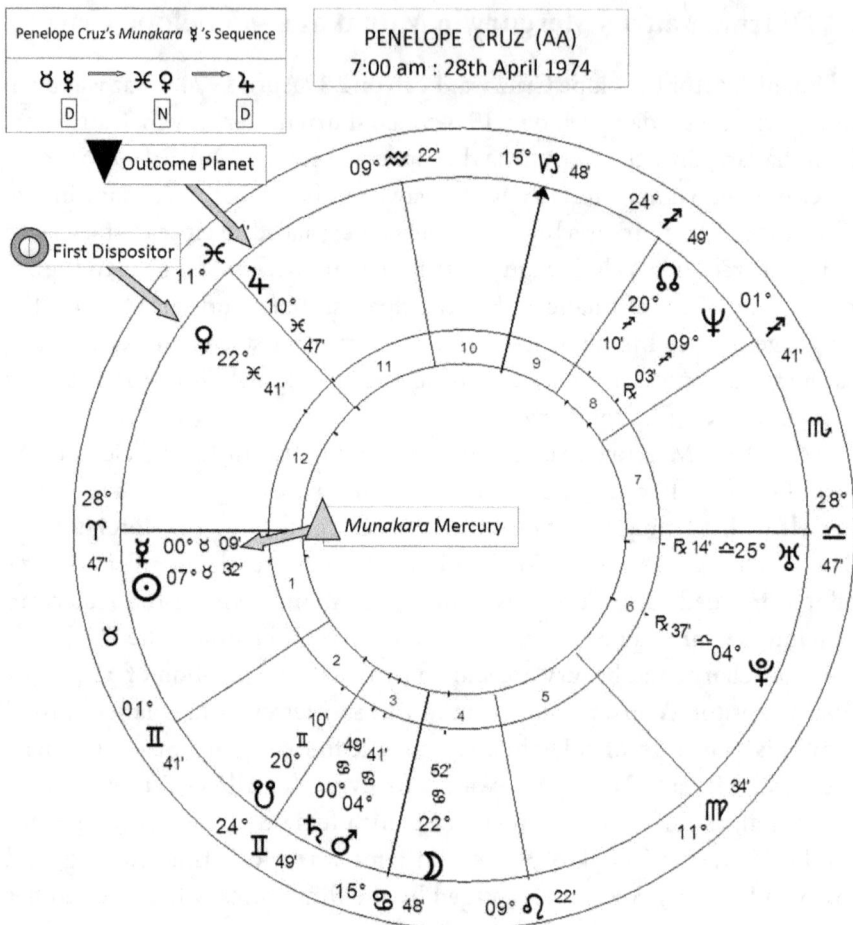

Fig 4.1: Penelope Cruz: Diurnal Mercury in Taurus in munakara

If Jupiter is involved in the sequence (as the outcome planet)

Jupiter as outcome planet for diurnal Mercury can cause a great deal of problems depending on which nocturnal planet sits between the two diurnal enemies. For instance, the Moon as first dispositor can focus diurnal Mercury on emotional issues or physical restraints that are exaggerated by Jupiter. The person may have high ambitions to achieve a goal but a physical impairment such as a speech impediment or a physical limitation can test Mercury's plan, and Jupiter's dream may be outside of the person's reach.

Chapter Four • *Mercury in Munakara*

Even when Venus' chances are slim for it to act as diurnal Mercury's first dispositor, it is possible (*Table 4.1, 4.3*) and actress Penelope Cruz' chart is one example of the obstacles placed in front of diurnal Mercury's steep climb to success when Jupiter's ambitions reach for the heavens. Venus as Mercury's first dispositor may indicate social barriers such as misunderstandings due to language, shyness and anxieties in social interaction. There may be a sense of unhealthy competition with women. Its enemy, Jupiter, can represent someone who takes umbrage at others' opinions and causes harm by broadcasting them or taking them out of context. Suddenly diurnal Mercury becomes socially outcast and this is damaging for reputations and bad for business.

Mars as the middle planet between diurnal Mercury and Jupiter is a volatile character at the best of times. To play this role Mars needs to be in Sagittarius (fire sign) or Pisces (water sign), and in either of these mutable elements, Mars is unpredictable, impulsive and easily stirred to anger. Small spats risk becoming huge dramas when Jupiter is the outcome planet. Neither Mars in Sagittarius nor Pisces is good for diurnal Mercury's tranquillity or peace of mind.

Example Charts:
- Caitlyn Jenner
- King Charles III

Nocturnal Mercury in Munakara

Diurnal Mercury may be inclined towards the advancement of research, education, commerce and networking, but nocturnal Mercury can also work to serve society in its own, more introspective way.

What does it mean when nocturnal Mercury is in a state of munakara?

The knowledge base and reasoning process for meeting goals differs between diurnal Mercury and nocturnal Mercury, which is highly attuned to the needs of the Moon. There are many ways to communicate besides spoken and written language, and nocturnal Mercury may be more attuned to pictures, images, symbols, body language and the cadence of voice rather than the words themselves. The last few dot points may be common challenges for nocturnal Mercury in munakara.

- Contending with rumours or gossip
- Cyber-bullying, misunderstandings or arguments
- Obstacles to clear communication, barriers in reading or writing skills
- Effort needed to stay focused, on task, or hold concentration
- Financial anxieties or frustrations in business undertakings
- Challenges in fine motor skills or movement
- Unresolved issues or conflict with siblings
- Creative or artistic disagreements that harm finances or contracts
- Questions on memory retention or challenges to events that others remember differently
- Social shyness or restrictions in speech or self-expression
- Desire to withdraw if feeling threatened or exposed in some way
- Need for clear definition between reality and fantasy
- Obsessive thought patterns or repeated conversations that lack resolution or closure to a situation

Table 4.7: Some possible expressions of nocturnal Mercury in munakara

Nocturnal Mercury in Munakara and Personal Challenges

Not every nocturnal Mercury dispoisted by a diurnal planet will end in munakara. The sequence might be broken when the first dispositor is in rulership, or is in Mercury's signs of Gemini and Virgo, or the first dispositor (diurnal) is in a sign belonging to another diurnal planet. Any of the three aforementioned situations will prevent the munakara sequence from occurring.

Nocturnal Mercury is usually well attuned to fulfilling the Moon's desire to provide an environment so that the individual feels nourished, loved and safe. Safety for the Moon is both physical and emotional and nocturnal Mercury is acutely aware of its role in supplying information to the Moon so that danger can be avoided, and emotional stress can be minimised. Unfortunately, Mercury and the Moon linked in a munakara sequence can often undermine Mercury's ability to provide that emotional assurance for the Moon. Nocturnal Mercury defends family or loved ones when it perceives them to be under attack but sometimes it needs to fact check its information, which is often subjective and based on perception rather than facts. Childhood is not the only time when nocturnal Mercury in contention might encounter learning or movement challenges as illness, accident or the aging process can slow the body's responses to the mind's requests.

Chapter Four • *Mercury in Munakara*

As one of the Moon's agents, nocturnal Mercury may display talents and skills that combine artistry with the physical body's abilities. However, a creative mind can become a mind plagued by obsession and nocturnal Mercury in munakara often needs the advice of a trusted friend or colleague to gain perspective and provide balance for their strong views. Despite being a trusted friend, munakara Mercury might be sensitive to criticism of their creativity or feel it is under-appreciated for its unique nature. Artistry is subjective, but if the dispute ends a relationship or ruins a business opportunity, then munakara Mercury may need to review its opinions. The first dispositor will be important to nocturnal Mercury's critical thinking process as the Sun, Jupiter or Saturn will deal with contention differently according to their condition in the chart.

Nocturnal Mercury in Munakara and Society's Challenges

Munakara Mercury is rarely interested in conformity, but nocturnal Mercury may need to be careful in placing itself too far outside of society's bounds. Isolation from others may be necessary to develop creativity and a unique view of the world, but it is not always healthy for nocturnal Mercury to remove itself from day-to-day dealings with others. Nocturnal Mercury in munakara may highlight a different process in memory retention, learning or reasoning, abstract thought, social behaviour or communication. These differences need to be encouraged rather than being seen as 'odd' or 'anti-social'. Part of the challenge for nocturnal Mercury in munakara is to guard and maintain one's individuality through design, artistry, humour, or writing, whilst still playing a participatory part in the community and in society. Individuals such as Kate Middleton, the wife of Prince William, may have to fulfil a role that is not necessarily suited to their nocturnal Mercury. However, if they can maintain their privacy in some way and have a healthy outlet for their munakara Mercury, then duty and personality should not be in conflict.

Some individuals with nocturnal Mercury in munakara may not have asked for fame or notoriety, but like Malala Yousafzai, they felt the need to overcome their natural reticence to speak out in condemnation of wrongs (in Malala's case, young women being denied their right to education). Others have been musicians and songwriters who have used their nocturnal Mercury in munakara to write contentious lyrics and music to ignite a generation and to record their own dissatisfaction with society.

Munakara in Theory

As with all planets in contention, there is usually a price to be paid for being outspoken, rebellious, critical or acutely observant and nocturnal Mercury is no exception to this rule. Finding one's healthy mental balance, searching for tranquillity, fighting one's demons at the same time as finding fame seems to be a part of nocturnal Mercury's challenges – challenges which are not always visible to the world.

Nocturnal Mercury's Sequence: Friends, Associates, and Enemies

Nocturnal Mercury's Table *(Table 4.8)* is an extract from al-Biruni's *Table of Friendship and Enmities* and shows Mercury's relationship with the other six planets.

D Diurnal / N Nocturnal	Essential Dignity Rulership / Exaltation (Mutual Damage)	Second Essential Dignity (Fall opposes Exaltation)	Second Essential Dignity — Borrowing Signs for Exaltation		
Munakara Planet △	Mutually Hurtful With (☿'s Two-Way Damage)	Injurious To (☿ Disposits Fall Sign)	Offering Friendship To (☿ Owns Exaltation Sign)	Asking Friendship From (Exalted ☿'s Dispositor)	Indifferent To ☿ - No relationship
△ [N] ☿	D Jupiter : Venus N ○ First Dispositor ▼ Outcome Planet	N Venus (♍) ▼ Outcome Planet	Neither Offers nor Asks For Friendship (☿ exalted in ♍)	Neither Offers nor Asks For Friendship (☿ exalted in ♍)	D Sun : Moon N ○ ▼ First Dispositor : Outcome Planet D Saturn : Mars N ○ ▼ First Dispositor : Outcome Planet

Table 4.8: *Nocturnal Mercury's Friends and Enemies (adapted from al-Biruni's Table of Friendship and Enmities)*

Associates of a nocturnal munakara Mercury: Sun, Saturn, Moon & Mars

If the Sun is involved in the sequence (as the first dispositor)

Munakara Mercury in any of the four fixed signs can be caught in repetitive thought patterns, and each element and sign ruler will have a different expression. The masculine fixed fire sign belongs to the Sun and Leo Mercury, regardless of whether it is munakara or not, can find itself digging deeper into fixed thought patterns, with the person refusing to back down when their knowledge or opinions are challenged. When this is also a nocturnal Mercury in Leo in munakara, then there are likely to be additional challenges which add to Mercury's distress. Nocturnal Mercury in Leo finds itself in a double bind as similar to Venus and Mars, nocturnal Mercury's job is to serve the Moon's requirements for emotional and physical comfort and security. Information gathered is meant to be for the benefit of the Moon, but when Mercury is in Leo it is in a sign belonging to the Sun and must show some solar qualities. Leo Mercury cannot help but speak out when there is injustice or misinformation, but this is very uncomfortable and sometimes dangerous for the individual with nocturnal Mercury in munakara. It is highly likely that when Leo Mercury is nocturnal, the Sun will be in Cancer in order for the Sun to disposit to a nocturnal planet – which is the case for all four example charts.

This particular sequence will bring the Moon back in play as nocturnal Mercury's outcome planet and perhaps it solves the question of whether nocturnal Mercury in Leo is meant to fulfil the Sun or the Moon's instructions. Should it stay true to the Moon, whose sect it shares, or follow the Sun's directives given that the Sun is the dispositor of its sign?

Either way, Mercury's contentious nature is likely to flare up when it witnesses a wrongdoing, and part of this particular sequence is the lesson that Leo Mercury's fiery nature must find an avenue by which it can find peace and be calmed once it has activated its passion to put things to rights. If nocturnal Mercury in Leo cannot do this as part of its self-protection mechanism, then it risks burning out and Leo Mercury is no use to either luminary. Nocturnal Mercury already has its internal dialogue but if in a state of munakara, it adds fuel to the fire and the individual may end up endlessly replaying old offences and insults to justify their actions in the argument. This is both exhausting and pointless, and fixed signs are not always well equipped to find fresh solutions to old patterns.

Example Charts:
- Edgar Degas (outcome planet, the Moon)
- Helen Keller (outcome planet, the Moon)
- Robin Williams (outcome planet, the Moon)
- Malala Yousafzai (outcome planet, the Moon)

If Saturn is involved in the sequence (as the first dispositor)

Aquarius is the fixed sign in the air element. Although the qualities of air are well suited to Mercury, there is still the problem of inflexibility as Aquarius's ruler is Saturn, a difficult planet at the best of times. Latching onto an idea but never allowing it to grow or develop is something which can stress nocturnal Mercury in Aquarius. Aquarius Mercury's mind-trap lies in its resistance to shifting ideas or incorporating new concepts to old or ineffectual theories.

If munakara is added to the mix, Aquarius Mercury disposits to Saturn, and Saturn uses its own nocturnal dispositor to fixate on where the thinking process went awry. If Saturn's dispositor is Mars, and Saturn is in Aries, then the combination of Saturn in fall and Mars as outcome planet, is extremely unsettling and challenging for Aquarian Mercury in its nocturnal state.

If Saturn, Mercury's dispositor, is in Cancer then the Moon will become involved and nocturnal Mercury completes its munakara sequence with the Moon as its outcome planet. However, Saturn is in detriment in Cancer, and Aquarius Mercury becomes awash with emotions that cloud its clarity, and affect its ability to be analytical, precise, and objective.

If Aquarius Mercury's sequence passes from first dispositor Saturn to Mars or the Moon, then Mercury is munakara, and the individual feels they have to fight relentlessly in order to defend their views. Stepping away from an argument is unthinkable, as ideas are concrete and real, and must be defended at all costs. The mind-trap deepens if hostility towards an idea sets in, and nocturnal Mercury may isolate or withdraw.

Venus is the third nocturnal planet, and Saturn in Venus's signs may be more diplomatic and provide an outcome where everyone wins and no-one feels slighted. Libra places Saturn in exaltation, and the individual may not be prepared to back down if Saturn's exaltation convinces them that they are justified.

It should be noted that nocturnal Mercury in Capricorn will still be disposited by diurnal Saturn, but nocturnal Mercury in Saturn's earth sign seems to avoid a few pitfalls that ensnare its air neighbour. Practical solutions and logical outcomes help Capricorn Mercury to avoid the Aquarian mind-trap, but other issues will arise for this nocturnal Mercury depending on whether the outcome planet is the Moon, Mars or Venus.

Example Charts:
- Neil Diamond (outcome planet, Venus)
- Chris McCandless (outcome planet, Mars)
- Dave Grohl (outcome planet, Mars)
- Cindy Sherman (outcome planet, Mars)
- Oprah Winfrey (outcome planet, Mars)
- Kate Middleton (outcome planet, Venus)

Chapter Four • *Mercury in Munakara*

If the Moon is involved in the sequence (as the outcome planet)

Any connection between Mercury and the Moon can produce a powerful and automatic physical response. That may be through the Moon in Mercury's signs or Mercury in Cancer – whether formed via aspect or munakara sequence. When nocturnal Mercury is in contention and its outcome planet is the Moon, any situation Mercury perceives as threatening or dangerous can provoke strong bodily reactions. Reactions such as increased heart rate, sweating, shaking and muscle tension are a warning to Mercury that something is not right and munakara Mercury needs to find a solution quickly to alleviate the danger.

The Moon was the outcome planet for Kurt Cobain's nocturnal Mercury's sequence. The lead singer of Nirvana experienced these physical warnings from a very young age. At age seven when his parents divorced, he developed acute stomach pains that dogged him throughout his life. Sadly, munakara Mercury's solution came through numbing the pain with painkillers, drugs, and alcohol. These may have contributed to his early death from a gunshot wound to the head, aged just 27.

Contention for nocturnal Mercury may be the inability to reconcile an idea that cannot come to pass on a physical level. Nocturnal Mercury completing its sequence with the Moon can mean challenges for the individual that involve the body's ability to either master, or relearn, any fine or gross motor skills. Illness or accident can be a part of the story for this munakara sequence as the Moon struggles to help Mercury find its equilibrium. Both Mercury and the Moon want the same thing – peace of mind and a safe place – but contention may upset the two nocturnal planets at either end of the sequence.

Example Charts:
- Edgar Degas
- Robin Williams
- Helen Keller
- Kurt Cobain
- Malala Yousafzai.

If Mars is involved in the sequence (as the outcome planet)

Mars is not one of Mercury's enemies, although it is capable of destroying the tranquillity nocturnal Mercury craves through Mars' capacity to create mental agitation. The diurnal planet in the centre of nocturnal Mercury's sequence will be in the signs of Scorpio or Aries, and its comfort in either of these signs may help to determine if Mars will be a help or a hindrance to Mercury. Nocturnal Mercury may not appreciate Mars agitating or inflaming a situation, but it may be necessary to go through some drama to resolve something that nocturnal Mercury is ignoring or procrastinating over. Mars is inclined to 'rip the bandaid off' and whilst contention is not pleasant for Mercury in some signs, it might be necessary for change to occur, or to make room for new ideas.

Example Charts:
- Chris McCandless
- Dave Grohl
- Cindy Sherman
- Oprah Winfrey

Enemies of a nocturnal munakara Mercury: Jupiter & Venus

Jupiter and Venus are judged as 'enemy' planets for Mercury because they rule signs detrimental to Mercury's nature. In the case of nocturnal Mercury, Venus and Jupiter have now swapped positions to those taken in the diurnal Mercury sequences. Jupiter is now the potential first dispositor, and Venus is an outcome planet.

If Jupiter is involved in the sequence (as the first dispositor)

Mercury in either Sagittarius or Pisces will be detrimental to Mercury, particularly if Jupiter is in a sign belonging to a nocturnal planet. Jupiter is the enemy. It creates problems for Mercury as the mutable fire sign and mutable water sign are inclined to fabricate their own version of reality. Nocturnal Mercury in munakara can already have an overactive imagination coupled with a tendency towards daydreaming. Munakara Mercury can be swayed by a rich internal world and when Jupiter is the storyteller, Mercury in Sagittarius or Pisces can begin to believe that the story is true. Nocturnal Mercury in Sagittarius expresses itself by the impulsive fire sign filling the story with flashes of drama or embellishing the facts to draw a bigger crowd. However, changing directions or altering the story midway is dangerous for munakara Mercury as it can lose track of the conversation and the individual finds themselves having to explain any discrepancies.

Nocturnal Mercury in munakara and out of sect (in a diurnal chart travelling with the Sun) may decide that communication is just too hard.

The individual with this statement in their chart will learn from past experiences that caution and keeping one's counsel is the safest way to avoid confrontation. The expected verbosity of Sagittarian Mercury is tempered by fears of being attacked or looking foolish. Mercury disposited by Jupiter is aware that a situation can escalate very quickly if the right words are not carefully chosen.

Under Jupiter's direction, Pisces Mercury (also in fall) explores the inner world of imagination, collective thought, emotive language and innuendo. For Mercury in munakara, contention means sifting through every conversation for missed clues as to what the other person was really saying. Information is subjective and all clues are examined. Body language, significant pauses, side-long glances, exaggerated facial expressions, silences, other people's reactions and comments – everything is under the microscope of debilitated munakara Mercury, ready to take offence, but not sure exactly where the nature of the offence lies.

Example Chart:
- Kurt Cobain (outcome planet, the Moon)

If Venus is involved in the sequence (as the outcome planet)

Venus' involvement in nocturnal Mercury's sequence is not restricted in the way that it is when it enters diurnal Mercury's sequence. A middle planet belonging to the diurnal sect will be in either Taurus or Libra. Venus can quite regularly be involved with nocturnal Mercury's sequence. Unfortunately, this may not be a good thing, given that traditional astrologers warned against the opposing natures of Mercury and Venus. *The Centiloquy of Hermes Trismegistus*, translated around 1262, is a collection of one hundred concise observations on astrology (aphorisms). Aphorism #6 states "Venus is the opposite of Mercury, who rules speech and learning, but she embraces pleasures and delights."[1]

Venus's sign of exaltation, Pisces, opposes Mercury's exaltation sign, Virgo. It perhaps explains the notion that learning and knowledge are incompatible with love and romance. Venus as Mercury's outcome planet can be a reminder that both planets are high functioning social planets, and that communication can sometimes go horribly wrong when one party is misunderstood by the other. Venus represents women, so may refer to comments which are belligerent, sexually suggestive, rude or unnecessarily personal. Nocturnal Mercury can sometimes seek to 'cover its tracks' with humour if inappropriate comments receive complaints. Bitterness can sometimes feature in these comments and the speaker, whether male or female, needs to evaluate if their opinions are coloured by some past hurt or incident.

Social isolation is not beneficial for nocturnal Mercury in contention, even if warranted by the individual's poor social skills. Venus as an outcome planet is likely to exacerbate any pre-existing anxiety, paranoia or mental health issues but sometimes nocturnal Mercury feels it is just too exhausting to connect with others socially and needs prompting, special care or support from loved ones to re-enter and engage with the community, the work environment, or society in general.

Example Charts:
- Neil Diamond
- Kate Middleton

Example of Nocturnal Mercury in munakara – King Henry VIII

Brief Biography of King Henry VIII

King Henry VIII of England was the second son of Henry Tudor (King Henry VII) and Elizabeth of York. He was born on 28 June 1491. He had an elder brother, Arthur, and two sisters, Margaret and Mary.

Henry's older brother Arthur was five years old when Henry was born, and little official attention was given to the second son's birth. Arthur was developing into a strong athletic child with good intelligence. All efforts were being made to mould him into a powerful future king. Henry, on the other hand, was christened and sent off to live with his mother and sisters in an all-female household far from his father's seat of power (Cancer Sun disposited by the Moon). He rarely saw his father or his older brother unless ceremony required his brief attendance.

In 1501, when Henry was 10, his brother Arthur married Catherine of Aragon. Arthur's sudden and unexpected death in 1502, when Henry was just 11 years old, placed Henry squarely in the unforeseen role as the future king. The following year in February 1503 his mother, Elizabeth of York, died giving birth to her seventh child on her 38th birthday. She and Henry VII had produced seven children, but only three survived to adulthood – Henry, and his two sisters Margaret, the future Queen of Scotland, and

Chapter Four • *Mercury in Munakara*

Mary, the future Queen of France. Henry, who had been raised by his mother, was devastated at losing her and an illustrated manuscript from the time, once belonging to Henry VII, shows the young Prince weeping into the sheets of his mother's empty bed.[2]

His father, Henry VII, was enveloped in his grief at the double loss of his first-born son, Arthur, and his wife and baby just six months later. Henry was closeted away and refused access to the court advisors who could have educated the untrained heir in his future role.

His father, Henry VII died in April 1509, meaning that Henry VIII became king at age 17. Henry was the first adult prince to inherit the throne peacefully from his father in almost 100 years.

Beginning his rule at age seventeen as a liberal king, Henry echoed the freedom of the Renaissance period. He encouraged fresh ideas, embraced art and architecture, learning and music. Henry himself was an accomplished musician and a composer. His 1518 Songbook contains over 20 songs and 13 instrumental pieces that he composed. However, what should have continued as a new Age of Enlightenment became instead a reign of fear, financial ruin, and religious persecution. Years of frustration and heartache fed Henry's mind and his suspicion resulted in him being increasingly isolated from his advisors. His decisions, unchallenged for fear of retribution, resulted in Henry's increasingly egotistical and tyrannical behaviour.

His first act as king was to marry his brother's widow, Catherine. At 23 years old, she was five years older than Henry. Catherine gave birth to a son, christened Henry, on 1 January 1511. The infant boy died within weeks. In 1516, Catherine gave birth to Princess Mary who later became Queen Mary I. In 1520, eleven years after their marriage, Henry and Catherine travelled to France for a two-week summit grandly named 'Field of Cloth of Gold' and recorded as one of the most extravagant and expensive European royal festivals in history.[3] Catherine turned 40 in 1525 and withdrew from court life.

Seven years later, Henry wished to divorce Catherine and marry Anne Boleyn. The Pope refused to annul the marriage, which drove Henry to break from the Roman Catholic Church and form his own Church of England, which permitted divorce. He divorced Catherine and married Anne in January 1533. Anne's first child, a daughter Elizabeth, was born on 7 September 1533. Less than three years later, Anne Boleyn was executed on 19 May 1536, having been found guilty of high treason against the king.

Munakara in Theory

She was accused of adultery and plotting to kill the king, both of which she denied until her death.

Henry's third wife was Jane Seymour, whom he married on 29 May 1536, just ten days after Anne's execution. Jane gave birth to the future king Edward VI on 12 October 1537 but died from post-natal complications twelve days later.

Henry's fourth choice for a wife was suggested by his chief minister Thomas Cromwell and Henry married the German princess, Anne of Cleves, in January 1540. The morning after the wedding night Henry called for an annulment and by July 1540 the marriage was over. On 28 July 1540, Henry had Thomas Cromwell executed for heresy and treason.

Henry married for the fifth time. This wife, 17-year-old Catherine Howard, was a first cousin to Anne Boleyn. Young Catherine was unfaithful to Henry and she and her two lovers were executed on 13 February 1542.

Henry married his last wife, the wealthy widow Catherine Parr in July 1543. Catherine helped reconcile Henry with his daughters, Mary and Elizabeth, and he reinstated them in the line of succession after Edward. Despite six marriages and many pregnancies, only one son and two daughters survived. Producing a male heir to the throne was a duty that weighed heavily on Henry, and he saw his difficulty doing so as a great personal failure and embarrassment.

Henry VIII died on 28 January 1547 at the age of 55, on what would have been his father's 90th birthday. His body was interred at Windsor Castle next to Jane Seymour. Henry was succeeded by his only surviving son, Edward VI who was nine years old at the time of Henry's death. In January 1553, at age 15, Edward fell ill and died of consumption on 6 July 1553.

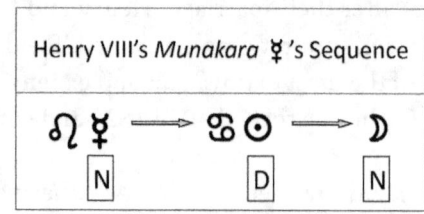

Table 4.9: *King Henry VIII: Nocturnal Mercury Munakara Sequence*

- **Key Questions:**
- What does King Henry VIII's Mercury contend with?
- What is its driving force?
- What is its trigger? What is its outcome?

Chapter Four • *Mercury in Munakara*

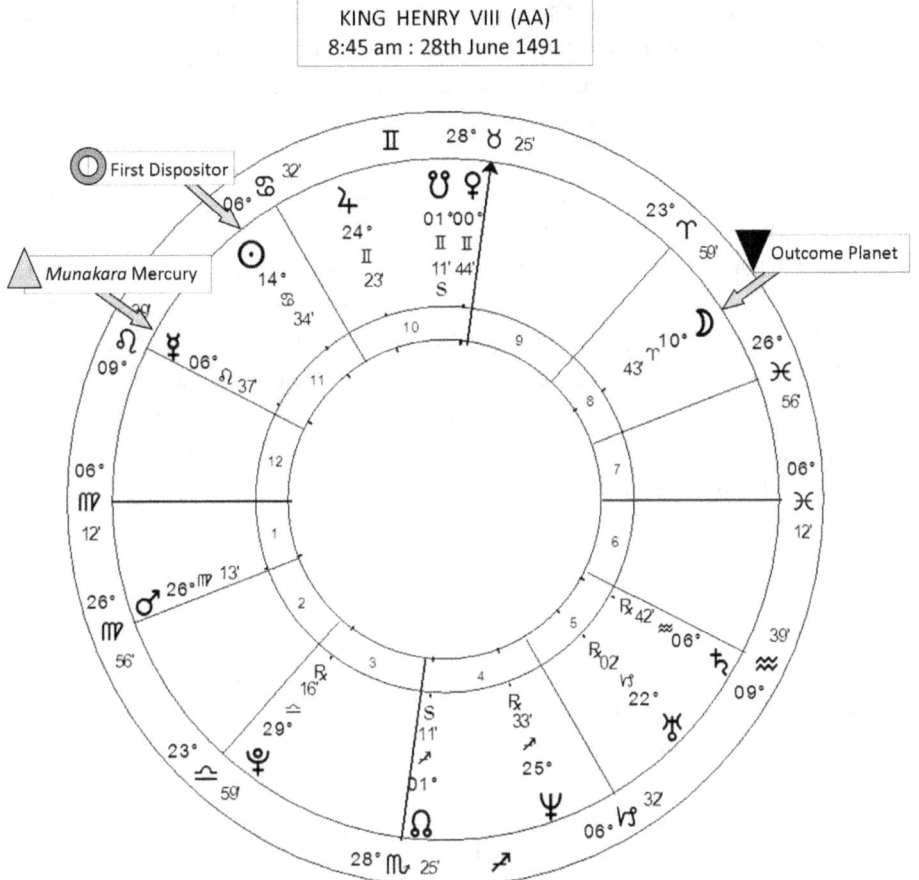

Fig. 4.2: King Henry VIII Natal Chart: Nocturnal Mercury in Munakara

King Henry VIII's munakara Mercury contends with his need to be loved and honoured, as opposed to his reality of being a king who is feared and ridiculed for not producing an heir for his kingdom. In another period a daughter would have sufficed, but in his time, it was a mark against his manhood, and a slap in the face from the God who had given him the divine right to sit on the throne.

Mercury is the ruler of Henry's Ascendant, and under a Whole Sign system, the angular signs/houses would be ruled by Mercury and Jupiter, both of which are planets in contention. Mercury in Leo is blind to its Ascendant sign of Virgo and has little or no control over its environment – not a good statement for a monarch in a land that depends on the King's good judgement. Jupiter's state of detriment in Gemini suggests that even though Henry roared like a lion, he mistrusted his own powers of reasoning, often ignored good advice, and wavered constantly, leaving his court in confusion, his Church without a leader, and his country in a state of religious and social devastation.

Henry VIII rarely took responsibility for his choices. Even though his chart carries Saturn in rulership and shows his determination to sire a male heir, Saturn's movement to the Whole Sign 6th house weakens its resolve, and its opposition to munakara Mercury (slipping into 12th house) demonstrates that hidden enemies were often influential in affecting Henry's decisions. The Moon as Mercury's outcome planet shows that Henry was not only too emotionally invested in carrying on his family name, but also too erratic, unreliable, easy to dissuade from wise counsel, and pompous (Mercury in Leo) to know when others were manipulating him to their own advantage.

Munakara Planet and Sect Condition – how comfortable is Mercury?

King Henry VIII's nocturnal Mercury is completely devoid of sect dignity (*Table 4.10*). Henry's obsession to have a son and heir (Saturn ruler of 5th opposes Mercury in contention) led his country into a civil and holy war, broke alliances across Europe, changed religious affiliations forever, and almost bankrupted England.

History records that Henry VIII directed the production of 55 new ships and created the beginning of England's permanent Navy. It shows that he successfully defended his country against French invasion in the last two years of his 38-year reign (1509–1547) even though he had provoked their attacks in the first place. Henry wisely delegated to three brilliant advisors, who best represented the strong Saturn in his chart. 'The Thomases' – Thomas Cromwell (Henry's Chief Minister), Thomas Cramer (Archbishop of Canterbury), and Thomas More (Lord High Chancellor) – were his three shrewd tacticians. It was their combined brilliance that saved Henry from losing his crown to foreign invaders.

King Henry VIII — ☿'s Sect Dignity			
Planet	Sect 1 Status	Sect 2 Hemisphere	Sect 3 Sign
♌ ☿	Day	With the Sun	Fire
N	D	D	D

Table 4.10: King Henry VIII: Nocturnal Mercury Sect Dignity

Chapter Four • *Mercury in Munakara*

There is no doubt that Henry was a headstrong ruler (dignified Saturn opposes Leo Mercury), but he was also an anxious, insecure man. He may have been better suited to a life of music, poetry, daydreaming, or hours of philosophical discussion rather than leading a country. In short, Henry's nocturnal Mercury would have made him a better second-runner prince, a 'spare to the heir' rather than pushing him into the limelight and expecting him to suddenly metamorphose into a mighty and powerful king.

Leo Mercury in munakara – King Henry VIII

"We are not only prince and king, but set on such a pinnacle of dignity that we know no superior on earth." – King Henry VIII describing himself in duality in a letter to William Benet (September 1530)

Nocturnal Mercury in Leo in munakara

Nocturnal Mercury can often have an introspective quality and can produce a creative and brooding individual immersed in a world of their dreams. Nocturnal Mercury serves the Moon and memories are linked to feelings, sounds, emotional experiences and images. When this Mercury is also munakara, opinions can be hard to shake, and early childhood impressions can affect reasoning and thought patterns into adulthood.

At the time of his father's death, still untrained and untested, Henry became the first English king in over 100 years to claim the throne without bloodshed. One of the reasons that Henry was unstoppable was that he made radical changes to the English Constitution, which greatly expanded royal power during his reign. Leo Mercury, disposited by the Sun, can be arrogant and self-serving if not reined in by humility or self-reflection. When manifested in a King who believes in his divine right to govern without question, his passions for a woman, who was not his wife, meant he ruthlessly abandoned the country's established religion.

Henry's munakara Mercury is within 1° of his 12th house, and this placement seems appropriate for a boy who unexpectedly found himself taken from virtual obscurity to ruling monarch. Mercury in Leo is in aversion to its sign of Virgo, the sign on Henry's Ascendant. Blindness between house and ruling planet can leave the person feeling as though they are invisible, or that their worth is unappreciated, or their words go unheard. Many of Henry's actions, particularly as he sickened and aged, escalated into erratic and unreasonable demands as he realised the male Tudor line could disappear with his death.

Initially Henry showed great promise and many of his contemporaries viewed him as charismatic, energetic, joyous and a welcome change from his serious and reserved father. Henry VII's withdrawal into grief at the deaths of his eldest son and wife meant that his presence was barely felt in the last few years of his reign and his son was seen as a vibrant young man who would re-energize the kingdom. However, the young new king's extravagances soon drained the royal coffers, and whilst he had a thirst for war, Henry's poor military skills meant defeat and significant financial strain from a trail of failed military campaigns.

Munakara Mercury is the ruler of Henry VIII's 1st house, and Saturn, ruler of the 6th house, opposes Mercury across the 6th/12th house axis. Henry's participation in an exhibition jousting competition in 1536 resulted in a serious accident which led to Henry's physical and mental deterioration. A leg injury refused to heal, becoming ulcerated and preventing him from the extreme physical exercise he enjoyed as a release from his royal duties and to remove the excess weight he gained from his large appetite.

Recent medical studies have theorised that Henry's behaviour in his later years could have been indicative of a traumatic brain injury, which it is believed he suffered as a result of that ill-fated joust. This theory may go some way toward explaining Henry's irrational mood swings, his inexplicable rages, and his paranoia, as his brain and body suffered from illness, advancing age, chronic injury, and disease (munakara Mercury and its outcome planet, the Moon).

First Dispositor: Sun in Cancer in 11th House

King Henry VIII's first official act as seventeen-year-old king was to marry Catherine of Aragon, his deceased brother's wife, who was five years his senior. The newlyweds were said to be well matched as they were both wildly extravagant and loved finery and displays of gold and silver. Henry's lavish tastes crippled the English treasury and his Cancer Sun – ruling the 12th house – shows the gathering of hidden enemies to plot his downfall.

Henry's chief minister, Thomas Cromwell, had been a prominent figure in engineering an annulment of his marriage to Catherine in 1533 so Henry could be free to legally marry Anne Boleyn. But this did not save Cromwell, when seven years later, he oversaw the king's disastrous marriage to Anne of Cleves in January 1540. Henry was bitterly disappointed that Cromwell had misled him about reports of her beauty, confiding in Cromwell that he had not consummated the marriage, saying, "I liked her before not well, but now I like her much worse."⁴ The marriage lasted six months and Henry had Cromwell arrested and executed for treason and heresy, later expressing regret for the loss of his chief minister, and blaming advisors for influencing his decision to have Cromwell put to death.

Henry VIII's Sun in Cancer disposits his munakara Mercury. Modern minds might not comprehend the urgency to produce an heir, but it should be remembered that this was the fledgling House of Tudor and recent history had only just placed this family on the English throne. The desperation to continue the bloodline led to Henry VII's six marriages and the old English nursery rhyme of *'Divorced, Beheaded, Died, Divorced, Beheaded, Survived'* has been handed down over the centuries recording the way in which the six wives of Henry VIII were dispatched.

The 11th house is the house of hopes and dreams. Henry's greatest wish should have been fulfilled through his Sun in the 11th house. But if his physical body was incapable of producing this desire (munakara Mercury in aversion to Virgo on the Ascendant), or his Moon (Mercury's outcome planet) is in T-square with Jupiter and Neptune) then all the wishing, beheading and divorces were never going to manifest in a male heir.

The outcome planet: Moon in Aries in 8th House

Mercury's dispositor, the Sun, is the second planet in aversion to its sign. The Cancer Sun is incapable of seeing the 12th house with Leo on its cusp. This aversion only adds to Henry's deepest fears that his name, and the House of Tudor, would die with him. A male heir was his one passion. The evidence of his wives' pregnancies, along with Henry's mental deterioration, has led historians to speculate that Henry suffered from McLeod syndrome, an X-linked recessive genetic disorder that affects the blood, brain, peripheral nerves, muscle and heart. Alternatively, Henry may have been Kell positive, which leads to autoimmune diseases that destroy red blood cells.

For all Henry's efforts to change his women, it seems that the physical fault lay with Henry. His Leo Mercury could never accept the fact that a ruler chosen by God could be the problem. It would have been blasphemy to suggest that Henry was the root of the problem in times when men held the power, and any country ruled by women was considered vulnerable to being acquired through marriage. In those times, the only way to secure sovereignty for the bloodline was to produce a male heir.

Gemini Jupiter in munakara – King Henry VIII

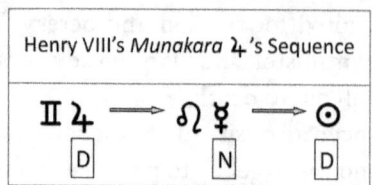

Table 4.11: King Henry VIII: Jupiter's Munakara Sequence

- **Key Questions:**
- What does King Henry VIII's Jupiter contend with?
- What is its driving force?
- What is its trigger? What is its outcome?

In the early years of his reign Henry VIII was hailed as 'a golden prince' and a 'universal genius'. Munakara Jupiter resides in the 10th house and is engaged in a T-square aspect with Neptune in opposition and Virgo Mars at the apex. On his ascension to the throne Henry was handsome and robust, competing and winning in the sports of the Tudor court; hunting, jousting, hawking, wrestling, swordplay and tennis. The fact that Henry was the first adult prince to inherit the throne peacefully from his father in almost 100 years was a miracle as far as the battle-weary English soldiers and his subjects were concerned.

Venetian Ambassador, Sebastian Giustinian, wrote in 1519 'He is the best dressed sovereign in the world: his robes are the richest and most superb that can be imagined.' With Jupiter elevated in the 10th house, Henry was eager to claim the title as the most powerful man in Europe. He loved pomp and ceremony and even his armour was etched with the figures of St George, the Virgin and Child, and exquisitely designed Tudor roses. Jupiter's detriment in the 10th house opposes Sagittarius at the base of his chart. For all his peacock strutting, Henry was ill-equipped to rule because his father (4th house) had overlooked the possibility that Arthur would die, and his second son might become king in his elder brother's place.

Physically, Henry was a giant amongst his people, not just because he was their king but because at 1.87m tall (6ft 2 in), he towered above most of his subjects. But beauty, adornment, and a strong physical presence were not enough to carry Henry successfully through his reign when Jupiter in Gemini disposits to another planet in munakara. Jupiter's sequence moves from debilitated Jupiter to nocturnal Mercury to the Sun, and for all Henry's swagger, history remembers him as a failure of a king, as well as the husband of six unfortunate women, and the father of two Queens with different religious affiliations.

All of these facts show Jupiter's presence in Henry's life. Henry must have felt a huge burden of responsibility given that his father had fought so hard to establish the dynasty, seizing the throne in 1485 at the Battle of Bosworth by defeating Richard III of the House of York. Henry VII had brought peace by marrying Richard's daughter Elizabeth but it was a fledgling and tenuous dynasty needing several male heirs to establish the lineage over time. Henry VIII ran out of time and opportunity. Henry's Cancer Sun, ruling 12th house, is Jupiter's outcome planet and Henry must have felt he was a terrible disappointment to his deceased father for failing to fulfil one simple task, that is, produce a son and a king-in-waiting.

Perhaps Henry would rest in peace knowing that the last Tudor monarch, his daughter Queen Elizabeth I, was a much better sovereign than he could ever be, despite being female and the daughter of Anne Boleyn, the woman who caused devout Henry to turn his back on the Catholic Church in Rome (munakara Jupiter in detriment). Elizabeth I outshone her father as a monarch, ruling successfully for 45 years, never marrying and handing her power over to a husband, despite pressure from several foreign suitors.

Munakara Planet and Sect Condition – how comfortable is Jupiter?

"God and My Right" – Henry VIII's royal motto

Henry's second munakara planet is Jupiter in Gemini in his 10th house. Jupiter rules the other two mutable signs of his four angular houses by Whole Sign – the 4th and also the 7th house of marriages. Henry's disastrous record of relationships makes sense given Jupiter's position in detriment and munakara. Jupiter's T-square in mutable signs with Neptune and Mars manifest in Henry's changing religious affiliations and his excommunication from the Catholic Church. Mars ruling the Placidus 9th house shows Henry's

King Henry VIII — ♃'s Sect Dignity			
Planet	Sect 1 Status	Sect 2 Hemisphere	Sect 3 Sign
♊ ♃	Day	With the Sun	Air
D	D	D	D

Table 4.12: King Henry VIII: Munakara Jupiter, Sect Dignity

determination to wage war on the Church, and his unique solution of appointing himself spiritual leader of his own Church of England. However, munakara Jupiter's square to Neptune shows the breakdown of structure, spiritual despair, confusion. It also shows Henry's aptitude for playing the roles of victim, saviour and persecutor, especially where his marriages were concerned. Henry felt he was the fatherless victim, persecuted by younger women, the perceived saviour of his people (at least in his mind), but also the persecutor of anyone who was loyal to the Roman Catholic Church.

Henry's feeling of being justified in his actions, no matter how cruel or destructive, is shown by Jupiter being in *hayz*, that is, complying to all three rules of planetary sect. Jupiter is completely supported in its sect condition and so far as Henry was concerned he had been ordained by God and any form of religion could be determined by him without interference from the Church or anyone else.

Further Delineations of Diurnal Mercury in Munakara
John Glenn, Caitlyn Jenner & Mark Ruffalo

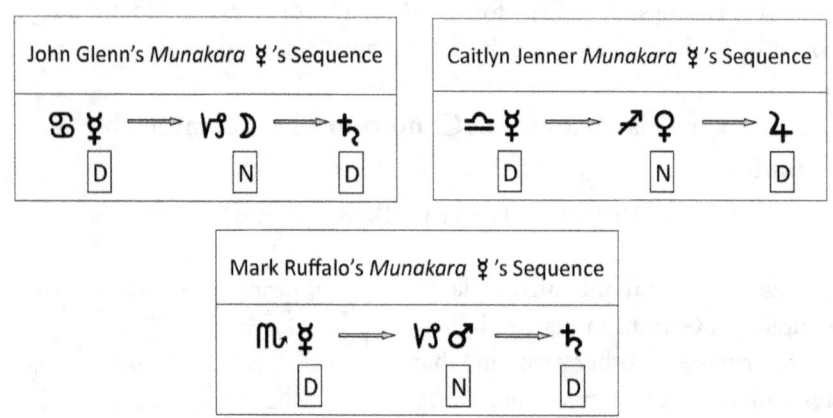

Table 4.13: *Munakara Tables for Diurnal Mercury*

Astronaut John Glenn, social media personality Caitlyn Jenner, and actor Mark Ruffalo have diurnal Mercury in three different signs ruled by three different nocturnal planets.

John Glenn has Cancer Mercury disposited by Capricorn Moon ending in Saturn as its outcome planet. Caitlyn Jenner has Libra Mercury disposited by Sagittarius Venus going to Jupiter. Mark Ruffalo has Scorpio Mercury disposited by Capricorn Mars with Saturn as the outcome planet.

All three individuals are groundbreakers for different reasons. Their names are household names, and fame has called them to play a unique role in society. Two first dispositors are in the sign of Capricorn, and for one planet, it signals debility, whilst the other celebrates its exaltation. Either way, both diurnal Mercury sequences finish with Saturn as diurnal Mercury's outcome planet.

All three of these delineations of diurnal Mercury in munakara can be found in Part Two of the book in Munakara Mercury's Delineations.

Further Delineations of Nocturnal Mercury in Munakara Kurt Cobain & Dave Grohl

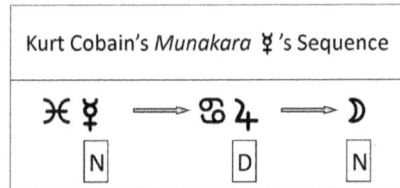
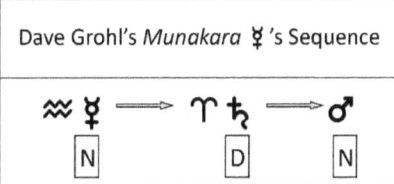

Table 4.14: Munakara Tables for Nocturnal Mercury

The two examples shown for nocturnal Mercury in munakara are the charts of creative individuals whose contentious Mercury helped to form their personality and tell something of their lives lived with Mercury in munakara. Both men are creative in their own way, but all will not be remembered in history for their creativity.

The 'spokesman of Generation X', musician Kurt Cobain, created iconic grunge music but had inner demons which destroyed his mental and physical health, and ultimately led to his death, aged just 27.

Musicians Kurt Cobain and fellow musician David Grohl were both members of the supergroup *Nirvana*. Together they created *Nevermind*, the 1991 album which became one of the most iconic albums in rock music history. Dave Grohl survived the breakup of *Nirvana* and avoided the same fate as his fellow band member, continuing his career in the music industry by forming his own group, *The Foo Fighters*.

Grohl's nocturnal Mercury is in the fixed air sign belonging to Saturn, and its sequence involves Saturn in fall disposited by Mars. At first glance,

Grohl's is a very troubling nocturnal Mercury's sequence, yet he is a good example of not allowing difficult astrological signatures to dictate one's life choices.

The charts of Kurt Cobain and David Grohl are examined in detail in Part Two in Munakara Mercury's Delineations.

CHAPTER FIVE
Venus in Munakara

What does it mean when Venus is in a state of munakara?

- A 'rebellious woman'
- Desire for popularity, social connection, or public acceptance
- Can be a separating force when peace-keeping attempts fail
- Perceived or genuine attacks or criticism from others
- Possible scandals, gossip, intrigues attracting attention
- Unwelcome advances of a sexual nature
- Complications in friendships or relationships
- Quest for pleasure accompanied by guilt or self-denial
- Misunderstandings with women, poor opinion or lack of trust of women
- Defender or custodian of women badly treated or shunned by society

Table 5.1: Some possible expressions of Venus in munakara

Munakara Venus and Personal Challenges

Venus represents the ability to negotiate in the face of conflict, preferring to make concessions and find a mutually beneficial solution through compromise. Whilst this is still true in theory for munakara Venus, finding a happy medium does not come easily to a planet in contention, and Venus is no exception. Munakara Venus tends to lose its flexibility when pressured by the two other planets in its sequence, and instead of calming troubled waters, it seems to inflame and worsen the situation. Venus in the signs of the Sun, Jupiter or Saturn can take an unpopular stand, and when a third planet is introduced through Venus' sequence, tranquillity is unlikely in its dealings with others.

As with all planets, munakara Venus will have different expressions in the charts of men and women. The male with munakara Venus may find himself in situations where he is challenged by strong or powerful women. He may find that past experiences or provocation overly colour his attitudes, which result in his behaviour or opinions being outdated or inflammatory.

In a woman's chart, munakara Venus can become complicated as the individual grows to feel comfortable with her body, safe to express her sexuality, and free to find her own version of femininity all within societal constraints. Women are not always kind to other women and life can be lonely for a woman with munakara Venus if she does not find others who are also willing to fight the unspoken code of 'how a woman is expected to behave'. Attacks from females who make judgements based on their own narrow views or the restrictions placed on them in their own lives are particularly hurtful for munakara Venus.

Munakara Venus is sensitive to social inconsistencies, either through personal experience or through observation of others being treated unfairly. Venus' sequence will influence the individual's experiences and observations with the outcome planet likely to show the response and the trigger for Venus' discomfort. For instance, comedian Billy Connolly has munakara Venus with the Moon as Venus' outcome planet. He uses comedy to soften the harsh edges of his observations about social inconsistencies. Entertainment has been his vehicle for finding his place where he is accepted and loved by audiences across the world.

In contrast, the adventurer Christopher McCandless (subject of the book *Into the Wild*), had Mars as Venus' outcome planet. He shunned intimacy and social engagement in his short life, yet one of his last messages was "Happiness is only real, when shared." McCandless' story spoke to a generation disillusioned by society's need to keep consuming and his choice to live outside the safety of society's rules struck a chord for many others who felt the same pressure to conform to familial or societal expectations. For McCandless his munakara Venus became a battle to survive (Mars as outcome planet) as this note in his diary shows: "It is the experiences, the great triumphant joy of living to the fullest extent in which real meaning is found. God it's great to be alive!"

Chapter Five • *Venus in Munakara*

Morning Venus and Evening Venus

Venus is a nocturnal planet, an agent of the Moon. It moulds itself to fill awkward or unsafe spaces with beauty, soft edges, laughter, colour and love. Venus makes the space worthwhile and gives it value, not value that fills bank accounts, but value through peace, harmony and kindness towards others. Venus will favour compliance, but it must be compliant by choice, otherwise all the joy leaves Venus and compliance becomes oppression. In the past these qualities have often been projected onto the female population as society expects women to be best equipped to meet Venus' requirements. But this is no longer the case in modern times and Venus can just as easily be expressed by any gender.

The relationship between Venus and the other planets is given below in the section on Friends, Associates and Enemies. Each one will hint as to how Venus will find and fill space to assist the Moon in its quest for physical or emotional security. Relationships are often described as 'complicated' and munakara Venus is the queen of complicated relationships.

Unlike Mercury, Venus does not shift sect alliance when placed ahead or behind the Sun, and it will always remain a nocturnal planet. However, Venus will have a more masculine expression when it rises ahead of the Sun and will be very feminine when it follows the Sun. According to Robert Hand,

> In Babylonian astrology, a morning star Venus was considered to be a warrior goddess (Ishtar of Akkad, a goddess of war), whereas the evening star Venus was the very feminine goddess of love (Ishtar of Uruk, goddess of the sensual life and priestess of the gods). This idea is preserved in later associations with Latin version of the Greek name for the morning star Venus, Phosphorus, which in Latin is Lucifer ('light-bringer').[1]

It may be that Venus, like Mercury, changes its focus and alters the expression of its munakara nature according to its position in relation to the Sun. Therefore, it is likely that morning star Venus will have a different experience of contention than its evening star counterpart. If this is true, then the expected behaviour for morning star munakara Venus will be to turn and fight its opponents, as its nature is more war-like. On the other hand, evening star munakara Venus may choose to solve its issues through more covert methods, keeping hidden or withdrawing into another world to escape, or using compromise rather than confrontation to deal with its contentious issues.

There are fourteen charts in the book with munakara Venus. Of these fourteen examples, munakara Venus is a morning star for eight charts and an evening star for six charts.

The eight morning star Venus charts belong to:

- (Prince Consort) Albert
- Tee Corrine
- John Glenn
- Christopher McCandless
- Cindy Sherman
- (Lord) Tennyson
- Amy Winehouse
- Oprah Winfrey

The six evening star Venus charts belong to:

- Kurt Cobain
- Billy Connolly
- (Prince) George
- LeBron James
- Janis Joplin
- Malala Yousafzai

For the purposes of this introductory work on munakara I have noted these differences but not fully explored them. I believe more work needs to be done on this subject of morning and evening Venus's in munakara.

Munakara Venus and Societal Challenges

*"It is better to live in a corner on the roof than to share a house with a **contentious** woman."* – Book of Proverbs, 21:09 and 25:24

While traditional societal gender roles for women vary around the world, many are strongly based on the importance of gentle, nurturing qualities and compliance with the decisions and actions of men in their lives (fathers, brothers, husbands, etc.). For a woman with munakara Venus, compliance and contention are principles at odds and she may find her behaviour invites unflattering labels such as 'shrewish', 'prickly', 'difficult', 'selfish', and most hurtful of all, 'unfeminine'.

In a man's chart, munakara Venus can present itself as a male who seeks these qualities in a woman, and is attracted to a strong-willed opinionated mate, or their partner is contentious because they differ from the women in his family. He may choose a same-sex partner thereby confronting the family's ideals of traditional relationships. Munakara Venus is drawn to challenge the bounds of familial or societal comfort, and Venus in contention is going to highlight the topic of women and relationships. Alternatively, it may see the individual carry negative views of women or their role in society. Their personal experiences of women may have resulted in rejection, bitterness, or disappointment. Interactions with powerful women may be tinged with fear, rather than respect.

Munakara Venus and Sect Dignity

In his writings al-Biruni makes it abundantly clear that sect dignity and munakara are inseparable, and for this reason, one technique cannot be examined without the other. Together they tell the combined story of a planet's capacity for its nature to be expressed through its most compatible environment.

It would make sense to say that Venus is highly sensitive to its environment given that Venus relies heavily on the five basic human senses that can be traced back to Aristotle's *De Anima* (*On the Soul*). Taste, smell, vision, hearing, and touch allow us to keep track of our body's relationship to space and as a nocturnal planet Venus is very much dependent on these five senses to aid the Moon's protection of its physical space.

Venus gains enormous pleasure from categorising taste into sweet, sour, bitter, salty or savoury. Venus abhors the sight of ugliness, disorder, or chaos and will do everything in its power to restore order, symmetry and beauty to its surroundings. Unpleasant smells disturb Venus and trigger a response to identify or mask the offending scent. Discordant sound irritates Venus, a lover of musical harmony and soothing tones. If something in Venus' environment does not feel 'right' Venus will instinctively recoil to remove itself from the distasteful object.

Problems start to arise for Venus when the Sun is high in the sky and Venus' close proximity to the Sun (maximum of 45–47° either side) means that mid-day births will automatically cause Venus to be out of sect. At its greatest elongation Venus is less than two signs away from the Sun and Venus in a diurnal chart (Sect Rule 1), travelling in the same hemisphere as the Sun (Sect Rule 2) is way out of its comfort zone. In response to an unfavourable environment, the goddess of war (Venus ahead of the Sun) becomes increasingly hostile and war-like. The goddess of love (Venus behind the Sun) has very little opportunity to express its more languorous side in a daytime chart and unfair accusations of laziness, daydreaming or self-indulgence abound for this Venus that prefers the night-time.

In his 1995 booklet *Night & Day*, Robert Hand states that ancient writers believed Venus in a diurnal chart "…behaved in a manner that was not appropriate to Venus (or to women either for that matter, at least from the point of view of the ancients)" and that it indicates "…a rather strong kind of feminine sexuality which in a traditional patriarchal society would incline a female native towards immorality and lascivious behaviour."[2]

Hand adds his own observations that he has seen no evidence of this, but that the modern translation is an out of sect Venus in a woman's chart is someone "…who would have difficulty accepting the traditional female role either in society or in sexual relationships."[3] According to Hand, Venus in sect [*that is, in a nocturnal chart (Sect Rule 1) and travelling in the opposite hemisphere to the Sun (Sect Rule 2)*] is "…the more traditional Venus, soft, feminine, etc.".

Twenty years after publishing the *Night & Day*, Robert Hand conducted a webinar that showed the evolution of his thoughts on planetary sect. In the 2015 webinar, Hand introduced a scoring system similar to the one for Essential Dignities and he recommended it as a possibility to define the degree of sect dignity for the planets. The more 'in sect' a planet was through conforming to the three rules of sect, the higher score it achieved in his number system.

Hand stated that when Venus scored highly by chart and hemisphere it enriched "…Venus' capacity for peace and harmony, its femininity, and its ability to draw people together in love."[4] However, according to Hand, when Venus scored poorly (severely out of sect) it was more masculine and in keeping with the Sun's principles. To quote Hand, "Venus in the day gives love on condition and is more self-centred, will be more interested in receiving love than giving it, and is the self-indulgent Venus."[5]

In other words, Venus scoring highly, in *halb* or *hayz*, is expected to be more yielding, more sensitive to others' needs, more 'feminine', more reflective of the mood at hand and keen to relieve tension or dispute.

Chapter Five • *Venus in Munakara*

But this description allows no expression if munakara Venus is a 'contentious' woman. The way in which we interpret Venus in sect needs to focus on Venus **in a place of comfort, a place of supportive environment,** rather than Venus in sect describing a woman compliant in nature and easily shaped to society's expectations. Nocturnality, whether by chart or hemisphere, should be complementary to Venus's expression and good sect dignity should show that the environment is one of comfort and acceptance and her surroundings give Venus the confidence to express her version of femininity.

Venus' Sequence: Friends and Enemies

Venus has connections to all remaining six planets. This says much about a planet that relies on connections, both easy and strained, to express its own nature. There are no 'associates' for Venus. Its two signs are taken up by other planets for their exaltation: the Moon takes Taurus and Saturn borrows Libra. Jupiter is a friend as Venus borrows Pisces for its exaltation.

Even though al-Biruni does not include the Sun as a planet that is injured by Venus, I have added it into the table as Libra is the Sun's fall sign. Mars is an enemy through the two planets' rulership signs and Mercury's animosity comes from the opposition of Pisces (Venus' exaltation sign) and Virgo (Mercury's exaltation sign).

D Diurnal / N Nocturnal	Essential Dignity Rulership / Exaltation (Mutual Damage)	Second Essential Dignity (Fall opposes Exaltation)	Second Essential Dignity — Borrowing Signs for Exaltation	
Munakara Planet △	Mutually Hurtful With (♀'s Two-Way Damage)	Injurious To (♀ Disposits Fall Sign)	Offering Friendship To (♀ Owns Exaltation Sign)	Asking Friendship From (Exalted ♀'s Dispositor)
△ N ♀	N Mars : Mercury D / N ▼Outcome Planet : D ○First Dispositor N ▼Outcome Planet	D *Sun (♎) ○ First Dispositor * al-Biruni does not list ☉ injured by ♀	D Saturn (♎) ○ First Dispositor N *Moon (♉) ▼ Outcome Planet * al-Biruni does not list ♀ offering to ☽	D Jupiter (♓) ○ First Dispositor

Table 5.2: Munakara Venus and al-Biruni's Table of Friends and Enemies

Friends of munakara Venus: Saturn, Jupiter, Moon

If Saturn is involved in the sequence (as the first dispositor)

Saturn, a diurnal planet, will be Venus' dispositor when Venus is in either Capricorn or Aquarius. Saturn befriends Venus, the owner of its exaltation sign, Libra, but the crossing of sect boundaries is not the only sign of tension between Saturn and Venus. The very nature of the two planets can be problematic given that Venus is geared to be highly sociable whilst Saturn often describes the loner, the outsider in social situations. By adding a third planet to the mix, unfair judgements or certain conditions may make socialising difficult, awkward or dangerous. Saturn can warn of restrictions, intolerance, hardships or bias against the individual and these conditions will test munakara Venus's patience especially if it struggles to find a place of belonging. Life may become tedious or feel humourless through Saturn's presence in Venus's sequence, and a close look at the outcome planet is a critical clue as to how a situation came about, and to determine how Venus lifts its saturnine mood.

The Moon as Venus's outcome planet can indicate challenges for the individual's health given that Saturn will be in detriment in Cancer in this sequence. Saturn rules afflictions of the physical body and its presence with the Moon may mean threats to survival, risky behavioural traits, or illnesses or restrictions that impact on personal or family relationships. Hopefully, illnesses will be brief and non-threatening given that friendships are trying to form between Venus and Saturn and some minor adjustments to life (through Saturn's discipline) may help the situation. Alternatively, Venus and the Moon should make for easier sequences when diurnal Saturn is Venus's first dispositor (Venus in Capricorn or Aquarius), as these two female planets are friendly towards each other through the lending of signs (Moon is exalted in Taurus).

Saturn in Aries will be in fall and Venus's outcome planet will be Mars. This munakara Venus fights against obstacles (particularly if Venus is a morning star) and Mars's placement in the chart, along with the houses it rules, will show the area of life in which the bloodiest of battles will take place. Chris McCandless known for pursuing a life of living completely detached from civilisation, became a generation's hero (Capricorn Venus) after becoming the subject of the book *Into the Wild*. Sadly, his Saturn in Aries showed foolhardiness rather than caution, and his death by starvation could have been avoided had he given more attention to Saturnian characteristics

Chapter Five • *Venus in Munakara*

such as common sense, preparation and self-care.

Other charts listed below also have Mars as their outcome planet. However, where Saturn is in Scorpio rather than Aries, these individuals have managed to use competition in their chosen career or sport as a form of discipline, a healthier expression for their munakara Venus dispositied by Scorpio Saturn.

Example Charts:
- Janis Joplin (outcome planet, Mercury)
- Chris McCandless (outcome planet, Mars)
- Cindy Sherman (outcome planet, Mars)
- Oprah Winfrey (outcome planet, Mars)
- LeBron James (outcome planet, Mars)

If Jupiter is involved in the sequence (as the first dispositor)

Even though they belong to opposite sect divisions, Venus and Jupiter are friends. Venus dispositing to Jupiter is more a warning to avoid excess than it is a serious issue. Too much of a good thing can becoming excessive and damages the body, especially as the Moon or Mars can be the outcome planet for munakara Venus. Even Mercury carries risks as Jupiter will be in detriment if nocturnal Mercury is Venus's outcome planet. Dabbling in illicit substances for recreational purposes can risk addiction, especially if there are underlying issues or no self-imposed boundaries.

Together Venus and Jupiter can produce good fortune by being in the right place at the right time. They may produce fame, popularity or adoration from the masses, but something needs to ground the individual and bring them back to reality. Venus in Pisces is in exaltation and if the individual is constantly being 'exalted' then there is a real danger that the person will come to crave the attention and will behave in a way that is increasingly outrageous. If Jupiter is in Cancer, it too is an exalted planet, and whatever hype surrounds the person is likely to keep building until there is a point of explosion in the person's life. Kurt Cobain had two planets in exaltation (Pisces Venus and Cancer Jupiter) and whilst Nirvana's *Nevermind* album is frequently ranked highly on lists of the greatest albums of all time, his planets' exaltation brought Cobain little happiness or peace of mind.

Comedian and comedic-singer, Billy Connolly's Venus is in Sagittarius so whilst his Jupiter is exalted in Cancer, he escapes the 'gift' of double exaltation that leads to munakara Venus. Both Kurt Cobain and Billy

Connolly have evening star Venus, and this may explain their love of music and their use of Venus in entertainment.

Example Charts:
- Billy Connolly (outcome planet, Moon)
- Kurt Cobain (outcome planet, Moon)

If the Moon is involved in the sequence (as the outcome planet)

The Moon borrows Venus's sign Taurus for its exaltation so they are friends. The Moon can add compassion to Venus's situation and the individual may gain great affection from those who idolise their skills in music, poetry or any creative pursuit. Both planets are feminine in gender, and they can have endearing qualities which draw people to them. However, they may also give a false sense of familiarity when the persona may be a facade that hides the person's insecurities or self-loathing. Millions of teenage girls adored Kurt Cobain and yet he felt himself to be so physically repulsive that friend and bandmate Krist Novoselic recalls "he [Kurt] talked about how ugly he thought he was all of the time. I remember one day he looked in a mirror and almost shed a few tears because he was so uncomfortable in his own skin. He was really insecure".[6] Cobain's munakara Venus is an evening star, and it seems sad that the adoration and love his fans felt for him and his music could not give him more self-love and self-appreciation.

When the Moon is the outcome planet for a munakara Venus, it will help the individual care for their own emotional needs, rather than constantly putting others' needs first. A Moon that is well-situated in the chart will help munakara Venus to ride waves of unpopularity, isolation or in times of difficult relationship issues. The Moon can also bring a more positive outcome to a distressed Venus that has lost its way, particularly if the body is well rested and healthy, and the mind is clear and calm.

Example Charts:
- Lord Alfred Tennyson
- John Glenn
- Billy Connolly
- Kurt Cobain
- Malala Yousafzai
- Prince George of Wales

Chapter Five • *Venus in Munakara*

Enemies of a munakara Venus: Sun, Mercury, Mars

If the Sun is involved in the sequence (as the first dispositor)

The sequence for munakara Venus in Leo can have two outcome planets, the Moon or nocturnal Mercury (*Table 5.3*). The signs either side of Leo, Cancer and Virgo, can produce a nocturnal outcome planet if Mercury is travelling behind the Sun. The maximum distance between Venus and the Sun is 45–47°, and even Gemini Sun is not out of reach provided Venus is in early degrees of Leo, and the Sun is in late degrees of Mercury's air sign.

Mars cannot be Leo Venus's outcome planet as the aspects from Venus in Leo to the Sun in Mars' signs are too wide (Leo squares Scorpio and trines Aries).

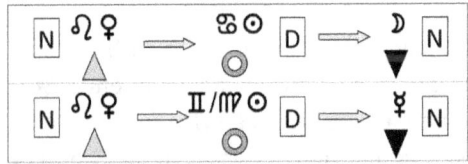

Table 5.3: Munakara Sequences for Leo Venus

Leo Venus in munakara is often an individual who takes a stand, defends a principle or protects their rights, particularly if they are female. Leo Venus in contention takes pride in being a champion for lost causes, in other words, doing the thing that everyone knows needs to be done but no one is doing. However, when contention is involved, there can be a blurred line between acting as a moral advocate and holding out for an impossible end result. We all admire defiance and grit in the face of huge obstacles but righteousness can border on obsession and gets boring when others have to listen to each tiny victory or defeat.

If the Sun, Leo Venus's dispositor, is placed in Gemini or Virgo, then Mercury will be the outcome planet, provided it is a nocturnal planet. Mercury is likely to get lost in the details and an audience, however sympathetic, soon tires of a monologue that places Venus at the centre as a superhero. The conversations get awkward and Leo Venus in munakara may clear the space to such a point that the individual feels isolated, uncomfortable or unpopular because others have moved to new topics, new causes, and new conversations.

Both Prince Albert and Amy Winehouse have Virgo Suns and morning star Venus's and when push came to shove they were willing to use their Leo

Venus to voice an opinion. A quote from the late Prince Consort Albert:

> Prejudice walking to and fro in flesh and blood is my horror, and alas, a phenomenon so common; and people plume themselves so much upon their prejudices, as signs of decision of character and greatness of mind, nay of true patriotism; and all the while they are simply the product of narrowness of intellect, and narrowness of heart.[7]

Amy Winehouse wrote lyrics that illustrated difficult themes such as heartbreak, depression, eating disorders, and addiction. "There's no point in saying anything but the truth. Because, at the end of the day, I don't have to answer to you, or my ex, or a man in a suit from the record company. I have to answer to myself."[8]

The Sun in Cancer will disposit to the Moon, and Venus will have included both luminaries in its munakara sequence. Sometimes this works well, as there can be balance between the solar perspective and the lunar landscape. For instance, success or popularity may be a desire for Leo Venus in contention, and the Sun might provide these benefits. At the same time, if the outcome is to gain empathy for a cause of a group of people ignored by society then Venus feels justified in bring this cause to light.

Malala Yousafzai used the BBC Urdu website as a platform for her Leo Venus in munakara to write on the denial of girls' education during the Pakastani Taliban invasion of the country. Malala's Venus is an evening star, and she had no desire to go to war against the Taliban, but circumstances escalated, and her life was almost forfeited as the price for her speaking out.

Example Charts:
- Prince Consort Albert (outcome planet, nocturnal Mercury)
- Malala Yousafzai (outcome planet, Moon)
- Amy Winehouse (outcome planet, nocturnal Mercury)

If diurnal Mercury is involved in the sequence (as the first dispositor)

The sequence for munakara Venus in Gemini or Virgo can have two outcome planets, the Moon or Mars (*Table 5.4*). The astronomical distance between Venus and Mercury at the maximum longitude is 76°, which allows for two-and-a-half signs between them. The only condition for diurnal Mercury is that it is travelling ahead of the Sun and can therefore be the first dispositor of Venus. If Mercury is nocturnal, it can only take the role of Venus' outcome planet.

Chapter Five • *Venus in Munakara*

Diurnal Mercury is an agent of the Sun, so it may be that Mercury takes the role of promoter of Venus's artistic or creative skills. However, as Venus is in munakara, it may need to read the small print where diurnal Mercury is concerned. The outcome planet will need to be examined as a creative Venus does not like to be hampered by terms and conditions when it is deep in its creative flow. Mars may want to break a contract that it feels is restricting munakara Venus and the Moon may find there are physical restraints or limiting expectations for meeting the delivery date. Gaining popularity or a reputation for your abilities is a good thing but in contention there are often strings attached when dealing with Mercury which is, after all, its enemy.

Diurnal Mercury follows the Sun's agenda and can be inclined to persuade Venus to ignore sexual innuendo or overlook discomfort or embarrassment. If Mercury is seeking promotion or advancement, it is willing to sacrifice Venus to reach its goal. These two planets are enemies and diurnal Mercury can encourage munakara Venus to make unwise, uncomfortable, or unsavoury associations for long-term benefit. If Venus does happen to be in fall, there are likely to be unpleasant results that involve the Moon or Mars. Either of these outcome planets will affect Venus's feeling of safety or protection from vicious commentary, or cruel personal vendettas.

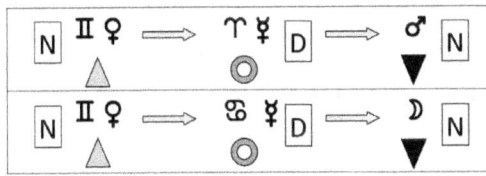

Table 5.4: *Munakara Sequences for Gemini Venus in diurnal Mercury's sign*

Gemini Venus does not suffer debility, but it does need to be careful of its words, and with whom it shares its secrets. Relationships, especially close ones, are based on trust and any indiscretions shared in private should not be shared with others as juicy bits of information. Unfortunately, munakara Venus in Gemini is not always discreet in its information sharing, especially where others are concerned. Munakara Venus likes to stir things up a bit so it can either sit back and enjoy the show, or more likely, offer its services as 'peacemaker'. The price for munakara Venus disposited by diurnal Mercury may be being ostracised from their friendship group for being an untrustworthy friend who meddles or spreads rumours for fun.

Munakara in Theory

Munakara Venus in Gemini can become easily bored in relationships and casts its eye around for something new and interesting. Boredom, predictability, or monotony is this Venus's kryptonite in relationships, and flirting with saucy double-entendre puns is its pleasure. The outcome planet will show where the problems of a broken relationship can occur. Whether it is the Moon (hurt feelings or emotional upheaval), or Mars (hot separations involving anger and accusations of betrayal and infidelity), it would be wise for munakara Venus to withdraw and contemplate its role in the heartbreak. Venus and Mercury can carry very 'young' energy, regardless of the person's age. If no accountability or responsibility is taken, then the problem of heartache may keep reappearing in their lives.

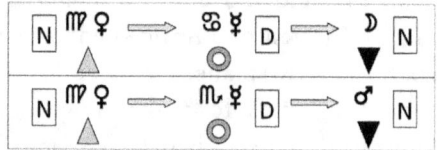

Table 5.5: Munakara Sequences for Virgo Venus in diurnal Mercury's sign

Virgo is Venus's fall sign and this Venus demonstrates a different disadvantage of being in the hands of an enemy. Munakara Venus in Virgo is inclined to dwell on comments made in jest or in unguarded moments of social interaction. What did the comment mean? Was it a friendly jibe or a harsh criticism wrapped in humour? Venus asks itself if it is being poorly judged, or if the statement was truly justified. Its behaviour will change according to the answer and perhaps also the outcome planet in its Venus's sequence – i.e., the Moon or Mars will react in its own particular way. The Moon will feel emotionally wounded and is likely to become defensive or withdrawn in the next social situation. This only compounds the problem as everyone starts to tiptoe around munakara Venus, especially since Mercury, the first dispositor in this sequence, will be in Cancer, the Moon's sign. Tears and emotional outbursts can add to munakara Venus in Virgo's distress, and the cycle gets locked into awkward silences and topics closed for discussion because of their sensitivity.

Virgo Venus in munakara can be overly critical of women in their behaviour, attitudes, or opinions. Venus's fall sign often indicates a woman who is critically judged by the community and even other women can be harsh if something about them offends or upsets society's expectations of their behaviour, their attire, or if the opinions they freely express are

Chapter Five • *Venus in Munakara*

alarming or confrontational in nature. This can be especially prevalent when Mars is the outcome planet. Mars loves to shock and create ripples of outrage wherever there is smugness or complacency. This is especially true when we consider that Mercury must be in Scorpio, two signs from Virgo, to produce a sequence that ends in Mars as an outcome for Virgo Venus in munakara. Scorpio Mercury is impassioned by principles and fascinated by revealing wrong-doings or revealing secret information. It also feels anger over injustice, especially when directed at a woman, and Mercury will give Mars ample ammunition to make others feel uncomfortable or defensive. Scorpio Mercury dispositing Virgo Venus is sure to break up a social gathering if Mars decides to call out bad behaviour, but as this is an outcome for munakara Venus, this kind of behaviour will cause Venus to feel embarrassed or lose friends who feel betrayed.

Example Charts:
- Lord Alfred Tennyson (outcome planet, Moon)
- John Glenn (outcome planet, Moon) (Morning star Venus in Gemini)
- Tee Corinne (outcome planet, Mars) (Morning star Venus in fall in Virgo)
- Prince George (outcome planet, Moon) (Evening star Venus in fall in Virgo)

If nocturnal Mercury is involved in the sequence (as the outcome planet)

Venus and Mercury may be at odds with one another, but nocturnal Mercury is a better supporter of Venus than its diurnal counterpart. Both nocturnal planets understand the need for retreat in order to heal, nourish, and replenish physical and emotional batteries. Nocturnal Mercury as the outcome planet for Venus is one way for contentious Venus to pour its energies into creative or artistic pursuits, but the middle planet in Venus's sequence may not help to bring these two energies together. Venus's first dispositor, whether it is Saturn, Sun, or Jupiter, will give insight into how Venus is challenged by contention. These options are discussed in the earlier paragraphs on diurnal dispositors for Venus.

Saturn in Mercury's signs may suggest shyness or social awkwardness for munakara Venus. The best way to deal with Mercury as the last planet in this sequence – Venus to Saturn to nocturnal Mercury – may be for the individual to find something practical to apply Mercury's creative gifts of song, verse, writing, or humour. When channelled towards addressing social issues, these creative avenues may also serve to alert others to a more widespread problem or to start the journey towards positive social change.

Jupiter in Mercury's signs will be to its detriment and can suggest that the planet known as the 'greater benefic' is struggling in some way to achieve its potential. Venusian projects may fail to get off the ground or get financial backing because Jupiter is not functioning on all cylinders. It may be that nocturnal Mercury is not suitably skilled at proposals, spreadsheets, or long-term visions to secure munakara Venus the fiscal help it needs to move the project forward.

Venus is often drawn towards expressing itself through an artistic outlet, but when nocturnal Mercury is the outcome planet there may be issues where money is scarce and artistic pursuits are hampered by a lack of funds. Alternatively, if munakara Venus represents a female experiencing periods of hardship, then Mercury, a mercantile planet, may be called upon to relieve the pressure by accessing funds or asking for help from siblings or close friends. Sometimes filling out the correct paperwork can generate income or a grant to assist munakara Venus to achieve its goals through some financial assistance. Creativity (Venus) may also go through a frustrating period of writer's block (Mercury) and the diurnal planet placed between nocturnal Venus and nocturnal Mercury may show what the individual needs to change in order free ideas and recommence their creative or productive activity.

All three example charts listed below were highly creative individuals who were challenged by their munakara Venus in different ways. American singer-songwriter, Janis Joplin was born with an evening star Venus, and she desperately wanted to be loved and accepted as a woman of worth and to have her talent recognised. She wanted to use her powerful voice to say something of relevance. Her teenage years were cruel years in which she was judged as unattractive and unpopular. Munakara Venus felt the scars of being unaccepted socially because Janis was different from the other girls in high school.

Amy Winehouse had a morning star Venus and she fought her detractors with comments such as "I don't care what people think about me. Never did, never will. Life is too short to be worrying about that shit."[9] Her music and lyrics reached many young women going through difficult circumstances, and perhaps her reality helped others to bridge their unhappiness and move to better times, kinder relationships, and healthier life choices.

The focus of Prince Consort Albert's munakara Venus was his all-consuming love and devotion to his wife, English monarch, Queen Victoria. Although Albert was a highly intelligent and sensitive man, he never gained

Chapter Five • *Venus in Munakara*

the respect or love due to him from Victoria's subjects. His munakara Venus' efforts to be accepted and appreciated for himself were met by derision and suspicion whenever he voiced an opinion in his German accent (Mercury as outcome planet). However, munakara planets are determined to meet any obstacle and Albert finally found acceptance through his Mercury's vision to create the first ever international exhibition of manufactured products, the 'Great Exhibition' in 1851.

Example Charts:
- Prince Consort Albert
- Janis Joplin
- Amy Winehouse

If Mars is involved in the sequence (as the outcome planet)

Venus and Mars are both nocturnal planets, and as such their role is to serve the Moon, the lunar luminary. However, they are natural enemies through the opposition of their rulership signs (Taurus opposing Scorpio and Libra opposing Aries).

Venus is about cohesion, it is constantly trying to connect and to keep that connectedness intact so that change cannot occur. Mars is the opposing force to Venus, endlessly motivated to destroy and drive a wedge in anything that has unity, so that something different and unexpected will happen. Both planets use their energy to either bring things together (Venus) or to drive them apart (Mars). Ancient Greek pre-Socratic philosopher Empedocles called these two energies love (Venus) and strife (Mars), denoting an eternal battle which ultimately neither force was capable of fully winning or losing.

The frustration for Venus is that ultimately Mars will win the contest as nothing is permanent in this world, in the elements or in life itself, so Venus must give way to Mars's demand to change. By placing diurnal planets Jupiter or Saturn between the two forces we start to see another barrier between the two planets that affects their battle in a different way. The Sun cannot be the middle planet in a Venus munakara sequence ending in Mars as the Sun will be too far away from Leo Venus in either Aries or Scorpio.

Jupiter in Mars' signs can add to thrill seeking qualities of a munakara Venus that includes these two planets. Jupiter does not hold back in Aries or Scorpio, a classic case of 'if the obsession does not kill you then perhaps it makes you stronger'. With Jupiter involved as the diurnal planet between them the potential extremes of Love and Strife at their absolute maximum and the personal cost to the individual has the potential to be devastating.

Cheyenne Brando, daughter of actor Marlon Brando, was born February 20, 1970 when Pisces Venus was disposited by Jupiter in Scorpio.[10] Her tragic story was one of violence and abuse, and her life was cut short at the young age of twenty five after she took her own life.

Venus in Saturn's signs, and Saturn in Aries or Scorpio will disposit to Mars, but Saturn in its fall sign (Aries) can be a dangerous intermediary for Venus and Mars, as a lack of caution or a respect for Saturn's rules can end in disaster. The story of the nomadic youth who shunned society and hiked across North America into the Alaskan wilderness in the early 1990s is told in the biographical book and film *Into the Wild*. The protagonist is Christopher McCandless and his munakara Venus sequence – Capricorn Venus to Aries Saturn to Mars – drives him to bind himself with nature (Venus), but it is a connection that cannot be physically maintained (Mars).

LeBron James's Venus sequence has the same three components as McCandless, but the story of basketball as his salvation is a much happier tale. His early life was exceedingly precarious (more Mars than Venus), but later in life his munakara Venus brought supportive friends and good people into his life through Saturn which is in Scorpio, not in fall in Aries.

The photographic artist Cindy Sherman and media personality Oprah Winfrey also have Scorpio Saturn and Mars in their Venus sequence and like James, their childhoods were tough, but the trio share qualities such as resilience, dynamism, and a passion that drove them to reach their goals.

Example Charts:
- Tee Corinne
- Cindy Sherman
- Oprah Winfrey
- Chris McCandless
- LeBron James

Queen Victoria and the 'Victorian Era'

England's Queen Victoria reigned for over 63 years and covered the last six decades of the 19th century (1837–1901). This period became known as the Victorian era and many of the stereotypes established in the Victorian era, especially for women, lasted much longer than the era itself. Despite the fact that Victoria was a powerful monarch in her own right, she nevertheless opposed the movement to give women the right to vote, calling it *"[m]ad wicked folly of women's right... forgetting every sense of womanly feeling and propriety."*[11]

Chapter Five • *Venus in Munakara*

Victoria believed in education for women but had mixed feelings about a woman's role in marriage, claiming "[t]here is great happiness in devoting oneself to another who is worthy of one's affection; still men are very selfish and the woman's devotion is always one of submission. Still the poor woman is bodily and morally her husband's slave. That always sticks in my throat."[12] The Queen's own example of her devotion to Prince Albert and her large family cemented the idea that a woman's responsibility was to love and respect her husband before anything else, and Victoria became an icon of late-19th-century middle- and upper-class femininity and domesticity.

Queen Victoria did not have munakara Venus, but her Moon was in contention and is explored in Part Two in the Moon's delineations. However, there were two men in her life who were unwavering in their support of her, and in echoing the beliefs, particularly on women, in her Victorian Era. Prince Albert, consort of the British monarch, was Victoria's first cousin and husband from 1840 until his death in 1861 at age 42. Prince Albert had Leo Venus in munakara state, situated in the 12th house and ruling his Taurus Mid-heaven and his chart delineation is featured below (*Fig. 5.5*). Albert's munakara Venus is a morning star and he worked tirelessly to protect and support Queen Victoria throughout their twenty-one-year marriage.

Lord Alfred Tennyson, was Poet Laureate during most of Queen Victoria's reign had Gemini Venus in contention, situated in the 1st house and ruling the 5th and 12th houses by Whole Sign. Lord Alfred Tennyson is one of the charts featured in Part Two in munakara Venus' delineations.

Chart Example: Albert, Prince Consort of Queen Victoria

Brief Biography of Prince Albert

Prince Albert of Saxe-Coburg and Gotha (1819–1861) was the husband of Queen Victoria from their marriage on 10 February 1840 until his death in 1861. He was the father of King Edward VII.

Albert was 20 years old when he married his cousin Victoria, with whom he went on to father nine children. The couple first met at Victoria's 17th birthday in April 1836 when she was already heir to the British throne. In their separate memoirs, both Albert and Victoria record that they almost instantly fell in love, but it was Victoria who would propose to Albert on 15th October 1839. His role as consort held no power or responsibility and rather than taking a public role, he was entrusted with running the Queen's household, offices, and estates.

Albert clashed regularly with Victoria's former governess, Baroness Lehzen, who, as private secretary and confidante, had enormous influence over Victoria before her marriage to Albert. Albert found Lehzen repellent, openly referring to her as "the hag", "crazy stupid intriguer" and the "House Dragon". He finally succeeded in having her dismissed in 1841 after the Princess Royal (Victoria and Albert's first child) fell ill under Lehzen's physician's care.

Albert was not popular with Victoria's court and Parliament refused her initial approach to grant him the title 'King Consort' due to anti-German sentiment and the reluctance to make Albert a peer. Victoria finally succeeded in granting him the title Prince Consort in 1857.

Prince Consort Albert created one of the marvels of the Victorian era, the Great Exhibition of the Works of Industry of All Nations in 1851 at the Crystal Palace in London. The Great Exhibition was an exhibition of culture and industry – Venus and Mercury in cahoots – held from 1 May to 15th October 1851 and was the brainchild of Price Albert and British inventor, Henry Cole. Albert worked tirelessly to bring his vision to fruition. The Great Exhibition was a self-funded exhibition, but much to Albert's relief it was a huge success financially, generating a surplus of approximately 200,000 English pounds. An excerpt from Albert's opening speech shows his enthusiasm for the project:

> Science discovers these laws of power, motion, and transformation; industry applies them to raw matter, which the earth yields us in abundance, but which becomes valuable only by knowledge. Art teaches us the immutable laws of beauty and symmetry, and gives our productions forms in accordance with them.[13]

Albert's support of emancipation plus his progressive ideas on science education, the welfare of working classes, reforms to universities, and modernisation of the military had an impact on Victoria and modernised many of her views. Victoria became more and more dependent on Albert's support and guidance during the years they were married, and she was devastated when he died at age 42.

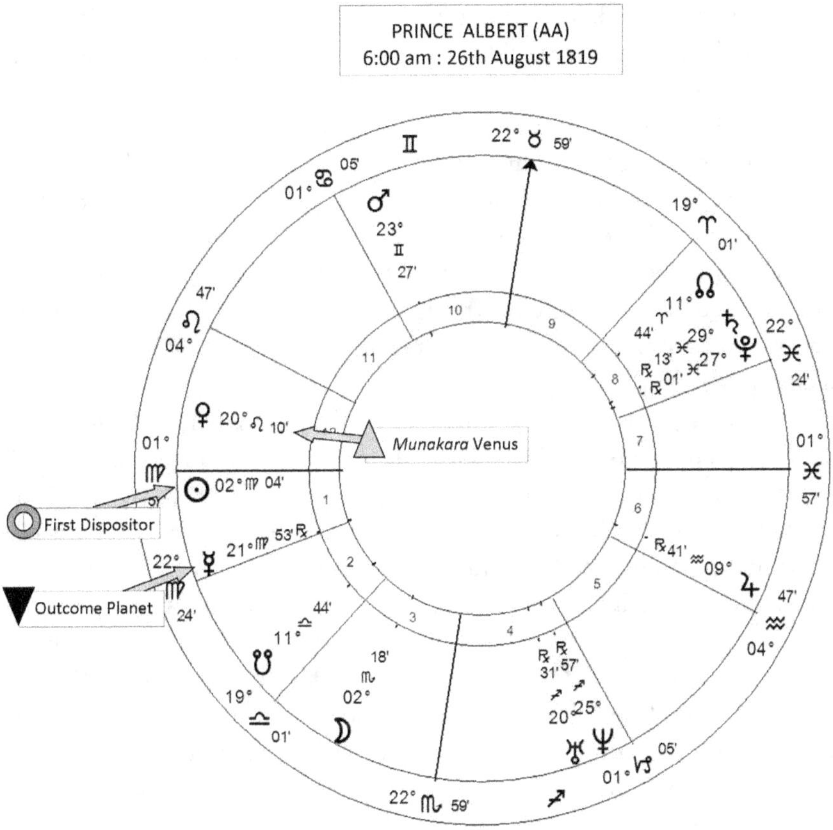

Chapter Five • *Venus in Munakara*

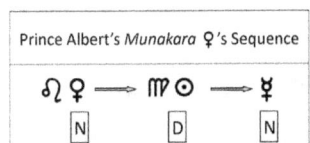

Fig. 5.1: Albert, Prince Consort Natal Chart – Munakara Venus

- **Key Questions:**
- What does Prince Albert's Venus contend with?
- What is its driving force?
- What is its trigger? What is its outcome?

Prince Albert's *Munakara* ♀'s Sequence
♌♀ → ♍☉ → ☿
N   D   N

Table 5.6: Albert, Prince Consort: Munakara Venus' Sequence

Albert's Leo Venus sequence for munakara is from the Sun (diurnal) to nocturnal Mercury. It presents as one of the difficult sequences for Venus. Its relationship to the Sun is strained by the fact that Venus' sign Libra is the

Sun's fall sign. Munakara Venus' outcome planet is Mercury, and it is not a great fan of Venus either, as both planets' signs are opposed to one another in their fall condition.

Prince Albert's first dispositor is his Virgo Sun which rules the 12th house. Albert collected a great number of enemies in England, though none were brave enough to show their faces and risk the Queen's displeasure. Most remained as hidden enemies who constantly tried to undermine his power over Victoria, but who could never outwardly oppose him. Albert was a diplomat and he was credited with persuading Victoria that the British royal family should remain above politics, resulting in Victoria winding back her open support for the Whigs party.[14]

The marriage in February 1840 to his first cousin must have created conflicting emotions for Albert. He truly loved Victoria and was immensely proud of her achievements, but his position in her court as Prince Consort brought with it hidden enemies, frustration at the loss of his own individuality, and a need to find purpose in his life as a separate identity from the Queen. Albert was a proud man and his contentious Venus craved acknowledgement for his skills, but with Virgo Sun on the Ascendant it must have been difficult for him to play second fiddle to his beloved Victoria. Secretly, he may have felt that ruling was a job better suited to a man (Venus in 12th house, Sun ruling 12th) but Albert was wise enough to know that his influence over Victoria would need to be carefully handled if he were to stay as her private advisor.

Mercury is Venus's outcome planet, and although Albert spoke perfect English (Mercury in rulership), his German accent was an easy target when the court wanted to label the Queen's husband as a foreigner. Virgo is Albert's rising sign, and Mercury is its ruler, so if for any reason for his English faltered – when he became angry, frustrated, or emotional – Albert became prey to others' spite and ridicule for something over which he had no control.

Prince Albert's Venus – Sect Dignity

Prince Albert's birth was recorded as 6:00 am so his Sun is less that a degree from his Virgo Ascendant. The Sun in this position makes it difficult to determine if it is a diurnal or nocturnal chart, given that it was almost autumn in Europe at the time of his birth. For this reason there is little point in discussing Venus's sect dignity in Prince Albert's chart if we cannot determine

Chapter Five • *Venus in Munakara*

the chart's sect. Venus dislikes its masculine sign of Leo, but we have no way of confirming if Venus was nocturnally placed (*halb*) in a nocturnal chart, or, if the Sun had risen and Venus was completely out of sect.

Leo Venus in Munakara: Albert, Prince Consort

"If you have succeeded in winning people's hearts by friendliness, simplicity and courtesy, the secret lay in this: that you were not thinking of yourself. Hold fast this mystic power; it is a spark from Heaven."
– Albert, Prince Consort

Munakara Venus in Leo in 12th House (Placidus and Whole Sign)

Prince Consort Albert was largely responsible for Lord Alfred Tennyson's appointment as Poet Laureate. Victoria became an ardent admirer after Albert's death, being soothed and comforted by reading Tennyson's *In Memoriam A.H.H.*. Tennyson was ten years older than Albert, but the two men shared a common theme: their fates were dependent on Queen Victoria, and both men had Venus in munakara.

Albert's Venus in Leo shows the nature of his wife's elevation, and although Victoria badly wanted her husband's title to be upgraded to 'king consort', the British government refused to introduce a bill to allow the title, simply because Albert was a foreigner and they had no desire to increase his power, even by title.

Victoria was born three months before Albert, on 24th May 1819, with Sun and Moon in Gemini conjunct her Gemini Ascendant. Victoria also had a planet in munakara: her Gemini Moon disposited to diurnal Mercury in Taurus, a sign belonging to Venus (*see Part Two in munakara Moon's delineations*).

Albert's Leo Venus in contention was well versed in diplomacy, and often he was better equipped to deal with foreign governments than Victoria, who was prone to using her Mars in Aries to bully her opponents, or to fly into a rage, when other countries refused to obey her orders.

The British Army was involved in two major conflicts during Queen Victoria's reign, the Crimean War (1853–56) and The Indian Rebellion (1857–58). By the 19th century, British monarchs had little power to call their country to war, but they had three great rights; to be consulted, to advise, and to warn, and aided and abetted by her hugely underrated husband, Victoria made full use of these rights to influence government policy. Albert served Victoria well when he convinced Queen Victoria to tone down her messages with both Prussia in 1856 at the conclusion of the Crimean War, and to curb her sharp response to the United States in 1861, thus ending conflict in the first case, and avoiding a new conflict. Her messages before his intervention were more an ultimatum than reasonable correspondence.

First Dispositor: Sun in Virgo conjunct the Ascendant

Munakara Venus rules Albert's Taurean Mid-heaven, and it soon became apparent to the court that Albert's advice was indispensable to Victoria, especially when he took the formal role as her secretary and the intimate role as her confidential advisor. The couple were reliant on each other practically, politically and emotionally and over their 21-year marriage they worked together as a highly efficient duo. Victoria was beyond distraught when Albert died in 1861, and for the remaining forty years of her life, Victoria mourned him by wearing black widow's weeds. Even after Albert's early death at age 42, Victoria made her important decisions based on what she thought Albert would have done.

Albert's meddling was extremely unwelcome so far as various government ministers were concerned, and his 12th-house Venus in contention with Virgo Sun ruling the 12th house, meant that Albert constantly battled the British aristocracy's covert efforts to ostracise him. Albert offended them with his severe moral code, his aloof professional manner, his artistic versatility and his desire to introduce scientific improvements at court. That they labelled him a German foreigner created the greatest tension (Venus rules the 9th house, 'the foreigner' by Whole Sign), with Albert able to do little to calm their fears or prejudices.[15]

Despite the upper echelon's considerable hostility and distrust of his 'foreign ways', Albert's guiding hand helped to mould the Victorian Era at a time when the British Empire grew to become the world's first industrial power as well as having revolutionary breakthroughs in the arts and sciences.

The Outcome Planet: Nocturnal Mercury in Virgo

Nocturnal Mercury shows Albert's sensitivity and artistic abilities as an accomplished musician, and as the amateur architect who remodelled Osborne House on the Isle of Wight. Venus rules Albert's 2nd house by Whole House, and by 1844, Albert had managed to modernise the royal finances to such a degree that he had acquired sufficient capital to purchase the property as a private residence for his family.

Munakara sequences can carry a phenomenal amount of energy. The Great Exhibition of 1851 was Albert's pet project, driven forward by his vision and passion, and was enormously successful and profitable for its six-month duration.

Prince Albert was often scoffed and privately ridiculed for his old-fashioned morals, and his puritanical attitude towards women (Leo Venus in contention). However, his attitude and disapproval of excesses and self-indulgence may have been in response to the circumstances of his childhood. Munakara Venus rules Albert's Mid-heaven and Mercury, its outcome planet, is the Whole Sign 10th-house ruler, so together they represent the house of mother. Albert's mother, Louise of Saxe-Gotha-Attenburg, was 16 years old when she married 33-year-old Ernst III. Louise was considered young, clever, and beautiful, but the marriage was not a happy union due to Ernst's many infidelities.

Louise demanded a divorce from her husband, but it did not go well for her, as Ernst exiled her from court and forced to leave her two sons, 6-year-old Ernst II and 5-year-old Albert, with their father. Louise secretly married her former lover, but their marriage was exposed in February 1831, and in the scandal she lost her children permanently. Sadly, six months later, Louise succumbed to cancer and died when she was only 30 years old.

Albert was very young throughout his mother's ordeal, but he loved her deeply, and perhaps he feared his own fate might be similar if the marriage to Victoria failed. Albert was said to have been extremely like his mother in looks, but the notoriety of his parents' sexual escapades left him with a strong moral compass that affected Queen Victoria, and helped to create a repressive Age that carried double standards on women and sexuality.

Further Examples of Munakara Venus: Lord Alfred Tennyson, Tee Corinne, Malala Yousafzai

Lord Alfred Tennyson was Poet Laureate during most of Queen Victoria's reign. His Gemini Venus is in contention, disposited by diurnal Mercury in Cancer. Munakara Venus is a morning star and is situated in the 1st house and ruling the 5th and 12th houses by Whole Sign.

Tee Corinne's Venus is a morning star, is in fall in Virgo, and Venus disposits to diurnal Mercury in Scorpio. Venus and Mars are not a good combination for first planet and outcome planet, and much of Corinne's

Munakara in Theory

artistic work is confrontational, focusing on female genitalia which is the basis of her artwork. Tee Corinne also has a diurnal munakara sequence, as her Scorpio Sun disposits to Mars in Gemini, with diurnal Mercury as the Sun's outcome planet.

Malala Yousafzai's Venus is an evening star in Leo and disposits to her Cancer Sun, resulting in the Moon being Venus' outcome planet. Venus and the Moon are friends in al-Biruni's Table of Friendships and Enmities, as the Moon borrows Taurus for its exalted sign. Malala Yousafzai has a second munakara sequence, and in fact, it is a duet with nocturnal Mercury also in Leo, and following in the same sequence as her Leo Venus: in this case, Mercury to Cancer Sun to Moon.

The natal charts of Lord Alfred Tennyson, Tee Corinne, and Malala Yousafzai are delineated in Part Two in the chapter on munakara Venus.

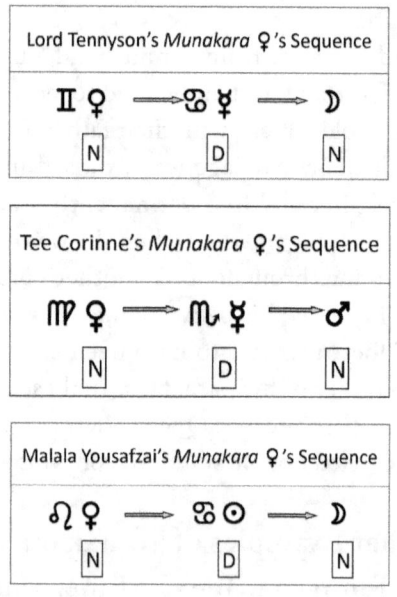

Table 5.7: *Munakara Sequences Tables for Venus Charts*

CHAPTER SIX
Sun in Munakara

What does it mean when the Sun is in a state of munakara?

- Perceived or genuine attacks on opinions, integrity or reputation
- Constant need to defend father's actions or feeling the compulsion to justify one's own actions
- Weakened energy levels or enthusiasm
- Difficulties in setting goals and maintaining focus, or achieving final successful outcomes
- Fear of criticism, public ridicule or humiliation
- Self-doubt concerning one's value to society
- Strong need to be praised or respected
- Issues with organised religion and/or questing for spirituality

Table 6.1: Some possible expressions of the Sun in munakara

Munakara Sun and Personal Challenges

First-century astrologer Vettius Valens begins Book One of his *Anthologies* with a description of the Sun and its areas of signification:

> In the nativity the all-seeing sun, nature's fire and intellectual light, the organ of mental perception, indicates kingship, rule, intellect, beauty, motion, loftiness of fortune, the ordinance of the gods, judgement,

public reputation, action, authority over the masses, the father, the master, friendship, noble personages, honours consisting of pictures, statues, and garlands, high priesthood, and rule over one's country and over other places.[1]

Put in simple terms, the Sun is the 'divine spark' that we all carry within us, a reflection of our own place where each of us acts as a tiny universe unto ourselves. The Sun in astrology is the energetic flame that warms our soul, gives us spirit and individuality and helps us to feel that our lives have a purpose.

Munakara Sun may challenge several representations that Valens listed. It may test the individual's physical or spiritual vitality, dulling the light and challenging the individual's sense of self-worth or self-identity. The individual with the Sun in munakara can find themselves feeling out of kilter with the world. Something seems off, almost as if the seasons are wrong. The light within struggles to shine with its full power and it can take a lifetime to separate one's own identity from the influence of family, friends, loved ones – in fact, every one whose opinions and behaviours have influenced the individual over a lifetime.

The struggle for authenticity is very real for the individual with munakara Sun. The questions; 'How can I be true to myself if I don't know who I am?' or 'How do I find myself without cutting all ties that influence my values or my beliefs?' can produce high levels of anxiety. Themes such as freedom and independence may pepper their conversations, especially where relationships or commitments are concerned, as munakara Sun values these ideals highly and is loath to forfeit them, even for a loved one. This internal discord may not be present all the time, but with munakara Sun there are likely to be periods when the individual feels uncertain about their identity. Frustration over the roles they are expected to play, uncertainty over their goals, or diminishing accomplishments, can be signs that munakara Sun is asking the person to pause and self-evaluate to move forward in their lives with a renewed confidence.

The Sun can be a representation of father, so Sun in munakara may add sensitivity to the subject of father, grandfather, or any male authority figures. If trust has been broken by a solar figurehead, then munakara Sun will feel bitter disappointment, not only in the person they trusted, but also at themselves for being in a position of vulnerability. Munakara Sun will hate the thought of others seeing them as the victim, as contention is generally a state of pro-active, rather than passive, behaviour. Munakara Sun will fight any labels imposed on it by others. For the Sun, munakara is the Sun's metaphorical journey from light (diurnal) to the acknowledgement of darkness (nocturnal) and then a return to light (diurnal). On a deep subconscious level, the individual with munakara Sun understands that the Sun's passage through the dark is an integral part of the solar experience during their lifetime.

Munakara Sun may frustrate the individual's aspirations, confuse their intentions or cloud their ambitions to the point that even they themselves are unsure of what it is they truly want. Munakara can dampen the Sun's light or decrease a natural enthusiasm or optimism for life. However, munakara Sun may also accentuate and exaggerate one's zest for life to a point where their energy exhausts those who are trying to keep up with the frenetic pace. Others cannot understand the driving force for such blind optimism, particularly in periods when extreme pressures of poor health or bad fortune would crush another's spirit.

Fighting to defend one's reputation can be the outward expression of Sun in munakara and a fall from grace, especially if the Sun is in Libra or Cancer (Venus or Moon as Sun's dispositor). Losing one's zest for life or the will to fight can also be common experiences for munakara Sun, as any of the nocturnal dispositors, whether the Moon, Mars, or Venus, are planets of passion who will test the Sun. A struggling Sun can be challenged when a particular passion wanes, or disappears entirely from the individual's life. Periods of depression or grief for a lost dream or a goal which is unobtainable may follow an energetic period, and munakara Sun will need the help of its two sequence planets to lift its spirits.

Munakara Sun and Society's Challenges

The individual with munakara Sun may choose to tone down their personality and forgo their independence in favour of a higher principle. Alternatively, duty or circumstances may set their destiny and their desires may not be allowed to rule their lives. For instance, both Queen Elizabeth II and her son and heir King Charles III have Suns in munakara: Elizabeth's chart has Sun in Taurus, and Charles' Sun is in the opposite sign of Scorpio (*Fig. 9.1*). Both monarchs have dedicated their lives to the service of their country and their British subjects. Normal adult identities are denied any queen or king, when their royal duties override their personal choices.

Munakara Sun can personify an individual grappling with feeling they have crossed a line somehow and need to justify themselves to society. Munakara Sun's battles may be spent in defending the individual's honour, reputation or good character and unfortunately, it is easier to lose one's reputation than to restore a good name once it has been lost. Society loves intrigues and scandals, and Sun in munakara can find itself the topic of much speculation and rumour.

Fame and celebrity status may follow a person with munakara Sun and the individual's ego can crave constant attention, but the risks of fame are that it will also bring insults, criticism, online trolling and vicious personal attacks. Sacrificing one's Sun to society's voracious appetite is a dangerous pastime, and even more so when the Sun is crossing sect boundaries, moving through enemy territory belonging to the Moon, Venus, or Mars, and coming out the other side to find itself in contention. Jupiter, Saturn, or diurnal Mercury will be possible candidates for the position of munakara Sun's outcome planet, and each of these planets will display their own characteristics when society tells the story of this person's life.

The Sun's Sequence: Friends, Associates, and Enemies

The Sun's natural enemy is Saturn. Both planets are diurnal, which means that any nocturnal first dispositor – Mars, Venus, or the Moon in either Capricorn or Aquarius – will result in Saturn being the Sun's outcome planet. Saturn is likely to create separation, hardship, self-doubt, or fear of failure for munakara Sun. It may bring disappointing results that highlight frustrations, restrictions, and small returns for significant efforts.

Saturn is also likely to carry impossibly high expectations. As both planets represent father – the Sun as father's warm guiding hand and Saturn as the stern disciplinary father – these expectations may reflect father at his most judgemental, or may be unfairly projected onto a father who is missing or incapable of showing pride in their child.

Identifying the intermediary nocturnal planet, *i.e.*, the first dispositor, plus the sign in which Saturn is situated, will give an indication as to the degree and the nature of the individual's self-criticism. It may also suggest how self-acceptance might be achieved through confidence, and the setting of realistic goals in the future.

Chapter Six • Sun in Munakara

D	Diurnal	Essential Dignity	Second Essential Dignity	Second Essential Dignity		
N	Nocturnal	Rulership / Exaltation (Mutual Damage)	(Fall opposes Exaltation)	— Borrowing Signs for Exaltation		
Munakara Planet △	Mutually Hurtful With (☉'s Two-Way Damage)	Injurious To (☉ Disposits Fall Sign)	Offering Friendship To (☉ Owns Exaltation Sign)	Asking Friendship From (Exalted ☉'s Dispositor)	Indifferent To ☉ - No relationship	
△ ☉ D	D Saturn ▼ Outcome Planet	N * Venus ☉ First Dispositor *al-Biruni cites ☉ as injurious to ♀. Their one connection is ☉'s exalted sign ♈, is ♀'s detriment.	—	N Mars ☉ First Dispositor	Mercury D D ▼ Outcome Planet D Jupiter : Moon N ▼ Outcome Planet : First Dispositor ☉	

Table 6.2: Al-Biruni's Friends and Enemies of the Sun

Friends and Associates of a munakara Sun: Moon, Mars, Mercury & Jupiter

If the Moon is involved in the sequence (as the first dispositor)

Cancer Sun dispositing to the Moon brings two luminaries together. Although this may bring empathy to the Sun's disposition, it also means the Sun has the potential to be munakara if the Moon disposits to a diurnal planet. The sect condition of the Moon will be critical to the Sun's heightened sensitivity as the resilience of an out-of-sect Moon can be questionable, and any discomfort the Moon feels will be automatically picked up by Cancer Sun.

The Moon as the Sun's dispositor adds emotionality to the Sun's agenda as it combines ambition and a desire for success (Sun's principles) with service, caregiving, nurturing or nourishment (Moon's principles). Without munakara, these two things can be achieved without much effort on the part of the individual with a Cancer Sun. But when the Moon disposits to a diurnal planet, munakara has occurred and will cause issues that frustrate the Sun. There may be family disputes, an expectation in following in father's footsteps or continuing the family business. Munakara tends to breed discontent, rebellion or resentment at expectations placed on the individual, especially when issues arise around individuality or maintaining one's autonomy. The Sun wants to do the 'right thing', but the Moon experiences guilt or becomes overly emotional when Sun takes action. The outcome planet, whether it is Jupiter, Saturn, or diurnal Mercury, becomes a trigger that sets off the planets in the Sun's munakara sequence and the Moon in the middle is left to suffer the consequences.

Example Charts:
- John Dee (outcome planet, Saturn)
- Edgar Degas (outcome planet, Saturn)
- Helen Keller (outcome planet, Jupiter)
- John Glenn (outcome planet, Saturn)
- Robin Williams (outcome planet, Jupiter)
- Princess Diana (outcome planet, Saturn)
- Prince George (outcome planet, Saturn)

If Mars is involved in the sequence (as the first dispositor)

Whether in Aries (in exaltation) or in Scorpio, the Sun is disposited by Mars, a nocturnal planet. Normally a good relationship exists between the Sun and Mars as they share a somewhat similar nature. Both planets love a challenge and admire qualities such courage, independence and an adventurous spirit. However, the Sun has a greater awareness of self-preservation. In a losing position the Sun will be capable of a strategic withdrawal in order to fight another day, ideally one when it has a greater advantage over its opponent. Mars, not so much. It will keep advancing trying to push for victory even when the cost is too great, the damage too severe and the prize barely salvageable once it is won. There is a potential that Sun in any of Mars's signs can achieve good, or even great, things so long as the Sun does not feel pushed or threatened by Mars.

Adding a third planet from the diurnal sect as Mars' dispositor creates a munakara sequence, which puts stress on the relationship between the Sun and Mars. Suddenly, the dynamics change, and one of the planets is stressed – either the Sun's plans become too grandiose for Mars to maintain its focus or energy, or Mars's incessant demands are too much for the Sun. As the relationship between the two sours, Mars's fight-or-flight responses become activated to every challenge, no matter how small. Munakara Sun fails to function under the stress, or makes terrible decisions based on paranoia or fear.

The outcome planet to Sun's munakara sequence will be a telling factor on the nature of the trigger that sends the individual into action. Saturn activates the Sun's fear of failure, Jupiter presents too many wild or infeasible plans, Mercury, which must be diurnal in Sun's sequence with Mars, is too unpredictable, mouthy, or opinionated. Rather than thinking its way out of the situation, diurnal Mercury in either the same sign as the Sun, or in the

Chapter Six • Sun in Munakara

sign preceding the Sun, is likely to make impossible promises that further humiliate or undermines munakara Sun's confidence.

Example Charts:
- Vincent van Gogh (outcome planet, Jupiter)
- Caitlyn Jenner (outcome planet, Mercury)
- King Charles III (outcome planet, Jupiter)
- Katy Perry (outcome planet, Saturn)
- Kelly Osbourne (outcome planet, Saturn)

The Impossibility for Nocturnal Mercury to be the Sun's Dispositor

It is impossible for the Sun in either of nocturnal Mercury's signs to be munakara, as Mercury must be placed behind the Sun in the order of the zodiac wheel for the Sun to make the first step towards contention (*Fig. 6.1*). If nocturnal Mercury is behind the Sun in Gemini or Virgo, but in the same sign as the Sun, it will be in rulership and does not progress to another dispositor.

There are a maximum of 28° between Mercury and the Sun, and any movement by nocturnal Mercury to a sign following Gemini or Virgo Sun will eliminate the possibility of munakara. For instance, the sign following Gemini is Cancer and nocturnal Mercury in Cancer would dispose to the Moon, another nocturnal planet, so no munakara. The sign following Virgo is Libra and nocturnal Mercury in Libra would dispose to Venus, again another nocturnal planet, so no munakara.

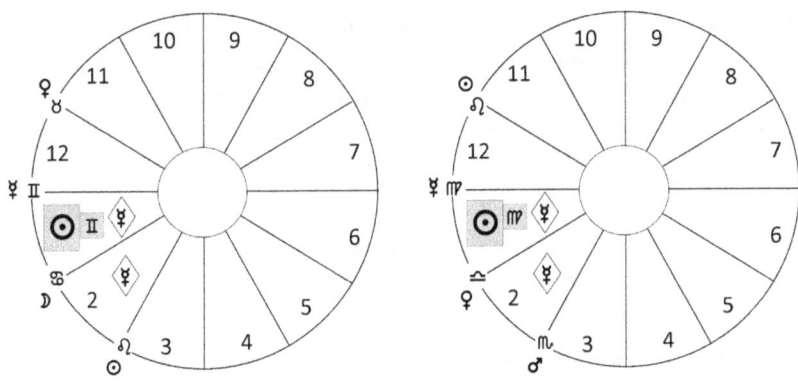

Fig. 6.1: Sun in Mercury's sign – no possibility for munakara Sun

If Diurnal Mercury is involved in the sequence (as the outcome planet)

The only way for Mercury to be involved in the Sun's sequence is for it to be a dispositor for the nocturnal planet that divides the Sun and diurnal Mercury. The Tables below (*Tables 6.3, 6.4, 6.5*) demonstrate the possibility for Venus, Moon and Mars to be in Mercury's signs and for diurnal Mercury to complete the sequence that results in the Sun being in a state of munakara.

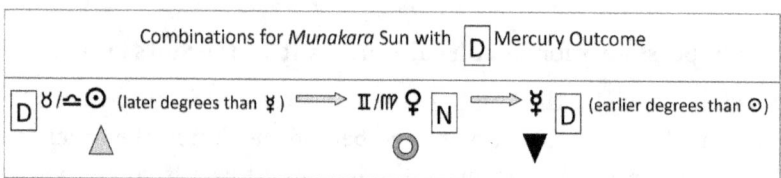

Table 6.3: *Munakara Sun dispositing to Venus in diurnal Mercury's signs*

In three example charts – Friedrich Nietzsche, Cher and Tee Corrine – Mercury is in an earlier degree in the same sign as the Sun. However, this doesn't always need to be the case as Mercury can be in the sign preceding the Sun's sign, as demonstrated by the chart of Caitlyn Jenner (Sun in Scorpio and diurnal Mercury in Libra).

There are certain conditions which must be in place if the three planets – Sun, Venus, and Mercury – are to form a sequence for munakara Sun. The first possibility is that the Sun can be in Taurus and disposit to Venus in Gemini, or, alternatively, it can be in Libra and disposit to Venus in Virgo. A second possibility carries its own level of complexity given that both the munakara planet and its first dispositor will be in their signs of fall: the Sun in Libra and Venus in Virgo. This combination of Sun and Venus in debilitated condition suggests adversity as the two planets struggle to achieve their potential. It may be that Mercury, as the outcome planet, is needed to change a negative perspective for this munakara Sun's sequence to find its own individuality or self-identity.

The fact that Mercury is diurnal, rather than nocturnal, can be a distinct advantage to the Sun as it means Mercury is willing to serve the Sun in its quest to earn respect. The problem for Libran Sun is that it often needs external validation, and if Virgo Venus is only attracting criticism or harsh remarks then munakara Sun's light starts to diminish and the individual loses the confidence that it spent so long building.

Chapter Six • *Sun in Munakara*

German philosopher Friedrich Nietzsche has this combination of Sun and Venus in fall and the tragic events in his life that express this fallen state are examined in Part Two of the Sun's delineations. The following quote is a lovely expression for his Libran Sun sequence: "One must still have chaos in oneself to be able to give birth to a dancing star."[2]

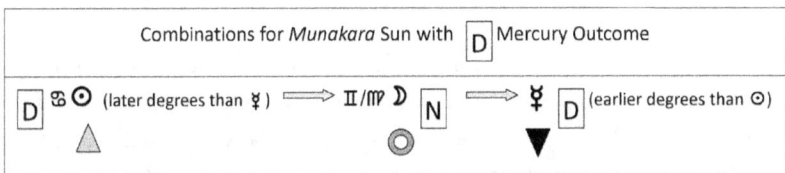

Table 6.4: *Munakara Sun dispositing to Moon in diurnal Mercury's signs*

Cancer Sun dispositing to the Moon in Gemini or Virgo will produce a sequence with diurnal Mercury as the outcome planet (*Table 6.4*). This particular sequence will be likely to concentrate on emotional issues or connections with family members. Alternatively, it may manifest in the individual's need to express their individuality through creativity, as the Moon is the original creative force. Diurnal Mercury will try to find a physical expression for this creativity and the sign and house of its placement in the chart will direct both the trigger and munakara Sun's possible outcome. A healthy expression for creativity can be achievable, so long as the two luminaries work together in harmony.

It should be remembered that the lunar phases will differ for the two signs – as Gemini Moon will be at the balsamic end of a lunar cycle to the Cancer Sun, whilst Virgo Moon will be separating from Cancer Sun and in either a new moon phase (less than 45° from the Sun) or a crescent phase (more than 45° from the Sun). This difference between waning and waxing lunar phases could be critical to the success of munakara Sun in Cancer. The Sun will need to judge whether the work has been done (Balsamic phase) and it is time to wrap up the project and look forward for new directions, or if it needs to put in future work as the Moon continues to move away from it (Crescent phase). Once diurnal Mercury finds its rhythm it will work to the Sun's advantage, but it needs to know when to rush headlong into a new enterprise and when to revisit one that may have been abandoned in the past and to attack it with renewed vigour and a fresh perspective.

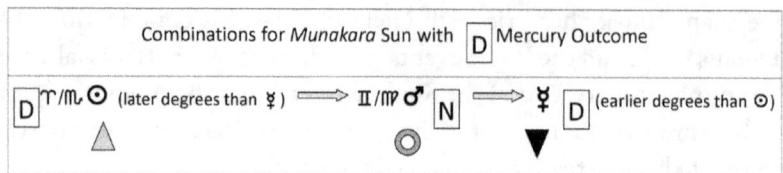

Table 6.5: Munakara Sun dispositing to Mars in diurnal Mercury's signs

Mars is similar to the Moon in that its orbit is not restricted by the Sun and both nocturnal planets can experience aspects as far away as an opposition of 180°. Mercury, the Sun's outcome planet will still need to be in earlier degrees than the Sun to keep its diurnal status, but there are no such restrictions on Mars. Aries Sun is an exalted Sun and in this situation Mars will be called upon to provide energy and passion for the Sun as it aims to reach a goal. However, adding munakara to the Sun is going to make Mars's job just that bit harder, especially when munakara Sun is likely to show the person's lack of self-confidence, drive or motivation. In this situation Mars (as first dispositor) can become frustrated with the Sun's hesitancy and take action to push the Sun more aggressively towards its goal.

Nocturnal Mars will be disposited by Mercury regardless of whether it is in Gemini or Virgo. However, its focus, attitudes and experiences will vary depending on its placement in either Gemini or Virgo. Gemini Mars may bring conflicts with siblings given that Mercury is the significator for brothers and sisters. Verbal disagreements may get out of hand and the Sun's sign – either Aries or Scorpio – will determine if the flare-up is simply a challenge to authority (munakara Aries Sun) or a deep wound that resists all attempts to heal (munakara Scorpio Sun). If its dispositor is Mars in Gemini, then this is a visionary Mars that is easily excited by big ideas, concepts and future plans. Adding munakara can frustrate both the Sun and Mars, particularly if Mercury is pragmatic and wants to know how 'pie in the sky' idealism can help manifest something into reality.

In Part Two of this book, under Venus's delineations, you will find Tee Corrine's chart. She has Mars in Gemini as her Scorpio Sun's first dispositor and her writing and artwork is edgy and confrontational. In her own words: "I believed that reclaiming labial imagery was a route to claiming personal power for women."[3] However it was as much a journey for her towards self-discovery as it was for women to understand that images of female genitalia should not be labelled as 'crazy' or 'bad'. Munakara Sun is a battler against authorities who believe they should have control over the individual.

Chapter Six • *Sun in Munakara*

Corinne battled printers who refused to print her books and artwork and art galleries who refused to exhibit her work. She battled authorities when her books were censored by the US government and the US Postal Service when they refused to handle her books through their delivery service.

Virgo Mars can still manifest in sibling conflicts but these are more likely to come from criticisms and complaints about childhood behaviours or broken promises. When Mars is caught between two diurnal planets it risks becoming an agitator and contention seems to come easily to a planet that understands combat and is constantly on the defensive. And Mars's ability to stir up the Sun or take Mercury's thoughts and turning them into irritations that end in explosive outbursts does little to help munakara Sun.

Example Charts:
- Friedrich Nietzsche
- Cher
- Tee Corinne
- Caitlyn Jenner

If Jupiter is involved in the sequence (outcome planet)

Jupiter as an outcome planet has the potential to complete munakara Sun's sequence with a planet that can bring big rewards and make the Sun's efforts truly worthwhile. The Sun in contention is naturally geared towards believing itself to be good and decent, but there is a fine line between the Sun's preference of being morally and justifiably 'right' and Jupiter's fervour of 'righteousness' that brooks no opposition and casts itself in the role of protector of the cause. Even if Jupiter is aiming for more mundane prizes such as good fortune, wealth, success, and notoriety, there can be shades of extremism. The individual needs to be careful that Jupiter is not leading munakara Sun towards behaviours or ideals that are excessive, prejudiced, or fanatical. Munakara Sun craves the gifts that Jupiter promises but overzealous Jupiter can get carried away and makes promises to the embattled Sun that it simply cannot keep.

Jupiter as the outcome planet for munakara Sun may bring spiritual issues as both planets are connected to religious or divine matters. There may be themes around high expectations or ambitions that risk deteriorating into ruthlessness, bitterness or envy over others who seem to have an easier journey through life. Complex issues such as selfishness or a sense of entitlement can be a challenge if the person is trying to overcompensate for feelings of inadequacy or insecurity.

The nocturnal planet that stands between the Sun in contention and Jupiter its outcome planet needs special attention as the Moon, Venus or Mars will all work to their own agendas. American author Helen Keller's Cancer Sun battled her body's illness and physical isolation through disability (the Moon) to emerge triumphant with Jupiter as the Sun's outcome planet. The charts of Queen Elizabeth II and her son and heir King Charles III have Suns in munakara. Elizabeth has Taurus Sun and disposits to Venus and Charles has Scorpio Sun ruled by Mars. Both regents have Jupiter as the Sun's outcome planet so there is an ingrained feeling of superiority in terms of class, education, social standing and wealth. Both monarchs use Jupiter for humanitarian and philanthropic interests, but their royal status places them in a unique position where they have little understanding of the freedom of decision-making as anonymous individuals, free from the obligations cast on them by their heritage.

Example Charts:
- Vincent van Gogh
- Helen Keller
- Robin Williams
- Queen Elizabeth II
- King Charles III

Enemies of a munakara Sun: Venus & Saturn

If Venus is involved in the sequence (as the first dispositor)

It is possible for Venus and Mercury to be involved in the Sun's sequence as we have seen earlier when diurnal Mercury was discussed as munakara Sun's outcome planet. The focus is then on Mercury and its role in the Sun's sequence which begins with either Taurus or Libran Sun.

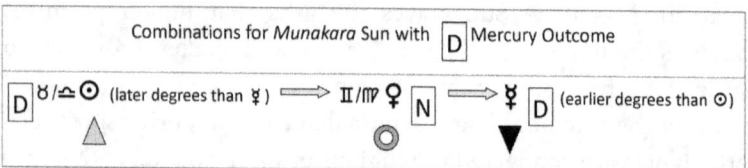

Table 6.6: *Munakara Sun dispositing to Venus in diurnal Mercury's signs*

Al-Biruni does not consider Venus to be injurious to the Sun even though the Sun is in Venus' sign Libra when it is in fall, which would indeed make it an enemy. For that reason, I have added Venus to Saturn as an 'enemy' of the Sun, even though its impact as 'enemy' is relatively less harmful when compared with Saturn.

Previously I spoke on the fall signs of the Sun (Libra) and Venus (Virgo) so for balance I will concentrate on Taurus Sun with Venus in Gemini as its first dispositor and diurnal Mercury as outcome planet. The Sun is in Taurus from late April to late May and this fixed earth sign (ruled by Venus) will add characteristics of comfort, beauty, earthiness, safe patterns and a dependable routine. Taurus Sun has two possibilities to end up in a state of munakara: Venus is either in Gemini and it disposits to a diurnal Mercury (*Table 6.6*), or Venus is in Pisces and it disposits to Jupiter (*Table 6.7*).

The two sequences will produce different outcomes but either way, Taurus Sun in munakara has lost its safety net and all of life's predictability has flown out the window. Gemini Venus will add to the instability of Taurus Sun, but this can happen anyway without Mercury's influence as outcome planet.

Diurnal Mercury adds to this potentially unstable Sun by throwing in dialogue that unsettles Venus which in turn upsets the Sun. Mercury loves change – it thrives on new, exciting and unpredictable and even if it is in Taurus, it will still seek to chase new possibilities and fresh ideas. Venus in Gemini will pick up on this and will feel stimulated by changes in the person's relationships and even their physical appearance is under threat from Venus and Mercury who think it's a great idea to 'freshen the look.' Too many ideas, too many possibilities, too much change is very destabilising for Taurus Sun in munakara. It leaves it feeling confused and uncertain about how to find authenticity or 'fit in' to be liked and accepted by others (a big thing for Taurus Sun).

The consummate entertainer, Cher, singer (she has 29 albums to her credit), actor (she has starred in 20 films), producer and presenter of numerous television specials has this combination – Taurus Sun to Gemini Venus to Mercury. As a performer Cher has not only reinvented her dress and style over the decades, but this amazingly talented artist has also multiplied her qualifications and shown the depth of her skills in over 60 years in the entertainment industry. Cher is a perfect example of how munakara Sun in Taurus deals successfully with her two ally planets in Sun's sequence. Rather than allowing Venus or Mercury to undermine or disrupt Taurus Sun, instead Cher has strengthened her self-identity and her personality so that she is rock solid in her true identity.

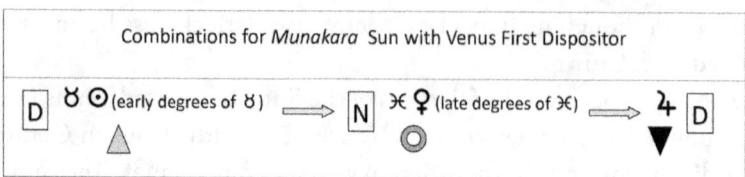

Table 6.7: *Munakara Sun dispositing to Venus in Jupiter's sign, Pisces*

The other option for Taurus Sun to be munakara is when Venus is exalted in Pisces. This is possible when the Sun is in early degrees of Taurus and Venus precedes it in late degrees of Pisces, the sign belonging to Jupiter. The Spanish actor Penelope Cruz has this munakara sequence and although I concentrated on her munakara Mercury in an earlier chapter, she also has Sun conjunct Mercury in Taurus and the two diurnal planets are a duet that share the same munakara sequence.

The chart of Queen Elizabeth II has Taurus Sun and Pisces Venus with Jupiter as the outcome planet. Exaltation can bring its own special challenges, but Elizabeth II has always showed nothing but her best side when in the public eye – perhaps why she was so loved by her subjects (Pisces Venus). Her son, King Charles III, also has Jupiter as his outcome planet for his munakara Sun in Scorpio. The long time waiting in the wings (and the inevitable frustration that must have caused) may have manifested in his middle planet of Mars. At the time of his coronation in May 2023, Charles was 73 years old, making him the oldest person to accede to the British throne after having been the longest-serving heir apparent and Prince of Wales in British history.

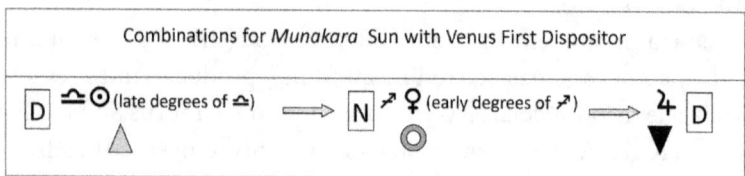

Table 6.8: *Munakara Sun dispositing to Venus in Jupiter's sign, Sagittarius*

A Sun in late degrees of Libra can disposit to Venus in early degrees of Sagittarius making Jupiter the outcome planet for munakara Sun. The Libran Sun in munakara may find satisfaction from Venus through a love of challenging oneself, or a love of adventure, pushing boundaries or seeking broader horizons. Jupiter as the outcome planet for munakara Sun will look for big expressions and grand gestures – and as long as Venus in the middle is loving the attention or doing something a bit 'edgy', then Sagittarius is likely no problem for the Sun's nocturnal dispositor. The signs of Libra and Sagittarius are both masculine and are located two signs apart, so if there is a sextile (60°) aspect between them, then whatever the person does is likely to gain positive attention and admirers along the way.

The one problem lies in the fact that munakara Sun in Libra is in its fall sign. Like Icarus from Greek mythology who flew too close to the sun, this combination may show someone whose ambitions were too great, who takes too many risks, is way too confident of their own abilities, and whose 'wax wings' melt as they fall back to earth with a bump.

The chart of American daredevil Evel Knievel has this Sun sequence – Libra Sun to Sagittarius Venus to Jupiter – and his antics bordered on self-destruction as he pushed himself past the limits to gain the admiration his munakara Sun so desperately sought for him to feel 'alive.' Every stunt became that little bit crazier, every Jupiterian risk pushed the limits that much more, but Knievel was addicted to the thrills and the crowds. Even when he fell with broken bones and horrendous internal injuries he would retreat and focus on healing to face the next great challenge.

"You can't ask a guy like me why I performed. I really wanted to fly through the air. I was a daredevil, a performer. I loved the thrill, the money, the whole macho thing. All those things made me Evel Knievel. Sure, I was scared. You gotta be an ass not to be scared. But I beat the hell out of death."4 – Evel Knievel in one of the last interviews before his death caused by respiratory disease in November 2007, aged 69.

Example Charts:
- Friedrich Nietzsche (outcome planet, Mercury)
- Queen Elizabeth II (outcome planet, Jupiter)
- Evel Knievel (outcome planet, Jupiter)
- Cher (outcome planet, Mercury)
- Penelope Cruz (outcome planet, Jupiter)

If Saturn is involved in the sequence (as the outcome planet)

Saturn is the Sun's enemy (Leo opposes Aquarius) so Saturn as its outcome planet is likely to prove a difficult challenge when munakara Sun is already nervous dealing with authority figures. Saturn is a sensitive trigger for the Sun as any relationship between these two planets, including the state of munakara, is going to be tense. The individual with munakara Sun can experience feelings of inferiority, fear of failure, or a deep insecurity – and unfortunately, Saturn can feed into these areas when it is the Sun's outcome planet.

Saturn may try to fortify the Sun by giving it a goal to chase but unfortunately many of Saturn's hints are themed by hardship, separation or a sense of isolation. Saturn's placement in the chart may show where the separation needs to take place before the Sun can move forwards towards its goal, but if the lesson is too hard or the individual with munakara Sun is not ready for the weight of responsibility, it may backfire and result in a different outcome instead.

The individual may adopt a scarcity mindset, in which while other people seem to get what they want, this person feels as though their basic needs will not be met throughout life. This mindset is not helpful to any Sun but when the middle planet is a nocturnal – Moon, Venus, or Mars – then the feeling is very strong that the physical world is against them. The Moon between Sun and Saturn can bring up emotional issues that the person is not ready to deal with. Alternatively, it can manifest in physical ailments which plague the individual and Saturn restricts from one side whilst the Sun in munakara lacks vitality on the other. Mars may fight hard but fighting might be the last thing that helps in this sequence and Venus may feel the effort is just too great and look for escape rather than resolution.

Example Charts:
- John Dee
- Edgar Degas
- John Glenn
- Princess Diana
- Prince George
- Mark Ruffallo
- Katy Perry
- Kelly Osbourne.

Munakara Sun – Katy Perry and Kelly Osbourne

Born two days apart, Katy Perry and Kelly Osbourne share many planetary similarities (*Figs. 6.2 and 6.3*). Both women have a stellium in Scorpio, dispositing to Capricorn Mars in exaltation.

Chapter Six • *Sun in Munakara*

The two-day difference in their births show a sign change in the Moon from Scorpio (Katy's Moon) to Sagittarius (Kelly's Moon). Both celebrities have Jupiter in its fall sign of Capricorn, and Pluto conjunct their Scorpio Sun. Saturn barely moves in the two-day interval and holds a prominent position in the Scorpio stellium.

Scorpio Sun is in munakara in both charts, as the sequence moves from diurnal Sun to nocturnal Mars in Capricorn back to diurnal Saturn:

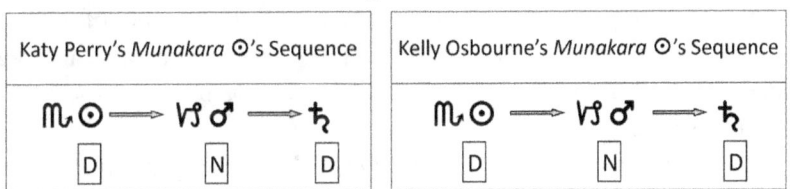

Table 6.9: *Munakara Sun Sequences of Katy Perry and Kelly Osbourne*

The backgrounds and experiences of these two women are vastly different, especially where their respective father figures are concerned. However, they also share a number of similarities.

Katy's father was a Pentecostal pastor who constantly uprooted his family across the US, chasing new pastoral territory for his church. Kelly spent her childhood touring the UK and the US with her family and her famous father, "Ozzy" Osbourne and his band Black Sabbath. She was on a kids' bus each summer chasing gigs and audiences from her birth until she was almost twenty.

Katy's family struggled financially, sometimes accessing the same food stamps as the more destitute members of their congregation. Kelly's family were not cash-strapped, but they struggled with the financial and emotional cost of Ozzy's addictions and a life on the road, which was constricted by the odd hours of a rock band, and exposed the young children in the family to many aspects of less than exemplary adult behaviour.

Both women's munakara Suns have close conjunctions to Pluto and the Sun Pluto aspect indicates a theme of father's power over the individual, particularly in their impressionable younger years. The feminine nature of Scorpio Sun can often indicate a strong matriarchal influence that overrides or counters father's control or eccentricities within the family unit. When the Scorpio Sun is munakara there can be a strong desire to rebel against the Sun figure, whether it is father or mother, so that one might establish their own sense of autonomy.

A desire to exercise the freedom over one's decisions is a constant theme for munakara Sun and often childhood is the starting place to exercise the right to make one's own choices. The problem lies in having the maturity for such independent actions. Both Katy and Kelly have experienced this in extremes in their early life. Katy received a strict religious upbringing where choices such as television viewing and even the brand of breakfast cereal (Lucky Charms were banned by her mother) were under the jurisdiction of her parents. Kelly's upbringing was often lacking in the types of boundaries most parents impose on their children as life was unpredictable and regular schedules such as bedtime or mealtime had little meaning for the three Osbourne children.

Munakara Scorpio Sun is disposited by Mars, and with Pluto present by conjunction there can be indications of outbursts and possible perceived and actual violence. Either way, life feels volatile and dangerous, particularly when Saturn is the outcome planet for the Sun's sequence. The presence of two malefic planets in the Sun's sequence can suggest a fight for survival and the Sun's energy is preoccupied with survival and keeping a low profile rather than drawing attention to oneself.

Katy Perry's Moon is also in Scorpio, and whilst the Moon is not munakara (the Moon and Mars are nocturnal planets), it is still in its fall. The double bind of both luminaries, one in contention (Sun) and the other in fall (Moon), is a difficult combination for someone who relies on bounce and positivity as her onstage persona.

Both young women have found themselves the subject of extensive public debate, and each of them has sought the limelight for different reasons. Over the years they have been cast in particular societal roles: Katy – the sweet, pretty girl with oodles of talent and hundreds of kooky costumes – has been raised to Pop Princess status, while Kelly was cast as the angry, foul-mouthed daughter of an aging rock star. But their roles have changed over the years. Several of Katy Perry's outfits at the 2024 Paris Fashion Week have been sensationally revealing, and one can only imagine how her conservative parents would view her new image. Kelly's life seems to have become more balanced with her new role as mother and with her determination to move away from drug and alcohol dependency. These projections of good girl/bad girl have haunted the two women since their teenage years, and their survival – and their ability to find their own self-identity – has depended on how they have been able to shape the narrative to become strong individuals who decide their own measure of self-worth.

Chapter Six • *Sun in Munakara*

Both women's birth time occurs at 8 o'clock Local Standard Time (LST), but one is a morning birth, whilst the other is an evening birth. Katy Perry was born at 8:00 am on 25th October, 1984, and with her Sun having risen over the Ascendant by the time she was born, so Katy has a diurnal chart.

Kelly Osbourne was born at 8:00 pm on 27th October 1984, giving her a nocturnal chart, as her munakara Sun had set by this time. Scorpio Sun is the only munakara planet in both women's charts.

Scorpio Sun in Munakara: Katy Perry

Brief Biography of Katy Perry

Katheryn Hudson, known professionally as Katy Perry, was born 25 October 1984 and is the middle child born to Pentecostal pastors Mary and Maurice Hudson.

Perry left home for Nashville at age 16 and recorded her first album *Katy Hudson* in 2001. Confusion over her name and that of actress Kate Hudson saw her change her name to her mother's maiden name, Perry.

After several false starts with various recording companies Perry signed to Capitol Records in 2007 and the release of her album *One of the Boys* in 2008 became the breakthrough album that launched Katy Perry into stardom. Perry toured extensively through 2008 and 2009 and hosted the MTV Europe Music Awards in both years.

Perry met future husband Russell Brand in 2009 and were married on 23 October 2010. On December 30, 2011, Brand announced they were divorcing after just 14 months of marriage. On 5 July 2012, Perry's autobiographical documentary *Katy Perry: Part of Me* was released to positive reviews and grossed $32.7 million worldwide at the box office. Perry's third album *Teenage Dream* was released in 2010 and was a huge commercial success.

Perry's fourth studio album *Prism* was released in 2013 with the themes of living in the present, relationships and self-empowerment. The album was praised for its more mature and personal lyrics and received generally favourable reviews from music critics. Her fifth studio album *Witness* was released in June 2017 to mixed reviews but it was a commercial success. Her sixth album *Smile* was released in August 2020. Perry began hosting a concert residency named *Play* at Resorts World, Las Vegas on December 29, 2021. *Play* ran until the final show on November 4, 2023. The residency grossed $46.4 million, becoming the 8th highest grossing female residency in the history of Las Vegas. Perry's seventh album *143* was released in September 2024.

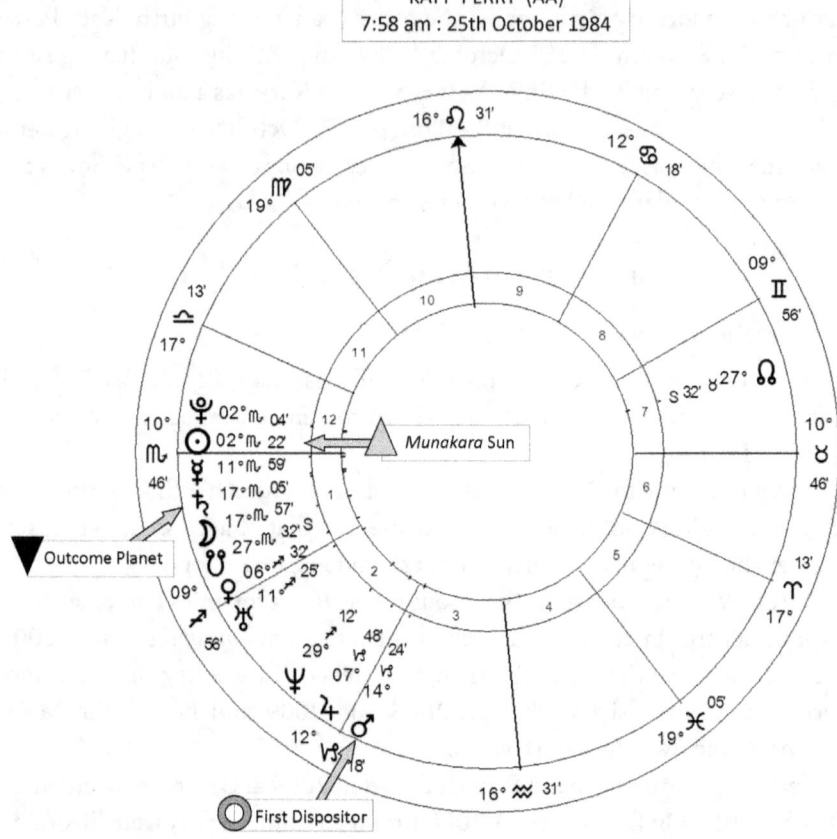

Fig. 6.2: *Katy Perry: Munakara Sun in Scorpio*

- **Key Questions:**
- What does Katy Perry's Sun contend with?
- What is its driving force?
- What is its trigger? What is its outcome?

Katy Perry's munakara Sun is indicative of Katy's high expectations – the Sun ruling Leo Mid-heaven and disposited by exalted Mars. However, its position on the Ascendant adds to her fragility when she is attacked by the media, or when anyone is critical of her work. Sun in munakara is bound to take harsh comments to the heart, and Katy's sensitivity crept through in 2017 when her fifth album *Witness* was panned by music critics. These were criticisms which triggered a period of depression and anxiety, with Perry

Chapter Six • *Sun in Munakara*

later admitting to having suicidal thoughts. "I started writing these songs when I was in my darkest place. I was clinically depressed, I wasn't even having bouts of depression, it was like I could not get out of bed."[5] Saturn is the Sun's outcome planet and in the same interview Perry stated "In 2017, my career didn't really meet my own personal expectations... I wasn't getting high off my own supply (of energy) anymore and then I was like, 'Oh wow, I've given all of the responsibility of my self-worth outward.'"[6]

Several civil court cases over the years have added pressure and threatened to harm Perry's reputation, including a 15-year legal saga when Sydney fashion designer Katie Perry finally won a case in April 2023 brought against the superstar for breach of trademark on merchandise sold during Perry's 2014 *Prism* tour in Australia. The confusion over rights to the name on leisurewear began in 2008 (the difference being the spelling of Katy or Katie) ended with the Federal Court Justice Brigitte Markovic describing the case as "[a] tale of two women, two teenage dreams and one name."[7]

This was not the first time Katy Perry had had to find a name for herself (munakara Sun) as her birth name, Katheryn Elizabeth Hudson, caused much confusion early in her singing career. Her debut studio album, *Katy Hudson* was released in March 2001 when she was 16, and sold only 200 copies as Red Hill Records went bankrupt before the album could be promoted. However, the similarity between her name and Kate Hudson, the famous daughter of singer Bill Hudson and actor Goldie Hawn was too close and Katy Hudson became Katy Perry (her mother's maiden name – 10th house is the house of mother) in 2003.

Saturn gives Perry the fortitude to maintain the high quality of her productions, but at the same time, Saturn still requires Perry to manage her off-stage responsibilities by lending her name and her energies to charitable organisations, as well as supporting a variety of social and political causes. Even without a Sun in munakara, a stellium in Scorpio is going to flex its considerable muscles, wanting to use its power and to have strong and passionate opinions.

"I'm never going to be lazy, because there are 500 other people waiting in line for this position."[8] – Katy Perry

Added to the Scorpio stellium is the impetus of her Sun's sequence – Sun, Mars, Saturn – which drives her harder than most of her peers to find meaning behind why she has been given this level of success so early in her life.

Munakara Sun searches for a link between the mundane and the spiritual and Perry's childhood was steeped in religious dogma and parental control over her environment. It is Perry's responsibility to find her own spiritual yardstick, her own truth and one that suits her in a high-octane profession where popularity is measured by the latest video, music awards, billboard hits, and audience and critics' approval. Capricorn Mars disposited by Saturn is probably the most grounded of all planets in exaltation, so Perry should be able to find solid ground and spiritual fulfilment if she puts the same amount of energy into this project as she has done for her career.

Munakara Planet and Sect Condition – how comfortable is the Sun?

Katy Perry's Sun is just 8° above the Ascendant, but it is enough to classify her chart as diurnal with the Sun's placement in the upper hemisphere of the chart. A diurnal chart is going to promote the principles of success, influence, visibility, and well-defined goals and accomplishments. The two other diurnal planets, Jupiter and Saturn, perform better in a diurnal chart, and lend their different skills to assist the Sun to achieve its desire for recognition, praise and worthiness. Mercury in Perry's chart is in later degrees of Scorpio, making it nocturnal in its sect condition. Perry describes herself as a "singer-songwriter masquerading as a pop star"[9] and nocturnal Mercury would confirm her talents for lyrics and "irresistible hook-laden melodies."[10]

Katy Perry — ☉'s Sect Dignity			
Planet	Sect 1 Status	Sect 2 Hemisphere	Sect 3 Sign
♏ ☉	Day	Sun Defines	Water
	D	D	D	N

Table 6.10: Katy Perry: Munakara Sun's Sect Dignity

Diurnality may ease the situation between two natural enemies of the same sect, that is, the Sun and its outcome planet Saturn, purely because Saturn is less cold and brittle in a daytime chart. According to Robert Hand, good sect dignity (diurnality) increases Saturn's energy levels, giving Saturn an ability to recognise limitations so that it can work around them, and improving its ability to define and set goals that are worthy, capable and realistic.[11] Katy Perry's munakara Sun sequence benefits from the fact that her two diurnal planets are in step with her diurnal chart, and even Mars, the Sun's dispositor, has good sect condition as it is travelling in the hemisphere opposite to the Sun (in *halb*).

Chapter Six • *Sun in Munakara*

Katy's Munakara Sun Pluto conjunct Ascendant

"I like to go out there looking like a strong woman, because I am strong. But I am also a woman who goes through all sorts of problems and highs and lows."
– Katy Perry, Interview with *Parade*

When the Sun is in a state of munakara it doesn't always know what the goals should be or even when the perceived goals are reached. It can be unsure of how to proceed to the next step higher on the ladder of success. Yearning, seeking, achieving, and then starting again are natural cycles for the Sun, as it gives the impression of mirroring the seasons of our year. But in truth, it's not the Sun that moves, it is the planets that revolve around it, and when the Sun is in contention, there can be a feeling that no matter how much the rest of the world revolves around the individual they still don't truly understand their purpose or how to 'become' themselves.

Pluto is the same degree as the Sun, and it seemed in 2010 that Katy would have it all professionally and personally – career and marriage to one of the English-speaking world's most eligible bachelors, commitment-shy Russell Brand. When Brand announced they were divorcing after 14 months of marriage, it seemed that Katy's perfect life was unravelling. Munakara Sun does not do well under constant public scrutiny, especially when some battles are not meant to be fought under such a brutal force of rejection. Brand claimed that Katy's rising fame was a major cause of the break-up. Perhaps her career over-shadowing his own waning popularity prompted jealousy and created a power struggle between them. It takes someone very secure in themselves to compete with the strength of munakara Sun, especially one that it determined to succeed, and whose owner is prepared to maintain a ferocious 'eye on the prize'. Perry certainly demonstrated her tenacity, having been dropped by three successive record labels before she found the right formula to succeed and gathered an army of fans to her fold.

Katy Perry's Scorpio Sun in munakara is part of a sizeable stellium in Scorpio – Pluto, Sun, Mercury, Saturn, Moon, and South Node – shows there is much greater depth to this pop princess than the image she shows to the world (munakara Sun rules the Mid-heaven). Perry has been quoted as saying: "I feel like my secret magic trick that separates me from a lot of my peers is the bravery to be vulnerable and truthful and honest. I think you become more relatable when you're vulnerable."[12]

Saturn is the outcome planet for Scorpio Sun's munakara sequence and some of this vulnerability is at the core of her success especially as Saturn is in partile (same) degree as her Scorpio Moon. The autobiographical documentary, released in July 2012 under the title *Katy Perry: Part of Me*, was a project filmed in the previous year when Perry was obviously feeling exposed and defenceless, answering questions in private interviews with her and her loved ones, and perfecting her performances and dealing with backstage dramas from her California Dreams Tour. In *Part of Me*, Perry talks candidly about the breakdown of her marriage to English actor/comedian Russell Brand, a marriage which ended via a text message from Brandt informing Perry that he was divorcing her.[13] The film received positive reviews and grossed US $32.7 million worldwide at the box office.[14]

The challenge to her munakara Sun to expose something so achingly private as the failure of her marriage (Sun/Saturn rules the 10th/4th house axis), at a time when everyone wanted 'a piece of her' (hence the title *Part of Me*), is a credit to someone who wanted to show that she had pain in her life, just like everyone else. Perhaps this is why her fans demonstrate such loyalty towards the singer.

A decade later, in a much happier space, Perry began hosting a concert residency in 2021, named *Play* (a great name for her munakara Sun) at Resorts World Las Vegas. The title is intended to convey to its audience that it is a light-hearted extravaganza. Its season ran from 2021 to 2023 and grossed US$46.4 million, becoming the 8th highest grossing female residency in the history of Las Vegas, and 18th overall.[15]

First Dispositor for Scorpio Sun: Mars in Capricorn

Katy's Capricorn Mars in 3rd House ruling Ascendant

Katy's exalted Mars is the Lord of her Ascendant and sextiles the most important angle in the chart. A fortunate aspect such as this placement gives great advantage, especially if the individual is willing to be courageous and fight for their place in the world. With only seven degrees separating Mars from Jupiter there is promise of great wealth and success (Jupiter rules 2nd house) if the recipient is willing to be tenacious, hard-working, and somewhat ruthless in their intention to succeed.

Mars also rules Katy's 6th house, and her sensitivity to harshness from music critics over her last two albums, have caused her some personal distress over her artistic choices. If munakara Sun relies solely on other's opinions of one's worth, then there are going to be some dark patches to get through in difficult times. Perry's Mars is in the 3rd house, showing natural talent if

Chapter Six • *Sun in Munakara*

she can stay focused, but it can also create burnout when that same planet connects the 1st house, with the 6th house of illness, exhaustion, and overwork.

In August 2016, Perry stated that she wanted to create an album with lyrics on self-empowerment and feminism, and when her fifth album *Witness* was released the following year, she described it as a '360-degree liberation' record, with 'purposeful pop' themes including political liberation, sexual liberation, and liberation from negativity. *Witness* was not met with the same enthusiasm as her earlier albums, as popular media (and her fans) were expecting the same light touch and bubblegum tunes that had earned her record-breaking sales from previous albums, *One of the Boys* (2008) and *Teenage Dream* (2010).

Despite a mental health hiatus after her fourth album *Prism* (2013) failed to rise in the billboard charts and was savaged by critics, Perry took another chance on *Witness* (2017) hoping it may be better received by fans and critics alike. Perry stated at the time that she was struggling with situational depression – an adjustment disorder with a psychosocial stressor or trigger which brings responses of intense emotional and behavioural reactions. Triggers included harsh reviews and negative public criticism, or the very public relationship break-up with her then-current partner Orlando Bloom.

Through the ups and downs on her career, Katy's Mars shows that while it may be in exaltation, it is still disposited by Saturn, a planet known for its connection to melancholia.

Katy has described her sixth studio album *Smile* (2020) as "her journey towards the light, with stories of resilience, hope, and love"[16] and explained that the title was about taking back your smile and "finding the light at the end of the tunnel."[17] *Smile* did not reach the billboard highs or the acclaim of her earlier albums but its theme is positive and uplifting – despite some critics have called the lyrics 'cringe-worthy'.

Ultimately Perry's journey is about her munakara Sun, not her ability to sit atop the popularity pole, and one cannot help but feel relieved that she is finding ways to express her Sun in munakara, rather than worrying about how her latest music will be received.

Munakara Sun's dispositor Mars (ruler of the Ascendant) is in a 7° conjunction with Jupiter (ruler of her 2nd house) and the critics can write what they please but it will not affect her income. Perry has amassed a fortune from the sales of her albums, her world tours over the years, her LA concert residency, a salary of $18–25 million for her appearances as a judge on *American Idol* when she joined the show in 2018. Her net worth in 2024 was estimated by Forbes at US$400 million. Forbes ranked Perry as the world' highest-paid female musician in 2015 and 2018 and she reportedly added $200 million in 2023 from the sale of her music catalogue.

Throughout the years her clever branding and endorsement deals with companies has meant her name *is* her brand and one can only admire the true grit of her munakara Sun as it has journeyed from the glare of fame to the darkness of self-doubt only to come through the light and be a shining icon to anyone who has experienced similar highs and lows that mark a planet in contention.

The outcome planet for Munakara Sun: Saturn in Scorpio
Katy's Saturn conjunct Moon in 1st House

"I come from a very non-accepting family, but I am very accepting." – Katy Perry, interview with *Vanity Fair*

Perry was brought up in a Pentecostal home with two parents who were pastors of the Church. With Saturn in same degree conjunction to the Moon, the ruler of her 9th house, their influence on her spiritual, philosophical and religious beliefs will have reinforced the idea that Fate is guided by something greater than mere good fortune.

Saturn with the Moon in Scorpio can suggest a combination of a domineering family patriarch (Saturn) with a mother who carries an emotional or physical wound (Moon in fall). But this assessment of dividing the conjunction into father (Saturn) and mother (Moon) is an oversimplification of Perry's childhood experiences. It is more likely that both parents share the aspect in some way, and the role of Saturn/Moon parenting was alternated between Katy's two nurturing figures.

Her mother may have been strict, or cold, or jealous of father's affection for his daughter, or her father may have been absent spending more time with his parishioners than with his family (Saturn rules 3rd and 4th houses). He may have felt his commitments to God were more important than his commitments to his family. Both parents chose the Church as adults to atone for what they described as 'a wild youth', and Saturn's inclination towards motives driven by guilt may have made the rules of their house extra harsh (Saturn rules 4th house), or unusual.[18]

Astrological statements in both Katy Perry and Kelly Osbourne suggest a mother's struggles, particularly where males or the girls' fathers are concerned. Both men, however different the story of their lives, felt they had a pathway to follow and the women who loved them learned to adapt, though it brought detriment and difficulty.

Sharon Osbourne may be the more famous of the two mothers but a common thread links them to choosing spouses who have let them fall into painful states at some stages in their lives. Katy's Moon is in fall, and in the same degree as her Saturn, and her mother's house, the 10th, is ruled by Katy's Sun in contention. By the time Kelly was born two days after Katy the Moon had moved out of its fall sign of Scorpio, and into Sagittarius, but it was now conjunct the unpredictable energy of Uranus, and her Sagittarian Moon is disposited by Jupiter, in its fall sign of Capricorn. Pisces is Kelly's tenth sign, so the ruling planet's state of fall reinforces her mother statement of difficulty and heartache, even when associated with a famous husband. Both daughters, Katy and Kelly, have been sensitive to their mothers' distress and have experienced a child's feeling of helplessness under the weight of a parent's sorrow or anxiety.

Katy has a daughter of her own, Daisy Dove Bloom, born in August 2020, and she is adamant that whilst she works 'a lot', she insists she will play a visible and active role in her daughter's life. "I have a wonderful nanny (for Daisy), but I feel that if I had a full-time nanny I would never be able to know how to care for my daughter."[19]

Saturn's strong sense of responsibility and its desire to be accountable for its actions will keep Katy Perry true to these words and make her a constant figure in her daughter's childhood. As Saturn is the timekeeper, it will ensure Perry does everything in her power to balance the heavy workload of her munakara Sun, in a diurnal chart, with her Saturnian commitment to her role as mother to a young daughter.

Perry's one risk to her maternal responsibilities is that Saturn can exhaust the Moon's capacity to nourish the body. The strain of Saturn through overwork, unrealistic schedules, or any demands placed on her by future touring may mean she cannot keep her promises, either to herself, or to her daughter. Perry's own expectations of excellence (munakara Sun) may bounce back on Mars, the ruler of her Scorpio stellium, and even in exaltation, Mars may not be able to keep running on empty, when it is not only the Ascendant Lord (her physical resilience) but also the ruler of her debilitating 6th house (illness and accident).

Scorpio Sun in Munakara: Kelly Osbourne

Brief Biography of Kelly Osbourne

Kelly Osbourne was born on 27 October 1984 and is the middle child of Ozzy Osbourne, heavy metal singer and television personality, Sharon Osbourne. Her father Ozzy was fired from Black Sabbath in 1979, five years before Kelly's birth, due to his alcohol and drug addiction problems.

Transforming into a solo artist, Ozzy released *Blizzard of Oz* in 1980, and a further 12 studio albums. Kelly and her siblings grew up travelling with her father as he went on tour during the 1980s and 1990s, living in more than 20 homes across the US and the UK. During this time Ozzy found great success as a solo artist, as well as briefly rejoining Black Sabbath at various points, including the opportunity to record the group's final studio album *13* in 2013 and touring with the band on a farewell tour that ended in 2017.

Ozzy's biggest financial success of the 1990s was a venture named Ozzfest, an annual music festival created and managed by his wife/manager Sharon. Since its beginning, five million people have attended Ozzfest, which ran most years from 1996 to 2018 and grossed over US$100 million.

Kelly first came to prominence while appearing with her family on the reality show *The Osbournes* (2002–2005). The series started when Kelly was seventeen and ended when she was twenty. Originally the camera crew were only supposed to be in their house filming for a few weeks but ended up staying for months as the series grew in popularity. Kelly's debut album *Shut Up* was released in 2002 by Epic records and her second album *Sleeping in the Nothing* was released in 2005.

In 2004 Kelly launched her own fashion line, Stiletto Killers, a rock-inspired line of t-shirts, hoodies and sweatpants and was a viable business until closing in April 2006. She has worked in television in acting and hosting roles and film since the early 2000s.

- **Key Questions:**
- What does Kelly Osbourne's Sun contend with?
- What is its driving force?
- What is its trigger? What is its outcome?

Kelly Osbourne's munakara Sun is more about testing her strength to survive than it is about her desire to achieve fame and glory, probably

Chapter Six • *Sun in Munakara*

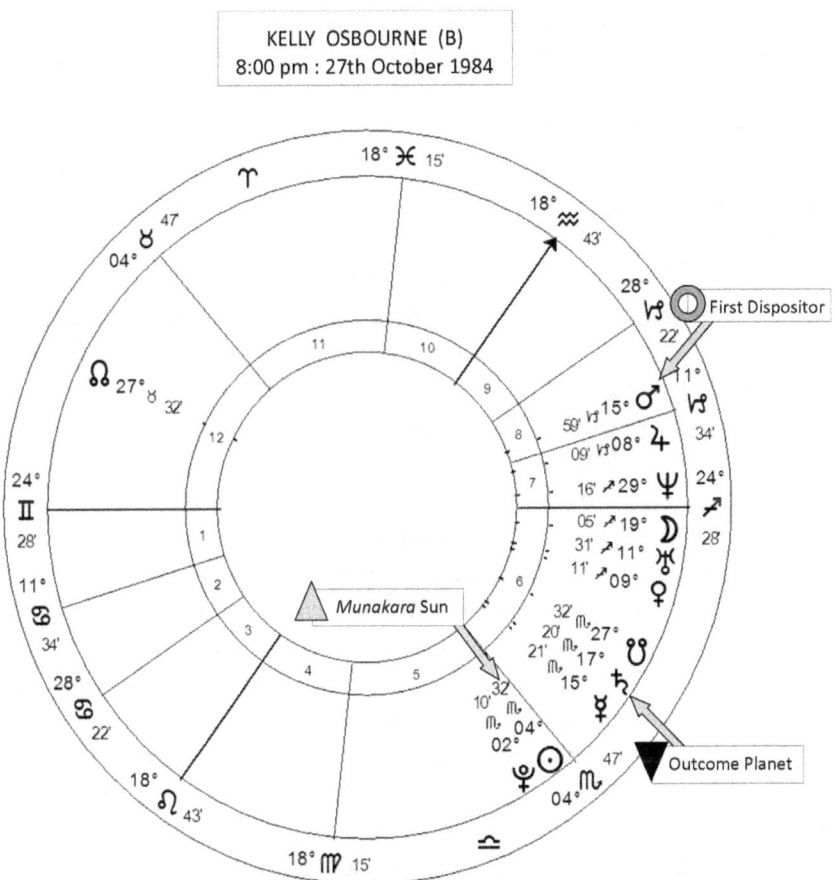

Fig. 6.3: Kelly Osbourne: Munakara Sun in Scorpio

because her Sun has lived with these themes for her entire life. Similar to Katy Perry's chart Kelly's MC and Imum Coeli (IC) are also ruled by Saturn and the Sun, but the signs are reversed and munakara Sun rules the IC and outcome planet Saturn, rules her Mid-heaven. Both women experienced transient childhoods, parents moving constantly across the US in search of something more, but unlike Katy Perry, Kelly was born into the world of music and entertainment, travelling most of her childhood in tour buses, and receiving her early education in transit.

The daughter of a famous but troubled rock star, Kelly's daily routine was high jacked by summer tours and constant dramas on the road as Ozzy's group toured the country. Munakara Sun conjunct Pluto was witness to the motto of 'living life large' and with munakara Sun ruling Leo on her IC (the opposite parental axis to Katy Perry), Kelly was accustomed to the extreme and sometimes violent behaviour of adults under the influence of alcohol and a concoction of drugs.

Sharon Osbourne, Kelly's mother, is represented by Saturn-ruled Aquarius on the Mid-heaven. Sharon shielded her three children as best she could from the mayhem, making sure they travelled in their own bus when on tour – a bus that was always parked discreetly away from other band members' mobile homes in case things got out of hand after the nightly concerts.

Any child's mental and physical stability would be questionable under these circumstances but munakara Sun ruling the IC took another leap forward into craziness when in 2000 the MTV reality show, *The Osbournes* brought around the clock camera crews into the family home where Kelly was living as a 17-year-old teenager.

The show was a tremendous success and went viral but the public's fascination with her family, the exploitation of Sharon's battle with cancer, and Ozzy's recovery from an ATV accident which nearly killed him, was too much exposure for Kelly's munakara Sun. To add extra spice to the viewing, Kelly was portrayed as a pint-sized, foul-mouthed, self-involved teenager in the series, and this one-dimensional view of her personality has taken her years to shed as she painfully and publically matured into adulthood. In hindsight the show exploited the Osbourne family in their own home (munakara Sun ruling IC) and made entertainment of their foibles, their weaknesses, their insecurities and their vulnerabilities.

Only one member, sister Aimee, a year older than Kelly and 18 at the time, was wise enough to self-protect by refusing to participate in the show. Aimee says: "Back then, I still felt I was trying to figure out who I was in the chaos of family life, so why on Earth would I want that portrayed on television? I wanted to protect myself, my parents, my siblings, too. They were very young, very impressionable."[20] Leo is the third sign in Kelly's Whole Sign chart and although the two girls are close in age (only 14 months separate them), Kelly's munakara Sun creates estrangement between the siblings with Kelly quoted saying: "We don't talk. We're just really different. She doesn't understand me and I don't understand her."[21]

Exalted Mars in Capricorn triggers the Sun's reactions, and its placement in the 8th house is more about chaos, drug and alcohol abuse, and Kelly's close calls with death, than it is about Saturn's sign of self-control and self-discipline. In her earlier years Kelly's munakara Sun (disposited by Mars) focused on pushing the boundaries constantly towards self-destruction, and her rehabilitation stints consumed social media sites in the first decade of 2000s, but Kelly is a survivor and her battle over dependency on medication and alcohol is a lifelong struggle.

Mars rules Kelly's 6th house, and Saturn resides there with Mercury two degrees away. Saturn's ability to survive under extreme situations has presented Kelly with many challenges, including accidents. When she fell down the stairs in her London apartment in November 2005, Kelly injured a nerve in her back, affecting her ability to walk. Poor health has also dogged Kelly due to a decade of undiagnosed Lyme's disease from 2004 to 2014, with a variety of symptoms such as fever, a constant sore throat, severe fatigue, depression, sleep disturbances, abdominal pain and seizures, and a skin rash. Much of her drug dependency during this period was not illicit drugs, but rather as a result of a string of drug treatments prescribed by puzzled physicians, who could find no suitable diagnosis for her wide-ranging symptoms.

Munakara Planet and Sect Condition – how comfortable is the Sun?

Kelly Osbourne's chart has a Rodden 'B-Rating' as her birth time was accessed from Todd Gold's book *Officially Osbourne: Opening the Doors to the Land of Oz* (Simon & Schuster, 2002). The book claims Kelly was born at 8:00pm. This time places her Scorpio Sun in munakara in a nocturnal position in the lower hemisphere of the chart.

Kelly Osbourne — ☉'s Sect Dignity			
Planet	Sect 1 Status	Sect 2 Hemisphere	Sect 3 Sign
♏ ☉	Night	Sun Defines	Water
D	N	D	N

Table 6.11: Kelly Osbourne: Munakara Sun's Sect Dignity

By the second rule of sect (travelling with or without the Sun) the solar planet defines its hemisphere, and therefore is never in a state of *ex conditione* (no sect dignity). However, a nocturnal chart coupled with a feminine sign does little to give the impression that Kelly's Sun has the same measure of comfort in is environment as did Katy Perry's Sun in her diurnal chart. By the time Kelly was born, her munakara Sun had moved two degrees further into Scorpio, putting a little more distance between Pluto and the Sun. In Kelly's Placidus chart, her Sun is in the same degree as her 6th-house cusp, so by both house systems, it would be considered to be a 6th-house Sun.

Munakara in Theory

A munakara Sun is always challenging for the individual's perception of their self-identity, and certain positions in a night-time chart add a little extra stress for the Sun. Kelly was born at night, and although we recognise the Sun's presence by placing it in the astrology chart, in physical terms the Sun is missing from the night landscape. Darkness creates a level of insecurity and an awareness of space needs to be cultivated to protect the physical body from harm and injury. This is the Moon's job and Kelly's night-time birth makes her Sagittarian Moon the main luminary in her chart. The Moon is not in debility (as is Katy's Scorpio Moon) but it still disposits to Jupiter in fall. The Moon opposes the Ascendant and this can add to the statement of illness or physical struggle to the individual's life.

Kelly's munakara Sun is situated in her 6th house and this placement is stressful for the luminary because it is difficult for the Sun to show its true brilliance in one of the darkest houses (bar the 12th house) in the chart. The 6th house represents a place which is dedicated to self-denial, duty, self-sacrifice, and preferred invisibility. Health issues often consume the Sun's energy in the 6th house, and this is not helped by Kelly's munakara Sun being in conjunction with Pluto. Add the Ascendant's lord, Mercury, also located in the 6th house, with Saturn (a natural health-destroyer), and then throw in the malevolent South Node in Scorpio, with the four planets in the same sign – all of which add to the health warnings in Kelly's chart.

Kelly's munakara Sun has an identical sequence to Katy Perry's Sun, as none of the two deciders from different sect camps – Sun and Mars – have changed their zodiacal sign in the two days between births. Saturn, the Sun's outcome planet, has not moved from 17° Scorpio from two days earlier, but it has changed from its partile conjunction to Katy's Scorpio Moon to conjunct Kelly's Mercury. The Moon's swift movement over the two day separation in birth dates has taken it away from Saturn's grip (Katy) and Mercury's degrees have increased, so that now it forms a closer conjunction to Saturn (Kelly).

Kelly's health issues have been mentioned above, and whilst the degree difference between Jupiter and Mars has remained at seven, the shift in sign position in a nocturnal chart means that Mercury (troubled by Saturn) rules the Ascendant and the Whole Sign 4th house, whilst Jupiter (in fall, in Saturn's sign) rules Kelly's 7th and 10th houses by Whole Sign. There is no aspect or recognition of the Ascendant by Mercury, with Mercury in Scorpio blind (in aversion) to Gemini. The Ascendant is therefore thwarted in its attempts to identify Kelly's immediate environment and Mercury is more likely to do her body harm from its position in her 6th house of illness, neglect, and accident.

Chapter Six • *Sun in Munakara*

Kelly's Munakara Sun Pluto in 5th House (Placidus)

"To make any kind of positive change, you have to accept yourself for who you are right now, not some imagined dream girl (or guy) who has zero wobbly bits and never needs to fart.... You will never be perfect, I will never be perfect, no one will ever be perfect, because perfection does not exist." – Kelly Osbourne, *There is no f*cking secret: Letters from a Badass Bitch*

Kelly's munakara Sun in 5th house was perfect fodder for a reality show, *The Osbournes*, which began filming in 2000 and ran from 2002–2005. The show ran during her puberty years, when no child welcomes scrutiny or needs to feel different from their teenage peers. The same year that Katy ran off to Los Angeles to be a singer, Kelly was exposed and vulnerable too, but for different reasons. Kelly's wrote her second autobiography *There is no F*cking Secret: Letters from a Badass Bitch* in 2017, and rather than following the usual format of chronological events in her life, Kelly's book is a series of random letters, written to different parts of her life about her struggle to find herself and gain independence from her famous family. The book is funny, raw, and incredibly honest, and I recommend taking the time to read it, especially if you are wondering what a Sun in munakara looks like from the perspective of someone who has truly played the role of a contentious woman.

In Whole Sign, Kelly's Sun slips from the 5th into the 6th house, and the journey towards Kelly 'finding herself' has led through some harrowing pathways of illness, drug and alcohol addiction, food issues and mental health concerns. The Sun has experienced highlights too, but with Leo on the IC, it has led back to Kelly's dichotomy between her fierce love and pride in her father's achievements, and her frustration with her father's habitual self-destructive patterns.

In the chapter entitled "Dear Rehab," Kelly says that reading a book on co-dependency was a turning point in her movement towards recovery.[22] Kelly began to recognise some of her own self-destructive attributes in the list of co-dependent traits: feeling responsible for solving others' problems, offering advice when unasked, poor understanding and communication of one's feelings and needs, chronic anger states, feeling used and unappreciated, and difficulty making decisions or adjusting to change. An acknowledgement of these traits within oneself is invaluable, especially when coming to terms with how Sun in munakara keeps crossing the boundary into nocturnal territory, and keeps falling into the same old patterns.

First Dispositor for Scorpio Sun: Mars in Capricorn
Kelly's Capricorn Mars in 8th House

Kelly Osbourne's Mars also rules her 6th house, but from the perspective of Mars's water sign, Scorpio, rather than its fire sign of Aries. Mars's placement in Kelly's 8th house shows she has tested the boundaries so far as taking risks with her life that may have ended badly. The company she kept in her earlier wild days did not help her Moon's spatial awareness, a concern when Kelly's chart is nocturnal, and the Moon is the prime luminary.

Kelly's munakara Sun is disposted by Mars which conjuncts Jupiter, Mars ruling the 11th house suggests friends with similar addictive habits and deep pockets to pay for these habits. Kelly and friends have had a Jupiterian good time with little concern for risk or repercussions.

Father Ozzy's duels with death are also shown by Kelly's 11th house in Whole Sign (4th house, father, plus eight, his death, is 11th house). With Aries on its cusp, Whole Sign 11th house is owned by Mars and perhaps for father and daughter, the fact that Kelly's Mars is exalted shows their joint resilience in surviving self-destructive habits.

As the dispositor for her Scorpio Sun, Kelly's exalted Mars has learnt from her mother how to manipulate social media, providing Kelly with a sizeable income as she has worked hard to create her own career away from her famous family. The exaltation may have opened doors but perseverance and an uncanny eye for popular street fashion has helped her to launch her own fashion line. Stiletto Killers was launched in 2004 and earned Kelly several hosting jobs, various acting roles, a spot on 2009 *Dancing with the Stars* series, and a role in 2011 as fashion correspondent with Joan Rivers on *Fashion Police*. It was on the set of *Fashion Police* in March 2013 that Kelly collapsed and suffered a seizure which led to a correct diagnosis of Stage 3 Lyme's disease, a serious level of infection, after ten miserable years of suffering from the neurological disease.

The outcome planet for Munakara Sun: Saturn in Scorpio
Kelly's Saturn conjunct Mercury in 6th House

> "The only thing I can do is be true to myself and think about what I post before I post it. I try to represent myself as honestly as possible, while most people put a lot of time and effort into constructing their social media presence to be the person they wish they were."[23]

Chapter Six • *Sun in Munakara*

Kelly's night-time birth makes her Sagittarian Moon the main luminary in her chart and although the Moon is not in debility (as with Katy's Scorpio Moon), it still disposits to Jupiter in fall. Jupiter's conjunction with Mars is a force to be reckoned with but appears to have manifested in years of addiction. In addition, both planets are disposited by Saturn, and Saturn's position in the 6th house indicates long-term health problems.

Kelly states in her book that she suffered for ten years from Lyme disease, a bacterial infection caused by a bite from an infected tick. Symptoms such as a rash, fever, fatigue and headaches are common, but the infection can become serious, spreading to affect the joints, heart and nervous system. Even with prompt diagnosis and immediate treatment symptoms can last for more than six months after treatment has been successfully completed. Lyme disease can also affect thinking, memory and cognitive skills, and with Kelly's Saturn conjunct her Mercury, these are the symptoms which Kelly says distressed her most with her experience of the infection. Kelly's case had gone undetected for ten years, often masked by bouts of drug use, and by the time it was finally diagnosed, she was told by doctors that she was six months away from having a heart attack, or ending up in a wheelchair.

Saturn as the outcome planet for the Sun is not going to make for an easy journey to find oneself. Feelings of inadequacy, insecurity, self-doubt and a fear of failure can mean that taking action to fix these issues is going to take time. It also requires a great deal of honest evaluation to correct these negative feelings, so it is encouraging to see Kelly's courage as she (literally) addresses her problems in her 2017 book *There is No F*cking Secret: Letters from a Badass Bitch*. Saturn also affects Kelly's self-esteem as Mercury, the lord of her Ascendant, is conjunct Saturn, and Kelly has been judged harshly on several occasions, when her online comments have been misrepresented or misconstrued.

> "Dear Mouth, On occasion, you've gotten me into real trouble. Sometimes you've spit out utterly the wrong words. But I am not racist. Never have been, or will be."[24]

Kelly announced her first pregnancy in May 2022, and perhaps taking responsibility for another human being (Saturn) will be a new growth in maturity and a step closer to self-actualization as Kelly takes on the new role of mother to her infant. Sharon will need to respect Kelly's need for privacy and to be careful that she does not overstep the mother/daughter boundaries, but it may be too late as she excitedly announced the new baby's arrival on daytime television, and then revealed his name, 'Sidney' – without Kelly's consent – on the January 3rd, 2023 episode, of her UK TV show *The Talk*. Kelly responded to her mother's indiscretion the next day on her Instagram page saying, "I am not ready to share him with the world. It is no one's place but mine to share any information on my baby."[25]

Kelly's Saturn, Sun's outcome planet, will be ferociously protective over her infant son, and Kelly will try to avoid the same mistakes her parents made in pursuing their own rise to fame and notoriety. Neither Sharon nor Ozzy have munakara Suns in their charts, so it may be hard for them to understand Kelly's need to be authentic to her own beliefs whilst at the same time dealing with the trappings of her famous family. Sharon may not give full weight to Kelly's need for boundaries, especially as they were missing in her childhood, but Saturn's relationship with Mars is solid given that the two planets in the Sun's sequence are in mutual reception and are in a sextile aspect with one another. This aspect between nocturnal first dispositor and diurnal outcome planet may be the protective factor Kelly has needed in her life, and the reason her munakara Sun has survived against all odds.

A Further Example of Munakara Sun: Friedrich Nietzsche and Vincent van Gogh

Philosopher and writer Friedrich Nietzsche's birth took place in 1844. He was the son and grandson of Lutheran Protestant pastors. The death of his father before his fifth birthday meant Friedrich was raised in a strongly religious matriarchal household, with a young widowed mother, his father's powerful mother, his father's two neurotic unmarried sisters, and a sister Elisabeth, who was two years younger than himself. Nietzsche had two planets in contention: his Libran Sun is munakara, disposited by Venus in Virgo, and Virgo Mars is munakara, disposited by diurnal Mercury in Libra.

Dutch Post-Impressionist painter Vincent van Gogh was born nine years after Nietzsche on 30th March 1853. Van Gogh was born into an upper-middle-class family and was a serious, quiet and thoughtful boy but showed signs of mental instability. He was the oldest surviving child of Theodorus van Gogh, a minister of the Dutch Reformed Church, and his wife, Anna Cornelia Carbentus. Van Gogh was given the name of his grandfather and of a brother stillborn exactly a year before his birth. On checking the

Chapter Six • *Sun in Munakara*

ephemeris it is interesting to note that his stillborn brother with the same name, born 30th March 1852, did not have Sun (or Saturn) in munakara as Mars was in Cancer a year before van Gogh's birth. Vincent van Gogh had two planets in contention: his Aries Sun is munakara, disposited by Mars in Pisces, and Taurus Saturn is munakara, disposited by Venus in Pisces.

The charts of Friedrich Nietzsche and Vincent van Gogh are delineated in Part Two in the chapter on Munakara Sun.

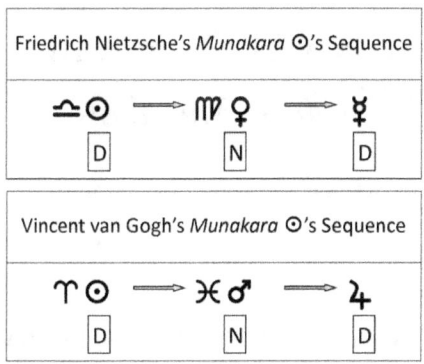

Table 6.12: *Part Two Munakara Sun Sequences: Friedrich Nietzsche and Vincent van Gogh*

CHAPTER SEVEN
Mars in Munakara

What does it mean when Mars is in a state of munakara?

- Suspicion about others' motives
- Defensive behaviour in the face of threats, whether real or perceived
- Experiences of bullying, confrontational or frightening behaviours
- Extremes of confrontation – either seeing challenges as full scale battles or avoiding confrontation at all costs
- Questioning one's bravery or courage
- Struggles over control or power
- Long-term battles, possibly involving chronic health issues

Table 7.1: Some Possible Expressions of Mars in munakara

Munakara Mars and Personal Challenges

Mars is a complicated planet when it comes to sect division. Mars belongs to the club of masculine planets and thus should sit alongside Saturn, Jupiter, and the Sun in sect alliance. Instead, it becomes the only masculine planet that belongs in the nocturnal sect with its female counterparts.

As a nocturnal planet, Mars must assist the Moon in identifying and protecting the space surrounding the individual. Mars is concerned with advancing into a space and once there, conquering, maintaining, and defending it. Mars's sect dignity in a chart plays a critical role in how it will go about protecting the space. Too diurnal of a placement and it risks becoming ferocious, aggressive and unpredictable. Any sign of nocturnality and Mars "gains a sense of compassion or feeling. ...The moisture of the night cools Mars down and connects it to other beings. Mars becomes a defensive, sustaining energy."[1]

Munakara is not a terrible disaster that should be feared if found in the chart. Rather, it is a special quirk that can bring defiance or the questioning of something that others take for granted. Munakara planets can test bravery and resilience in the face of setbacks or hardship. The contention at the heart of munakara can manifest as the desire to assert an opinion, to present a hypothesis with enthusiasm, to ardently affirm a particular stand, or strongly proclaim a statement backed by a belief or doctrine.

When challenged, munakara Mars throws down the gauntlet. The individual is often surprised when others agree but do not have the same conviction to fight for their beliefs. Munakara Mars can be merciless if any weakness is shown by allies or opponents, particularly if it is an out of sect Mars. If munakara Mars displays contempt for its allies because they lack the same 'do-or-die' attitude then it is left to fight the battle alone and the individual's anger is not only aimed at its enemies, but also at those who have betrayed and abandoned them.

Mars is already a fighter and Mars in munakara feels like an extra dose of provocation. Mars is a planet of passion and strong emotions, sometimes bordering on obsessive in its focus and its execution. Even when it is forging ahead, at the same time, it builds its defences in case it is attacked. Munakara Mars has problems with the planets in its sequence as it truly understands the term 'enemy territory'. Mars is proficient in 'hot' separations – fast releases brought about by anger, rage, argument, resentment, anguish – and when munakara is present, Mars lives in a constant state of planning its strategy, ready to move to the battlefield and engage with the enemy.

The other two planets in munakara Mars's sequence need careful attention, so that when circumstances present themselves Mars can use its energy in a productive manner rather than as a weapon. Mars will use anything at its disposal, and that includes its dispositor as a weapon, whether it is control or an abuse of power (Saturn), flattery, money or influence (Jupiter), emotive words or persuasion (Mercury), or the bluff of authority (Sun) to gain an advantage.

Mars's outcome planet will describe what it is protecting, or what power or advantage it expects to gain by its conquest. The other nocturnal planet at the other end of Mars's sequence will also be conscious of space, and Mars will defend or destroy through its outcome planet. Venus signifies women, popularity and privilege. The Moon is the family or the 'heart impulse', but sometimes heartache and revenge if separations are painful and circumstances have left no closure for the Moon to commence its healing process. Nocturnal Mercury will have its own plans for Mars, and these need constant review and modification because Mercury is fickle and changes direction with little warning.

By understanding the nature of Mars's diurnal first dispositor, and its nocturnal outcome planet, munakara Mars may choose a less destructive option. Triggers such as money problems, constant blocks or mounting frustration, exhaustion, illness, differences of opinion or family tensions, can set munakara Mars in motion. Identifying the triggers through the ruling planet or its location in the chart can ease Mars's distress and convince it to stand down.

Some individuals with munakara Mars choose to rebel through harnessing the power of the pen rather than wielding the sword. Alice Ann Bailey, founder of Esoteric Astrology, was the author of thirty books on metaphysical subjects, and one of the first writers to use the term 'New Age'. Bailey's chart has Leo Mars dispositing to Gemini Sun to nocturnal Mercury and the fact that an accurate birth time is questionable does not alter munakara Mars's sequence. Bailey states in her autobiography that she prefers Pisces as her rising sign (midnight birth), although other astrologers believed her Ascendant to be Leo or Virgo (birth in the late morning).[2] Mercury as Mars's outcome planet shows her prolific writings, and Bailey's Jupiter and Saturn in Aries are also munakara (Aries Jupiter/Saturn to Leo Mars to Sun).

Perhaps it was her munakara Mars – first dispositor for Jupiter and Saturn – which lent Bailey the courage to leave the safety of her wealthy British middle-class family, travel to India, and then migrate to the United States with husband Walter Evans. Munakara Mars made her brave enough to divorce Evans in 1915, when the marriage failed, and to work in a sardine factory to support her three young children on a single mother's wage. Bailey joined the Theosophical Society in 1918 and quickly rose to a prominent position in the American Section. Her battles with Annie Besant, president of the Theosophical Society (1907–1933) were legendary, with Besant ejecting Alice and her second husband, Foster Bailey, from the organisation. Long after the deaths of the three women whose energies moulded The Theosophical Society – Helena Petrovna Blavatsky, Annie Besant, and Alice A. Bailey –

Chapter Seven • *Mars in Munakara*

the controversy rages on and as recently as 2015 an article titled, "14 Good Reasons To Question The Alice Bailey Teachings" was published on a website on Theosophy.[3]

Others with munakara Mars take a more direct route and choose to place themselves on a course towards confrontation and strife. Canadian-American conservation and environmental activist, Paul Watson, is the founder and former CEO of Sea Shepherd Conservation Society, an anti-poaching and direct action group focused on marine conservation activism which has been active for 45 years since its inception in 1977. Watson's munakara Mars has upset a number of countries, and led to legal action from authorities in the United States, Canada, Norway, Costa Rica, and Japan. In spite of his brushes with law enforcers, and outstanding warrants for legal infringements, Watson has never been imprisoned, perhaps due to the fact that both Mars in Capricorn, and Saturn in Libra, are both located in their exalted signs. Venus is Watson's outcome planet for his munakara Mars and it is his lifelong love of the sea and his ability to rally others who volunteer their time and energy to his cause that makes him a true 'rainbow warrior.'

Australian hacker and information warrior, Julian Assange, is the founder of WikiLeaks. Wikileaks released documents in 2007 showing apparent war crimes in Afghanistan and Iraq by the US military, which led to Assange's confinement and imprisonment for a total of 12 years from June 2012 to June 2024. It is interesting to note that Assange also has Jupiter in munakara and Assange's fight for freedom lasted a dozen years – a full Jupiter cycle. His chart is discussed in the following chapter on Jupiter in contention. Julian Assange's battle for freedom began in the Ecuadorean embassy in London where he was granted asylum in 2012. Assange was, however, taken into custody in April 2019 and moved to Belmarsh Prison for breaching his bail conditions. The pressure was immense as US authorities fought in court to extradite him to America to face charges under US law, and if convicted, to serve a life sentence in prison. His release from prison and his flight to Australia on June 24, 2024 was swift and unexpected as he pleaded guilty to one count of breaching the Espionage Act and in return was allowed to walk free and return to Australia. Similar to Paul Watson, Assange's Mars disposits to Saturn, but neither planet is exalted, as Mars is in Aquarius, and Saturn is in Gemini. Mercury is Assange's outcome planet for munakara Mars and his unwavering belief that any and every government should be held accountable for its actions (Saturn in Gemini) brought about the release of thousands of secret documents that were never meant to see the light of day.

Florence Nightingale is another individual with munakara Mars. Mars took her to the Crimean War (1853–1856), aged in her early thirties, where her campaign to improve hygiene standards in the temporary hospitals at Constantinople significantly reduced the death rate in wounded soldiers. "The Lady With the Lamp" would become a legendary symbol for compassion, fortitude and courage under extremely difficult circumstances. Unfortunately, munakara Mars meant that Nightingale's own health suffered from the experience and she spent the last 50 years of her life as an invalid. Being bedridden did not restrict her determination and she continued to write and publish on nursing standards when her poor health permitted. Florence Nightingale was ahead of her time as a pioneer in statistics, and she was a social reformer, not just in nursing and health care reforms, but in improving the plight of women in poverty, helping to abolish harsh prostitution laws, and creating better opportunities for women in the workforce. Her birth time is unknown but Mars does not leave Leo and Nightingale was born on a day when the Sun was in Taurus. Munakara Mars follows a sequence which sees Leo Mars disposit to a Taurean Sun, and Venus, the significator of women, is the nocturnal outcome planet for her Leo Mars.

Paul Gauguin was an outsider who could have lived a comfortable life with his wife and family in Paris had he remained as a wealthy stockbroker in the mid-1880s. But instead, he followed his passion for painting and paid the price by living an isolated life in poverty in the Polynesian islands. His art was ridiculed, his family abandoned, his wealthy friends refused to pay for his commissioned work. His artistic friend, Vincent Van Gogh, cut off his own ear and mailed it to Gauguin, after a drunken argument between the pair became violent. Gauguin could have had an easier life on the Islands as he owned a beautiful piece of land and planned to build his dream home from commissions for his work from the French authorities on the island. However, his commission was revoked and he was thrown off his land after he had rallied the local indigenous people to fight against the same authorities who were his employers. Gauguin could have swallowed his pride and returned chastened to his wife's wealthy family and resumed his comfortable lifestyle, but he chose starvation, tropical illness, and isolation to pursue his passion to become an artist of note. When Gauguin died, legend has it that a chest full of his artwork was thrown into the sea and his painted canvases were cut up by the locals to make shoes. Paul Gauguin had Mars in munakara in the same sequence as theosophical writer Alice Bailey, even though there was over 30 years between their respective births

Chapter Seven • *Mars in Munakara*

(Leo Mars to Gemini Sun to nocturnal Mercury in Cancer) and whilst he lived the life of a tortured artist – a true example of *Melencolia I* – his vibrant works of island life are a testament to the fact that he believed that following his passion was his only choice.

It is important to remember that munakara Mars may not always display the feisty nature of noise and bluster. Munakara Mars can also be a quiet battle of a more secret nature. Bravery is not always about drawing attention to oneself or promoting one's passion, but may also be quiet acts of dignity, determination and restraint, where the challenges are private, and sweet victories are personal, not meant for disclosure or bragging rights. Finding inner peace and a place of healing are equally valid. Learning to identify one's reaction to provocation and to direct munakara Mars towards non-confrontational reactions is an important lesson for an individual coming to terms with Mars in the state of munakara.

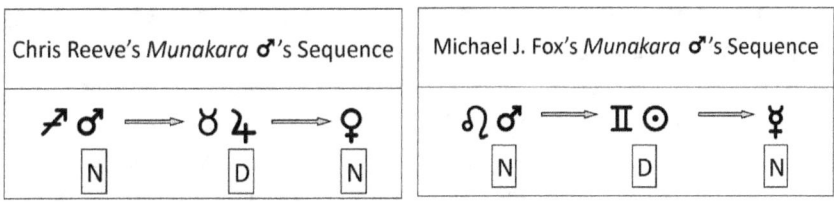

Table 7.2: Munakara Mars's Sequences for Christopher Reeve and Michael J. Fox

The chart of actor Christopher Reeve has both Moon and Mars in munakara. His chart is featured in Part Two on munakara Moon's delineations. Fellow actor, Michael J. Fox also has munakara Mars in a fire sign but his Mars sequence differs from Reeve's planets. Fox's chart is featured in Part Two on munakara Mars's delineations. Through either accident or illness, both men have needed their Mars to bear the strain of living with quiet dignity, courage and in the knowledge that they were not alone in suffering misfortune. Reeves and Fox have used their fame and influence to speak out for a cure, better treatment, or improved knowledge to educate the public. Both actors were, and are, activists for their respective causes, and have demonstrated dogged determination in overcoming the constant string of struggles placed before them.

The adversity visited upon these two men is not solely the expression of munakara Mars. The event itself might incorporate munakara but it does not end there. Rather, it shows a fighting spirit that combines tenacity with optimism, the type of optimism that is required to gain maximum benefit from life, *despite not because of* the challenge which has been presented to them. Both men believe/d in the possibility of a cure, or at the very least, an improved quality of life for themselves and others who suffer the same fate. Chris Reeve and Michael Fox have poured energy, time and resources into building foundations and institutions which bear their names, and financially and emotionally support thousands of others who share their disabilities. Sadly, Christopher Reeve did not live to see the miracle he hoped for, the ability to walk again. Michael J. Fox may not find the cure for Parkinson's Disease in his lifetime, but their generosity of spirit will mean that others can continue to benefit from their passion and optimism and the belief that science will eventually find an answer.

Munakara Mars and Society's Challenges

An individual with munakara Mars has several outlets for Mars's energy. This condition can be incredibly useful in solving issues which stretch society's resources or create societal strife and disharmony. Working in areas that alleviate societal stress or which strengthen resilience, can be something that occupies Mars in munakara on a professional level. Syphoning off some of munakara Mars's excess energy at work or in a community may be beneficial. For example, a career strengthening community resilience to natural disasters such as flooding, drought, fire or environmental damage can enthuse and captivate some of the restlessness or agitation created by munakara Mars. Redirecting Mars and providing it with a structure that builds on its energy may help it to focus on a practical outcome.

> *"The foundation of a free country is that your freedom to swing your fist ends where someone else's nose begins. That is, someone else is free to do what they like until it interferes with your physical body and space."*[4]

Mars in munakara values its ability to act as a free spirit, making its own decisions and mistakes, as it progresses through life. However, with freedom comes risk, and Mars in contention needs to learn to take responsibility for its actions, as there are often consequences if a risk is too great, or it infringes on other people's rights, or endangers their safety. An explanation of cause and effect may help Mars to understand that its behaviour affects others, that not all change is good, and that there can be unintended or negative consequences.

Chapter Seven • *Mars in Munakara*

German philosopher, Friedrich Nietzsche (1844–1900) lived a tortured life, but his ideas have become the basis of modern theologians, psychologists, poets, novelists, and philosophers of the twentieth century. Nietzsche had both his Sun and Mars in contention, and these are explored in Part Two of munakara Sun's delineations. Nietzsche's theory on the Last Man (featured in his *Thus Spoke Zarathustra*) is relevant to both planets, but the desire to create mayhem comes closer to the concept of Mars rather than the Sun which searches to find the meaning of its existence.

Nietzsche warned that if society did not change its ways, it was headed for a decaying system based on nihilism (Latin, meaning 'nothing'), and that its citizens would succumb to the belief that life has no meaning or purpose. He feared human civilization would simply focus on avoiding pain using the tools of comfort, convenience and risk reduction. He called this condition 'The Last Man' because he saw it as a return to an animal-like state of existence.

> "*Man is a rope, tied between beast and overman – a rope over an abyss. A dangerous across, a dangerous on-the-way, a dangerous looking-back, a dangerous shuddering and stopping.*"[5] – Friedrich Nietzsche, *Thus Spoke Zarathustra*

In Nietzsche's philosophy The Last Man (the beast) was in constant conflict with The Super Man (*Übermensch*) who was fearless, rebellious, wilful, ambitious and immune to failure, exhaustion or hardship. Nietzsche's Super Man was free to take action and conquer all obstacles with bravery and moral strength.

Without being aware of his two contentious planets, Nietzsche was celebrating the idealism of munakara Sun and Mars. Whilst his own mental frailty prevented him ever achieving this Super Man status for himself, his legacy is the concept of battling against the apathy of nihilism, and striving towards nobility of spirit and individuality. Sadly, during World War II, Hitler perverted Nietzsche's *Übermensch*, manipulating him to become a hideous image of Hitler's ideal Arian soldier.

Nietzsche hated antisemitism and distrusted German nationalism, and yet his words were used posthumously to serve Hitler's purposes and left a smear on his character, against which he was helpless to defend himself. The curse of being misunderstood or misinterpreted, whether deliberately or by accident is something that any planet in munakara can suffer, but when Mars is such a volatile energy, and is the representative for war and conflict, it is ripe for such a curse. The German philosopher's reputation took a battering through his words being distorted and misconstrued. This should be no surprise considering Mercury features in both his Sun and Mars sequencing; diurnal Mercury is the outcome planet for his Sun, and the first dispositor for his Mars in Virgo.

Mars's Sequence: Friends, Associates, and Enemies

The excerpt for Mars from al-Biruni's Table (*Table 7.3*) shows Mercury to be the only planet that does not take status as either friend or enemy to Mars.

D Diurnal / N Nocturnal	Essential Dignity Rulership / Exaltation (Mutual Damage)	Second Essential Dignity (Fall opposes Exaltation)	Second Essential Dignity — Borrowing Signs for Exaltation		
Munakara Planet △	Mutually Hurtful With (♂'s Two-Way Damage)	Injurious To (♂ Disposits Fall Sign)	Offering Friendship To (♂ Owns Exaltation Sign)	Asking Friendship From (Exalted ♂'s Dispositor)	Indifferent To ♂ - No relationship
[N] △ ♂	Jupiter : Venus [D] [N] First Dispositor : Outcome Planet ☉	[N] Moon (♍) ▼ Outcome Planet	[D] Sun (♐) ☉ First Dispositor	[D] Saturn (♑) ☉ First Dispositor	Mercury [D]/[N] [D] ☉ First Dispositor [N] ▼ Outcome Planet

Table 7.3: Al-Biruni's Table for Mars: Difficult Sequences for Munakara Mars

Friends and Associates of a munakara Mars: Sun, Saturn, & Mercury

If the Sun is involved in the sequence (as the first dispositor)

Leo Mars will disposit to the Sun, and the Sun will need to be in a sign belonging to a nocturnal planet, for munakara Mars in Leo to complete its sequence. Even though they belong to opposite sect divisions the Sun and Mars are quite compatible. They are both masculine planets and their natures feed from the desire to achieve a goal, the more unreachable the better. They loath safety and boredom and they share the need to conquer new territory. The Sun may pause a little longer to bask in the glory than Mars, who is impatient to move on, but both planets are naturally proactive masculine energies that need competition and a test of bravery.

It might be easy to confuse the nocturnal Mars with diurnal Sun but it should be remembered that Mars is an agent of the Moon and as such is as protective in its nature as it is proactive. If its dispositor (Sun) gives

Leo Mars respectability, praise or promotion along the way then Mars will not reject these solar benefits. Despite this, Mars's key role is to move into enemy territory in order to fight for and protect the individual's physical and emotional state (the Moon's domain). There may be rumours or scandals of failure along the way but if munakara is concerned with seeing the fight through to the finish, then these setbacks only fuel munakara Mars to fight harder or smarter in the future.

Leo Mars will take on some solar principles such as the need for autonomy as self-government, giving Mars the freedom to follow its own path. Munakara Mars may use physical challenges or highly unusual circumstances (see example charts below) to beat its way to success or to recognition or social change. However, this is Leo Mars in munakara and there will be another nocturnal planet as the third identity to complete Mars's sequence.

If the Sun is in Cancer, the Moon will be Mars's outcome planet. What better way for the Moon to witness Mars's courage than to take a ringside seat and keep testing Mars's loyalty and dedication to the task. If loved ones become part of the scenario then Mars and its dispositor, the Sun, will feel it is a matter of pride to defend something or someone the individual loves.

Nocturnal Mercury is likely to take a more direct method to provoke Mars into action and will feed it with thoughts, plans, language and sometimes outrageous schemes to invite Gemini or Virgo Sun into the contest. Taurus or Libra Sun will bring Venus into the picture as Leo Mars's outcome planet and defending one's honour or good name may involve women or women's roles in society.

Example Charts:
- Florence Nightingale (outcome planet, Venus)
- Paul Gauguin (outcome planet, Mercury)
- Alice Bailey (outcome planet, Mercury)
- Helen Keller (outcome planet, Moon)
- Cher (outcome planet, Venus)
- Dennis Rodman (outcome planet, Venus)
- Michael J. Fox (outcome planet, Mercury)
- Amy Winehouse (outcome planet, Mercury)

If Saturn is involved in the sequence (as the first dispositor)

Mars will be in either Capricorn or Aquarius if Saturn is the first dispositor for Mars. Similar to the Sun, they share the same gender and a friendly relationship when Saturn lends its sign to Mars for its exaltation. This will be where the similarities end as these two malefic planets are extreme in their temperaments and are going to create separations in order to get the job done. Aphorism #90 from Hermes Trismegistus' *Centiloquy*, states: "Saturn produces evil with slowness, but Mars produces it suddenly; and therefore Mars is reputed to be worse in harming."[6]

The *Centiloquy* uses the term 'evil' in its judgment, but in truth, 'separation' is a more accurate term, to describe the difference between Saturn and Mars. These two planets are extreme in their qualities. Both planets are extreme dryness, Saturn couples this with extreme cold, Mars with extreme heat. They are planets that practice the art of severance and their respective natures are driven to separate physically and metaphorically, in order to create change.

Saturn separates through coldness – lack of convenience, lack of contact, missed opportunities, poor timing or time-poor. A Saturnian separation will seem as though a close connection, project or friendship gently winds down through lack of common interest, a change in priority, neglect, or discomfort in one another's company. A reduction in energy, effort or availability over a period of time results in coldness where once there was warmth. This leads to apathy, disinterest, alienation, or disconnection which makes it feel as though the energy or interest that kept it together has been exhausted, and so it is time to move on to something new and exciting. A Saturn separation is often accompanied by feelings of regret and sometimes guilt, as neglect or diminishing commitment has probably played a role in its demise. Saturn's separations are separations of time and place no longer working to nourish a friendship or relationship. Shared experiences dwindle and the opportunity to spend time together often requires too much effort and contact diminishes into memories of the past. There is sadness and regret and even guilt over not maintaining contact, but the separation is 'cold', it feels like whatever connected you to the other person has run its race and it is time to move on.

Mars is a planet of heated arguments, bitter recriminations, anger and hurt feelings of betrayal and mistrust. A Mars separation is therefore completely different. The planet of extreme heat produces an angry confrontation, a heated exchange of harsh words, and mutual home-truths, words and actions that cannot be forgotten or forgiven. Mars's separations are bridges burned, where feelings of rage, betrayal, indignation and pain remain. The heat of Mars's separations is easily rekindled when thoughts of the injury arise. The

Chapter Seven • *Mars in Munakara*

initial feelings of anger can cool, but instead of dissipating, the scorched ground becomes lava fields of bitterness, and powerlessness.

Sometimes munakara Mars pre-empts a Saturn separation by finding fault or picking fights because there is a fear that a slow malingering death to the friendship/relationship is much worse that a clean break of tears and tantrums.

When munakara Mars is disposited by Saturn there will likely be both types of separation. Saturn gifts Mars with direction, purpose and discipline and if nocturnal Mercury is the outcome planet, then ideas are feverishly constant but not always reliable or practically manifested. This is the test for Mars in munakara – to be fresh and innovative but not crazy and confrontational. Saturn warns munakara Mars that there *will* be a price to pay for rebellion or anarchy but Mars in contention is not listening to Saturn, it is obsessed by Mercury who whispers that anything is possible if you are brave enough.

When munakara Mars is disposited by Saturn there may be constant obstacles or restrictions which keep bobbing up for Mars but as both of these planets are concerned with control issues – as in some authority/company/administration should be doing something but is corrupt or negligent – then the outcome planet (Moon, Venus, or Mercury) will trigger Mars's sequence to respond through the planets' house placements or the houses their signs rule in the chart.

Example Charts:
- Paul Watson (outcome planet, Venus)
- Elon Musk (outcome planet, Mercury)
- Julian Assange (outcome planet, Mercury)

If diurnal Mercury is involved in the sequence (as the first dispositor)

Mars in Gemini or Virgo will disposit to Mercury. This will only be the first step in the sequence if Mercury is travelling ahead of the Sun and is therefore diurnal in sect condition. Regardless of its sign, diurnal Mercury is a promoter of the Sun, and will do its best to inspire munakara Mars through innovative ideas, daring concepts and conversations that border on rebelliousness or lively discussions that quickly become loud or personal.

Munakara Mars dispoiting to Mercury can indicate communication difficulties, learning or speech difficulties. This can lead to social shyness (Venus as outcome planet), or emotional distress as a result of physical impairment (Moon as outcome planet) as Mercury rules the body's fine and gross motor skills. Even without these physical challenges, diurnal Mercury can feel the need to fight for or protect an idea or opinion, and Mars in Gemini or Virgo is more than happy to become involved in the intellectual struggle. As Mars is in munakara, heated discussions can get out of hand and deteriorate into personal slurs on the individual's character and the outcome planet – Moon or Venus – will indicate where the individual feels the most vulnerable.

Sometimes Mercury brings scandals for Mars to ruminate over, or some secret or hidden knowledge comes to light and the person must defend their honour or justify their actions. Getting a reputation as a trouble-maker is never easy to shake off particularly if the person with munakara Mars in Mercury's sign is the one who stirs the pot and does not walk away from insults or abuse. Mercury is the significator for siblings so there can be friction and old wounds of jealousy from the past that rear their head and lead to one of Mars's hot separations.

Munakara Mars in Mercury's signs has an urge to speak out and tell its truth, often upsetting the status quo or embarrassing someone who wishes to stay silent in the background. King Charles III's late ex-wife, Princess Diana, and his current wife, Queen Consort Camilla, have munakara Mars in diurnal Mercury's sign and ending in the Moon as the outcome planet. The battle was ultimately over a male monarchy-in-waiting (Charles) and both women used their Mars to great effect to influence his choice of partner.

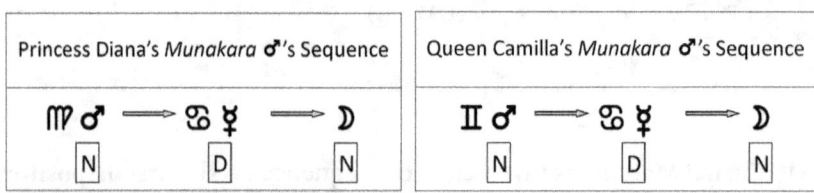

Table 7.4: Princess Diana and Queen Camilla: Munakara Mars's Sequence

Diana's munakara Mars is in her 8th house in Placidus but moves to the 10th sign in Whole Sign and is elevated with Pluto in her most public house after the Ascendant. Diana's motives to champion confrontational or uncomfortable Martian-themed causes – HIV/AIDS sufferers, landmine eradication programs, leprosy hospitals, children's cancer wards, mental health and addiction to name just a few – was certainly from a place of compassion and empathy (Moon as outcome planet). But Virgo Mars in munakara (with Mercury in 7th house) may have been trying to prove

Chapter Seven • *Mars in Munakara*

to Charles that she was the more appealing choice, particularly when it came to gaining the love and admiration of his subjects. Unfortunately, munakara Mars was a little too successful in this area and Charles found himself competing (Virgo Mars) and losing the media's attention (Cancer Mercury) to his vivacious and passionate young wife. Diana's munakara Mars rules her IC, and the staff to the Royals were more loyal to Charles than they ever were to her. The 4th house (IC) is also mother-in-law (ten houses from the 7th house) and as the marriage began to show stress, Diana turned to the Queen for guidance but Elizabeth was ill-prepared to deal with her emotionally vulnerable daughter-in-law. 'As the cracks between Charles and Diana emerged, so did those between the Queen and Diana,'[7] wrote Rachel Burchfield in *The Independent* (2022).

Camilla's munakara Mars is elevated too, but in the 11th house in both systems, and Camilla came from an aristocratic background that was more familiar and comfortable for the shy eldest son of Queen Elizabeth II. Had Camilla been available at the time the Royal Family were searching for a suitable mate for Charles (Moon as outcome planet), they might have considered Camilla, although it was rumoured that the family had caused the breakdown of their relationship nearly a decade before Diana came onto the scene. Camilla had gone on to marry Peter Parker Bowles in 1973.[8] Gemini Mars forms unions, speaks the same language, often has the same values and links its alliances through humour and attitudes that are reflected in the other person. Diana, 12 years Charles' junior, didn't have a chance against Camilla's Mars but she kept fighting for Charles' attention, that is, until the disastrous interview with BBC identity Martin Bashir in November 1995 when Diana admitted to her mental health struggles and Charles's affair with Camilla, stating, "There were three of us in this marriage, so it was a bit crowded."[9] In true Mars style, documents published in 2021 showed that Diana was tricked into the interview when she was presented with forged bank statements proving her affair with army captain James Hewitt, and the unethical actions of the BBC pushed Diana into a corner from which she felt there was no escape. Munakara Mars rules Diana's Whole Sign 12th house and Diana was fighting hidden enemies as well as those individuals in the Royal Family (Moon, outcome) who openly opposed and criticised her.

Example Charts:
- Princess Diana (outcome planet, Moon)
- Queen Camilla (outcome planet, Moon)
- Caitlyn Jenner (outcome planet, Venus)

If nocturnal Mercury is involved in the sequence (as the outcome planet)

Mars and Mercury are associates rather than friends or enemies – they neither benefit not harm each other. Therefore, the result of having nocturnal Mercury as munakara Mars's outcome planet is going to depend on how the individual uses Mercury as the 'solution' to Mars's state of munakara. Nocturnal Mercury often has an artistic side as it taps into the Moon's creative energy and allows the individual's thought processes to link to words, artwork, language, rhythm, movement, or music as a form of personal expression.

In the case of munakara Mars, nocturnal Mercury may be the impetus to create in a situation where Mars feels the need to separate in order to be independent or feel free to follow their own path. There is an element of this in the example charts below: Alice Bailey's search for enlightenment, Paul Gauguin's break from his comfortable life to pursue his dream as a painter, Chris McCandless' rejection of society to find adventure, Elon Musk's vision of travelling to Mars to start a new colony, and Julian Assange's technical brilliance in hacking and information distribution to the masses.

Nocturnal Mercury should perhaps think carefully about the consequences before taking inappropriate action or dangerous risks, especially where Mars is concerned. However, it seems that in the charts mentioned here that Mercury is more likely to feed Mars's craziness than to calm it down.

The diurnal planet placed between the two nocturnals will give some indication as to what interests both munakara Mars and nocturnal Mercury. If the middle planet is Jupiter then it will be in detriment in either Gemini or Virgo and any battle Mars engages in may feel unwinnable. The opponent is too strong, too clever, too well prepared for the battle or too powerful – this was the case for Chris McCandless when he opted out of society and chose to roam the country, free of obligations and duties.

When Saturn is the middle planet there is likely to be a battle with authority. The determination to speak out against an injustice that involves discrimination, abuse, corruption or exploitation. Mars in Saturn's signs can have a strong urge to change the system, but if the individual becomes overwhelmed by the sheer size of the problem, then they can be caught up in their own mental battles and nocturnal Mercury's path can be a journey into depression or anxiety. Elon Musk and Julian Assange have both encountered the darker side of a munakara Mars sequence involving Saturn and Mercury as there have been times in their lives where obstacles have been insurmountable and Saturn's vision has been bleak. It is all very well to encourage Mercury to break new ground, to be innovative and to challenge old patterns and old beliefs, but when everything seems to be working against you then exhaustion and doubt can creep in.

The Sun as the diurnal planet is going to encourage personal expression in some way as Leo Mars will look for independence or fight to express itself artistically or creatively. When nocturnal Mercury is the outcome planet for Leo Mars then individuality and authenticity become battlefields and the person feels they have something to champion and a reason to keep fighting – whether it is for independence, the right to make one's own decisions, or to have a say in their own destiny (Alice Bailey, Paul Gauguin, Amy Winehouse). Even the ability to speak can become a battle all on its own as the chart of actor Michael J. Fox demonstrates in his munakara Mars sequence of Leo Mars to Gemini Sun to Mercury in Cancer.

Example Charts:
- Alice Bailey
- Paul Gauguin
- Michael J. Fox
- Chris McCandless
- Elon Musk
- Julian Assange
- Amy Winehouse

Enemies of a munakara Mars: Jupiter, Moon & Venus

If Jupiter is involved in the sequence (as the first dispositor)

Mars in Sagittarius or Pisces will make Jupiter the first dispositor in a munakara Mars sequence. Jupiter suggests the battleground is large or the battle itself produces significant upheaval with repercussions. Jupiter prompts Mars to take risks, encouraging over-confidence or giving Mars the false impression that gambling with something that Mars cannot afford to lose is a good idea. In the heat of the battle Mars disposited by Jupiter will leave things to chance in the hope that things will go in their favour.

Munakara Mars with Jupiter as first dispositor will fight for a principle or spend its energy reserves on big visions, but commitment is hard for this combination and Mars may be unable to maintain the level of its interest and energy, particularly if there are responsibilities or restrictions.

Rather than making Mars dynamic and courageous, Jupiter adds recklessness and speed with a touch of ruthlessness, arrogance, and lack of caution. Mars in munakara does not need this kind of encouragement from

Jupiter if it is in Sagittarius or Pisces. Sagittarius adds to Mars's fiery nature and makes it unpredictable and dangerous, whilst Pisces Mars lacks control and has a feeling of being on the edge of madness. If Jupiter then deposits to a second nocturnal planet – Moon, Venus or nocturnal Mercury – then these behaviours become even more erratic.

In olden times Mars ruled wars, bloodshed and sudden death whilst Jupiter was representative of the king, his court and his ability to rule his subjects with wisdom and tolerance. Connecting them through aspect was either dangerous for the ruling classes who risked losing their power, or indicative of a cruel and malevolent ruler, whose unpredictability brought ruin to their subjects. The combination of Mars and Jupiter was a dire warning of danger, most likely to accelerate conflict and end in disaster.

The outcome planet for Sagittarius or Pisces Mars may soften the effects of munakara Mars. However, whatever risks are taken, the outcome planet will need to be ready to deal with foolish actions or risky behaviour. Venus is an opponent to Mars so it may be that the individual is robbed of something they love, and this loss is deeply felt when Mars separates through grand 'Jupiterian' gestures.

Example Charts:
- Neil Diamond (outcome planet, Venus)
- Janis Joplin (outcome planet, Moon)
- Christopher Reeve (outcome planet, Venus)
- Chris McCandless (outcome planet, Mercury)

If the Moon is involved in the sequence (as the outcome planet)

The Moon has very little power to harm Mars but the fact that their respective signs are not beneficial – Moon in Scorpio is in fall, Mars in Cancer is in fall – is a warning that the Moon has its own ways of disrupting munakara Mars when it is the outcome planet. Both nocturnal planets are sensitive conduits for emotions, and they use intuition to assess danger. The Moon can highlight feelings of isolation or rejection and Mars will respond with anger, defensiveness or feigned indifference.

Mars's role as the Moon's protector can be strained by the two planets belonging to the same sequence as Mars is on the alert for danger and the Moon, as the outcome planet, is hitting every trigger it can to activate a Martian response. The sensitivity felt by both nocturnal planets at either end of Mars's sequence will be picked up by the diurnal planet which separates the two forces. This munakara Mars sequence is about finding a safe haven,

Chapter Seven • *Mars in Munakara*

receiving sanctuary, being physically and mentally at peace with oneself.

The middle planet, the diurnal Sun, Saturn, Jupiter or Mercury, will show what torments the individual and indicate what it is they are trying to achieve through Mars. The Sun may be a search for autonomy and the right for independence despite physical restrictions (Helen Keller). Jupiter may be a larger-than-life dream to succeed against all odds and ease the pain of social rejection (Janis Joplin). Mercury may be the right to speak out and be accepted for who you really are and not who you're perceived to be (Princess Diana) or to shake off the memory of a beloved deceased rival who you will be compared against until the end of your days (Camilla). Munakara Mars with Moon as the outcome planet shows the wound is deep and healing may feel impossible, but Mars is a fighter and never gives up or backs away from the challenge no matter how hopeless, exhausting or painful the quest may seem.

Example Charts:
- Helen Keller
- Janis Joplin
- Princess Diana
- Queen Camilla

If Venus is involved in the sequence (as the outcome planet)

The nature of two oppositions – Aries to Libra, or Taurus to Scorpio – produces bitterness between the ruling planets of these signs. When Venus becomes Mars's outcome planet in its munakara sequence there are issues in crossing gender boundaries between the masculine animus (Mars) and the feminine anima (Venus). Two charts which demonstrate the challenge of trying to successfully balance these diverse energies are the charts of Caitlyn Jenner (*see p. 275*) and basketball legend, Dennis Rodman (*see p. 589*).

The tension created by these opposing forces has taken these individuals on journeys where they find themselves at odds with society's expectations, and it has required strength of character, courage and enormous willpower to stand up and live with honesty and integrity whilst refusing to compromise on what gender means for them.

Ptolemy's Aphorism #12 reads, "Love and hatred prohibit the true accomplishment of judgments; and, inasmuch as they lessen the most important, so likewise they magnify the most trivial things."[10]

These two nocturnal planets are passionate emotive energies. If Venus is Love that tries to bind all things together, forever, then Mars is Hate that uses all its energy to drive them apart. Planets in munakara struggle to make good judgements based on logic and reason, especially when heated. The more heated they become the more unlikely they are to hold the problem at a distance and things become distorted, magnified, overwhelming in their complexity. Munakara Mars is no exception to this and is perhaps the planet most likely to react from an emotional base of Love or Hate – 'I love this, so I will defend it to my last breath', or 'I hate this so much, I will not rest until it has been destroyed'. In that reaction, it creates a perfect atmosphere for change within the individual and even within society. Sometimes a person's fame and bad fortune will magnify the problem, and they become a figurehead, or projection for something the public will no longer tolerate in its midst. Sometimes, their fate illuminates a problem that is forgotten or seen as too hard to address, and their fight becomes a battlefield for the collection of large resources to enable advancement in research or changes to political or social stagnation.

Venus is the symbolic representative for women and munakara Mars often becomes the champion of women, whether that individual is a female who chooses to fight for their gender through the example of their own life, or they have a desire to express their femininity in their own individual way.

Example Charts:
- Florence Nightingale
- Friedrich Nietzsche
- Cher
- Christopher Reeve
- Paul Watson
- Dennis Rodman
- Caitlyn Jenner
- Neil Diamond

Munakara Mars: Janis Joplin

Brief Biography of Janis Joplin

Janis Joplin was an American singer and songwriter born in Port Arthur, Texas on January 19, 1943. The eldest child of Dorothy and Seth Joplin, she began singing blues and folk music in high school. In 1963 Joplin hitchhiked from Texas to San Francisco with a friend. She recorded a few blues songs that were released long after her death as the bootleg album *The Typewriter Tape*.

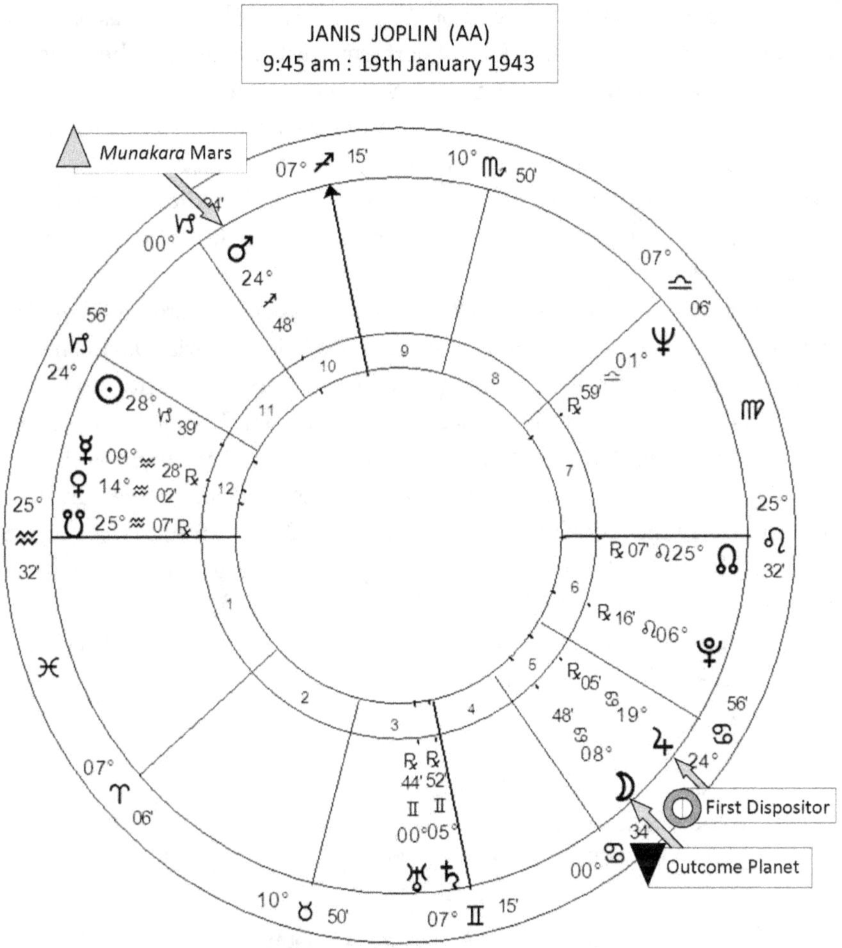

Chapter Seven • *Mars in Munakara*

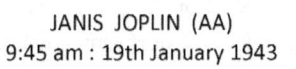

Fig. 7.1: Janis Joplin: Munakara Mars in Sagittarius

In the two years that she lived in San Francisco, Joplin's drug use increased dramatically. In 1965, friends worried about her physical decline persuaded her to return to her family in Port Arthur. But in 1966 Joplin returned to San Francisco to join the band Big Brother and the Holding Company, touring in that year and recording tracks for an album in Los Angeles. By the following year they were getting regular gigs, and their breakthrough came in June 1967 at the Monterey Pop Festival. By 1968 Joplin was becoming famous and her voice featured on their second album *Cheap Thrills*. Joplin's last performance with the band was in December 1968. She formed a new backup group, the Kozmic Blues Band in January 1969 and toured with them to Europe.

Joplin appeared at Woodstock on 17 August 1969 but she was forced to wait ten hours backstage and did not perform until 2:00 am. By then, she had been using heroin and drinking alcohol for hours and whilst the audience loved her, she did not perform at her best. Her singing was not included in the 1970 documentary film or the soundtrack for *Woodstock*, at her insistence that she was unhappy with her performance. Joplin's addictions continued to affect her stage work and her final concert at Madison Square Gardens in December 1969 was a disaster.

In February 1970 Joplin travelled to Brazil where she stopped her drug and alcohol use. She met and fell in love with American tourist David Niehaus who urged her to continue travelling with him. But Joplin returned to US and her old habits and joined the Canadian band, Full Tilt Boogie Band, playing the first session in April 1970 and touring in the summer months through Canada with the all-star Festival Express tour. The Full Tilt Boogie Band's last public performance took place on 12 August 1970 in Boston, Massachusetts. In September 1970, Joplin and Full Tilt began recording a new album in Los Angeles. Though Joplin died before all the tracks were fully completed, there was still enough usable material to compile the LP, *Pearl*. Janis Joplin died on 4 October 1970, from a heroin overdose at just 27.

- **Key Questions:**
- What does Janis Joplin's Mars contend with?
- What is its driving force?
- What is its trigger? What is its outcome?

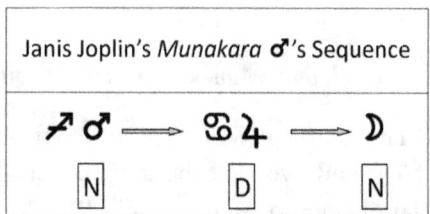

Table 7.5: *Janis Joplin: Munakara Mars's Sequence*

Janis Joplin's munakara Mars was magnetic and her raw energy drew others to her like a magnet. However, Mars is still the planet of 'hot' separation and is inclined to give the person a sense of invincibility, lulling them into a false sense of security that they are the ones in control of their destiny. Fame, in the form of munakara Mars, is a double-edged sword as the more one rises to become a shooting star, the greater the separation between the ordinary and the extraordinary. For all her fame, Janis Joplin was a very lonely person. She was famous for saying that she made love to 25,000 people on stage, but still went home alone.

Joplin's munakara Mars contends with the artist's ferocious need to be noticed and accepted as a 1960s female rock icon. During the 1960s in a male-centric industry where female artists, song writers and instrumentalists were largely ignored, Janis Joplin dominated as a performer who was not afraid "to write candidly about her life, beliefs and feelings, directly challenging the men that dominated their industry."[11] Until her one-woman revolution, the roles of the two genders in the industry were clearly defined – male rock stars publicly performed, and females showed their appreciation by being their fans, buying records, merchandise, concert tickets and making up the majority of screaming audience members.

Joplin's Mars was driven by the combination of exalted Jupiter and its dispositor Moon in rulership. She knew she was good and regardless of her gender; she knew she deserved a spot in the upper echelon of 1960's rock gods. The raw honesty of Janis Joplin's lyrics and her grating and penetrative voice gave vent to her emotions and frustrations. Her live concerts were cathartic for both the artist and her audience. Jupiter in exaltation and the Moon in rulership may not have benefited Janis emotionally, but watching her performances today is just as moving as it was almost sixty years ago.

Eleven degrees separates Janis' Moon in Cancer from retrograde Jupiter in exaltation. The Moon is applying to Jupiter giving Mars's first dispositor and outcome planet a conjunction in Janis' Placidus 5th house of creativity and entertainment. Mars's sequence shows how Joplin's performances were received by her audience who adored her raunchiness, her frenetic energy and her anti-establishment rantings. However, the conjunction moves to Janis' 6th house by Whole Sign, and the regular use of stimulants keeping Mars charged and energised exacted a high toll from her body (Cancer Jupiter Moon) and eventually led to her premature death at just 27.

Munakara Planet and Sect Condition – how comfortable is Mars?

Mars belongs to the nocturnal sect but it is a masculine planet so it prefers a fire or air sign which complements its gender and nature. However, Mars is not agreeable in a daytime chart and in addition, it does not fare well travelling in the same hemisphere as the Sun. Mars will burn hot and bright, but risks incinerating everything around it and burning itself out in the process.

Aquarius is the sign on Janis Joplin's Ascendant. Ten signs away is Scorpio (by Whole Sign) and munakara Mars would be the ruler of Joplin's career and public status. Aside from its state of munakara, Mars is significantly out of sect and good manners are not part

Janis Joplin — ♂'s Sect Dignity			
Planet	Sect 1 Status	Sect 2 Hemisphere	Sect 3 Sign
♐ ♂ ⃞N	Day ⃞D	With the Sun ⃞D	Fire ✓

Fig. 7.6: Janis Joplin: Munakara Mars's Sect Dignity

of Mars's nature when it has nothing to cool it down or give it perspective. Robert Hand says in *Night & Day*: "The daylight only makes Mars more active and less feeling. The perfectly diurnal Mars is one that is ferociously active.....It is a raw, instinctual energy that is never really conscious."[12]

Janis's fans would not have recognised the shy, intelligent misfit who wanted love and acceptance but whose munakara Mars reflected the cruelty of others who taunted her in her childhood and adolescence. Instead, they saw Janis's stage persona. They saw a loud, foul-mouthed individual who screamed through a microphone to get her point across to the audience, and this is the woman they worshipped.

Sagittarius Mars in Munakara – Janis Joplin

"I'm a victim of my own insides. There was a time when I wanted to know everything. It used to make me very unhappy, all that feeling. I just didn't know what to do with it.

But now I've learned to make that feeling work for me. I'm full of emotion and I want a release, and if you're on stage and if it's really working and you've got the audience with you, it's a oneness you feel." – Janis Joplin (1967)

Munakara Mars in 10th House (Placidus)

Janis's munakara Mars is her most elevated planet in the chart and literally stands alone with no viable aspect to tone down its random on-off energy or provide perspective or distraction when it becomes too painful. Her fixed Ascendant/Descendant commands a fixed fourth and tenth sign in the Whole Sign system, with Venus becoming the 4th house Lord and Mars, its opponent, commandeering the 10th house through the fixed water sign of Scorpio. Mars may be elevated still, but it moves to the eleventh sign of Sagittarius, and adds aversion to its list of woes when Sagittarian Mars cannot see Scorpio.

In one biography by Myra Friedman titled *Buried Alive*, she describes Janis as "[e]cstatic on stage and emotively sublime, going through life like a superbly visible comet streaking across the sky: quick, brilliant, gone."[13] It has been over 50 years since Janis Joplin's death from an accidental overdose of heroin. It is presumed that it was not Janis's intention to take her own life but that the heroin she injected into her veins was particularly potent, as several of her drug dealer's other customers died on the same weekend on 4 October 1970.[14]

Mars in Sagittarius describes Janis' dynamic performances on stage, particularly at the 1967 Monterey Pop Festival, where she and her band Big Brother & the Holding Company really came out to the world. As one journalist recalls "[h]er enduring influence and popularity can be attributed to her raw, unadulterated, fearless performances"[15] and once the wildness and ferocity of her munakara Mars was unleashed there was no holding back. All the years of insults and abuse, of being ignored and ridiculed became the fuel that lit her fire. Music critic and author Joel Selvin describes Joplin's change in persona after the documentary of the 1967 Monterey Pop Festival, when she began to be noticed in the male dominated music scene in San Francisco. He says she became this outlandish, extravagant hippie queen, and in his words, "[a]n invention of her own arrogance which was a very thinly applied layer over a vast insecurity that you could see right through the ego to see that scared, fearful little girl."[16]

This astute comment by an observer gives voice to the feeling of not knowing where one is going in life, and the motto, 'fake it till you make it', is a dominant theme for the aspirations of a munakara planet in the 10th house. Certainly, Mars's movement to 11th house (Whole Sign) does not disrupt Mars's energy and the combination (Placidus and Whole Sign) describes Joplin's ability to command and control a huge audience. The pure masculine force of her Mars meant that she rose above other female singers of the 1960 and remains a pioneering force for female pop stars despite the brevity of her career, spanning eight years from 1962 until her death in 1970.

Mars rules the 3rd house by Whole Sign as well as the 10th and her sister Laura was one of Janis' greatest defenders. Laura Joplin wrote *Love, Janis* in 1992, the first major biography in two decades. In an interview in the 2015 documentary film *Janis: Little Girl Blue*, Laura says: "I think Janis is someone who opened doors, kicked them open, and the more she got thousands of people on their feet stamping, saying, 'come on, respond, be with me, show me', the more she made people (particularly women) come to a sense of their own inner challenge."[17]

The 3rd house is the place of early learning experiences, and Janis suffered the other side of adoration when she was a child. She was bullied and ostracised by her peers as they sensed she was different from them and they punished her for physical and behavioural differences. The names they used to humiliate her were based on her weight and the fact that her skin was scarred by acne. Her brother Michael recalls, "She rocked the boat in a very small conservative town. There were 'white' and 'coloured' restrooms. She spoke up against that. And in that town, that was tough."[18]

Janis quipped on the Dick Cavett Show in 1970, "They laughed me out of class, out of town, out of the state."[19] Her sister Laura commented on her early years saying, "I remember her having social issues with people at school; she'd come home in tears and frustration."[20]

Janis was brutally honest when she spoke of those early years, and her munakara Mars was more than a little proud of how far she had risen in the world:

> There was nobody like me there. It was lonely, those feelings welling up and nobody to talk to. I was just 'silly crazy Janis.' Man, those people hurt me. It makes me happy to know I'm making it and they're back there, plumbers just like they were. People aren't supposed to be like me...but now they're paying me $50,000 a year to be like me.[21]

One year of college at Texas University did little to raise her self-esteem (Mars rules Placidus 9th house). Teenagers were no kinder to Janis than her former classmates had been in the younger grades. One can only imagine the humiliation Janis must have felt when the fraternity boys got together and published her photo with the title 'the ugliest man on campus' in the college magazine. She left university and Texas for San Francisco in 1963, "Just to get away because my head was in a much different place."[22]

First Dispositor: Jupiter in Cancer in 5th House (Placidus), 6th House (Whole Sign)

Two weeks prior to her death, lying back on a motel bed discussing Jim Morrison's addiction, Janis told one of her band members concerned over

Chapter Seven • Mars in Munakara

her safety: "It's not going to happen to me. My people are pioneer stock. They came across the country to Texas. They're tough. I've got those genes and nothing's going to happen to me."[23]

Jupiter is exalted in Cancer and the ruler of Janis's Mid-heaven. She certainly experienced adoration, fame and success, but Jupiter is also conjunct its own dispositor, the Moon and Janis's feelings of displacement grew proportionally with her fame. The two remaining planets in Mars's sequence are Jupiter and the Moon in conjunction in Cancer – the greater benefic is exalted and the night luminary is in rulership – so whilst she performed to alleviate her loneliness, her talent only served to create a greater chasm between herself and the rest of the world.

Switching between two house systems (Placidus and Whole Sign), the 2nd house of wealth is ruled by either her munakara Mars (Aries: Placidus) or by Mars's dispositor Jupiter (Pisces: Whole Sign). Janis was born into a middle-class working family so the sudden surge in wealth might be explained by Jupiter's rulership, or it may be that munakara Mars gave Janis the wealth to afford copious amounts of Southern Comfort and supported her expensive US$200-a-day heroin habit.

Whole Sign 6th house has Cancer on the cusp, so whilst the entertainment business is expressed by the Moon and Jupiter in the 5th house in Placidus, both planets move to the darker 6th house – the destruction of health – when Whole Sign becomes the chart's model for Janis's life. In 6th house the two planets in dignity become 'effective' but not positive in their influence on to Janis's health in this house, as their powerful presence is magnified by a house where negative or excessive patterns can become chronic illness or addictive habits.

Part of Janis's inability to deal with the demons presented by munakara Mars may have been that her daily life (6th house) possessed very little stability or normality. The fact that after the Monterey Pop Festival Janis was in great demand and her erratic lifestyle as a rock star constantly saw her on the road, performing night after night before enormous crowds with her expected style of fever-pitch energy. Superhuman levels of energy – Mars to Jupiter to Moon – require legal and illegal additives to strengthen and maintain this high velocity of energy. Calming medication is then also necessary to reduce high energy after performances so the spiral of up and down (Jupiter) continues until the body (Moon) can no longer tolerate the strain or successfully process the additives without doing permanent damage to the body.

The outcome planet: Moon in Cancer in 5th House (Placidus), 6th House (Whole Sign)

"Take this lonely heart from one lonely girl,
Reaching too high, babe, can't helped from getting burned."
– Lyrics found in Janis' diary[24]

The Moon is making an applying aspect to retrograde Jupiter. The 5th house of entertainment and creativity works well for these two planets as they underpin munakara Mars's comet-like flash in an industry that encourages comets, only to exploit them before they burn up and another one takes their place. After Monterey, prestigious Columbia Records (exalted Jupiter) took over the band's contract and Janis's visibility on stage, on television screens, and in recording studios increased dramatically as she was convinced to leave her band and record as a solo artist.

In February 1970 Janis vacationed in Brazil and whilst there met David Niehaus, a college graduate who was travelling around the world. Niehaus was perhaps Janis's healthiest love relationship, although it barely lasted a summer due to his dislike of her heroin habit. Niehaus knew Janis perhaps better than her long-term band members. On the morning after her death on 4 October 1970, a telegram from David arrived on the front desk of her hotel, telling her how much he missed her and begging her to join him in Kathmandu in late October.

Speaking in the documentary film *Janis Joplin: Little Girl Blue* Niehaus said: "She felt everyone's pain. That's what she felt when she sang the blues. That's basically why she did heroin. So she didn't have to be involved with everyone else's life. Most people can be oblivious to what's going on around them but Janis couldn't block it out."[25]

Perhaps the very last letter she wrote to her family back home[26] is a testament to the complicated nature of her Mars in contention and Janis' burning desire to succeed, not only for herself, but in order to gain acceptance from her loved ones:

> *Dear Family,*
> *I'm awfully sorry to be such a disappointment to you, but I really do think there's an awfully good chance I won't blow it this time. There's really nothing more I can say right now, guess I'll write more when I have more news. Until then, address all criticism to the above address and please believe that you can't possibly want for me to be a winner more than I do.*
> *Love, Janis*

Janis' last album *Pearl* was released three months after her death. It sold 4 million records. *Me and Bobby McGee* remains her biggest single.

Aquarius Venus in Munakara – Janis Joplin

The campus newspaper at the University of Texas at Austin, *The Daily Texan*, ran a profile on Joplin in the issue dated July 27, 1962, headlined "She Dares to Be Different." The article began, "She goes barefoot when she feels like it, wears Levi's to class because they're more comfortable, and carries her autoharp with her everywhere she goes so that in case she gets the urge to break into song, it will be handy. Her name is Janis Joplin."[27]

- **Key Questions:**
- What does Janis Joplin's Venus contend with?
- What is its driving force?
- What is its trigger? What is its outcome?

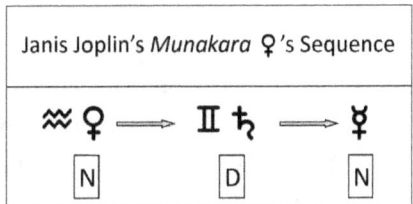

Table 7.7: Janis Joplin: Munakara Venus's Sequence

Janis Joplin's munakara Venus is the story of a rebellious woman with incredible talent, but one who felt isolated, insecure and alienated for most of her life – except in those rare moments when she could communicate to the audience through her voice and her lyrics. Venus's sequence sees Aquarian Venus travel to diurnal Saturn in Gemini, and then back to nocturnal Mercury, five degrees away from its starting point planet, Venus.

Janis's Saturn is an influential planet in her chart and traditional astrologers would have remarked on the melancholic nature of her chart. With Saturn hugging her MC/IC axis at the bottom of the chart, and ruling her Capricorn Sun in late degrees, plus Aquarian Mercury, Venus, South Node, and Ascendant, Janis truly had the temperament of an artist misunderstood by the world. Perhaps Janis feared that her popularity was temporary and that she would eventually be discarded and returned to the anonymity of her adolescent years. With Saturn in Gemini is disposited by

Mercury, Janis would perhaps have chosen infamy over being ignored or forgotten.

Munakara Venus's dispositor, Saturn is conjunct Uranus, and the new synodic cycle which had begun eight months earlier, in May 1942, at 29 Taurus (Venus's sign). In the time between the conjunction and Janis's birth in January 1943, the two planets had both moved into Gemini and it is this movement that places her Venus in a state of munakara.

The year of Janis's birth certainly reflected the craziness of the Uranus Saturn conjunction as the effects of WWII were being felt across the world and technological advancements were escalating in a bid to gain the greatest advantage over the enemy. The war had been raging for several years, and women were needed in employment, factories, sports arenas, and transport to take the place of the men on the warfront.

Janis became a role model to many young women born in the same era and her music reflected the frustration of female teenagers who wanted change and were willing to fight for new freedoms and a woman's independence from society and its male members.

Nocturnal Mercury is Venus's outcome planet in its munakara sequence and Janis Joplin's voice was unlike any other female vocalist of her time. It wasn't soft, it wasn't melodious, and it wasn't gentle. It was a roar of protest, a scream of frustration, a siren that unsettled men. But it reached the core of a new generation of 'Uranus Saturn in Taurus' women who demanded a new place in society, a breakdown in the patriarchal system, and equal rights for women. Socially Venus and Saturn describe Joplin's place in the two great US concerts, the Monterey Pop Festival (1967) and Woodstock (1969), billed as 'an Aquarian Exposition: 3 days of Peace and Music' with 32 acts that attracted more than 460,000 attendees.[28]

On a personal level munakara Venus represented the women who influenced Janis Joplin. It describes Joplin's adoration for blues singer Bessie Smith (1895–1937) whose gravestone she financed at the singer's unmarked grave.[29] It describes the relationship with her younger sister, Laura Joplin, who published her own biography, *Love, Janis* in 2005, which includes a series of previously unpublished letters by Janis herself written to her sister and her family. It describes Peggy Caserta, founder of famous multi-million-dollar Haight-Ashbury clothing boutique Mnasidika in 1965. Caserta became Joplin's best friend and lover with famous footage of the two women arriving by helicopter at Woodstock. After Caserta published the notorious 1973 bestseller *Going Down With Janis*, she was hated, betrayed and self-exiled.

Chapter Seven • *Mars in Munakara*

Caserta claims Joplin introduced her to heroin: "I didn't know anything about heroin because I was a pot-smoking acidhead. It's a whole different high, different world. But once I started doing heroin with her, it really took the edge off. It just made us feel normal. We didn't do heroin because we were miserable, we did it for fun."[30] Caserta refuses to believe that Janis died from a heroin overdose. She believes she tripped and fell on a bedside table, breaking her nose and resulting in a death from asphyxiation. Castera was luckier than Joplin – she survived heroin addiction, society's rejection after her tell-all book on Janis, rehab, and prison and came out the other end with her 2018 redemption book, *I Ran Into Some Trouble*.

Munakara Planet and Sect Condition – how comfortable is Venus?

It is no surprise that Janis Joplin's Venus is completely without sect dignity. All Robert Hand's predictions of "[a] woman behaving in a manner not appropriate for Venus" are true. Indications of a strong kind of feminine sexuality would certainly describe Janis, as would "[a] female native inclined towards immorality and lascivious behaviour."[31] Janis's two nocturnal planets in contention – Mars and Venus – made her a

Janis Joplin — ♀'s Sect Dignity			
Planet	Sect 1 Status	Sect 2 Hemisphere	Sect 3 Sign
♒ ♀	Day	With the Sun	Air
N	D	D	D

Table 7.8: Janis Joplin: Munakara Mars's Sect Dignity

force to be reckoned with, and if they were uncomfortable planets in their environment, then imagine how uncomfortable others were in the whirlwind space Janis Joplin created around herself when she was in full Mars or Venus mode.

Janis Joplin's two munakara planets are Mars and Venus. They do not intersect in any way – no aspect connects them, their munakara sequence has no mutual planet, they share no dispositor – and yet, together the two planets in munakara are champions that combat gender and social inequalities. Together, they tell the story of a woman who refused to compromise, who was in her own way a leader in equal rights for women and the disenfranchised. Had she survived, Janis may have become the right woman with the power, voice and attitude to lead the revolution into the next millennium.

Further Examples of Munakara Mars
Dennis Rodman & Michael J. Fox

The charts below are two further examples of Mars in contention, with Leo Mars disposited by the Sun in Taurus and Gemini. NBA basketball player Dennis Rodman and actor Michael J. Fox were both born in 1961, and their charts reflect some similarities given the two men were born four weeks apart in early May and June respectively. The two charts are featured in Part Two in the chapter on munakara Mars's delineations.

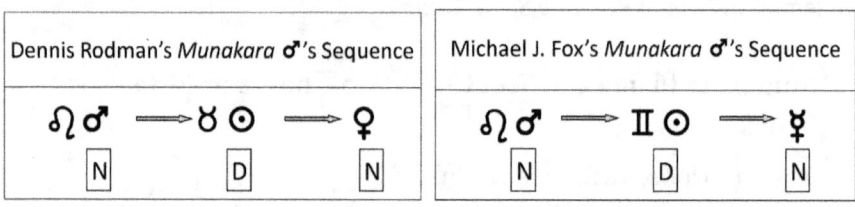

Table 7.9: Munakara Mars's Sequences

CHAPTER EIGHT
Jupiter in Munakara

What Does it Mean when Jupiter is in a state of munakara?

- Physical, social or financial risk taking
- Excessive behaviour or indulgences which have potentially harmful or addictive consequences
- Tendency for exaggeration or resentment when challenged by others
- Obstacles or constant setbacks in achieving success, recognition or ambitions
- Difficulty with children or money
- A feeling of being unprotected or unlucky
- Quick rise to fame, but quick fall to oblivion too
- Seeks to impress but mannerisms can be exaggerated or fanatical in nature
- Zealous opinions which alienate people or create larger rifts between divided sides

Table 8.1: Some possible expressions of Jupiter in munakara

Munakara Jupiter and Personal Challenges

Traditional astrologers called Jupiter 'the greater benefic', and writers such as 1st-century astrologer, Claudius Ptolemy, reinforced Jupiter's elevation above the other planets in glowing descriptions such as this:

Jupiter, if he should be lord alone, will thoroughly improve and benefit all things. Among mankind, in particular, this planet promotes honour, happiness, content, and peace, by augmenting all the necessaries and comforts of life, and all mental and bodily advantages. It induces also favours, benefits, and gifts emanating from royalty, and adds greater lustre to kings themselves, increasing their dignity and magnanimity: all men, in short, will share in the prosperity created by its influence.[1]

How then do we reconcile an interpretation of Jupiter such as Ptolemy's with what we might expect from Jupiter when it is munakara? If munakara shows a planet that is struggling in some manner, then how does a contentious Jupiter manifest?

Of particular challenge when the delineating munakara Jupiter, is the irony/paradox of using prominent or celebrated people as examples of individuals suffering from feelings of invisibility, publicly shame or disgrace, or bitter sadness of unfulfilled hopes.

Is it contradictory to talk about the frustrations of not being acknowledged or the feelings of being ignored and unappreciated that can be associated with Jupiter in munakara, only to find it present in the charts of eminent individuals who *have* gained attention and notoriety? If it is, I hope you will forgive me for this contradiction!

Throughout the book I have used examples charts of famous individuals with various planets in munakara. The assumed familiarity we have with these people, added to the amount of information available to the public, grants the opportunity to look at the technique of munakara and see it working in their individual histories.

In these charts and individual histories of Jupiter in munakara, we can observe a wide array of examples, ranging from bitter disappointment that 'expected' gifts are never received, to brilliance which goes unrecognised and unrewarded, to inflated judgement of their talents and abilities, to unrealistic expectations of good fortune, privilege and wealth.

In some of the chart examples munakara Jupiter is the mark of royalty. We find Jupiter in munakara in the charts of Empress Catherine the Great; King Henry VIII, two of Queen Victoria's children; Arthur and Louise, her granddaughter, Czarina Alexandra of Russia and her son, Prince Alexei Romanov (both assassinated in the Russian Revolution); and more recently, Queen Camilla; Meghan, Duchess of Sussex; and two of Prince William's children, Princes George and Louis.

Chapter Eight • *Jupiter in Munakara*

In the charts of commoners – those not born to royalty – munakara Jupiter can show a brilliant rise followed by an equally spectacular fall. This fall may be in popularity, in reputation, or even in freedom as in the case of alchemist John Dee and social activist Julian Assange. Others were challenged early in life by obstacles such as poverty (singer Neil Diamond), disability (author and political activist Helen Keller), fractured family relations (media proprietor Oprah Winfrey) or the exploitation of their early talents (composer Wolfgang Mozart).

In truth, munakara Jupiter comes with a warning: it can indicate a fast and glorious rise in status, fortune, benefit, infamy, but just as quickly, it can strip reputations, create great dramas and cause monumental misery. There is always a price to be paid for munakara Jupiter, and on some level the chart owner knows that – instinctively believing that all good fortune is temporary and impending disaster is right around the corner.

An individual with munakara Jupiter can be described by others as self-righteous, pompous, arrogant, self-indulgent, or inconsiderate. All these descriptions can be valid for a munakara planet bent on achieving its own way, disregarding other people's needs in the process.

Munakara Jupiter is inclined towards gambling with the hope of gains, gain which may not always and only be financial benefits. It can show the individual who is addicted to the adrenaline rush of living life on the edge, constantly taking risks that are dangerous, excessive or unnecessary. These risks can be harmful to the body as well as the individual's peace of mind. Temperance (in thought, action, or speech) does not come easily to munakara Jupiter, and this lack of restraint can be part of the problem when it is spiralling downwards.

When fortune turns against munakara Jupiter the individual can turn belligerent or nasty, attacking opponents or blaming others for their own bad luck. This does not endear munakara Jupiter to those who may be trying to help ease a tense situation and the person with munakara Jupiter can quickly change from a hero to a villain in other people's eyes. If the tide of popularity does turn against them, munakara Jupiter needs to be careful it does not fall into personifying a negative stereotype.

The individual with munakara Jupiter can appear arrogant if they believe they have the only possible solution to a difficult situation. If their mannerisms are patronising, or their opinions are offered in a condescending way, then arguments and resistance are likely, no matter how brilliant or insightful they feel they have been. No-one takes well to being treated with condescension and the individual with munakara Jupiter needs to be very conscious of how they are presenting an idea or a proposal. They need to read the room and change their approach to a more sensitive one if they are offending others with high-handed behaviour. Jupiter also represents the zealot, the fanatic, the dogmatist, or the fatalist, so the presence of munakara can elevate or exaggerate this type of social labelling if the individual is not willing to compromise or to ease back on any fanatical behaviour.

Munakara Jupiter and Society's Challenges

Jupiter is a planet of ambition and munakara Jupiter's ambition is often driven by the haunting memory of past failures or restrictions. Jupiter is the antithesis of Saturn (the greater malefic) but the two visible outer planets often share early experiences of hardship, disruption and isolation. Munakara Jupiter works hard to change the past and may indicate an individual who is ruthlessly ambitious or fixated on climbing the ladder to success in an attempt to prove themselves to others.

> *"When you wish upon a falling star, your dreams can come true. Unless it's really a meteor hurtling to Earth which will destroy all life. Then you're pretty much hosed, no matter what you wish for. Unless it's death by meteorite."*[2]
> – Quote from a framed poster in Elon Musk's SpaceX headquarters in Hawthorne, California

The examples of past royals with Jupiter in munakara show that some have had the power to topple governments, champion new philosophies, or influence social trends, overriding the laws, language and beliefs of previous regimes. But a royal lineage is not always necessary to shake society's foundations and individuals with munakara Jupiter can have great influence on the important issues that captivate the opinions, attitudes and beliefs of society in their lifetimes.

Munakara Jupiter's three-planet sequence can give indications of how this power might be used. Often the outcome planet shows both the trigger and the result achieved by the individual whose endgame is to increase their power, gain advantage or advancement, or to take control of a situation.

Munakara Jupiter is often compelled to defend the individual's ideology, whether it is based on political views, power structures, economics, social, or religious freedoms. Jupiter holds knowledge and wisdom in great regard,

Chapter Eight • *Jupiter in Munakara*

but if munakara means Jupiter has lost its way and the individual's opinions or actions are promoting falsity, prejudice, hatred, inequality, or incitement to mob rule, then society needs to be discerning about who it promotes as a the 'ideal' spokesperson for its standards of freedom.

The assumption that someone with munakara Jupiter will always act valiantly and wisely is not always true as sometimes Jupiter in contention appears in the individual who is actively creating dissent in a group or within society. Munakara Jupiter is not always compelled to act honourably, as chaos and change can be the catalyst for an individual's rise to power, with social advancement and political gain possible side benefits arising from the ruins of revolution.

Jupiter's Sequence: Friends, Associates, and Enemies

Subject to al-Biruni's Table of Friendships and Enmities (*Table 8.2*), Jupiter's sequence would rather avoid the following combinations which involve planets hostile towards Jupiter, namely, Mercury, Mars, and Saturn. So far as sign rulerships go, Jupiter is indifferent to the Sun even though it belongs to the Sun's sect category. Jupiter is friendly towards Venus and the Moon as there are signs shared between Jupiter and the two female nocturnal planets.

D Diurnal / N Nocturnal	Essential Dignity Rulership / Exaltation (Mutual Damage)	Second Essential Dignity Fall (opposes Exaltation)	Second Essential Dignity — Borrowing Signs for Exaltation		
Munakara Planet	Mutually Hurtful With	Injurious To	Offering Friendship To	Asking Friendship From	Indifferent To ♃ - No relationship
	(♃'s Two-Way Damage)	(♃ Disposits Fall Sign)	(♃ Owns Exaltation Sign)	(Exalted ♃'s Dispositor)	
△ D ♃	[N] Mars ☉ First Dispositor / Mercury [D]/[N] [D] ▼ Outcome Planet [N] ☉ First Dispositor	Mercury (♓) [D] ▼ Outcome Planet [N] ☉ First Dispositor [D] * Saturn (♑) ▼ Outcome Planet * ♃ Injured By ♄	[N] Venus (♓) ☉ First Dispositor	[N] Moon (♋) ☉ First Dispositor	[D] Sun ▼ Outcome Planet

Table 8.2: Al-Biruni's Table of Friendships and Enmities

Friends and Associates of a munakara Jupiter: the Moon, Venus & the Sun

If the Moon is involved in the sequence (as the first dispositor)

The Moon is the fastest moving nocturnal dispositor so its movement through the signs will determine if Jupiter in Cancer is in a state of munakara. Jupiter's exaltation in the Moon's sign of Cancer complicates a judgement on munakara Jupiter's condition – as exaltation enhances Jupiter's powers but munakara contention suggests there will be challenges, difficulties and heartache involved. Together the Moon and Jupiter rule the Ascendant of the Thema Mundi chart, the Birth-chart of the Universe. They are a combined life-force, originally describing vegetation that is abundant, vigorous, dense and teeming with life. The shift to interpreting this prolific energy to personal use in a natal chart is the feeling of growth that occurs without structure and results in too many choices that can overwhelm the individual. Exalted Jupiter in contention needs guard rails, otherwise opportunities get wasted or momentum is lost because the person struggles to focus – or gain advantage – from one particular theme.

The Moon's fast sign turnover every two days means that each time Jupiter is in Cancer it risks being in munakara as the next Moon's sign belonging to a diurnal planet introduces a new dispositor to the mix. Munakara Jupiter in Cancer can have prolific talents and the potential to rise to great heights, if circumstances allow the individual to benefit from munakara. However, there can be negatives, as exalted Jupiter in the Moon's sign can bring with it family issues from childhood, or even further back in the family's history which occurred before the person was born. It is possible that the child born with exalted Jupiter in munakara becomes the trigger for the family to confront some past trauma if the Moon (as Jupiter's dispositor) indicates Jupiter has shown little restraint in a caregiver's behaviour, and instead, has indulged in harmful or destructive vices. If exalted Jupiter happens to represent a force 'larger than life', then childhood might be a miserable time for the individual with munakara Jupiter, with little safety, and no accountability of the adults who should have protected, rather than exploited, the child.

Two of the three examples are for men who have munakara Jupiter in exaltation in their charts. Both Billy Connolly (*Fig. 10.2*) and John Dee (*Fig. 10.13*) have Jupiter in munakara and their stories are featured in the chapter dedicated to multiple munakara planets.

The third example is the United Kingdom's Prince George, a young child

Chapter Eight • *Jupiter in Munakara*

at the time of writing. Prince George – the eldest son of William, Prince of Wales, and Catherine, Princess of Wales, and the first grandson to King Charles III – is the second in the line of succession to the British throne behind his father, and his family situation may play a significant part in his munakara Jupiter over the coming decades. Jupiter in Cancer is not the only planet in munakara in Prince George's chart. He has a total of five planets in contention – Sun, Moon, Mercury, Venus, and Jupiter. His Chart is also featured in the chapter on multiple munakara planets.

Example Charts:
- John Dee (outcome planet, Saturn)
- Billy Connolly (outcome planet, Mercury)
- Prince George (outcome planet, Saturn)

If Venus is involved in the sequence (as the first dispositor)

Jupiter in Taurus or Libra will be disposited by Venus. Without a third planet's presence to complete the munakara sequence, the connection between the greater and lesser benefic planets should bring good fortune and a smooth passage in life. However, the very nature of munakara is contention so Jupiter in munakara means that good fortune requires considerable talent and hard work, and smooth passage requires constant vigilance and upkeep. Jupiter's ability to be in the right place at the right time can only carry the individual's good luck so far and Venus will need to look to its own sign's dispositor to see how it can assist munakara Jupiter to hold onto that luck.

American entertainers Neil Diamond and Cher have spent a lifetime honing their skills and changing their style to produce albums and concerts that have drawn audiences over the decades. But they have had periods in their careers where they were considered obsolete, old-fashioned or out of step with current musical trends. Popularity, social acceptance and sometimes female solidarity are all under the heading of Venus. When you are a public figure and have Venus as munakara Jupiter's dispositor, you need all the support you can get to retain your popularity.

Example Charts:
- Wolfgang Amadeus Mozart (outcome planet, Saturn)
- Cher (outcome planet, Mercury)
- Neil Diamond (outcome planet, Saturn)
- Meghan, Duchess of Sussex (outcome planet, Mercury)

If the Sun is involved in the sequence (as the outcome planet)

Jupiter and the Sun are both diurnal planets so the Sun will act as the outcome planet when the nocturnal between them is in the sign of Leo. In some traditional texts Jupiter was called a 'spear-bearer' to the Sun and its role was to bring honour, respect and advantage to the solar luminary's need for success and power. The Sun should always benefit from Jupiter's efforts, but if Jupiter is munakara, there may be a problem that neither diurnal planet can resolve. Jupiter is naturally a risk-taker but when it is in a sign belonging to a nocturnal planet there may be challenges that even the 'greater benefic' (Jupiter's tag) cannot resolve.

In Greek mythology Zeus was Jupiter's Greek counterpart. Whenever Zeus moved out of his masculine domain and into the unfamiliar world of the feminine, he brought violence, death and despair. He couldn't understand why his strength didn't bend women and goddesses automatically to his will, and so he resorted to trickery, cruelty and force to win his way. It rarely worked well for Zeus, and individuals with munakara Jupiter need to be careful to avoid following in Zeus' ways – especially if the Sun is their outcome planet – otherwise femininity may be their undoing.

Munakara Jupiter with the Sun as its outcome planet may indicate an individual who seeks to impose their will or choices on someone else. If Jupiter in munakara succumbs to arrogance, selfishness or high-handedness, then any of their hard-won benefits can end up melting away like the Sun's last rays at sunset. Munakara Jupiter needs to be generous with any benefits it gains from its good fortune, as what can be given by the gods can be taken away just as easily. A trap of having the Sun as munakara Jupiter's outcome planet is that the individual may believe that their rise to prominence was entirely through their own efforts, brilliance, or divine spark (Sun), which is simply not true.

Example Charts:
- King Henry VIII
- Edgar Degas
- Helen Keller

Enemies of munakara Jupiter: Mars, Mercury & Saturn

If Mars is involved in the sequence (as the first dispositor)

Although Aries or Scorpio's placement is not a debility sign for Jupiter, the animosity between the two planets causes extra tension: "Jupiter is the

Chapter Eight • *Jupiter in Munakara*

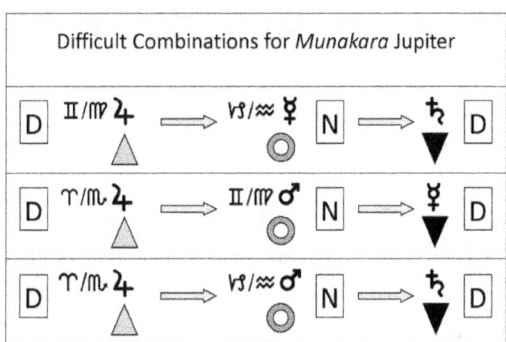

Table 8.3: Munkara Jupiter's Enemies

opposite of Mars, the former indeed wishes for mercy and justice, but the latter [wishes for] impiety and cruelty."[3]

Mars belongs to the nocturnal sect and can only take the position of first dispositor in Jupiter's munakara sequence. By their nature alone, Jupiter and Mars are at loggerheads, and the essential dignity known as "exaltation" adds extra tension to their relationship. Cancer is Jupiter's sign of exaltation, but is Mars's fall sign. In the reverse, Capricorn is Mars's sign of exaltation, and Jupiter's fall sign.

Jupiter in Moon or Venus's signs can amplify munakara Jupiter's feelings of superiority; especially if the individual was born into wealth or privilege or achieved success early in life. In contrast, munakara Jupiter disposited by Mars shows a different side to Jupiter, one that has a sense of urgency, a taste for danger or risk-taking, or displays a special skill that draws admiration or raises them above others. Struggle, competition, or a sense of danger are likely to be common themes when Mars is Jupiter's dispositor.

Table 8.3 shows Jupiter's two possible sequences when Mars is involved as first dispositor. Mars in Mercury or Saturn's signs will complete the sequence, but both are problematic for Jupiter, given that Jupiter is in detriment in Mercury's signs and in fall in Capricorn, one of Saturn's signs.

Example Charts:
- Helen Keller (outcome planet, Sun)
- Queen Camilla (outcome planet, Mercury)
- Elon Musk (outcome planet, Saturn)
- Julian Assange (outcome planet, Saturn)
- Prince Louis (outcome planet, Saturn)

If nocturnal Mercury is involved in the sequence (as the first dispositor)

Jupiter's two rulership signs, Sagittarius and Pisces, square one another and oppose Mercury, Gemini and Virgo. Therefore, together the two planets rule the four mutable signs.

Jupiter and Mercury share a hostile relationship, as they are in detriment in each other's signs. Regardless of its sect, Mercury will be a problem for munakara Jupiter, but the reasons *on why it is a problem* will differ according to whether it is diurnal or nocturnal. If Mercury is diurnal it can play the role of outcome planet in Jupiter's munakara sequence. However, if Mercury is nocturnal, then it will be Jupiter's dispositor if Jupiter is in the signs of Gemini or Virgo. (*Table 8.3*).

Jupiter in Gemini or Virgo places Jupiter in detriment, and Jupiter tends to make mistakes that are specific to each of Mercury's mutable signs of air (Gemini) and earth (Virgo). Jupiter in Gemini tends to make sweeping generalisations and grandiose statements based on few facts. It falls into traps from poor information gathering or from snatching random pieces of data and turning them into knowledge. If munakara is a further issue for Gemini Jupiter, the individual may get called out on their weak evidence base and will lose credibility if this happens too often. Talk show host Oprah Winfrey has made a small fortune from her Gemini Jupiter in munakara (Jupiter's outcome planet Saturn rules 2nd house). However, Jupiter sits in Oprah's 7th house ruling her Ascendant she has also made some spectacular mistakes possibly because someone in her team wasn't doing their research properly. She has also had more than her fair share of rumours and fake stories published about her personal life (and her weight issues), another possible expression of munakara Jupiter in the 7th house.

Jupiter in Virgo tends to suffer the opposite fate in that it easily becomes bogged down in the details and rather than synthesising excess information, Jupiter obsesses about it and makes mistakes trying to address everything at once. Freedom of information is Jupiter's catchcry but in the case of Virgo Jupiter, freedom *from* information is needed. Otherwise, Jupiter risks being overwhelmed by statistics, data and procedures. Jupiter in detriment in Virgo risks compulsive fact-checking to the point where it doesn't end up circulating the information. Virgo Jupiter in munakara risks burying itself in depressive thoughts by believing that *everything* is wrong – and it may need perspective to see that whilst everything is not perfect, that is part of life. The chart of American college drop-out and adventurer Chris

Chapter Eight • *Jupiter in Munakara*

McCandless has Virgo Jupiter in munakara. His refusal to work within societal structures led him across the US in search of freedom, independence and a sense of belonging. Unfortunately, Virgo Jupiter did not equip him with the necessary survival skills for his journey and his demise was a sad and lonely consequence of its failure.

Example Charts:
- Edgar Degas (outcome planet, Sun)
- Chris McCandless (outcome planet, Saturn)
- Oprah Winfrey (outcome planet, Saturn)
- Cindy Sherman (outcome planet, Saturn)

If diurnal Mercury is involved in the sequence (as the outcome planet)

If Mercury is diurnal and is a player in Jupiter's munakara sequence then it will be Jupiter's outcome planet (*Table 8.3*). In this scenario diurnal Mercury and Jupiter will have a joint role to fulfil – and that is to help the Sun to achieve brilliance. To this end, munakara Jupiter is going to take financial risks, display excessive character traits or exaggerate. However, when diurnal Mercury is its outcome planet there will be times when the vision is greater than the possibility – and whatever Mercury is selling, munakara Jupiter finds it impossible to deliver. In many ways these two rulers of the mutable signs share some similarities. They tell stories, pedal dreams and make promises – both to the individual who wholeheartedly believes their own rhetoric – and to the collective, which loves a bit of flashy showmanship.

Munakara Jupiter with diurnal Mercury as its outcome planet can describe an individual who is larger than life, someone who embellishes the truth and entertains through a clever turn of phrase, a sharp intellect, good comedic timing, or the ability to present a fascinating persona to the world. This charismatic personality can find success selling an idea or opinion to others, as long as they are not fact-checked too many times. This munakara sequence may make for a wonderful salesperson, but the individual needs to remember that overkill will make others' doubt your sincerity and you can lose friends just as quickly as you made them.

Example Charts:
- Cher
- Billy Connolly
- Queen Camilla
- Meghan, Duchess of Sussex

If Saturn is involved in the sequence (as the outcome planet)

Jupiter's fall sign of Capricorn is owned by Saturn, and therefore Jupiter is nervous of the greater malefic. Saturn is a fellow diurnal planet, and therefore can only take the position of outcome planet in Jupiter's sequence (*Table 8.3*).

The two diurnal energies at either end of munakara Jupiter's sequence are very different in nature and Jupiter will likely resent Saturn's interference. Saturn is often concerned with accountability and this dour concept is a dampener for munakara Jupiter's enthusiasm and natural effervescence. Saturn as outcome planet to Jupiter's munakara sequence means there will be a time in which Jupiter's statements or commitment are tested and if found wanting, Saturn will extract payment in its own severe way.

Saturn is the lord of Time, and no matter how much positivity munakara Jupiter exudes, or how far into the future it projects its promises, the passing of time will measure Jupiter's sincerity and bring Jupiter down with a bump if whatever it promises is actually impossible or highly improbable.

Example Charts:
- John Dee
- Wolfgang Amadeus Mozart
- Chris McCandless
- Neil Diamond
- Oprah Winfrey
- Cindy Sherman
- Elon Musk
- Julian Assange
- Prince George
- Prince Louis (Kate/William)

Jupiter in Munakara: Elon Musk and Julian Assange

Brief Biography of Elon Musk[4]

Elon Musk (born June 28, 1971) is a South African-born American entrepreneur and allegedly, the richest man on the planet.[5] Born to a South African father and Canadian mother, in 1988 Musk obtained a Canadian passport and left South Africa to avoid compulsory military service and for the greater economic opportunities available in the United States.

In 1995, Musk founded Zip2, a company that provided maps and business directories to online newspapers. In 1999, Zip2 was bought by the computer manufacturer Compaq for US$30 million, and Musk then founded an

Chapter Eight • *Jupiter in Munakara*

online financial services company, X.com, which later became PayPal, which specialising in transferring money online. The online auction site eBay bought PayPal in 2002 for $1.5 billion.

Musk has long been convinced that for life to survive, humanity must become a multi-planet species. However, he was dissatisfied with the huge expense of rockets. In 2002, he founded Space Exploration Technologies (SpaceX) to make more affordable rockets. The Super Heavy – Starship system, a spacecraft designed for providing fast transportation between cities on Earth and building bases on the Moon and Mars, was first launched in 2020. SpaceX is contracted to build the lander for the astronauts returning to the Moon by 2025, as part of NASA's Artemis space program.

Musk was also one of the first significant investors in, as well as the chief executive officer of, electric car manufacturer Tesla. In 2006, Tesla introduced its first electric car, the Roadster, which could travel 245 miles (394 km) on a single charge. Unlike most previous electric vehicles, which Musk thought were 'stodgy' and 'uninteresting',[6] the Roadster was a sports car – it could go from 0 to 60 miles (97 km) per hour, in less than four seconds. Model X luxury SUV went on the market in 2015, and two years later the Model 3, a less-expensive vehicle, went into production and became the best-selling electric car of all time.

Musk joined the social media service Twitter in 2009 and became one of the most popular accounts on the site, with more than 85 million followers as of 2022. In October 2022, Musk purchased Twitter for $44 billion. Among Musk's first acts as Twitter owner was laying off about half the company and allowing users to purchase the blue check-mark verification for $8 a month, which had previously been bestowed by Twitter upon notable figures. In addition, he disbanded Twitter's content-moderation body and reinstated many accounts that had been banned. Advertising revenue fell sharply as many companies withdrew their ads from the platform and Musk changed the name of the company from Twitter to X in July 2023.

Brief Biography of Julian Assange[7]

Julian Assange (born July 3, 1971) is an Australian computer programmer who founded the media organisation WikiLeaks. As a teenager Assange demonstrated an uncanny aptitude for computers. Using the hacking nickname 'Mendex', he infiltrated a number of secure systems, including those at NASA and the Pentagon. In 1991, Australian authorities charged him with 31 counts of cybercrime. He pleaded guilty to most of the counts.

In 2006 Assange created WikiLeaks to serve as a clearinghouse for sensitive or classified documents. Practising what Assange called 'scientific journalism' (providing primary source materials with a minimum of editorial commentary), WikiLeaks released thousands of classified documents originating from a variety of government and corporate entities, including details on the US military's detention facility at Guantanamo Bay in Cuba, a secret membership roster of the British National Party, internal documents from the Scientology movement, and private emails from the University of East Anglia's Climatic Research Unit.

In 2010, WikiLeaks posted almost half a million documents obtained from US Army intelligence analyst Bradley Manning (later called Chelsea Manning) – mainly relating to the US Wars in Iraq and Afghanistan. While much of the information was already in the public domain, President Barack Obama's administration criticised the leaks as a threat to US national security. In November 2010, WikiLeaks began publishing an estimated 250,000 confidential US diplomatic cables, dating mostly from 2007 to 2010, but some dated as far as back as 1966. Reaction from governments around the world was swift, with many condemning the publication. Assange became the target of much of that ire, and some American politicians called for him to be pursued as a terrorist.

In May 2011, Assange was awarded the Sydney Peace Foundation's gold medal, an honour that had previously been bestowed on Nelson Mandela and the Dalai Lama, for his exceptional courage in pursuit of human rights.

In June 2012, after his extradition appeal was denied by the Supreme Court, Assange sought refuge in the Ecuadoran embassy. He spent nearly seven years living in the Ecuadoran embassy in London in an effort to avoid prosecution, and an additional five years in British prison fighting extradition to the United States.

In June 2024, Assange was freed from British custody as part of a deal with the US Department of Justice. In exchange for pleading guilty to a single count of illegally obtaining and disclosing national security information, Assange was sentenced but in lieu of time already served (five years in Belmarsh Prison). After which he was permitted to return to Australia.

Elon Musk is the elder of the two men (*Fig. 8.1, biwheel's inner chart*), with the business magnate born on 28th June 1971 in Pretoria, South Africa. Julian Assange is five days younger than Musk (*biwheel's outer chart*) with his birth date on 3rd July 1971 in Townsville, Australia.

Chapter Eight • *Jupiter in Munakara*

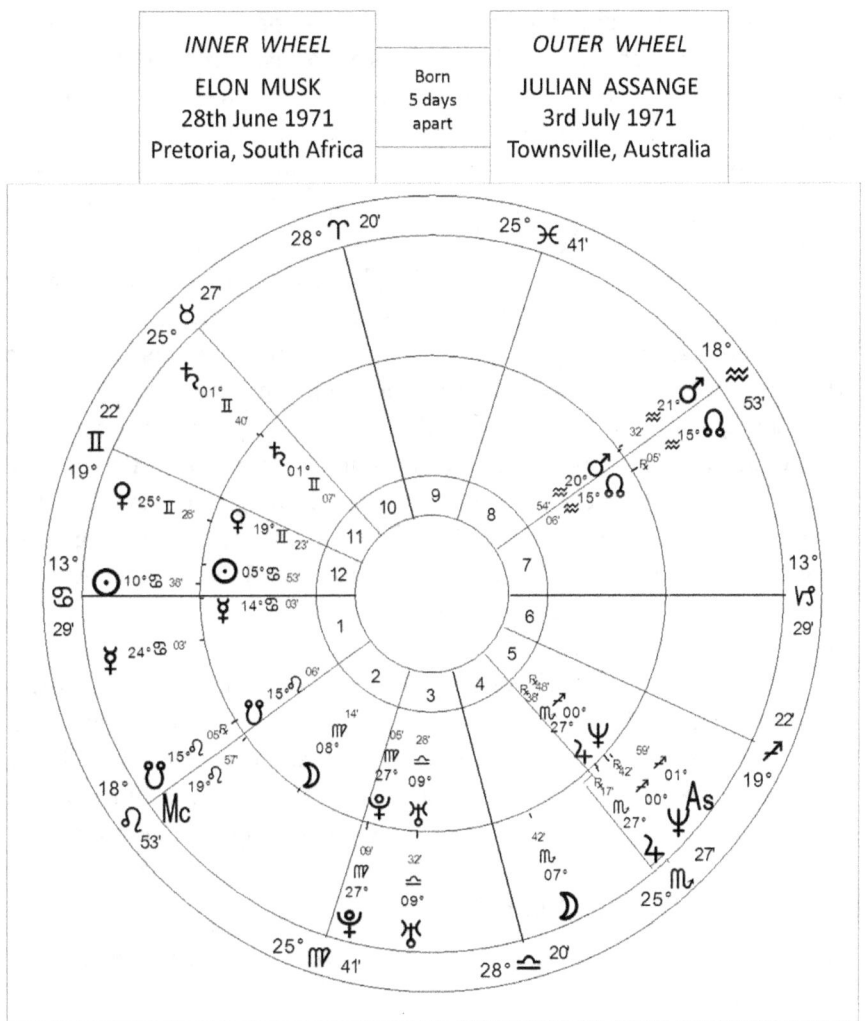

Fig. 8.1: BiWheel for Elon Musk and Julian Assange

The biwheel shows their Cancer Suns with a 5° separation to mark the the days between their births. It also shows a sextile aspect between Musk's Moon in Virgo and Assange's Scorpio Moon in fall. There are a few degree differences between their fast-moving planets Mercury and Venus, but the remainder of their planets show very little difference in degrees. Musk's Mercury lies on his Ascendant, whilst Assange has Neptune on his Ascendant and Saturn opposing it on the Descendant. Musk's Saturn Neptune opposition lies across his 5th- and 11th-house axis in the Placidus house system.

In their own way, both men are outlaws. They appear to make their own rules, are unapologetic in breaking the laws of normal society, and their true motivations are clouded in mystery. They use social media platforms for self-promotion, though whether that is to feed their egos and their idealism is unclear. Musk bears the label of 'the wealthiest man in the world' and, at the time of writing, has just donated a sizeable amount to an anti-immigration group working to put Donald Trump back into the White House for a second term.[8] Donald Trump has three planets in munakara (Sagittarius Moon to Libran Jupiter to Venus; Cancer Saturn to Sagittarius Moon to Jupiter: Leo Mars to Gemini Sun to nocturnal Mercury) so perhaps it is no great surprise that the two would work together, either openly or covertly.

Assange, on the other hand, fell afoul of several government agencies, particularly the US Government, as he fought a 12-year battle to avoid extradition to United States to face numerous charges under their 1917 Espionage Act. Assange forfeited his own freedom to make hidden agencies accountable for their actions, and whilst he has a penchant for the limelight, the years from 2012 to 2024 have been difficult, restrictive, and damaging for his physical and mental health.

Both Musk and Assange have a diurnal munakara planet and a nocturnal munakara planet – Jupiter and Mars – but their planets' house placements and house rulerships differ in their respective natal charts. In both charts, the two planets in munakara are in aspect to one another: Jupiter in the fixed water sign, Scorpio, squares Mars in the fixed air sign, Aquarius.

Munakara Jupiter – Elon Musk

"Being an entrepreneur is like eating glass and staring into the abyss of death."
Elon Musk

- **Key Questions:**
- What does Elon Musk's Jupiter contend with?
- What is its driving force?
- What is its trigger? What is its outcome?

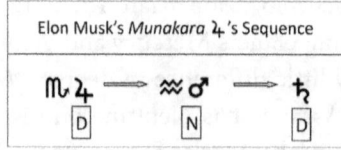

Table 8.4: Elon Musk: Munakara Jupiter's Sequence

Chapter Eight • *Jupiter in Munakara*

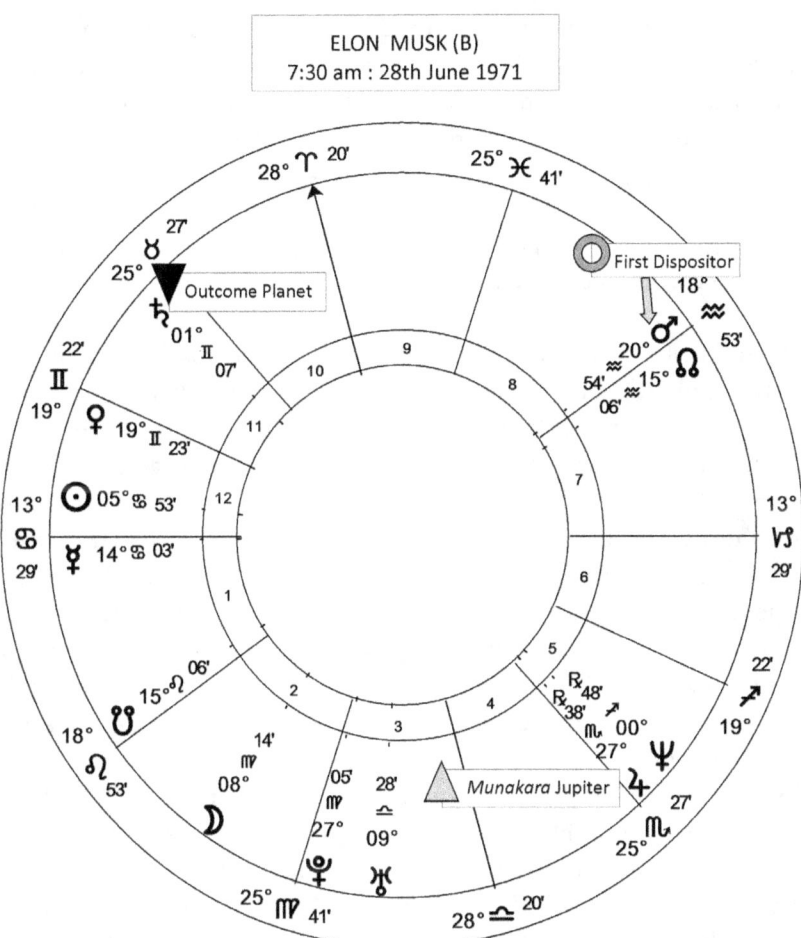

Fig. 8.2: Elon Musk, Natal Chart: Jupiter in Munakara

In both Elon Musk and Julian Assange's charts munakara Jupiter forms a square aspect to Mars (also in munakara). This aspect suggests the two planets will not compromise their principles and has the potential to feed long-lasting feuds that can flare up at any moment. These relationships can be bitter and rancour-filled, potentially harming those involved.

Elon Musk likes to sign his posts on his social platform X (formally known as Twitter) with the phrase "Vox Populi, Vox Dei" meaning "The voice of the people is the voice of God." A sweeping statement reminiscent of Jupiter's association with divinity and somehow suggesting that the people's popular opinion is backed by the power of God.

However, as is typical of munakara Jupiter, Musk's media grab for attention is misleading and the four words he uses so freely are not the full quote. The phrase is borrowed from a letter written by Saxon scholar and teacher Alcuin to Emperor Charlemagne in 798 which reads:

> "And those people should not be listened to who keep saying the voice of the people is the voice of God ('Vox populi, vox Dei'), since the riotousness of the crowd is always close to insanity."

Elon Musk relishes the opportunity to spread his 'sacred message' across the globe and unfortunately, with munakara Jupiter in the water sign of Scorpio, and its dispositor Mars in an air sign, it creates a voice of malice, stirring his followers into a type of righteous rage. Musk is the epitome of the online 'troll', provoking others to emotional responses, acting as a bully and a provocateur, and adding his own special brand of hatred, distrust and dissent through social media. Musk often defends his posts as a 'joke'. An example of this is an online post after Trump's second assassination attempt at his golf course in early September 2024. After taking his post down Musk said "One lesson I've learned is that just because I say something to a group and they laugh doesn't mean it's going to be all that hilarious as a post on X."[9]

Saturn is not a beneficial outcome planet for Jupiter and if the individual does not maintain integrity or honesty (Saturn) then hardship and restriction are likely to follow. In Musk's chart Saturn ties the 7th and 8th houses together through the rulership of signs Capricorn and Aquarius. Relationships, open enemies and joint resources are connected through Saturn's rulership of these houses. In an article published in September 2024 Tesla investor Ross Gerber told *The Washington Post* that he has invested less than $1 million in the company X but now considers the stake worthless.[10] Gerber believes the company has lost 90% of its value since Musk bought it out, "Elon's done a tremendous amount of wealth destruction since he's purchased Twitter. For the people who put capital into (Elon) for any amount, trying to explain to people how he lost so much money is not a fun conversation."[11] The article continues with the statement that Jack Dorsey, Twitter's founder, remains one of the platform's largest investors. But even Dorsey has lost an estimated $720 million, according to the *Post*. "It all went south," Dorsey said, referring to the acquisition.[12]

Chapter Eight • *Jupiter in Munakara*

Munakara Planet and Sect Condition – how comfortable is Jupiter?

Jupiter is a diurnal planet that enjoys its allegiance with the Sun, so when the chart is diurnal Jupiter will produce its best manifestations of success, power, wealth and good fortune. However, Robert Hand does warn that if "a malefic [planet] aspects a diurnal Jupiter its benefits are reduced somewhat but not eliminated."[13] In Musk's case, Jupiter is opposed by Saturn and this aspect could spoil Jupiter's ability to achieve workable or realistic goals, or keep strong, protective boundaries. Even the square from malefic Mars may damage some of Jupiter's power and wealth, and the involvement of both malefics in munakara Jupiter's sequence plus their direct damaging effects through square and opposition aspects may potentially take their toll on the lasting effects of Musk's greater benefic in munakara.

Elon Musk — ♃'s Sect Dignity			
Planet	Sect 1 Status	Sect 2 Hemisphere	Sect 3 Sign
♏ ♃	Day	No Sun	Water
	D	D	N	N

Table 8.5: Elon Musk: Munakara Jupiter's Sect Dignity

Scorpio Jupiter in Munakara – Elon Musk

"The reason I acquired Twitter is because it is important to the future of civilization to have a common digital town square, where a wide range of beliefs can be debated in a healthy manner, without resorting to violence."
– Elon Musk, October 27, 2022

Munakara Jupiter in Scorpio in 5th House

On October 27, 2022, Elon Musk strode into the Twitter Headquarters in San Francisco brandishing a bathroom sink and posting on his newly acquired platform, "Entering Twitter HQ – let that sink in!"[14] In the year that followed the takeover and rebranding of Twitter (to X), Musk gutted content moderation, restored accounts of previously banned extremists, and allowed users to purchase account verification.

Musk's munakara Jupiter is found in his 5th house of leisure activities. Whilst X has been used by many subscribers for entertainment, amusing banter, and social connection, it was also a relatively safe forum for human rights activists to exercise their freedom of speech in countries under harsh totalitarian regimes. Twitter is now under new management and Musk's leadership exposes these advocates. They are no longer safe from persecution when their identities and whereabouts can be sold by Musk to the highest bidder. "Musk's lack of regulation has opened the floodgates for hate speech against marginalized groups and misinformation."[15]

Just under a year of its purchase, on October 11 of 2023, the European Commission warned Musk in writing that he needed to cease and desist from publishing disinformation, fake news, and old and misleading images on X, otherwise he risked being fined 6% of his revenue or receiving a total blackout ban in the EU.[16]

> "My children didn't choose to be born, I chose to have children. They owe me nothing, I owe them everything."[17] – Elon Musk

Jupiter, the significator of children, lies in Musk's 5th house. Musk has fathered fourteen children, and counting. Whilst experts warn of the dangers of Earth's increasing climate change and the burden placed upon it by over-population, Musk's Jupiter in contention has swung to the other side of the argument, claiming instead that the world is under threat of a potential population collapse, a problem that he swears is a bigger risk to civilization than global warming.[18]

Munakara Jupiter in Scorpio ruling 6th House

Jupiter in munakara may have provided a large number of children for Musk, but as Jupiter is also the ruler of his 6th house, Musk has suffered a number of poor health, medical mishaps over the years. In true munakara Jupiter style, Musk tried to throw a 350-lb sumo wrestler to the ground a decade ago, something he said: "cost me smashing my c5-c6 disk and eight years of mega back pain."[19]

> "Work like hell. I mean you just have to put in 80 to 100 hour weeks every week. This improves the odds of success. If other people are putting in 40 hour workweeks and you're putting in 100 hour workweeks, then even if you're doing the same thing, you know that you will achieve in four months what it takes them a year to achieve." – Elon Musk

Musk drives himself relentlessly putting in 120-hour weeks,[20] often working seven days a week and only takes "two or three" truly workless vacation days per year.[21] He suffers from insomnia, anxiety and depression, as well as having PTSD from a turbulent childhood. In an Interview with CNN in March 2024 Musk discussed his use of the medication ketamine and added that he had a prescription for the drug. He denied that he overuses the medication, saying, "if you use too much ketamine, you can't really get work done. I have a lot of work, I'm typically putting in 16-hour days...so I don't really have a situation where I can be not mentally acute for an extended period of time."[22] Ketamine is an FDA-approved anesthetic that was developed fifty years ago but it also has a reputation as an illicit party drug that is known to cause hallucinations and a relaxed, disconnected feeling.[23] (Jupiter in contention in 5th house, ruling 6th house).

Elon Musk appeared in public on 3rd November 2023 in an interview with British Prime Minister at the time, Rishi Sunak at the AI Safety Summit.[24] Musk's two munakara planets could not be more evident as he made the prediction of a time when humans will no longer need to work (Jupiter ruling 6th house, Mars in 8th house): "We are seeing the most disruptive force in history here. There will come a point where no job is needed. You can have a job if you want ...but the AI will be able to do everything."[25] Musk, who co-founded the ChatGPT developer OpenAI, and has launched a new venture called xAI, seems to feel he can profit from AI, despite at the same time describing AI as "one of the biggest threats to humanity", adding that it was "not clear we can control such a thing, but we can aspire to guide it in a direction that is beneficial to humanity."[26]

First Dispositor: Mars in Aquarius in 8th House

"I would like to die on Mars. Just not on impact." – Elon Musk

Musk's Jupiter in the 5th house squares its dispositor Mars in the 8th. It seems ironic that the man who wants to pioneer and colonise Mars should have the same planet in a state of munakara in his chart. Nothing could be more symbolic of Mars's hot separations than the blasting off of rockets into the atmosphere to find new planets to conquer. Musk fervently believes that the only way in which humanity can survive is for it to become a multi-planet species[27] and he seems hell-bent on turning his dream into a reality.

Twenty years ago, Musk founded Space Exploration Technologies (SpaceX) to make more affordable rockets, designed to move streams of people and goods across the universe. Musk's Jupiterian fantasy is of a cosmic Silk Road, but instead of connecting East to West, his vision connects galaxies and shrinks the universe into a profitable highway to benefit a few powerful merchants. Musk's funding for his Space Odyssey comes from the sale of PayPal, an online money transfer company, for $1.5 billion dollars in 2002 and a true indicator of Martian activity in the 8th house of joint resources. Munakara Mars resides in the house of 'other people's money' and rules (and sextiles) Musk's Mid-heaven in Aries – and is the ruler of his 5th house of children, entertainment, and social media engagement.

The outcome planet: Saturn in the 11th House (12th House in Whole Sign)

Saturn is the outcome planet for munakara Jupiter and Musk seems intent on removing the barriers which separate common decency from mob rule. In early January 2023, two months after purchasing Twitter, Musk laid off thousands of Twitter staff working within the platform's Trust and Safety sector whose job specifications were to handle misinformation, global content moderation, hate speech, and harassment.[28]

Musk's Saturn rules his 7th and 8th houses and the outcome of munakara Jupiter's desire to fight heroically for free speech and an interplanetary future is costing Musk a small fortune. In February 2023, Musk tweeted "Last three months were extremely tough, as had to save Twitter from bankruptcy, while fulfilling essential Tesla and SpaceX duties. Wouldn't wish that pain on anyone."[29] A year on from the purchase of X (formerly Twitter), the platform's value had fallen from US$44 billion to US$19 billion.[30] Still a grand sum in the scheme of things, but Saturn is no friend of Jupiter and even for the world's richest man there may be a bottom to the money pit.

Jupiter's outcome planet has connection to the two houses representing one's enemies. Saturn rules the 7th house, the place of one's open enemies, and Saturn's Whole Sign placement is in Musk's 12th house, the house of hidden enemies. Musk's public feuds with powerful people – Jupiterian figures as large and colourful as Musk himself – are more in the nature of 7th-house enemies as their spats take the form of verbal abuse shouted across 'the digital town square'.

For instance: animosity between Amazon founder Jeff Bezos and Musk over leasing rights to NASA's launchpad in 2013, a feud with Mark Zuckerberg in 2016 after a SpaceX test went haywire and destroyed a Facebook satellite, and a quarrel with Bill Gates in 2022 when Musk accused Gates of not taking climate change seriously by shorting Tesla's stock. Musk has incurred

Chapter Eight • *Jupiter in Munakara*

the wrath of an entire political party by changing his allegiance with the Democrats to the Republicans, after accusing the Democrats of being a Party of "division and hate." Donald Trump was not happy in November 2022 when Musk publicly backed Ron DeSantis, Trump's rival at the time, and a potential threat to his own presidential campaign. In a tweet on Musk's own social media platform, Trump described Tesla vehicles as "driverless cars that crash" and SpaceX as "rocket-ships to nowhere." In the same week as endorsing DeSantis, Musk also reinstated Trump's account with Twitter after a ban was placed on Trump for the January 6 attack. Former Twitter officials posted at the time Trump's posts "were highly likely to encourage and inspire people to replicate the criminal acts that took place at the US Capitol."[31]

However, the fences appear mended between Musk and Trump. "Elon Musk Becomes Donald Trump's Kingmaker" was the heading of a Bloomberg article, released after the announcement of Musk's promised monthly contribution of US$45 million to Donald Trump's Super Pac, the group in charge of Trump's campaign for the next Presidency.[32]

Saturn rulership of the 7th and 8th houses is a reminder of how influential Musk can be when he puts large amounts of money on the table, and he wants something in return for his investment.

Aquarius Mars in Munakara – Elon Musk

"I wouldn't say I have a lack of fear. In fact, I'd like my fear emotion to be less because it's very distracting and fries my nervous system." – Elon Musk

- **Key Questions:**
- What does Elon Musk's Mars contend with?
- What is its driving force?
- What is its trigger? What is its outcome?

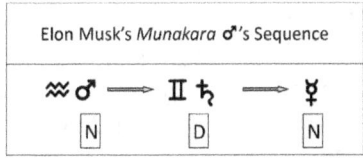

Table 8.6: Elon Musk: Munakara Mars Sequence

In July 2024 European regulators charged X with breaching the Digital Services Act – for misleading its users, non-compliance in key transparency areas, and cheating on the 'blue checks' that are meant to show trustworthy sources of information. At the time of writing, the EU is threatening to impose a fine on X of up to 6% of its global annual turnover, an amount which will run into the millions should it be issued.[33] The EU investigators launched the investigation in December 2023, and at the time of writing this book, are now looking into X's content moderation practices to assess whether the company has breached the Digital Services Act over dissemination of illegal content and failing to fight misinformation.

Munakara Mars disposited by Saturn is a direct connection between the two malefic planets, and although these two extreme forces are not enemies (as Mars is exalted in Saturn's other sign of Capricorn), separation is a theme any time these two planets meet in a sequence. Saturn may convince the individual with munakara Mars that they are in control of the situation, but the crossing of sect boundaries is a hint that this is likely not the case. Mars's outcome planet, a second nocturnal companion, will describe what Mars is protecting, or what power or advantage it expects to gain by its conquest.

In Musk and Assange's case, nocturnal Mercury is Mars's outcome planet. Whilst both men's recorded IQ rating is well above the average of 100 – Musk's is reputed to be 155 whilst Assange's IQ is believed to be above 170 – intelligence and self-preservation are not the same thing, and Mercury may not be able to contain Mars's self-destructive qualities.

Mars plays a role in Jupiter's munakara, as it is the first dispositor in the diurnal planet's sequence. However, Mars also has its issues as it too is in a state of munakara. Mars is in the later degrees of Aquarius and as such, it does not aspect its dispositor, Saturn, even though the two planets are in air signs. Perhaps the more interesting aspect is Mars's trine to Venus, not because Venus is involved in munakara, but because Mars and Venus, always share two consecutive axes in any given chart.

In Musk's case, Mars rules the MC at the chart's zenith, and Venus rules the Imum Coeli (IC) at the nadir. Together, they also jointly rule the 5th- and 11th-house axis and a trine between two nocturnal planets, despite one of them in munakara, can bring great good fortune and advancement to the individual. Unfortunately, trines can be fickle too, and a fall can come as quickly as a rise. Saturn, as first dispositor to Mars, may be able to hold fast to Mars's shooting star, but Saturn has its own issues being embattled with Neptune and munakara Jupiter, through its opposition to both planets.

Mars is a nocturnal planet and whilst Saturn is its dispositor for the sign of Aquarius, Musk and Assange's final planet in Mars' munakara sequence is nocturnal Mercury. In Musk's case, it is also conjunct his Ascendant.

Chapter Eight • *Jupiter in Munakara*

A prominent Mercury rising at birth often denotes an individual who gains notoriety and who creates a brand-name in their own right. However, when Mercury becomes the outcome planet for munakara Mars, there is a sharpness of the brain which creates a steady flow of ideas and opinions, but also may give rise to outrageous statements. Musk was excellent at self-promotion when he was a subscriber to Twitter, but the ownership appears to have unbalanced him as he encourages division, hate and extremism on the newly named platform. On the eve of the first anniversary of X, Musk's 'humour' turned on Wikipedia, the open source website used for sharing references and knowledge on a global scale. "He saw a collective resource that people prized and he wanted to hurt it,"[34] wrote *Guardian* journalist Zoe Williams. Musk challenged Wikipedia's request for small donations to keep it afloat, posting on X that he would donate $1bn if it would change its name to *'Dickipedia.'*

A second important factor comes with the realisation that whilst Musk and Assange share Mercury in Cancer, both disposited by the Moon, the five days between them has shifted Mercury's dispositor from Virgo (Musk's Moon) to Scorpio (Assange's Moon). Musk's Mercury is in mutual reception with the Moon, indicating a cunning, craftiness to Mercury's actions on the Ascendant, especially when it comes to stirring others' emotions for one's own purpose. Assange's Moon on the other hand is in fall, and this jeopardises the individual's safety if they speak out with passion (Cancer) rather than with caution – and Mercury's recklessness further accentuates the quincunx to munakara Mars.

There is no doubt that both men are risk-takers, but perhaps Musk has the foresight to pull back in time to self-preserve, whilst Assange pushes on regardless of the consequences, his munakara Mars believing that he is a truth-warrior and he has justice (in the form of munakara Jupiter) on his side when it comes to the disclosure of sensitive information.

Munakara Planet and Sect Condition – how comfortable is Mars?

If Musk's publicly available birth time is to be trusted, then his Cancer Sun has risen over the horizon and the chart can be classified as diurnal. The discomfort that nocturnal Mars experiences travelling in the same hemisphere as the Sun in a diurnal chart makes Mars an extremely hot, volatile and destructive force. Robert Hand calls Mars in this situation "belligerent, competitive and selfish in its effects; it wants to win at all costs and likes to fight for the sake of fighting."[35] Mars is the ruler of Musk's Mid-heaven and Musk is ruthless when it comes to destroying his competitors and using any means possible to gain the advantage in the cut-throat business world.

Hand claims that daylight only makes Mars "...more active and less feeling. The perfectly diurnal Mars is one that is ferociously active, but has its feelings completely in check so that it can with perfect discipline and order create mayhem. It is therefore unlucky and unfortunate."[36]

Elon Musk — ♂'s Sect Dignity			
Planet	Sect 1 Status	Sect 2 Hemisphere	Sect 3 Sign
♒ ♂	Day	With the Sun	Air
N	D	D	✓

Table 8.7: Elon Musk: Munakara Mars Sect Dignity

The square aspect between Musk's two planets in contention is unlikely to control an out of sect Mars's destructive nature or rationalise its extreme behaviour. In the reverse, Jupiter is likely to agitate Mars even further, adding to rash judgements and lack of damage control. Munakara Mars in Saturn's sign will make its own rules and justify any aggressive move that helps it to win and with Mercury as its outcome planet, big ideas, no matter how insane, will over-ride caution or accountability. Out of sect Mars is driven to crush the enemy, even if there is nothing to salvage at the end of the battle.

Munakara Jupiter – Julian Assange

In December 2006, just after the launch of WikiLeaks, Julian Assange created a dating profile on the website okCupid under the username Harry Harrison. Assange posted this invitation:

> *Passionate, and often pig-headed activist intellectual directing a consuming, dangerous human rights project looking for a siren for a love affair, children and occasional criminal conspiracy. Such a woman should be spirited and playful, of high intelligence, though not necessarily formally educated, have spunk, class & inner strength and be able to think strategically about the world and the people she cares about.*[37]

Whilst this description was light-heartedly intended to pique the interest of a new love, it says much about Assange's two planets in contention. Mercury, ruler of 7th-house relationships, forms a water trine to munakara Jupiter, and a quincunx to munakara Mars. Mercury is also the outcome planet for Assange's munakara Mars.

Chapter Eight • *Jupiter in Munakara*

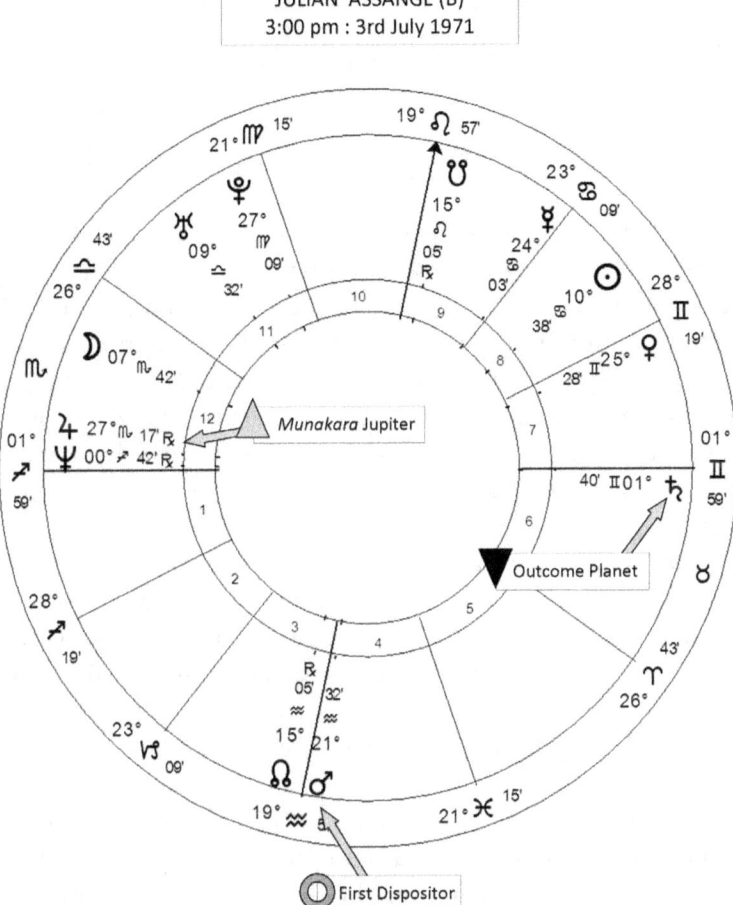

Fig. 8.3: Julian Assange Natal Chart: Munakara Jupiter's Sequence

- **Key Questions:**
- What does Julian Assange's Jupiter contend with?
- What is its driving force?
- What is its trigger? What is its outcome?

"We must all look to ourselves and understand whether what we are doing is right and just, not just according to the views of our superiors but according to the long view of history, according to human rights and to our feelings of compassion."[38] – Julian Assange, *In His Own Words* autobiography, published April 2022

Munakara in Theory

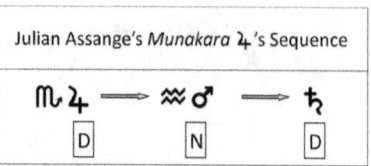

Table 8.8: Julian Assange: Munakara Jupiter's Sequence

Julian Assange's munakara Jupiter lies in his 12th house, and he has made many formidable hidden enemies during his time as the head of not-for-profit website WikiLeaks. Even as a youth Assange used his contentious Jupiter to work in secrecy, infiltrating and exposing weaknesses within thousands of systems including the US Pentagon[39] (Saturn on the Descendant is Jupiter's outcome planet). Even as a 16-year-old skilled hacker in 1987, Assange, using the name *Mendax* (from Latin 'nobly untruthful') to cover his identity, had a self-imposed set of ethics: he did not damage or crash systems he hacked, and he shared information.[40]

Munakara Jupiter in Scorpio is in aversion to its Sagittarian sign on the Ascendant, and although there have been many claims that Assange is in this for the fame, notoriety, and global attention, this astrological statement questions these allegations. Rather, Assange (and munakara Jupiter) has always been blind to the fact that his actions are dangerous, have the potential to rob him of his freedom and his legal rights, and may ultimately be life-threatening.

Assange's munakara Jupiter contends with his abhorrence of injustice, a position he has held since he was a young child. In Australia in December 1996, at the age of 25, Assange faced a theoretical sentence of 290 years in prison for 31 counts of crimes relating to hacking. The judge sentenced him to a fine of A$2,100 and released him on a A$5,000 good behaviour bond because of his "disrupted childhood and the absence of malicious or mercenary intent."[41] The light sentence may have been helped by the fact that three years prior to his trial, Assange had provided technical advice and support to help the Victorian Police Child Exploitation Unit to prosecute individuals responsible for publishing and distributing child pornography.[42] His drive to expose 'the truth', and his belief in 'privacy for the weak, and transparency for the powerful', has been the philosophy that makes his every move contentious, and incites fear in those governments and corporations that hide the truth, and bury unpleasant, unpalatable, or dangerous activities.

Chapter Eight • *Jupiter in Munakara*

Assange's weapon is WikiLeaks – his Mars in Aquarius drives Jupiter forth to fight corrupted authorities, secret institutions and military powerhouses. When his house arrest in 2010 at Ellingham Hall restricted his movements, he explained the need for WikiLeaks to change its tactics:

> WikiLeaks had always been a guerrilla publisher. We would draw surveillance and censorship in one jurisdiction and redeploy in another, moving across borders like ghosts. But at Ellingham I became an immoveable asset under siege. We could no longer choose our battles. Fronts opened up on all sides. I had to learn to think like a general.[43]

Saturn in Gemini is Jupiter's outcome planet and Assange's hope and desire is to build a better society. In his autobiography, Assange states:

> It is from the revelation of truth that all else follows. Our buildings can only be as tall as their bricks are strong. Our civilization is only as strong as its ideas are true. When our buildings are erected by the corrupt, when the cement is cut with dirt, when pristine steel is replaced by scrap – our buildings are not safe to live in. And when our media is corrupt, when our academics are timid, when our history is filled with half-truths and lies – our civilization will never be just. It will never reach to the skies.[44]

Munakara Planet and Sect Condition – how comfortable is Jupiter?

Assange's chart is diurnal with the Sun above the horizon and Jupiter travels with the Sun (in the diurnal hemisphere); therefore Jupiter has a high level of comfort in Julian Assange's chart. This fact tends to suggest that even under the sometimes difficult conditions of munakara, Jupiter feels justified in transforming its ideals into actions, and that it is capable of forming a philosophy that suits Assange's needs. However, Jupiter's position in apparent retrograde motion creates problems of repetition, with learning and moving forwards with newly acquired wisdom a challenge for him. By being retrograde his

Julian Assange — ♃'s Sect Dignity			
Planet	Sect 1 Status	Sect 2 Hemisphere	Sect 3 Sign
♏♃	Day	With the Sun	Water
D	D	D	N

Table 8.9: *Julian Assange: Munakara Jupiter's Sect Dignity*

Jupiter runs the risk of repeating its mistakes, or not even understanding that mistakes have been made at all. After escaping a severe sentence in 1996 Assange told the judge that he (the judge) had been "misled by the prosecution in terms of the charges" and that "a great misjustice has been done." The judge told Assange "you have pleaded guilty, the proceedings are over" and advised him to be quiet.[45]

One of the most consistent criticisms of Julian Assange – apart from the obvious releasing of secret documentation – and one that created friction within the WikiLeaks camp, was that 'he doesn't plan ahead.'[46] However, this organisational failing also served him well by baffling his opponents in the outside world, as they never knew where his next move was likely to be. His girlfriend in 2005 (at the time of WikiLeaks website registration) was a fellow Melbourne university student, and she remembers the randomness of their lifestyle, saying, 'He's very good at going on adventures, because his whole life is an adventure.'[47]

From 2007 to 2010, Assange travelled continuously on WikiLeaks business, visiting Africa, Asia, Europe, and North America. Assange truly is a citizen of the world, and his ease in a nomadic lifestyle suits munakara Jupiter in good sect condition. Andrew Fowler, author of *The Most Dangerous Man in the World* comments "Assange's ability to get help from strangers was both charmingly naive and mildly exploitative. It would become a constant theme of his nomadic days as the head of WikiLeaks."[48]

Jupiter's first dispositor is Assange's second munakara planet, Mars, and diurnal Jupiter in munakara squares its nocturnal dispositor in the fixed air sign of Aquarius. Mars's munakara sequence is shown below, and it too involves Saturn as its own first dispositor. Saturn in Gemini is Jupiter's outcome planet, and all three planets – Jupiter, Mars and Saturn – are deeply influential, and present in Assange's life. The trio cling to angles: Jupiter, Ascendant ruler, is four degrees from the Ascendant's degree, Mars opposes the Mid-heaven, and Saturn opposes the Ascendant on the other side of the chart, at the same degree as the Gemini Descendant.

Scorpio Jupiter in Munakara – Julian Assange

"Transparency and accountability are moral issues that must be the essence of public life and journalism." – Julian Assange, quoted by John Pilger in a speech outside the Old Bailey, September 7, 2020

Chapter Eight • *Jupiter in Munakara*

Munakara Jupiter in Scorpio in 12th House

AstroDatabank gives Assange's 3:00 pm birth time a 'B' rating under the recommendation of Lois Rodden, quoting the time from *Julian Assange: The Unauthorised Autobiography*.[49] This birth time results in a Sagittarius Ascendant, ruled by Jupiter in Scorpio, in the 12th house.[50] Prior to this, an anonymous source cited a birth certificate for 2:05 pm. This is odd because Australian birth certificates do not record time of birth, and the registry could not have had the information. The earlier 2:05 pm birth time produces a Scorpio Ascendant, ruled by Mars in Aquarius. Either way, a munakara planet would be the lord of Julian's Ascendant, regardless of whether it was Scorpio or Sagittarius.

My personal preference is the Sagittarian Ascendant with the 3:00pm birth time, as this would mean Jupiter is in aversion to its sign, and I believe Assange demonstrates a number of personality traits associated with the ruler, Jupiter in Scorpio, being blind to Sagittarius. Traits such as the need for drama, grand gestures, erratic behaviour, and a level of almost narcissistic tendencies seeming to compensate for feelings of being ignored, misunderstood or discontented with injustice. Jupiter also being in a state of munakara adds to the feeling of 'it's me against the world', with the addition of Neptune conjunct Jupiter, both on the Ascendant, contributing with the three roles of victim, saviour, and persecutor. The two planets oppose Saturn on the Descendant, and open enemies accumulate on this point in the chart, further exacerbating munakara Jupiter's image of itself as saving the world or being a victim, unjustly persecuted for their beliefs.

First Dispositor: Mars in Aquarius conjunct IC

WikiLeaks has created a huge amount of embarrassment and rage within the ranks of political parties, military institutions and governmental agencies throughout the world, and its founder, Julian Assange, has been described by the media as 'the heart and soul of this organisation, its founder, philosopher, spokesperson, original coder, organiser, financier, and all the rest.'[51] But Julian sees his role differently, "We always expect tremendous criticism. It is my role to be the lightning rod....to attract the attacks against the organization for our work, and that is a difficult role. On the other hand, I get undue credit."[52]

Munakara Mars in Aquarius certainly may be the 'lightning rod' that draws attention and power, but also generates society's need to punish, control and silence dissidents, and those who would disrupt the workings of governments, the security of the armed forces, or threaten the profits of organisations and large corporations. Writer and director Angela Richter says: "I hardly know anyone who says "I" as reluctantly as Assange." Karen Sharpe, complier and editor of *Julian Assange in His Own Words* adds, "In the many talks, interviews, and documentaries I watched in compiling material for this book, it was "we" that prevailed over "I" so many times over....By paying tribute to the contribution of others, Julian deflects attention from his own importance."[53]

Munakara Mars in Aquarius – power to the people. Assange states that: "It is only the people working with the press that holds powerful groups like states to account. That system of scrutiny of the state is so sacrosanct in preventing democracies going astray that it must be kept open, and people must be kept free to exchange knowledge with each other, and the press must not be censored."[54]

The outcome planet: Saturn in Gemini

The two diurnal planets, munakara Jupiter, and its outcome planet Saturn, face off against one another across the relating axis known as the Ascendant/Descendant line. This line is the imitation of Earth's horizon and breaks the zodiac circle into two hemispheres. Likewise, Jupiter and Saturn mark unseen boundaries between expansion and reduction. In Assange's chart, the greater benefic (Jupiter) and greater malefic (Saturn) face one another in animosity. In reality, the more Assange became celebrated as a shining beacon for freedom of information (Jupiter), the greater was the need for authority (Saturn) to punish his audacity in exposing their weaknesses and mistakes.

The United Nations Special Rapporteur on Torture Nils Melzer examined Assange in Britain's Belmarsh Prison in 2019 and stated: "In 20 years of work with victims of war, violence and political persecution I have never seen a group of democratic States ganging up to deliberately isolate, demonise and abuse a single individual for such a long time and with so little regard for human dignity and the rule of law. The collective persecution of Julian Assange must end here and now!"[55]

Aquarius Mars in Munakara – Julian Assange

- **Key Questions:**
- What does Julian Assange's Mars contend with?
- What is its driving force?
- What is its trigger? What is its outcome?

Chapter Eight • *Jupiter in Munakara*

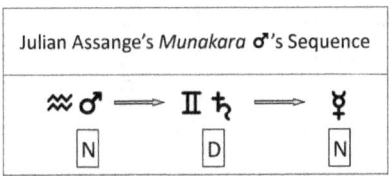

Table 8.10: Julian Assange: Munakara Mars's Sequence

Munakara Mars sits on Assange's IC opposite his Mid-heaven. Its two-degree conjunction to the North Node is tighter than Musk's same union, which is almost six degrees apart. Perhaps munakara Mars's conjunction to North Node is Assange's compulsion to play the role of freedom fighter, and that especially under the conditions of war, he pursues those in power whom he feels must be held to account for their actions.

Mars has just crossed over the 4th-house cusp in the Placidus system but it would stay in the 3rd house in his Whole Sign chart. This position may better suit Assange's inner dialogue as his contentious Mars has made him a warrior in the pursuit of secret data (Mars rules his Whole Sign 12th house). Assange's Ecuadorian embassy period (2012–2019) saw his munakara Mars on the IC challenged by his restricted living conditions within the embassy. For seven years Assange was constrained within a living space of roughly 360 square feet, an office space converted to hold a bed, telephone, sun lamp, computer, shower, treadmill and kitchenette. Cameras and listening devices were secretly installed and every conversation and meeting was taped and sold to various interested parties, including the CIA, by Assange's diplomatic hosts.[56]

In both charts Mars's dispositor Saturn is in opposition to Neptune. Whilst this aspect may be interpreted as Musk's motives in spreading misinformation, Assange has always been clear in his objectives. Saturn plays a major role in both munakara sequences – as outcome planet for Jupiter, and as first dispositor for Mars – and any input from Saturn will bring Neptune as its tag-along companion. The Neptune trifecta of victim/saviour/persecutor manifests through Saturn's involvement with Jupiter and Mars, but the placement of the opposition across Assange's Ascendant/Descendent line suggests he will play the role of each character regardless of whether he chooses them or they are chosen for him.

Much to the US government's chagrin, public pressure to release Assange and cancel the charges against him continued to grow,[57] even after he was seized and imprisoned in the notorious HM Prison Belmarsh. Twelfth-house Jupiter (in munakara) ruling the Ascendant kept reminding the world of his unjust incarceration and in aspect to Mars (in munakara) on the IC, the wheels of justice and politics[58] kept moving relentlessly towards a solution. When his release came in June 2024, it was fast – it was an admission of guilt, to save face for the US authorities, and a victorious moment for all those who had campaigned for his freedom.[59]

Julian Assange's munakara Mars contends with his distrust of warmongers and those who profit from other people's misery. He has been nominated for the Nobel Peace Prize eight times, but rejects the idea of accepting the prize, as it means that his name is associated with other Nobel Prize laureates, such as Barack Obama, Henry Kissinger, and Menachem Begin, all of whom he believes have accelerated conflict and spread bloodshed through war.

His driving force is the desire to build a better world based on forcing authorities to admit to their actions, and munakara Mars works hard to reveal the truth, with full disclosure and accountability, no matter how uncomfortable it may be for those in power. He applies what he calls 'scientific journalism' to WikiLeaks, to try to ensure they do not publish wrong information.

> *Everything we do is like science. It is checkable, independently checkable, because the information which has informed our conclusion is there. Just like scientific papers which are based on experimental data must make their experimental data available to other scientists and to the public, if they want their papers to be published. It's our philosophy that raw source material must be made available so that conclusions can be checkable.*[60]

Assange's Saturn in Gemini follows through on its principles and Assange believes that information pertinent to the public should be freely available through what he calls "The Fourth Estate." In the Fourth Estate context, the people who acquire information are sources; the people who work on information and distribute it are journalists and publishers; and the people who may act on it includes everyone.[61]

Julian Assange's munakara Mars has shown resilience, determination and courage under fire. During the seven years in which Assange was confined to the Ecuadorean embassy – from June 2012 to April 2019 – with no Internet facilities or telephone connections in the final year, he still somehow managed to help to publish 5 million documents, produce 3 books, launch more than 30 publications, and give 100 talks.[62]

Elon Musk's Mercury has not moved close enough to Mars's degree to create a quincunx between first and third planet in Mars's sequence. However,

Chapter Eight • *Jupiter in Munakara*

five days later, at the time of Julian Assange's birth, Mercury had moved to 24 degrees Cancer, forming a quincunx to Mars at 21 Aquarius.

This type of 'non-aspect' shows an aversion between the two planets' signs, Cancer and Aquarius, which have nothing in common and therefore the planets work independent of each other. A quincunx, or aversion, means the planets are unwittingly causing damage to each other, and in the case of Assange, Mars's munakara sequence is likely to be more detrimental than Musk's because of the aversion between Mars and Mercury.

> *"People often ask, 'What can I do?' The answer is not so difficult: Learn how the world works. Challenge the statements and intentions of those who seek to control us behind a facade of democracy and monarchy. Unite in common purpose and common principle to design, build, document, finance and defend. Learn. Challenge. Act. Now."*[63] – Julian Assange, 2020

Munakara Planet and Sect Condition – how comfortable is Mars?

Munakara Mars lies at the base of Assange's chart, at the IC, and belongs to the nocturnal hemisphere, travelling in the opposite hemisphere to the Sun (in *halb*). Its removal from the Sun's light and heat provides Mars with an externally calm and patient demeanour, coupled with a more compassionate point of view, than when Mars travels with the Sun. Aquarius is a masculine sign, and in sharing the same gender, it suits Mars. Concepts, ideas, communication and like-mindedness attract Mars and fires its energy and enthusiasm, even when Saturn is the owner of the air sign.

Julian Assange — ♂'s Sect Dignity			
Planet	Sect 1 Status	Sect 2 Hemisphere	Sect 3 Sign
♒ ♂	Day	No Sun	Air
N	D	N	✓

Table 8.11: Julian Assange: Munakara Mars' Sect Dignity

Saturn adds planning, intelligence, purpose and control to Mars's nature and Mars has no issue with being in battle or facing off against a challenge, even when the odds seem against it, as is often the way when it is in a state of munakara.

There is a cunning quality added to Mars's contentious character when nocturnal Mercury is its outcome planet. Speech is passionate and idealistic, and Mercury can bring others around to supporting outrageous or unusual thought processes. Nocturnal Mercury is not always clear on its motives or the next move it intends to make, and often involves the soul of a poet or a revolutionary. Julian Assange is both, and whilst he believes he has good intentions, when Mercury is the outcome planet for Mars these intentions can be misconstrued or used to turn others against him. There is no doubt that Assange is courageous in the face of great and powerful opponents, but his mind is not unbreakable, and the constant pressure of incarceration likely took its toll on both nocturnal planets.

Julian Assange's Facebook message to his supporters, published July 1, 2024:

> *Dear Friends,*
> *I write to you with immense gratitude and joy in my heart. Finally after 14 long years I'm free. This freedom is not just mine, but it belongs to all of you who supported me in my darkest moments.*
>
> *Your unwavering support, your letters, your prayers and your belief in me have kept my spirit alive. Each day, your love has given me strength to persevere and have hope through this day. There are no words to express the profound gratitude I have for each and every one of you.*
>
> *Thank you for being my rock my light and my hope. I can't wait to embark on this new chapter of life and I'm excited to share it with all of you. Together we overcome and together we will move forward."*
> *Julian Assange*

Further Examples for Munakara Jupiter
Wolfgang Amadeus Mozart, Cindy Sherman, and Oprah Winfrey

The chart of Wolfgang Amadeus Mozart (born 27 January, 1756) has two planets in munakara: Jupiter in Libra and the Moon in Sagittarius. Mozart was a brilliant child who excelled in composition and played in the courts of Europe's Emperors from the young age of just 6 years old. Mozart's story is one of brilliance and excess, and his chart is featured in Part Two of Munakara Jupiter's Delineations.

American photographer and artist, Cindy Sherman, was born on 19th January 1954 at 4:27 am. Media host and businesswoman, Oprah Winfrey, was born ten days later, also in the early hours of the morning. The two

Chapter Eight • *Jupiter in Munakara*

women's charts are remarkably similar, both with Sagittarius rising and munakara Jupiter as the Ascendant Lord. They share a number of planets in close proximity, except for the fast-moving Moon, but these too have some connection as both are in early degrees of fire signs, and trine one another in Leo (Sherman), and Sagittarius (Winfrey).

Jupiter is not the only planet in munakara for these two women, and the combination of three planets in munakara combine to create their own unique individuality, and to provide the passion to speak out against oppression, discrimination and violation, particularly where women are concerned. Mercury and Venus form a duet in both women's charts, and this nocturnal sequence adds depth and direction for munakara Jupiter. Both women share concerns for women's issues, and although they take different paths in different mediums, they share a sense of being compelled to tell the stories of women, and to shine a light on the exploitation of women in today's modern society. The charts can be found in Part Two in Munakara Jupiter's Delineations.

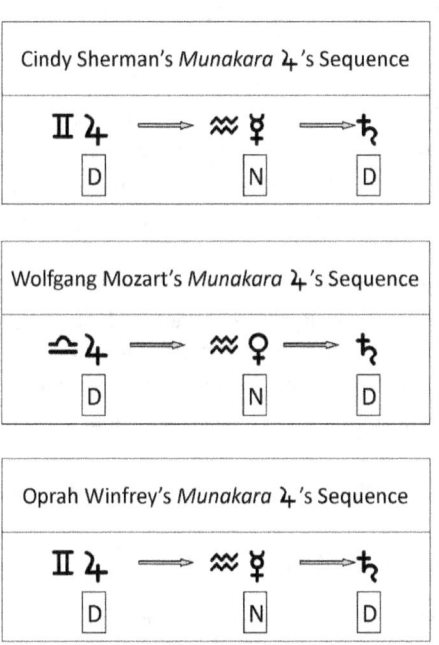

Table 8.12: Munakara Jupiter's Sequences

CHAPTER NINE
Saturn in Munakara

What does it mean when Saturn is in a state of munakara?

- Feeling constantly under attack from authority figures
- Having one's authority, expertise or integrity challenged by others
- Fearful, disparaging or negative attitude towards father figure or authority
- Fascination with secret dealings, or a belief in conspiracy theories
- Strong desire for autonomy, belief in the right of self-government
- Rebellion at having to comply with, or be controlled by unfair or unjust rules or a system not respected, the feeling of being above the rules
- High expectations for authority figures in terms of integrity, honesty, transparency, accountability, honourable behaviour or fairness
- Deep disappointment when expected standards are not met
- Impossibly high expectations of one's own behaviour and standards

Table 9.1: *Some possible expressions of Saturn in munakara*

Munakara Saturn and Personal Challenges

More so than other planets, Saturn in munakara often brings questions like 'Who finds me contentious? Am I a bad person? What do I find contentious in my life? Am I a good person experiencing bad things?'

Part of the reason for this dichotomy of 'good verses bad' is the fact that Saturn's normal compulsion is to follow directions, obey the rules,

Chapter Nine • *Saturn in Munakara*

trust in the process of justice, believe that disobedience leads to chaos, and emphatically agree with the statement that 'no-one is bigger than the institution'. Munakara seems to be the antithesis of Saturn as Saturn lays emphasis on authority, hierarchy, order, duty, tradition, responsibility and sacrifice. In contrast, munakara Saturn often rebels against these principles, wanting to incorporate ideas such as freedom, reform and radical change.

Saturn in a state of munakara tends to produce an individual who is highly sensitive to criticism which they perceive to be undermining their actions or opinions. This often results in the individual feeling under threat, particularly from figures in authority or power. Saturn's already reserved nature becomes more closed, and mistrust intensifies for officialdom, management, government agencies, bureaucracy, the police, or anyone in a position of power or control. Saturn in munakara strongly values the individual's right to self-govern, especially when the individual believes the rules do not apply to them or do not make sense. Munakara Saturn resists being swayed by those it deems to be unethical, deceitful or amoral. A sense of losing control can be a big trigger for munakara Saturn, and the person will fight to maintain control over their own decisions.

Difficulty can arise if the individual with munakara Saturn tries too hard to influence others and bring them under their control. Munakara Saturn values honesty above all else, yet the person is not always honest about their own insecurities. The ruling planet of Saturn's sign will give indications as to where it fears its greatest weakness lies, and each of the nocturnal planets will differ in their expression and effect on Saturn's munakara behaviour.

Every one of us can look back and evaluate our separations in life, and with the wisdom of 20/20 hindsight, we can see the difference between our Saturn separations (slow and cold) and our Mars separations (hot and fast), and this is particularly true when we find either of these planets in munakara. NBA superstar, LeBron James has Saturn in munakara and his separation from the Cleveland Cavaliers for the first time in 2010 was controversial. LeBron wanted to be a part of the super-group of players forming in the Miami Heat, and he made the announcement that he would be joining them in the following season in a nationally televised special titled *The Decision*. As far as James was concerned, it was a simple separation born from the desire to move on and try something new in his career. However, his Saturn in Scorpio disposits to Mars, and his fans reacted strongly when they found their hero was jumping ship before winning them an NBA championship. In other words, what started as a simple Saturn separation flared into fans burning his jersey and a backlash of hatred with all the anger and malice of a Mars separation. James re-signed with the Cavaliers in 2014, but it took a further two years until he was forgiven, and then, not until he had led his former club to victory in the 2016 Championship Finals. LeBron's munakara Saturn sequence ends with outcome planet, Jupiter, so all ends well, but LeBron has been haunted by *The Decision*, and every so often the topic reappears to embarrass and humiliate him. LeBron James' chart is featured in Part Two in the chapter on Munakara Saturn's Delineations.

In Greek mythology Cronos (Saturn), is the old god terrified of being usurped by younger, more virile versions of itself. Cronos swallows his children as they are birthed because he is haunted by the guilt of his creator father's castration by his own hand. The terror of history repeating itself is so great that he would rather consume his own children than risk their acts of betrayal and the destruction of his power. In the act of swallowing his children, Cronos represents Time. In this clever and cruel myth we find the analogy of Saturn using Time to consume human life from the moment of birth; turning babes to children, youths to adulthood, and adults to old age. Time can seem to be an enemy, especially for those individuals with munakara Saturn. There is never enough of it, it drags in periods of sorrow, boredom or physical pain, it speeds up in moments of happiness, pleasure or contentment, and it cannot be controlled, avoided or pressured to change its constant path through life.

Munakara Saturn feels the jaws of Cronos nibbling, gnawing and sucking at the marrow, swelling the joints and snapping at brittle bones. All the while asking 'What control do I give away as I age? What authority or power will I lose as society no longer deems me useful or relevant? As each year progresses, what knowledge, skill or strength will slip away from me? How old will I be when I know I am feeble, vulnerable, weakened, ridiculed, or ill?'

As much as an acute awareness of time passing can feel a curse to munakara Saturn, it can also galvanise its chart owner into action with the belief that 'the time in nigh', and that some matters must be addressed at a particular moment. Saturn in munakara is a signature for those who believe their duty lies in protecting the principles of fairness, honour and justice, and correcting wrongs perpetrated by powerful individuals, corporations, or government agencies.

Chapter Nine • *Saturn in Munakara*

Munakara Saturn and Society's Challenges

'Group harmony' is a modern term used to describe a lack of disagreement and discord in a social group such as a society, community, organisation or workplace. The "perfect" group harmony is one in which the members interact peacefully, are in agreement with one another, and whose members avoid conflict at all costs. In theory, group harmony looks ideal as it appears to benefit all members of society, particularly when it subscribes to the belief that the group's needs override the needs of the individual. However, in practice group harmony carries heavy penalties for some – such as individuals with munakara Saturn, who question the rules and who find its benefits too suffocating or too high a price to pay for social stability.

In order to maintain group harmony it is considered inappropriate and disruptive to act in one's own interests, and the group's status quo is highly valued. There is a lack of tolerance for disagreement and even if group decisions must be respected, even if irrational and the individual knows them to be wrong. There is no place for dissidents, risk takers, or independent thinkers in group harmony.

Needless to say, an individual with munakara Saturn is unlikely to see the benefits of group harmony and will be incapable of staying quiet or tolerating injustices. They will rail against mediocrity, and ignore social etiquette, even if being insistent means that people are embarrassed, uncomfortable, or shocked. Alternatively, frustration can solidify into cold silence for Saturn in munakara where the person withdraws completely and uses isolation or passive hostility as their weapon. Munakara Saturn takes its unofficial role as society's guardian very seriously. Even when there are repercussions Saturn in contention is unlikely to back down under the threat of disapproval or social isolation.

Munakara Saturn does not suffer fools, but its behaviour can be insufferable, especially if it bullies others, or tries to control their decision-making processes. Heavy-handed behaviour is usually met by resistance, and munakara Saturn risks painful experiences of separation, isolation, and bitterness if it does not learn to proceed with caution. The individual must learn to move from Cronos-like brutal solutions, to gentler ways of cultivating the soil until new growth springs forth and nurturing it as it grows. This will prove a much kinder method for munakara Saturn, and which method will come more easily will depend on the nature of the other planets in munakara Saturn's sequence.

Some individuals with munakara Saturn have fought against group harmony and amongst their number is the French military leader and former President of France, Charles de Gaulle. A decorated officer of the First World War, General de Gaulle fled to England after refusing to accept his government's armistice with Germany in June 1940. A military court in France sentenced de Gaulle to death for treason but undaunted he persevered in building a Free French movement against Nazi Germany in World War II.

Mary Wollstonecraft Shelley (1797–1851) was the second daughter born to feminist philosopher, educator and writer Mary Wollstonecraft and the first child of the philosopher, novelist and journalist William Godwin. Shelley is best known for her 1818 work *Frankenstein; or, The Modern Prometheus*. Shelley was 18 years old when she experienced her "waking dream" that led to what has been described as the first published work of science fiction. To quote a major exhibition produced by the National Library of Medicine in 1997–1998: "[S]he (Shelley) posed profound questions in her novel about individual and societal responsibility for other human beings. To make her point, she used the scientific advances of her era and the controversy surrounding them as a metaphor for issues of unchecked power and self-serving ambition, and their effect on the human community."[1]

The American novelist Louisa May Alcott (1832–1888) was born 35 years after Shelley and she too was born with Saturn in munakara. Her father, Bronson Alcott, founded an abolitionist society in 1850, and Alcott's childhood home, The Wayside residence in Massachusetts was a stop for fugitive people in the Underground Railroad. Alcott wrote her famous novel, *Little Women*, in 1868 for a publisher who agreed to publish her father's book on philosophy only if she wrote a novel for girls. Similar to Shelley, Alcott's early life was shadowed by her father's debts and although both fathers were idealists, educators and philosophers, they had no idea on how to provide financially for their families.

Saturn's Sequence: Friends, Associates, and Enemies

In terms of Saturn's friendships and enmities (*Table 9.2*), the Sun and Moon are hostile to Saturn but it is unlikely that they will cause much damage to Saturn's situation in the chart. Saturn, as the greater malefic, creates problems for the two luminaries, but the opposite is not true as the Sun and Moon do nor inflict harm on Saturn.

Chapter Nine • *Saturn in Munakara*

If either the Sun or Jupiter are Saturn's diurnal outcome planet, then their grievances are slight but worthy of note. Particularly in situations where munakara Saturn makes an aspect to them in the chart, as this will reinforce Saturn's contentious nature.

D Diurnal N Nocturnal	Essential Dignity Rulership / Exaltation (Mutual Damage)	Second Essential Dignity Fall (opposes Exaltation)	Second Essential Dignity — Borrowing Signs for Exaltation		
Munakara Planet △	Mutually Hurtful With (♄'s Two-Way Damage)	Injurious To (♄ Dispositis Fall Sign)	Offering Friendship To (♄ Owns Exaltation Sign)	Asking Friendship From (Exalted ♄'s Dispositor)	Indifferent To ♄ - No relationship
D ♄	D Sun : Moon N ▼ Outcome Planet ○ First Dispositor	D Jupiter (♌) ▼ Outcome Planet	N Mars (♑) ○ First Dispositor	N Venus (♎) ○ First Dispositor	Mercury D/N D ▼ Outcome Planet N ○ First Dispositor

Table 9.2: Al-Biruni's Table: Saturn's relationships

Friends and Associates of a munakara Saturn: Venus, Mars, Mercury

If Venus is involved in the sequence (as the first dispositor)

Saturn in Taurus or Libra will be disposited by Venus. Taurus and Libra differ in two major ways: their elemental quality (Taurus is earth, whereas Libra is air) and in the list of essential dignities (Taurus is the Moon's exaltation sign, whereas Libra is Saturn's exaltation sign).

Where munakara Saturn is disposited by Venus, issues such as unfairness, social inequality or poor treatment of a marginalised group is going to make Saturn's hackles rise. There may be issues around gender or sexism (Venus is female/femenine), race, class, or religious freedoms being restricted or denied. Saturn in Venus's signs will want to rally others and may act as a leader to gather like-minded people together and organise them to fight together.

It can indicate an individual who is a vocal, inspiring speaker and communication can be a powerful weapon for Saturn to sway public opinion in its favour. Popularity can be one of the benefits of Saturn's exaltation but words will not be enough if the person's actions do not show integrity or are not authentic in following through on their mission. Munakara Saturn in exaltation can show a sudden rise in social status, but with it can come accusations of being high-handed, arrogant, or unfit for the new elevated role.

Promises or pledges made by munakara Saturn must be backed by a practical plan, and as the true astrological Time-Lord, Saturn needs to set out schedules for anticipated goals and honour these schedules if it wants to make plausible progress. Saturn's outcome planet may give some indication on how true progress can be made, as Jupiter or the Sun can bring success so long as Saturn is not distracted by negativity or harsh criticism. Accountability and honesty are high ideals for Saturn to keep maintaining and sometimes near impossible if Jupiter or the Sun are looking for personal glory rather than following Saturn's direction. Diurnal Mercury will be keen to voice disappointment regarding social injustice or unfair treatment of women, but it may lose its audience if Saturn in Venus's signs become too morose or touch on subjects which are taboo or uncomfortable for the audience.

Example Charts:
- John Dee (outcome planet, Mercury)
- Paul Watson (outcome planet, Jupiter)
- Gordon Brown (outcome planet, Jupiter)
- Meghan, Duchess of Sussex (outcome planet, Mercury)

If Mars is involved in the sequence (as the first dispositor)

Saturn and Mars have a rather complicated relationship given Mars borrows Capricorn for its exaltation, but is also the ruler of Aries, which is Saturn's sign of fall. Aries and Scorpio will produce different outcomes when involved in the sequence, as the cardinal fire sign (Aries) creates problems for Saturn. Aries increases Saturn's hot and dry qualities, meaning its actions are more likely to be unpredictable, rash, volatile and potentially dangerous. Munakara will in turn amplify and inflate Saturn's reactions, especially if authority figures are seen as threatening to the individual. Aries Saturn in munakara with Mars as the first dispositor is going to need a safety valve to release tension. Otherwise it has the potential to build to a climax that is likely to end in destruction.

The outcome planet may be critical in allowing munakara Saturn to channel its frustrations to a more positive expression. In the examples listed below, two charts – Helen Keller and Chris McCandless – have Aries Saturn in munakara but their outcome planets differ. Helen Keller's munakara Saturn sequence ends in the Sun. Until light – in the form of knowledge and language – was cast on her isolated world of darkness, the only outlet for her fear and isolation (Saturn) was her rage – 'kicking and screaming when she felt angry', with her 'highly erratic behaviour' causing many of her relatives to believe she should be institutionalised[2] (munakara Saturn). Chris McCandless's munakara Saturn has Jupiter as the outcome planet for his sequence, so freedom and independence were a natural choice for him when he rejected society's authority.

Saturn and Mars are planets that focus on separation and for this reason Mars may not be an 'easy' planet to have as first dispositor for munakara Saturn. Control is a big issue for Saturn but being in a state of munakara can mean that Saturn is anything but in control of situations. The more control that is forced upon munakara Saturn, sometimes in the form of responsibility or guilt, the more likely it is that it will rebel. The combination of Saturn and Mars can bring implied or actual violence as a consequence of separation or rejection, in the form of noise, sudden action and unexpected aggravation.

Munakara Saturn in Scorpio can indicate internalised anger, repression of emotions or a genuine fear that the person's rage cannot be controlled. The individual may look as though they are in command of their emotions but there needs to be an outlet for this repressed energy otherwise its release can be more dangerous than Aries Saturn simply because non-one is prepared for its brutal force. The outlet might be physical activity but even then its needs direction, or at least a long-term goal, or a central focus to draw Mars's energy towards something which is productive, rather than destructive.

Example Charts:
- Antonio Salieri (outcome planet, Sun)
- Helen Keller (outcome planet, Sun)
- Chris McCandless (outcome planet, Jupiter)
- Amy Winehouse (outcome planet, Sun)
- LeBron James (outcome planet, Jupiter)
- Prince Harry (outcome planet, Jupiter)

If nocturnal Mercury is involved in the sequence (as the first dispositor)

Munakara Saturn will be in either Gemini or Virgo for nocturnal Mercury to be Saturn's first dispositor. Values and belief systems are an important foundation for munakara Saturn in Mercury's signs, but forcing others to share the same views is only going to make Saturn more open to antagonism or ridicule, which will not sit well with Saturn. If attitudes towards the individual are disrespectful, or if opinions are not listened to or given merit, then munakara Saturn in Gemini may become caustic or use sarcasm to be heard. Unfortunately, this type of response on Saturn's part is likely to isolate it even more, or worse, risks not having its views or suggestions taken seriously. It might be important for Gemini Saturn in munakara to heed the words of Stoic philosopher, Epictetus, who said: "We have two ears and one mouth so that we can listen twice as much as we speak."[3]

To follow Saturn's munakara sequence, Mercury must be nocturnal. This may be part of Saturn's frustrations if its nocturnal dispositor is too shy or too self-conscious to defend Saturn's views. It may be that Saturn in Gemini manifests in a speech impairment, or learning difficulties, either in childhood or in adult life through accident, illness or injury. Gemini Saturn's munakara may be experienced through isolation, embarrassment or insecurity where communication or self-expression is concerned. Mercury also rules fine and gross motor skills so when munakara Saturn is in either of its signs, it may manifest in physical restrictions or complications in the body responding to the brain's commands.

In order for sect boundaries to be crossed in the sequence, Mercury must be nocturnal (*i.e.*, from diurnal Saturn (first planet) to nocturnal Mercury (the dispositor/second planet) then to either the Sun or Jupiter (outcome planet). Gemini Saturn may be able to hide nocturnal Mercury's sensitivity, but Virgo Saturn will be acutely aware of any shortcomings that cause the individual to feel different. Often characteristics which are celebrated and admired as an adult can be the source of much anguish in childhood where the individual feels odd or strange. Once more Saturn becomes the planet of separation as gifts which are remarkable in the fullness of time, are targets for bullying by other children. Virgo Saturn in munakara may use clever language, self-expression, writing, humour or dry observation as protection from hurt or rejection. Suppressing emotions is not a good solution for munakara Saturn as it is likely to lead to illness given that Saturn rules so much of the physical body. Nocturnal Mercury's involvement with this Saturn sequence can also lead to depression, anxiety or challenges to mental health. In this case, the outcome planet becomes critical in understanding how sensitivity and professional help can ease the pain that Saturn may be enduring in silence.

Example Charts:
- Louisa May Alcott (outcome planet, Jupiter)
- Charles de Gaulle (outcome planet, Jupiter)
- Robin Williams (outcome planet, Sun)
- Richard Branson (outcome planet, Sun)

Chapter Nine • *Saturn in Munakara*

If diurnal Mercury is involved in the sequence (as the outcome planet)

From the perspective of the Essential Dignities, Saturn and Mercury are neither friends nor enemies. When they are in aspect, Saturn may curb Mercury's enthusiasm and make it more cautious or inclined to check its facts. However, as both planets are diurnal, they can work together to promote the Sun's interests and to help the Sun achieve its objectives of success, respect and social advancement.

Diurnal Mercury as munakara Saturn's outcome planet is an instrument through which munakara Saturn will express its displeasure and discuss Saturn's themes of integrity, fairness, honesty and accountability. If munakara Saturn is disgruntled, diurnal Mercury can give voice to its grievances and may even sway others to join it in the fight to change something for the better.

If munakara Saturn is struggling to find its moral compass, diurnal Mercury (as its outcome planet), can be of great benefit if the individual collects their thoughts or reaffirms their beliefs when they are questioned or challenged by others.

The nocturnal planet – the Moon, Venus, or Mars – which separates Saturn from diurnal Mercury will give some indication as to what grabs Saturn's attention and makes it irate and need to express its disapproval. The nocturnal planet in either Gemini or Virgo will express its dispositor, Mercury, in a different way.

The Moon in Mercury's sign will mean munakara Saturn is in detriment in Cancer and the deep emotions felt by munakara Saturn will need expression. Four of the examples listed below – Wordsworth, Kennedy, Van Morrison and Parton – have the Moon as the interim planet between munakara Saturn and diurnal Mercury and expression is very important, whether their medium is poetry, politics or music.

Example Charts:
- John Dee
- William Wordsworth
- John F Kennedy
- Van Morrison
- Dolly Parton
- Meghan, Duchess of Sussex

Enemies of a munakara Saturn: Moon, Sun, Jupiter

If the Moon is involved in the sequence (as the first dispositor)

For the Moon to be the first dispositor, munakara Saturn will be in detriment in the sign of Cancer. Saturn in detriment takes two forms: firstly, being in the hands of an enemy (Moon) and secondly, being in a water sign, which is a foreign element for Saturn. The Moon is the significator for the physical body, and in more modern times, the Moon shows the individual's emotional landscape.

The Moon represents indulgence and abundance whilst Saturn represents quite the opposite, replacing abundance with scarcity, restraint and deficiency. There is conflict for Cancer Saturn as the Moon is trying to produce abundance while Saturn is simultaneously cutting back. Situations tend to arise where the individual is making inconsistent decisions based on emotions rather than on logic or reason. Saturn is the lord of boundaries and water knows no boundaries. This is particularly relevant for Cancer Saturn as it is often changes the rules for self-gratification or to please someone it loves or wants to impress.

Saturn goes into detriment when it cannot be fair, just and even-handed in its decisions, and Saturn in munakara significantly magnifies Cancer Saturn's inability to be impartial. While the individual with munakara Saturn is incensed by displays of corruption or deliberate mismanagement, they can also be the person provoking the breakdown of order and instigating riots and chaos. Munakara Saturn in Cancer shows misused authority ("the rules don't apply to me" attitude) Munakara Saturn in Cancer also brings together the planet responsible for health (Moon), with the planet that destroys health (Saturn). Part of the challenges the individual may face can include movement and vitality in periods when the body is suffering from Saturn's effects.

Saturn in munakara in Cancer may also manifest as abandonment; either separation at an early age (particularly from parents) or as an adult with separation or estrangement from partners or children. Saturn's jurisdiction includes the passing of time and things outside of one's control, and there can be genuine angst, guilt and heartache if the individual feels they have allowed too much time to pass, or the reason for separation was within their control. William Wordsworth's Virgo Moon (Saturn's first dispositor) conjuncts his MC and opposes Mercury (Saturn's outcome planet) and his poems were themes on loss, death, separation, abandonment and grief.

Chapter Nine • *Saturn in Munakara*

Example Charts:
- William Wordsworth (outcome planet, Mercury)
- Mary Shelley (outcome planet, Jupiter)
- Van Morrison (outcome planet, Mercury)
- Dolly Parton (outcome planet, Mercury)

If the Sun is involved in the sequence (as the outcome planet)

Perhaps the most hostile of oppositions is the battle between darkness (Saturn) and light (Sun) – often represented in myth as stories of the battle between good (Sun) and evil (Saturn/Satan).

The individual with the three-planet sequence that begins with Saturn and ends with the Sun is likely to have experiences that parallel mythic stories of darkness and light. However, it would be too simplistic to say that the path will always run from Saturn (darkness) to the Sun (light). The story of Helen Keller's release from isolation and silence through Anne Sullivan's dedication and lifelong loyalty is an exceptional example of munakara Saturn's sequence ending in the Sun. But that does not mean that her Sun's path was always a lantern to Saturn, or that she did not know darkness again in her adult life.

Another example, Italian composer Antonio Salieri – who was accused of poisoning his German rival, Wolfgang Amadeus Mozart – had his reputation (Sun) ruined over the centuries by malicious gossip and innuendo, and it has only been since the turn of the 21st century that the claims have been shown to be false. Comedian Robin Williams, entrepreneur Richard Branson and singer Amy Winehouse have all had their dark times and bouts of depression despite incredible fame and success in their respective fields.

The Sun is intrinsically good so it does not set out to harm Saturn but damages are naturally incurred when these two diurnal planets are linked through the munakara sequence. A fall from grace can occur to Saturn in munakara and with the Sun as the outcome planet, the defences are up, and rebuilding may be the last thing on the person's mind.

Saturn's first dispositor will be a nocturnal planet in the sign of Leo (Sun as outcome planet) and so there is always going to be something to prove or justify, or an attempt to gain attention, even if that attention is ultimately destructive in nature. Munakara Saturn's energy may be taken up by the individual defending themselves against rumours or subtle attacks from detractors who lurk in the shadows.

Example Charts:
- Antonio Salieri
- Helen Keller
- Robin Williams
- Richard Branson
- Amy Winehouse

If Jupiter is involved in the sequence (as the outcome planet)

When Jupiter is munakara Saturn's outcome planet the individual can experience a sudden rise in fame. This idea of fortune smiling on the person with munakara Saturn can create an extremely productive period, so long as Saturn is prepared to work hard and make the commitment to keep producing quality work. However, this may be where contention comes into play if the person feels they cannot maintain or repeat this level of excellence. Then munakara Saturn becomes 'a one-hit wonder' and no matter how much effort or time is invested by Saturn, the moment has passed, and Jupiter cannot reach the same high level.

Munakara Saturn can experience 'imposter syndrome' or feeling like a fake or fraud despite having achieved success in the past. Jupiter may keep providing opportunities to munakara Saturn but if the person has lost their confidence or is experiencing writer's block or a creative equivalent, then Saturn is likely to hesitate or buckle under the pressure. Self-doubt is something very familiar to Saturn in any chart, but when combined with the additional pressure of munakara, plus Jupiter as the outcome planet (a planet which inherently adds more pressure), then difficult emotional states such as anxiety or depression may be the result.

Once munakara Saturn decides that it can use success as a springboard for future advantage then some of this pressure eases off, but until then Jupiter is no friend to Saturn as it keeps promising much but delivering little. Saturn is injurious to Jupiter due to Capricorn being Jupiter's fall sign. On the surface it looks as though Jupiter does very little to harm Saturn, however, some of the individuals listed below have stretched their luck or resources too far and have paid the price by being ostracised from society. Some have been (and will be) judged harshly by history as the Lord of Time, Saturn, will record both their successes and their follies.

Even more so than regular Saturn, munakara Saturn feels the necessity to be the authority figure. When Jupiter's expansion mode is too rapid or

Chapter Nine • *Saturn in Munakara*

lacks order things become chaotic and munakara Saturn tends to go into micromanagement mode. This rarely helps anyone and the outcome tends to be that others choose freedom (Jupiter), looking for new horizons or independence. This leaves munakara Saturn with feelings of failure, isolation, separation and abandonment.

Each of the individuals listed below have had their moments of victory (Jupiter) but they have also experienced times of hardship, pain and loss. Saturn's natural desire to separate becomes a little less cold and detached when Saturn is in munakara. By its very nature munakara contention means dissent, argument, conflict and discord, so when Saturn is losing control and separating the friction created adds more heat and more emotional involvement than Saturn is usually able to invest.

Saturn rules signs which are not particularly familiar with feelings or emotional states. In contrast, Jupiter's signs belong to the category of highly emotive elements of fire and water. When Jupiter is Saturn's outcome planet it will force munakara Saturn to experience 'hot emotions' such as excitement, enthusiasm, hostility, anger and passion – or 'wet emotions' such as empathy, kindness, happiness, tenderness, sadness, regret and despair. The nocturnal planets (either the Moon, Mars, Venus or nocturnal Mercury) will separate the two diurnal planets (Saturn and Jupiter). It will be in Jupiter's fire sign, Sagittarius, or its water sign, Pisces and the first dispositor will bring this fiery or watery emotion to bear in Saturn's process of separation.

Example Charts:
- Mary Shelley
- Louisa May Alcott
- Ferruccio Lamborghini
- Charles de Gaulle
- Paul Watson
- Gordon Brown
- Donald Trump
- Chris McCandless
- LeBron James
- Harry, Duke of Sussex

The 21st Century Firm

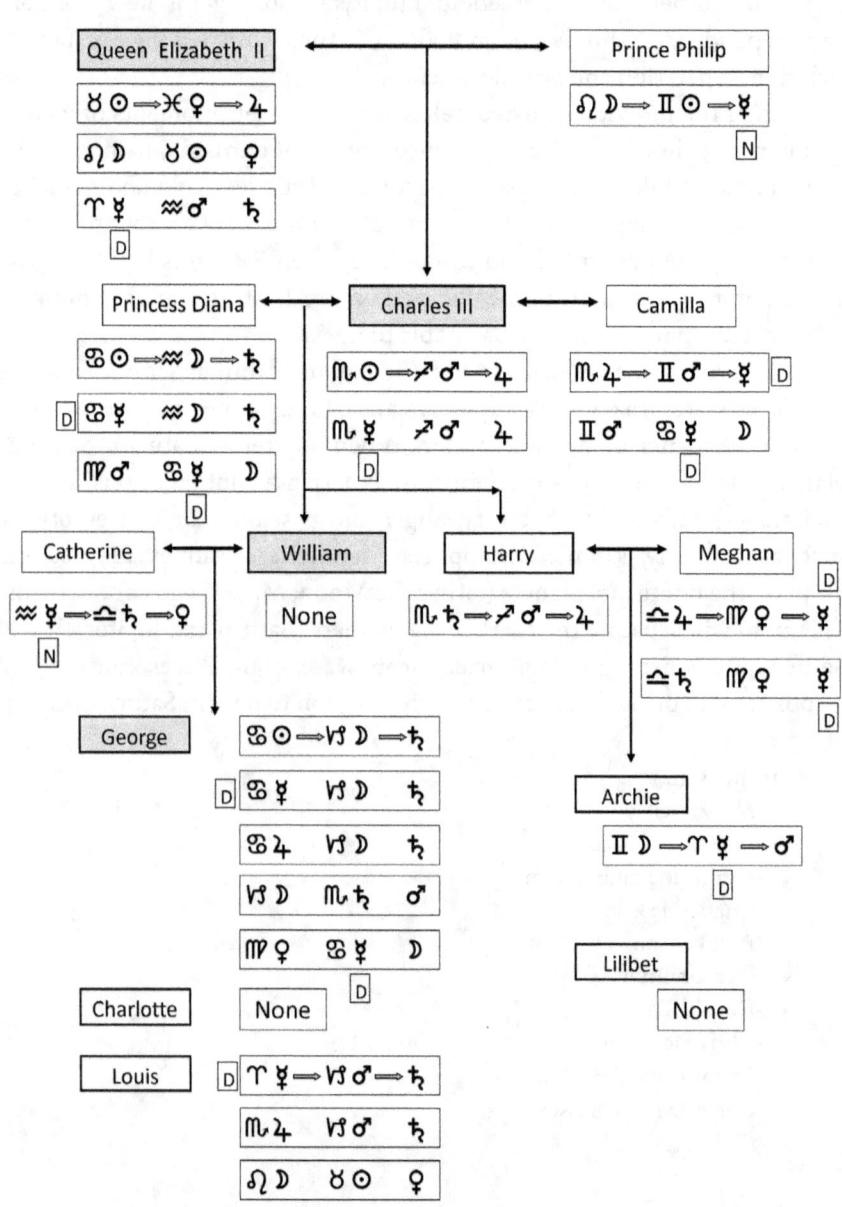

Fig. 9.1: The 21st Century British Royal Family

Chapter Nine • *Saturn in Munakara*

Munakara and the Modern British Monarchy

The British Royals have a history of family members with munakara planets. Henry VIII's chart was examined in an earlier chapter on Mercury, and Henry's grandfather, Edward IV, his father, Henry VII, and his mother, Elizabeth of York, all also had planets in munakara.

Father Henry VII seized the crown on 22 August 1485 and married the daughter of his enemy, Edward IV, to end the War of the Roses (1455–1487) and become the first king of the House of Tudor. Henry VIII's first daughter Mary I and his son Edward VI (who died age 15) each had two planets in munakara.

In later generations Queen Victoria (last monarch of the House of Hanover) had Moon in munakara and her husband Prince Consort Albert had Venus in munakara. Queen Victoria's chart features in Part Two on munakara Moon delineations, whilst Albert's chart can be found in an earlier chapter on Venus. Eight of their nine children (Leopold being the exception) had at least one planet in munakara.

The House of Windsor was founded in 17 July 1917, and there have been five Windsor monarchs since then: George V, whose eldest son, Edward VIII (munakara Sun), abdicated the throne on 11 December 1936, George VI (munakara Saturn), Elizabeth II (munakara Sun, Moon, Mercury), and Charles III (munakara Sun and Mercury). The 'Firm', a nickname describing the British royal family, saw the passing of Queen Elizabeth II on 8 September 2022, and Charles III's coronation taking place on 6 May 2023, eight months after her death at 96 years of age.

The following page is a family tree for the 21st-century Firm, beginning with Elizabeth II and Prince Philip, both living at the turn of the century, and running through the British royal family in the order of succession. Princess Diana is included in this list, even though she perished three years before the new millennium in a car accident in 1997.

The family tree shows fourteen members of The Firm and underneath their names are the list of munakara planets in their charts. Their natal charts have not been included in the diagram, but all dates and times can be found in the online *Astro-Databank* website, and munakara planets can be verified from the charts on the website.

Perhaps the biggest surprise in the line of succession is William's first-born son, George, who has five planets in munakara: both of his luminaries, nocturnal Venus, and the two diurnal rulers of his MC/IC axis, Mercury and Jupiter in Cancer. (*See p. 323*)

The example charts for munakara Saturn follow the British royal family's tree and these belong to Harry, Duke of Sussex, and his wife Meghan, Duchess of Sussex.

Harry was born the second son to parents King Charles III and Diana, Princess of Wales, on 15 September 1984. He was given the British royal title of Prince Henry of Wales and he is currently fifth in the line of succession to the British throne. Harry served in the British Army for ten years (2005–2015) and launched the Invictus Games in 2014 as founding patron and remains involved in a non-royal capacity.

Harry and American actor Meghan began a relationship in mid-2016 and their engagement was announced on 27 November 2017. Harry was made Duke of Sussex prior to his wedding on 19 May 2018. Harry and Meghan stepped down as working royals on 31 March 2020, and moved to Southern California where they launched Archewell Inc, a mix of for-profit and not-for-profit (charitable) business organisations. Harry's memoir *Spare* was published in January 2023.

Munakara Saturn: Harry, Duke of Sussex

"I know at the end of the day, she chooses me. I choose her. Whatever we have to tackle will be us together as a team."[4] – Harry, Duke of Sussex on his wife, Meghan

The year 2020 was a big year for 'The Firm' as Harry and Meghan, Duke and Duchess of Sussex, stepped down as senior members of the British Royal Family. The couple were born three years apart, and although Saturn had moved to the next sign when Harry, the younger of the two was born, both charts have Saturn in munakara.

Harry's munakara Saturn has completely different goals and expectations from Meghan's Saturn. They did not share the same social and political background as children and young adults, and their perceptions of authority come from very different positions in society. Both have struggled to connect with their respective Saturnian father figures, as Harry is estranged from his father King Charles III, whilst Meghan has had no contact with her father, Thomas Markle, since the days before her wedding in 2018.

With munakara Saturn on the Mid-heaven, Harry's chances of rebelling and marrying outside of the circle of British aristocracy were always high, especially after the history of his own mother. Princess Diana Spencer married Charles, Prince of Wales (now King Charles III) in July 1981, and

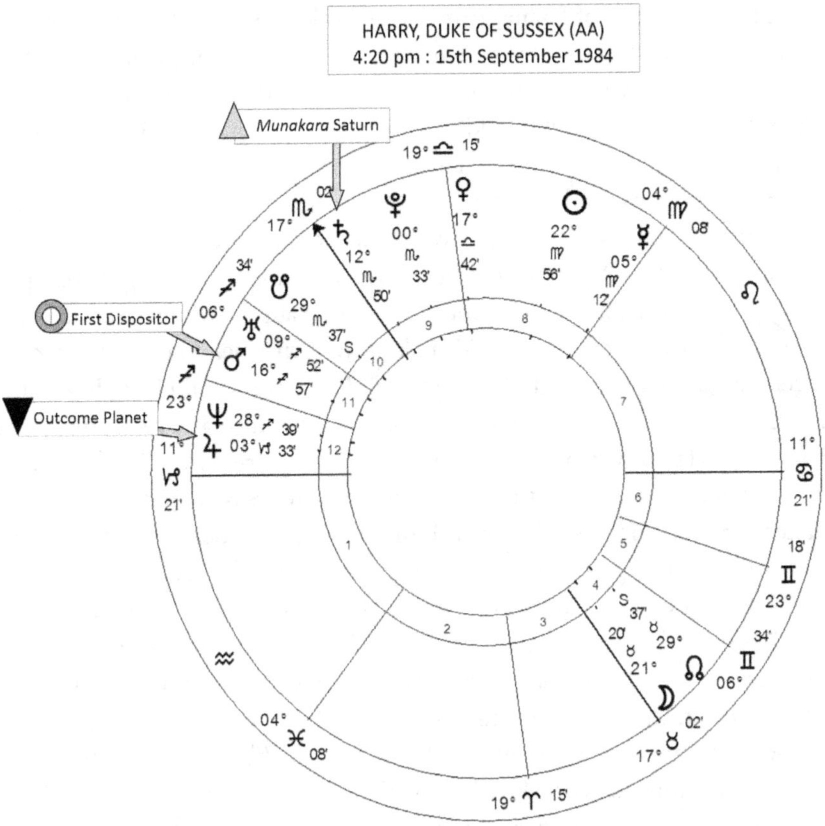

Chapter Nine • *Saturn in Munakara*

HARRY, DUKE OF SUSSEX (AA)
4:20 pm : 15th September 1984

Fig. 9.2: Harry, Duke of Sussex Natal Chart: Munakara Saturn's Sequence

- **Key Questions:**
- What does Harry's Saturn contend with?
- What is its driving force?
- What is its trigger? What is its outcome?

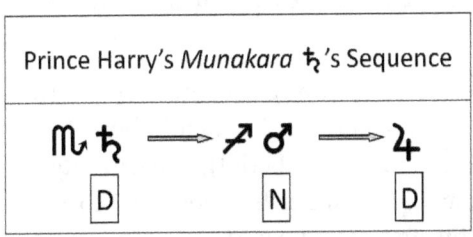

Table 9.3: *Prince Harry: Munakara Saturn's Sequence*

took the official title of Diana, Princess of Wales. The royal couple had two sons, William and Harry, but the marriage was not a happy one, and they separated in 1992, eleven years after exchanging wedding vows. Their marital difficulties were widely publicised, and the couple divorced in 1996. In August 1997, Diana died in a car crash in Paris, France.

Harry has an exalted Moon moving away from an opposition to Saturn, with nine degrees separating the two planets on his MC/IC axis. However, the aspect tells the tragic story of Princess Diana and Prince Charles despite the degree difference between the planets in Taurus (Moon) and Scorpio (Saturn) on the parental axis. Munakara Saturn rules Harry's Capricorn Ascendant, and the exalted Moon rules his 7th house – and Harry has stated that he does not want a repeat of his mother's loneliness and rejection by the British Royal family to be revisited on his wife's experiences of his family.

Mars in Sagittarius is Saturn's dispositor and Mars is conjunct the volatile planet Uranus. This aspect supports munakara Saturn's desire to rebel against authority and to upset the status quo, particularly if he feels they have too much control over his life and he needs to be independent of them. Harry has described himself as agoraphobic (fear of unsafe environments)[5] and believes his mental health issues stem from "the pain or suffering that perhaps my father or my parents had suffered."[6] Harry believes his anxiety and panic attacks began in his late 20s with the heavy load of official visits and functions (munakara Saturn on the Mid-heaven) that eventually "led to burnout" and that his request for help from his family were met with "total silence and total neglect."[7] Jupiter is munakara Saturn's outcome planet and its position in Capricorn shows its debility in Saturn's sign indicating a fall from grace. Jupiter in fall is the trigger that Harry needed to leave the comfort and security of his past and to forge a new future free of the restrictions placed upon him by being a part of the British Royal family.

Munakara Planet and Sect Condition – how comfortable is Saturn?

Harry was born during day-light hours and Saturn's elevated position on the MC is a place of comfort for a child born into royalty, especially given that his grandmother, Elizabeth II, also had Saturn conjunct her Mid-heaven. William, his older brother, has Jupiter in Scorpio on his Mid-heaven. Harry claims in his book titled 'Spare' that on the day of his birth (then) Prince Charles jokingly said to his wife, "Wonderful. Now you've given me

Chapter Nine • *Saturn in Munakara*

an heir and a spare, my work is done."⁸ With the arrival of their second son, it seemed The Firm would be set up for future decades to come with two male heirs standing by to replace Harry's father, Charles III, and grandmother, Elizabeth II.

Saturn in a daytime chart is also travelling in the same hemisphere as the Sun and both sect conditions will aid Saturn even though it is under

Prince Harry — ♄'s Sect Dignity			
Planet	Sect 1 Status	Sect 2 Hemisphere	Sect 3 Sign
♏ ♄	Day	With the Sun	Water
	D	D	D	N

Table 9.4: Prince Harry: Munakara Saturn's Sect Dignity

the trying conditions of munakara. Harry's financial situation (Saturn rules his 2nd sign) will not be too bleak given that it is rumoured he inherited 8.5 million pounds from a trust set up by his grandmother when he turned 40 in September 2024.⁹

Mars is Saturn's first dispositor, and Mars is uncomfortable in a diurnal chart and travelling in the same hemisphere as the Sun. Its fire sign Sagittarius saves Mars from complete sect ruin, but fire is a hot, dry energy and this sign does little to calm Mars's rage or temper its impetuous behaviour. "Without question, I was so angry with what happened to [Diana] and the fact that there was no justice at all. Nothing came from that. The same people who chased her into the tunnel, photographed her dying on the backseat of that car."¹⁰

Harry's Mars slips into the 12th house by Whole Sign and its placement in the house of hidden enemies becomes obvious when in his memoir (*Spare*) Harry revealed that he had killed 25 members of the Taliban whilst serving in Afghanistan, and that he had viewed them like pieces on a chessboard (presumably, rather than as people). His comments sparked criticism from top military figures and prompted Afghan families to call for his prosecution.¹¹

Jupiter is Saturn's final planet in its munakara sequence, and Jupiter in fall enters the 1st house in the Whole Sign system. Jupiter's position is eight degrees from the Ascendant, but by rising before Harry's birth means that it is in good sect dignity in a diurnal chart, in the same hemisphere as the Sun. Jupiter may be *halb*, but it is not *hayz*, as Capricorn is a feminine sign. Jupiter brings benefits, but its position in fall is going to be a problem for Harry when Jupiter is the final planet in Saturn's munakara sequence.

Munakara Saturn: Harry, Duke of Sussex

"Part of my role and part of my job is to shine a spotlight on issues that need spotlight, whether it's people, whether it's causes, issues, whatever it is."[12]
– Prince Harry, Sept, 2019

Munakara Saturn in Scorpio conjunct MC

In an echo of his late grandmother, Elizabeth, Harry has Saturn conjunct his Scorpio Mid-heaven. Elizabeth's Saturn and MC were in later degrees of Scorpio, and Saturn was not one of her three planets in munakara. Queen Elizabeth II's chart is featured in the following chapter on multiple munakara planets. Perhaps Harry understands the cost of his grandmother's dedication to her role more than anyone else in the family given that Elizabeth committed to more than seventy years of service to the British monarchy.

Munakara Saturn on the Mid-heaven is going to make its presence felt, and the constant media attention throughout Harry's life has meant that he has borne criticism, speculation, positive and negative commentary throughout his entire life. Harry's contentious nature has been rich fodder for photography, video, biography, podcasts, interviews, parody and vicious rumour, and still Harry was expected to maintain a jovial good-natured attitude towards all things public.

However, munakara Saturn struck back after a four-year legal battle with Mirror Group Newspapers when in December 2023, the English High Court ruled that Harry had been a victim of unlawful information gathering, including phone-hacking by journalists on the Daily Mirror, Sunday Mirror and Sunday People tabloids with the knowledge of their editors.[13] Harry has been quoted as saying that the legal battles with the British tabloid press had been a 'central piece' of the breakdown of his relationship with the royal family.[14]

Munakara Saturn opposes Harry's exalted Moon in Taurus and he has been quoted as saying that losing his mother at age 12 shut down all of his emotions, and that for the past 20 years this emotional disconnection affected his personal life and his work.

Saturn's opposition to the Moon highlights the separation from his mother, and through the joint rulership of his Capricorn Ascendant and Cancer Descendant, his fears for Meghan are an echo of his anguish and loss of Diana.

Chapter Nine • *Saturn in Munakara*

It's incredibly triggering to potentially lose another woman in my life, but the list is growing. And it all comes back to the same people, the same business model, the same industry. My father used to say to me when I was younger, he used to say it to both William and I, 'Well, it was like that for me. So it's going to be like that for you.'[15]

Harry, it appears, will not take the risk of losing Meghan and there is no doubt in his mind that there is a connection between the two women he has loved in his life. Harry has been quoted as saying, "If my mother was here now, she and Meghan would be thick as thieves."[16]

His distrust and hatred for the media, whom he holds responsible for Diana's death, resurfaced after his marriage to Meghan when the British press began publishing cruel and spiteful comments about the new Duchess of Sussex. "My mother was chased to her death while she was in a relationship with someone who wasn't white, and now look what's happened. You want to talk about history repeating itself, they're not going to stop until Meghan dies."[17]

Dubbing her 'Duchess Difficult' when reporting snipes from Palace courtiers, or rumours that one senior royal referred to her as 'Harry's showgirl', or stories of tears and rifts between the royal sisters-in-law, have done nothing but alienate Harry's Saturn in munakara and to create contention by severing ties with his family (Saturn opposing the Moon).

Harry's Saturn in munakara rules his Capricorn Ascendant, and Harry needs to feel he has purpose and relevance in this world. Therefore taking a minor role in The Firm is not going to give him the satisfaction he craves from Saturn's position at the culmination point of his chart. The problem with Saturn (on the MC) ruling both the 1st and 2nd houses, is that money needs to be made through personal appearances and actions, which keeps the individual constantly in the public eye and mind. The deals that the Sussexes made with Netflix and Penguin Random House are reported to be in the arena of $120 million with the first book of a four-book deal published in late November 2022, exposing his life within The Firm.

The Royal and VIP Executive Committee (RAVEC) are an independent Home Office body responsible for allocating taxpayer-funded bodyguards for the royal family and British and visiting VIPs from other countries. Since 2020 and the Sussexes withdrawal from royal duties, RAVEC downgraded its level of security for his family when they are in the UK. This must have terrified Harry's munakara Saturn as it meant that he would no longer have automatic police protection and the fear that his family is not safe runs very deep for Harry. At the time of writing, he is locked in a legal battle with RAVEC but in April 2024 he lost an initial appeal against a high court decision which ruled in favour of RAVEC's decision to withdraw security.[18] Fighting the RAVEC ruling has allegedly cost Harry more than $1.9 million, added to the expense of hiring his own bodyguards – who are not permitted to carry firearms – when he, or his family, are in the UK.

Harry's munakara Saturn has had other problems with authorities in the US since he changed his country of residence from UK to US in legal documents in June 2023, when Frogmore Cottage, given to him by Elizabeth II after his marriage, was taken away by his father, Charles.[19] However, this could be problematic for Harry as his admission of recreational drug use as a youth in his book *Spare* has led to the Heritage Foundation initiating a lawsuit to strip Harry of his US residency, accusing him of dishonesty and receiving preferential treatment. Applicants for US residency must disclose any history of drug use on their application forms. Failure to do so can result in deportation, and President Elect, Donald Trump, indicated that he would cancel Harry's visa if elected to office in November 2024. Trump has since taken office, yet the pursuit of this threat remains unclear.[20]

By his own admission in his memoirs (Saturn rules 1st house) Harry has brought this Saturn drama down on himself, as he often fails to realise that he is still a figurehead (munakara Saturn on MC) who will be criticised or praised according to his behaviour and the values that he displays to the world. Having Saturn's outcome planet (Jupiter) conjunct the Ascendant denotes his privileged upbringing, but Jupiter's state in fall (Capricorn) implies Harry never quite fits in, or that he receives an adequate amount of praise from his father (Saturn). Jupiter on the Ascendant is tied to Harry's sense of self-worth but when it is disposited by his munakara Saturn (and Saturn's outcome planet) then all he is inclined to feel is his father's disapproval and disappointment in his second son.

First Dispositor: Mars in Sagittarius in 12th House (Whole Sign)

The first and last verses of the poem "Invictus" by William Ernest Henley seem fitting for Harry's Saturn in contention, particularly for a lost royal who seeks his own path in life removed from an establishment that doesn't encourage independence.

Chapter Nine • *Saturn in Munakara*

"Invictus" by William Ernest Henley (1895)
Out of the night that covers me,
Black as the pit from pole to pole,
I thank whatever gods may be
For my unconquerable soul.
....
It matters not how strait the gate,
How charged with punishment the scroll,
I am the master of my fate,
I am the captain of my soul.

The Invictus Games is an international multi-sport event for wounded, injured and sick servicemen and women, both serving and veterans. They are held at approximately eighteen-month intervals, but The Hague 2020 Invictus Games were postponed until April 2022, Dusseldorf 2023 took place in September 2023, and at the time of writing, the fifth games are due to take place in Vancouver and Whistler in British Columbia, Canada in February 2025.

The Invictus Games was an initiative of The Royal Foundation of the Duke and Duchess of Cambridge (William and Kate) and Prince Harry, in partnership with the Ministry of Defence. Prince Harry is credited as the driving force behind the inaugural Invictus Games in 2014, after he witnessed a similar event for return ex-service personnel in 2013 at the Warrior Games in the US.

> *"I have witnessed first-hand how the power of sport can positively impact the lives of wounded, injured, and sick Servicemen and women in their journey of recovery."*[21] – Harry, Duke of Sussex

Once more Harry's munakara Saturn showed its contentious nature with negative feedback on his acceptance of the Pat Tillman Award for Service at the 2024 Excellence in Sports Performance Yearly Awards (ESPY). The award is named after Patrick Tillman Jr. an American professional footballer who left his sports career and enlisted in the US Army. Tillman died at age 27 in 2004 whilst serving in Afghanistan. The late hero's mother was highly critical of the choice stating: "I am shocked as to why they would select such a controversial and divisive individual to receive the award."[22]

This is not the only controversy that surrounds Harry and the Invictus Games, as the Foundation's chief executive Dominic Reid, stood down from his position within days of Harry accepting the award. His sudden departure left the preparations for the 2025 Games in disarray, and organisers are blaming Harry for Games' problems.[23] It has also been reported that around 2,000 ex-servicemen have left the Invictus Games citing that the event had *"lost its original meaning"* and that Harry should step down as Patron to the Foundation as a mark of respect to veterans.[24]

Whilst Harry's Saturn on the MC might empathise with war veterans, its dispositor, Mars, is conjunct Uranus and this aspect keeps throwing Harry into controversies, so perhaps a quiet and dignified withdrawal from his association with the Invictus Games might be the best option for both the event, and for Harry's dignity (Saturn in munakara).

Harry's removal from any involvement with the British military was instigated by his father and adds one more barrier between Charles and himself given that Mars rules Harry's Whole Sign 4th house. Charles asking for the keys back to Frogmore Cottage within 24 hours of Harry's memoir *Spare* did little to help the situation.[25] Before the birth of his daughter Lilibet, Harry spoke to American actor Dax Shepard about his strained relationship with his father: "There is no blame. I don't think we should be pointing the finger or blaming anybody, but certainly when it comes to parenting, if I've experienced some form of pain or suffering because of the pain and suffering that perhaps my father or my parents had suffered, I'm going to make sure I break that cycle so that I don't pass it on, basically."[26] This type of public statement about Charles as a father, rather than a monarch, is unlikely to aid in healing the rift that exists between father and son and Charles has only met his youngest grand-daughter Lilibet (named after his own mother) once in 2022.[27]

The outcome planet: Jupiter in Capricorn in fall

"We don't see each other as much as we used to, but, you know, just as (all) brothers, you have good days, you have bad days." – Harry in an interview with Tom Bradby, *Harry and Meghan: An African Journey* (2019)

Jupiter in fall is the third planet in Saturn's munakara sequence, and its movement between the 12th house in the Placidus chart and its eight degrees from the Capricorn Ascendant brings Jupiter into the angular 1st house. This may reflect one of the reasons why Harry's position in the royal family is so precarious at this time when there is a change in the monarchy from Queen Elizabeth II to King Charles III.

Chapter Nine • *Saturn in Munakara*

The trouble with Jupiter – Saturn's outcome planet – is that not only is it in fall in Capricorn (munakara Saturn is its dispositor), but it is also conjunct his Capricorn Ascendant. Harry does not look like his father (munakara Saturn on MC), nor does he look like his brother William (Jupiter rules 3rd house of siblings), and this fact always leads to conjecture about his royal parentage. Amongst all the speculation, innuendo and rumours about Harry's physical differences from Charles and William (who look very similar), it seems Saturn's aging process has brought him closer to looking like his late grandfather, Prince Philip. For Harry to turn around and reject his lineage after a lifetime of being accused of not truly belonging to it seems a cruel twist on the part of munakara Saturn.

Jupiter rules both the difficult 12th house and the 3rd house of siblings in the Whole Sign system. Harry's older brother, William, appeared protective over Harry after their mother's untimely death, and the brothers were presumed to present a united front. However, the introduction of Kate as William's wife seemed to make Harry 'a third wheel' at official functions. The Golden Couple were always first, and Harry trailed somewhat behind them, so his release from the succession to the crown when Kate produced an heir meant that he was free to play the role of a rogue and renegade prince. According to Dylan Howard, author of *Royals At War*: "In many ways Harry lived a life free of the shackles of becoming king one day. There was nothing wrong with that in the eyes of the House of Windsor because it made him more relatable, and it also modernised the monarchy."[28]

A close trine between Harry's Jupiter and Mercury highlights the rulers of the 3rd- and 9th-house axis representing his brother (3rd) and the house opposite, his brother's wife (9th house). For Harry, this would mean William becomes a symbol for his Jupiter in fall, and Mercury, ruler of the ninth, is Kate – William's wife. William's advice to Harry to "…slow the relationship"[29] with Meghan would not be taken well by Harry. With Pluto sitting at the midpoint of the Jupiter Mercury trine, Harry has naturally seen William's coolness towards Meghan as a betrayal (Pluto) and has provoked a need to protect the woman he loves. Jupiter is unlikely to back down with aspects to Pluto and Mercury, so a stalemate is the natural way for Pluto to 'dig in' even when Jupiter in fall (ruler of 3rd house) makes Harry feel excluded through a traumatic rift with the family.

Munakara Saturn and Jupiter Duet: Meghan, Duchess of Sussex

"I've never wanted to be a lady who lunches – I've always wanted to be a woman who works. And this type of work is what feeds my soul and fuels my purpose."[30] – From *Elle* UK essay, "With Fame Comes Opportunity, But Also A Responsibility"

The intention, feeling, and expression behind Meghan's munakara Saturn sequence is completely different to Harry's Saturn in contention for two critical reasons. Firstly, Meghan was born three years before Harry, and her Saturn is in the sign of Libra, which places it in exaltation. Saturn in exaltation presents different challenges for the planet, as idealism or lofty principles often accompanies Saturn's experiences of contention and grievances of 'unfairness' or the lack of 'a level playing field' are part of its contentious nature.

Secondly, unlike Harry's Saturn, Meghan's munakara Jupiter joins Saturn in a duet and Jupiter is likely to amplify Saturn's feelings of outrage when issues of contention arise. Separately, Jupiter and Saturn have different agendas when they find themselves in a state of munakara. Jupiter in munakara strives for success, is ferocious in its ambitions, lives larger than life and has big visions of what it would like to achieve. Saturn in munakara is resistant to authority figures, including father, and is often acutely sensitive to criticism or accusations of inadequacy, incompetence or inferiority.

Meghan's munakara duet of Saturn and Jupiter is disposited by Venus, but Venus struggles in Virgo and in a woman's chart Venus in fall may indicate that Meghan suffers from harsh or critical judgements which may be unfair (Saturn) or unjustified (Jupiter). Saturn often believes that obstacles can be overcome with a good work ethic, grit and determination, but Meghan may have found that she was no match for the resistance she met when she joined her husband's family. Constant comparisons by the media between the two brothers' wives – Kate (Venus in Aquarius) and herself (Venus in fall) – were unavoidable. When Meghan could not fight this one-sided comparison and her comments and actions were deliberately misconstrued, then Mercury, as Meghan's outcome planet for Saturn and Jupiter, is likely to trigger the anxiety and depression Meghan spoke of in her interview with American media personality Oprah Winfrey in 2021.[31]

Chapter Nine • *Saturn in Munakara*

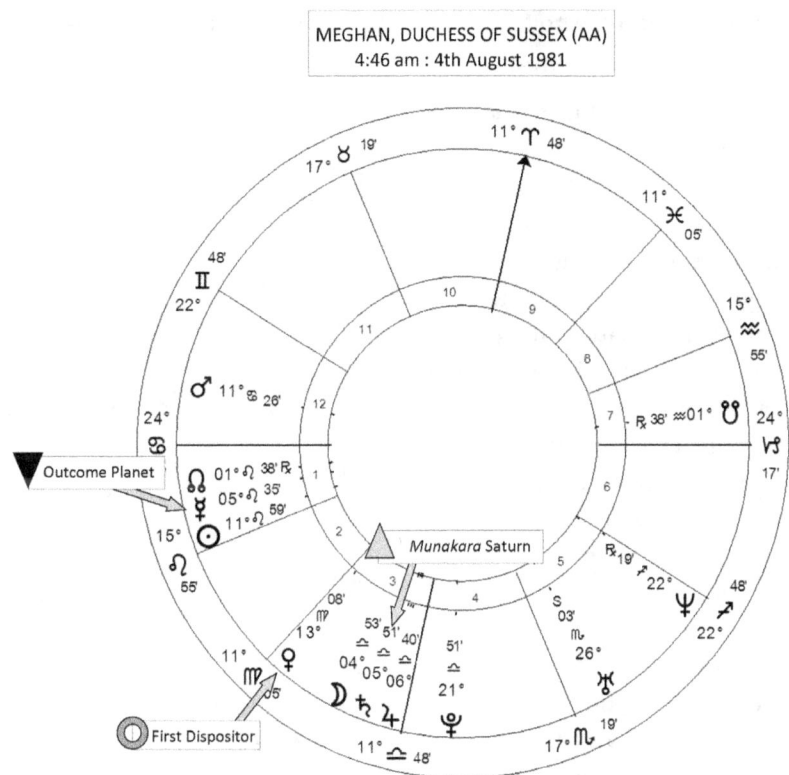

Fig. 9.3: Meghan, Duchess of Sussex Natal Chart:
Munakara Saturn/Jupiter Sequence

- **Key Questions:**
- What does Meghan's Saturn and Jupiter Duet contend with?
- What is their driving force?
- What is their trigger? What is their outcome?

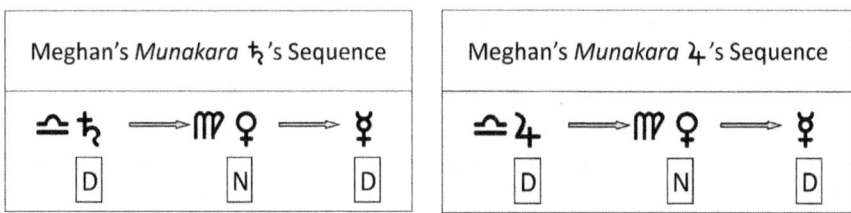

Table 9.5: Meghan, Duchess of Sussex: Munakara Saturn and Jupiter Sequence

Munakara Planet and Sect Condition – how comfortable is the Saturn and Jupiter Duet?

Meghan was born during the early hours of the morning when the Sun was still beneath the horizon, and as such, hers is a nocturnal chart. This means the Moon is the prime luminary of her chart and her two munakara planets, Saturn and Jupiter, are conjunct her Libran Moon, giving it strength and fortifying its nurturing principles. Both planets are travelling in the same hemisphere as the Sun as all three diurnal planets – Saturn, Jupiter and Sun – are situated in the lower hemisphere of the chart. This position will give her munakara planets sect dignity according to the second rule of sect (diurnal planets in the same hemisphere as the Sun).

Saturn and Jupiter are in Libra, a masculine air sign, and Saturn is in dignity by being in exaltation in Libra. Both diurnal planets are disposited by Venus, but Meghan's Venus in fall indicates a woman who suffers from 'falling' in some way – it may be socially unacceptable or is judged harshly by others or is unpopular with other women. The fact that Meghan now has a greater social platform (Saturn and Jupiter in munakara), that is, more visibility, more wealth and more power since her marriage, means that more eyes are upon her, and more voices are raised against Venus (Mercury is Saturn and Jupiter's outcome planet).

Meghan's nocturnal chart suits Venus, the dispositor for Saturn and Jupiter's sign, and the feminine sign of Virgo brings a second advantage in sect dignity. Venus often travels in the same hemisphere as the Sun, but this is not a huge disadvantage for Venus when the chart is nocturnal. Venus's dispositor is Meghan's diurnal Mercury in Leo, and similar to the other two diurnal planets, Mercury is in sect dignity by travelling with the Sun, and placed in a masculine sign.

Meghan — ♄'s Sect Dignity			
Planet	Sect 1 Status	Sect 2 Hemisphere	Sect 3 Sign
♎♄	Night	With the Sun	Air
D	N	D	D

Meghan — ♃'s Sect Dignity			
Planet	Sect 1 Status	Sect 2 Hemisphere	Sect 3 Sign
♎♃	Night	With the Sun	Air
D	N	D	D

Table 9.6: Meghan, Duchess of Sussex: Munakara Saturn and Jupiter Sect Dignity

Chapter Nine • *Saturn in Munakara*

"Make a choice: continue living your life feeling muddled in this abyss of self-misunderstanding, or you find your identity independent of it. You push for color-blind casting; you draw your own box. You introduce yourself as who you are, not what color your parents happen to be."[32] – Meghan Markle

Munakara Saturn and Jupiter in Libra in 3rd House

Meghan has Cancer as her rising sign and the Moon, the ruler of her Ascendant, is conjunct munakara Jupiter and Saturn. The Moon is the dominant luminary in a nocturnal chart and becomes even more relevant when it is the ruler of the Ascendant. Meghan's Libran Moon adds emotionality to the two munakara planets and pulls the Moon between the emotional extremes of being lovingly embraced (Jupiter) or cruelly rejected (Saturn) because of her mixed-race ethnicity. Meghan has said, "My dad is Caucasian, and my mom is African American. I'm half black and half white. Being biracial paints a blurred line that is equal parts staggering and illuminating."[33]

Andrew Morton states in his 2018 biography *Meghan: A Hollywood Princess* that at the time of her marriage in 2018 Meghan's website, *The Tig*, contained intelligent and well-written essays about gender equality and race, but that the palace had ordered the website "to be scrubbed from the World Wide Web."[34] In his Introduction to the book, published just prior to their wedding, Morton states: "[i]n the last important royal wedding for a generation, Prince Harry's glamorous bride will be the first bi-racial divorcee ever to marry a member of the British royal family. Their union, blessed by Her Majesty the Queen, will make the monarchy seem more inclusive and relevant in an ever-changing world."[35] Morton's prediction for a smooth transition from old traditions (munakara Saturn) to a new DEI (diversity, equity and inclusion) framework represented by munakara Jupiter was a painful process as Meghan became the personal representative of this idealised notion (her Moon conjunct Saturn/Jupiter duet).

This very public representation continued to plague Meghan after her wedding and into the period before the couple left The Firm. In *Oprah with Meghan and Harry*, a 2021 television special hosted by American media personality Oprah Winfrey, the couple admitted that several comments had been made privately to Harry by an unidentified member of the royal family over the skin colour of their then-unborn child.[36] The contentious nature of these comments would have been extremely hurtful and distressing for Meghan during her first pregnancy and would have added to dispositor Venus's fall state and outcome planet, Mercury's anxiety.

The fear of not being emotionally or physically safe is not an imagined fancy, but a real threat as Meghan's Moon struggles to feel safe and secure in every new environment (Cancer Ascendant) and this is not helped by her two munakara planets that bring contention whenever they are activated. Saturn rules Meghan's 7th house (partners) and Jupiter rules her 9th house (my partner's siblings) and the conjunction between the two planets in munakara shows that Meghan is drawn into the dramas and the publicity surrounding Harry and William's relationship. Third-house placement for three planets (four, if Venus is included) indicates a huge amount of media attention is focused on Meghan. This exposure is likely to cause Meghan to feel even more protective in herself (Moon rules Ascendant), and now that she has become a mother (Moon), to extend that same level of protection to Archie and Lilibet.

Meghan's Saturn rules the 7th and 8th houses – the relationship and its financial resources – and part of the public discussions on her marriage to Harry included speculation over their joint resources as a couple. Even though this subject would be taboo for any ordinary pair, it garnered a great deal of interest in newspapers and on social media sites. Meghan is often blamed for the rupture between Harry and his family and perhaps she has played a part in it (Moon and munakara Saturn rule her Ascendant/Descendant axis), but the fact that Harry also has munakara Saturn shows his own dissatisfaction with the protocol and restrictions that accompanied his former role as a royal.

When Meghan married Harry she made the statement that she would "[h]it the ground running in her work to empower girls and women in the UK."[37] At the time it was a courageous statement made by her Leo Mercury (outcome planet for Saturn and Jupiter) trying to be brave and it was misjudged as an arrogant statement rather than a hopeful, exuberant one, as she hit a brick wall when she thought she would be an exciting new 'change-maker' for the royal family.[38] Meghan's munakara Jupiter rules her 6th house of duty and her 9th house of idealism (or foreign influence) and the tantalising idea that she would bring a fresh new perspective to old traditions is a statement made by her Jupiter in munakara. Rather than the royals embracing her exotic style (Jupiter), The Firm closed ranks against her (Saturn) and Meghan was left out in the cold.

Andrew Morton, author of *Meghan: A Hollywood Princess* (2018) says in his book that Meghan has very strong political opinions and that she has always liked to control her own publicity. In her role as Harry's wife, Norton

Chapter Nine • *Saturn in Munakara*

says that Meghan feels very stifled by not being allowed to address criticisms levelled against her or respond to any false statements made in the press.

Morton is protective of Meghan and thinks very highly of her, considering her to be very intelligent and a sincere humanitarian.[39] He believes there have been faults on both sides, stating in 2020 at the height of the royal crisis: *"More is at stake than just Meghan Markle. Her response affects the whole House of Windsor and (The Firm's) narrow-mindedness goes a long way to explaining why they left the family."*[40]

There is little room for doubt when Harry said he was concerned for Meghan's mental health at the time of her first pregnancy when anxiety and depression[41] were a real threat at a time when Meghan's detractors were becoming increasingly hostile and two conflicting energies in munakara where increasing the tension on her Libran Moon (her physical and emotional state). The Moon ruling her Ascendant saw her defending every action, and when all three planets are disposited by Venus in Virgo, then something had to change in order for Meghan to redefine her equilibrium and feel safe again.

First Dispositor: Venus in Virgo in fall

"I don't want to be loved, I want to be heard."[42] – Meghan, Duchess of Sussex

Meghan is an outspoken independent woman who unwittingly became the personification for the extraction of Harry from The Firm. 'Megxit' (a play on 'Brexit' when the UK left the European Union) is the term used by the British media to lay the blame squarely at Meghan's feet, and to confirm the idea that Venus in Virgo is a dangerous woman. Harry's rebellious antics were fodder for British tabloids long before Meghan's arrival on the scene, but the British public's tolerance of Harry's behaviour did not extend to forgiving his new wife when she appeared to step out of line.

In echoes of the story of Edward VIII, Harry's great-granduncle, who abdicated the throne in 1936 to marry American divorcee, Wallis Simpson, the British public found it much simpler to believe that a 'wicked woman' stole him, rather than accept he would desert them of his own volition. The Sussexes's original idea of stepping away and reducing their duties rather than stepping down was rejected by the royal family, and when Meghan broke the royal rule 'never complain, never explain', there was no other option but to expel them from the ranks.

Meghan's Venus in fall rules her 4th house, and the strained relationship between herself and her father has not always helped her cause of being accepted by The Firm. In December 2021, UK courts ruled in Meghan's favour after she sued Mail on Sunday for publishing private letters written to her father, Thomas Markle. Meghan penned the five-page letter to her estranged father in the lead-up to her wedding in May 2018 asking him to desist from talking to the media, as Prince Harry was being subjected to constant berating from the royal family. In an insulting settlement payment, the British tabloid was ordered to pay one pound in damages. What hurt the Mail more is the fact that they were required to pay a 'substantial amount' for copyright infringement, rather than for privacy, as well as being responsible for Meghan's $2 million legal fees.[43]

Whilst Meghan is justified in protecting her privacy – even though it was Thomas Markle who gave the letters to the tabloid – Meghan has committed some missteps that show Venus in Mercury's sign is bound to set up a fall if the wisdom is lacking, and this will reverberate back to the two planets, Saturn and Jupiter in munakara. In April 2022 Meghan's company submitted a trademark application the claim the word "archetypes" – a word in use since the 16th century – for the title of her new Spotify podcast. The trademark application sought to prevent others from using the word in various entertainment services, such as podcasts, on-demand streaming media, live stage performances and webcasts. The trademark would also apply to services "…[i]n the fields of cultural treatment of women and stereotypes facing women."[44] Even if this was a publicity stunt designed to promote the upcoming podcast, it was destined to backfire on her as the media poured scorn on it as a perceived act of stupidity. The podcast debuted on Spotify on August 23, 2022, but by June 2023, Spotify and Archewell Audio had released a statement confirming they had agreed to part ways.[45] The application to trademark the podcast's name *Archetypes* was withdrawn in September 2023.[46]

The outcome planet: Diurnal Mercury in Leo

"Women don't need to 'find a voice'. They have a voice. They need to feel empowered to use it, and people need to be encouraged to listen."[47] – Meghan Markle, commenting on *#MeToo* at the 2018 inaugural Royal Foundation Forum

Chapter Nine • *Saturn in Munakara*

Meghan has diurnal Mercury conjunct her Leo Sun in the 1st house in Placidus, but it moves to the 2nd house of finances in the Whole Sign system. Leo Mercury is the outcome planet for both Saturn and Jupiter, and its movement to the house of finances highlights the sequence for both planets, but particularly for Saturn in munakara.

Mercury in Leo rules Meghan's 3rd and 12th houses in her chart and whilst she is outspoken and has strong opinions, it has created hidden enemies. For instance, when Harry's statement to the Press in November 2018 implored them to cease and desist from harassing Meghan, he caused a terrible gaffe by hijacking the media's attention from Prince Charles and Camilla's diplomatic tour overseas. Meghan may have had no influence over the release of Harry's statement, but she bore the brunt of the blame because it caused a media frenzy by Harry inadvertently confirming that she was officially 'his girlfriend'.

Royal Editor of the *Daily Mirror*, Russel Myers, comments that the royal family has strict protocols in place to make sure they do not overshadow each other's work, and says about Harry's statement, "It was catastrophic. It torpedoed Prince Charles' tour of the Middle East which went down like a lead balloon in the palace."[48]

Meghan's changed status from celebrity to a senior member of The Firm may be where she seriously miscalculated the impact it would make on her two planets in munakara. Leo Mercury, as the sequence's outcome planet, was overawed by the duties she was expected to perform as a new member of the royal household (Moon, Saturn, and Jupiter in Libra). Meghan's appeals to Kate for help fell on deaf ears (Jupiter rules Kate's house), and her first official function with the Queen at the opening of the Mersey Gateway Bridge in June 2018 shows an awkward, confused Meghan making a series of unfortunate mistakes, ones that could easily have been corrected if she had been properly schooled in the appropriate rituals and expected protocol of the establishment.

Further Delineations for Munakara Saturn
Paul Watson, Gordon Brown & LeBron James

Eco-warrior Paul Watson[49] and Scottish politician Gordon Brown were born within three months of each other and have munakara Saturn in Libra. Both Watson and Brown have Venus in signs belonging to Jupiter, the third planet in Saturn's sequence.

The third chart in Part Two for munakara Saturn belongs to NBA basketball player LeBron James, who was born during the third turn of Saturn's ingress into Scorpio, born two months after Harry, Duke of Sussex, and with the same three planets in Saturn's sequence, Saturn, Mars, Jupiter. Harry was born in mid-September 1984 with Mars in the earlier sign of Sagittarius, whilst LeBron's Mars had moved to Pisces by the time of his birth in late December 1984.

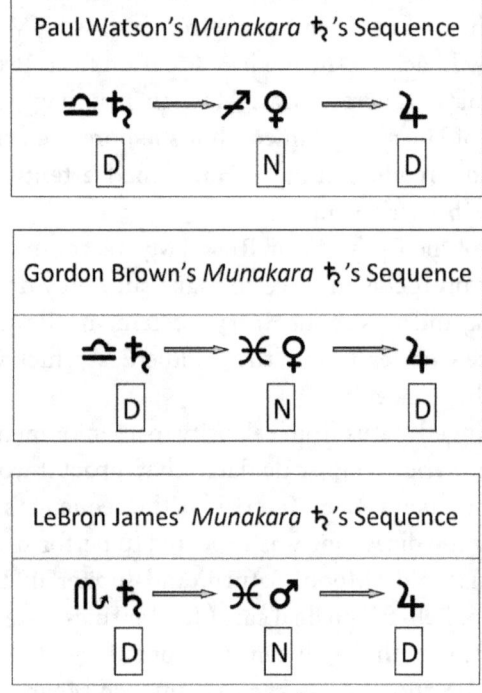

Table 9.7: Munakara Saturn's Sequence

CHAPTER TEN
Multiple Munakara Planets

By their very nature munakara planets are planets which are incompatible or discordant with their surroundings. They experience discomfort in certain circumstances which trigger a planet's specific reaction to conflict according to their nature, and their significations. Accompanying a planet in munakara is the feeling of not belonging, of being out of place, and this means that individuals with munakara planets are highly sensitive to situations where they feel different or at odds with others' behaviour or opinions. When everyone else goes right, they go left: many speak about being the black sheep of the family, or that they attract attention for behaviour or actions that embarrasses them, or that they are misunderstood or their motives are misinterpreted by others. The actions that they believe deserve praise or acknowledgement are the ones that go unnoticed, or are claimed by someone less deserving than themselves. They voice opinions that are unpopular, inflammatory or provocative in nature, but they may also silently punish themselves if they stay mute when they know they should speak up. And it seems that the greater the number of planets in munakara, the more out-of-step a person is likely to feel within themselves, and yet, not understand why exactly this is happening to them.

The complexity of addressing three or more planets in contention means that a new approach is required in order to understand how these combinations may work in a chart and in the life of the individual with multiple munakara planets.

Multiple munakara planets often display a pattern of their own and sometimes a reoccurring planet is involved in several sequences, moving between the three positions of munakara planet, first dispositor, and outcome planet. For instance, Billy Connolly has three planets in munakara (*Fig. 10.2*) and his Gemini Moon is an active participant in all three: it is munakara, it is first dispositor for Cancer Jupiter, and it is the outcome planet for Venus. Similarly, Caitlyn Jenner's Libran Mercury plays triple roles in her three sequences (*Fig. 10.4*): diurnal Mercury is munakara, it is first dispositor for Mars, and is the outcome planet for her Scorpio Sun. In both of these examples, one particular planet – Moon for Connolly and Mercury for Jenner – is a major contributor (or recipient) in each munakara sequence. This type of multiple munakara highlights a key planet dealing with several issues at once – the need to determine the nature of what it contends with – plus the role of being either a first dispositor for another munakara planet, or being the second dispositor, and therefore taking on the role of outcome planet.

Not all multiple munakara sequences will produce a neat division between the three roles of first, second, and third planet in the munakara sequence. Some planets may not be in munakara themselves, but they pop up as either the dispositor of the first planet, or the dispositor of the second planet, *i.e.* the outcome planet, as in the case of Venus in Cher's chart (*Fig. 10.3*). In Empress Catherine the Great's chart (*Fig. 10.6*), Mercury is involved in all four sequences but Mercury, in itself, is not a munakara planet. Its role as a repeat dispositor does not mean it is powerless. Rather, it signifies that the same planet has a level of significant control in the unfoldment in the munakara planets' stories and experiences, and the reader needs to pay attention to its sect dignity, position, aspects and rulership houses in the chart.

When examples of charts with more than three munakara planets – four, five, or even six sequences that end in munakara as is found in the charts of John Dee (*Fig. 10.13*) and Helen Keller (*Fig. 10.14*) – there is a tendency to focus on what has gone wrong in their lives and what levels of difficulty they have experienced for one reason or another. Perhaps in these cases the focus should shift instead to their ability to survive so much contention and yet still display brilliance, inventiveness, compassion and courage as they follow their destiny and change attitudes through contributions that move society forward towards tolerance, kindness and acceptance of anyone who looks or acts outside the narrow models of normality.

Chapter Ten • *Multiple Munakara Planets*

When I have found charts of individuals with multiple munakara planets whose lives seem extreme, difficult, or painful, I also want to point out that their planets in contention have brought with it their own brand of uniqueness, brilliance and resilience, and as with all things astrological, you cannot change any one thing without changing everything! For those clients, students, peers, and family members who I have counselled over the past few years on their munakara planets I have found the majority to be intensely proud and protective towards their planet (or planets) in contention, understanding with wisdom that whilst presenting them with adversity at times, the planet/s in contention have tested their mettle and brought opportunities and benefits, as well as challenges into their lives.

Munakara Sequences where all Three Planets are in Contention

Multiple munakara sequences occur because more than one or two planets are found in signs that belong to other planets, and these other planets belong to the sect of a different persuasion, *i.e.* diurnal to nocturnal sect, or vice versa. At first view munakara sequences can seem random but increased practice shows patterns between planets and the signs they occupy in the chart. As the number of munakara planets in a chart rises, there is the potential for another pattern to occur – *the pattern of all three planets in a sequence being in contention*. The three planets are the original planet *plus* the first and second dispositor. This fact is not a given when looking at multiple munakara sequences, but it does become more pronounced as more munakara sequences occur, and nine of the fourteen charts in this chapter show sequences where all three planets involved are munakara.

For instance, Billy Connolly (*Fig. 10.2*) and Caitlyn Jenner (*Fig. 10.4*) each have three munakara sequences. But the last one in the trio has been bolded because in Connelly's chart Venus's munakara sequence contains its two previous munakara planets (Moon and Jupiter). Likewise, Jenner's Sun's sequence contains two planets (Mercury and Mars) which are also munakara planets.

Edgar Degas (*Fig. 10.7*) has a chart with four munakara planets and two of these – Mercury and Jupiter – have sequences with three munakara planets. Robin Williams (*Fig. 10.9*) also has a chart with four munakara planets, and two of these – Mercury and Saturn – have been bolded because their sequences contain three munakara planets. Lastly, Amy Winehouse

(*Fig. 10.10*) has a chart with four munakara planets and one of these – the Moon – has a sequence containing three munakara planets (the Moon *plus* two dispositors).

Prince George (*Fig. 10.12*) has a chart with five munakara planets and one of these – Venus – has a sequence with three munakara planets (Venus *plus* two dispositors). Christopher McCandless (*Fig. 10.11*) has a chart with five planets in munakara, and all five sequences have been bolded because all of the planets in their sequences are in contention. McCandless's Leo Moon and Aquarian Sun are not munakara, but neither do they play a role in any of his five-planet sequences.

This pattern is repeated in the charts of John Dee (*Fig. 10.13*) and Helen Keller (*Fig. 10.14*), both of whom have six planets in munakara. All six of their planets' sequences are bolded because they are made up of planets which are also munakara planets. It would be easy to assume that this will be the case when the number of munakara planets is high, but this is not always true. Similar to Christopher McCandless, Prince George has five planets in munakara, but only one planet, Venus, has a sequence with two other planets in the state of munakara.

The question becomes: does this matter? How does two other dispositor planets in contention affect the first planet in munakara? The best way I can answer these questions is to examine the lives of the nine people who have this situation and to see how the munakara planets may have manifested in their lives.

This idea is explored in greater detail in the following delineations, but simply put, I would suggest that a munakara planet with two members in contention in its sequence is a planet that becomes a driving force in the individual's life.

For instance, Venus is Billy Connolly's munakara planet with three planets in contention in its sequence. Munakara Venus takes precedence and demonstrates Connolly's driving need for popularity, acceptance, and love from his audiences, as well as showing the importance of his strong loving bond with his wife Pamela Stephenson and the influence she has had over his life. The Sun in Caitlyn Jenner's chart is the munakara planet with three planets in contention. Jenner's Sun outweighs the challenges presented to her Mercury and Mars as her battle for identity and her need to be authentic – for the world to accept her for who she truly is – is a powerful incentive for Jenner's munakara Sun to follow its destiny and it becomes a dominant theme in her life.

Chapter Ten • *Multiple Munakara Planets*

Mercury and Jupiter are the two planets in Edgar Degas's chart that conform to the pattern of three munakara planets in a sequence. These two munakara planets show Degas's drive for perfection (not fame) was relentless, as was his utter contempt at being labelled with other artists of his time as being an 'Impressionist'. Mercury and Saturn are the two planets in Robin Williams's chart with sequences of three munakara planets. Together Mercury and Saturn describe the pace of his brilliant mind, his dry observations on human behaviour, his originality when his humour reached new heights of absurdity, as well as his mind's darkness and depression that plagued him throughout his life, particularly encapsulating the last two years before his death. The Moon in Amy Winehouse's chart is the singular munakara planet with three planets in contention. An accentuated munakara Moon provides insight into Winehouse's self-consciousness about her body *"I'm ugly,"*[1] the abuse her body suffered through continued battles with addiction and bulimia, and her desperate need for emotional stability – all of which are red flags for her most embattled munakara planet. Venus is Prince George's one munakara sequence with three planets in contention and it is difficult to make any judgements about how this super-stressed planet may impact on his future life so far as his need for popularity, stability in his relationships, and acceptance from others is concerned.

The extremity of the last three charts whereby *all of their munakara sequences contain three planets in contention* has led me to believe that the lives of Chris McCandless John Dee, and Helen Keller – all vastly different in time periods, experiences, and chart details – shared certain things in common which are not easy to see at first glance.

In terms of munakara planets – particularly multiple munakara planets – at different times in their life the individual is confronted by conflicting choices that will place them in an untenable position where a satisfactory or successful outcome is an unlikely expectation. They face severe criticism from external sources and are subjected to harsh judgements that are often unfair, totally intolerant, or lacking in compassion for their situation. The lives of all three people – McCandless, Dee, and Keller – were full of contradictions and each one made decisions which were counter-productive to any easy or comfortable pathway. Often their vulnerability, or their personal views, left them open to manipulation by others and less scrupulous people took advantage of either their adversity, or their passion. When they were offered help or advice, they refused it, especially if it was contrary to their own opinions or if it might sway decisions already in play.

They battled through situations that caused them to constantly make compromises, and made choices that from an outside view looked hypocritical to their beliefs or showed petty behaviour – common to everyone – but they were somehow expected to be 'above' such pettiness. The three people answered to their own version of a higher power but were hurt when others questioned their character, beliefs or motivations. Each one was challenged to sacrifice their principles in order to find practical solutions, and all three became an enigma after their deaths.

These three charts are the last of the fourteen charts in this chapter, and whilst the number of multiple munakara planets are extreme, it should be remembered that many hundreds of other people born on the same day, may not have been famous, but they will have experienced their own versions of difficult munakara multiples acting out within the bounds of their own lives.

Munakara Multiples: Three Planets in Contention

EXAMPLE ONE: QUEEN ELIZABETH II

Three Planets in Contention

A Brief Biography:

Elizabeth II (April 21, 1926 – September 8, 2022) was Head of the Commonwealth and the Queen of the United Kingdom of Great Britain and Northern Ireland from February 6, 1952, until her death in 2022. Her reign of 70 years and 214 days is the longest of any British monarch or female monarch, and the second-longest verified reign of any monarch of a sovereign state in history. Elizabeth was the elder daughter of Prince Albert, duke of York, and his wife, Lady Elizabeth Bowes-Lyon. As the child of a younger son of King George V, the young Elizabeth had little prospect of acceding to the throne until her uncle, Edward VIII (afterward duke of Windsor) abdicated in 1936, making the ten-year-old Princess Elizabeth the heir presumptive When her father, King George VI, died in February, 1952, Elizabeth – then 25 years old – became queen of seven independent Commonwealth countries. In November 1947, she married Phillip Mountbatten, a former prince of Greece and Denmark. Their marriage lasted 73 years until his death in 2021.

QUEEN ELIZABETH II (AA)
2:40 am ; 21st April 1926

♉☉ ⟹ ♓♀ ⟹ ♃	♌☽ ⟹ ♉☉ ⟹ ♀	♈☿ ⟹ ♒♂ ⟹ ♄
D N D	N D N	D N D

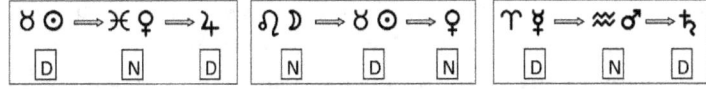

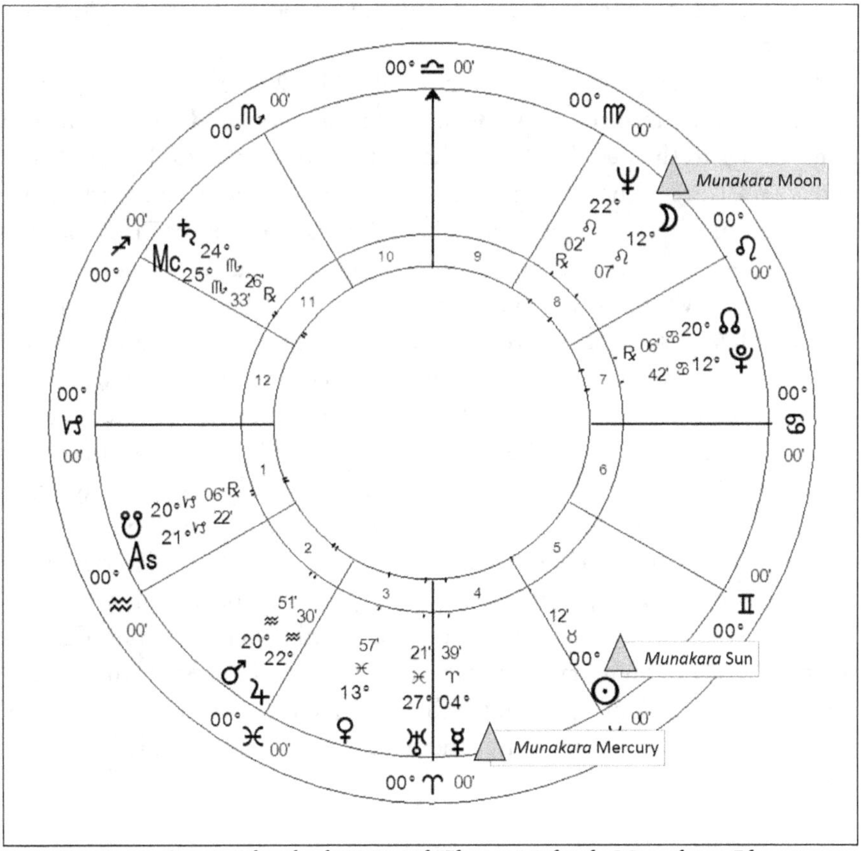

Fig. 10.1: Queen Elizabeth II Natal Chart: Multiple Munakara Planets

"I declare before you all that my whole life, whether it be long or short, shall be devoted to your service and the service of our great imperial family to which we all belong." – Princess Elizabeth on her 21st Birthday (April 21,1947), Cape Town, South Africa

Four years after making her famous declaration to serve the Commonwealth throughout her lifetime, 25-year-old Princess Elizabeth of York became queen regent on the death of her father, King George VI. Princess Elizabeth was ten years old when her uncle abdicated from the throne, and her father became King in his place. When asked as a child what she wanted to be when she grew up, Princess Elizabeth answered: "I should like to be a horse."[2] Elizabeth's sense of service and duty was not a taught lesson, but rather an innate quality born from three planets in munakara. Munakara Sun puts aside its independence and autonomy for the sake of Jupiter (the royal family).

Elizabeth's munakara Sun sits in the Placidus 2nd house, not surprising as her image is imprinted on all British coin and notes, and is proof that her Sun belongs to the people. Venus, the Sun's dispositor, is exalted in Pisces and is a measure of the level to which the Sun rises in power and influence.

However, when the Sun is munakara, Venus' position in Pisces speaks more of personal sacrifice, especially if obligation and responsibility is its driving force. Venus moves to the 3rd house in the Whole Sign system, and part of Elizabeth's skills were her diplomacy, grace and natural charm, particularly in any formal situation when she represented the Crown.

In the first degree of Taurus, the Sun moves into the Whole Sign 5th house, and as much as Elizabeth was regent, her children were a necessity to ensure the House of Windsor lives on. Elizabeth passed away on 8 September 2022, and her first-born son – munakara Sun in 5th house – was crowned King Charles III at his coronation on 6 May 2023. Charles is the longest-serving heir apparent, and at age 74, will become the oldest person in history to accede to the British throne. Similar to his mother, Charles has both Sun and Mercury in munakara, so it will be interesting to see what impact Charles will bring as monarch given that his two munakara planets in Scorpio reside in his 4th house, and his contentious Sun is the lord of his Leo Ascendant.

> "It has been women who have breathed gentleness and care into the harsh progress of mankind. The struggles against inhuman prejudice, against squalor, ignorance, and disease, have always owed a great deal to the determination and tenacity of women."[3] – Queen Elizabeth II, Christmas Broadcast 1966

With cardinal signs on her horizon, Venus – first dispositor for her Taurus Sun and outcome planet for her Moon – is the ruler of Elizabeth's Whole Sign 10th house, and its exaltation describes the nature of a monarch who was loved and respected by her people throughout her long reign. Venus' trine to Pluto shows her passion and dedication, necessary virtues if you are to reign over a country for seven decades, whilst sacrificing your own individuality for the sake of others, and molding your personality to reflect your country's stability. Elizabeth has been quoted as saying *"We have to be seen to be believed"* and her constant appearances in public only diminished as she advanced into her 90s. Countless tours to the Commonwealth have been carried out with Venusian poise, and great diplomatic success, witnessed by the fact that even those countries who have chosen to leave the Commonwealth still have strong ties to England and this has much to do with Elizabeth's skills in diplomacy.

"Family does not necessarily mean blood relatives but often a description of a community, organisation or nation."[4] – Queen Elizabeth II

Munakara Moon can sometimes be misunderstood particularly when it describes someone who has an iron-grip control over their emotions. From an outsider's view Moon in contention is misrepresented as the person having little emotional depth, a cold heart or someone lacking in compassion. When crisis strikes, munakara Moon appears as though the person is shutting down emotionally, or drawing attention to an unexpected, and sometimes inappropriate way of dealing with pain, grief, or heartache. Elizabeth's Moon in fiery Leo disposits to her munakara Sun, and with both luminaries and Mercury in contention, there are going to be times when she is at odds or in conflict with those she loves, especially within her private family circle. Elizabeth's Moon rules her 7th house, and whilst most often it represents the individual's partner, Elizabeth's 7th house would also describe the monarch-prime minister relationship with her governmental counterpart. Winston Churchill was the incumbent prime minister of the United Kingdom when Elizabeth became queen, and there were fifteen prime ministers under her reign, with the last, Liz Truss, being appointed two days before Elizabeth's death.

Weekly meetings between the Queen and whoever holds the position of current prime minister took place ever since Elizabeth became monarch in 1952, with the only exception being the fifteen months of Covid-19 lockdown, beginning on 11 March 2020. For the first time, cameras were invited in to record the recommencement, and then Prime Minister Boris Johnson, met the Queen once more in person, on a Wednesday for their weekly chat. Her munakara Moon acts as a sounding board for the leader of the British parliament, and in a 1992 documentary, the Queen said prime ministers feel like they can release the pressure they face when speaking to her.

> "They tell me what is going on or if they have any problems, and sometimes I can help in some way as well. They know I can be impartial and it is rather nice to feel one is a sponge."[5]

Ex-PM David Cameron once said he found the meetings "very valuable", and John Major said he could discuss "absolutely anything" with the Queen, whilst former PM Harold Wilson, believed to be one of her favourites, said it was the only meeting the details of which he could guarantee would not be leaked.[6]

The relationship between Charles' first wife, Princess Diana, and the Queen is difficult to ascertain from the Queen's point of view, and the only record comes from Diana's own comments.[7] However, Diana's Aquarian Moon (*Fig. 10.5*) – such an active participant in her munakara trio of planets – is in similar degrees to Elizabeth's Jupiter Mars conjunction, and the same Aquarian Moon squares Elizabeth's Saturn, and Mid-heaven in Scorpio.

Elizabeth's diurnal Mercury in Aries is munakara, with Mars as its first dispositor, and Saturn is the diurnal outcome planet. Charles – Elizabeth's first-born child – will have partners who are represented by Elizabeth's 11th house, seven houses from her 5th house. Elizabeth's 11th house is ruled by Mars, and contains both her Saturn and Mid-heaven by Whole Sign, and 'Diana's house' shows the strain of Mercury in munakara, when its dispositor rules this house. Elizabeth was heavily criticised for her coldness and unemotional response to Diana's death by remaining at her country home Balmoral (munakara Mercury in the 4th house), and not rushing back to Buckingham Palace to publicly mourn her ex-daughter-in-law.

> "When life seems hard, the courageous do not lie down and accept defeat; instead, they are all the more determined to struggle for a better future."[8]
> – Queen Elizabeth II, Christmas Broadcast 2008

Munakara Mercury's involvement with the two malefic, Mars and Saturn, is perhaps Elizabeth's most volatile sequence, and suggests that under a calm exterior – munakara Sun and Moon – lurks a quick temper, impatience or little tolerance for fools or time wasters, and possibly a sharp

Chapter Ten • *Multiple Munakara Planets*

or caustic tongue that was well-hidden from the public. This version of Elizabeth's Mercury may have been far more familiar to the closed circles of her relatives, loved ones, servants, or most trusted friends. Part of Mercury's contention is the inability to truthfully voice one's opinions, and the two remaining munakara sequences of Sun (duty), and Moon (family commitments), would have outweighed the more impetuous or rebellious nature of Elizabeth's Aries Mercury in munakara.

Netflix's controversial hit series *The Crown* is a fictitious interpretation of the British royal family, but the release of its fifth series at the end of 2022 was critical, given that it was programmed to show between the passing of the Queen and the coronation of King Charles III. Elizabeth's grandson and Diana's second son, Harry has also shaken the British royal family with the release of his autobiography *Spare*, in January 2023. Harry's book, and the fictional series, *The Crown*, will be a further embarrassment for 'The Firm' as no doubt, both book and series have focused on the events surrounding the breakdown of Charles and Diana's marriage.[9] Diana's famous interview from the 1990s will be aired once more, and it will be interesting to read how Queen Elizabeth II will be portrayed by her grandson in his book, and by the scriptwriters of the series.

"Work is the rent you pay for the room you occupy on Earth."[10]
– Queen Elizabeth II

There is little doubt that Elizabeth 'paid her rent' as her workload was enormous, her self-control through countless hours of obviously boring and repetitive public duties was legendary. Her strict adherence to the correct protocol was instilled in her at a very young age and these are key factors that will be remembered from Elizabeth's long reign, especially as Saturn, the ruler of her Ascendant, is placed squarely on the MC.

Will Saturn be enough to protect Elizabeth's legacy, when it is the outcome planet for her munakara Mercury? Al-Biruni associates the 4th house with those things which follow death, and what happens to the dead, whilst Lilly says 4th house is the determination, or the end of matters.[11] With munakara Mercury in Elizabeth's 4th house, its dispositor Mars, ruling her Mid-heaven, and Saturn as Mercury's outcome planet, it would be a shame if a fictitious series, or a disgruntled grandson, had the last word on a woman who kept her opinions to herself and was always the perfect model of dignity and decorum.

EXAMPLE TWO: BILLY CONNOLLY
Three Planets in Contention
A Brief Biography:

Sir William Connolly CBE (born 24 November 1942) is a retired Scottish comedian, actor, artist, musician, and television presenter. He is sometimes known by the Scots nickname the Big Yin ("the Big One").[12] Known for his idiosyncratic and often improvised observational comedy, frequently including strong language, Connolly has topped many UK polls as the greatest stand-up comedian of all time.[13] In the 2003 Queen's Birthday Honours, Connolly was appointed a Commander of the Order of the British Empire (CBE) for "services to Entertainment." In October 2017, Connolly was knighted at Buckingham Palace by Prince William, for services to entertainment and charity. Connolly announced his retirement from comedy in 2018, and in recent years he has established himself as an artist. In 2020, he unveiled the fifth release from his *Born on a Rainy Day* collection in London,[14] followed by another instalment later that year and has subsequently issued another five collections. In 2022 he received the BAFTA Fellowship for lifetime achievement from the British Academy of Film and Television Arts.

> *"Do what makes you happy. Be what makes you happy. If others disapprove tell them to rearrange these words into a popular Fraser saying, 'Yourself F*** Go."*
> – Billy Connelly, opening line, *Windswept and Interesting* (2021), Winner of the 2022 British Book Awards Audiobook of the Year: Non-Fiction

Sir William Connolly CBE has three munakara planets: diurnal Jupiter, and nocturnal Moon and Venus. Jupiter's exaltation in Cancer means his Moon is its first dispositor, and when Jupiter becomes first dispositor for Venus, then the Moon moves to the third position of outcome planet. Billy's Moon plays a significant role in his chart as the ruler of his Mid-heaven, and the dispositor of his Jupiter as it conjuncts the MC.

The Moon is close enough by aspect to be a personal statement of the Saturn/Uranus cycle which began earlier in May 1942. The opposition of his Sun and Venus in Sagittarius to his Gemini planets completes the Moon's involvement in the chart, although it also trines Billy's Ascendant at 13 Libra. The Moon's aspects and its relevance as an angle Lord is quite enough information to absorb, but when its activity in his three munakara

Chapter Ten • *Multiple Munakara Planets*

sequences is taken into account, the Moon becomes a critical factor in examining his life. For this comedian munakara Moon in Gemini sharpens his skills in observing human traits and turning them into humour as his audience relates to his observations and finds connections in their own lives to his shared experiences.

Moon in Gemini disposits to his diurnal Mercury in Scorpio and the Moon's sequence ends with Mars (an enemy of the Moon). The battle ahead is one that will require courage as it will be his Moon's final battle. Mars has dealt Billy some hard blows in the past, but its position in rulership – and its rulership of the 7th house – has also given him a strong and supportive partner in Pamela Stevenson, his wife of 33 years, a trained psychologist, actor, writer and comedian, who wrote his biography *Billy* in 2002.

Billy, gave up drinking almost four decades ago, commenting at the time on his decision to stay sober, "If Pamela goes away, I'm on my own. There's nothing. There's only me and '**it**' (his addiction to alcohol). So the choice becomes very apparent."[15]

Billy narrates his latest autobiography *Windswept and Interesting* (2021) in Audible Books "It's the first time I've done this. Other people have written about me – or for me – but this time, it's just my own life in my own words."[16] His voice is scratchy, and he sounds old and exhausted. You can hear both his struggle to concentrate and his determination to deliver his story in his own words before Parkinson's Disease robs him of the opportunity to speak freely. The timbre in his voice no longer holds its rich and smooth musicality, and a bit of the laughter is missing from his voice, but it is still Billy, with his raw honesty, and his candid sense of humour.

Billy's Moon spends a great deal of time contending with his painful past, and for a man who spent his life making others laugh, it is sad to hear him confess, "I suspect happiness is having a liking for yourself and having a joy in being with yourself and I'm not sure I have it. I think I might have been happy before my mother left (when I was four)."[17]

But his Gemini Moon has also brought more than laughter to his audience. Through Billy's stories he has allowed them to identify with his pain, and to heal some of their own, particularly if they have shared similar fractured upbringings that echo his own childhood experiences. By laughing at his jokes, his stories, his memories, his quirky way of expressing himself with sheer honesty, and without any guile or affectation, Billy Connolly has reinvented the idea of family bonds that exist through shared experiences, rather than bonds of blood and accidents of birth.

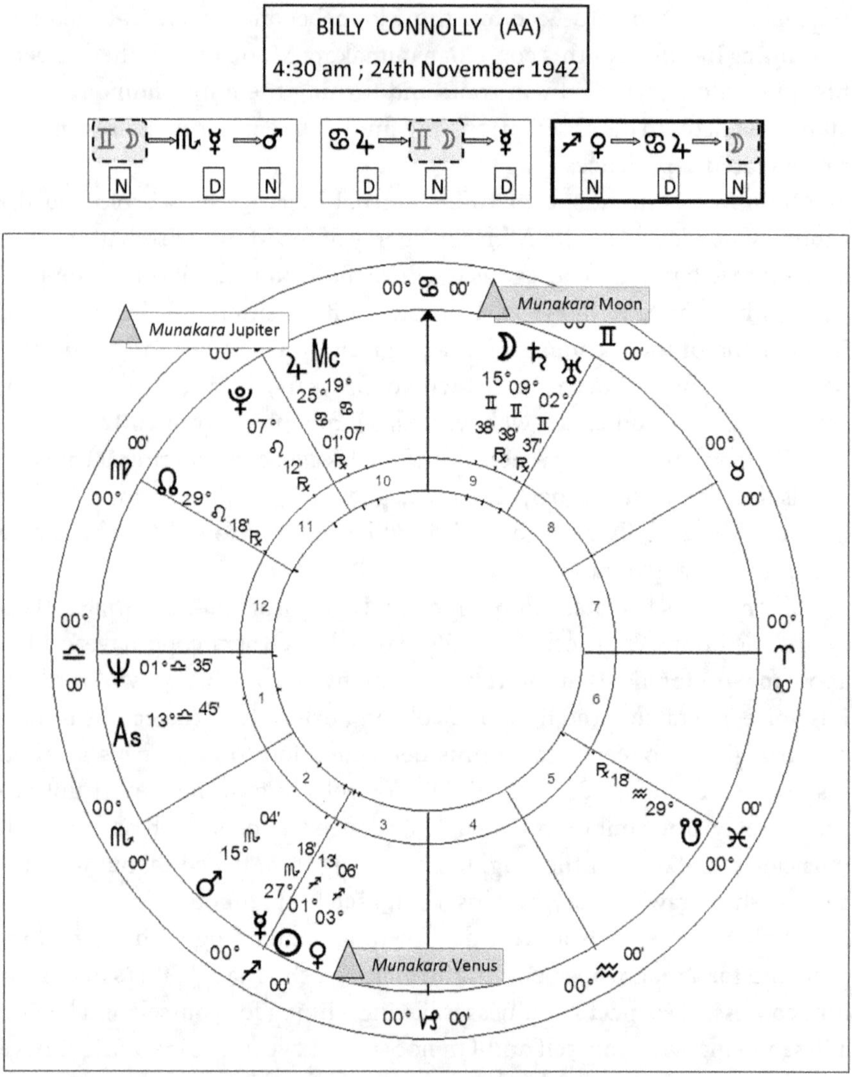

Munakara in Theory

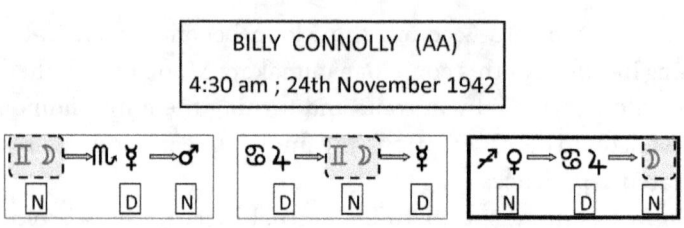

Fig. 10.2: Billy Connolly Natal Chart: Multiple Munakara Planets

Exalted Jupiter in munakara describes his rise in fame and wealth that goes way beyond his expectations as a boy suffering the harsh trifecta of poverty, cruelty and abuse. Jupiter in contention conjuncts Billy's Midheaven and trines Mercury, its outcome planet, and Billy's Scottish accent, wild unruly locks, and his signature beard – often dyed in all the colours of the rainbow – have made him instantly recognisable on the work stage. Munakara Jupiter is the dispositor for both his Sagittarius Sun and Venus, but

Chapter Ten • *Multiple Munakara Planets*

only Venus is munakara as the Sun disposits to Jupiter, another diurnal planet. Venus's outcome planet is the Moon, and this means that all three planets are munakara.

Venus is the lord of Billy's Libran Ascendant and his 8th house and the combination of these two houses, plus Venus's sensitivity to contention, could have meant that his early childhood experiences could have led to an early death after years of violence or conflict. However, the planet involved is Venus, not Mars or Saturn, and instead Billy was lucky to find a life partner who has loved and supported him for over four decades. Munakara Venus is driven to please others, to gain approval and affection, and Billy Connolly has been fortunate to have the artistic and comedic skills to make sure that when he tells his 8th house stories of despair and heartache, he is loved and accepted by his audiences because others identify his struggles with their own. He is a survivor, and if he can use humour to heal his wounds then there is hope for others who witness his courage and munakara Venus (and its two buddies) has done its job.

Munakara Venus rises above these terrible conditions experienced by the Moon and Jupiter, and it creates fellowship between Connolly and his audience, many of whom may find shades of his life within their own difficult beginnings. As his Ascendant's ruler munakara Venus represents Connolly's gift for relating to others and bestowing a sense of a camaraderie – if only for a few hours – as it has the ability to offer healing through turning tears into laughter and loneliness into comradeship.

If a planet is munakara, the chaos it creates may in fact be a part of the individual's survival mechanism, designed to buy more time as it reacts to adversity or challenge from an outside source. Crossing boundaries in sect means going into enemy territory, and self-protection can take the form of verbal attacks, destructive habits, or 'prickly' mannerisms that are designed to push other people away in order to feel safe (and alone) within one's environment. But Connelly chose different mannerisms to cope with his pain, facing his demons through music, laughter, humility, super-expressive language, and clownishness.

Venus is a planet of connection, utilizing kindness, artistic expression, love and close affinity with others, enough to bring joy and lighten dark moments for his audience. Along with its planetary offsiders Venus has delivered much contention into Connelly's life and often his salty language offends and confronts people's sensibilities but there is no doubt that he has a big heart and a true appreciation of life's beautiful moments.

Billy Connolly weathered a hard childhood – his Moon is present in all three of his sequences – and the love and protection normally afforded a young child were not a part of his early experiences. Throughout his adult life Billy has punished his body through excesses in alcohol, and poor management of his physical health, and for each of these 'body punches' munakara Moon pays a price. Sadly, Billy's diagnosis of Parkinson's disease in 2013 brought the decision to curtail his public appearances and force his retirement from live performances five years later as he admitted he could no longer continue his fast-paced repertoire on stage, while also dealing with the disease's progression. A double diagnosis of cancer in 2018, adds further to his munakara Moon's struggles to maintain the energy that he needs to commit to his current passion for drawing, painting, and sculpture.

EXAMPLE THREE: CHER
Three Planets in Contention
A Brief Biography:

Cherilyn Sarkisian (aka Cher), born May 20, 1946, is an American entertainer who parlayed her status as a teenage pop singer in the 1960s into a successful multi-genre career, projecting an image that is altogether tough, vulnerable, outspoken, and resilient.[18] Known for having a devoted fan base, Cher is a cultural icon who continually reinvents herself. Her struggle with undiagnosed dyslexia as a youth made her education an unhappy experience. At age 16 she left school and moved to Los Angeles, where she met entertainer and songwriter Salvatore ("Sonny") Bono, whom she married in 1964. The couple began singing together, and their first big pop hit came in 1965 with "I Got You Babe", which sold more than three million copies. During the early '70s Cher's solo singing career flourished. Cher and Sonny divorced in 1974, and she developed a successful nightclub act. Moving into acting in the 1980s Cher had some movie hits, receiving an Academy Award nomination in 1983 for her supporting role in *Silkwood*. In 1988 she won an Oscar for her starring role in the romantic comedy *Moonstruck*. Cher released two successful albums in 1987 and 1989. Her career seemed to be waning until the release of *Believe* in 1998. Cher's enduring popularity across generations was evident with a successful and elaborate Las Vegas residency (2008–2011). Her later albums include *Closer to the Truth* (2013), *Dancing Queen* (2018) and *Christmas* (2023). In 2018 Cher was named a Kennedy Center honouree. In 2024 she was inducted into the Rock & Roll Hall of Fame.[19]

Chapter Ten • *Multiple Munakara Planets*

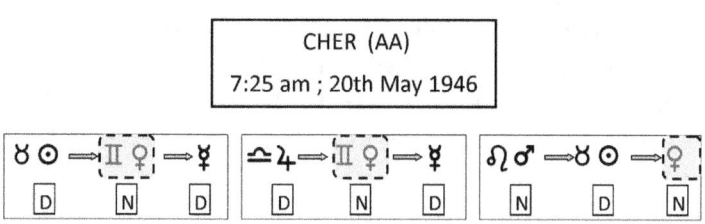

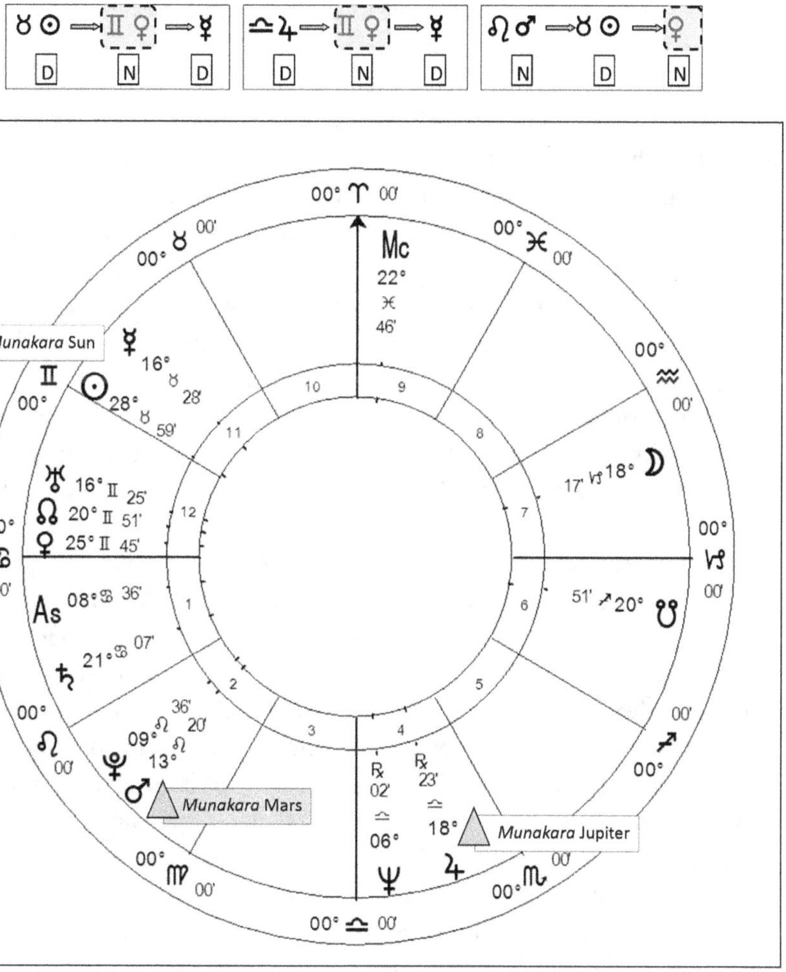

Fig. 10.3: Cher Natal Chart: Multiple Munakara Planets

"Women have to harness their power – it's absolutely true. It's just learning not to take the first 'no'. And if you can't go straight ahead, you go around the corner."[20] – Cher

Cher, 'Goddess of Pop', is an American singer, actress and television personality who has Sun, Jupiter and Mars in the state of munakara. At first glance the two diurnal planets have an identical sequence of first dispositor

(Venus) and outcome planet (Mercury). However, there is no duet here, as the planets are in two different signs belonging to Venus.

Although it is tempting to try to make the duet happen, at this stage in munakara research, it is far simpler to stay with same sign and the aspect of conjunction as a duet rather than reach across the chart for like-engirdling signs belonging to the same ruling planet.

The two diurnal planets in Venus' signs are Jupiter and the Sun, and in a diurnal chart where the individual seeks fame, attention, success and reputation, these are gifts that see the two planets working towards the same objectives. However, their contention shows that nothing will be handed to them on a silver platter.

With all the wealth Cher has accumulated over her 60-year career, it is easy to forget that earlier in life, munakara Sun (ruling 2nd house) manifested in struggles with money. Contrary to her current bank balance, Cher carries memories of financial insecurity and the fear of sudden deprivation. These marks are indelibly left on the psyche, and not helped by munakara Mars conjunct Pluto in the 2nd house, a stark reminder of how quickly and dramatically everything can be removed from within her grasp.

The Sun represents father, and Cher was denied the stability of a protective guiding father figure during her formative years. Her father had drug and gambling problems, and her parents divorced when Cher was ten months old. Her mother remarried, but by the time Cher was nine, the second marriage had failed, leaving a single mother to support Cher and her younger half-sister, by working multiple jobs to make ends meet. At one point, her mother was destitute, forced to leave her daughters at an orphanage for several weeks while she sought work further afield. Years later, Cher was a single mother with two children, and although her circumstances were never as dire as her mother's situation, munakara Sun instinctively reacts to feelings of failure. With the combination of munakara Sun ruling the 2nd house and munakara Mars in the 2nd house (ruling 5th house), these astrological indicators signify Cher's fear of being incapable of financially supporting her children.

The desire and ability to share one's wealth with others gives Taurean Sun purpose and direction and paves the way for the Sun's dispositor Venus to make important social connections and loyal friendships. Venus has nothing to prove in Cher's chart – it is not munakara – so the choices Cher makes are her own, regardless of social norms or expectations of 'normal' loving relationships. Both munakara Sun and munakara Jupiter (through dispositor Venus) end their sequences with Mercury and as of 2022, Cher has four million

Chapter Ten • *Multiple Munakara Planets*

Twitter followers; amazing for a woman who is four years away from being an octogenarian. The paparazzi are falling over each other to photograph Cher with her new 36-year-old beau, or when she pops up in a surprise appearance at the Balmain show in Paris, following Olivier Rousteing's presentation of the French atelier's 2023 collection, saying, "the stage was calling me to come home."[21]

Cher's Sun in contention sits in the 11th house, and anyone who gains Cher's approval when she graces their stage, or attends their opening, or presents at their social functions counts themselves to be a success by association with this amazing star. However, there have been times in Cher's six decade career – as there should be for anyone with this longevity – when munakara Sun and Jupiter, disposited by Venus, have missed the mark, and Cher's bankability suffered from choices made in the arenas of management or partnerships. Her munakara Sun in 11th house has not always loved the attention, and whilst Cher's dream to be famous was a constant aim, she was incredibly shy and insecure when she first started her singing career with Sonny Bono. Sonny's original intention was to promote her as a solo artist, but her stage fright was crippling (munakara Sun in 11th house) and he began to join her onstage so that she could focus on him rather than on the audience.

Cher's munakara Jupiter is at the apex of a T-square with Saturn and the Moon, both in their detriment and opposing one another, and much of Jupiter's contention involves being caught in this tense mythic opposition of debilitated planets. Neither the Moon, nor Saturn, feature in Cher's munakara sequences, but the aspect to Jupiter, which is in contention, is crippling for a planet that yearns for freedom (Jupiter), at the same time as carrying past emotional wounds and fearing rejection and abandonment (Saturn / Moon). Venus repeats its role as first dispositor, and Mercury as Jupiter's outcome planet, so much of Cher's down periods have materialized through being a woman who is underestimated and undervalued. Whilst popular culture was busy writing Cher off and consigning her to the 'has-beens' pile, Cher's trio of munakara planets were fighting to reclaim the limelight and using her multiple talents to conquer not one, but several fields of entertainment.

Munakara Jupiter rules Cher's MC, and she has had to face hostility from the public over various issues to which she was deeply committed, no matter how unpopular (Venus disposits Jupiter), or potentially harmful to her career (munakara Mars sextiles Jupiter). Cher's munakara Mars does not back down from a fight, does not alter an opinion even if it causes her harm or unpopularity, and she will stand to defend something that the public views as threatening or socially unacceptable (Mercury as outcome planet rules 12th house). Long before issues such as LGBT rights and HIV/AIDS prevention, poverty, elder rights, animal rights became popular catch-cries, Cher was bringing them to the forefront and forcing people to acknowledge they were social responsibilities rather than individual problems. During Covid-19 she launched CherCares Pandemic and Response Initiative (CCPRRI), an initiative that distributed $1 million to chronically neglected and forgotten people during the Pandemic and munakara Jupiter – in its T-square to Saturn and Moon – is driven to educate and improve social conditions for those with no voice, value, or visibility so far as society is concerned.

Cher's Jupiter by its state of munakara and its position at the apex of the Saturn/Moon opposition are warnings of possible health conditions, and chronic illness has drained Cher's vitality over the years. The Moon is her Ascendant ruler and with Saturn in detriment in this house from where it opposes Capricorn Moon, contentious Jupiter (ruling her 6th house) acts as a pivotal mid-point in this dangerous scenario. Cher has battled ill health for a number of years, surviving a killer virus picked up in the 1980s which led to chronic fatigue syndrome in the 1990s. A serious virus affected her kidneys and singing voice in 2021, and she contracted pneumonia in 2022, but it is her plastic surgery which often draws the media's greatest attention to her body's condition and encourages often vicious attacks on her physical appearance.

'Her plastic surgery is not merely cosmetic. It is hyperbolic, extreme, over the top....Cher has engaged in transformational technology that is dramatic and irreversible," says author Grant McCracken.[22] Echoing munakara Jupiter's dispositor Venus, are criticisms from author, Caroline Ramazanoglu, who believes Cher has compromised her own unique beauty, by replacing her strong, ethnic look with "a conventional and ever-youthful version of female beauty. Her normalised image now acts as a standard against which other women will measure, judge, discipline and 'correct' themselves."[23]

> *"I feel like a bumper car. If I hit a wall, I'm backing up and going in another direction. And I've hit plenty of f***ing walls in my career. But I'm not stopping. I think maybe that's my best quality: I just don't stop."*[24] – Cher

Munakara Mars has provided Cher with the strength of purpose and her passion to fight her own battles, in order to find a place to be an independent woman in a male-dominated industry. She has been dismissed a number of times, but she fights not only for herself (Sun disposits Mars), but also for any woman (Venus as outcome) with the courage to follow their dreams and prove their critics wrong, by creating their own niche in the music industry.

We can all agree that Cher's career has been long and fruitful, but there are signs of her triple munakara planets being out of step with her peers and the public. Her career nearly didn't get off the ground because her first commercial single in 1962, "Ringo, I love you", was rejected by many radio stations because they refused to believe Cher's voice was that of a woman, and instead that it was a male homosexual, declaring his love for Ringo Starr.

In 1965 when Cher teamed with Sonny Bono, the duo were advised by the Rolling Stones to move to England as the US 'just didn't get them'. Their fashion and music were an instant hit in the UK, but by the end of the 1960s the same music was considered 'bland', and they were considered 'square', at a time when the sexual revolution made them look like an old married couple, and their anti-drug stance aligned them with parents, not with the US youth who were at the height of the drug culture.

Unsuccessful albums, movies and other projects that failed to inspire the public, and the breakdown of her marriage to Sonny was a dark time, only alleviated by some success with television variety shows. The late 1970s saw Cher decline in popularity, but her shift from disco music to rock in the 1980s saved her once more from oblivion. Cher's acting career followed in the mid 1980s but the Hollywood establishment would not take her seriously as an actor, and once more, Cher was out of step with her environment. However, by 1988 had become one of the most bankable actresses of the decade, commanding $1 million per film.[25] The early years of the 1990s were again years of struggle for Cher, illness, negative film reviews, declining music successes, but then she resurrected her career for the fourth time with her album *Believe* in 1998, and the rest, as they say, is history.

EXAMPLE FOUR: CAITLYN JENNER

Three Planets in Contention

A Brief Biography:

Caitlyn Jenner (born October 28, 1949) is an American decathlete who won a gold medal at the 1976 Olympic Games in Montreal and in 2015 became the most prominent athlete to publicly come out as transgender.[26] After the 1976 Olympic triumph, Jenner became active as a network television sports commentator and made television commercials, lectured, and published several books.

In 1991 Jenner married Kris Kardashian, and the gold medallist later gained a new type of fame by becoming one of the central figures in the popular reality show *Keeping Up with the Kardashians* (2007–21), a program following the exploits of the couple's family. The pair divorced in 2014, and in April 2015 Jenner announced that she identified as a woman, two months later revealing that she wanted to be referred to as Caitlyn Jenner. Jenner's public shift from a male gender identity to a female one turned her into a cultural icon.[27] Her efforts to raise the visibility of transgender people were both widely praised and heavily scrutinized. Her memoir, *The Secrets of My Life*, was published in 2017.

> *"I'm saying goodbye to people's perception of me and who I am. But I'm not saying goodbye to me. This has always been me. When you think of me, please be open-minded. I'm not this bad person. I'm just doing what I have to do."*
> – Caitlyn Jenner, Diane Sawyer Interview, April 2015

Earlier in life, before her transition, Jenner excelled at testing the mind and body to their limits, as munakara Mars in Virgo (Sun's ruler) disposits to Mercury. In 1976, Jenner mobilized her three munakara planets – Sun, Mars, and Mercury – to win a gold medal at the Olympic Games in Montreal, with a record score of 8,618 points. This gained her attention and public acclaim, which satisfied her munakara Sun, as well as challenges to overcome and subsequent success that her munakara Mars enjoys. However, it brought little peace of mind for her munakara Mercury.

> *"My brain is much more female than it is male. It is hard for people to understand that but that is what my soul is."* – Caitlyn Jenner in the Diane Sawyer Interview, April 2015

The sequence for Jenner's munakara Sun involves her two other planets in contention, and this highlights the dilemma that Jenner says herself says is a dichotomy between a 'female brain and soul' that was trapped within a male body. Munakara Sun in Scorpio is disposited by Mars in munakara (the male) and its outcome planet is Mercury (female mind and soul). Therefore, trying to be authentic and true to oneself is constantly compromised by how the world views this individual, who appeared to be so successful and fulfilled.

Chapter Ten • *Multiple Munakara Planets*

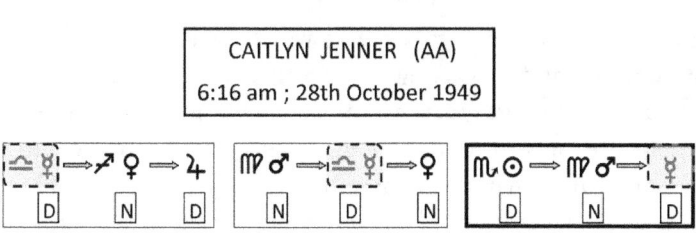

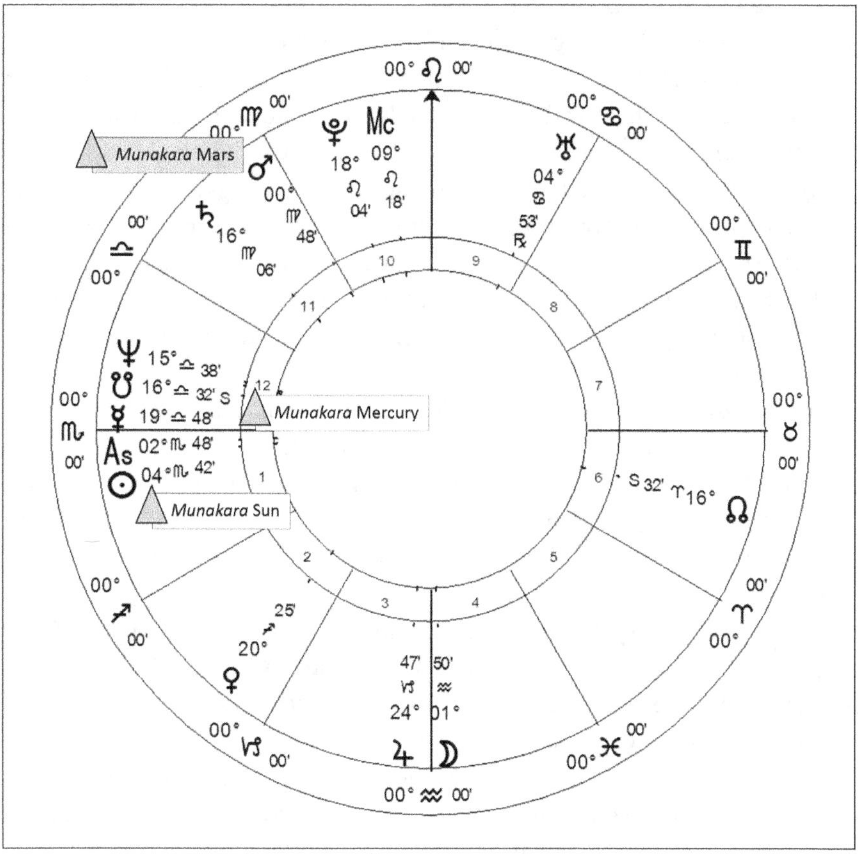

Fig. 10.4: Caitlyn Jenner Natal Chart: Multiple Munakara Planets

Munakara Sun sits on the Ascendant, in aspect by square, and rules Jenner's Mid-heaven in Leo. All three planets in the Sun's sequence are munakara planets, making them unpredictable, stressed and challenged. Munakara Sun is further stressed by its dispositor Mars (also munakara) and its outcome planet Mercury (also munakara).

Munakara in Theory

Munakara Sun has several aspects which add to its skills in covering Jenner's true identity by using subterfuge as a form of self-protection. Scorpio Sun is in sextile aspect to its dispositor, Mars. Playing the role of elite athlete, both planets in munakara made sure that no-one could question Jenner's masculinity, with her competitive nature and strong male physique. To the outside world (Leo Mid-heaven) Jenner was a supercharged hero and a picture of perfect manhood. Frank Litsky wrote in *The New York Times* on the morning after the gold medal win, "Bruce Jenner of San Jose, Calif., wants to be a movie or television star. After his record-breaking victory in the Olympic decathlon today, he probably can be anything he wants."

Munakara Sun squares Moon in Aquarius, and whilst the Moon is not a player in the three munakara sequences, the aspect suggests a tension and the concept of freedom and personal expression is strongly reinforced by this aspect. Munakara Mercury is the Sun's outcome planet and its conjunction to the South Node (a malefic in traditional texts) is an indication of its discomfort and the feeling of being 'dishonest' so far as one's identity is concerned.

Although the marriage to Kris Kardashian took Jenner's fame to new heights via TV reality stardom, Jenner was trapped by that fame (munakara Sun on the Ascendant), and unable to pursue her dream of becoming a woman (munakara Mercury rules 11th house). In the end it took almost forty years for Jenner to achieve that dream – finally transitioning in 2015, at the age of sixty-six.

Jenner's Mercury in munakara is an active participant in all three sequences of her munakara trifecta. Libran Mercury indicates the importance for Jenner to alter her designated birth gender and become the woman she knew herself to be.

Mercury is the planet which signifies thought, memory, communication and opinions, and even though it took six decades for Jenner to be authentic to her true self, her statement to Diane Sawyer shows Mercury's dilemma throughout Jenner's life.

This cautious, self-protective Mercury hid Jenner's secret, masking her true identity, and learning from a young age to mimic a masculine psyche. Observation, calculation and imitation was munakara Mercury's brief, and by observing the boys and men in Jenner's environment, she was able to portray the exact opposite to the image she held as her true self.

Given Jenner's journey through life and experiences as a child who felt herself to be so different from other children, it makes sense that Mercury, in

Chapter Ten • *Multiple Munakara Planets*

the sign of Venus, tended to isolate her from social interaction, and to keep her own counsel concerning her identity and sexuality.

> *"If you are dyslexic, your eyes work fine, your brain works fine, but there is a little short circuit in the wire that goes between the eye and the brain. Reading is not a fluid process."* – Caitlyn Jenner

Jenner's dyslexia added to Mercury's feelings of combat brought about by munakara. She suffered from embarrassment and feelings of failure when it came to reading aloud in the classroom as a child. She turned to compensating for her academic weaknesses and low self-esteem through challenging the smart boys to a race, knowing she could dominate them on the athletics field.

Libran Mercury sits in the sign preceding Jenner's Scorpio Sun and both diurnal planets are munakara. This suggests a waiting game for society's attitudes to change before she could openly identify as a woman. Jenner's two diurnal planets experienced the unnerving feeling of being vulnerable and susceptible to victimisation, a result of which was her third munakara planet. Mars covered her private insecurities and she trained relentlessly to become an elite athlete in a male body that was totally incongruous with her mind (munakara Mercury) and her spirit (munakara Sun).

Mercury is as much about honing one's fine and gross motor skills as it is about mental agility, and Jenner's athletic prowess was tested by a male body, and the choice to enter athletics through the vehicle of the gruelling decathlon. As a young athlete, decathlon training worked as a distraction for her gender dysphoria, as did other sports after the Olympics, but nothing seemed to ease the pain. "You always think in the back of your mind, I can live with this. I can fix this... If I just do this it's going to be OK." Jenner told Buzz Bissinger in the 2015 article in *Vanity Fair*.[28]

Jupiter is Mercury's outcome planet, but it is in Saturn's sign and in fall, meaning it must travel a long lonely road to achieve the freedom to finally drop Mercury's mask and to reveal to the world the true nature of her identity. Jupiter is just over 90 degrees from its munakara planet, and the cardinal square between first and last planet in Mercury's sequence has brought Mercury an outlet for its frustrations – bestowing many athletic gifts on Jenner including childhood athletics, college football, water-skiing championships, decathlon, and after the Olympics, tennis, car racing, and a pilot's licence.

Venus plays a role in two of Jenner's munakara sequences – as first dispositor to Libran Mercury and as the outcome planet for Mars – and whilst mutual reception between Mercury and Venus protects Venus from munakara, it is still a big player in the story of Jenner's transformation from male to female. Years of hiding, depression and failed relationships (Venus rules 7th and 12th houses) convinced Jenner that her life would not be authentic, and she could not be truly happy, until she took steps to live her life as a transgender woman.

Unfortunately for Jenner, her new sense of freedom from the Kardashian family loosed her tongue and released munakara Mercury, leading to a public feud when she claimed that her gender change was the show's one true real story and that *KUWTK* owed its popularity to her involvement with the show. She further stated that, as opposed to her, the Kardashians were 'publicity-hungry' and described her marriage to Kris as 'acrimonious misery', thereby further alienating her from the family.

Her opinions as a transgender woman have also drawn criticism from many LGFBTQ+ activists[29] and it seems her three munakara planets will continue to create havoc for her so long as she stays in the media limelight.[30]

EXAMPLE FIVE: PRINCESS DIANA
Three Planets in Contention
A Brief Biography

Diana, princess of Wales (July 1, 1961 – August 31, 1997) was the former consort (1981–96) of Charles, Prince of Wales (later Charles III); mother of the heir apparent to the British throne, Prince William, and his younger brother Prince Harry, duke of Sussex. On February 24, 1981, her engagement to Charles was announced, and her beauty and shy demeanour made her an instant sensation with the media and the public.[31] The couple married in St. Paul's Cathedral on July 29, 1981, in a globally televised ceremony watched by an audience numbered in the hundreds of millions. "Princess Di" rapidly evolved into an icon of grace, elegance, and glamour. Exuding natural charm she used her celebrity status to raise awareness of her numerous charitable causes, and her changing hairstyles and wardrobe made her a fashion trendsetter. Behind the scenes, Diana struggled with severe postnatal depression, low self-esteem, eating disorders, and the mounting strain of being constantly pursued by both the official media royal-watchers and the tabloid press. The royal couple formally separated in 1992, and their divorce became final in August 1996. Diana's popularity continued after the divorce and she used her celebrity to great effect in promoting her charitable work, but the media were often intrusive in uncovering her private life. While attempting

Chapter Ten • Multiple Munakara Planets

to evade pursuing journalists in Paris, Diana and her companion Dodi Fayed and their driver were killed in an automobile accident in 1997.[32]

"I do things differently, I don't go by a rule book, I lead from the heart, not the head, and albeit that's got me into trouble in my work, I understand that."[33]
– Diana, Princess of Wales

Diana Frances Spencer was aptly named after the Roman Moon goddess given that her Moon in Aquarius features in all three of her munakara sequences. The Moon is the dispositor for her duet planets, Sun and diurnal Mercury in Cancer, and the Moon is also the outcome planet for her munakara Mars in Virgo. A duet often talks about two planets being harnessed together as a team to achieve a joint purpose which will benefit both planets. Depending on the planets involved – in this case, Sun and Mercury – a munakara duet indicates the manner and description by which burdens will be shared as they fight in unison to achieve their separate aims. The Sun has no issue with Mercury, but the two planets in contention tie together image, vocation, and reputation (Sun) with the need to vocalize, communicate and share information (Mercury). Diurnal Mercury is a servant of the Sun, and in a munakara duet the shared aim is to have one's name and face easily identifiable, and for the public to recognise the individual. Together these two planets 'imprint' on the public psyche and the more recognisable one becomes, the more successful the planets in contention see themselves. It makes little difference to munakara planets if the imprint they make is positive or negative, and with Saturn as the outcome planet for Diana's duet, she was always likely to experience both sides of fame.

Saturn in Capricorn is in rulership in Diana's chart, but it is also retrograde and forms a square aspect to her Mid-heaven in Libra. Venus in rulership is Diana's MC lord, and the air trine between Libran MC and Aquarian Moon gave her the natural ease to relate to others, and to quickly earn their trust, love and loyalty.

Diana's ability to shine in any public arena that required royal attendance became an issue for The Firm as her warmth, spontaneity, compassion, social ease, and sense of fun placed Charles (ruled by munakara Mercury in her chart) firmly in the shadows, as she demonstrated everything that was missing in the royal family.

Her Aquarian Moon, active in her trio of munakara planets, squares Venus in Taurus, and as her public support grew, so did her problems with other

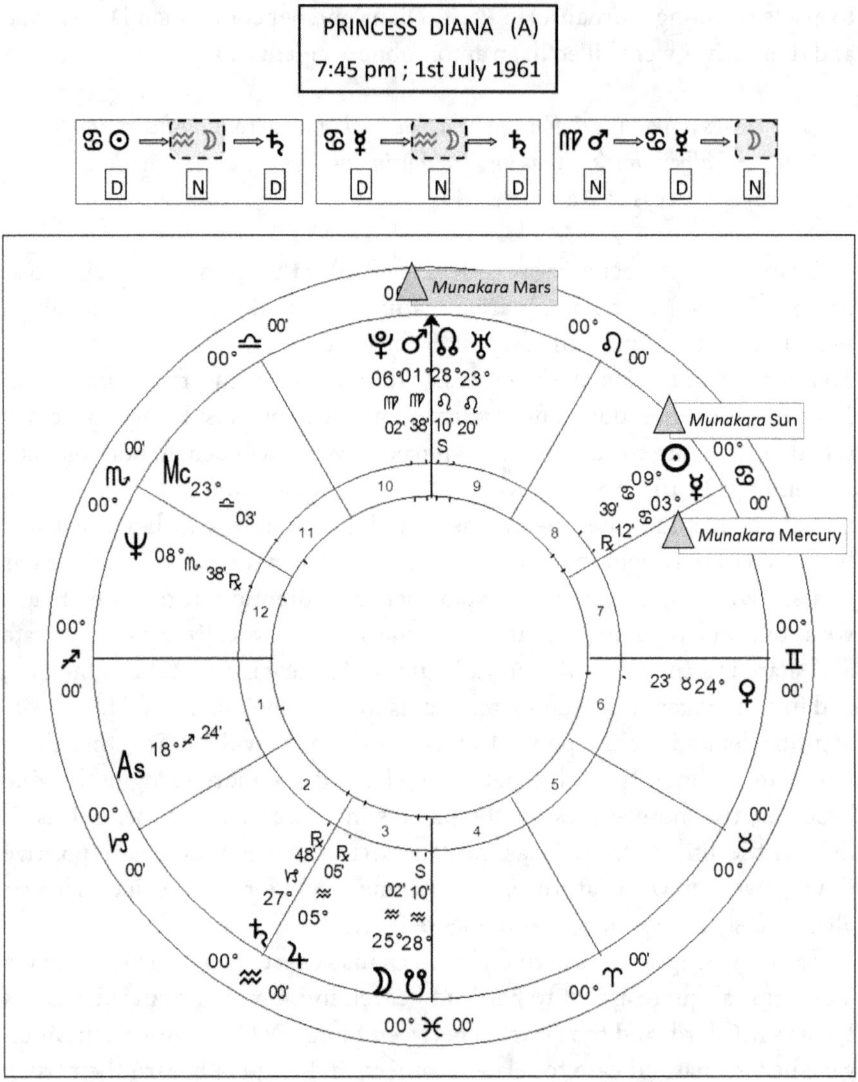

Munakara in Theory

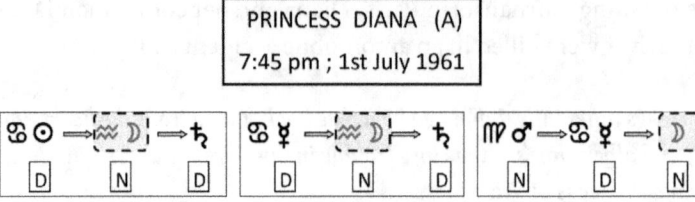

Fig. 10.5: Princess Diana Natal Chart: Multiple Munakara Planets

more staid members of the British Royal family, who believed she was far too familiar with her royal subjects. The gap between public and royalty was narrowing under her influence, and this agitated both Charles (7th house) and The Firm (munakara Mars Virgo in Whole Sign 10th house).

Diana's three munakara planets are in aspect to one another: a conjunction between Sun and Mercury and a sextile to Mars in the 10th house. Initially shy and hesitant about her capability to perform her new

Chapter Ten • *Multiple Munakara Planets*

royal duties (munakara Mars in Virgo), Diana's duet in Cancer began to win hearts, but the two planets in contention – Sun and Mercury – had their own battles with her mental frailty, as Diana's marriage to Charles began to break down, and her loneliness became a major factor in her unhappiness. Munakara Sun and Mercury sit in an awkward position in the difficult 8th house, and their independent house rulerships give an indication as to how they were battling to maintain a brave front, when life was becoming increasingly difficult for Diana.

Cancer Sun rules the 9th house, but unfortunately, it is blind to Leo, and Diana's total unpreparedness for the personal and professional development she would need to put into overdrive in order to fit in to royal life, is shown by the way in which the Sun is in aversion to its house of rulership. As a child Diana may have been comfortable as a part of the royal family's private life when her family lived next door to Sandringham, but she was totally ill-equipped to understand the public commitments of the same family she had known in her childhood. What was totally familiar to the royal family felt as private as living in a goldfish bowl, especially when the press became obsessed with her, and her every move was photographed, broadcast to media outlets across the world, and commented on (not always kindly) by the press.

So many things should have been red flags for anyone caring to look into Diana as a future queen of England. Diana's Mercury in contention rules her Whole Sign 7th and 10th houses – 7th house belongs to Charles as her partner, and 10th belongs to her mother, her step-mother, and her father-in-law. The battles with Charles, dealing with his emotional coldness, and the revelation of his marital betrayal, show some of munakara Mercury's discord. Eventually Diana came to the realization that her marriage was more about promoting the royal family's popularity and delivering heirs to the throne, than possessing a close loving bond with her husband. Diana's isolation from her new family, who could not comprehend (or tolerate) her emotional outbursts and her fragile mental health, is a statement of her trio of planets in contention: Mars in Mercury's sign, and Sun and Mercury in the Moon's sign.

Diana broke the secret royal maxim, "never complain, never explain", on November 20, 1995 in her interview for BBC Panorama with Martin Bashir, where she confessed that she had suffered from post natal depression after William's birth, and rather than receiving compassion and support, others in The Firm labelled her as unstable, hysterical, and mentally unbalanced (munakara Sun rules 9th house, the house of my husband's siblings, three houses from the 7th house). Her infamous statement "there were three of us in this marriage, so it was a bit crowded", is a comment on the role of Camilla Parker Bowles as Charles's lover. In the interview Diana's three munakara planets went into overdrive, calling the media (who had now turning against her) "abusive" and condemning their "harassment" of her as she tried to build a new life away from her husband's family.

In 2020, it was revealed the her interviewer, Martin Bashir, had used forged bank statements to imply that Diana's former private secretary had been paid for spying on her. BBC Director-General Tim Davie apologised to Earl Spencer, Diana's brother, but the damage had been done years before this fact was public knowledge. In truth, Diana was once more manipulated by forces outside her control (Saturn is Sun/Mercury's outcome planet), and when speaking with Bashir in a public forum, Diana was tricked several times by Bashir into making a number of unguarded comments that revealed more than was allowable by traditional standards when protocol protects other members of the royal family in interviews with the press.

Mercury rules the tenth sign of Virgo, where munakara Mars resides by Whole Sign, and Diana's relationships with those who represented the tenth sign – official press members, the paparazzi, official and informal events, celebrations – were often fraught with disappointments, disapproval, arguments and misunderstandings, as one would expect from a munakara planet *in situ* (Mars), ruled by another planet in contention (Mercury).

Munakara Mars rules Diana's 5th house of children, and the 12th house of hidden enemies, and Diana was fiercely protective over her two boys. Prince William was reported to have been "overcome with a feeling of dread" as soon as he saw the interview, while Prince Harry initially refused to watch it, and later blamed Bashir for asking personal invasive questions, and not his mother for answering them.[34]

Diana's relationship with her mother Frances was difficult, and reports describe Frances as jealous, angry, and often spiteful towards her own daughter.[35] The two women were estranged at the time of Diana's death, but perhaps knowing that three munakara sequences balance on Diana's Aquarian Moon, gives some insight into the tension between mother and daughter. In a 2020 interview with People's Maria Pasquini Diana's younger brother, Charles, said "Our father was a quiet constant source of love, but our mother wasn't cut out for maternity. Not her fault, she couldn't do it. While she was packing her stuff to leave, she promise Diana (then aged five) she'd come back to see her. Diana used to wait on the doorstop for her, but she never came."[36]

Chapter Ten • *Multiple Munakara Planets*

Frances may have been called a snob and a bad mother by Diana when she was alive, but Frances converted to Catholicism after Diana's death, and became a humanitarian and philanthropist who cared for bereaved families and handicapped children.[37] It is almost as if Frances took on the roles which had been most important to Diana, but roles which Diana was no longer alive to fulfil herself.

Diane was the fourth of five children, and the third living daughter of a family that desperately wanted a male heir. The Moon is first dispositor for Diana's Cancer Sun and Mercury, and Diana's greatest fault may have been that she was born the wrong gender, into a titled British family that desperately yearned for a son to claim his father's title, 9th Earl Spencer, and to inherit Althorp, the family's ancestral seat in Northamptonshire. One year before Diana was born, Frances was jubilant with the arrival of a son, John, but the baby died shortly after his birth, and when Diana was born as the third daughter to two older sisters, she was an automatic disappointment for her parents. It took a week to find the interest to name the new baby, and whilst the birth of a son, Charles, three years after Diana fulfilled the dynasty's necessary requirement, the marriage was under too great a strain, and headed for divorce.

Diana was separated from her mother at age five, when her father gained full custody of Diana and her younger brother Charles, when Frances' own mother testified against her daughter as an unfit mother. Diana's father remarried a few years later, but Diana's relationship with her step-mother, Raine, was no improvement in providing a close motherly bond. Diana accused her step-mother of being a bully, and on one occasion, pushed Raine down the stairs after a particularly heated argument. If Diana's Moon had hoped for a supportive loving relationship with Charles' mother, then this too was denied her when she joined the royal family. With three planets in munakara (and two with Saturn as the outcome planet) it is easy to understand why Diana was constantly out of step with the fussiness and formality expected by the British royal family. By the end of her relationship with The Firm, Diana's munakara Mars in Virgo was defiant, rebellious, outspoken and often, ill-mannered towards the family who had rejected her and closed ranks on her to protect her husband Charles. Whether her death was an accident or a deliberate act of violence is impossible to deduce, but Princess Diana paid the ultimate price for her rebellion against one of the world's oldest and most traditional families. Diana was no match for the 'super-tanker' known as The Firm and even her three planets in contention failed to fortify her mental health and her emotional strength. A miserable childhood and an unhappy marriage compromised Diana's belief in herself and undermined her confidence in her own capabilities, and inevitably, it weakened her will-power. Her munakara planets may even have led to her untimely death at an early age (munakara Sun and Mercury in the 8th house) before she truly had the opportunity to find happiness and fulfilment in her life.

Munakara Multiples: Four Planets in Contention

EXAMPLE ONE: CATHERINE THE GREAT

Four Planets in Contention

A Brief Biography:[38]

Catherine II (2 May 1729 – 17 November 1796) was born as Princess Sophia Augusta Frederica von Alhalt-Zerbst-Dornburg in the Kingdom of Prussia. She became the empress of Russia (1762–96) after overthrowing her husband, Peter III. With her ministers Catherine reorganized the administration and law of the Russian Empire and extended Russian territory, adding Crimea and much of Poland.

In 1739, when Sophia was 10, she met the second cousin who would be her future husband, grandson of Tsar Peter the Great and heir to the throne of Russia as the Grand Duke Peter III. In 1744 Catherine arrived in Russia, where she immediately began to study Russian and Orthodoxy, with the end result of abandoning Lutheranism for the Russian Church, being re-christened Yekaterina – Catherine.[39] She assumed the title of Grand Duchess Catherine Alekseyevna when she married her young cousin the following year. Her husband was a great disappointment to everyone. The marriage was a complete failure and the following 18 years were filled with humiliation for her.

At the time of their marriage Russia was ruled by Peter the Great's daughter, the empress Elizabeth, whose 20-year reign greatly stabilized the monarchy. Devoted to much pleasure and luxury and greatly desirous of giving her court the brilliancy of European court, Elizabeth prepared the way for Catherine.

Catherine, however, would not have become empress if her husband had been at all normal. He was extremely neurotic, rebellious, obstinate, perhaps impotent, nearly alcoholic, and most seriously, a fanatical worshipper of Frederick II of Prussia, the foe of the empress Elizabeth. Catherine, by contrast, was clearheaded and ambitious. Her intelligence, flexibility of

Chapter Ten • Multiple Munakara Planets

character, and love of Russia gained her much support. The empress Elizabeth died on Christmas Day 1761, while Russia, allied with Austria and France, was engaged in the Seven Years' War against Prussia. Shortly after Elizabeth's death, Peter, now emperor, ended Russia's participation in the war and concluded an alliance with Frederick II of Prussia. He made no attempt to hide his hatred of Russia, and in fact, could barely speak the language; discrediting himself endlessly by his foolish actions, he also prepared to rid himself of the wife ha hated and to whom he had been wed for almost two decades.

Catherine had only to strike: she had the support of the army, the court, and public opinion in both capitals (Moscow and St. Petersburg). She was also supported by the 'enlightened' elements of aristocratic society, since she was known for her liberal opinions and admired as one of the most cultivated persons in Russia. On July 9, 1762, she led the regiments that had rallied to her cause and had herself proclaimed empress and autocrat in the Kazan Cathedral. Peter III abdicated and was assassinated eight days later. In September 1762, she was crowned with great ceremony in Moscow, the ancient capital of the tsars, and began a reign that was to span 34 years as empress of Russia under the title of Catherine II, until her death in November 1796 at age 67.

"You philosophers are lucky men. You write on paper and paper is patient. Unfortunate Empress that I am, I write on the susceptible skins of living beings."[40] – Empress Catherine the Great

Catherine II's chart has four planets in munakara: the Moon and Venus are nocturnal planets in the same degree of Gemini and are in a duet, and the Sun and Jupiter are diurnal planets in contention.

"I am one of the people who love the why of things."[41] – Catherine the Great

Whilst Catherine's diurnal Mercury is not in munakara, it is common to all four of her sequences by being the dispositor for the Moon and Venus, and the outcome planet for the Sun and Jupiter. There is no doubt that Catherine was a highly intelligent woman but she was a woman who held western European philosophies (she was friends with French writers and philosophers Voltaire and Denis Diderot), and she wanted to surround herself with like-minded people in Russia. Her goal was to modernise Russia and to do this she appointed Ivan Betskoy as her advisor on educational matters.[42]

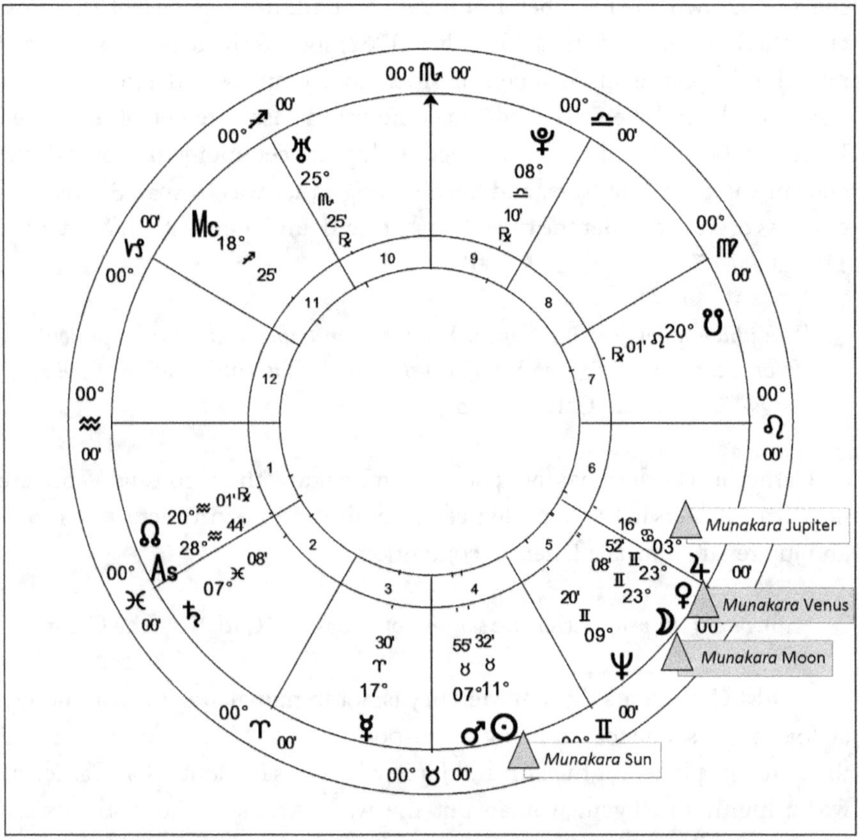

Munakara in Theory

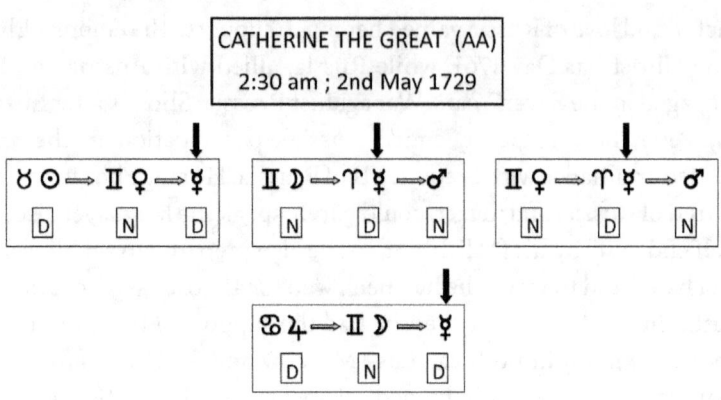

Fig. 10.6: Empress Catherine the Great Natal Chart: Multiple Munakara

Chapter Ten • Multiple Munakara Planets

"I may be kindly, I am ordinarily gentle, but in my line of business I am obliged to will terribly what I will at all."[43]

Catherine's munakara Sun in Taurus sits with Mars in the 4th house and its rulership of the 7th house show her family connections (4th) which make her suitable as the bride (7th) to future emperor, Peter III. However, both the Sun and Venus, its dispositor, are planets in munakara and this suggests that things are never as simple as they seem at first sight.

Two powerful women played a huge role in Catherine's destiny: her mother Joanna (munakara Moon) and her husband's aunt, Elizabeth (munakara Sun), the second daughter of Peter the Great, and sister to his mother who had died shortly after his birth (10 houses from the 7th house is the partner's mother).

Peter's aunt Elizaveta Petrovna (Empress Elizabeth), had seized the throne with the military's support in 1742 and had declared her nephew, 14-year-old Peter, as her heir. However, she needed to secure a bride for the teenager and for this she and Joanna arranged Grand Duke Peter's marriage to Sophia/Catherine. Initially the relationship between the two women was friendly as Elizabeth had been betrothed to Joanna's brother who had died of smallpox before the wedding took place.

Catherine's munakara Moon is in a duet with Venus (Sun's dispositor) and historical accounts portray Joanna as a cold, abusive woman who loved gossip and court intrigues. Fifteen-year-old Joanna married thirty-seven-year-old Prince Christian August of Anhalt-Zerbst but the marriage was a mismatch because of their large age gap and different personalities. Joanna's soldier husband was a sober and simple man who lived in a small townhouse whilst his young wife loved to socialize in the luxurious courts of Northern Germany. There were rumours of questionable paternity when Sophia (Catherine) was born two years into Joanna's marriage and the fact everyone had hoped the first born would be a son and heir to his father meant Joanna was bitterly disappointed in her daughter. The labour was intense and life-threatening for Joanna, who had to lie in bed for 19 weeks to recover from Sophie's birth. She handed her child over to nurses and servants and did not show the child any affection. According to Sophie's memoirs, her mother was often violent and angry towards her for no reason[44] (Mars in detriment rules mother's house, the 10th, and conjuncts munakara Sun), and perhaps the loving bonds that were lacking between mother and daughter (munakara Moon) give some insight into Catherine's strained relationship with her own son, Paul, who was born in 1754.

Catherine's 5th house is ruled by Mercury, but it is the house where her munakara nocturnal planets, Moon and Venus, reside in Gemini, and in an echo of her mother's experience of childbirth, controversy over Paul's paternity surrounded his birth as most believed the royal couple were incapable of producing an heir, given that Catherine and Peter had been married over eight years before Paul's birth. There was much speculation that Peter was unable to consummate the marriage and Catherine's first lover, Sergei Saltykov, was believed to be Paul's biological father. Records of Catherine's delivery show that the room in which she gave birth was drafty and no attempt was made for hours to clean, warm, feed, comfort, or give medical attention to the young Grand Duchess. Instead, she bled, sweated from the chill of open windows but lacked the strength to call for help or return to her room.[45] Her new son was whisked away from her by Empress Elizabeth who raised the child as her own, allowing Catherine only brief encounters with her son. The child had, in effect, become a ward of the state and, in a larger sense, the property of the state.[46] Paul was alternatively smothered with affection by his childless great aunt, and neglected at the same time when her interest in him waned. His caretakers did not take time to form his character, and his diet was nutritionally deficient, in spite of his family's wealth. Deprived of the opportunity to bond with either parent – his father was assassinated when Paul was eight – he reached adulthood as the ignored, but highly necessary, son of the reigning Tsarina, Catherine the Great.[47]

Joanna may have bore Catherine little affection – Catherine's only surviving sibling was a boy, Frederick, born five years after her – but Joanna's hunger for fame centred on her daughter's prospects of becoming Empress of Russia (Mars in detriment rules mother's house, the 10th, and conjuncts munakara Sun). She travelled with Catherine to Russia to prepare for the royal wedding ceremony and was intent on residing in Elizabeth's court. However, once there her meddling became too much for Elizabeth and on the accusation that she was spying for Prussia's King Frederick, Joanna was banned from the country in 1747.

Catherine's education reformer, Ivan Betskoy, was well known to both Elizabeth and Joanna. He played a major role in Elizabeth's *coup d'etat* and in gratitude the new Empress made him General Major. He had known Joanna two decades previous, their intimacy giving rise to rumours that Catherine was his biological daughter (munakara Sun in father's house; Sun conjunct Mars in detriment, ruler of mother's house). When Joanna was ordered from Saint Petersburg Betskoy went with her, and the two lived in Paris until Peter

Chapter Ten • *Multiple Munakara Planets*

III recalled Betskoy to Russia and put him in charge of imperial palaces and gardens. Betskoy renewed his acquaintance with his purported daughter (Catherine), and rather than staying loyal to the new Tsar, her alleged father was a major influence in helping her to depose Peter in 1762.

Catherine's munakara Sun in the 4th house describes both her love affair with her adopted country, and her frustration with its backward ways. She waited in the wings for 18 years to become Empress and wanted desperately to drag Russia into the Enlightenment that was occurring in Europe's royal courts; but instead she was trapped in a loveless marriage, humiliated, bored, and regarded with suspicion in Empress Elizabeth's court.

Munakara Sun in the 4th house, ruling the 7th house (the house of partners and open enemies), encapsulates the hostility that existed between herself and Grand Duke Peter, a man she describes with loathing in her memoirs as an 'idiot' and a 'drunkard from Holstein' and saying of her marriage 'there is nothing worse than having a child-husband'.[48] Peter's hatred of his wife was intense but he appears to have believed that Paul was, in fact, his son and legitimate heir to the Russian throne. Nothing would have given him greater pleasure than denouncing Catherine as an adulteress and calling for her banishment or execution. Several facts support this belief: there was a strong resemblance between other Romanovs and Paul and there were numerous physical and personality similarities between Paul and Peter III.[49] It has been claimed that Catherine the Great was one of the world's most skilful politicians. Her position at the time of Paul's birth was shaky and her only hope for advancement was to perpetuate the Romanov dynasty.[50] It would be unlikely that she would foolishly jeopardize her dreams to become Empress of Russia. Peter was her only way to secure her own position, especially whilst Elizabeth was still on the throne, and she would not have wanted to give Peter any excuse to get rid of her.

"I cannot live one day without love."[51] – Catherine the Great

There is no doubt that Empress Catherine II would have been described as 'a contentious woman', and Venus in munakara with the Moon in the 5th house lends itself to crazy misogynistic myths that cast one of the most powerful players as a nymphomaniac with bizarre tastes in bestiality and voyeurism. Munakara Venus rules Catherine's 4th and 9th houses and surrounding countries were exceedingly nervous of Russia's expansion of borders during Catherine's thirty years in power. Munakara Venus often puts a woman on the wrong side of society's approval and Catherine the Great was no exception. Historians often describe Catherine as "taking many lovers" but in truth, from 1752 to 1796, a span of 44 years, Catherine was involved in 12 romantic relationships, with most lasting for more than two years each. Like England's Elizabeth I, Catherine recognized that to marry meant to relinquish her power, and so instead she chose partners with whom she usually had a good working relationship.[52]

Munakara Venus rules the 9th house and often it was foreign powers who fed these salacious rumours about Catherine's promiscuity. For instance, in France – which Catherine had such affinity with its philosophers – they turned on Catherine when she showed no support for the French Revolution in 1789 and she became a vilified representative of the repressive royal order with the same pornographic libels that were being circulated against the French queen, Marie Antoinette.[53] Catherine's greatest rival throughout her reign, King Frederick II, ruler of Prussia, said about her, "A woman is always a woman and, in feminine government, the …. (a woman's genitalia) has more influence than a firm policy guided by straight reason."[54] The British presses depicted Catherine as prey to her voracious sexual appetite in obscene political cartoons, such as *An Imperial stride!* published in 1791, showing seven 'European Powers' gazing up at her (the Doge of Venice, the Pope, the King of Spain, France's Louis XVI, Britain's King George III, her son Paul, and the Turkish Sultan) passing lewd remarks as she strides across the European continent increasing her power.[55] In truth, they were terrified of this female monarch and they chose her gender (Venus in munakara) to ruin her reputation and reduce her to their level.

> "I shall be an autocrat: that's my trade. And the good Lord will forgive me: that's his."[56]

Jupiter in exaltation is Catherine the Great's fourth planet in munakara. Jupiter sits in her 6th house in the Whole Sign system and rules her 2nd and 11th houses. It aspects Saturn, the ruler of her Ascendant, trines Saturn, and is Saturn's dispositor, given that Saturn is in Pisces. Munakara Jupiter also squares Pluto in the 9th house.

At first glance it can be difficult to imagine how an exalted Jupiter might express itself in Catherine's 6th house, particularly when Catherine appears to have had an excellent constitution and to have suffered very little illness until the stroke that led to her death at age 67.

Chapter Ten • *Multiple Munakara Planets*

However, there are several instances which might describe this diurnal planet in contention. Firstly, Catherine's 6th house is Peter III's house of hidden enemies (twelve houses from the 7th house) and he obviously did not anticipate his wife overthrowing him six months after he, the rightful heir, had been crowned Emperor of Russia. His lineage came from his grandfather, the infamous Peter the Great, and his royal blood was from the house of Romanov. Peter could not have anticipated that Catherine, an outsider, would have the courage, the resources, or the capability to muster the military (army and navy) to mutiny against him, or that the nobles would support her. Even the general populace hated him and armed with sticks and stones they pelted Peter to prevent him from returning to the capital city.[57]

When Catherine was declared Empress of Russia she worked tirelessly (munakara Jupiter in 6th house), dedicating long hours to establish a reign of order and justice, spreading education and dreaming of establishing a court to rival Versailles, and developing a national culture that would be the envy of all European courts.[58] This was her dream, but unfortunately, exalted Jupiter is in contention and her attempts at reform were constantly thwarted by the fact that Russia was not ready for the Enlightenment and for all her efforts she met opposition at each turn. In 1767, six years into her reign, Catherine prepared a document – Instruction of Catherine the Great – which recommended liberal, humanitarian political theories for use as the basis of government reform and the formation of a new legal code.[59] Exalted Jupiter ruling her 11th house (trine her Ascendant ruler, Saturn) was in play when Catherine organised a commission composed of delegates from all the provinces and from all social classes, with the exception of serfs, to gather for the purpose of ascertaining the true wishes of her people and to frame a new constitution. But exalted Jupiter is munakara, and as is typical of a planet in contention, nothing came of Catherine's Instructions as it was considered too liberal for publication in France and it remained a dead letter in Russia.

"I am an aristocrat, it is my profession."[60]

Whilst Catherine had been desperate for reform in Russia, she was appalled at the violent events marking the French revolution from 1787 to 1799. The execution of France's Louis XVI in 1793 frightened and appalled the crowned heads of Europe and Catherine was no exception. She (and munakara Jupiter) had no intention of relinquishing her own power and privileges, and when Poland started to agitate for a liberal constitution, Catherine sent in troops in

1792 under the pretext of forestalling the threat of revolution. The next year Russia annexed most of western Ukraine while Prussia helped itself to large territories of western Poland.

> "A great wind is blowing, and that gives you either imagination or a headache."[61]

Exalted Jupiter in Cancer can have lofty ideas, especially when it comes to being protective or liberal in its views. However, when Jupiter – and its dispositor, the Moon – are both planets in munakara, then ideals can be sacrificed for the sake of practicality. Catherine's original plans to emancipate the serfs were formed when Empress Elizabeth was in power, and as Empress, she soon found her plans to be deeply unpopular with the noble class who relied on free labour for their wealth. Catherine needed the nobles' support and Russia, which was 95% agricultural, needed serfs to function as a country. Rather than easing some reform, Catherine (via munakara Jupiter) went completely in the other direction. She strengthened a system that she herself had condemned as inhuman, and increased the numbers by imposing serfdom on the Ukrainians who had until then been free. In order to buy loyalty from the nobles and her ministers, she re-distributed crown lands to them and gave them hundreds of serfs to work the land. Catherine's immense expenditures on her ever-growing economic, military, and cultural projects of which she was so proud, were financed by the misery of forced labour and virtual slavery of the masses.

Catherine's liberal views did not extend to the serfs and it was her loathed son, Paul I, who would be the first tsar to limit the work required of the most unfortunate members of Russian society. Munakara Jupiter is disposited by the Moon in 5th house (Catherine's son) and whilst Paul did not abolish serfdom, on his own lands he educated their children, lent them money, instituted a system of free medical care, gave them more land for their use, and upgraded agricultural technology to ease their working life.

EXAMPLE TWO: EDGAR DEGAS
Four Planets in Contention
A Brief Biography:[62]

Edgar Degas (19 July 1834 – 27 September 1917) was a French painter, sculptor, and printmaker who was prominent in the Impressionist group and widely celebrated for his images of Parisian life. Degas was famous for

Chapter Ten • *Multiple Munakara Planets*

his studies of laundresses, cabaret singers, ballet dancers, milliners, and prostitutes of his Impressionist period.

Degas was often described as an Impressionist, but he hated the title which clumped him together with artists he felt were inferior to him, and very different from his own style of painting. Impressionists were famous for landscapes painted out of doors by their artists, but in true munakara fashion, Degas thought this a silly practice, and preferred to stay in his studio and work from memory. His ballet dancers modelled for him in his studio and his famous racecourse paintings were never painted at the track.

It was not until after Degas's death that the wealth of his output was revealed in a succession of vast public sales in Paris in 1918 and 1919. Thousands of his previously unexhibited works on paper and canvas were sold, and some of the later, less naturalistic examples distressed even his most loyal admirers. Certain aspects of his achievement gained prominence for the first time, principally the wide range of his printmaking. In the early 1920s, when the first series of posthumous bronze casts were unveiled in Europe and the United States, Degas's sculpture provided a further revelation to the art world.

Degas is now counted among the most complex and innovative figures of his generation, credited with influencing Pablo Picasso, Henri Matisse, and many of the leading figurative artists of the 20th century.

"There is a kind of shame in being known especially by people who don't understand you. A great reputation is therefore a kind of shame."[63]

"I should like to be famous and unknown."

Degas' Cancer Sun is munakara, and his hatred of being easily classified is something he fought against throughout his life. Before his twentieth birthday, Degas was a registered copyist at the Louvre by 1853, and travelled in Italy for three years, to learn by copying the works of Michelangelo, Raphael and Titan. He might have remained a wealthy man who dabbled in art, but the death of his father in 1874 plunged him into debt, and for the first time, Degas was forced to become dependent on his artwork for income.

Degas' Sun in contention rules his 7th house, and whilst he admitted he was lonely in his older years, and urged others to take a wife to avoid loneliness, his reply to his choice of bachelorhood was, *"I, marry? Oh, I could* never bring myself to do it. I would have been in mortal misery all my life for fear my wife might say, 'That's a pretty little thing,' after I had finished a picture."[64] Yet, it has been observed that Degas' portraits are notable for the psychological complexity and their portrayal of human isolation.[65]

In his natal chart Degas's Sun in Cancer is in a wide opposition to his Moon in Capricorn and both luminaries are in a state of munakara. Degas' Capricorn Moon is located in the 12th house and rules his 6th house. Whilst his Moon in detriment and munakara describes his eventual blindness and his overall health concerns, it also encompasses his loneliness and his unsociability. Munakara Sun and munakara Moon are present in munakara Mercury's sequence; the Sun is its dispositor and the Moon is its outcome planet and Mercury's position in the 7th house is made abundantly clear in Degas's statement above.

Degas surrounded himself with women and yet had no desire to form a lasting relationship with any one woman, preferring instead to treat them as 'subjects ' for his art's purpose rather than engage with them, either intellectually (Sun) or emotionally (Moon). Sadly, 7th-house munakara Mercury with luminaries in contention left him a sad and lonely man because of his belief that "the artist must live alone, and his private life must remain unknown."[66] The famously misanthropic, cantankerous and misogynistic Degas grew even more isolated in his later years, becoming morose and withdrawn, partly due to his deteriorating eyesight. His artist friend Pierre-Auguste Renoir observed, "All his friends had to leave him; I was one of the last to go, but even I couldn't stay til the end."[67] He remained a bachelor throughout his life and was not known to have any romantic entanglements; Manet noted that Degas was "not capable of loving a woman." Degas died in 1917, childless and alone.[68]

Regardless of his talents, Degas must have been an infuriating friend and no doubt his munakara Mercury in 7th house describes both his friends and his enemies. In 1868 Degas painted *Monsieur and Madame Edouard Manet* and gifted it to the couple. The painting depicts Manet reclining on the sofa as his wife plays the piano. As the story goes, the next time Degas saw the picture, it had been slashed right through Mme Manet's face. Degas was furious, and took the painting back. While it is unclear what provoked such a reaction in Manet, historians have speculated that he objected to the depiction of marital disharmony.[69] Perhaps Manet felt slighted by Degas's observation of his friend's unhappy marriage, and Degas's view of marriage in general.

Chapter Ten • *Multiple Munakara Planets*

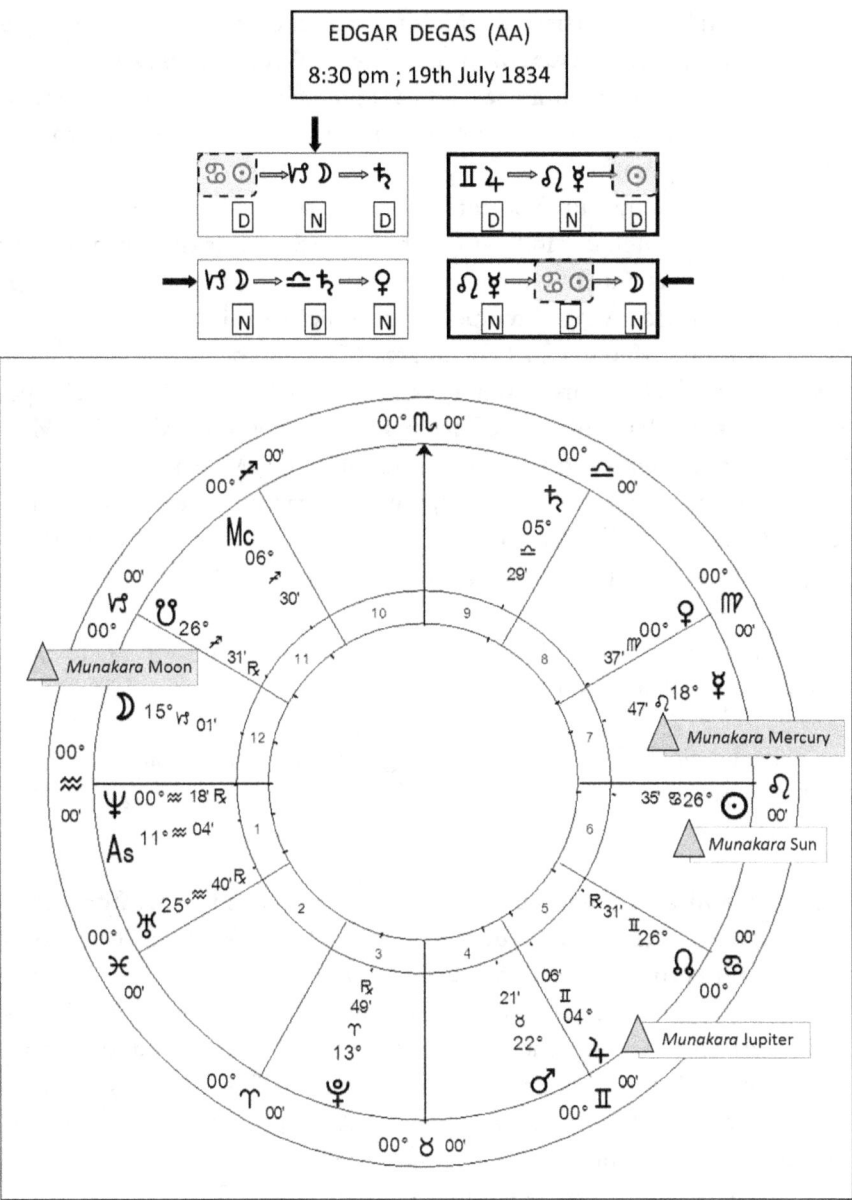

Fig. 10.7: Edgar Degas Natal Chart: Multiple Munakara Planets

Art dealer, Ambroise Vollard – his close friend and informal biographer – knew that Degas's admirers would not understand that the painter used rudeness and disdain to push others away, and that he was really a timid man who doubted his own artistic talent. It was common knowledge that Degas had poor eyesight (munakara Moon), and he would often pass associates and friends in the street, claiming he could not possibly recognise them because the daylight hurt his eyes, yet Volland says his sight was never a problem when criticising another's work, or gaining fine detail in his own art.

Degas' munakara Sun also interacts with two of his other planets in contention; Leo Mercury following behind the Sun, sees the Sun as its first dispositor, and as outcome planet for Gemini Jupiter in detriment. Degas had a reputation for being ill-tempered, and quick to fly into an uncontrolled rage (munakara Mercury in Leo squares Mars and opposes Uranus), but Vollard's recollections are about a man who was fond of his housekeeper Zoe, and more than tolerant of her many shortcomings. One day when Vollard commented on this saying "Did you know, Monsieur Degas, that most people think you very hot-tempered?" Degas answered, "I want them to think me so." and Vollard pursued, "But you really are good-hearted." Degas countered with "I don't wish to be good-hearted."[70]

"Do it again, ten times, a hundred times. Nothing in art must seem to be an accident, not even movement."[71]

"You must aim high, not in what you are going to do at some future date, but in what you are going to make yourself do today. Otherwise working is just a waste of time."[72]

Perfectionism is often seen as a Saturnian trait, and certainly meeting high standards one has set for oneself is part of Saturn's role as dispositor of Degas' Capricorn Moon, and the ruler of his Aquarian Ascendant. However, munakara Jupiter also has its issues with perfectionism, particularly in Degas' case where his Jupiter is joined by two other planets (Mercury and the Sun) in munakara. The desire to reach to the heavens and reproduce something only the gods would appreciate is somewhat blasphemous for mortal man to emulate, and may be one of the reasons the Renaissance painters were so obsessed with re-enacting religious themes in a visual form. The Jupiterian ideal can sometimes be so lofty that the ability to reach these heights and bring something to fruition can feel impossible, and Jupiter in Gemini keeps adjusting and fiddling so that the project does not reach completion, and the door is always open for more improvement. Reality can be too final, and then the individual has to deal with the gap between conception and

Chapter Ten • *Multiple Munakara Planets*

completion, or it may fall too short of the mind's expectations, and Jupiter's disappointment is crushing, and final in its extreme.

Degas's munakara Jupiter is the ruler of his 2nd house, and resides in the 5th house of creativity, and a major crisis for him was the commitment to pay his father's debts after his death (munakara Sun). In order to pay the debts Degas was forced to part with an extensive collection of art that he had initially inherited from his father (5th house is the personal wealth of my father – second from the 4th house). Both planets – Jupiter and Mercury are munakara – and Degas became increasingly embarrassed when prices asked for his art work, grew in proportion to the rise in his popularity, as he genuinely believed they were not worth the money, and that he did not have the talent of Delacroix or Ingres, two painters whom he idolised. He was a perfectionist, and he was always 'correcting' his work, or abandoning it because it did not meet his rigorous standards.

Jupiter rules Degas' Sagittarian Mid-heaven, and opposes it by tight degree, and his perfection did not stop with the painting itself. Degas insisted on choosing the frames of what he called his 'articles', and if a collector substituted his frame with a more expensive gold frame to increase its value, Degas would refund their money and take their picture back. This happened numerous times, even once when Degas arrived for a dinner party and saw his painting in an alien golden frame. He is alleged to have removed it from the frame with the aid of a coin, and returned home with it under his arm, all whilst his dinner patrons were waiting for him to return to the table. Degas had a mania for adding final touches to his pictures, even after they had left his studio and been sold. One collector friend was known to fasten one of his works he had purchased to the wall with chains, so Degas could not remove it, particularly after Degas had visited him once, and commented on the fact that the subject's foot 'needed just one more little touch.'[73]

Vollard mentions that it was a custom for Parisian artists of that period to show friendship and support for one another by exchanging their works, but that Degas would become enraged if he found his 'exchange' had been put up for sale by the reciprocating artist. To show his displeasure at their deceit, Degas would bundle up their gift to him, leave it on their doorstep and ignore them from that moment onwards.[74]

"Only when he no longer knows what he is doing does the painter do good things."[75]

Munakara Jupiter is in detriment in Degas's 5th house (ruled by munakara Mercury) and the painter is often described as a hater of children, women, dogs, cats, and flowers on a dinner table – and whilst the last one is true – Vollard, cites examples of children who were his friend, his politeness towards several women, and a number of occasions where he tolerated other people's domestic pets. In private he called ballet dancers 'the rats of the Opera' but he honoured them in his work, giving them poise, grace and beauty even in their resting poses. Vollard's book *Degas: An Intimate Portrait* was originally published ten years after Degas' death by Greenberg in 1927, and republished by Crown, New York in 1937. There are many critiques and explanations on Degas' style, his preferred mediums of oil, pastels and clay, and even discussions on the choice of his topics, but there is little written that talks about his sensitivity, or the many contradictions of his complex personality. Vollard's book is a fabulous insight into the private artist, and luckily, the book is available online and can be easily accessed through *Internet Archive*.[76]

"There is a kind of success that is indistinguishable from panic."[77]
– Edgar Degas

EXAMPLE THREE: NEIL DIAMOND
Four Planets in Contention
A Brief Biography

Neil Diamond (born January 24, 1941) is an American singer-songwriter. He began writing pop songs for other musicians and then launched a solo recording career that spanned more than five decades. He has sold more than 130 million records worldwide, making him one of the best-selling musicians of all time[78] He has had ten No. 1 singles on the US Billboard Hot 100 and thirty eight songs have reached the top 10 on the Billboard Adult Contemporary charts. He has also acted in films, making his screen debut in the 1980 musical drama film *The Jazz Singer*.

In 1972, Diamond performed for 20 consecutive nights at the Winter Garden Theater in New York City.[79] The theatre had not staged a one-man show since Al Jolson in the 1930s. It made Diamond the first rock-era star to headline on Broadway.

Diamond was inducted into the Songwriters Hall of Fame in 1984 and into the Rock and Roll Hall of Fame in 2011, and he received the Sammy

Chapter Ten • *Multiple Munakara Planets*

Cahn Lifetime Achievement Award in 2000. In 2011, he was an honouree at the Kennedy Center Honours, and he received the Grammy Lifetime Achievement Award in 2018.

In January 2018, Diamond announced that he would stop touring after he was diagnosed with Parkinson's disease. An announcement on his official website said he was not retiring from music and that the cancellation of the live performances would allow him to "continue his writing, recording and developments of new projects."[80] In April 2021, the *New York Times* reported that *A Beautiful Noise*, a musical based on Diamond's life and featuring his songs, would open in Boston in the summer of 2022. The musical opened on Broadway on December 4, 2022 and grossed more than $1 million at the box office in the week leading up to its Broadway premiere.[81]

> *"I have a love-hate relationship with song writing. I love it because it's so satisfying....when it works. I hate it because it forces you to dig inside yourself. It is without question the most difficult thing I do. Performing, on the other hand, is the most joyful and happiest thing I do. The bigger the audience the more anticipation, the more excitement."*[82] – Neil Diamond, 1977

> *"I am, I guess, a little over the top generally. I don't know if that's a good or bad thing but it's true. I'm a super-sensitive kind of person; I can be very emotional about things."*[83]

Neil Diamond has four planets in munakara. The Moon and nocturnal Mercury share the same sequence, but are not a duet, as they are in different signs belonging to Saturn. Venus, the lord of the Ascendant, is an integral part of his quartet of 'battlers', but it is not in munakara itself, because it is in mutual reception with Saturn.

Neil Diamond's statement in an interview in 2012 with Chrissie Iley from *The Telegraph* confirms his dilemma in finding a balance between solitude, and a lifetime spent writing and touring "50 years on the road" but separated from his family, "this drive has been cited as the reason for the break-up of his first and second marriages."[84]

One of Neil Diamond's first commercial successes, *Solitary Man*, was written in 1966, and was written about the lonely years when he was broke and spent much of his time alone, "I portrayed myself as a Solitary Man in the early part of my career because the writing process is a very solitary process, and that was my frame of mind. But as I grew up and learnt about myself, I've realised I like having people around."[85] Munakara Moon in Capricorn is in

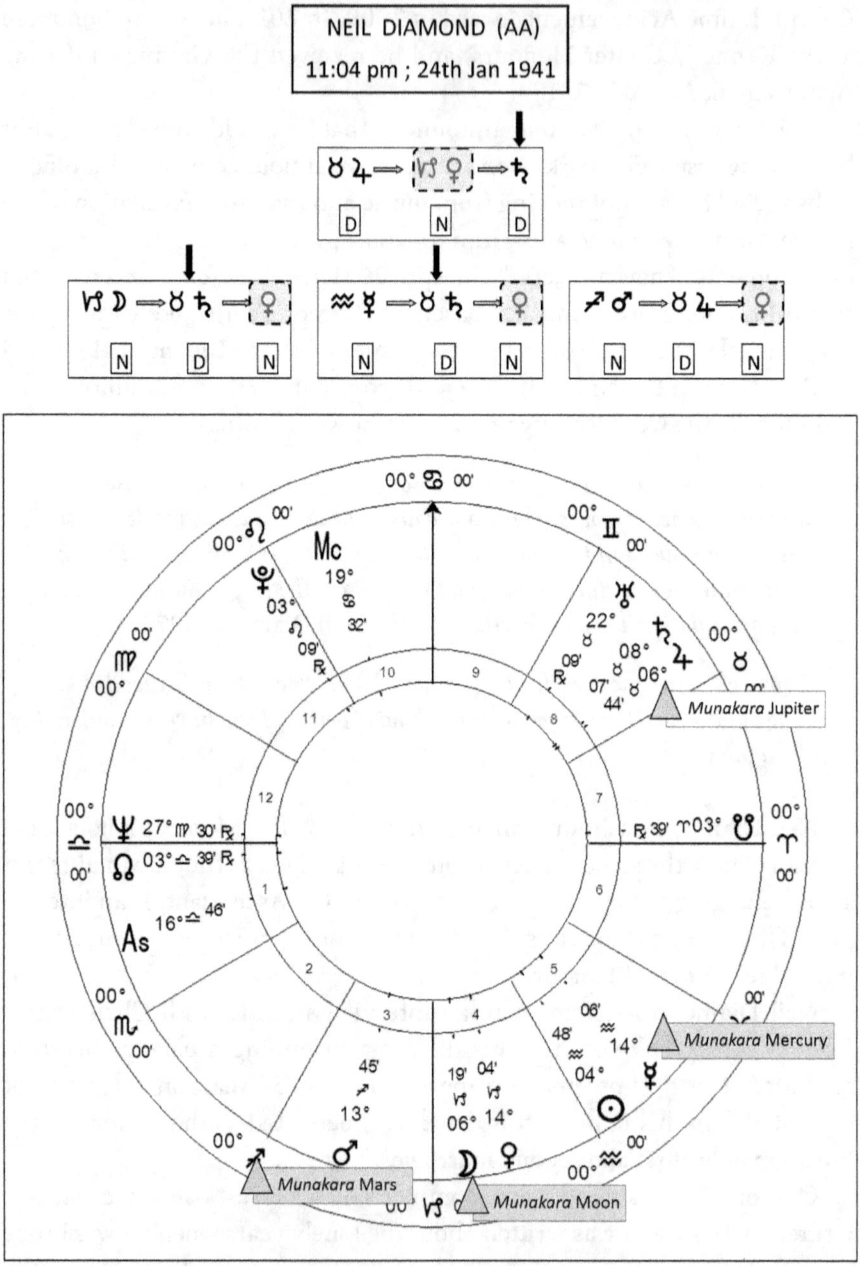

Munakara in Theory

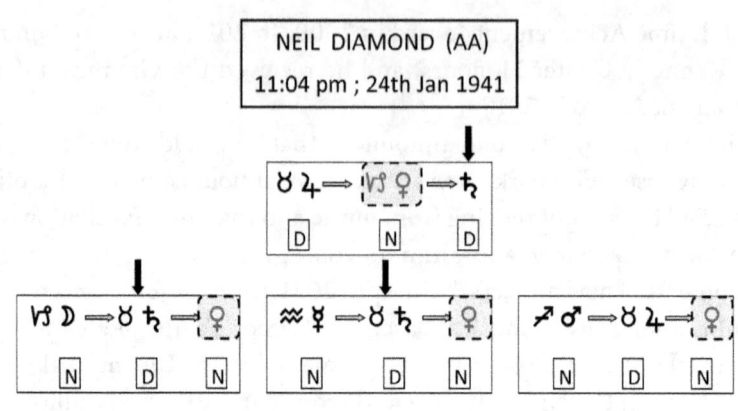

Fig. 10.8: Neil Diamond Natal Chart: Multiple Munakara Planets

Chapter Ten • *Multiple Munakara Planets*

detriment and is the ruler of Diamond's Mid-heaven. Venus is conjunct the Moon at the base of his chart and both planets trine munakara Jupiter and Saturn (present in three of Diamond's sequences). Even a so-called 'easy' aspect can accelerate feelings of sadness and loneliness. When Saturn plays such a dominant role as dispositor for the Moon and Mercury, and is the outcome planet for Jupiter then it will accentuate the pressure of not fitting in, or cause sensitivity to rejection and public ridicule.

In an interview from 2006 titled "Another Sad Lament"[86] Diamond spoke candidly about his battle with melancholy even whilst celebrating the surprising success of his latest album *12 Songs*. Munakara Mercury is in Aquarius, and squares its dispositor Saturn, and Mercury in contention may be responsible for a negative mindset, or issues with mental health. Saturn's placement alongside munakara Jupiter (Saturn is Jupiter's outcome planet), may also lend itself to difficult periods when life feels hard, or anxiety weighs down the mind.

Perhaps his melancholia was born from being a child embarrassed by his poor background, and Saturn ruling his home with Moon and Venus present in the 4th house. This may indicate why he says he felt he could never bring friends from school to his room above the butcher's shop where he remembers the sound of mousetraps setting off in the night would wake him. But also with munakara Moon's presence here, Diamond may not have wanted to share his private space with other children who might make negative comparisons to their own homes, or expose his humble dwelling to others at school. Diamond admits in the interview that his two hours on stage take him out of himself but that afterwards, "You have to come down. There's only one second between the wild adulation of your audience and the moment when you're entirely alone. It's a lonely kind of thing. They're two entirely different situations. In one, you're totally alone. In the other, you're social and extrovert and everything you ever wanted to be."[87]

Diamond acknowledges his melancholy has been present for a large percentage of his life, and says it has been a part of his nature, and he supposes he was 'born that way'. He was the black sheep of the family, a quiet kid in contrast to his parents who were very extroverted individuals. His interviewer asks him if his state of mind is getting better as he gets older, and Diamond's 2006 answer to the question is, "*It's pretty much the same. I've tried to deal with it, to get rid of it, but it's part of me at this point. I've accepted what I am. I'm content, but there's always a cloud that's hovering over me that threatens rain at any moment. When good things happen, I don't take them too seriously. I feel maybe they'll be taken away. I feel good about my career, but it hasn't changed what I am as a person. You're stuck with that old model. I don't fight it."*[88]

Diamond's Mercury in Aquarius is in contention, and has been part of his growing awareness that he really does enjoy, and need, the company of others. Moon in Capricorn also disposits to Saturn, and as much as the Moon closes down for emotional self-protection, his songs have universal appeal as they connect with those mourning a lost love, and listening to his songs is more likely to be a form of self-therapy and healing, than a joyous celebration of love.

Mars in Sagittarius rules Diamond's 7th house of partners and relationships, and also the 2nd house of finances, but it too is munakara, disposited by diurnal Jupiter, with Venus as its outcome planet. Diamond was married to his second wife, Marcia Murphey, for a quarter of a century, and he admits that he feels guilty about the years they spent apart. In 1996, when they divorced without lawyers' involvement, the media speculated that she received the biggest settlement in the history of divorce, but Diamond argues that the amount suggested was falsely exaggerated. "I told my former wife, 'Honey, I wish it were true. I'd love to give that to you.' But musicians don't make that kind of money. Businessmen and thieves make that kind of money."[89]

Munakara Mars sextiles Diamond's Ascendant, and also sextiles his Mercury in contention, and he has not always been so positive in his outlook on life. Mars and Mercury have different munakara journeys – Mars disposits to Jupiter and Mercury disposits to Saturn – but they seem to end up in similar places, as Jupiter and Saturn are in partile conjunction in Taurus, and Venus is the outcome planet for the three nocturnal planets, the Moon, Mercury, and Mars. Contention robs some of the optimism from Jupiter, as part of the issue in having to fight for something is not a natural impetus for Jupiter, a planet that expects to make gains with little effort rather than battle its way to good fortune, or claw its way to success in an undignified manner. Jupiter likes its privilege to come with ease and grace, not from years of sweat, tears and disappointment.

It seems surprising give the length and success of Neil Diamond's career, but he was not inducted into the Rock and Roll Hall of Fame until 2011, when at the age of 70, his peers decided that maybe he had contributed to the success of the music industry. In an interview held three years prior to the lateness of the event, Diamond admitted her was both hurt and puzzled by his omission. "It makes me wonder. I've paid my dues and I think I've done

Chapter Ten • *Multiple Munakara Planets*

good work. I'd like to be in there with my peers. Maybe I just have to keep doing it and hopefully I'll get in some day."[90]

For a musician who reinvented his career in 2006 at age 65, Neil Diamond has been treated as a bit of a joke around the music industry. His 2006 album *12 Songs*, was voted one of the best albums of that year, and praised by music critics as "the best work he has done in 30 years". Two years later, Diamond followed it up with the even more highly acclaimed album *Home Before Dark* in 2008, and he continued to capitalize on his revival with a sell-out concert at the Hollywood Bowl, seven years later in 2015. Yet his credibility as a serious musician, performer, and songwriter has been questioned over the years, and often, merely because he seems to be out of step with the times. In 1966 after *Solitary Man*, and a seven years apprenticeship writing songs that other artists snatched up, Diamond signed a recording deal, and arrived on the scene looking like Elvis, but ten years on from Elvis' prime popularity. In the Seventies when it was cool guys like Stevie Wonder, James Taylor, Barry White, Eric Clapton and Elton John that were the rage, for Neil Diamond it was gaudy shirts and copious amounts of chest hair. Jupiter in contention, alongside Saturn, just could not get the look right, but Diamond admits he needed the outlandish shirts, because they transformed him from shy young boy, to superhero of the stage: *"I have to have the uniform or I can't fly."*[91]

Diamond says that for better or worse, the shirts created an image in people's minds of what he was, rather than who he was. "My clothes designer started to make these fantastic shirts and they got more fantastic as time went on. We probably stayed with it too long. Then the shirts became a rebellion for me, a way of removing myself from a group that would not accept me anyway. It was, 'You don't like it? I'll take another dozen.'"[92]

Venus shines through as a ray of hope in all four of Diamond's sequences, whether it is first dispositor for diurnal Jupiter, or as outcome planet, because Jupiter and Saturn are both in Taurus. A much happier version of Neil Diamond has developed since 2012, when he married his third wife, Katie McNeil, saying in 2014, "My life with Katie has brought me a kind of satisfaction that I don't think I've ever experienced in my life."[93] His third marriage has certainly brought him joy, and hopefully lifted some of his melancholy, particularly if he now believes he is no longer travelling life's journey alone.

EXAMPLE FOUR: ROBIN WILLIAMS
Four Planets in Contention
A Brief Biography[94]

Robin Williams (21 July 1951 – 11 August 2014) was an American comedian and actor known for his manic stand-up routines and his diverse film performances. While undoubtedly a successful comedic actor, Williams was equally adept at more sober roles. Williams studied political science at Claremont Men's College, where he began taking courses in improvisation. He then attended the College of Marin to study acting but later received a scholarship to study at the Juilliard School in New York City. Williams eventually moved back to California, where he began appearing in comedy clubs in the early 1970s. After guest appearances as the alien Mork on *Happy Days*, Williams was given his own show, *Mork & Mindy* (1978–82). The series offered Williams the opportunity to transfer the enthusiasm of his stand-up performances to the small screen and provided an outlet for his prolific improvisational talents. *Mork & Mindy* proved an immense success and was instrumental in launching William's film career.

As his career progressed, Williams continued to take both comedic and serious roles. In just a few of his dramatic roles Williams played a distressed former professor in *The Fisher King* (1991) and a psychiatrist who mentors a troubled but mathematically gifted young man in *Good Will Hunting* (1997) for which he won an Academy Award for his role. He starred as a doctor who attempts to heal his patients with laughter in *Patch Adams* (1998) and portrayed a psychotic photo-lab technician who stalks a suburban family in *One Hour Photo* (2002).

A 2002 stand-up performance led to the hugely successful *Robin Williams: Live on Broadway* (2002), which was released as both an album and a video. Williams was sidelined with heart problems in early 2009, but he returned to work shortly thereafter, promoting his films and resuming his Weapons of Self-Destruction comedy tour.

Williams was active with a number of charities, including Comic Relief and the Christopher and Dana Reeve Foundation, an organization founded by his lifelong friend, dedicated to curing spinal cord injury. During his career, Williams suffered from substance abuse and instances of severe depression. He was found dead at his California home in August 2014, at age 63.

In 2018 HBO Documentary Films produced a film by Marina Zenovich, titled *Robin Williams: Come Inside My Mind*.[95] The film is almost two hours

Chapter Ten • *Multiple Munakara Planets*

in duration and dips in and out of different time periods in Williams' life. Much of the commentary in the film is voice-overs from the past, and the hundreds of interviews and stand up routines performed by Robin Williams. The film is readily available online, and is a treat for anyone wanting to revisit the absolute manic joy that is Robin Williams.

> *"Everyone you meet is fighting a battle you know nothing about. Be kind. Always."*[96]

Williams has four planets in munakara, two of which are diurnal, and two that belong to the nocturnal sect division. Cancer Sun and Saturn in Virgo are his two diurnal planets, and both can show discord with the father, or some difficulty as a result of father's behaviour. As an only child whose family moved regularly to accommodate his father's work, Williams was often alone and friendless during his childhood. Williams once said, *"My father's laughter introduced me to the comedy of Jonathon Winters. My dad was a sweet man, but he was not an easy laugh."*[97]

Sun in Cancer is involved in three of the four munakara sequences – as a munakara planet, as a first dispositor for his nocturnal Mercury, and as the outcome planet for Saturn. His birth time places munakara Sun at the top of his chart, and Leo is his tenth sign for a Scorpio rising chart. However, it is munakara Mercury (conjunct Pluto) that sits on Robin Williams's MC.

> *"My childhood was lonely. Both my parents were away a lot, working, and the maid basically raised me. And I think that's where a lot of my comedy comes from. Not only was the maid very funny and witty, but when my mother came home I'd use humor to try and get her attention. If I made mommy laugh, then maybe everything would be all right. I think that's where it started."*[98]

The two diurnal planets (Sun and Saturn) in munakara are in a sextile aspect, and usually there is an expectation that a 'tame' aspect like this will not cause distress for the individual. But when Saturn and the Sun are both munakara – and rule the 4th- and 10th-house axis – then any contact between the two planets in contention can jog painful memories or activate negative connotations of their contact with one another, Sun to Saturn aspects activate feelings of isolation, loneliness, fears of failure, or insecurities about the person's identity or their value to the community. It seems Williams was not immune to these feelings which may have stemmed from an unhappy childhood.

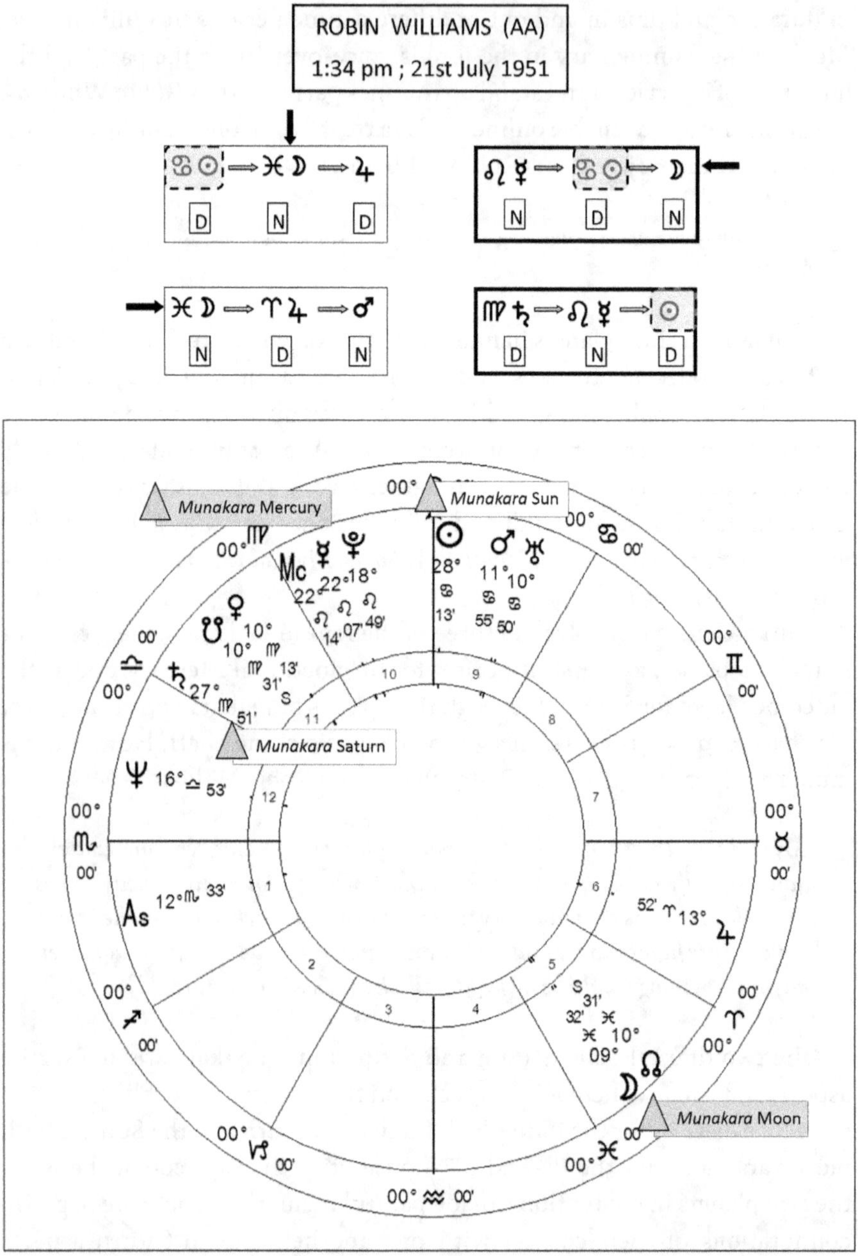

Munakara in Theory

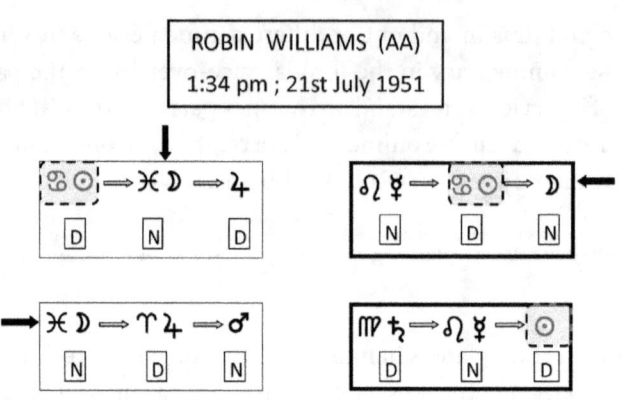

Fig. 10.9: Robin Williams Natal Chart: Multiple Munakara Planets

Chapter Ten • *Multiple Munakara Planets*

Two sequences are bolded in *Fig. 10.9* to draw attention to the fact that all three planets in Saturn (Saturn, Mercury, and Sun) and Mercury's (Mercury, Sun, and Moon) munakara sequence are munakara themselves, and this factor has significant impact in calling out the two most difficult sequences in Williams's munakara foursome.

> *"The imagination functions on its own. I grew up as an only child, so the imagination was a necessity, like a survival mechanism."*[99]

Mercury in contention is the culminating planet at the same degree as Williams' Mid-heaven and Pluto's presence adds to his genius. Williams' chart has a nocturnal Mercury in Leo, disposited by the Sun, but still connected to Saturn as Saturn is in Mercury's sign of Virgo. For Williams imagination and depression went hand in hand and his brilliant mind had little respite or tranquillity when Pluto took degrees next to munakara Mercury in Leo and Jupiter in Aries formed a volatile trine to the same planet. Fame and notoriety plagued nocturnal Mercury on the MC (totally out of sect) as his fans and the public expected Williams's zaniness to always be on tap. *"....People use (cocaine) to relieve the pressure, and for me it was about getting numb and forgetting. I did coke so I wouldn't have to talk to anyone. For me it was a true sedative, a way to pull back from the world."*[100]

Frenetic Mars (disposited by munakara Moon) conjuncts Uranus, with Mars (the Ascendant ruler) trining 12 Scorpio, and munakara Moon bringing in the third water sign at 9 Pisces. Whilst Mars itself is not munakara, it is the Moon's outcome planet, and Williams's struggles with cocaine addiction came early in his career, as he never sought to hide his depression and alcoholism from his fan base. Williams' honesty in creating routines around his addictions created a safe place for others to cope with their own, and to bring humour to a humourless and distressing topic.

Similar to the Cancer Sun, Williams' Moon also takes all three positions in munakara sequences – as first planet it is in contention, as first dispositor for Cancer Sun, and as outcome planet for nocturnal Mercury in Leo – makes his final two years a heartbreaking outcome, for a man who gave willingly, and lovingly to others. His Moon is closely aligned with the Nodal axis and the opposition to Venus in fall says much about the dilemma between his need to be private (Venus rules 12th house) and his desire to be loved and accepted when Venus rules his 7th house of relationships with 'others'. Many of his one-liners revealed so much truth about this man, so when Venus is disposited by his munakara Mercury and he says, "The truth is, if anything, I'm probably addicted to laughter."[101] you know you are hearing a planet in contention express itself.

Many tributes to this amazing comedian and decent human being speak of Williams' desire to serve others, and this seems to be a common thread when both luminaries are in contention. Sun and Moon in munakara brings the overwhelming need to sacrifice one's own emotions or personality to relieve the suffering of others. But to then feel threatened (or consumed) by the collective's demands to constantly meet their needs. Robin's Saturn in Virgo is also munakara so keeping clear or protective boundaries are something that he struggled with throughout his adult life. His prominent nocturnal Mercury on the MC must play two roles – that of a munakara planet, and also as a first dispositor for Saturn – so his story becomes even more poignant when Robin Williams lost control over his incredible brain as it began to disintegrate from Lewy body disease (LBD).

Robin's Wish: *"I just want to help people to be less afraid."*[102]

Robin's Wish[103] is a 2020 documentary on Robin Williams produced by Tylor Norwood, titled *Robin's Wish*, and concentrates specifically on the last two years of Robin's life and his battle to understand what was happening to him. Norwood's documentary is the story of a man whose mind is not only collapsing, but a man who possesses the will-power, strength and self-sacrifice, to hide it from his family, his friends, and his colleagues, in order to spare them distress, and is a story of selfishness and deep compassion for others.

Robin's Wish is also the story of his four munakara planets, and I would suggest a couple of viewings are necessary in order to comprehend the complicated nature of multiple planets in contention. Another YouTube viewing I would recommend is Tylor Norwood's hour-long interview with Matthew Sherwood, host of Factual America Podcast on November 10, 2020.[104] Norwood talks about his interviews with seventeen people who witnessed Williams' mental and physical decline, and yet who protected his privacy from the rest of the world because they loved him, and could see that he was suffering.

His third wife, Susan Schneider Williams, wrote an open letter in late 2016 in the medical journal *Neurology*[105] as an honest appraisal of her experience as Williams' carer at the end of his life. The article is titled *The terrorist inside my husband's brain,* and is worth taking the time to read the article, if only to comprehend the impact of LBD on Williams during the last two years of his life. Robin Williams filled so many lives with joy and there are countless examples of his humility, kindness and compassion. There are so many wonderful observations, and truthful moments that he shared with others. I have chosen just a few Robin Williams's quotes that I believe cut to the heart of his four planets in munakara, and as nocturnal Mercury is one of Williams' planets in contention, it seems fitting that he expresses his thoughts in his own words.

Robin Williams Quotes[106]

"Life's a tragedy to those who feel and a comedy to those who think. So it can be a curse in that you find something funny in even the darkest thing."

"It's amazing that medical science can develop a drug to give you an erection, but can't develop a drug to give you mental clarity."

"I think the saddest people always try their hardest to make people happy because they know what it's like to feel absolutely worthless and they don't want anyone else to feel that."

"I used to think that the worse thing in life was to end up alone. It's not. The worse thing in life is to end up with people who make you feel alone."

"I don't know how much value I have in this universe, but I do know that I've made a few people happier than they would have been without me, and as long as I know that, I'm as rich as I ever need to be."

"You're only given a little spark of madness. If you lose that, you're nothing."

EXAMPLE FIVE: AMY WINEHOUSE

Four Planets in Contention

A Brief Biography[107]

Amy Winehouse (14 September 1983 – 23 July 2011) was an English singer-songwriter who skyrocketed to fame after the release of her critically acclaimed multiple Grammy Award-winning album *Back to Black* (2006). However, her tempestuous love life and substance abuse stalled her recording career even as they made her a favourite subject of tabloid journalism. Winehouse was born in north London to a Jewish family. She and her elder brother, Alex, were raised primarily by their mother, a pharmacist, who divorced their father, when Winehouse was 9 years old. At the prestigious BRIT School (a school for the performing and creative arts), Winehouse showed ability as an actor as well as a singer, and by age 16 she was performing with jazz groups.

On her critically acclaimed debut album, *Frank* (2003), Winehouse proved herself to be a shrewd, caustic lyricist, and her smoky, evocative vocals drew comparisons to jazz and rhythm-and-blues legends Sarah Vaughan, Dinah Washington, and Billie Holiday. Yet Winehouse was vocal about her dislike for the album, telling *The Guardian* that she did not even own a copy of it herself.

A series of tumultuous romances followed for Winehouse, none more fevered than her on-again, off-again relationship with Blake Fielder-Civil, about whom many of the heartbreak songs on her next album, *Back to Black*, were written. The album was honoured at the 2008 Grammys with five awards. In November 2008 Winehouse was named Best Selling Pop/Rock Female at the World Music Awards. An *Entertainment Weekly* reviewer wrote of the album, "It's precisely Winehouse's lyrics – smartass, aching, flirty, and often straight-up nasty – that raise this expertly crafted set into the realm of true, of-the-minute originality."[108]

After marrying Fielder-Civil in May 2007, Winehouse began behaving increasingly erratically and cancelling shows. Despite Winehouse's many troubles, her remarkable musical talent was regarded as undeniable by fans and critics alike. However, her life seemed to continue to spin out of control. Although she entered rehab, she did not remain long, and reports of substance abuse continued to follow her. In July 2009 she and Fielder-Civil divorced. Two years later Winehouse attempted a comeback tour, but it was cancelled after the singer appeared to be intoxicated at the opening concert. Her very public slide into personal chaos – marked by dramatic weight loss (Winehouse struggled with bulimia), drunken performances, an arrest in Norway for marijuana possession, and the incarceration of Fielder-Civil after a bar fight – ended in her death from alcohol poisoning in July 2011.

"*I don't regret anything.*"[109] – Amy Winehouse

Amy Winehouse (1983–2011) burst onto the UK charts at the beginning of the last millennium, heralded as one of the UK's premier singers during the early 2000s, with the release of her debut album *Frank* in 2003 in homage to her (and her father's) idol Frank Sinatra. Amy was like a burning comet,

Chapter Ten • *Multiple Munakara Planets*

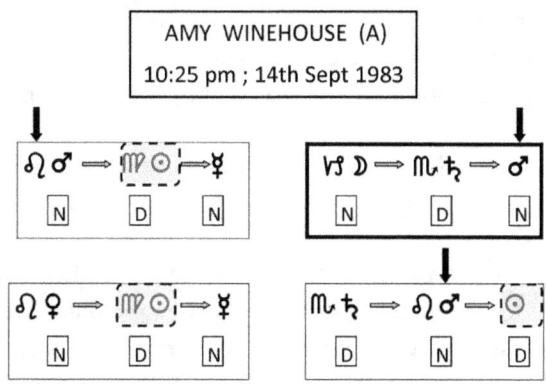

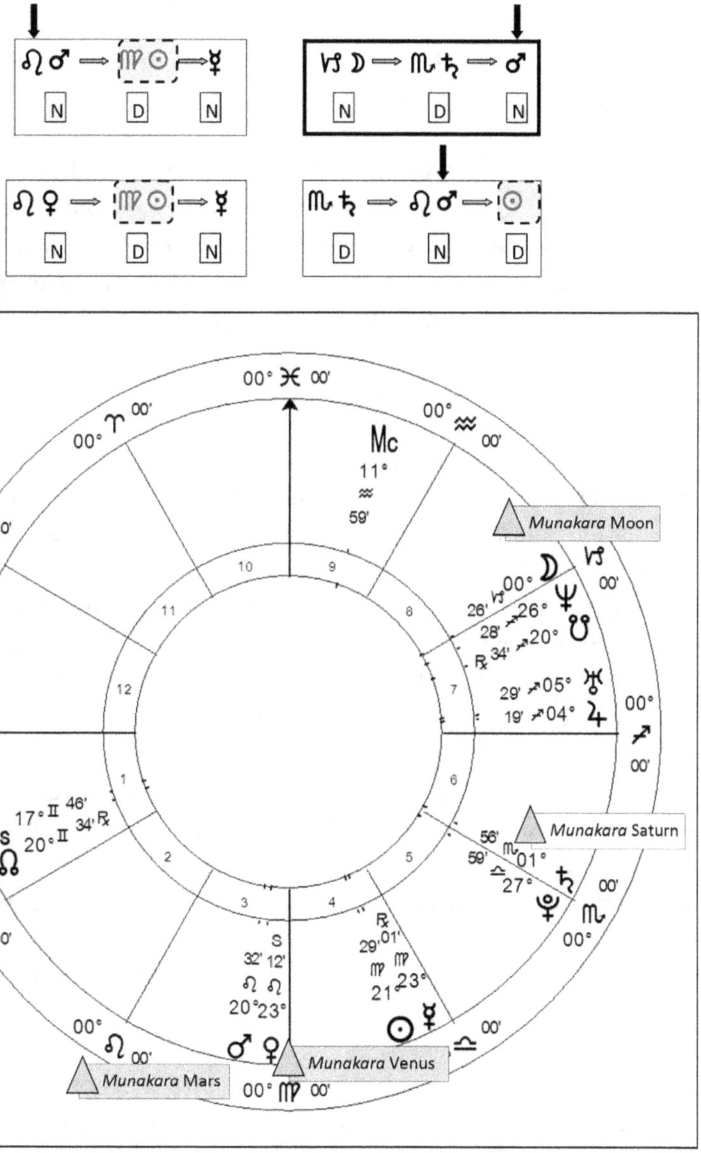

Fig. 10.10: Amy Winehouse Natal Chart: Multiple Munakara Planets

famous for delivering dynamic and brilliant performances when she was switched on, but towards the end of 2000's first decade, the comet had become self-destructive, and tragically burnt itself out by the beginning of the second.

> *"I don't think your ability to fight has anything to do with how big you are. It's to do with how much anger is in you."*[110]

Winehouse's Mars in Leo features in three of her four munakara sequences – it is first planet, dispositor for Saturn and outcome planet for the Moon – and whilst she dreamed of fame and fortune as a teenager attending Sylvia Young Theatre School, the constant badgering she received from the press added to her feelings of being trapped within a virtual goldfish bowl.

> *"I feel love is somehow killing me."*[111] – Amy Winehouse

Mars and Venus are always a volatile combination when in close proximity to one another and their conjunction (plus a munakara duet) was likely to produce both great disharmony, and a dynamic flow of creativity to this chart.

Unfortunately, Mars and Venus's natural state of animosity through their signs' rulerships makes for an extremely uncomfortable combination, especially for Venus, a planet that struggles to deal with the antagonistic qualities of Mars. This discomfort moves to a whole new level of hostility when both nocturnal planets find themselves yoked together in a state of contention.

Maintaining healthy relationships is always hard work, but when the astrological archetypes for male and female psyche are in contention, the individual (in this case, Amy Winehouse) battles to establish strong boundaries between self-love (Venus), ambition (Mars), and infatuation with a potentially dangerous partner (Venus/Mars combination). Winehouse was ill-equipped to deal with the destructive and violent forces that drove her passionate infatuation for Blake Fielder-Civil, who introduced her to hard drugs such as crack cocaine and heroin.[112] Winehouse's Capricorn Moon is munakara and Mars as the Moon's outcome planet shows the level of despair Winehouse suffered when Fielder-Civil, in his words, "set her free"[113] and filed for divorce after two years of marriage. She spiralled into a world of alcohol and drug abuse to relieve her pain despite the fact that Fielder-Civil was serving a prison term for a year during their marriage when he was convicted of assaulting a bar owner.

Chapter Ten • *Multiple Munakara Planets*

Part of Amy's pull towards the charismatic Blake was grounded in her desperation to be noticed and praised by her father, Mitchell Winehouse. Amy often described herself as "Daddy's Girl" and even sported a tattoo on her left shoulder with these same words. But, Mitch's manipulation, and his control over his daughter during her successful years,[114] is rooted in poisoned soil as Amy constantly relived her feelings of being deserted by him as a nine-year-old child, and was terrified of losing him again, as she had when her parents divorced.

Virgo Sun is the dispositor for Amy's munakara duet of Mars and Venus, and Mercury in Virgo is the outcome planet for the Sun. Sun and Mercury in Virgo lie in Amy's 4th house, the house of father, and Amy tried constantly to receive Mitch's approval, but perhaps he was incapable of providing Amy with the reassurance and the protection she so desperately needed to feel safe, and to feel good about herself. The documentary film *Amy* released in 2015 portrays Mitch Winehouse as greedy and uncaring and in one interview he is asked if he loved the attention he gained from being Amy's father to which he answers, "Yeah, right, well, they should have been there to see how enjoyable it was having fights with drug dealers. No, it was not enjoyable."[115]

Amy's initial break up with Blake in 2006 generated the necessary angst and heartbreak to provide the creative material on her second and final studio album *Back to Black*. The title song describing Amy's misery when Blake left her to return to an ex-lover. Throughout the album the songs explore themes of guilt, grief, infidelity and trauma in a relationship – in short, all perfect fodder for her four planets – Moon, Saturn, Mars and Venus – in a state of munakara. Amy's lyrics were clever, relatable and modern, and the combination of her soulful voice with emotion-charged words highlighted the conjunction of Virgo Sun and Mercury in a powerful gambit and resulted in the release of five singles from the album which gained instant commercial success.

The sequence for Amy Winehouse's Moon has been bolded because the Moon's dispositor Saturn is munakara, as is the Moon's outcome planet, Mars. In some ways, above all else, this singular munakara sequence indicates a battle which exacerbates the most painful issues in her short life. Three munakara planets tied together in sequence is likely to increase the ability to obsess over the areas that the first planet, the Moon, has jurisdiction: areas such as care and maintenance of the body, emotional stability, and the security that emotional and physical needs will be met.

Triple munakara planets – two of which are first and second dispositors – are likely to respond by focusing on not just how the planet meets the individual's needs represented by that planet, but also to catastrophize when these needs are not met.

For this reason, Winehouse's munakara Capricorn Moon in detriment becomes more inflamed as her physical and emotional state deteriorate through her obsession with of Blake Fielder-Civil, and the addictions she shared with her husband. Their divorce in 2009 did not galvanize Amy to pull herself back from the brink of self-destruction, or create a new healthier lifestyle, by curbing her drinking or by dealing with her bulimia, which saw her body diminishing and becoming more skeletal with each public appearance. Munakara Saturn's role as the Moon's dispositor, did not helped Amy to remove herself from the past, or move forwards to learn the art of self-appreciation and emotional independence. But this is not surprising given that Saturn is the fourth planet in Amy's chart which is in munakara status.

"I don't write music when I'm happy...I write music when I've got nothing."
– Amy Winehouse

Munakara Mars is the Moon's outcome planet and its duet with Venus is a reminder that no matter how creative and unique Winehouse's talents were, she could never find self-love, self-esteem or self-protection through the outlet of her considerable artistic abilities.

In an interview two years after Amy's death in June 2011, her older brother Alex said, "She suffered from bulimia very badly. That's not, like, a revelation – you knew just by looking at her...She would have died eventually, the way she was going, but what really killed her was the bulimia...I think that it left her weaker and more susceptible. Had she not had an eating disorder, she would have been physically stronger."[116]

The reasons behind eating disorders are complex and diverse, but the outcome is a denial of the body, as nourishment is withheld through purging or fasting, and Amy's body – and her munakara Moon – could not cope with her bulimia in combination with excessive alcohol consumption. Amy was warned by doctors that she needed to take better care of herself, but her battles went way beyond physical comfort, or concerns over her body shape and weight, and seemed more about punishing her body, than stretching its limits through substance abuse.

Chapter Ten • *Multiple Munakara Planets*

Moon in detriment is never easy, given that it is the planet that signifies emotional strength and stability, as well as a healthy discipline over the physical body. In Amy's case, Saturn is also munakara, and therefore, has its own battles to contend with: battles such as learning integrity, self-reliance, responsibility for one's actions, and the ability to draw boundaries and maintain them for honour and self-respect. Being overwhelmed by guilt or self-loathing does little to improve the situation, or to make inroads towards less destructive habits. Amy's song "Rehab" is one of her catchiest tunes, but the lyrics are an echo of Saturn in contention when it comes to being controlled by others, or trusting others to solve problems that are beyond the individual's capacity. Saturn in Scorpio disposits to Amy's Mars, and both malefic planets are constantly in a state of separation, conflict and denial when they are dealing with their worst munakara moments.

Amy's munakara Moon also incorporates Amy's relationship with her mother, Janis Winehouse, and a Moon in contention can show mother's battles as well one's own difficulties with the Moon. Janis was diagnosed with multiple sclerosis (MS) a year after her son Alex was born in 1979. She was counselled by doctors to not strain her body through another pregnancy for the sake of her health, but Janis ignored their advice, and Amy was born three years later in 1983. It would be another twenty years before the disease became pronounced in 2003, after a viral infection hospitalized Janis and the resulting MRI exam found lesions on her brain. Amy's distress for her mother, or perhaps her awareness of her mother's MS history prior to her birth, would have added to Amy's feelings of guilt. That, plus her father's abandonment of her mother to live with his girlfriend, added to Amy's desperation to hold onto Blake, and she was determined that she would not repeat the pattern of her mother's failed marriage.

Amy Winehouse was out of sync with the world in so many ways. Her most beloved music genre belonged to the era of Tony Bennett and Frank Sinatra, and she would have been much happier crooning in a dark bar and getting paid in drinks for the night. Like her fellow Club 27 member, Kurt Cobain, Amy had longer to be famous, but both she and Kurt realized too late that they loved the music far more than they loved the attention. Both were shy introverted people in private, but the world in which they moved expected the same behaviour from them off the stage as when they were in entertainment mode. That meant drugs and alcohol were necessary to morph the shyness into loud, fun party goers and to cover deep insecurities they shared about their bodies and their musical talent. Both members of the tragic

27 Club fostered disastrous relationships with partners just as destructive as themselves – Courtney for Kurt and Blake for Amy – partners who could not supply them with the steadiness and love they so desperately needed to drive away their despair or provide them with a sense of self-worth.

> "I really thought I was on the way out. My husband Blake saved my life. Often I don't know what I do, then the next day the memory returns. And then I am engulfed in shame."[117]

Munakara Multiples: Five Planets in Contention

EXAMPLE ONE: CHRISTOPHER McCANDLESS

Five Planets in Contention

A Brief Biography[118]

Christopher McCandless (12 February 1968 – 6 September 1992) was an American adventurer who died from starvation and possibly poisoning, at age 24, while camping alone on a remote trail in Alaska. His death made him a figure of controversy, admired by some as an idealist but disparaged by others as self-destructive. His father was an aerospace engineer who – in partnership with his second wife, Christopher's mother – became a successful entrepreneur. Soon after receiving his bachelor's degree in May 1990, McCandless donated his savings to a charity, cut off communication with his family, and drove to Arizona, where his car was disabled by flash flood in the vicinity of Lake Mead.

For the next two years McCandless travelled widely in the western United States as a self-styled tramp finally reaching Fairbanks via the Alaska Highway on April 25, 1992. Three days later he hitchhiked a ride southwest to the Stampede Trail in Alaska. McCandless's original plan was to hike westward to the Bering Sea, but he ended up sheltering in an abandoned bus – Fairbanks City bus #142 – on the little-travelled trail. Forced to live on a substandard diet McCandless weakened and died in mid-August 1992. His body, which weighed only 67 pounds (30.4 kg), was discovered by hunters on September 6, 1992. The cause of death was officially reported as starvation.

> "The very basic core of a man's living spirit is his passion for adventure. The joy of life comes from our encounters with new experiences, and hence there is no greater joy than to have an endlessly changing horizon, for each day to have a

Chapter Ten • *Multiple Munakara Planets*

new and different sun." – Christopher McCandless, last letter to his friend 'Ron Franz', April 1992, *Into the Wild*, p.58

Christopher McCandless's name may not be instantly recognizable, but his story is, and most people have either read the book *Into the Wild* (1996) by Jon Krakauer, or watched the 2007 movie adaptation directed by Sean Penn. The book has been listed on high school curriculums in the US for years, perhaps as a lesson in the dangers of living your dreams unconditionally, and in the process, alienating yourself from loved ones and society.

All five munakara sequences are rotations of planets that are also in contention. His Leo Moon and Aquarian Sun are not in munakara, nor do they play in part in his five-planet sequences. Nocturnal Mercury and Venus are not conjunct, but they are both in signs belonging to Saturn and have identical munakara sequences. Munakara Mars (their outcome planet) opposes the Uranus Pluto conjunction present in the charts of those born in the late 1960s, and Mars is the first dispositor for Saturn.

Both diurnal planets, Jupiter and Saturn, are in signs of debility: Jupiter is in detriment in Virgo, and Saturn is in fall in Aries. As luck would have it, they are each other's outcome planet – this fact gives little comfort that events triggered by the last planet in the sequence with augment well for both planets in debility. Together, Jupiter and Saturn rule difficult houses; Saturn rules Chris' 6th house where the nocturnal Venus in munakara resides, whilst Jupiter rules the dark house of the 8th, where nocturnal Mars in munakara resides by Whole Sign.

As can be expected from five intensely integrated munakara sequences, opinion was deeply divided when details of Chris McCandless' Alaskan escapade were released to the public. Hunters and residents of Alaska judged his actions foolhardy and dangerous and viewed his death as the inevitable result of the actions of an ill-equipped, ignorant, and overly confident youth. Whether acting on poor advice or making the choice himself, McCandless foolishly entered untamed territory without a compass or proper navigational map, with no axe, and carrying only a light-bore rifle and a ten-pound bag of rice. In response to this criticism, author Jon Krakauer points out that in fact, Chris did survive 112 days fending for himself in the wild, and that it was only a couple of terrible mistakes in the end that led to his demise.

For instance, McCandless falsely believed that he could leave the wildness whenever he chose to move on with his travels. This belief was based on conviction rather than sound knowledge of his environment and the dangers

Munakara in Theory

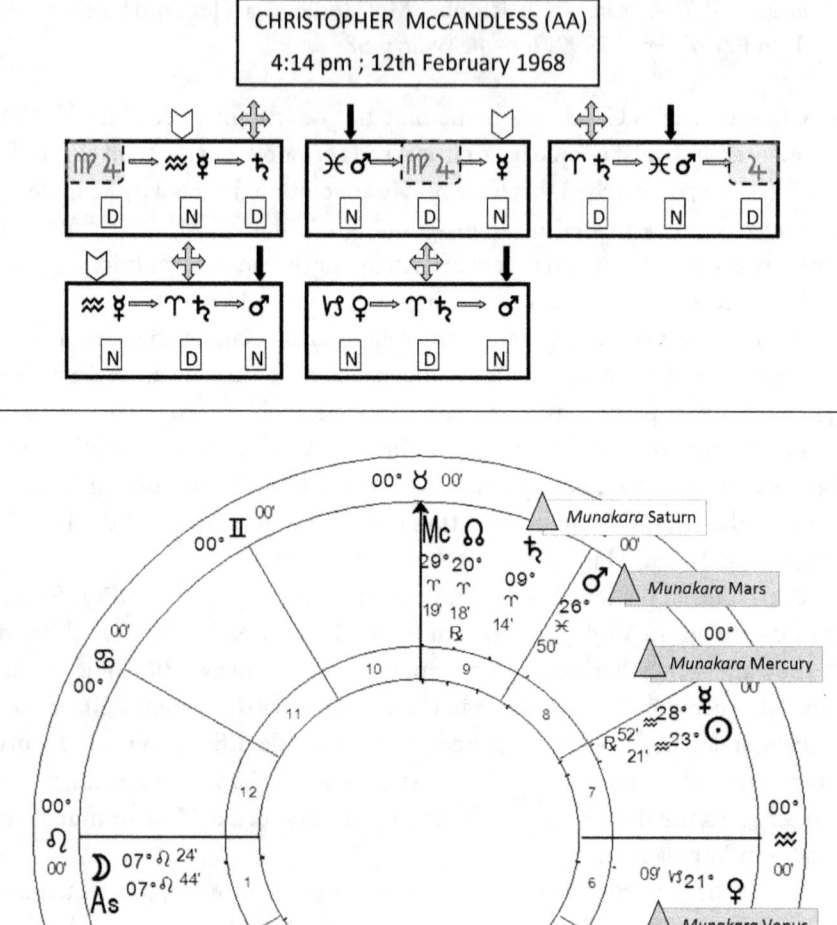

Fig. 10.11: *Christopher McCandless Natal Chart: Multiple Munakara Planets*

Chapter Ten • *Multiple Munakara Planets*

that it could pose for someone as inexperienced as himself. McCandless had originally waded through the Teklanika River at the end of April to follow the Stampede Trail, but it had allegedly become a raging torrent in the late-summer runoff and was swollen with rain and snowmelt from glaciers high in the Alaskan Ranges.

But even this fact has been called into question as Alaskan journalist Craig Medred wrote in 2016: "Krakauer (biographer, *Into the Wild*) claims McCandless 'noted in his journal that it rained for a week straight.' The journal contains no such note. Krakauer claimed it was this period of rain that caused flooding and prevented McCandless from crossing the Teklanika River and walking to safety. Weather records for nearby Denali National Park and Preserve show no heavy rains for what Krakauer specifies as the period of time in question."[119]

According to Krakauer McCandless decided that his one option was to retrace his steps and spend the next few weeks in the bus, foraging as he had done during the previous months, and waiting for the water to subside for a safe crossing. In his journal he wrote "Disaster... Rained in. River looks impossible. Lonely, scared."[120]

Had McCandless carried a topographical map of the region he would have seen that just half a mile (800 m) downstream was a hand-operated cable car that could have carried him safely across the river, swollen or not, and he could have been on his way out of the wilderness.[121] Instead he returned to the bus, posting the following message in the vain hope that someone would venture past and save him:

> *Attention Possible Visitors. S.O.S. I need your help. I am injured, near death, and too weak to hike out. I am all alone, this is no joke. In the name of God, please remain to save me. I am out collecting berries close by and shall return this evening.*
>
> *Thank you, Chris McCandless. August?*[122]

Mercury, Mars, and Venus are his three nocturnal planets in munakara. Mercury and Venus share the same munakara sequence involving Saturn and Mars, and Mars's sequence ends with Mercury. All three nocturnal planets form aspects to Neptune and it is interesting to note that when McCandless started a journal of his adventures he began by writing in the third person, always referring to himself as 'Alex', continuing this practice throughout the journal's use until his death. On the first page he wrote: *"No longer would he* answer to Chris McCandless: he was now Alexander Super-tramp, master of his own destiny."[123]

For instance, when he crossed into Mexico by paddling through the Morelos Dam's open floodgates and shooting down the spillways below, he writes in his journal "Alex looks quickly round for signs of trouble." Or "Canals break off in a multitude of directions. Alex is dumbfounded...Alex is crushed." and later when he is shown a route through the canals, "Alex is overjoyed and hope bursts back into his heart."[124] It is as though McCandless distances himself from his adventures through the contact with Neptune by making his alter ego 'Alex Super-tramp' the hero of his story. Perhaps this was his self-protection against five extreme and passionate munakara planets that constantly challenge 'Alex' (and leave Chris in peace), who in hero mode, bravely conquers all obstacles and grows stronger and more confident with each new experience. It is noteworthy that McCandless's final plea for rescue posted on the 142 bus was not signed 'Alex' but rather, signed in his own name, perhaps in a lucid moment when he realized that his alter ego would not save him this last time.

Munakara Jupiter opposes its dispositor Mercury with a three degree orb, but Mercury's late position in Aquarius takes its journey from Saturn to Mars. Most of these planets have issues with their end-product planet, ranging from discomfort to outright hostility, and these may give clues as to why this particular young man became a projection of youth at the end of the last century. His rejection of a life mapped out for him by parents, schooling, and society is the impetus for his journey across America, and in many ways, it outlined Western youth's desperate loss of identity, and their disillusionment and rage at society's inability to provide them with a sense of purpose.

McCandless was an intelligent and articulate young man, but he burned with indignant and somewhat self-righteous rage. Pisces Mars disposits to munakara Jupiter and for many in society who judged him, he was a selfish, ungrateful brat (Mars) who turned his back on loving and supportive parents (Jupiter). However, the true story – like his munakara planets – is far more complicated. Munakara Mars rules Chris' 4th house, and his relationship with his father, Walt, was strained. Krakauer says, "Both father and son were stubborn and high-strung. Given Walt's need to exert control (munakara Saturn) and Chris' extravagantly independent nature (munakara Jupiter), polarization was inevitable."[125]

In 1986, four years before he disappeared, Chris drove down to his old neighbourhood during his summer holidays, hoping to visit some old friends

Chapter Ten • *Multiple Munakara Planets*

from his childhood. Instead he discovered secrets about his father's past and any respect he had for Walt was completely destroyed. Chris had believed that Walt's second marriage to his mother, Billie, was a happy marriage when he was born as the first child of their union. But Walt had continued his first marriage and unknown to his two wives, had secretly maintained both households (munakara Mars trine Neptune, munakara Mercury square Neptune in 4th house). Two years after Chris was born Walt fathered a son by his first wife Marcia, and eventually Walt's double life came to light with the second family (Walt, Billie, Chris and Carine) forced to leave the district to escape the scandal.

In 2015, more than twenty years after Chris' death, his sister Carine wrote a book titled *The Wild Truth*, in which she exposed the siblings' traumatic childhood at the hands of two alcoholic parents and a father with a violent temper.[126] Munakara Mars opposes the synodic cycle of Uranus Pluto, and although the exact conjunction took place in 1966, two years prior to Chris' birth, there is still a connection accommodated by Pisces Mars, that links the two volatile outer planets. The history of Walt's alcohol-fuelled rages that were familiar to Chris as a child, added to the explosive secret he uncovered as a teenager, are signs of contentious Mars in distress, so when Chris decided to suddenly cut from his family in a way that only Mars, Uranus and Pluto can, it makes sense when previously unknown facts are added to his story.

The shared ruler of munakara Venus and Mercury incorporates Saturn and Mars as first dispositor and outcome planet respectively, and whilst Chris was in his self-imposed years of separation, he devoted much of his time to living a life true to the teachings of his favourite authors (munakara Jupiter in Virgo). Together, the trio of Venus, Mercury and Jupiter allowed him to live what he considered to be through the philosophies of writers such as Tolstoy and Thoreau, both of whom chose chastity over physical contact and intimacy. McCandless was very skilled at being friendly, sociable, communicative and popular, yet he could not allow himself to be vulnerable, or to rely on another person for his well-being. He often met female travellers, free spirits like himself along the way, but he never permitted himself to fall in love and although, many people talked about the impact he had made on them during their short acquaintances on his travels, he seems incapable of returning their feelings.

Chris' Venus in Capricorn disposits to Saturn, ruler of his 7th house, but this then leads to Mars and is a reminder of his broken relationship with his father. With Chris' trust issues it is easy to see why chastity and moral purity were personally an easier path for him, and an idealistic choice to follow in the footsteps of his literary heroes. Several of his beloved books contained passages on celibacy as a chosen way of life; Tolstoy's *The Kreutzer Sonata* and Thoreau's *Walden* has a passage circled by McCandless "Chastity is the flowering of man; and what are called Genius, Heroism, Holiness, and the like, are but various fruits which succeed it."[127] Krakauer notes in *Into the Wild*, "Like not a few of those seduced by the wild, McCandless seems to have been driven by a variety of lust that supplanted sexual desire. His yearning, in a sense, was too powerful to be quenched by human contact. McCandless may have been tempted by the succour offered by women, but it paled beside the prospect of rough congress with nature, with the cosmos itself."[128]

The last book Chris McCandless was believed to have read is the tragic romance, *Doctor Zhivago* by Boris Pasternak, as there is an entry dated 28th July 1992 in Chris' handwriting, next to the passage that reads "And so it turned out that only a life similar to the life of those around us, merging with it without a ripple, is genuine life, and that an unshared happiness is not happiness..."[129] The realization that he had chosen a lifestyle so very different from others, and especially in separation from his loved ones, must have hit Chris hard, as his note reads "And this was most vexing of all", followed by the phrase in uppercase handwriting *"HAPPINESS ONLY REAL WHEN SHARED."*[130]

With five planets in munakara and all of them playing a significant role in each others' sequences, it should be little surprise that the story of Chris McCandless's adventures has taken on fable-like qualities as he becomes a representative for disenchanted youth at the end of the last century. The book and film *Into the Wild* inspired numerous people from various countries to attempt visits to Bus 142, and many would-be pilgrims were as ill-equipped as McCandless and were required to be rescued by locals. After the deaths of two such seekers in 2010 and 2019, Alaska state authorities had the bus removed in 2020 and taken to the Museum of the North in Fairbanks.[131]

Christopher McCandless has stayed in the minds of many who remember his story and Eddie Vedder, singer and songwriter for *Into the Wild* made this observation at his *Water on the Road – Full Concert* in February 2017, ten years after writing the soundtrack for the movie.[132]

> "It's pretty incredible to see the impact made by somebody who wasn't trying it on, just on his own and how inspiriting it was. It's interesting to see who wants to designate him as foolhardy and reckless, but he was out there trying to find

the truth, or some kind of essence that's beyond normal, or what we consider normal. They called him insane but sometimes I think it's what people consider normal – that could be insane."

EXAMPLE TWO: PRINCE GEORGE
Five Planets in Contention
A Brief Biography

Prince George of Wales (born 22 July 2013) is a member of the British royal family. He is the eldest child of William, Prince of Wales, and Catherine, Princess of Wales. George is the eldest grandchild of King Charles III and second in the line of succession to the British throne behind his father. George was born in London during the reign of his paternal great-grandmother, Queen Elizabeth II, and was third in line before her death.

"My dad will be king so you better watch out."[133]
– 9-year-old George's warning to his peers

George's parents, William and Kate, have publicly discussed that they chose the time (George's seventh birthday in 2020) as a "controlled moment of their choice" to tell George that he would be king in the distant future. Apparently the same measure of care was not extended to William, as the Royal parents have commented on "William's unhappiness at the haphazard fashion in which the whole business of his royal destiny had buzzed around his head from the start."[134]

Saturn's first square at age seven, seems such a critical time to tell a child about his intended future, and whilst Saturn is not one of George's planets in munakara, it does feature as outcome planet to George's three diurnal planets in contention. Saturn is the dispositor of George's Capricorn Moon, a Moon that is not only in munakara status, but also features in all five of his planets' sequencing patterns.

Five planets in contention is a lot to take in. But the trio of diurnal planets in Cancer – Sun, Mercury and Jupiter – has created a situation where they share a common dispositor, the Moon, and it is in a sign belonging to an alternate diurnal planet (Saturn). The Moon in detriment is also munakara, and unfortunately, its sequence involves its two enemies, its dispositor Saturn, in Scorpio, and Mars, its outcome planet.

Both of George's luminaries are in a state of munakara, and as George was born at full moon (the Sun and Moon oppose each other). Note that the chart (*Fig. 10.12*) is Whole Sign and whilst the luminaries may look as if they are close to the MC/IC axis, this is not true. Both Sun and Moon are in the final degrees of their signs, approaching the fixed signs of Leo (MC) and Aquarius (IC). Therefore, their position gives a false interpretation that they are at the highest (Sun) and lowest (Moon) part of the chart.

Venus's trio of munakara planets has been bolded to draw attention to the fact that its dispositor (Mercury) and its outcome planet (Moon) are also munakara planets. George's other munakara sequences involve Saturn or Mars and neither of these two planets are in munakara state. Saturn in Scorpio disposits to Mars, but Mars in Cancer is disposited by the Moon so neither sequence proceeds for the two malefic planets.

The two planets which represent mother or the female – Moon and Venus – are not only munakara but are also in both in poor condition in George's chart: the Moon is in detriment and Venus in Virgo is in fall. As George is still a young child, the difficulties presented to these planets is likely to manifest through George's mother, Catherine, and her eldest child will be very aware of the health issues his mother has struggled with throughout 2024. Mother's house is the 10th house (ruled by munakara Sun) and her house of illness – 6 houses away – is George's 3rd house with Capricorn on the cusp and containing his munakara Moon. In January 2024 Catherine underwent abdominal surgery for an undisclosed medical condition[135] and the palace announced on March 22 that she had been undergoing chemotherapy since late February 2024.[136] In September 2024 Catherine revealed that she had completed her chemotherapy treatment and that she was looking forward to resuming public engagements in the coming months.[137]

Munakara Mercury rules George's Mid-heaven in Virgo, his munakara Sun is in the final degree of Cancer, and its dispositor, the Moon in detriment, opposes it in similar degrees. Jupiter, the planet of royalty, is exalted in Cancer, but like the Sun, it is munakara and disposited by a Moon which is also in contention. Both luminaries aspect George's late degree Ascendant at 27 Scorpio, and the Ascendant's ruler, Mars is the second of two planets which is not in contention (the other one is Saturn), but Mars is in fall in Cancer, and lies between two munakara planets – Jupiter and Mercury – in George's chart.

Saturn rules the 4th house of father in George's Whole Sign chart, but like the Ascendant, it too is disposited by Mars in fall. Saturn is in the first sign by

Chapter Ten • *Multiple Munakara Planets*

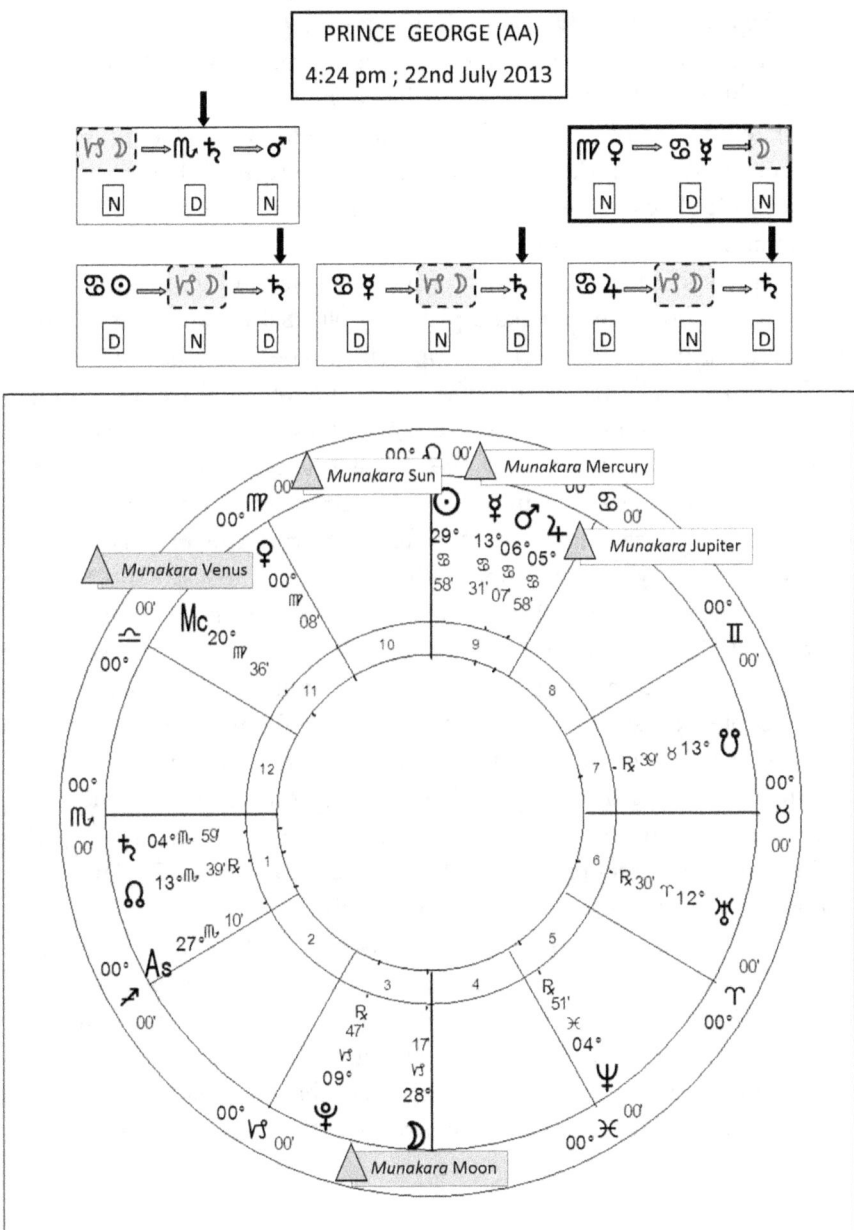

Fig. 10.12: Prince George Natal Chart: Multiple Munakara Planets

Whole Sign, but it will move to the 12th house in any of the quadrant system of houses, as Saturn is in lower degrees of Scorpio than the Ascendant's degree. George's father, William, is the next in line to the throne, and William's Midheaven degree is at 2 Scorpio, only a couple of degrees from George's Saturn at 4 Scorpio. William's Ascendant is in the sign directly following his MC's sign, and with late degrees of Sagittarius rising, William's MC will fall into his 12th house by Whole Sign.

Young George has only just started his journey in life, so little can be deduced over how five munakara planets – plus Saturn and Mars – might play out in his future, but an article appearing in the magazine Marie Claire, in November 2022 titled 'Prince George will never be King, according to history writer',[138] shows there are already rumbles over whether George will ever ascend to the British throne. The article is designed to be controversial and to sell magazines, but in light of George's 'ferocious fivesome', it is interesting to see the following quotes from author and history writer, Dame Hilary Mantel, saying that Prince William will be the last King, and she believes Prince George will never take the throne. Mantel told *The Times* in early 2021, that she thinks "it's a fair prediction given that it's very hard to understand the thinking behind the monarchy in the modern world when people are just seen as celebrities."[139] George's parents have been open in stating that they would modernise the monarchy when they are rulers, making themselves more approachable during official events, and doing away with many formal traditions, but one cannot help but wonder if this will be enough to secure George's fate as the next King of England when William passes the monarch to his first born son.

Five planets in munakara makes for a fascinating story when every move made is scrutinised and privacy is sacrificed by duty, but hopefully George finds fulfilment through his 'five wild cards'. As George grows into his munakara planets it may be that his feelings of being out-of-sync are a by-product of being a royal without a kingdom, or the last remaining figurehead for a custom that holds little value or purpose in the modern world.

Chapter Ten • *Multiple Munakara Planets*

Munakara Multiples: Six Planets in Contention

EXAMPLE ONE: JOHN DEE
Six Planets in Contention
A Brief Biography[140]

John Dee (13 July 1527 – 1608 or 1609) was an English mathematician, natural philosopher, astronomer, astrologer, occultist, and alchemist.[141] He lifted astronomy from obscurity, taught mathematics, and developed navigational systems that later would help to establish England's naval superiority.[142] His father Roland was a mercer (trader of textile goods) who sent his son to Cambridge at age 15 and who was familiar with the intrigues of Henry VIII's court where he served as a minor gentleman courtier providing expensive and lavish materials for men and women alike. Once at college, young Dee's appetite for knowledge was insatiable, allowing himself only four hours of sleep at night, and spending his many waking hours studying Greek, Latin, geometry, mathematics, astronomy, navigation, scripture, law, medicine and cryptography – the art of writing codes.[143]

As a scholar, scientist and astrologer, John Dee was a trusted advisor to both daughters of Henry VIII, even though the two step-sisters were sworn enemies. In 1555 Dee was arrested and cast into jail for 'calculating', *i.e.*, constructing the natal horoscopes of Mary and her half-sister Elizabeth. The charges were raised to treason against Queen Mary, but Dee pleaded his case so well that Mary's Catholic bishop convinced her to invite Dee to join her court. In 1556 Dee presented Mary with a visionary plan for preserving old books, manuscripts and records and suggested founding a national library in her honour.[144] The plan never came to fruition so instead Dee expanded his own personal library at his home, acquiring books and manuscripts in England and on the Continent. Dee's library, a centre of learning outside the universities, became the greatest in England – boasting some 2,670 manuscripts, as opposed to Cambridge's 451 and Oxford's 379.[145]

When Elizabeth succeeded to the throne in 1558, Dee became her astrological and scientific advisor. He chose her coronation date and even switched religions from Mary's Catholicism to become a Protestant, the religion favoured by Elizabeth I. For 20 years from 1558 to 1578 Dee was Elizabeth's court astronomer spending much of his time on alchemy, divination, and Hermetic philosophy. As her political advisor, he advocated the foundation of English colonies in the New World to form a "British Empire", a term he is credited with coining.[146]

By the early 1580s Dee's influence in Elizabeth's court was waning and Dee was becoming discontent with his progress in learning the secrets of nature and frustrated by his diminishing influence in court circles. He began to turn his hopes towards the supernatural as a means to acquire knowledge and when Dee met charlatan and petty criminal, Edward Kelley in 1582 he felt he had met the man who could answer his prayers. Kelley convinced Dee that he could converse with angels and spirits on Dee's behalf. Together the two men travelled throughout Europe conducting spiritual conferences, a fact that Queen Elizabeth used to her own advantage as she convinced Dee to act as spy for the English throne. Dee sent information back to Elizabeth, but rather than incriminating himself by using his signature instead he signed the letters with '007'. The two circles symbolised the eyes of Queen Elizabeth ('for your eyes only') and seven was the alchemist's lucky number.

In 1583 Dee, Kelley and their families left England for Poland, with Dee entrusting his house and library to the care of his brother-in-law. While away, his home was ransacked, and his manuscripts were burnt or stolen. Then, shortly after Dee and his family returned to England, plague swept the country, and Dee was blamed for the spread of the disease. The plague took his wife and four of their eight children. Kelley gained fame in Europe selling his skills as an alchemist, and Queen Elizabeth pressured Dee to persuade Kelley to return and ease England's economic burdens through alchemy (turning lead into gold).[147] When Dee refused to contact Kelley, Elizabeth appointed him Warden of Christ's College in Manchester in 1995 which provided him with a small stipend for his living expenses.

Dee's circumstances worsened when Queen Elizabeth died in 1603 and he lost all royal patronage as her successor James I was highly critical of occult practises to the point that he personally supervised the torture of women accused of being witches.[148] Dee spent his final days alone and in poverty, selling his remaining books and casting astrological charts to survive. He died at the age of 82 and was buried at his home in Mortlake. His gravestone has disappeared and there is no resting place to mark the life of this most learned and unusual scholar.[149]

> "There is nothing (the works of God only set apart) which so much beautifies and adorns the soul and mind of man as does knowledge of the good arts and sciences." – John Dee

Chapter Ten • *Multiple Munakara Planets*

John Dee's six-planet sequencing has three major players, the Moon, Mercury, and Saturn. Together this trio dictates the nature of the man and his obsession for knowledge and power. Mars in Scorpio is the single planet that escapes contention, and as Mars is not a dispositor for any of Dee's other planets (no planets in Aries or Scorpio), it plays no role in their munakara sequences. For this reason, all six sequences are bolded because all six munakara planets are involved in each other's sequences.

The exact time of John Dee's birth is unclear as two charts exist: one chart is set for the time 4:02 am, allegedly discovered by Elias Ashmole who inherited Dee's library, and one is in the British Library set for a birth time at 4:40 pm. Legend has it that Dee drew both AM and PM charts "in his own hand," perhaps to cast deliberate confusion over his birth data, and to protect himself from his enemies and detractors who may themselves, have been astrologers. On 13th July 1527 the Moon on the day changes sign during the time from AM to PM birth time, but this fact does not save Dee's Moon from contention as the sign change is from Capricorn to Aquarius, two consecutive signs that share Saturn as their ruler. Both 4:40 am and 4:02 pm charts contain six munakara sequences for Dee's planets, with Mars in rulership being the exception. The difference in the two charts means that the planets' house placements and house rulerships are unreliable, and a true delineation cannot be conducted to ascertain how the planets worked in a way specific to the natal chart's layout. However, aspects between the planets can still be analysed as only the Moon's movement affects its aspects over the twelve-hour period between the morning and late afternoon charts.

Mars forms a powerful trine to Dee's Cancer Sun and there is little doubt that, even without six planets in munakara, Dee was an ambitious man who was determined to win a prominent position in politics, and to fully immerse himself in two English Courts ruled by powerful women of opposing religious persuasion.

Dee's Moon – whether in Capricorn or Aquarius – is involved in five of his six munakara sequences. So too is its dispositor, Saturn, and the 4:02 pm birth chart shows a close square between the two planets in fixed signs. Saturn is the outcome planet for three diurnal planets, the conjunction of Jupiter and Mercury, and the Sun in Cancer. This same chart indicates a full moon on the day of Dee's birth, with Saturn as the apex planet of a T-square involving the Sun and Moon opposition.

Munakara in Theory

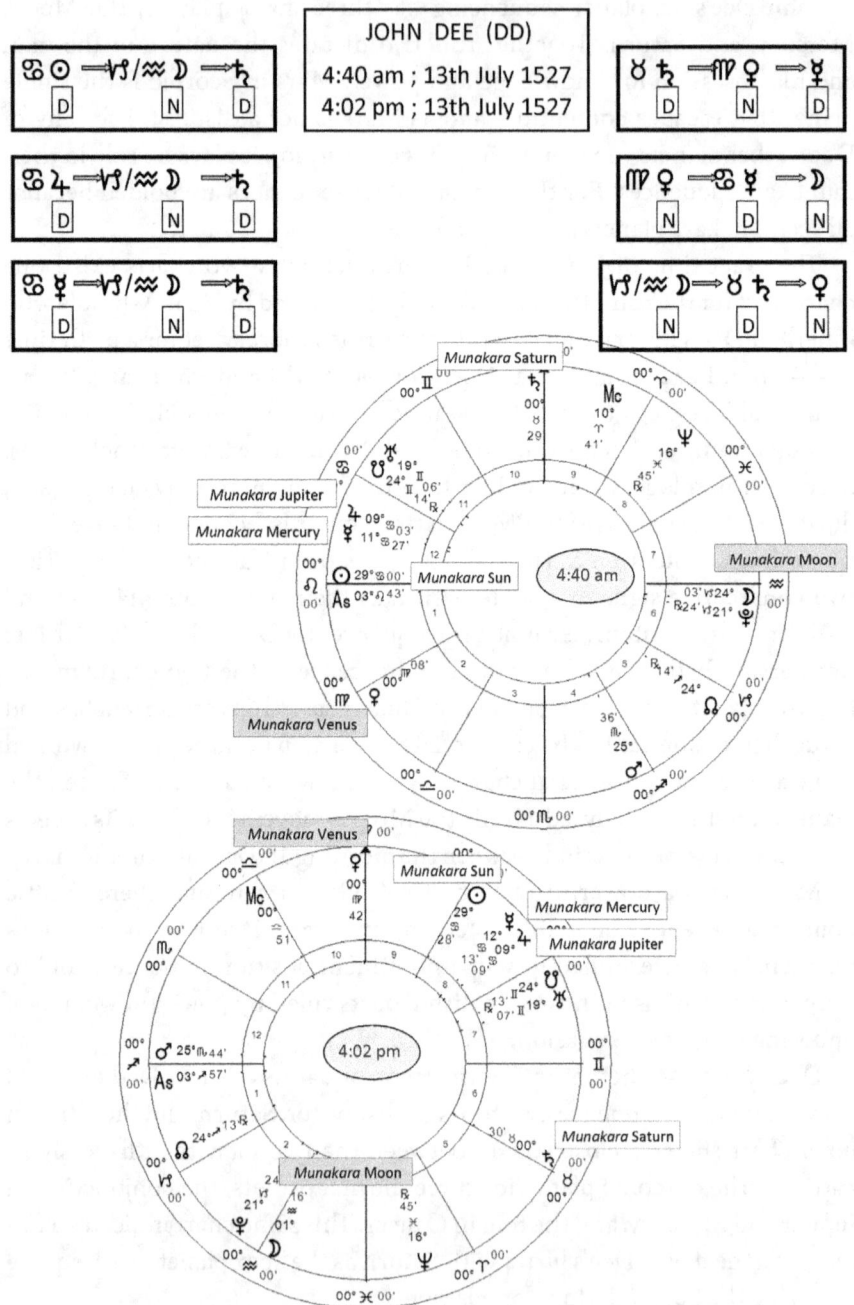

Fig. 10.13: John Dee Natal Chart: Multiple Munakara Planets

Chapter Ten • *Multiple Munakara Planets*

"I have from my youth up, desired and prayed unto God for pure and sound wisdom and understanding of truths natural and artificial, so that God's wisdom, goodness, and power bestowed in the frame of the world might be brought in some bountiful measure under the talent of my capacity."
– John Dee

Dee's Cancer Sun, Mercury, and Jupiter share identical munakara sequences and perhaps these three planets are paramount in convincing Dee of his superiority above all men, and his conviction that he alone would be the one to possess the skills and knowledge to communicate with angels. His vast library, the largest in England, would have contained hundreds of esoteric texts and manuscripts that may indeed have convinced his trio of planets in Cancer that he was rightfully born to be the true guardian of divine secrets.

Saturn, the planet signifying the seas, and the god responsible for the safe passage of ships and benefactor of sailors, served Dee well in his role as advisor to Queen Elizabeth I. When the Spanish Armada stood off the English coast Dee's ability to cast meteorological charts predicting great storms caused him to advise Elizabeth to hold her fleet from entering deep waters and rather than incurring English losses through battle, to allow the foul weather to destroy Spain's fleet for them.

Mercury features in three of Dee's munakara sequences, and there is no doubt that Dee was a genius in his lifetime. He was a mathematician, who in his 20s lectured throughout Europe, packing university halls and introducing the public to the glyphs of addition (+), subtraction (-), multiplication (x), and division signs for the first time.[150] But Dee's contentious opinions were evident even as a precocious 28-year-old when at his Saturn Return he was offered a readership in mathematics at Oxford University which he declined, citing as offensive English universities' emphasis on rhetoric and grammar (which together with logic, formed the academic *trivium*) over philosophy and science (the more advanced *quadrivium*, composed of arithmetic, geometry, music, and astronomy).[151] At the time Dee was employed as a lowly rector at Upton-upon-Severn but he refused to compromise his principles even to his own advantage.

Dee developed navigational systems, again with the aid of his munakara planets (Saturn, Jupiter, and Mercury), which provided him with the ability to think beyond the restrictions of his time, systems which were utilized to establish England's naval superiority later in history, long after Dee's popularity had risen and then fallen out of favour within the royal circle.

Munakara in Theory

Six planets in munakara – all with sequences involving planets in contention – is going to produce unusual characters who imprint on society in their own unique way. Dee and Kelley practiced Enochian magic (from *The Book of Enoch*),[152] a series of rituals and ceremonies designed to evoke angelic and other spiritual entities. Dee recorded these communications in a language he called Enochian and a script which was indecipherable, and accompanied by tables of magic correspondences. Despite modern fiction that depicts Dee as a magician conspiring with evil spirits, in truth Dee was a deeply religious man. His drive to communicate with the angels was a heartfelt belief that with their guidance he might be able to heal the deep and serious rifts between the Roman Catholic Church, the Reformed Church of England, and the Protestant movement in England.[153] When Dee entered into his spiritual conferences he did not do so lightly: he followed strict Christian rituals to achieve maximum purity of body and soul through intense periods of purification, prayer and fasting.[154] Nor can Edward Kelley be simply dismissed as an opportunist who took advantage of Dee's vulnerability as Kelley's angelic communications, documented by Dee over the five years the two men travelled together, are remarkable for the scope of their volume, intricacy and vividness.[155] With Dee's vast knowledge of esoteric matters and keen intellect it would have been impossible for Kelley to maintain his subterfuge for this period of time had he truly been a fraud. Kelley allegedly spoke in a special angelic or Enochian language which Dee recorded in his journals believing that angels dictated enough useful information through Kelley to fill several books on esoteric knowledge.[156]

An examination of any planet in munakara can suggest alienation and misinterpretation for the individual, but with six of seven planets in contention, the fall from grace can be spectacular. History seems to remember Dee as a deluded old fool who lost his wealth and reputation through his association with tricksters and charlatans. But he was a brilliant man, perhaps a true Renaissance man, proficient and talented in many fields of study, caught in a time 200 years after the Renaissance, and born several hundred years before his brilliance could be properly utilized.

Ten years after Dee's death, the antiquarian Robert Cotton bought land around Dee's house and began digging for papers and artefacts. He found several manuscripts, mainly records of Dee's angelic communications. Cotton's son gave these to the scholar Meric Casaubon, who published them in 1659, with a long introduction critical of their author.[157] As the first public revelation of Dee's spiritual conferences, the book was popular because of its sensationalist topic. Casaubon, who believed in the reality of spirits, argued in his introduction that Dee was acting as the unwitting tool of evil spirits when he believed he was communicating with angels. This book is mainly responsible for the image, prevalent for the next two-and-a-half centuries, of Dee as a dupe and deluded fanatic.[158] Of course the deceased Dee could not defend himself and the ruin of his reputation continued as he became a less reputable figure of the Elizabethan era, not cast in the same honoured light as fellow scientists and colleagues Flemish geographer, cosmographer and cartographer, Gerardus Mercator, and Danish astronomer, Tycho Brahe.

A revaluation of Dee's character and significance came in the 20th century through the work of the historians Charlotte Fell Smith and Dame Frances Yates.[159] Both brought into focus the parallel roles of magic, science, and religion in the Elizabethan Renaissance and spoke highly of Dee's many valuable contributions to its success.

Fell Smith writes in 1909: "There is perhaps no learned author in history who has been so persistently misjudged, nay, even slandered, by his posterity, and not a voice in all the three centuries uplifted even to claim for him a fair hearing. Surely it is time that the cause of all this universal condemnation should be examined in the light of reason and science; and perhaps it will be found to exist mainly in the fact that he (Dee) was too far advanced in speculative thought for his own age to understand."[160]

EXAMPLE TWO: HELEN KELLER
Six Planets in Contention
A Brief Biography

Helen Adams Keller (June 27, 1880 – June 1, 1968) was an American author, disability rights advocate, political activist and lecturer. Born in Tuscumbia, Alabama, Keller became ill with a fever at 19 months old, resulting in vision and hearing loss. She then communicated primarily using home signs until the age of seven, when she met her first teacher and lifelong companion Anne Sullivan. Sullivan taught Keller language including reading and writing. After an education at both specialist and mainstream schools, Keller attended Radcliffe College of Harvard University and became the first deaf-blind person in the United States to earn a Bachelor of Arts degree.[161]

After college, Keller read Braille translations of works by Karl Marx, H.G. Wells and William Morris. She joined the Socialist Party of America (SPA) in 1909, and became a member of Industrial Workers of the World (IWW) shortly after, supporting strikes, walking picket lines, giving lecture tours and writing articles for publications like *The Liberator*. She noticed the close relationship between disability and poverty, and blamed capitalism and poor industrial conditions for both. As Keller told the New York *Tribune* in 1916, blindness was "often caused by the selfishness and greed of employers."[162]

Keller was a prolific writer, writing 14 books and hundreds of speeches and essays on a wide range of topics, campaigning for those with disabilities, for women's suffrage, labor rights, and world peace. She supported the National Association for the Advancement of Coloured People (NAACP), founded in 1909, and in the same year, she was a founding member of the American Civil Liberties Union (ACLU), created to protect striking workers from jail and deportation.[163] She opposed World War I on the grounds that it served capitalist interests, and her radical views made her a target of FBI surveillance for most of her life.[164]

Despite these activities, Keller is more commonly remembered for the forty years (from 1924 to 1964) that she spent fundraising and doing advocacy work on behalf of the American Federation for the Blind (AFB), a largely apolitical organization. Keller died in her sleep on June 1, 1968 at the age of 87.

Aside from the digital Helen Keller Archives on the AFB website, very few personal details remain on her remarkable life. Anne Macy (nee Sullivan) burnt her own diaries and other private material before her death. John Macy, the editor of several of Helen's books (and Anne Sullivan's ex-husband) left virtually nothing of his records as her editor, and the bulk of Helen's letters, notes and records were burnt in a house fire in 1946. The destruction of hundreds of thousands of letters written to Keller by deaf, blind, and deaf-blind people from around the world is a colossal loss as so much could have been learned on the everyday lives of people with disabilities during the early to mid 20th century.

In 2020, documentary film-maker, John Gianvito, directed a beautiful and unusual film titled *Her Socialist Smile*[165] intended to capture Helen Keller's political life during her young adult years, from her first public speech in 1913, to the time when she became the public spokesperson for the American Foundation for the Blind (AFB) in 1924. In several interviews to promote his film, Gianvito tells of his long-standing desire to make the film, but the frustrations he encountered made it a project that looked impossible for many years, given that there was a total lack of images or audio recordings of Keller's speeches during this eleven-year period.

Chapter Ten • *Multiple Munakara Planets*

Gianvito cites two major reasons for this obstruction to the usual avenues open to documentarians. Firstly, when Helen became involved with the AFB, there was concern over her Communist leanings, and Helen's image needed to be sanitized. All political opinions and references to Socialist Parties were removed by the AFB, and in order for Helen to become their major fundraiser, much of the material had to simply 'disappear'. Secondly, the Helen Keller International Archives was destroyed in September 11, 2001 with the collapse of the Twin Towers, where the archives were stored. It seems ironic that there should be so little information available on a woman who played a major role in American history in the last century, and whose lifetime achievements went way past the depiction of her childhood and the 'water-pump moment' that changed the direction of Helen Keller's life.

"Security is mostly a superstition. It does not exist in nature, nor do the children of men / as a whole experience it. Avoiding danger is no safer in the long run than outright exposure. / Life is either a daring adventure, or nothing."
– Helen Keller

All six planets in Helen Keller's sequences contain other planets which are also in the state of munakara. Similar to the two previous charts of Christopher McCandless and John Dee, Keller's life contained a series of contradictions and so many unfair judgements of a child/woman thrown into the limelight, often without her knowledge or her consent.

Helen Keller has two duets in her chart; nocturnal Mercury and Mars in Leo disposited by Sun in Cancer, and Jupiter and Saturn in Aries, and disposited by Mars in Leo. Her Cancer Sun has the maximum amount of activity in its involvement in five (of six) sequences. It is a Sun in munakara, as well as a first dispositor to Helen's Mercury/Mars duet in Leo, and also, the Sun is the outcome planet for the Jupiter/Saturn duet in Aries.

Pisces Moon is munakara, and is the first dispositor for Helen's Cancer Sun, as well as being the outcome planet for the nocturnal duet of Mercury and Mars. Leo Mars holds down four positions; it is munakara, plus first dispositor (twice) and outcome planet (once). Aries Jupiter claims the full set by being in munakara, first dispositor for Pisces Moon, and outcome planet for Cancer Sun.

In all six scenarios, the planet in contention is in a sign belonging to another stressed planet in a similar condition. So the sequencing is not so much about friends and enemies as it is about planets in similar states of stress, contradiction, and tension, whereby their principle needs are ignored, compromised, or misunderstood by the individual and others who interact with them.

> *"What a strange life I lead – a kind of Cinderella-life – half glitter in crystal shoes, half mice and cinders! But it is a wonderful life all the same."*[166] – Letter to Mrs. Carrie Fuld, ca. 1933

Throughout Helen Keller's life she was surrounded by misunderstanding, often misquoted or misrepresented by the press, and often society carried a distorted image of Keller and her disability. In 1897, when Helen was seventeen years of age, one newspaper reporter described Helen's physical attributes, "Her chin is beautifully formed, the mouth and teeth are good, her complexion is clear and healthy and the expression of her face wonderfully attractive in its bright alertness", but the tragedy was that "looking at the face you are struck first, of course, by the pathos of the eyes that show all too plainly their affliction. Aside from these there is nothing to sadden one in Helen Keller's appearance."[167] Comments such as these frustrated and irritated Keller when so much focus was given to her physical appearance, rather than her accomplishments or her intelligence. Only a trusted few really understood her, and they were her female companions – this should be no surprise as Venus stands apart from her planets in contention, and Venus plays no active role in any of the six sequence patterns of her munakara planets. Venus in Cancer disposits to Helen's Moon, but as both are nocturnal planets, Venus goes no further towards contention. Likewise, none of Helen's visible planets are in Venus' signs of Taurus and Libra, so Venus is never first dispositor or outcome planet for any of her other planets' sequences.

Venus is conjunct Keller's South Node/Cancer Sun, and Venus is the ruling planet of her chart's 7th and 12th houses. Given Venus' position in her chart (and its lack of contention) Keller voiced her immediate connection with Anne Sullivan calling March 3, 1887, 'her soul's birthday', to mark the day that Sullivan arrived at her home for the first time. Venus is not in a state of munakara and is free from the constraints of contention. Helen and Anne's first meeting was the beginning of a 50-year relationship that began as teacher and pupil, and became a close and loving companionship as both women matured and grew into adulthood.

Until Helen formed an attachment to Anne, her mother was her whole world and she would only ever allow her mother to touch her or hold her

Chapter Ten • *Multiple Munakara Planets*

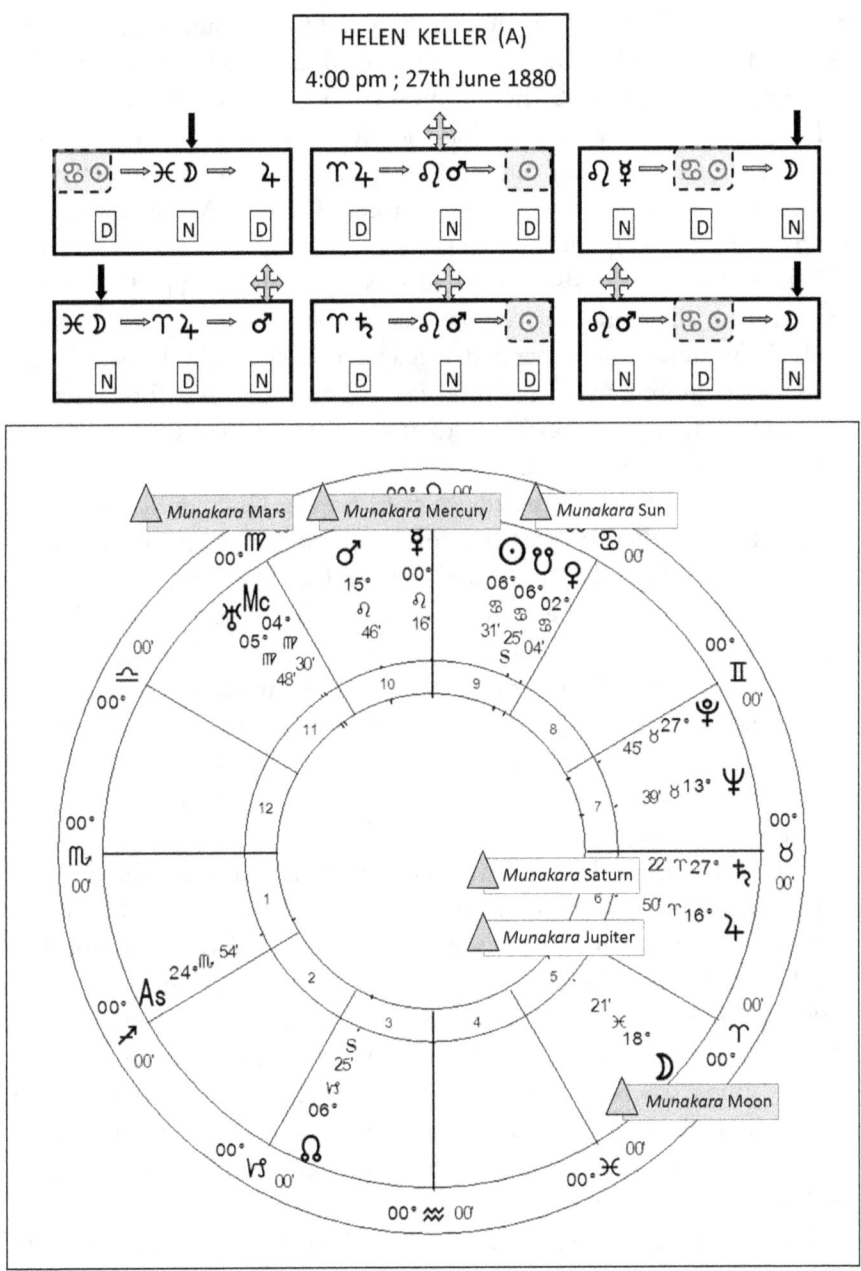

Fig. 10.14: *Helen Keller Natal Chart: Multiple Munakara Planets*

in an embrace, "My mother succeeded in making me understand a good deal...Indeed, I owe it to her loving wisdom all that was bright and good in my long night." Helen's 10th house (mother's house) contains her Mercury and Mars munakara duet which has the Moon (mother) as their outcome planet. The Sun is Mercury and Mars's dispositor and the Sun rules the 10th house with Leo on its cusp. Mars is the ruler of Helen's Ascendant and the dispositor for both Jupiter and Saturn.

When Helen's baby sister Mildred was born, Helen tipped the cradle over because she could not comprehend that her beloved doll's bed was suddenly occupied by another body. Helen's mother caught the baby before it fell to the ground, but the family was nervous of Helen's future actions towards the infant, and they began their search to find a solution to Helen's erratic behaviour before it ended in tragedy.

Keller's parents sought the advice of Alexander Graham Bell, who sent the family to the Perkins Institute for the Blind. Bell rejected the idea of referring the Kellers to the School for Deaf in Hartford, Connecticut, because he did not approve of their use of sign language. Munakara Jupiter and Saturn are in Aries in Keller's 6th house, and many of the people chosen by either Helen or her family, to be her close confidantes, guides or teachers often created controversy or drew negative comments from the public arena. Munakara Mercury and Mars in Leo are a duet in Keller's 10th house and one duet connects to the other through the trine aspect of Leo to Aries (Jupiter and Saturn).

Keller was constantly drawn into issues that she had little influence over, and her friendship with Alexander Graham Bell was one such instance where she was condemned by association. Keller recalled her first meeting with Bell with great affection saying, "You held out a warm hand to me in the dark...I did not dream that that interview would be the door through which I should pass from darkness into light."[168] However, her loyalty towards Bell and the Blind Association drew criticism from those in the deaf community who felt that she had publicly supported Bell's cause to promote oralism (oral speech) over sign language as the preferred form of communication for deaf people.

Katie Booth, author of *The Invention of Miracles: Language, Power and Alexander Graham Bell's Quest to End Deafness* says: "I can't even begin to express the deep, deep, deep trauma that so many people still carry from those educations." Booth's book, released in April 2021 compiles years of her research into Bell's letters and other archival material.[169]

Chapter Ten • *Multiple Munakara Planets*

Perkins Institute for the Blind was under the directorship of Michael Anagnos and it was he who sent 20-year-old visually impaired Anne Sullivan as an inexperienced young woman with no formal education to teach Keller. Anagnos was an ambitious young man who wanted desperately to advance his career through Sullivan's success and a year after Sullivan's arrival Anagnos was sending exaggerated reports to the papers making ridiculous statements such as 'Helen demonstrates problems in geometry by means of her playing with blocks'. Accounts like this made any accurate record of Sullivan's successes obsolete, as the papers wanted a 'miracle child', and controversy constantly surrounded any factual or fanciful reports concerning Helen Keller's story. Incredulous disbelief, professional jealousy from other teachers, and efforts to discount or disprove Sullivan's statement followed Helen's progress, and Sullivan bore the brunt of hostility and resentment against both herself and her young pupil.

Controversy followed Keller throughout her life and often through others' manipulation she found herself the subject of debate or the recipient of anger and intolerance. The rising tide of public anger turned against Keller, Sullivan, and Anagnos in 1891 with the incident that became known as "The Frost King", a story written by 11-year-old Helen as a birthday present to Michael Anagnos, about King Frost and his fairies whose task it was to change the colours of the leaves at fall. Anagnos converted it from a private letter to a public event, and when by a series of events it was published nationally, Keller was accused of plagiarism. As her teacher, Anne Sullivan faced public accusations of being a fraud, and the fallout discredited the Perkins Institute by association.

Helen was devastated and deeply upset at being accused of lying, as she had no memory of having a similar story, *Birdie and his Fairy Friends* by Margaret T. Canby, being read to her. It was later discovered that Sophia Hopkins, a teacher at Perkins, had read Keller the story while she was on vacation in Cape Cod. However, without sight to discriminate between the two teachers, Keller made the mistake of confusing Hopkins with Sullivan, and both child and teacher were brought before a tribunal at Perkins to explain her confusion. The panel's hostility rattled Sullivan, and embarrassed her about her own "imperfect education", but for Helen, she felt she had disgraced herself, and noted the incident in her book, *The Story of My Life*, writing "no child drank deeper from the cup of bitterness than I did."[170]

Writer Mark Twain was a friend of Keller and Sullivan, latently defending them in the Frost King fraud, and writing to Helen in 1903, declaring the

"Plagiarism Court" a collection of decayed human turnips. But the whole incident had a devastating effect on Helen, as it robbed her of her confidence, and tormented her on the origins of her thoughts, and her reliance on her own memories.[171]

Helen's recollections begin in *The Story of My Life*,[172] from the time she met Anne Sullivan to her 21st birthday. Helen's three nocturnal planets, Moon, Mercury, and Mars, give testament to Helen's rage and confusion over her constant state of darkness. Helen's reference to herself as the 'Phantom' before Sullivan's arrival, reflects her feelings that she had no visible presence in the world, and that her only means of connection was through alternating between withdrawal and clinging to her mother, to extreme acts of will-power to demonstrate her frustration.

Helen's nocturnal Mercury and Mars duet was in constant turmoil until she was given the opportunity to communicate through finger-spelling and lip reading by holding her hand across a speaker's mouth to understand the spoken word. But whilst Helen was learning at an incredible speed in her own private world with Anne Sullivan, her Mercury/Mars duet in the tenth sign at the top of her chart was in contention, with the rest of the world reporting, discussing, forming opinions, criticising and attacking in any manner that seemed fit to sell newspapers.

In 1909, Helen had surgery to remove her eyes and replace them with blue-tinted glass eyes. Prior to this operation, Helen's left eye protruded, and she only appeared in profile in photographs. From this point forward, front-facing photographs of her were common. Those close to her, her household, and members of her family were sworn to secrecy, and Helen became so adept at blinking and giving the appearance of animation, that 30 years later a reporter praised her blue eyes, saying they had "none of the lack-lustre look usual to the blind. When she talks, they take on animation; and they gaze at you with what seems a seeing glance."[173]

Helen knew she was constantly under observation, but her blindness gave others 'permission to stare' at her without the usual social constraints of good manners, consideration for others' feelings or politeness, and she therefore fought to look as 'normal' as possible in order to negate her disability. But the nature of contention often means that what you fight so hard to disallow, ignore or invalidate, becomes a defining factor in how you are assessed by society, the community and family members. By Helen's efforts to appear non-disabled, she reinforced her public persona and increased her fame by accentuating the miracle of 'overcoming' her disabilities with sheer will-power. In this way she was trapped in her own story, and one of her closest confidantes for over 30 years, Nella Braddy Henney, wrote in 1947, "Helen wants to be free and tries to be but is actually one of the least free people on Earth."[174]

In 1909, at age 29, Helen Keller joined the Socialist Party of America, and when America made its Declaration of War on April 7, 1917, she publicly defended the radical International Workers of the World (IWW), and strengthened her support for the SPA, to protest against what they believed to be "a crime against the people and they would not sacrifice one life or one dollar towards the war effort". Helen Keller was a pacifist who fought against the government's rousing speeches for young American men to sign up and become soldiers to fight a war, she felt had no relevance to the working classes.

"Any intelligent person can see that peace cannot be left to governments. Governments are founded on force, and in order to defend and extend their power they inevitably resort to militarism." – Helen Keller

In truth, Helen was in a bind, as her lofty principles were in conflict with the need to secure her own financial independence. She ran a household of several able-bodied women, with the addition of John Macy, when he was married for several years to Anne, all of whom were financially dependent on her. In 1910, when one of America's wealthiest industrialists, Andrew Carnegie, offered her a regular pension income, Keller cited her principles as an opponent to capitalism to turn the offer down. But three years later, her finances had worsened, and she gave up hope of supporting herself through her writing. In 1913 she wrote to Carnegie, "I was ambitious to earn my own living and to make things easier for those that I love. But I did not understand until now that in order to carry out this idea I should have to lay another burden upon the dear shoulders of those who were already heavily burdened." Keller received a Carnegie pension for decades, but never wrote on its conflict with her socialist ideals.[175]

In 1896 Keller converted to Swedenborgianism, a Christian group established by the Swedish spiritual leader Emanuel Swedenborg, who preached the belief that the soul and the body were separate, and that there was a spiritual body with perfect senses which existed within, and independent from, the material body. Helen's munakara Sun lies in her 9th house, and its ruler is her munakara Moon in Pisces. Under the precepts of her unusual religion, her deaf-blindness mattered very little, and instead its lack of distraction from material sights and sounds was an advantage, and she believed allowed for a deeper sense of spirituality which would reveal "a world infinitely more wonderful, complete, and satisfying" than the one that focused on her disabilities.[176]

A lifetime lived with six out of a possible seven planets in munakara is not likely to be a lifetime lived without misunderstanding, frustration and misinterpretation. For Helen Keller, whether intentional or not, her fame sprang from the misconception that she was the 'perpetual overcomer', and all that was needed by others with similar disadvantage, was to follow her example, and they too could move past the barriers of their physical disabilities. The *New York Times* wrote in 1955, that Helen had "a quality of courage that enables a few gifted and benign souls to overcome their own handicaps and to give themselves to humanity and for humanity." The majority of the public considered disability a personal problem, and those who could not triumph over it, were seen as disadvantaged individuals who lacked the fortitude to get on with their lives with quiet dignity and a minimum of fuss and to stop burdening society with their problems.[177]

There are those who argue that history portrays a romantic image of Helen Keller, and that rather than championing for the disabled, "Keller rarely explored the political dimensions of disability, adopting beliefs that were often seen as conservative, patronizing, and occasionally repugnant."[178]

Purely because her life was lived as an exception, rather than the norm of disability, Helen Keller supported the belief that disability was a problem to be conquered, and once conquered, a problem left behind. Kim Nielson argues in *The Radical Lives of Helen Keller*[179] that with her strong socialist views Keller had the power and the public attention to make radical change for all those with disabilities, but that she did very little to improve the political attitudes and laws of her time. Even though she had the opportunity and a belief in social equality, Keller did not campaign against laws that discriminated against disabled people, laws denying them the right to marriage, education, employment, citizenship, and even the right to access to public space and participation in public events.

Nielson maintains that Helen Keller grew up with the notion that she was special, and her isolation from others with disability helped her to maintain the illusion that she was stronger, braver, better, and more determined than other people with disability. Nielson concludes that by buying into this falsehood, Helen Keller missed the opportunity to successfully politicize

Chapter Ten • *Multiple Munakara Planets*

disability as an issue of rights, prejudice, or discrimination, instead choosing to ignore the segregation and exploitation of the disabled through sheltered workshops that paid a minimum wage.[180]

With all of these conflicting opinions of Helen Keller as a heroine, as a child plagiarist, as a socialist, as a media celebrity, as a fundraiser, and as a person who could have educated the public on legal rights for the disabled, it seems only fair for Helen to have the last word when it comes to defining herself:

"I am not a perfect being....I have more faults than I know what to do with. I have a naughty temper. I am stubborn, impatient of hindrances and of stupidity. I have not in the truest sense a Christian spirit. I am naturally a fighter. I am lazy. I put off till tomorrow what I might better do today. I do not feel that I have been compensated for the two senses I lack. I have worked hard for all the senses I have got, and always I beg for more."[181] – "A Message from the Hand, or from Darkness to Light (Another Beginning)," draft of speech, 1928.

CHAPTER ELEVEN
Al-Biruni's Chronocrators: Munakara and the Time Lords

Firdaria is a predictive technique believed to have originated in 1st-century Persia. Firdaria is a system which divides the human life into periods of years (and months) governed by one of the seven original planets. The planets run in the Chaldean Order, starting with Saturn as the planet closest to the heavens (the fixed stars) and ending with the Moon as the closest planet to Earth. The Firdaria patterns are dependent on whether the chart is diurnal or nocturnal and have different commencement points – beginning with the Sun if the chart is diurnal, or beginning with the Moon if the chart is nocturnal.

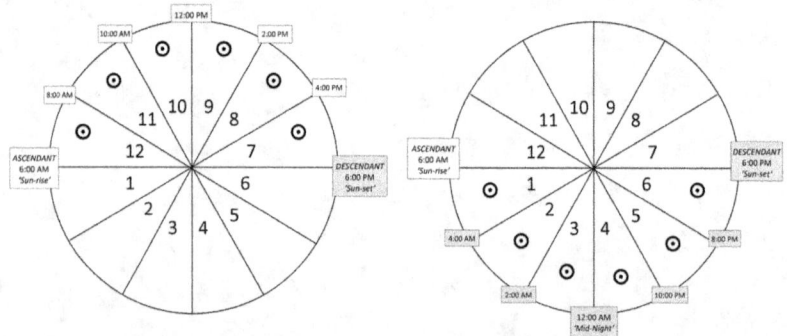

Fig. 11.1: A Diurnal Chart begins the Diurnal Firdaria with the Sun. A Nocturnal Chart begins the Nocturnal Firdaria with the Moon.

Chapter Eleven • Al-Biruni's Chronocators: Munakara and the Time Lords

Al-Biruni's Notation #395, 'Firdaria of Planets', describes this system and calls the planets Time Lords or 'Chronocrators'. The text in bold is mine and shows the first period belongs to one or the other of the luminaries in accordance with the nature of the chart.

> *The years of a man's life according to a Persian idea are divided into certain periods (firdar) governed by the lords of these known as Chronocrators (Time-Lords). When one period is finished another begins.* **The first period always begins with the sun in a diurnal nativity and with the moon in a nocturnal one;** *the second with Venus in the one case, in the other with Saturn, the remaining periods with the other planets in descending order.*[1]

In a diurnal chart the seven periods of life up to the age of seventy will begin at the Sun for 10 years and then pass to Venus for 8 years, followed by Mercury for 13 years. At age thirty one, the Moon will rule for 9 years and at age forty, Saturn will become the Firdaria lord for 11 years. Jupiter will follow for 12 years and the seventh and last planet in the diurnal sequence will be Mars which rules for 7 years. At the age of seventy, the Nodal years will begin with the North Node for 3 years followed by South Node for 2 years. The diurnal cycle of Firdaria begins once more with the Sun at seventy five years of age, and will follow in identical order as the first series of Diurnal Firdaria.

In a nocturnal chart the seven periods of life will begin with the Moon for 9 years and will move at the top of the Chaldean Order to Saturn for 11 years and will run down the planets until all seven periods are completed. Jupiter will follow Saturn for 12 years, and at age thirty two, Mars will be next planet to rule for 7 years, followed by the Sun at age 39 for 10 years, and then Venus for 8 years. Mercury will be the final planet before the 5-year period of the Nodes and Mercury will rule for 13 years from the age of 57 to 70 years of age.

Figs. 11.2 and 11.3 show the order of diurnal and nocturnal Firdaria listing the periods and the ages which each 'major' lord (long-term) covers during its governing period. The final three chapters in my book *A Tiny Universe's Companion* (2018) are dedicated to Firdaria: these chapters describe each sub-period Firdaria and include a modern interpretation of the texts by 1st-century astrologer Vettius Valens, and 16th-century writer Johannes Schoener on the topic of Time Lords.[2]

Munakara in Theory

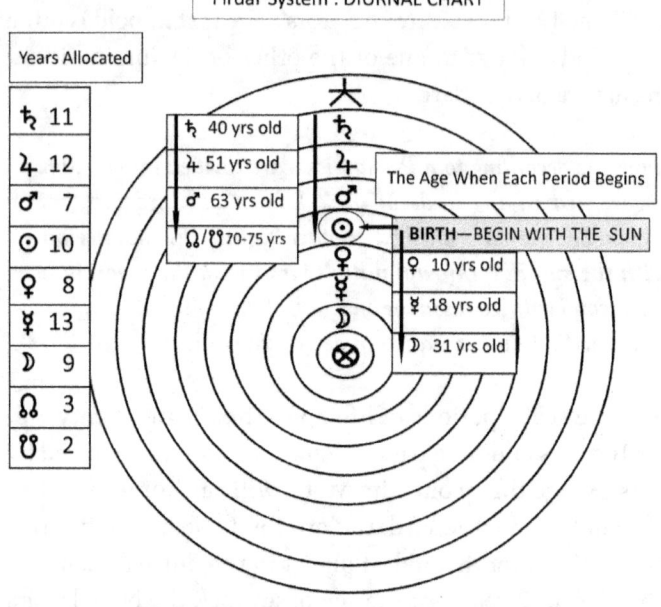

No.	Ruler	Period	Age Span
1	☉	10 yrs	Birth—10 yrs old
2	♀	8 yrs	10—18 yrs old
3	☿	13 yrs	18—31 yrs old
4	☽	9 yrs	31—40 yrs old
5	♄	11 yrs	40—51 yrs old
6	♃	12 yrs	51—63 yrs old
7	♂	7 yrs	63—70 yrs old

Fig. 11.2: Diurnal Firdaria: The Seven Periods (Years) belonging to each Planet

Al-Biruni's Table on Firdaria: Notation #438–439

Notation #395 continues to describe Firdaria with the breakdown into smaller sub-Firdaria periods consisting of months rather than years. This is achieved by dividing the year periods by seven (the number of planets) and allocating months to the planets, starting with the long-term ruler and then proceeding in the Chaldean Order. The long-term periods and short-term periods are identical in diurnal and nocturnal Firdaria, and only the age of the person and the order of the various major Time Lords differ (*Figs. 11.2; 11.3*) according to whether the chart is diurnal or nocturnal.

Chapter Eleven • Al-Biruni's Chronocators: Munakara and the Time Lords

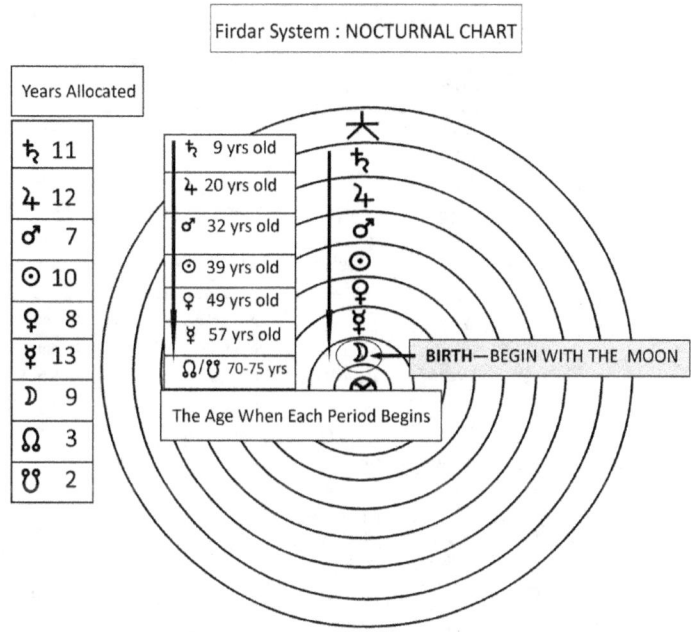

Fig. 11.3: Nocturnal Firdaria: The Seven Periods (Years) belonging to each Planet

No.	Ruler	Period	Age Span
1	☽	9 yrs	Birth—9 yrs old
2	♄	11 yrs	9—20 yrs old
3	♃	12 yrs	20—32 yrs old
4	♂	7 yrs	32—39 yrs old
5	☉	10 yrs	39—49 yrs old
6	♀	8 yrs	49—57 yrs old
7	☿	13 yrs	57—70 yrs old

> The years of each period are distributed equally between the seven planets, the first seventh belonging exclusively to the chronocrator of the period, the second to it in partnership with the planet next below it and so on.[3]

Al-Biruni provides a table in Notation #438–439, Firdaria and their Association Times[4] and *Fig. 11.4 (next page)* is a replication of this table along with al-Biruni's text: "Periods of life (firdaria) controlled by the planets as chronocrators, 438, and the times of association, 439, (seventh of the periods) of the other planets with the general chronocrators, 395."

Munakara in Theory

Period	Chronocrators In diurnal nativities	Chronocrators In nocturnal nativities	Times of associations in last six sevenths	
1	Sun 10 years	Moon 9 years	In Sun's period / In Moon's period	1y. 5m. 4d. 7h. / 1y. 3m. 12d. 21h.
2	Venus 8 years	Saturn 11 years	In Venus' period / In Saturn's period	1y. 1m. 21d. 5h. / 1y. 6m. 25d. 17h.
3	Mercury 13 years	Jupiter 12 years	In Mercury's period / In Jupiter's period	1y. 10m. 8d. 7h. / 1y. 8m. 17d. 7h.
4	Moon 9 years	Mars 7 years	In Moon's period / In Mars' period	1y. 3m. 12d. 21h. / 1y. 10h.
5	Saturn 11 years	Sun 10 years	In Saturn's period / In Sun's period	1y. 6m. 25d. 17h. / 1y. 5m. 4d. 7h.
6	Jupiter 12 years	Venus 8 years	In Jupiter's period / In Venus' period	1y. 8m. 17d. 7h. / 1y. 1m. 21d. 5h.
7	Mars 7 years	Mercury 13 years	In Mars' period / In Mercury's period	1y. 10h. / 1y. 10m. 8d. 7h.
8	Dragon's head 3 years Whether day	Dragon's Tail 2 years Or night	The Dragon's Head and Tail have no association times with the planets	

Fig. 11.4: Al-Biruni's Table on Firdaria (#438–439): Chronocrators of the Day and Night

A Modern View of al-Biruni's Firdaria Tables:

	Diurnal Firdaria Ruler of Years		Age Span	Nocturnal Firdaria Ruler of Years		Age Span
1	☉	10	Birth—10 yrs old	☽	9	Birth—9 yrs old
2	♀	8	10—18 yrs old	♄	11	9—20 yrs old
3	☿	13	18—31 yrs old	♃	12	20—32 yrs old
4	☽	9	31—40 yrs old	♂	7	32—39 yrs old
5	♄	11	40—51 yrs old	☉	10	39—49 yrs old
6	♃	12	51—63 yrs old	♀	8	49—57 yrs old
7	♂	7	63—70 yrs old	☿	13	57—70 yrs old
	☊	3	70—73 yrs old	☊	3	70—73 yrs old
	☋	2	73—75 yrs old	☋	2	73—75 yrs old
1	☉	10	75—85 yrs old	☽	9	75—84 yrs old
2	♀	8	85—93 yrs old	♄	11	84—95 yrs old

Fig. 11.5: The Seven Long-term Periods of Firdaria: Diurnal Firdaria begins with the Sun, Nocturnal Firdaria begins with the Moon

Planetary Sect, Firdaria, and Munakara

Fig. 11.6 shows the number of years allocated to each planet and it is noteworthy that diurnal planets get slightly longer years (total of 33 years), whilst the nocturnal planets have less years of influence with a combined total of 24 years. Mercury has the longest period – 13 years – regardless of whether it is diurnal (rising before the Sun) or nocturnal (rising after the Sun) in the chart.

The time periods allocated to the planets remains the same in the Firdaria system (*Fig. 11.5*), but what becomes very clear is the fact that the Firdaria system is completely dependent on the divisions of sect dignity. The whole Chronocrator (Time Lord) system relies on knowing whether the chart is diurnal or nocturnal as this information is vital to the starting point of the correct Firdaria at the native's birth.

DIURNAL PLANETS Major Time Periods (Yrs)		NOCTURNAL PLANETS Major Time Periods (Yrs)	
☉	10	☽	9
♄	11	♀	8
♃	12	♂	7

BOTH DIURNAL AND NOCTURNAL Major Time Period (Yrs)	
☿	13

Fig. 11.6: Long-term (Major) Periods allotted to the Planets in Firdaria

The connection to the accidental dignity known as sect division plays a major role in determining several important factors. Sect is a major factor in identifying a planet's possibility of being in a state of munakara. The sequence from diurnal to nocturnal to diurnal (or vice versa) is determined by a planet's natural division into diurnal or nocturnal sect.

The sect dignity tables provided for each planet in munakara adds depth to the delineation of the planet in contention and aids in determining whether the planet in munakara is able to express in a more positive way in the individual's life. Generally speaking, the greater the level of sect dignity, the more the munakara planet's environment will support and reward its efforts by offering opportunities for the planet in contention to fulfil its purpose. Good sect dignity diminishes a planet's distress and circumvents its frustrations in either failing to find a direction for its contention, or alternatively, being overwhelmed by a hostile environment that does little to relieve stress and increases the planet's experiences of alienation. Good sect dignity offers a munakara planet a greater sense of achievement, a more creative expression or a less negative experience. However, poor sect dignity adds greater discomfort for the planet in munakara, often accelerating confrontation or defensive behaviour, increasing agitation, and offering a less satisfactory outcome for the planet in contention.

Planetary sect is the fountainhead for the Firdaria system with the first period reinforcing the power and influence of the dominant luminary – the Sun for the diurnal chart, and the Moon for the nocturnal chart – as the first decade belongs to the prime luminary in each sect. The following chart examples in this chapter show periods of time when a munakara planet has been either the long-term or short-term Chronocrator (Time Lord) in each individual's life.

Periods in Life when Chronocrators (Time Lords) are Munakara Planets

The four example charts with munakara planets were chosen to demonstrate both long-tem Firdaria periods (LeBron James and Frida Kahlo), as well as short-term Firdaria periods (Harry, Duke of Sussex and Julian Assange) when the planet in munakara was acting as Chronocrator.

American NBA professional basketball player, LeBron James, has two planets in the state of munakara. His chart is featured in Part Two in the chapter on munakara Saturn, but he also has Venus in contention and for this reason the long-term Firdaria period of Venus is examined in the first example of a munakara planet's role in Firdaria.

LeBron James (*Fig. 11.7*) has a diurnal chart and munakara Venus was the lord of his second Major Firdaria period, taking charge for eight years from the time that LeBron turned ten, to its completion on his 18th birthday. The example shows a general overview of James's Venus Firdaria rather than an in-depth examination of munakara Venus' interaction with each of the remaining six planets in its sub-periods.

Mexican artist, Frida Kahlo is the second example of a munakara planet's involvement in Firdaria. Kahlo's chart has nocturnal Mercury in Leo in contention (*Fig. 11.10*). Her birth took place during the daylight hours, and as a day-time birth, Mercury becomes the third Chronocrator (after the Sun and Venus), and rules for the longest period of thirteen years in her life. Mercury is Time Lord from the age of 18 years to 31 years of age, and each of the seven periods has been catalogued in Kahlo's munakara Mercury's long-term Firdaria.

Robert Hand states in his article on Firdaria (my bold in text):

Chapter Eleven • Al-Biruni's Chronocators: Munakara and the Time Lords

*There is a planet which has a long period rulership over the 'major period' which is often referred to as a 'major ruler'. This major period in turn is subdivided further into sub-periods or 'minor periods', which are also assigned to rulers of their own, often referred to as 'minor rulers'. However, we have discovered from Greek sources that such designations may not be appropriate as in those systems **the 'minor ruler' is often more important than the 'major ruler'**. We do not know at this time whether that is true in firdar(ia).*[5]

It seems likely that the planet which rules for the shorter period of time – months not years – is considered to be the planet which shows the most activity. It is the short-term lord whose nature is deeply imprinted on the period of months in which they are the Chronocrator overseeing the individual's life. When that planet is also munakara there will be noteworthy times in life where decisions and actions take one road over another. A munakara planet's role in Firdaria creates turning points that are often born from friction or antagonism, but they will also be times when conviction plays a major role in determining the individual's choices.

Harry, Duke of Sussex, is the third example of a munakara planet's impact on Firdaria, but in this case, the planet in contention is the sub-period (short-term) Firdaria lord. Harry has Saturn in munakara, and the time periods examined in his life are times when Saturn has been his short-term Chronocrator, starting with his first Sun Firdaria at birth, and continuing to the age of forty when Saturn becomes his Major Time Lord (*Fig. 11.15*).

The fourth chart under consideration belongs to whistleblower, Julian Assange, who has two planets in munakara, Jupiter, and Mars (*Fig. 11.16*). Both Firdaria periods of long-term lords (years) and short-term lords (months) will have these two planets in succession in the Chaldean Order. Mars will always follow Jupiter, and for this reason, the sub-periods for these two planets in contention will be in a consecutive order. Their time allocations will be identical (set by the long-term ruler) but the events and flavour of Jupiter's sub-period, followed immediately by Mars' sub-period, will differ greatly according to their conflicting natures and their relationship with the long-term ruler. Julian Assange's Firdaria example begins with his first Sun Firdaria, lasting ten years, and examines Jupiter and Mars' sub-periods in the diurnal Firdaria series to the age of 51 years.

Munakara in Theory

LeBron James: Munakara Venus Firdaria (8 years)
Two Football Coaches, Two Basketball Coaches, and the "Fab Four"

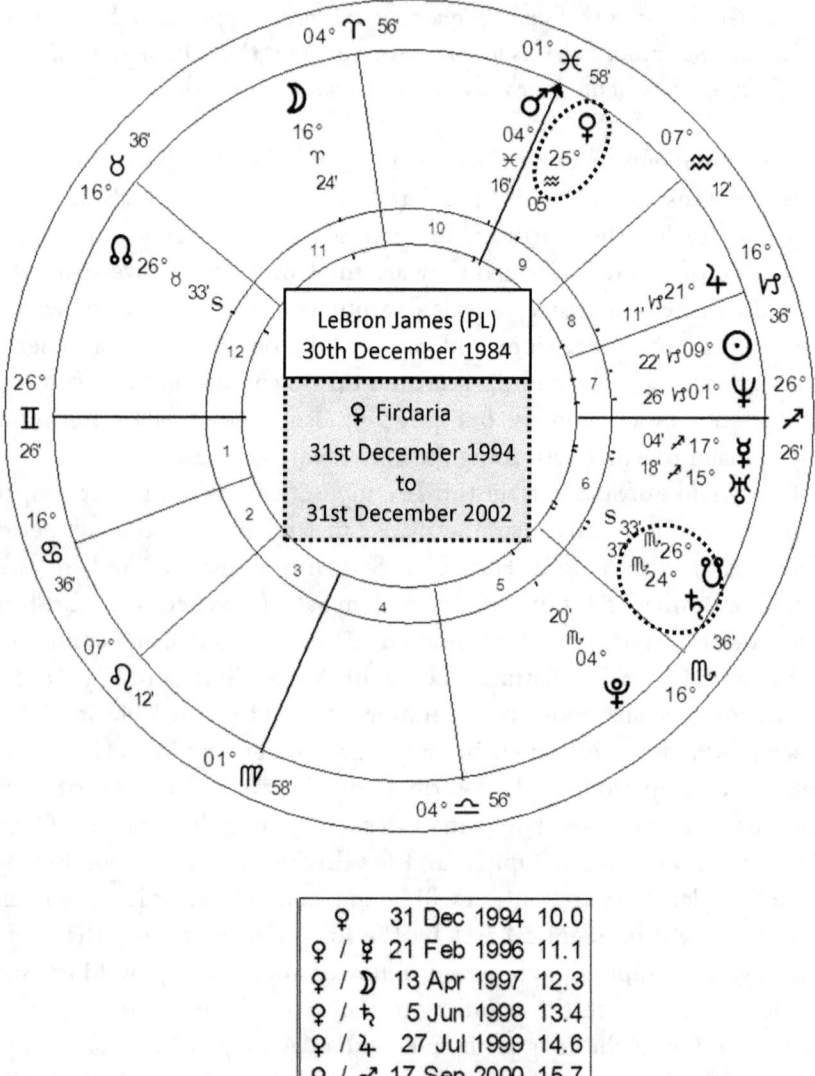

Fig. 11.7: LeBron James Natal Chart: Venus Firdaria

Chapter Eleven • *Al-Biruni's Chronocrators: Munakara and the Time Lords*

On November 13, 2005, a few weeks before his 21st birthday, LeBron James became the youngest player in NBA history to score 4,000 career points beating out fellow high-school prodigy Kobe Bryant. Known as "King James", LeBron was arguably the most talked-about NBA draft pick – and definitely the most-talked about high-schooler – but his road to glory does not begin with him as first pick in the 2003 NBA draft – rather, it began with his Venus Firdaria, the eight year period of munakara Venus as his Chronocrator between the ages of ten and eighteen.

LeBron's two munakara planets, Venus and Saturn, are examined in Part Two in the chapter featuring Saturn as a planet in contention and Saturn continues to play a major role in LeBron James' basketball career: father and son made NBA history by playing together in the same game for the Lakers on the opening night of the 2024/2025 season against the Minnesota Timberwolves.[6] However, munakara Venus is the planet that provided good fortune, friendship and a safe haven for James during his teenage years. Venus brought opportunity for positive change in his life and taught lessons that went far beyond skills on a basketball court. Munakara Venus taught him to trust others, to find something that would bring him pleasure and self-satisfaction, it taught him to love, to enjoy the comradeship of brothers when he was an only child, and to find peace, acceptance and self-love.

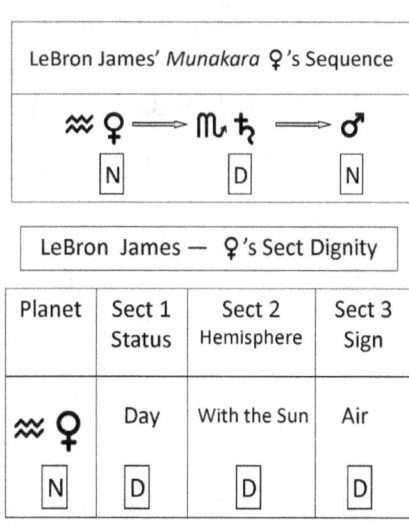

Fig.11.8: LeBron James' Munakara Venus' Sequence and Sect Dignity

Prior to the arrival of Venus' Firdaria, LeBron's first decade – Capricorn Sun's Firdaria – was a lesson in survival: a hostile world where poverty, violence, homelessness and despair were the constant companions of a young single mother and her son. LeBron's mother, Gloria, was only 26 when her son's Venus Firdaria began, and Jupiter in fall ruling 10th house brought run-ins with the law while her son was growing up; contempt of court, disorderly conduct and criminal trespassing.[7]

Saturn (on the South Node) is LeBron's other munakara planet, and the dispositor of his Venus in Aquarius. Munakara Saturn can indicate difficulty with a father figure and good male role models were missing during LeBron James' first ten years. The lack of safe, watchful or responsible father figures, protective male mentors, law-abiding men, stable and reliable influencers, men of wisdom, strength and integrity – all of these were missing from his early years when he was raised by a single mother with very few resources and little protection for Gloria or her child. However, Venus' Firdaria began to bring these types of men into his life to protect and teach him, not just the rules of the game, but to guide him in the rules of life which had been so desperately missing before munakara Venus began to work its magic.

Overview of Munakara Venus Period: 10 to 18 years old

Two Football Coaches

James' Venus Firdaria begins with LeBron's tenth birthday on the last day of 1994. The two years leading up to LeBron's Venus Firdaria were tough years. He and his mother were sleeping on other people's couches, they had no permanent residence and LeBron involuntarily missed 80 (some references cite 100) days of his 180-day schooling year in the fourth grade, because he simply had no transport to get him to classes in a school that was miles away from his constantly changing accommodation.

In 2018 LeBron opened his foundation's "I Promise School" in Akron, Ohio, and when asked about his own hard years in lost schooling he answered: "It was challenging. It was mentally challenging. Sometimes you think about a kid being in the third grade at that age – being 8, 7 years old or in the fourth grade – having responsibility. Or having stress. No kid at 8 and 9 should have stress. And I was one of those kids. So I know exactly what these kids today are going through."[8]

Bruce Kelker was the first coach to arrive on the scene just prior to LeBron's Venus Firdaria which began on the last day of 1994 with LeBron's tenth birthday. Kelker was putting together a youth football team when he first met the Jameses. He offered them a home and stability, and LeBron joined his football team.

LeBron came to the attention of a second youth football coach, Frank Walker, and he offered the boy a home with his family. Walker recalls his own son and LeBron fooling around in the backyard, and noticing that when the boys were shooting hoops James 'really had something.' Soon he had LeBron enrolled in a basketball team, and in an interview held in 2003, three months before the NBA pick, Walker told the journalist, "His gift is that you can teach

Chapter Eleven • Al-Biruni's Chronocators: Munakara and the Time Lords

him something and he catches on real quick. Show him something once or twice and he picks it up. With other kids, it takes a lot longer. That's his gift."[9] Munakara Venus sits in the 9th house where new skills are challenged, practised and perfected so that they become second nature.

Venus' rulership of the 5th house (sport, leisure and good fortune) is easy to see when, in the same interview, James acknowledges the gift of Coach Walker in his life at a time when things were tough: "My life changed. I had shelter and food. I'll never forget what the Walkers did for me, especially Frank. He doesn't get the recognition he deserves because he's real quiet but he was the first one to give me a basketball and the first one to show a real interest."[10]

Two Basketball Coaches

"I believe that things happen for a reason. I believe it was Karma that connected me to Coach Dru."[11] – LeBron James

Coach Dru Joyce was a father who had been drafted into coaching basketball because his son, Little Dru, had so desperately wanted to play the game, but was considered too small to be picked by other teams. Coach Dru started looking in Recreation Centres to build a team around his son's talents and saw James, visiting him at Frank Walker's home to convince Gloria to allow her son to join the Shooting Stars. Coach Dru found Sian Cotton at his local church, and the band of three (James, Little Dru and Sian) formed the basis of the Shooting Stars – starting out in 1995 in fifth grade in a tiny gym with a linoleum floor – and going on to qualify for the national Amateur Athletic Union (AAU) tournament in Cocoa Beach, Florida, a 20 hour road trip 1,187 miles away from Akron. Willie McGee was the fourth piece of the dream, and completed the "Fab Four" in the seventh grade (1997). In the following year when the boys were in eighth grade (1998), Coach Dru was made assistant basketball coach at Buchtel, mainly because of his success and his influence over the boys. Eighth grade try-outs at Buchtel, "open gyms", were indicating that there was only room for the bigger boys, Cotton, McGee, and James, and there would be no place on the squad for Little Dru – too short, too scrawny, too little of everything[12] – so the four boys, unknown to their parents, started looking for other options.

The second basketball coach who would influence James during Venus's Firdaria years was one whose reputation was in tatters, and who was the epitome of Venus in contention: misrepresented, misunderstood, disgraced and highly unpopular. Keith Dambrot had, after asking permission from the

African-American members of his team, used a racist word in the team's locker room at halftime to rouse his players to victory. He unwisely used the word to describe "a person who is fearless, mentally strong and tough", but someone overheard him and reported him to the disciplinary board. Subsequently, Dambrot lost his coaching position and any chance of re-entry to the arena of college basketball coach. When Coach Dru took his son and James to the Jewish Community Center where they met him, Dambrot's only contact with basketball was as a voluntary coach teaching kids on Sunday evenings.

In 1998, Dambrot came in from the cold, and he was offered the head coaching position at St. Vincent-St. Mary High School. When Little Dru heard this news, he started to make plans to follow him there in the following year, 1999, in the boys' ninth grade, and their freshman year of high school. Little Dru was determined to make his high school's basketball team, and his height would have eliminated him from the team at Buchtel, even though his father was assistant coach there. Coach Dru had been given the position because he was expected to deliver the Fab Four to Buchtel, so they could bring honour to the school's basketball team. The other boys tried to change his mind, but Little Dru's mind was set, and they decided the only thing they could do, was to join him at St. V.'s (as it was known locally).

St. Vincent-Mary's was a Catholic school with a 13% minority population of African-American students, whereas Buchtel was 97% African-American students with 40 % of its 700 students economically disadvantaged. The boys and their coach were heavily criticised in the neighbourhood for 'deserting' Buchtel to attend another school especially since St. V.'s best sport was football, not basketball, but Little Dru was adamant that his only chance to play varsity basketball was at St.V's. As James says, "A pact is a pact after all, and brothers are brothers if you define brothers by love and devotion and loyalty."[13] Coach Dru quit his coaching position at Buchtel, and joined the boys in freshman year in 1999 at St.V's, a decision that made him as unpopular as his former Shooting Stars team, as many in the black community believed he had influenced the boys' choice to change high schools.

> "It was Karma that put me with a high-school coach who had been a Division I college coach and had seen players who had gone off to play in the NBA. His experience told him, even in those early days of my high-school career, that I had a chance if I learned how to respect the game and played with the mentality of a warrior."[14]

Chapter Eleven • *Al-Biruni's Chronocators: Munakara and the Time Lords*

This is the second time in the Vanity Fair article that James mentions the term 'karma' – once for each of his critical coaches during the duration of Venus Firdaria's eight years. Coach Dambrot is an unconscious reference to Aquarius Venus' sequence: paraphrasing Dambrot 's, 'respect the game' (Saturn, Venus' first dispositor), and 'playing with the mentality of a warrior' (Mars as its outcome planet). St. V.'s team – basically the Shooting Stars – went on to win its first state championship in 2000.

LeBron's Band of Brothers (The Fab Four)

The 2009 documentary *"More Than a Game"* is largely footage shot by 21-year-old first-time director Kristopher Belman, who filmed four Akron high school basketballers and followed their season, thinking 'they were something special.' The year 2000 was Mars's sub-period for Venus and Mars is the outcome planet for munakara Venus. The year 2000 was also the boys' sophomore year and the four boyhood friends – LeBron James, Sian Cotton, Willie McGee and Dru Joyce III (Little Dru) – were joined by their fifth member, an angry young man named Romeo Travis.

Initially, fitting in with the "Fab Four" was not easy. Travis had not shared the childhood memories of Shooting Stars, had not faced the initial discomfort of moving into an alien atmosphere at St. V.s'. Travis had also not experienced the nurturing hand that Coach Dru had provided for the younger boys when they were children starting their basketball training with the basics. Like James, Travis had grown up in a poor neighbourhood, but unlike James who had a close relationship with his mother, Travis had done it alone, and did not understand the need to rely on anyone other than himself. James' comments in *Vanity Fair*,

> *Like me, he (Travis) went to a variety of different schools growing up. But I had found Little Dru and Sian and Willie. They were my body and soul; they kept me going no matter how hard times got. Romeo never had that, and the concept of lasting friendship was silly and wasteful in his eyes. 'You could be my friend today and you could be gone tomorrow' was how he put it. He had no use for us, and he made that clear.*[15]

Once more, the group of friends faced resentment from Akron's Black community when yet another skilled player moved to the white Catholic school. Coach Dambrot's ambitions to revive his career made him a coach who always played his best team. This meant more bench-time for less-talented members who were excluded from the expanded 'Fab Five'. More contention, more difficulty, more battles to fight, more pressure to win – even under the umbrella of Venus – munakara is still going to carry the seeds of injustice, prejudice, animosity, and resentment during its time as Firdaria lord.

In James' sophomore year (2000) with Travis as the last piece, St. V. won back-to-back state championships. The hype was beginning to grow for James and as he entered his Junior year in 2001, rumours began to circulate that he would go straight to the NBA as soon as he completed his Senior year in high school. But even Venus can sting when it is in munakara, and Coach Dambrot left St. Vincent without a word to the boys when he was offered an assistant's job at the University of Akron.

When they returned from summer holidays as Juniors in September 2001 – James was in a Venus/Mars sub-period – Dambrot was gone, and the five boys felt bitter and angry at the way he had used them to resurrect his coaching career. His betrayal cut deep, and for some of the boys who had been deserted by errant fathers, this was yet another blow at the hands of a deceitful and self-serving adult. Mars is munakara Venus' outcome planet and the two nocturnal planets often show a painful period in a Firdaria where both planets are involved as major and minor Firdaria lords.

Once more, Coach Dru stepped in and filled the gap, becoming their new coach in Junior year (2001–2002). It was a disaster, but the fault did not lie in his coaching; 'too much media attention, too little attention to basketball.' The boys and their coach had settled by Senior year (2002–2003), and in the last year playing together as high school friends, they won the last game to finish the season as the No. 1 ranked national champions.

Frida Kahlo: Nocturnal Mercury in Munakara

A Brief Biography[16]

Frida Kahlo (6 July 1907 – 13 July 1954) was a Mexican painter known for her many portraits, self-portraits, and works inspired by nature and the artefacts of indigenous Mexicans. Her brilliantly coloured self-portraits deal with such themes as identity, the human body, and death. In addition to her work, Kahlo was known for her tumultuous relationship with Mexican muralst Diego Rivera (married 1929, divorced 1939, remarried 1940).

Kahlo was born to a German father and a Mexican mother of Spanish and Native American descent. As a child, she suffered a bout of polio that left her with a slight limp, a chronic ailment she would endure throughout her

Chapter Eleven • *Al-Biruni's Chronocators: Munakara and the Time Lords*

life. Although Kahlo took some drawing classes, she was more interested in science, and in 1922 she entered the National Preparatory School in Mexico City with an interest in eventually studying medicine. While there she met Rivera, who was working on a mural for the school's auditorium.

In 1925 Kahlo was involved in a bus accident, which so seriously injured her that she had to undergo more than 30 medical operations in her lifetime. During her slow recovery, Kahlo taught herself to paint, and she read frequently, studying the art of the Old Masters.

After her convalescence, Kahlo joined the Mexican Communist Party, where she met Rivera once again. She showed him some of her work, and he encouraged her to continue to paint. She and Rivera were married in 1929 and Kahlo changed her personal style where she began to wear the traditional Tehuana dress that became her trademark.

The couple travelled through the US for three years (1930–33) and Kahlo began to develop her own painting style while Rivera completed commissions for mural from several cities.

Her first solo exhibition took place in New York in 1838, and it was a great success. The following year she travelled to Paris to show her work. The Louvre acquired one of her works, *The Frame* (c. 1938), making Kahlo the first 20th-century Mexican artist to be included in the museum's collection.

Kahlo underwent several surgeries in the late 1940s and early '50s. often with prolonged hospital stays. Her ill health caused her to attend her first solo exhibition in Mexico in 1953 lying on a bed. She died a year later, the official cause documented as a pulmonary embolism.

Nocturnal Mercury in Munakara Firdaria (13 years)

Frida began her long-term Mercury Firdaria on her eighteenth birthday. Two months later, on 17 September, 1925, she suffered a horrific bus accident which would cause her lifelong pain and change the course of her life from that moment forward. Mercury would be her long-term Firdaria lord for thirteen years, and each of the seven planets (including Mercury) would be her short-term Firdaria lords for a period of approximately 22 months.

Frida Kahlo was born during the daylight hours so her diurnal Firdaria begins with the Sun for ten years followed by Venus for eight years. Mercury will rule for thirteen years, then the Moon for nine years, Saturn takes eleven years, Jupiter is next for twelve years, and finally, Mars completes the series with the shortest term of seven years.

Frida's munakara Mercury will be the planet that rules the longest period in her life, from age 18 to 31. During these years her planet in contention will not only produce her most important work, it will see her most challenging years and contain the two 'great accidents in her life.' Every day was a battle of pain, restricted movement and frustration, yet a total of 72 major works were painted during Frida's 13-year Mercury period.

It has been said that Kahlo made herself through her paintings into "the main character of her own mythology, as a woman, as a Mexican, and as a suffering person....She knew how to convert each into a symbol or sign capable of expressing the enormous spiritual resistance of humanity and its splendid sexuality."[17]

Frida Kahlo's Mercury is in the state of munakara: nocturnal Mercury in Leo disposits to Sun in Cancer with the Moon as Mercury's outcome planet in its sequence. Mercury is in the 12th house in her Placidus chart (Fig. 11.10), but moves to the 1st house in Whole Sign as Leo is the sign on her Ascendant. Aspects are scarce for Kahlo's Mercury, and its fixed sign position creates problems for the rulership of Virgo as the two signs, Leo and Virgo, cannot see each other. Virgo is on the 2nd-house cusp, and the security of one's finances is often part of the struggle when the ruling planet is in aversion, as well as being in the state of contention. Munakara Mercury's other rulership house is the 11th house with Gemini on the cusp and no-one loved to party more than Frida Kahlo. Her work was once described by French writer Andre Breton as 'a ribbon around a bomb,'[18] but the description might as well have described Frida herself. Whenever she could move her body without excruciating pain (Mercury in 1st house), Frida would fill the Blue House with lively conversation, music, copious amounts of alcohol, high jinks, laughter, bawdy jokes, and her own special brand of frenetic energy.

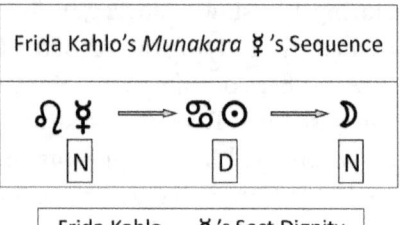

Fig. 11.9: Frida Kahlo's Munakara Mercury Sequence and Sect Dignity

Frida loved to be the centre of attention (Leo rising ruled by Cancer Sun) and even when she was immobilized by pain she would instruct the

Chapter Eleven • *Al-Biruni's Chronocators: Munakara and the Time Lords*

strongest men present to fetch her and her bed so that she would not miss the fun (Mercury rules her 11th house). Many of Frida's paintings were focused on her own image and depicted periods in her life marking both happy times (her marriage to Diego) and times of grief (her miscarriages) but always set by munakara Mercury in Leo to show her as an image of an alluringly beautiful indigenous woman.

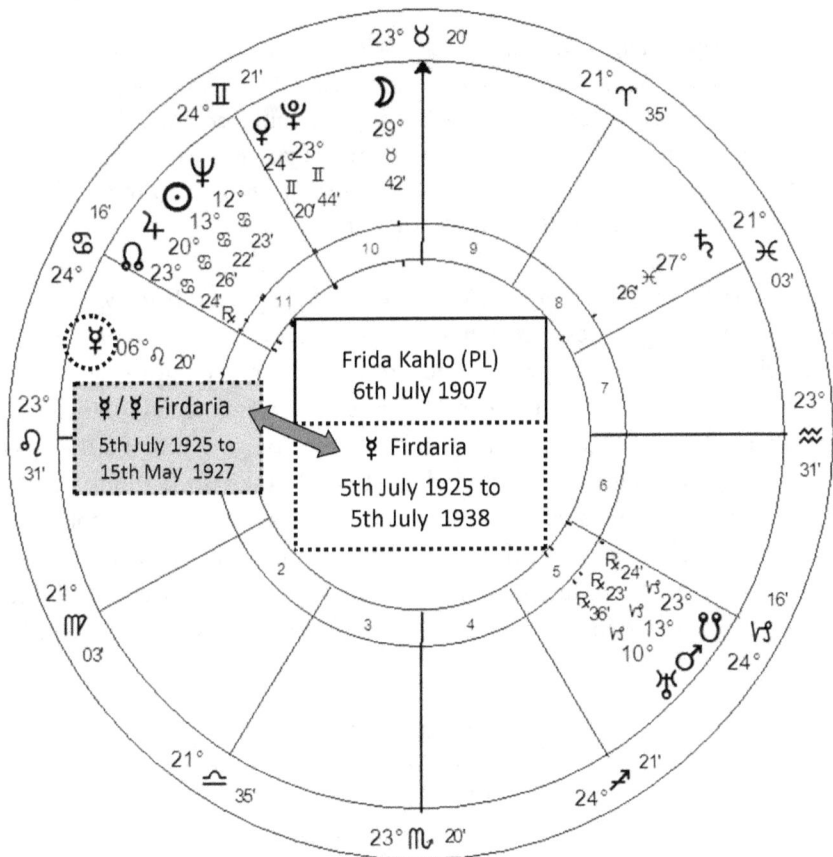

*Fig. 11.10: Frida Kahlo's Placidus Natal Chart:
Munakara Mercury in 12th House*

The sequence for munakara Mercury in Leo leads to both luminaries – Sun in Cancer to Moon – and Frida Kahlo grew up in a home with a mother who was constantly ill, often depressed, and emotionally unavailable (Moon, outcome planet), and a father who was emotionally violent (Leo Mercury's dispositor). Her father was an epileptic prone to physically explosive and unpredicted episodes, and it fell to his 'favourite daughter' to keep him engaged and to cajole him out of his dark moods. Frida's sister, Cristina does not seem to have captured her father's attentions, but there is no written proof of her relationship with their father.

American photographer Edward Weston described his first meeting with Frida Kahlo on December 14, 1930:

> *I photographed Diego again, his new wife – Frida – too: she is in sharp contrast to Lupe (Guadalupe Marin, Rivera's second wife), petit, – a little doll alongside Diego, but a doll in size only, for she is strong and quite beautiful, shows very little of her father's German blood (Mercury's dispositor). Dressed in native costume even to huaraches, she causes much excitement on the streets of San Francisco. People stop in their tracks to look in wonder.*[19]

Rivera's biographer, Bertram Wolfe, wrote "Diego and Frida were feted, lionized, spoiled. Parties everywhere, streams of invitations to teas, dinners, week-ends, lectures with great audiences coming to get a glimpse of them and listening, astounded, to Diego's words on art and social questions."[20] Frida's munakara Mercury was gaining attention, but not in the ways she so desperately wanted and needed. It would take until 1953 – during her Saturn/Venus Firdaria and months before her death in the following year – for Frida's first solo exhibition to be granted in her beloved Mexico, and she must have felt deeply hurt that her art was recognised and valued everywhere, except the place where she needed the most validation for her talents.

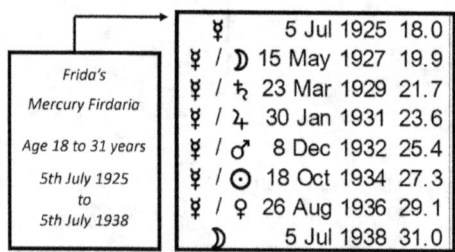

Fig. 11.11: Frida Kahlo's Mercury Firdaria

Overview of Munakara Mercury Period: 18 to 31 years old
Frida Kahlo's Two Accidents

DIURNAL CHARTS Time Lords for Daytime Births	☿ 13 year MAJOR Period * 1 yr 10 months MINOR Period	Example Chart Frida Kahlo: 6th July 1907 Time Periods
1	☿ / ☿	18.0 – 19.9	From 5th July 1925 to 14th May 1927
2	☿ / ☽	19.9 – 21.7	From 15th May 1927 to 22nd March 1929
3	☿ / ♄	21.7 – 23.6	From 23rd March 1929 to 29th Jan 1931
4	☿ / ♃	23.6 – 25.4	From 30th Jan 1931 to 7th Dec 1932
5	☿ / ♂	25.4 – 27.3	From 8th Dec 1932 to 17th Oct 1934
6	☿ / ☉	27.3 – 29.1	From 18th Oct 1934 to 25th Aug 1936
7	☿ / ♀	29.1 – 31.0	From 26th Aug 1936 to 4th July 1938

Fig. 11.12: Frida Kahlo's Munakara Mercury Firdaria:
Major and Minor Firdaria Periods

MERCURY/Mercury: 5 July 1925 to 14 May 1927

On September 17, 1925 Frida Kahlo and her boyfriend Alexandro Gomez Aria spent the afternoon after school wandering around the street stalls of downtown Mexico City before catching a bus to take them home to Coyoacan. The bus was nearly full and the two teenagers found seats together near the back of the bus. A street trolley approached as the bus was about to make a turn and the bus driver believed he could make the turn before the trolley reached it. This is Alex's recollection of the accident:

The electric train (streetcar) with two cars approached the bus slowly. It hit the bus in the middle. Slowly the train pushed the bus. The bus had a strange elasticity. It bent more and more, but for a time it did not break. It was a bus with long benches on either side. I remember that at one moment my knees touched the knees of the person sitting opposite me. I was sitting next to Frida. When the bus reached its maximum flexibility it burst into a thousand pieces, and the train kept moving. It ran over many people.

I remained under the train. Not Frida. But among the iron rods of the train, the handrail broke and went through Frida from one side to the other at the level of the pelvis. When I was able to stand up, I got out from under the train. I had no lesions, only contusions. Naturally the first thing that I did was to look for Frida.

Something strange had happened. Frida was totally nude. The collision had unfastened her clothes. Someone in the bus, probably a house painter, had been carrying a packet of powdered gold. This package broke, and the gold fell all over the bleeding body of Frida. When people saw her, they cried, 'La bailarina, la bailarina!' With the gold on her red, bloody body, they thought she was a dancer.

I picked her up....and then I noticed with horror that Frida had a piece of iron in her body. A man said, 'We have to take it out!' He put his knee on Frida's body and said, 'Let's take it out.' When he pulled it out, Frida screamed so loud that when the ambulance from the Red Cross arrived, her screaming was louder than the siren. Before the ambulance came, I picked up Frida and put her in the display window of a billiard room. I took off my coat and put it over her. I thought she was going to die. Two or three people did die at the scene....others died later.[21]

Frida spent a month in hospital, and a further three months immobilized in full body plaster casts. Her father (first dispositor, the Sun) gave her a small lap easel and hung a mirror above the bed so that Frida could pass time by painting the only thing she can see – her own image (munakara Leo Mercury in 1st house).

Frida's first painting was "Self-Portrait in a Velvet Dress", painted from her bed in 1926 as she was convalescing. She painted it as a gift for Alexandro, to win him back after he abandoned her, accusing her of being 'too liberal' before the accident. Under the first sub-period belonging to Mercury, Frida recaptures Alexandro's heart with the painting (Sept 1926), but loses him the following year (March 1927), a few months before the Moon's sub-period, when his parents send him to Europe to remove him from her considerable influence. They remained friends throughout Frida's life, but the romance was never rekindled.

Chapter Eleven • *Al-Biruni's Chronocators: Munakara and the Time Lords*

MERCURY / Moon: 14 May 1927 to 22 March 1929 (Munakara Planet and Outcome Planet)

"I paint my own reality. The only thing I know is that I paint because I need to, and I paint whatever passes through my head without any other consideration."

In 1928 during the Moon sub-period Frida meets Diego Rivera for the second time (he visited her school when she was 14). Frida had joined the Communist Party in late 1927 and they moved in similar circles, attracted to the same political philosophies. Frida's Moon is void-of-course at 29° Taurus and is conjunct her Mid-heaven. The Moon rules her 12th house, and her marriage to Diego certainly gave her fame and immediate status, but it was often a toxic relationship that caused Frida a great deal of emotional pain. Frida is quoted as saying to a friend, *"There have been two great accidents in my life. One was the trolley, and the other was Diego. Diego was by far the worst."*

MERCURY / Saturn: 23 March 1929 to 29 January 1931

Marriage to Diego Rivera takes place (21 Aug 1929) during Saturn's sub-period. Saturn is the ruler of Kahlo's 6th and 7th houses and squares Gemini Venus and Pluto.

"Diego began to fall in love with me. My father didn't like him because he was a Communist and because they said he looked like a fat, fat, fat Breughel [Peter Breughel, 16th C. Flemish painter]. They said it was like an elephant marrying a dove. Nevertheless, I arranged everything in the Coyoacan town hall for us to be married on the twenty-first of August, 1929."[22]

Frida was 22, Diego, 43. Frida's mother refused to attend the wedding, but her father approved the marriage because Diego was considered to be successful and affluent and would have the finances to afford to pay for Frida's medical bills and the many operations she would need in the future. Her father warned Diego that he is marrying *un demonio* – a devil.

"I borrowed petticoats, a blouse, and a rebozo [fringed shawl] from the maid, fixed the special apparatus on my foot so it wouldn't be noticeable, and we were married. Nobody went to the wedding, only my father, who said to Diego, 'Now, look, my daughter is a sick person and all her life she is going to be sick. She's intelligent but not pretty. Think it over awhile if you like, and if you still wish to marry her, marry her, I give you my permission.'"[23]

Frida described her mother as 'calculating, cruel and fanatically religious,'[24] and there was rarely affection between mother and child, yet Frida adopted indigenous Mexican dress and her mother's culture after her marriage to Diego and remained true to this style for life. The couple left Mexico and moved to San Francisco in November 1930 for Diego's wall mural commissions in US.

MERCURY / Jupiter: 30 January 1931 to 7 December 1932

In New York in 1931 Frida's Mexican style drew attention and comment but she lived in Diego's shadow and seemed to be in awe of him. "I don't want anything to hurt him, nothing to bother him and rob him of the energy he needs for living, for living as he likes, for painting, seeing, loving, eating, sleeping, being by himself, being with someone....but I would never want him to be sad. If I had good health, I would give him all of it, if I had youth, he could take it all."

In 1931, under her Jupiter sub-period Frida, painted several portraits including *Frieda [she later dropped the 'e' in her name] and Diego Rivera* from a wedding photo. A San Francisco newspaper dismissed its artistic worth claiming it was "valuable only because it was painted by the wife of Diego Rivera." The couple moved to Detroit in early 1932, and Frida suffered her second miscarriage. Exalted Jupiter is situated in Frida's 12th house and rules her 5th house (her creativity and desire for a child) and her 8th house (near-death experiences). The move to Detroit centred around Diego painting murals for the Detroit Institute of Arts. Frida's fluency in English is far superior to Diego's, and on her arrival to the city, Frida tells interviewers that she is the greater artist of the two of them: "Of course he (Rivera) does well for a little boy, but it is I who am the big artist."[25] She began a number of important works but did not complete them until her Mercury/Mars Firdaria.

MERCURY / Mars: 8 December 1932 to 17 October 1934

During her Mars sub-period Frida completed four of her most harrowing works – *Frida and the Caesarean Operation, Henry Ford Hospital, My Dress Hangs There,* and *My Birth.* Capricorn Mars is exalted but it lies in Frida's 6th house and opposes her Sun, the dispositor for her Leo Mercury in munakara. Diego says of this period "Frida began work on a series of masterpieces which had no precedent in the history of art – paintings which exalted the feminine quality of truth, reality, cruelty, and suffering. Never before had a woman put such agonized poetry on canvas as Frida did at this time in Detroit."

Chapter Eleven • Al-Biruni's Chronocators: Munakara and the Time Lords

In March 1933 during Mars' sub-Firdaria the Riveras move to New York City. After three years in the United States, Frida was homesick and increasingly disillusioned by America's social decay and the wide divide between wealthy clients and impoverished workers. She began work on *My Dress Hangs There* and there is increasing tension between the couple, as Rivera loves the attention and lifestyle he enjoys in America, but Frida is miserable, misses Mexico and feels alienated from her culture and her country. Mars rules the 4th house (home) and the 9th house (foreign or alien countries) and Mars adds to munakara Mercury's agitation when the two planets' energies are combined.

Both take lovers but stay together. Frida's 1932 painting *Self-Portrait on the Border between Mexico and the United States* places Frida in a virginal white dress at the centre, on her left is the natural beauty of her beloved Mexico, and on her right side is the industrialized ugliness and brutality of American capitalism. Diego loses his commission in New York to paint a mural for the Rockefeller Center when he includes Lenin in his mural. Instead Diego is hired to paint a mural for the New Workers School, and whilst he wishes to stay in the United States to pursue more commissions, he is pressured by Frida to return to Mexico after the mural's unveiling in December 1933.

MERCURY / Sun: 18 October 1934 to 25 August 1936
(Munakara Planet and First Dispositor)

Cancer Sun in the 12th house is the ruler of the Ascendant and this is a particularly painful period in Frida's life. The pair returned to Mexico but Diego misses the adulation he received in America, and perhaps in response to Frida's control over him, he begins an affair with Frida's younger sister, Cristina. Frida discovered the affair early in 1935 and moved out of their family home, considering divorce as an option. The affair was a particularly cruel blow for Frida (Mercury signifies siblings) as Cristina was her closest confidante, and she felt betrayed by the two people she loved most in the world. Gaining Rivera's attention may have been a triumph for Cristina as she has lived in the shadow of her talented sister, their father's favourite, throughout her childhood and adolescence.

Frida suffered depression as a result of the affair, plus a second abortion, an appendectomy, and surgery on her foot to remove gangrenous toes. She eventually forgave her husband and sister and moved back home in late 1935. *A Few Small Nips* ('*unos cuantos piquetitos*') was painted in 1935 during

Frida's isolation from her family and depicts a painting of a husband holding a knife over the naked and bloodied body of his murdered wife. The title are the words spoken during the trial of a man who killed his wife for being unfaithful, claiming to the judge that he had only inflicted a 'few small nips'. Frida's rage at the hypocrisy of Mexican patriarchal society is evident in this painting, and Diego's infidelity is still a painful memory.[26]

Frida Kahlo resumes her political activities in 1936, joining the Fourth International (founded by Leon Trotsky), and becoming a founding member of a solidarity committee, to provide aid to the Republicans in the Spanish Civil War.

MERCURY / Venus: 26 August 1936 to 4 July 1938

Venus rules Frida's 3rd house with Libra on its cusp and Cristina is the indirect subject of Frida's *Memory, the Heart*, a reflection on her pain at Cristina's betrayal with Diego. The 1937 self-portrait shows Frida with a metal rod piercing through an empty space in her chest, placed higher in her body than the one from her accident, but creating greater pain because of its subject matter.

Venus is the ruler of the 3rd house (siblings) and the MC lord. Venus squares Saturn, the ruler of the 7th house (partners). Frida's sister, Cristina, was one of Diego's favourite models, and alongside Frida, she and her two children are featured in one of his most famous murals *The History of Mexico: The World of Today and Tomorrow*. Cruelly, Diego paints Frida as 'statuesque' whilst Cristina appears 'lively' – his wife lies peacefully alongside his lover – and the inclusion of Cristina's two children in the mural are a constant cruel reminder to Frida that she is barren, whilst her sister is fertile.

Frida's painting *Mi Nodriza y yo* (*My wet-nurse and I*) was also painted in 1937 (the same year as *Memory, the Heart*), and records the fact that Frida was taken away from her mother to be breastfed by a wet nurse because her mother was pregnant with another baby, her sister Cristina.

Taurus on Frida's Mid-heaven places Venus as its ruler, and during Venus's sub-period, French Surrealist artist André Breton visited Rivera in April 1938, but was more impressed by Frida's work. Breton arranged for her first solo exhibition at the Julien Levy Gallery in New York in 1938 – the exhibition was a success and led to a second exhibition in Paris in 1939. One New York art critic for *Time* wrote "Little Frida's pictures....had the daintiness of miniatures, the vivid reds, and yellows of Mexican tradition and the playfully bloody fancy of an unsentimental child."[27]

Chapter Eleven • *Al-Biruni's Chronocators: Munakara and the Time Lords*

During the Mercury/Venus period Frida and Diego successfully petition the Mexican government to grant asylum to former Soviet leader Leon Trotsky, and opened their home for he and his wife as a residence in Mexico. The exiled couple arrived in January 1937, and lived with the Riveras for over two years. An argument with Diego, possibly after another attempt on Trotsky's life, forced them to move out and live independently. Soon after his arrival in Mexico, Frida and Trotsky became lovers for a brief period, and remained friends until his death in August 1940 in Mexico City.

Frida Kahlo: Mercury Firdaria
Second Time Around (2002–2013)

Fame is an interesting phenomenon, particularly when it does not require the physical presence of someone whose body is no longer bound to the Earth. Frida Kahlo died seven days after turning 47 on 13th July 1954 during her Saturn/Venus Firdaria. The official cause of death was pulmonary embolism but her nurse reported that Frida had taken an overdose of painkillers on the night she died.

The diurnal Firdaria begins a second ten-year term for the Sun between the ages of 75 and 85 years of age, and for Frida Kahlo, these ages would have occurred between the time period of 5 July 1982 (75 years old) and 5 July 1992 (85 years old). Frida's Cancer Sun is munakara Mercury's dispositor and the reawakening of Frida's fame began in the 1980s when art historian Hayden Herrera published his international bestseller, *Frida: A Biography of Frida Kahlo*,[28] in 1983. In May 1982, the Whitechapel Gallery in London opened an exhibition of her paintings and photographs of Frida which later travelled to Sweden, Germany, the United States, and Mexico.

The commercialization of her image – coined 'Fridamania' begun in the mid-1980s – has led many scholars and cultural commentators to mourn that the brilliance of her art has been overshadowed by the tragedy of her accident, and the life-long physical agony she suffered as a result of her injuries.

Herrera's book was re-released in 2002 to coincide with the release of the Hollywood film *Frida* – released in 2002, the same year as the commencement of Frida's Mercury/Mercury Firdaria. The film starred and was co-produced by Mexican actress, Salma Hayek as Frida. The film was based on Herrera's biography and was a financial and artistic success, grossing US$56 million worldwide and earning six Academy Award nominations, including Hayek's nomination for Best Actress (the first Mexican actress to receive this honour).

American art historian and former chief curator of MoMA, Kirk Varnedoe, opines on Frida's posthumous success, his words encapsulating her munakara Mercury in Leo: *"She (Kahlo) clicks with today's sensibilities – her psycho-obsessive concern with herself, her creation of a personal alternative world carries a voltage. Her constant remaking of her identity, her construction of a theatre of the self are exactly what preoccupy such contemporary artists as Cindy Sherman or Kiki Smith, and on a more popular level, Madonna."*[29]

When a planet, particularly Mercury, is munakara there are constant reminders that misinformation, misdirection, and misrepresentation are ongoing sources of irritation. Even though Kahlo has passed from this world, her artwork often defies labelling, being classified as 'surrealist', 'realist' and the current classification as 'magic realism' where her compositions are irrational, strange, and magical.[30] Frida's Leo Mercury in her Whole Sign chart craved attention. It was evident in her brightly coloured clothing, her accentuated makeup, her elaborate hairstyles, her jewelry, all so different from other women of her period screamed 'look at me'. But her Placidus Mercury in munakara lies in her 12th house, and she hid her most intimate thoughts and her emotions within the iconography of her art, and protected herself through her flamboyant indigenous dress style.

An article in 1998 in *Women's Art Journal* under the title, "Fashioning National Identity: Frida Kahlo in "Gringoland", comments that In the United States she acted as an unofficial ambassador of post-revolutionary Mexico, and that "Kahlo was keenly aware of the ability of clothing to communicate information about the tastes, principles, character, and moods of her nation", right down to the "ribald Mexican sayings" embroidered on her petticoats.[31]

The Diary of Frida Kahlo: An Intimate Self-portrait was written during the last ten years of her life (1944–1954), years after Frida's Mercury Firdaria was over. Yet *The Diary* was begun around the time when munakara Mercury was the sub-period Firdaria lord for the Moon (Moon is Mercury's outcome planet) and continued into her Saturn Firdaria when her health deteriorated after her right leg was amputated at the knee in August 1953, her dependency on painkillers escalated. Together, the two planets rule her rising and setting degrees and Saturn rules her 6th house of illness. Frida's final drawing in the diary is a black angel accompanied by the last words she wrote, "I joyfully await the exit – and hope never to return – Frida."[32]

The Diary's richness and emotional depth is a testament to the singular planet which is munakara in her chart. Her Mercury is nocturnal and the journal reflects the nocturnality of a chaotic and creative mind, one that has few boundaries when it comes to fulfilling the reader's expectations of literary competence or logical thought processes. Instead, her diary is a collection of doodles, poems, letters, sketches and phrases, and notes that make little sense to anyone but the writer. It is half-writing and half-image.

The introductory essay by Sarah M. Lowe begins with the words, *"Reading through Frida Kahlo's diary is unquestionably an act of transgression, an undertaking inevitably charged with an element of voyeurism. Her journal is a deeply private expression of her feelings, and was never intended to be viewed publicly. As such, Kahlo's diary belongs to the genre of the 'journal in time', a private record written by a woman for herself."*[33]

The Diary of Frida Kahlo was released to the public in 1995 – in her second Venus/Moon Firdaria – and its publication re-marketed her personality and re-energised her munakara Mercury in Leo (Moon is Mercury's outcome planet). The diary introduced her work to a new generation of women who heralded her as a 21st-century folk hero for her courage in the face of adversity as much as for her artistic works. Of her almost 200 paintings, 55 are self-portraits, and women especially, have identified with her self-portraits that openly displayed deeply personal and emotional issues, especially those that explored themes such as pain, sexuality, and cultural identity. Frida has been embraced by modern feminists, the LGBTI community, the art world and unfortunately, the commercial world too. A reincarnated Frida might be appalled by the copious amount of copied and modernised merchandise in shops, boutiques, clothing stores, airports and chain-store outlets, but there is no doubt that her munakara Mercury in Leo has placed her as one of the most recognisable faces in this century.[34]

In Frida's *Diary*, Carlos Fuentes, a Mexican novelist and essayist, shares that "I only saw Frida Kahlo once. But first, I heard her." Fuentes says the *Diary* exemplifies Kahlo's love of language and endless play with words, her "ribald, punning, dynamic genius for humorous language.... Her voice, all who knew her tell us, was deep, rebellious, punctuated by *'caracajadas'* – belly laughs – and by *'leperadas'* – four-lettered words."[35]

Munakara in Theory

Harry, Duke of Sussex: Munakara Saturn

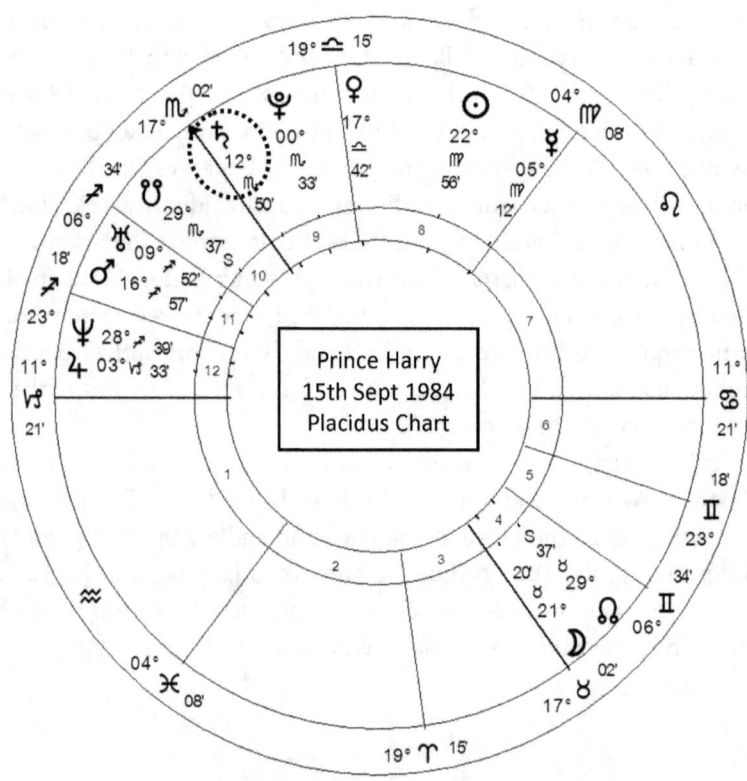

Fig. 11.13: Prince Harry's Munakara Saturn Sequence,
Sect Dignity, Chart Placement in Placidus Chart

Chapter Eleven • *Al-Biruni's Chronocrators: Munakara and the Time Lords*

Prince Harry: Munakara Saturn, Short-Term Firdaria Lord
Periods differ according to Long-term Firdaria Lord's Years

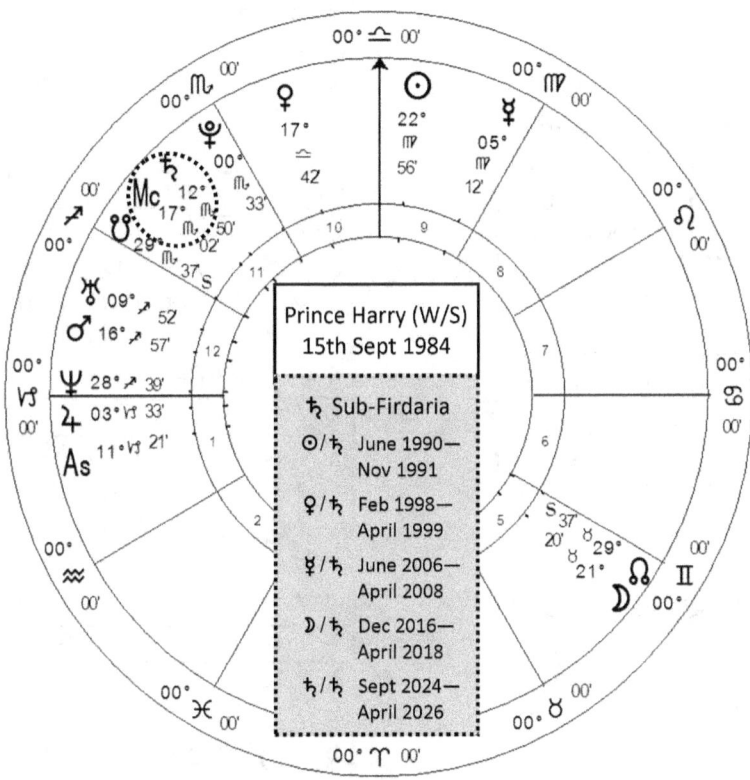

Fig. 11.14: Prince Harry's Whole Sign Natal Chart: Saturn's Placement and Saturn's Sub-Firdaria Periods

Sun/SATURN: 3 June 1990 to 6 November 1991 (Age: 5.7–7.1 yrs)

Prince Harry's his first long-term Firdaria lord will be his Sun as his birth took place during daylight hours. The Sun in Harry's chart sits in Whole Sign 9th house, and the Sun's position in Virgo means that it is blind to the 8th house with Leo on its cusp. Even from a young age his Virgo Sun is collecting information and storing it away for future use. His Sun is disposited by Mercury in rulership and any new or unusual experiences (9th house) will be measured and collated. When something totally unexpected happens and situations change suddenly (8th house) the Sun will use reason and practical knowledge to understand its new challenges.

Munakara in Theory

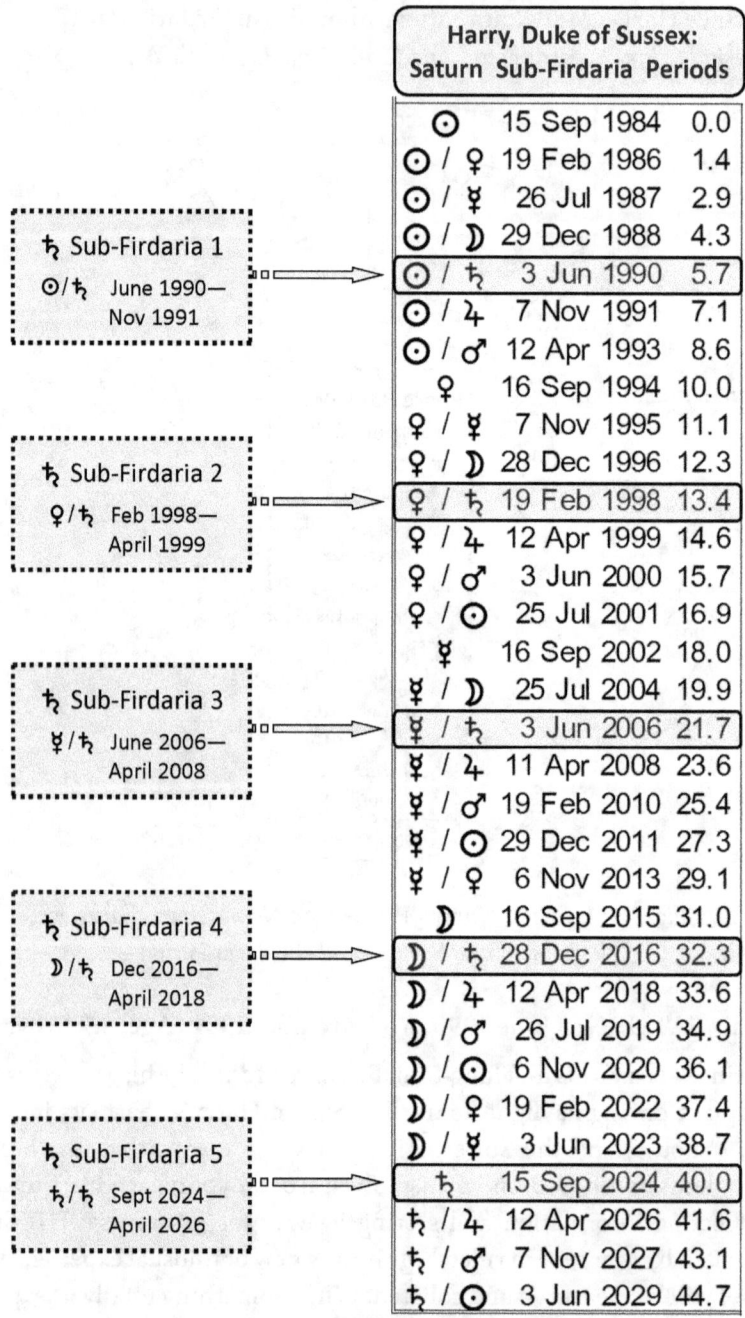

Fig. 11.15: Prince Harry's Munakara Saturn Sub-Firdaria Periods: Saturn as Chronocrator of the Months

Chapter Eleven • *Al-Biruni's Chronocators: Munakara and the Time Lords*

The Sun and Saturn are both planets that symbolize the father (or the dominant male) but in different forms, and with different messages. The Sun shines light on the child with praise and admiration and represents the warm protective parent who gently teaches by example. Saturn, on the other hand, is the father who disciplines, who sets boundaries and expectations, and whose criticism, withdrawal of affection, or punishment is the end result when the child displays poor behaviour or disobedience.

Young Harry was between the ages of five and a half and just over seven years when Saturn was the Sun's sub-period lord. Both planets are diurnal, but they are not friends as their signs oppose one another in the Thema Mundi chart. Saturn as Sun's agent is often harsh and uncompromising, sometimes providing unpleasant examples of parenting by the father figure, with coldness or withdrawal in father's behaviour, or describing an experience of separation in some form.

Saturn is Harry's Ascendant lord and the young child may have felt it was his behaviour, or something about his actions or appearance which were creating this experience with his father. In truth, Harry's parents and their marriage were under extreme scrutiny at this time, and rumours of his father's affair with Camilla Parker-Bowles were beginning to surface in the media. In 1989 Diana confronted Camilla at a family gathering, noting, "I was terrified of her." Diana recalls, "I said, 'I know what's going on between you and Charles and I want you to know that. Don't treat me like an idiot." Diana said Camilla responded to her accusation with the words, "You've got everything you ever wanted. You've got all the men in the world falling in love with you and you've got two beautiful children, what more do you want?" to which Diana replied "I want my husband."[36]

Public appearances of the couple in 1990 and 1991 showed them looking strained and distanced, no eye contact or loving embraces, and body language that suggested anger and resentment on both sides. Rumours of Diana's romantic liaison with Major James Hewitt had not yet appeared, but the press were beginning to notice and comment on the physical differences between Harry, and his older brother, William.

Venus/SATURN: 19 Feb. 1998 to 11 April 1999 (Age: 13.4–14.6 yrs)

Princess Diana's death preceded Saturn's second sub-period by a few months before its arrival in February 1998. Harry's grief at losing his beloved mother whom he adored is shown by Venus in rulership (Libra) in the 10th house of mother in the Whole Sign chart. Saturn's dispositor is Mars in the 12th house, and it would be hard to believe that Harry did not hold his father, and his father's family, somehow responsible for her death. His parents' divorce had become official a year before Diana's fatal car accident, but she had remained close to her two sons, particularly Harry, who was barely into his teenage years when he lost his mother.

Saturn's sub-period for Venus coincides with Saturn cycle's first opposition around age fourteen, and this point in the cycle is often connected with loss or a traumatic event that ends childhood and marks a painful or abrupt entrance into adulthood. Transiting Saturn was also opposing Harry's Venus during the period of Diana's death, and the combination of transit, cycle, and Venus/Saturn Firdaria period, demonstrates the difficult of munakara Saturn as Harry struggles with grief and must deal with the distress of losing Diana, the mother, and Diana, the ideal concept of feminine beauty (10th house Venus in Libra). For Saturn to be opposing Venus by transit it would have been passing through Harry's 4th house (father and home) and Charles, his father, may have been incapable of comforting his teenage son.

Adding to Harry's sense of separation and emotional isolation from his father was the fact that he was packed off by Prince Charles to Eton College – during Saturn's sub-period – to become an away-from-home boarder in September 1998, a year after he had lost his mother. A less rigid father (Saturn in munakara) might have taken Harry's circumstances into consideration, and ignored tradition, recognising Harry's sensitivity (Venus Firdaria) and knowing that he would be ill-equipped to join his older brother at Eton. But Charles' own traditional upbringing (Charles has a munakara duet, Sun and Mercury, in Scorpio), had cemented Charles's attitudes as regimented, disciplined, and possibly insensitive to Harry's need to be close to home in his time of grief. Charles' own schooling experience saw constant separation from the Queen and Prince Phillip, and perhaps the thought never occurred to him to offer a different mode of education for Harry.

Jupiter in Capricorn is munakara Saturn's outcome planet, and a certain level of harshness and inflexibility can accompany Jupiter in its fall sign. Prince Charles' infidelity had once more re-surfaced with Diana's death, and the press and public were harsh in judging him as a husband and father. Perhaps he thought the cloistered conditions of Eton would protect his boys from the media and create an easier solution for Charles, by placing distance between himself and his sons, at least during school terms.

Chapter Eleven • *Al-Biruni's Chronocators: Munakara and the Time Lords*

Mercury/SATURN: 3 June 2006 to 10 Apr. 2008 (Age: 21.7–23.6 yrs)

"Anyone who says they don't enjoy the Army is mad – you can spend a week hating it and the next week it could be the best thing in the world and the best job you could ever, ever wish for. It has got so much to offer." – Harry, Duke of Sussex

Diurnal Mercury and Saturn belong to the same sect, and are in a sextile aspect to one another in Harry's chart, so this time is possibly his happiest experience of Saturn as sub-period Firdaria lord. This period includes the time when Harry is commissioned as an Army officer on April 12, 2006. Virgo Mercury in rulership sits in Harry's Whole Sign 9th house, and in 2007–2008, he served for over ten weeks in Helmand Province, Afghanistan. He would have served a further two months n Afghanistan, but a news embargo was broken on February 28, 2008 by German, Australian, and US Internet sites (Mercury/Saturn). Harry was immediately removed from his unit (Saturn) and the foreign country (Mercury) in a covert operation as his superiors feared his regiment may be targeted and he would become an easy target and a potential propaganda triumph, for the Taliban if they had managed to kill, or capture him.37

Saturn also reminded Harry of the earlier loss of his mother during this period, as the ten-year Memorial Concert for Diana was held on June 30, 2007. Once more, the media relived the experience of his mother's death, and conspiracies and rumours were selling papers like hotcakes, in the month between Diana's Memorial Concert in June, and her Service of Thanksgiving on the anniversary of her death on August 31, 2007.

Moon/SATURN: 28 Dec. 2016 to 11 April 2018 (Age: 32.3–33.6 yrs)

Moon and Saturn are not friends as their signs, Cancer and Capricorn, are in opposition, so there can be major upheavals when Saturn is required to become a representative for the Moon. Saturn's nature is to separate slowly through coldness, and often there is a long war of attrition involved in its methods to extricate itself from emotional attachments. Given that this is the period when Harry meets his future wife Meghan Markle – the alleged catalyst for Harry's later desertion – then it makes sense that he should fall in love and marry during Saturn's sub-period for the Moon.

Mutual friends introduced Harry to Meghan in July 2016, Harry later saying that he was instantly smitten and that it was love at first sight for both of them. In November 2016, weeks before Saturn's sub-period firdaria, the Palace's Communications Secretary sent a letter to the press outlining Harry's concerns for Meghan's safety stating he "is deeply disappointed that he has not been able to protect her."[38] Harry accused the press of 'crossing a line' by exposing Meghan to a wave of abuse and harassment, using racial undertones in their comment pieces, constantly harassing her mother, offering payment to her former lovers, and 'the bombardment of nearly every friend, co-worker, and loved one in her life'. In 2017, the Press eased down a little on its attacks on Meghan, especially as it seemed that Meghan was a possible candidate for marriage. Relations between the press and Harry became friendlier when they published articles of Meghan's relationship with William and Kate, and speculated on the Queen's acceptance of Meghan as Harry's bride of choice.

In April 2017 Harry appeared on Bryony Gordon's podcast *Mad World* and acknowledged his mental health with the support of his brother (Saturn's outcome planet Jupiter rules 3rd house) " I sought counselling after 20 years of not thinking about the death of my mother, Diana, and two years of total chaos in my life."[39] He added that he had struggled with aggression and felt anxious at royal engagements, and that he had taken up boxing as a way of coping with mental stress and "letting out aggression."[40] Mars is munakara Saturn's dispositor and conjuncts Uranus in the 12th house so Harry's Saturn on the MC finds an outlet through boxing. Harry also says in the interview conducted in his Moon/Saturn Firdaria that what he had experienced after his mother's death "was very much" post-traumatic stress disorder (PTSD).[41]

The Press covered the couple's travels to Africa to celebrate Meghan's 36th birthday in August 2017, and by late November 2017, no-one was surprised when the couple announced their engagement. Wedding plans now filled the newspapers as dresses, flowers, guests and pageantry were discussed in great detail. The wedding date was announced as May 19th 2018, a month after Saturn's sub-period had ended, and as Jupiter (Saturn's outcome planet) replaces Saturn in Firdaria order, another royal wedding was broadcast worldwide, and the royal couple was celebrated by all who agreed they made a wonderful couple.

However, this was still a Moon/Saturn Firdaria and behind the happy scenes cracks in the royal family were beginning to appear. William was questioning his brother and cautioning him against the speed of the relationship and its rapid escalation to a serious long-term commitment, and relations between Meghan and Kate were becoming frosty as the wedding date approached.

Chapter Eleven • *Al-Biruni's Chronocators: Munakara and the Time Lords*

Prince Harry's Separation from the British Royal Family

The Moon's Firdaria is the major period in which Harry's rebellion against the royal family became known to the outside world. In January 2020, under the **Moon/Mars Firdaria**, Harry and Meghan were retiring from public duties as representatives of the Crown. Mars is Saturn's dispositor and rules Harry's 4th house (father and family) and his Midheaven in Scorpio. The decision to sever ties with his family after a stressful Christmas gathering at the end of 2019 led to the Duke and Duchess's office being moved to Buckingham Palace in the New Year and the office was officially closed on 31 March 2020 when the Sussexes ceased "undertaking official engagements in support of the Queen."[42] Harry's Moon resides in his Whole Sign 5th house and in May 2019 (two months before Mars' sub-period) the couple welcomed their first child, Archie. Harry's role as a new father may have triggered his desire to protect his family (Moon rules 7th house) and to create a better relationship with his son than the one he shared with his father, King Charles III (Mars rules 4th house).

Harry's **Moon/Sun Firdaria** begins in November 2020 and covers the period when they moved to Canada and then settled in California in the US. Harry's two luminaries are in trine aspect in earth signs – Taurus Moon and Virgo Sun – and it should be noted that both luminaries' dispositors (Venus for Moon and Mercury for Sun) are in rulership, suggesting strength of purpose and indicating dispositor-planets not easily swayed by others' opinions. Their move to live overseas (Sun in 9th house) removed them from the English tabloids but their interview with Oprah Winfrey in 2021 during the Sun's sub-period revealed private details on the couple's need to leave a toxic relationship with Harry's family. Their second child, Lilibet, named after Queen Elizabeth II, was born during this same period in June 2021.

Harry's book *Spare* was published in the **Moon/Venus Firdaria.** Venus in Libra resides in Harry's Whole Sign 10th house and rules the 5th house as well as the 10th house. Venus's elevated position in rulership shows Harry's desire to expunge unpleasant memories through his autobiography. The title of his book, *Spare*, is a reference to the term 'an heir and a spare' meaning the need to have a backup plan if William, his older brother, had died young, or been unable to bear children to carry on the royal line. It is a hint that Harry felt the burn of being a second child and somewhat superfluous once William married Kate and they produced three children to secure the bloodline. Both the Moon and Venus represent Meghan, his wife, and there can be no doubt that she strongly supported his choice to share his memories. Venus ruling 5th and 10th house suggests Harry undertook this task for his children, as much as for himself. The 10th house is also the house of mother (Diana) and perhaps Harry wanted to give his version of his mother's life after so much time had passed since her death.

Saturn/SATURN: 15 Sept. 2024 to 11 April 2026 (Age: 40–41.6 yrs)

The time gap between the last Saturn sub-period ending in 2018 (Moon/Saturn) and the next beginning in 2024 (Saturn/Saturn), has seen a multitude of separations, changes, and burnt bridges between Britain's royal family, and the two renegades (Harry and Meghan) with Saturn in munakara. Myriads of Tweets, numerous podcasts, startling interviews with Oprah, revelations in Netflix docu-series and unforseen claims in autobiographies, have destroyed any chance of Harry returning to the fold. It will be interesting to see how this major Firdaria of a munakara planet turns out for the Windsor's black sheep. Saturn will take eleven years of Harry's life, and will rule the first short-term period from his 40th birthday until April 2026.

Harry's munakara Saturn is in conjunction on his Scorpio Mid-heaven and he will need to find a way to give his Saturn purchase, especially if he wants to move away from the role of 'victim' in his famous family. He has been uprooted – by his own choice – and now he needs to set down foundations that are not built on resentment, past regrets, recriminations or accusations of foul play on the part of his relatives. His grandmother, Queen Elizabeth II, has passed on and freed him of his closest ties with The Firm. She too had Saturn conjunct her MC, and whilst Elizabeth did not baulk at her responsibilities – Elizabeth's Saturn was not munakara – she would understand that Harry's life needs to have a Saturnian direction and purpose. Elizabeth's fate was set when her father became King and she took his role on his death; her death has granted Harry freedom, but the costs are great, both financially and personally, when munakara Saturn rules the 1st and 2nd houses. Earning an income worthy of a prince will not be easy, nor will he ever lose sight of his royal lineage, even if he is stripped of his title.

His beloved connections with the British Army have been taken from him, perhaps more out of spite than necessity (Mars, Saturn's dispositor in 12th house ruling 4th house), and touring a speaker's circuit could activate his anxiety and simply replace his royal duties, but he may need to follow this course for economic practicalities, earning a living by appearance, as munakara Saturn rules both his 1st (one's physical presence in the environment), and his 2nd house (wealth) by Whole Sign.

Chapter Eleven • *Al-Biruni's Chronocators: Munakara and the Time Lords*

Saturn in contention is inclined to say 'no man is my master', but this will be a hard lesson for Harry to learn as he enters the eleven year period belonging to Saturn's Firdaria, which will take him into middle age from 40 to 51 years of age. Saturn in munakara meets challenges involving the individual's integrity, their honesty and their ability to take responsibility for actions (whether they be good or bad). Harry's Saturn is in good sect condition (diurnal chart and diurnally placed) so perhaps after some false starts, Saturn in contention will use Mars (its dispositor) in 12th house to build a future where he feels proud of his choices to stand independent from his famous family and to gain the greatest benefit through his outcome planet, Jupiter, in the 1st house.

While some royal watchers have happily blamed Meghan for Harry's break away from the British royals, with Harry's Saturn in munakara it is likely that other circumstances during his Saturn Firdaria would have created exactly the same outcome. Prince Harry was bound to clash with the Firm's conservative views and traditions, and his rebellion against the protocol and restrictions imposed by his royal family was just a matter of time given that Saturn – the lord of time – is in contention in his chart. His marriage to Meghan and the poor treatment she received at the hands of the media may have hastened his decision to break free of the Firm, but it was always his acute awareness of his family's lack of respect towards him that would be the catalyst to ignite his munakara Saturn.

Julian Assange: Munakara Jupiter and Munakara Mars

Julian Assange is the fourth example for munakara planets in Firdaria periods, and like the three preceding charts, his chart is diurnal, and the lord for his first long-term Firdaria period will be the Sun, the chart's main luminary. Assange's Cancer Sun resides in his eighth house and father figures came and went as Julian lived a nomadic lifestyle with his mother, and later his younger brother. The Sun and Moon are connected in Julian's chart as the Moon disposits his Cancer Sun and the two luminaries are in trine position in the water signs of Cancer and Scorpio. The Moon is in fall in Scorpio and whilst his mother was a free spirit with few inhibitions, her choice in relationships (munakara Jupiter rules her derived 7th house) had a deep impact on her two sons' childhood years.

Munakara in Theory

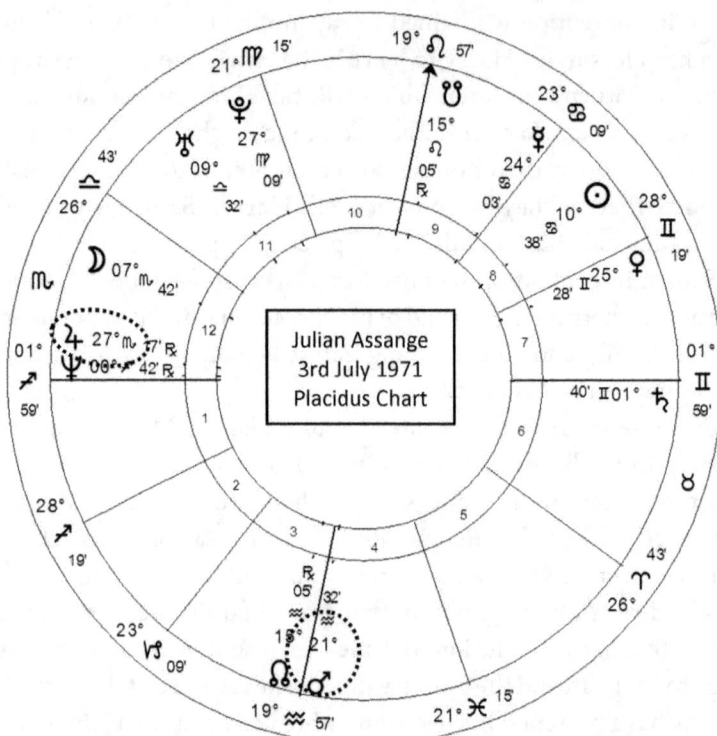

Fig. 11.16: *Julian Assange Placidus Chart : Munakara Jupiter square munakara Mars*

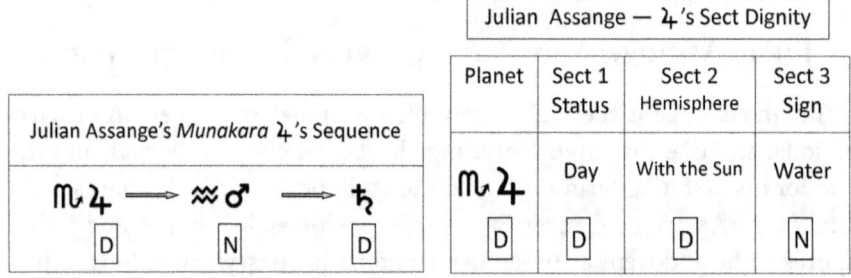

Fig. 11.17: *Julian Assange: Munakara Jupiter's Sequence and Sect Dignity*

Munakara Mars: Short-Term Firdaria Lords

Julian Assange has two planets in munakara, diurnal Jupiter and nocturnal Mars, and one planet follows the other in the Chaldean Order of the Planets. For this reason, when the longer periods of Firdaria are divided

Chapter Eleven • Al-Biruni's Chronocators: Munakara and the Time Lords

by seven (the number of planets in total) then the Jupiter sub-period will always be followed by the Mars sub-period. Both planets are in munakara status, but both planets will express themselves differently according to their nature and their circumstance in the chart. Their sequences also differ (*Fig. 11.17: 11.18*), and whilst there is some commonality – Mars features in Jupiter's sequence as it is the first dispositor for Jupiter in Scorpio – the outcome planet differs as Jupiter has diurnal Saturn as its outcome and Mars brings nocturnal Mercury to complete its three-step process.

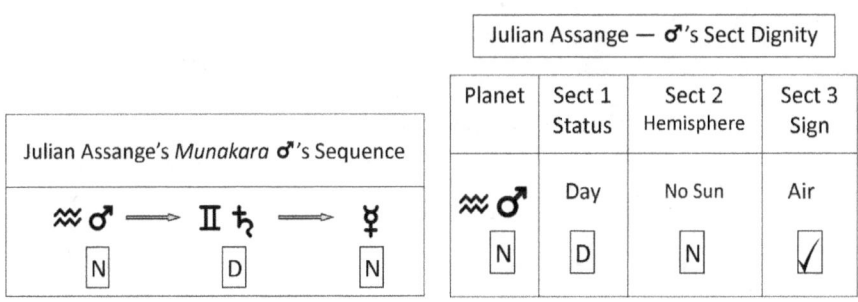

Fig. 11.18: Julian Assange: Munakara Mars' Sequence and Sect Dignity

A further complication in separating one sub-period from the other is the fact that in Julian Assange's chart the two planets are in square aspect in fixed signs. This means that when Jupiter is the sub-period lord it pulls in the aspect to Mars, and when Mars is the sub-period lord it will pull in the aspect to Jupiter as part of the experience as a minor period Time Lord.. There is also some debate over the correctness of Julian's birth time as some cite the time as one hour earlier, giving him a rising sign of Scorpio and an Ascendant lord of Mars. The 3:00pm birth time gives an Ascendant degree of 2 Sagittarius, so it is questionable whether it is Jupiter or Mars which is his Ascendant lord. The Ascendant lord governs the individual's physical body, vitality, and relationship with their environment and either of these planets in munakara will affect these significations, particularly when the Ascendant lord is the sub-period Firdaria lord.

Munakara in Theory

Munakara Jupiter and Mars as Short Term Firdaria Lords
Periods differ according to Long-term Firdaria Lord's Years

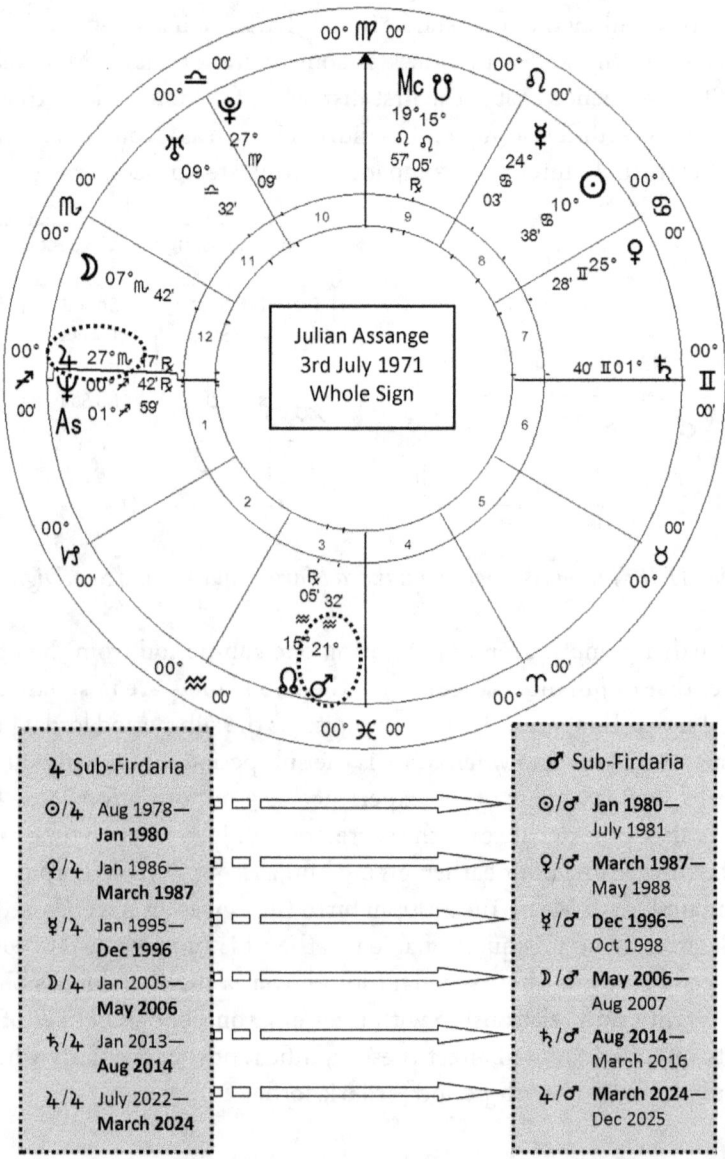

Fig. 11.19: *Julian Assange Whole Sign Chart: Munakara Jupiter and Mars' Sub-Firdaria Periods*

Chapter Eleven • Al-Biruni's Chronocators: Munakara and the Time Lords

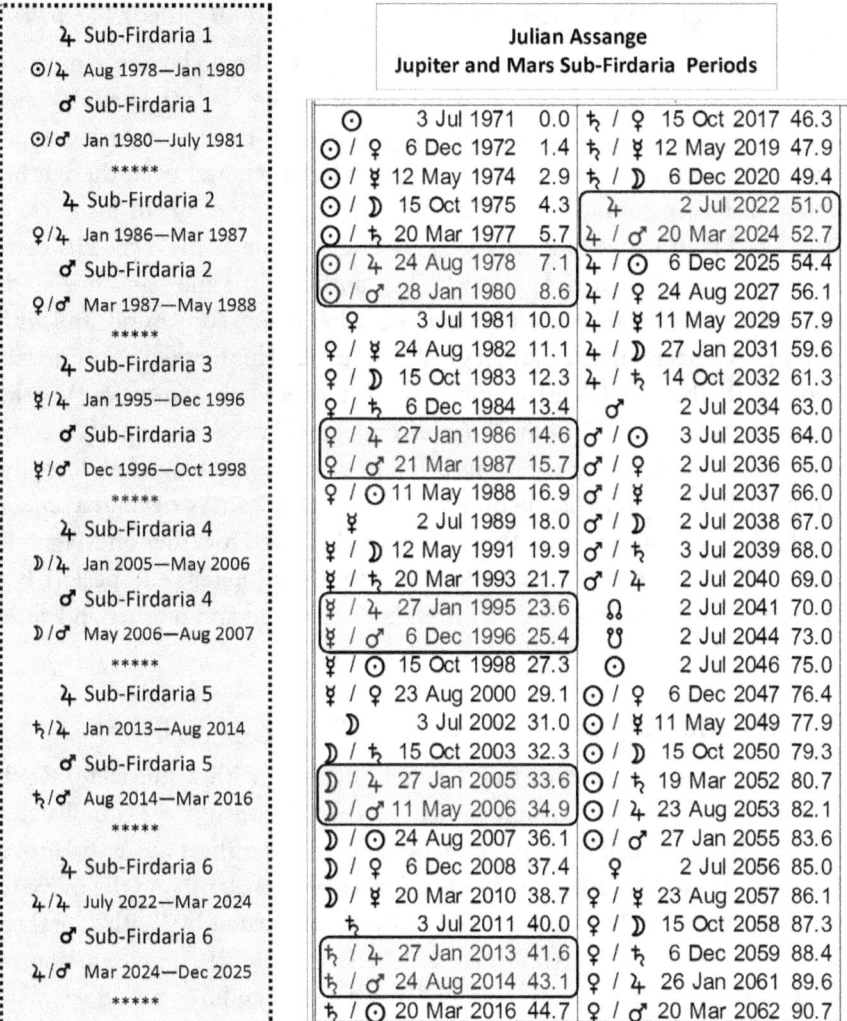

Fig. 11.20: Julian Assange Munakara Jupiter and Mars' Firdaria Sub-Periods

JUPITER and MARS Sub-Firdaria periods in SIX Long-Term Firdaria

"What is a gentleman?....The importance of being honourable, and keeping your word, and acting like a gentleman. It's someone who has the courage of their convictions, who doesn't bow to pressure, who doesn't exploit people who are weaker than they are, who acts in an honourable way...(This) describes an ideal I believe men should strive for."[43] – Julian Assange, 2021

Sun/JUPITER: 24 August 1978 to 28 January 1980 (Age: 7.1–8.6 yrs)

The experience of Jupiter as sub-lord for the Sun should be one of growth, learning and self-confidence, arriving just after the seventh birthday and coinciding with Saturn's first square. In Julian's life, this is the period when Brett Assange played the role of his substitute father, and even though his biological father, John Shipton, has played a supportive role in his current situation, Julian chose to legally take Assange's name as his own. His early education was random and eclectic as his mother Christine was a free spirit and believed a formal education would stifle her young son's mind, and with his Sun in Cancer, Julian's mother greatly influenced his first ten year Firdaria belonging to the Sun. Christine encouraged his overwhelming curiosity in the world and nourished his desire "to overcome barriers to knowing."[44] At eight years of age Julian devoured dozens of books on mathematics and philosophy, and munakara Jupiter absorbed information on topics way beyond a child's usual interests. Julian, his mother and stepfather lived together on Magnetic Island, off the north-east Queensland coast during Jupiter's sub-period, but by the end of 1979, Christine and Brett had separated and mother and child moved south to Lismore.

Sun/MARS: 28 January 1980 to 3 July 1981 (Age: 8.6–10 yrs)

During this period Christine became involved with a musician, Keith Hamilton, and they had a son together, but the relationship was tumultuous, and by 1982, the relationship had broken down. Hamilton was a disturbed young man, and Christine and her two boys were constantly on the move to avoid detection by The Family, a cult movement created by Keith's mother, Anne Hamilton-Byrne. Anne believed herself to be the 'reincarnation of Jesus Christ', and her secretive cult collected young children to indoctrinate them into the cult.[45] The Assange family escaped the devastating impact of The Family, and Julian was never inflicted with Anne's inhumane conversion techniques, but it was a time of fear, hiding, and constant, sudden upheavals in his young life.

Venus/JUPITER: 27 Jan. 1986 to 21 March 1987 (Age: 14.6–15.7 yrs)

Jupiter's second sub-period occurs during Venus' eight year Firdaria and the two lords have an inconjunct aspect that shows separation, isolation and an unusual social infrastructure. Venus rules Julian's 6th house of potentially poor health, and in the period prior to Jupiter's sub-period (belonging to

Chapter Eleven • Al-Biruni's Chronocators: Munakara and the Time Lords

Saturn – Jupiter's outcome planet) Julian had suffered from an illness similar to glandular fever. Christine removed him from the bullying atmosphere at high school – where other students teased him as 'The Prof' – for eighteen months, and Julian's academic life began to flourish without the restrictions of a formalized school programme. By the time he rejoined school, Julian had taught himself machine code – a computer programming language, and Jupiter's sub-period saw the creation of Mendex, his nom de guerre in the hacking world. The *New Yorker* likes to claim that Assange borrowed the name Mendex from the Roman poet Horace's 'splendide mendex' or 'notably untruthful', but Assange's biographer Andrew Fowler believes he borrowed the name from the 1920s Australian science fiction character Major Mendax created by Erle Cox. Major Mendax is an eccentric inventor who experiments with 'matter transmission, invisibility, and the extraction of gold from seawater.'[46] Venus/Jupiter's Firdaria period taught Assange something critical, 'it allowed him to interact with the outside world, without having to personally engage with those he contacted.'[47]

Venus/MARS: 21 March 1987 to 11 May 1988 (Age: 15.7–16.9 yrs)

Venus and Mars are not good companions so there is likely to be trouble brewing when Mars becomes sub-period lord in Venus's major Firdaria period. Mars looks for danger and the two planets are in quincunx position in Assange's chart. Whatever mischief Mars is making as the ruler of the 5th and 12th houses is likely to bring disharmony and agitation for Venus. In other words, what starts as risky and exciting is likely to have long-term and potentially serious consequences.

In 1987, Assange modified his computer and transformed it from a game-playing console to 'a supercharged device that could link directly to other computers.'[48] Assange's munakara Mars has nocturnal Mercury as its outcome planet, and Assange desperately wanted to find the key into the late 1980s version of existing computer networks and telecom systems. This is the time before World Wide Web, and the Internet and high-speed cables and wireless interactions were still twenty years away.

Along with two others, 'Trax' and 'Prime Suspect', Assange formed a hacking group they called 'International Subversives' and cheap local calls in Australia made it possible for them 'to develop their skills and training without paying for it'.[49] They used bulletin boards (BBS) to post messages, and soon decided that if they were to be classified truly as 'international' they need to break into systems outside of Australia. They needed more processing power to hack into overseas systems, and when they applied for access codes to the Royal Melbourne Institute of Technology (RMIT) and they drew the attention of the Australian Federal Police (AFP).

Mercury/JUPITER: 27 Jan. 1995 to 6 Dec 1996 (Age: 23.6–25.4 yrs)

Five years prior to Jupiter's sub-period, Cancer Mercury's Moon sub-period begins with the Australian Federal Police (AFP) knocking on Assange's door, with a warrant for his arrest in October 1991. Assange's desire to be recognised within the hacking community as 'the best' had meant that his bragging (Jupiter/Mercury), and conversations detailing his exploits and his illegal operations, had been recorded by the AFP since the beginning of Mercury's Firdaria.

Rather than quietening him, it turned him into a minor star in his cloistered 12th-house world, and munakara Jupiter, in the 12th house, and Mars (in square aspect), ruling the 12th house, had become the information warriors that Assange believed them to be in his own imagination. Assange wanted to use his notoriety to promote an open and free system of communication (Mercury), where 'collective action and community benefit always came before cash.'[50]

His court case was originally set for May 1995 – during Jupiter's sub-period – and his case was presented to the Supreme Court of Victoria but the court did not take the case, and it was sent back to the County Court. While waiting for his trial to begin, Assange fell into a deep depression and checked himself into a psychiatric hospital and then spent six months sleeping in the wilderness around Melbourne.[51]

During Jupiter's sub-period Assange formed the Cypherpunks, an elite club of hackers, mathematicians, nonconformists, and activists. Their manifesto claimed the individual's right to privacy should be protected in the electronic age, but that governments, corporations, and other faceless organizations (Saturn is munakara Jupiter's outcome planet, and munakara Mars' first dispositor) would do everything in their power to destroy the individual's privacy. It was therefore the Cypherpunks' duty to protect this privacy, by creating a new system of communication, which would ultimately become the precursor to Facebook and other social networking sites.

In June 1996 American John Young, celebrated his first year of membership with the Cypherpunks by setting up Cryptome, a website specifically dedicated to freedom of speech, exposing 'government impropriety' and hosting leaked government documents – the precursor to WikiLeaks.

Chapter Eleven • *Al-Biruni's Chronocators: Munakara and the Time Lords*

Mercury/MARS: 6 Dec. 1996 to 15 Oct. 1998 (Age: 25.4–27.3 yrs)

In 1997 – during the combination of munakara Mars and its outcome planet – Julian Assange operated one of the Usernet's first chat rooms, a place where many speakers could gather to express ideas and communicate with one another simultaneously. Titled 'Suburbia' it was an open forum with reoccurring topics such as various governments' control over free speech, the possibility of nuclear war, the role of US military bases overseas (including Australia), and collective information-sharing on cracking computer encryption codes. During this same period Assange developed the Strobe port scanner, a device capable of scanning hundreds of thousands of computers at any one time to find their weaknesses. The Strobe could open a 'door' for the Cypherpunks to read emails, bank statements, and sensitive information as well as finding passwords and keys to other computers.

Mars' sub-period began with Assange's criminal trial proceedings on December 5 1996. Of his experience in court, Assange later told Andrew Fowler, "It's an unusual experience in court when the judge says 'the prisoner will rise' and no-one else stands up."[52] Although there were 26 charges brought forward, the judge was exceedingly lenient on Assange, taking into account the unstable nature of his childhood, and the fact that he had not financially benefitted from the hacking, rather that he had 'merely hacked into computers to access material that would empower him.' The judge completed his sentence with the opinion that Assange was highly intelligent and that it was 'very unlikely that you will come back (to court).'

In October 1998, at the end of his Mars sub-period, Julian Assange posted an email inviting members to meet him in person as he travelled across the globe 'looking for meetings with kindred spirits and recruiting members to build a team for what was to come.'[53] For perhaps the first time in his life, Assange was searching for physical and intellectual support, and he needed to meet people face to face to determine if they were fit material for his new agenda. Assange needed to materialize his vision and he signed off his cryptic invitation with the words of Antoine de Saint-Exupery: *"If you want to build a ship don't drum up people together to collect wood and don't assign them tasks and work, but rather teach them to long for the immensity of the sea."*[54]

Moon/JUPITER: 27 Jan. 2005 to 11 May 2006 (Age: 33.6–34.9 yrs)

Julian Assange's Moon and Jupiter are both placed in Scorpio, the sign belonging to Mars. This fact not only makes Mars (also a planet in contention) the first dispositor in Jupiter's munakara sequence, but also places the Moon in its sign of fall. Assange's Moon/Jupiter period is the incubation period of WikiLeaks, and perhaps it is noteworthy that this has been the reason, and the driving force, behind Julian Assange's downfall, public disgrace, and subsequent imprisonment as both planets are placed in his Whole Sign 12th house. The Moon rules Assange's 8th house, and the combination of Ascendant ruler (Jupiter) with 8th-house ruler (Moon) has meant that enormous financial and political resources have been at work to destroy this man's reputation, sanity, health and freedom.

Assange was studying physics and mathematics at the University of Melbourne during his Moon / Jupiter Firdaria and began a relationship with another student. They moved in together, and she recalls that in the second half of 2005 she came home to find a huge whiteboard installed in their bedroom with just one word written on it: WikiLeaks. Assange had been secretly working on the concept for weeks and he explained to his girlfriend that WikiLeaks would be a place where 'anyone in the world can post documents, anonymously.'[55]

Moon/MARS: 11 May 2006 to 24 August 2007 (Age: 34.9–36.1 yrs)

In 2006, Assange reached out to John Young, creator of Cryptome, to register the WikiLeaks.org site on his behalf, and on October 4 2006, the site became live. Assange's Scorpio Moon is disposited by his munakara Mars and the birth of his Internet whistleblower site would go on to challenge the mainstream media, and expose the secret documents of governments and corporations worldwide. Munakara Mars in Aquarius truly becomes a contentious planet during this period as Assange sets up the vehicle by which he believes he can make Saturnian institutions accountable for their actions, most of which are conducted behind closed doors and excluding the general populace (Mars rules 12th house).

> "WikiLeaks has become the rebel library of Alexandria. It is the single most significant collection of information that doesn't exist elsewhere, in a searchable, accessible, citable form, about how modern institutions actually behave. And it's gone on to set people free from prison, where documents have been used in their court cases; hold the CIA accountable for renditions programs; and feed into election cycles....Our civilization can only be as good as our knowledge of what our civilization is. We can't possibly hope to reform that which we do not understand."[56] – Julian Assange, *In His Own Words*, 2021

Chapter Eleven • *Al-Biruni's Chronocators: Munakara and the Time Lords*

Saturn/JUPITER: 27 Jan. 2013 to 24 Aug. 2014 (Age: 41.6–43.1 yrs)

Julian Assange's eleven year Saturn Firdaria began on his 40th birthday on 3rd July 2011. Saturn is involved in both Julian's munakara sequences – Saturn is the outcome planet for diurnal Jupiter, and is the first dispositor for Mars in Aquarius – and for this reason its Firdaria period is likely to manifest many of the problems associated with his Jupiter and Mars in contention. Saturn also opposes his Ascendant degree and his Neptune – the symbol for victim, saviour, persecutor – on his Sagittarian Ascendant.

In the five year interim between the registration of WikiLeaks, and Saturn's Firdaria in 2011, the website created a huge amount of embarrassment, consternation and panic within the ranks of political parties and governments throughout the world. Publications on drone strikes in Yemen, corruption across the Arab world, extrajudicial executions by Kenyan police, Tibetan unrest in China, a serious nuclear accident at the Iranian 'Natanz' nuclear facility, exposure of corruption in Swiss banking, and Peru's oil scandal are just a few examples of WikiLeaks' exposures. The site had already had far-reaching effect, and confirmed the nature of its contributors' dedication to releasing information, normally hidden and unavailable, as scores of documents reached the international public domain. However, the US did not escape scrutiny either as WikiLeaks leaked damaging emails during the 2008 United States presidential campaign, more damaging material followed with the release of the *Collateral Murder* video in April 2010, the Afghanistan War logs in July 2010, the Iraq War logs three months later in October 2010, followed soon after by the "Cablegate" files in November 2010.

Something had to be done to control WikiLeaks and its leader, and Saturn's Firdaria provided the perfect opportunity. WikiLeaks continued to publish throughout 2011 and 2012 (Saturn/Saturn Firdaria) – the Guantanamo Bay files leak in April 2011 and the Syria Files in July 2012. After an international warrant was issued by Sweden for Assange's arrest in late September 2010 for unlawful coercion and multiple cases of sexual molestation,[57] Assange breached bail in June 2012 and sought refuge at Ecuador's Embassy in London and was granted asylum The majority of his Saturn Firdaria's eleven years would be spent in the Ecuadorian embassy, and both munakara sub-periods of Jupiter and Mars, would encapsulate his struggle to avoid criminal charges from Swedish authorities (most of which were dropped in August 2015 because the statute of limitations had expired, and then the investigation itself was abandoned in May 2017), and to fight against extradition to the United States to face charges for conspiracy to commit computer intrusion.

Chelsea Manning, a former US Army intelligence analyst and whistleblower, had leaked classified information to WikiLeaks, and her court-martial took place in the summer of 2013, when munakara Jupiter was Assange's sub-period lord for Saturn. Manning was charged with 22 offences, and she pleaded guilty to 10 charges in February 2013. Manning was convicted in July 2013 of violations of the Espionage Act, after disclosing nearly 750,000 classified, or unclassified but sensitive, military and diplomatic documents to WikiLeaks, and she was imprisoned from 2010 to 2017, when her sentence was commuted by President Barack Obama. In 2013, Assange and others in WikiLeaks helped whistleblower Edward Snowden, to flee US law enforcement, and Assange continued to communicate from the embassy and influence decisions, even though he was physically contained within its limited space. Also in Jupiter's sub-period during 2013, Sweden had tried to drop the Assange extradition to face charges of sex allegations, but it was revealed later, that the English Crown Prosecution Service dissuaded them from doing so.[58]

Saturn/MARS: 24 Aug. 2014 to 20 March 2016 (Age: 43.1–44.7 yrs)

Saturn is munakara Mars' First Dispositor

Mars' sub-period accentuates Assange's physical and mental deterioration during his asylum period in the Ecuadorian embassy in London. In July 2015 he wrote to French President Francois Hollande requesting refugee status, but it was refused. During Mars' sub-period Assange was accused of gathering information inside the embassy, and that he had compromised their communications system by using a briefcase with a listening device to record diplomatic proceedings. In fact, the opposite was true, and it was Assange himself who was under constant surveillance without his knowledge, or his consent.

The British Government were spending 4 million pounds a year on watching the embassy and those entering and leaving the building, whilst In 2015 the Ecuadorian embassy employed Undercover Global (UC Global) to install a hidden surveillance system in Assange's quarters, to spy on their visitor. The following year UC Global began selling their accumulated information from video and audio surveillance secretly to US intelligence, a fact which was only discovered in April 2019, when UC Global approached WikiLeaks to sell the information yet again, to a third party. WikiLeaks notified the British police and the embassy was stormed the following day, when Assange was removed, and taken to HM Prison Belmarsh, a prison used in high-profile cases,

Chapter Eleven • *Al-Biruni's Chronocators: Munakara and the Time Lords*

particularly those concerning national security. Within Belmarsh's grounds is the High Security Unit (HSU), which has 48 single cells, as is regarded to be the most secure prison unit in the United Kingdom. Assange was held in the HSU until an ITV documentary revealed conditions in Belmarsh, and Assange's legal team managed to have him moved to another part of the prison in January, 2020 (Saturn/Mars Firdaria – Assange's munakara Aquarian Mars rules 12th house).

Jupiter/JUPITER: 2 July 2022 to 20 March 2024 (Age: 51–52.7 yrs)
Munakara Jupiter is Julian Assange's Long-term Time Lord for 12 years

Munakara Jupiter's twelve year Firdaria follows on from Saturn's long-term Firdaria, and its twelve year stint started on Julian Assange's 51st birthday. Jupiter began the round of sub-period lords for the first nineteen months of its long-term dozen years invoking its powers from July 2022 to March 2024. Assange's legal proceedings limped through Saturn/Moon's year of 2021 and half of 2022 by witnessing various events: Judge Baraitser's ruling that Assange could not be extradited to the United States, citing concerns about his mental health and the risk of suicide in a US prison (January 2021),[59] and US prosecutors' immediate appeal against the denial of extradition, the exposure of fabricated allegations in the US indictment (June 2021), the High Court's decision to allow the US appeal (August 2021), the two-day appeal (October 2021), the High Court's ruling in favour of the United States (December 2021).[60]

Munakara Jupiter's Firdaria begins in mid 2022, and the tide began to turn back in favour of towards Assange in January 2022 when Assange was granted permission to petition the Supreme Court of the United Kingdom for an appeal hearing. In March 2022, the court denied permission for an appeal, but in the months between, Assange's supporters had raised the equivalent of around $52.8m in cryptocurrency, money raised for Assange's legal defence. Concern for Assange deepened on April 20, 2022, when Westminster Magistrates Court formally approved the extradition of Assange to the US, and on June 17 2022 (two weeks after Assange's 51st birthday), the British Home Secretary Priti Patel approved the extradition.[61] Two weeks later (July 1 2022), Assange lodged an appeal against the extradition in the High Court, following it with a further lodgement in late August 2022, and in November 2022, his legal team made a further appeal to the European Court of Human Rights.[62]

The year 2023 continued to see legal banter between British courts, and US prosecutors' desire to pull Assange away from the public eye and bury him in US penal subjugation. Invisibility, control and retribution were strong motivators for the US government, and UN special rapporteur Nils Melzer maintains that the 'Assange case sets a dangerous precedent: once telling the truth becomes a crime, censorship and tyranny will inevitably follow.'[63]

Jupiter/MARS: 20 March 2024 to 6 Dec. 2025 (Age: 52.7–54.4 yrs)

Munakara Jupiter is Assange's Long-term Time Lord, munakara Mars is his Short-term Time Lord

On February 20, 2024, the High Court of Justice in London began a two-day hearing after Assange's legal team requested leave to appeal the extradiction order signed in 2022. Assange was too ill to attend the hearing as his wife, Stella, described the 52-year-old's health as "in decline, physically and mentally."[64] On May 20, 2024, two High Court judges gave Assange leave to appeal against extradition.[65]

In the meantime, the Australian government under newly elected Prime Minister Anthony Albanese was working quietly through diplomatic channels towards preventing Assange's extradition to the US. On 14 February 2024, the Australian House of Representatives passed a motion – by a vote of 86 to 42 – calling for Assange's immediate release and return to Australia.[66]

On 24 May 2024 – two months after the Jupiter/Mars Firdaria had begun – the UK High Court ruled Assange could bring a new appeal to his extradition. US attorneys were advised by their British lawyers that this time, Assange's appeal would be successful and this triggered a breakthrough in plea negotiations.[67]

On 24 June 2024, a plea bargain was agreed and Assange was released from HM Prison Belmarsh. He was immediately flown by charter flight to Saipan (a territory of the US in the western Pacific Ocean) where he was required to attend the federal courthouse. On 26 June Assange pleaded guilty to a charge under the US Espionage Act of 1917 of conspiracy to obtain and disclose national defence information. The judge accepted Assange's guilty pleas and sentenced him as planned to 62 months time served.[68] Assange left the courthouse and returned to the charter flight that would take him to Australia as a free man.

Chapter Eleven • *Al-Biruni's Chronocators: Munakara and the Time Lords*

Jupiter and Mars are Assange's two planets in munakara and as can be expected, Julian Assange is not a repentant man. Even in retrospection of the dozen years he has forfeited in his life, there is little doubt that he believes his actions were honourable and justified (munakara Jupiter) and that the long battle was truly worth the effort (munakara Mars) . In his first flight out of his homeland on 1 October 2024, Assange flew to Strasbourg, France, to address the Committee on Legal Affairs and Human Rights of the Council of Europe. In his first public appearance since his release from prison Assange stated that he had "pleaded guilty to journalism (not espionage) and that he had chosen freedom over justice."[69]

PART TWO

Munakara in Practice

Chart Delineations

Part Two expands on the theory of munakara (contention) introduced in Part One of the book. The chapters in Part One show munakara from the perspective of one planet (*i.e.*, the Moon or Mercury or Venus, etc.), explaining the nature of contention and what an astrologer might expect to see when they find a planet with a munakara sequence in a chart.

The chapters in Part One look at the impact of sect dignity on the planet in munakara, and also explore the relationship a munakara planet might have with the other two planets in its sequence. Finally, one or sometimes two, charts are provided so that the reader might follow the process of munakara sequencing through these examples.

Munakara is a technique which will be unfamiliar to most astrologers, so I felt it could be beneficial to increase the number of chart examples, but to do it in such a way as to avoid swamping the theory presented in Part One.

The additional example charts were particularly chosen because the people are famous, so there is a large amount of readily available information relating to how their lives have played out. If you, or your client, have the same munakara sequence as one of the example charts, seeing the sequence in practice may provide some insight into how the same munakara planet might work in your or your client's chart.

Munakara in Practice

The purpose of Part One is to explain and demonstrate how this old technique that al-Biruni calls 'munakara' functions as a useful tool in astrology. The purpose of Part Two is to present what I believe to be, are clear examples of munakara planets working in the charts of well-known people whose story resonates with our own, people who we admire, or who we passionately dislike – but want to know more – and to encourage more astrologers to adopt this technique, even if it is because they like the person in the example.

The additional charts in Part Two have one, two, or even more, munakara planets, and I have chosen to delineate them according to the influence of one of the planets in munakara. Similar to the chapters in Part One, I have arranged the chapters in Part Two beginning with charts that have munakara Moon, and finishing with charts where Saturn is in munakara.

The charts were chosen for their diversity, for an insight into the period in which the individual lived, for their level of fame or notoriety, and for the interesting ways in which I believe their munakara planet or planets have presented themselves in the individual's life.

CHAPTER TWELVE
Munakara Moon Delineations

Queen Victoria

A Brief Biography of Queen Victoria

Princess Alexandrina Victoria, daughter of Prince Edward, Duke of Kent and Princess Victoria of Saxe-Coburg-Saalfeld was born on 24th May 1819 at Kensington Palace. At the time of her birth Victoria was fifth in line to the throne after the four eldest sons of George II.

Victoria described her childhood as "rather melancholy" as her mother was extremely protective and raised Victoria in isolation and away from the company of other children. The "Kensington System" was a strict and elaborate set of rules implemented by the Duchess (Victoria's mother) and designed by her to prevent her daughter from interacting with people she considered to be 'undesirable'. In truth it was a system of exclusion that was tailored to maintain the child's total dependency on her mother.[1] Victoria was never allowed to be apart from her mother, her tutor or her governesses, and even when she was an adult, Victoria shared a bedroom with her mother every night. Every action was monitored and recorded by her mother's attendant Sir John Conroy, and reported back to her mother, even small details such as being banned from walking down the stairs without holding someone's hand. Victoria's lifelong habit of keeping journals and making copious entries into her diaries (she wrote an average of 2,500 words a day)[2] most probably began with the requirement that each day she record an analysis of her daily behaviour – how well or how badly she had behaved – in her 'Behaviour Book.'[3]

On 20th June 1837 Victoria was told that her uncle, King William IV, had passed away the night before, and she was now Queen. Victoria had just turned 18. Victoria's coronation took place one year later on 28th June 1838 as approximately 400,000 people lined the streets to see the new Queen. On her accession, Buckingham Palace became the Queen's official residence and Victoria was the first Sovereign to use the palace as her home. Victoria reigned for 63 years, seven months and two days, a reign only surpassed by her great-great-granddaughter Elisabeth II.

Even after Victoria became queen she was still required by social convention to live with her mother as she was an unmarried young woman. At the conclusion of her wedding ceremony Victoria shook hands with the Duchess and promptly evicted her from Victoria's rooms and moved the Duchess into a remote apartment in Buckingham Palace. She often refused the requests from her mother to see her, rarely visited her mother in her apartment and remained cold and distant from her.[4]

Victoria was close to Whig prime minister, Lord Melbourne, and when she complained that her mother's proximity promised "torment for many years" Melbourne suggested the problem would be solved by her marriage to which Victoria replied that marriage was a "shocking alternative" to the irritations created by her mother.[5]

Victoria's journal entry on 15th October 1839 (the day on which she proposed to Albert), reads "I told Albert that it would make me too happy if he would consent to what I wished (to marry me): we embraced each other over and over again, and he was so kind, so affectionate: oh! To feel I was, I am, loved by such an angel as Albert, was to great a delight to describe."[6]

The couple married on 10th February 1840 and the first of their nine children was born on 21st November 1840. Victoria hated being pregnant,[7] viewed breast-feeding with disgust,[8] and thought newborn babies were ugly.[9] Victoria lost her mother and her beloved Albert in the same year, 1861. The Duchess died in March 1861 and unexpectedly, Victoria was heart-broken. Albert took over many of her official duties as Victoria was overcome by an intense and deep grief at the loss of her mother.[10] Albert became unwell and died on 14th December 1861. Victoria was inconsolable, avoiding public appearances and preferring to stay secluded in Windsor Castle or Balmoral Castle in Scotland.

Chapter Twelve • *Munakara Moon Delineations*

Queen Victoria died aged 81 on 22nd January 1901 and her eldest son, Edward VII became the next English monarch.

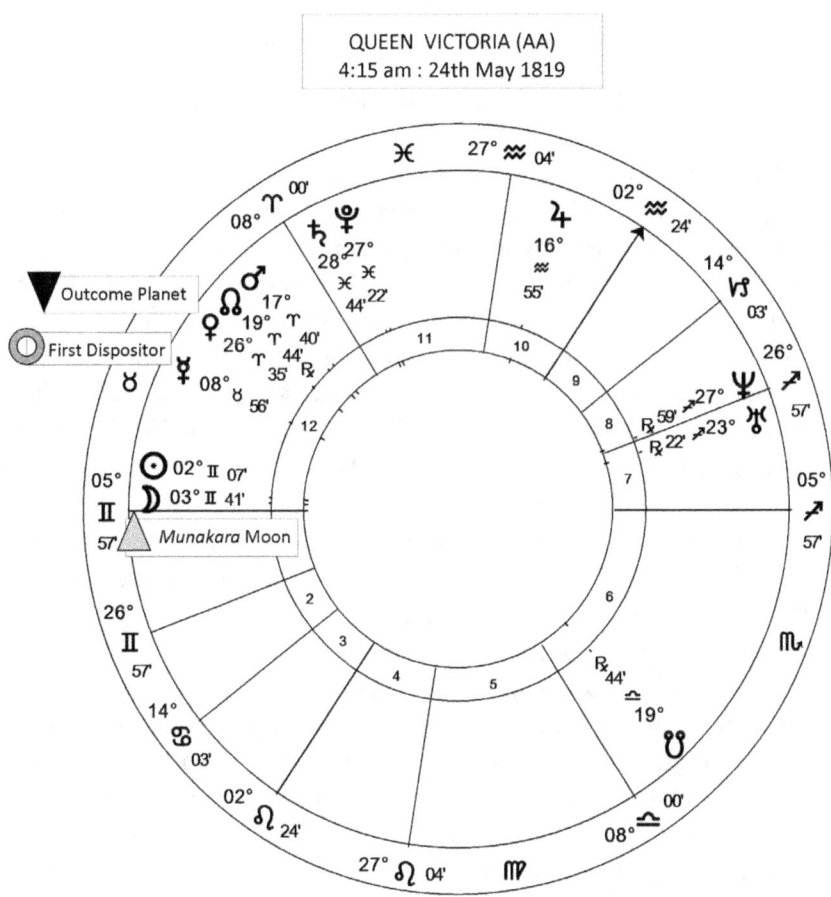

Fig. 12.1: Queen Victoria of England Natal Chart – Munakara Moon

Gemini Moon in Munakara: Queen Victoria

- **Key Questions:**
- What does Queen Victoria's Moon contend with?
- What is its driving force?
- What is its trigger? What is its outcome?

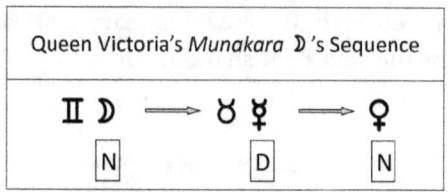

Table 12.1: Queen Victoria: Munakara Moon's Sequence

Victoria had munakara Moon – Gemini Moon disposits to diurnal Mercury in Taurus with Venus as the Moon's outcome planet – and Victoria made no secret of her feelings on pregnancy, motherhood and children.

Victoria was pregnant or nursing for 16 years of her adult life, calling pregnancy the "*Schattenseite*," or shadow side of marriage. She warned her adult daughter that childbirth was "a complete violence to all one's feelings of propriety which God knows, receives a shock enough in marriage alone." In private correspondence in the late 1850s to her first-born daughter Vicky, who was expecting her first child and was determined to be positive about the experience, Queen Victoria wrote: "What you say of the pride of giving life to an immortal soul is very fine, dear, but I own I cannot enter into that; I think much more of being like a cow or a dog at such moments; when our poor nature becomes so very animal and unecstatic."

In truth, it was pregnancy and childhood that Victoria hated, not her brood of nine children. Her husband, Albert, died when he was 42 and even though her position meant the relief from financial hardship, Victoria was a single mother to her nine children for over four decades. She was a slight build and constant pregnancies wreaked havoc on her tiny frame (munakara Moon) and constant pain caused her to suffer from post-natal depression.

Victoria's biggest crime was being outspoken about motherhood (munakara Moon) at a time in the 19th century when motherhood was idealised as sacred, and the fact that pregnancy and childbirth was actually frightening, debilitating and potentially fatal for both mother and child, was largely ignored by those who glorified the act of giving birth. Unlike other noble or affluent women of her time, Victoria believed that a core part of a child's upbringing was to spend as much time with the parents as possible, and even though she was a working mother with huge time commitments, Victoria saw her new babies so frequently that her ladies-in-waiting commented on it.[11]

Victoria' repulsion at being pregnant and her dislike of motherhood are well recorded as she saw them as a distraction not only from her role as monarch,

Chapter Twelve • *Munakara Moon Delineations*

but they also interrupted her relationship with Albert, as she felt he gave the children the loving attention which was stolen from her. Her munakara Moon also displayed itself as a spontaneous, or '*de novo*' mutation (a change in the DNA sequence of a gene, one that has not appeared in previous generations), and Victoria is considered to be the source of the disease haemophilia amongst her descendents in the European royal families which followed her reign. Two of her female children, Princesses Alice and Beatrice, inherited the haemophilia gene from their mother and became carriers for the mutant gene which affected their own children, whilst Leopold, her youngest son, suffered from the disease and died at age 30 from haemorrhaging as the result of a fall from a horse. Prince Leopold had two children, a daughter Alice named after her late aunt, and a son Charles. Alice was a carrier of the haemophilia gene like her namesake but Charles, who was born four months after the death of his father, did not inherit the disease from Leopold.

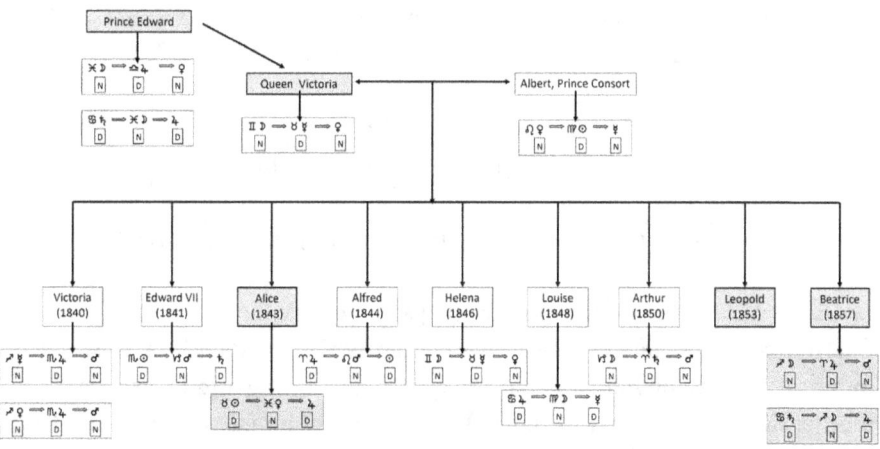

Fig. 12.2: Queen Victoria and Albert, Prince Consort: Children. Shaded names indicate originator of gene mutant haemophilia (Prince Edward), female carriers (Queen Victoria, Alice, and Beatrice) and haemophiliac (Leopold).

Prince Edward – Victoria's father
(2nd November 1767 – 23rd January 1820)

The question as to why the mutated gene that created haemophilia was present in Victoria's descendants, but not her ancestors, has been a topic of modern speculation over the decades. One theory is that her biological father was not the Duke of Kent, but instead was the result of a liaison between her mother and a haemophiliac lover.[12] However, this seems improbable given that it was a race between Edward and his four older brothers to produce a legitimate heir to the throne. Her mother, Princess Victoria, is recorded as being 'scandalised by the presence of the illegitimate children of Edward's older brother, William, at court' so it is unlikely that she would invite questions over her child's legitimacy by taking a lover.[13] She would not have risked the crown over some uncertainty that Edward was not her child's father. "It is more likely that the mutation arose spontaneously because Victoria's father (Edward) was over 50 at the time of her conception and haemophilia arises more frequently in the children of older fathers.'[14] This type of spontaneous mutation accounts for about a third of cases.[15]

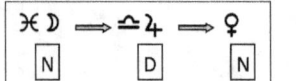

Table 12.2: Munakara Sequences for Prince Edward, father of Queen Victoria

Pisces Moon disposits to Jupiter (royalty) with Venus (daughter) as the final outcome planet. Prince Edward died when his daughter was eight months old, leaving her to be raised by her controlling and overprotective mother. Munakara Moon is in the Whole Sign 3rd house of siblings and as the youngest of four boys and only son to produce an heir, the Moon rules 7th house of marriage partner (the Duchess).

Munakara Saturn in Cancer is situated in Whole Sign 7th house and disposits to the Moon (also munakara) in the 3rd house, with Jupiter as the outcome planet for Saturn. Jupiter is elevated in the Whole Sign 10th house in Libra. Prince Edward, a confirmed bachelor, married Victoria's mother, a widowed German princess with two children in 1818 at age 51, after his father's only legitimate heir and his niece, Princess Charlotte, died in 1817 at age 21, during the delivery of a stillborn son.

Chapter Twelve • *Munakara Moon Delineations*

Victoria, Princess Royal (Vicky) – Victoria's first born child
(21ˢᵗ November 1840 – 5ᵗʰ August 1901)

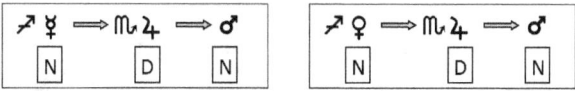

Table 12.3: Munakara Sequences for Princess Victoria, Queen Victoria and Albert's first born child

The munakara duet (two planets in conjunction with identical sequences) are conjunct the chart's mid-heaven and Victoria's gender (Venus) was a disappointment from birth. When the physician delivering the baby exclaimed sadly to the new mother: "Oh Madame, it's a girl", the queen replied: "Never mind, next time it will be a prince!"[16] If Vicky had been born a male with the same chart she may have been a better regent than her younger brother Edward. Her Mercury Venus duet was conjunct Saturn on the MC, but Edward VII, his three brothers, and their male children, were in line for the throne before the eldest sibling, a girl, had a chance to take the throne after her mother's death.

Vicky was educated by her father, Prince Consort Albert (also with munakara Venus), to embrace a politically liberal environment, and these views were shared by her husband Prince Frederick of Prussia whom she married at age 17. The royal pair hoped that Prussia (later the German Empire) would become a constitutional monarchy based on the British model. Her father Albert was always seen as a foreigner by his wife's subjects, and unfortunately his daughter suffered the same fate as German Empress Consort, Victoria (Vicky), was criticised for being foreign-born (with an English mother, Queen Victoria), and Vicky was ostracised by her husband's family and the powerful members of the German dynasty (House of Hohenzollerns).

Their plans could not become manifest as she was Empress for only a few months. Her husband, Frederick III, died from laryngeal cancer in 1888 – only 88 days after his accession. Their son, Wilhelm II, became king but he was much more conservative than his parents who had inadvertently chosen an educator with staunch conservative views to educate their two sons, rather than someone who shared their own liberal views. Wilhelm II was their first born child but the delivery had gone badly, and after four days of labour the nerves to his left arm were damaged and left him with a withered left arm fifteen centimetres shorter than the other. The difficult birth also caused Wilhelm some fetal distress and there is speculation that the future emperor was deprived of oxygen for eight to ten minutes which may have brought on neurological problems that made him an unstable ruler.[17] When Vicky's husband, Frederick III, became ill she wrote to her mother voicing her fears that she and ailing husband were "shadows ready to be replaced by William (Wilhelm)."[18]

Frederick III's mother died in 1890, two years after her son, and Empress Frederica (Vicky's new title) had hopes to succeed her mother-in-law as patron of the German Red Cross and the Association of Patriotic Women. Her son, the German Emperor, refused her request causing a deep bitterness and rift between mother and son.[19] Wilhelm II isolated her completely from public life, purging all institutions and removing from office any people close to his parents. On his father's death Wilhelm II had ordered the occupation of the imperial residence by soldiers and had insisted that his mother and siblings move elsewhere, preferably leaving Germany permanently, but Empress Frederick (Vicky) was persistent and moved instead to the countryside in Hesse. There she built a castle in honour of her husband, maintaining her own court and entertaining like-minded liberals.

Controversy constantly surrounded the Empress: she was only 17 and homesick when she married and her plans for an English-style garden were mocked and refused by her in-laws. She was accused of leaking sensitive information to her parents which was then published in British newspapers. She was blamed for her first-born son's withered arm, the nerves of which were damaged during the birth. She was blamed for taking her husband Frederick III to Britain when he was terminally ill and then admonished because she continued on to Italy – in a desperate hope for a cure – rather than returning home to Germany so he could die in his homeland.

Empress Frederica (Vicky) was not a carrier of the haemophilia gene, but when her second son, Prince Henry, married his first cousin Irene (her sister Alice's daughter and a carrier of the regressive gene), two of her three grandsons were born with haemophilia. The third child of Queen Victoria and Albert, Princess Alice (*Fig. 12.2*) bore three children who would be affected by the disease: her son Friedrich who died at age two, and two daughters, Irene and Alix, who were carriers of the regressive gene. Alix married Tsar Nicholas II of Russia and their only son Alexei was a haemophiliac who was treated by the infamous monk, Rasputin.

Princess Beatrice – Victoria's ninth and last child
(14th April 1857 – 26th October 1944)

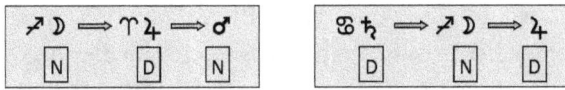

Table 12.4: Munakara Sequences for Princess Beatrice (carrier),Queen Victoria and Albert's last born child

Three of Queen Victoria's children 'inherited' a munakara Moon from their mother – her third daughter Helena (born 1846), her third son Arthur (born 1850), and her fifth daughter Beatrice (born 1857). Beatrice also had Saturn in munakara, as did her grandfather, Prince Edward, and their munakara Saturn shared the same sequence of planets (Saturn, Moon, Jupiter).

Princess Beatrice was the youngest child of Victoria and Albert and was the last of Queen Victoria's children to die, nearly 66 years after the first, her elder sister Alice. Beatrice was born seventeen years after her sister, Vicky, the first of Victoria and Albert's nine children, all of whom achieved adulthood. Controversy surrounded the birth when it was announced that Queen Victoria would use chloroform during the delivery of her last child. At the time chloroform was considered to be dangerous to mother and child and was frowned upon by the Church of England and the medical authorities.[20]

Beatrice's munakara Moon is in her 4th house, and although her childhood was overshadowed by the death of her father when she was four years old, Beatrice enjoyed a different relationship with both Victoria and Albert before his death. Vicky, the elder favoured child, was leaving home to start her married life when Beatrice arrived, and the new baby filled a gap when she left for Germany to marry Frederick III. Queen Victoria disliked most babies yet she considered Beatrice to be attractive and even enjoying bathing Beatrice, a task she had left to the servants for her older children. The Queen commissioned paintings of Beatrice with her long golden hair, and she once remarked that Beatrice was "a pretty, plump and flourishing child....with fine large blue eyes, a pretty little mouth and very fine skin."[21] Albert too, was enamoured with his youngest child, who was both intelligent and affectionate towards her father.[22]

When Queen Victoria's mother died in March 1861 and when reading her personal letters and journals, Victoria discovered that her mother had, indeed, loved her. Without perhaps understanding why on a logical level, Victoria would allow only two of her daughters, Alice, and young Beatrice, to enter her private apartments to console her on the loss of her mother. These were her two daughters who like herself, were the carriers of the haemophilia gene. When Albert's death followed nine months later in December 1861, once more Victoria chose Alice and Beatrice in her bereavement, and isolated herself from her other children. It was recorded that Victoria often took Beatrice from her cot, hurried to her bed, and "lay there sleepless, clasping to her child, wrapped in the nightclothes of a man who would wear them no more."[23]

Queen Victoria intended for Beatrice to remain a single woman, a perfect lifelong companion to her in her old age. However, Beatrice fell in love with Prince Henry of Batterberg and spent a year trying to persuade her mother to approve the marriage. Victoria refused to speak to her youngest daughter for seven months, choosing instead to communicate through notes passed back and forwards, even though the two women remained working side by side.[24] Victoria finally relented and granted Beatrice her permission on the condition that the couple live with her, and Beatrice would continue her duties as unofficial secretary to her mother. Beatrice bore four children to Prince Henry of Battenberg, and although the eleven-year marriage was short, it was a happy one.

Beatrice carried the haemophilia gene, passing it on to her own daughter Victoria, who became a carrier and passed the gene to her own children. Beatrice's two sons, Leopold and Maurice, suffered from the disease. Her second son, Lord Leopold Mountbatten died at the age of 32 during a hip operation, and his younger brother Maurice died at age 23, killed in action in World War I. Her eldest son, Alexander, was not affected and lived to be the last surviving grandson of Queen Victoria, passing awing in 1960 at 71 years of age.

Beatrice's Saturn is also munakara and she stayed true to her word, remaining at Victoria's side until her death in 1901. Beatrice was forty four when Queen Victoria died and apart from Henry, her adult life was taken up by the demands of her mother yet she wrote these words two months after Victoria's death "...you may imagine what the grief is. I, who had hardly ever been separated from my dear mother, can hardly realise what life will be like without her, who was the centre of everything."[25] Beatrice became

Chapter Twelve • *Munakara Moon Delineations*

her literary executor and devoted the next 30 years to editing her mother's journals. Victoria had instructed Beatrice that on her death her daughter was to remove any private material that might be hurtful to living people. Beatrice removed so much material that the edited journals are only a third as long as the originals.[26] Beatrice would copy a draft from the original and then copied her draft into a set of blue notebooks. Both the originals and the first drafts were destroyed and the surviving 111 notebooks are kept in the Royal Archives at Windsor Castle.[27]

Munakara Moon: Albrecht Dürer

A Brief Biography of Albrecht Dürer

Albrecht Dürer (21 May 1471 – 6 April 1528) was a painter, printmaker, and theorist of the German Renaissance. He was born in Nuremberg, Germany, to a successful goldsmith, Albrecht Dürer the Elder, and his wife Barbara. His parents' union produced eighteen children, but only three survived to adulthood. By his twenties Dürer was a master in various forms of his art, and the Italian Emperor Maximilian I, was his patron from 1512 until the emperor's death in 1519. Dürer's work covered a vast array of techniques including engravings, altarpieces, portraits and self-portraits, watercolours and books.

Dürer travelled throughout Europe for the four years between 1490 and 1494 but he was forced to stop his grand tour when he was ordered home to marry the daughter of a prominent Nuremberg citizen. In July 1494 he married Agnes Frey, and although he honoured the agreement in respect for his father's wishes, it was not a happy match.

The Northern Hemisphere of the Celestial Globe (1515)

In 1515 Dürer and Maximilian I's court astronomer Johannes Stabius created the first world map on a solid geometric sphere.[28] Together they also produced the first planispheres of both southern and northern hemisphere, as well as the first printed celestial maps, which prompted the revival of interest in the field of celestial cartography throughout Europe.[29]

By 1521, at the age of 50, Dürer was becoming concerned that the deterioration of his sight and the stiffness in his hands would affect his work and he completed few commission in the last seven years of his life. He died at age 57 in 1528, possibly as a result of a malarial infection he contracted in 1521 when he contracted the disease whilst visiting Zeeland to see a stranded whale. Whilst dealing with his illness, Dürer became increasingly interested in the mathematical proportions of the human body, and he published two books *The Four Books on Measurement* (1524) and *Fortification* (1527) before his death in April 1528, and a third book *The Four Books on Human Proportion* (1528) was published just months after his death.

Some of Albrecht Dürer's Important Works

Four Self-Portraits at ages 13 (1484); age 22 (1493); age 26 (1497); age 28 (1500)

In 1500, at the beginning of a new century, painter, draftsman, printmaker and writer Albrecht Dürer painted his fourth and last self-portrait at the age of 28. His first self-portrait at 13 years of age was scratched out in silverpoint, an extremely difficult medium as it allowed for no mistakes. By the time he was twenty two, his next self-portrait shows the same side-on pose – known as the three-quarter view – but it is richly painted and Dürer holds a flower famed as an aphrodisiac – this portrait is a present for his bride-to-be, Agnes Frey. In Dürer's next self-portrait at 26 (1497), he is dressed as a wealthy man and the background shows an Italian landscape, a place where he felt more at home than Germany. This portrait is also painted as a three-quarter view and the four ages – 13, 22, 26, and 29 – show a similar attitude moving from childhood to early adulthood and depicting improved wealth and social status.

Nemesis (The Great Fortune) (1501)

The year after his last self-portrait Dürer engraved *Nemesis (The Great Fortune)* a combination between Nemesis, the Greek goddess of divine retribution and the winged Fortuna, the Roman goddess of victory and fortune. Nemesis/Fortuna is shown crossing the heavens by balancing on her wheel of Fortune, and carrying her instruments of good and bad luck in her hands. Below Fortuna lies a city and its inhabitants who are oblivious to the fickle goddess passing overhead.

Between 1507 and 1511 Dürer worked on some of his most celebrated paintings: *Adam and Eve* (1507), *Martyrdom of the Ten Thousand* (1508), *Virgin with the Iris* (1508), the altarpiece *Assumption of the Virgin* (1509) and *Adoration of the Trinity* (1511). In 1514 created his three most famous engravings and the trio became known as his *Meisterstiche* (Master Engravings): *Knight, Death and the Devil* (1513), *St. Jerome in His Study* (1514) and *Melencolia I* (1514).

Meisterstiche (Master Engravings) (1514)

The Master Engravings of 1514 consist of three interrelated works that examine a spiritual theme. In his first Master Engraving, titled *The Knight, Death and the Devil*, the knight's two adversaries are almost caricatures in comparison to the noble knight riding by. Death's face shows the ravages of the plague but it has a grovelling and pitiful appearance and the goat-headed devil is more cartoonish than frightening.

The second Master Engraving, titled *St. Jerome in His Study*, is the one whose interpretation seems the most straightforward. Saint Jerome, translator of the Bible into Latin, is the perfect example of the Christian scholar, working diligently at his desk, whilst his lion and dog slumber peacefully in the foreground. The sunlight pouring in through the windows highlights the halo of light around his head, and the engraving has a sense of studious effort balanced in harmony with repose and religious dedication.[30]

The third Master Engraving, titled *Melencolia I*, shows a winged personification of Melancholy, who is seated dejectedly with her head resting on her hand. She holds a calliper and is surrounded by other tools and assorted objects associated with geometry, the one of the seven liberal arts that underlies artistic creation. On the wall behind her appears a numbered magic square in which each row and column add up to thirty-four. Beside her, a putto sits on a milstone while writing on a tablet. A comet punctures the sky in the background.[31]

The three engravings are quite different in their execution, but there are several items which keep reappearing; a companion dog in several poses, active in *The Knight*, resting in *St. Jerome*, and a starving and deathly looking beast in *Melencolia I*. An hourglass, the bell, and skulls or skull-like figures feature in all three pieces, all reminders of the shortness of life. The knight's face wears the same grim look as the angel in *Melencolia I*, and some art critics have described him as a 'robber knight' rather than a noble Christian knight off to win glory at the Crusades. In Greek legend a fox's tail wrapped at the top of a weapon (alance or spear) is a symbol representing the animal's odious characteristics of 'greed, cunning and treachery, as well as lust and whoring.'[32]

Melencolia I (1514)

Renaissance thought linked melancholy with creative genius. *Melencolia I* is a depiction of the intellectual situation of the artist and is thus considered, by extension, a spiritual self-portrait of Dürer.[33] Dürer borrowed much of his symbolism from Italian philosopher Marsilio Ficino (1433–1499) for the third Master Engraving titled *Melencolia*. Ficino's book on astrology titled *Book of Life*, drew from the world view of Neoplatonism by linking the heavens to humankind's behaviour and destiny. Symbols for Saturn abound in *Melencolia I*:

- the bat belongs to Saturn as it is symbolic of evilness let loose in the night.
- the emaciated dog at the feet of the angel is a reference to his mother dying from a wasting disease.
- The dark skinned winged figure (a medical indication of black bile, melancholy's humor).
- the ocean in the background (Saturn is the Lord of the sea).
- the hourglass (Saturn as the lord of Time).
- the seven-stepped ladder to heaven (Saturn in the Chaldean Order at the highest level closest to God).
- the scales of Libra (Saturn's exalted sign).
- the keys draped at her waist "keys signify power, the purse means wealth."[34]
- the death bell tied to rope (traditionally attached to the toe of the deceased during the plague so that it would ring if the buried awoke from a coma).
- the tools of tradesmen, such as carpenters (Saturn rules stone, wood, agriculture and geometry).
- the compass in the angel's hand depicts geometry.
- The tombstone in the shape of a polyhedron (Saturn rules geometry) with the image of Dürer imprinted on the stone.
- the grindstone (Saturn rules agriculture) with the fringed cloth atop which sits a putto (cherub) busy scribbling as the only figure showing animation in the engraving.

Gemini Moon in Munakara: Albrecht Dürer

- **Key Questions:**
- What does Albrecht Dürer's Moon contend with?
- What is its driving force?
- What is its trigger? What is its outcome?

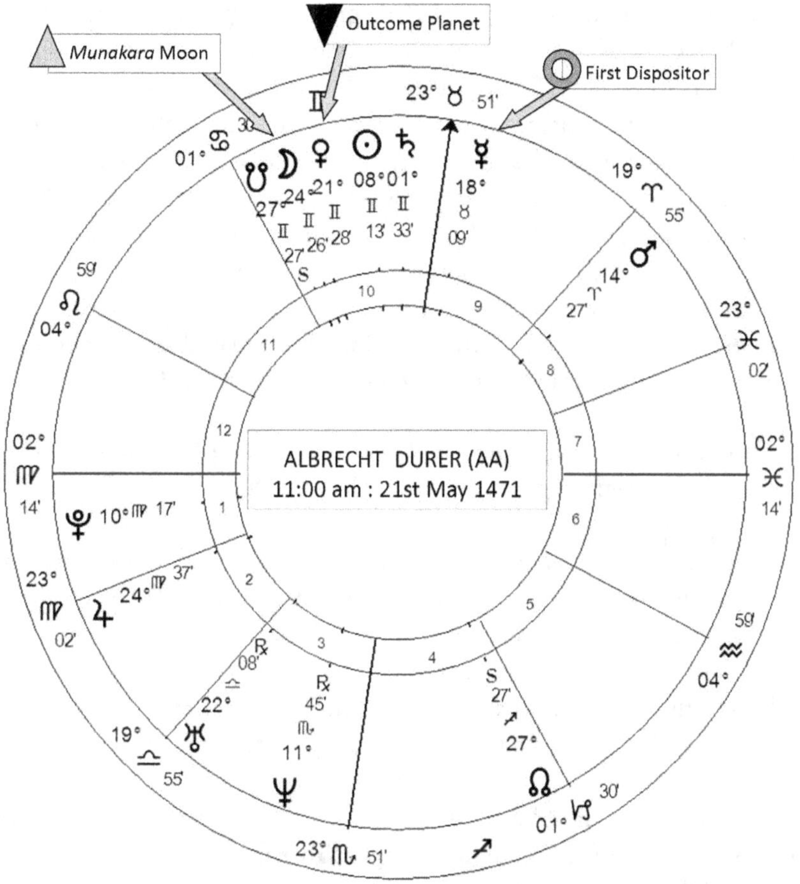

Chapter Twelve • *Munakara Moon Delineations*

Fig. 12.3: Albrecht Dürer Natal Chart: Moon in Munakara

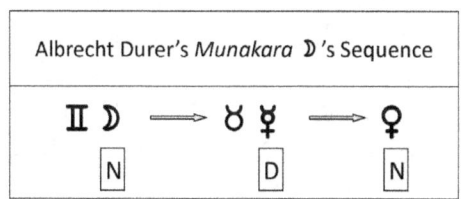

Table 12.5: Albrecht Dürer: Munakara Moon's Sequence

Albrecht Dürer's munakara Moon expresses itself in the scope of his artistic genius, the detail and precision of his work when drawing or etching animals or humans, and later in life, his fascination with the proportions of the human body. As first dispositor, Taurus Mercury gifts the Moon with steady hands and balances mental agility with physical skill to perfect Dürer's knowledge of the mathematical dimensions of the human body and to display them perfectly in his artwork. Dürer's munakara Moon struggled with his fear and repulsion of the physical body's inevitable deterioration through age or illness. His munakara Moon could not contend with any physical form that was not perfect, or was susceptible to the sudden changes of Fortuna – his 1501 painting *Nemesis (The Great Fortune)* – through illness, poverty or accident. Even the natural process of the body's aging through the passage of time was abhorrent to Dürer. A deeply religious man, Dürer struggled to reconcile his faith in a God that created the perfection of mathematical proportions with the imperfection of the aging process.

"The lie is in our understanding, and darkness is so firmly entrenched in our minds that even our groping will fail." – Albrecht Dürer

During the Renaissance period, melancholy was believed to be closely linked to creative genius. The roots of the 'tortured artist' who eases their own emotional anguish through finding a medium that reaches out to others, shares suffering as a collective experience and eases pain through the soothing gifts of music, prose, art or religious symbolism. German author Cornelius Agrippa classified melancholic inspiration into three ascending levels; the lowest Level (One) governed the imagination and belonged to the realm of artists, the middle Level (Two) controlled the reason of scientists and physicians, whilst the highest Level (Three) governed the spirit and intellect of theologians such as himself. Dürer uses the Roman numeral 'I' in the title of his *Melancolia I* to describe Level One, the lowest classification of melancholy to which he felt he belonged as an artist.

Dürer's identification with his own mental frailty (Gemini Moon disposited by Mercury) led him to suffer bouts of depression with the completion of each new piece of art. His exhaustion went far beyond his physical limitations, but his obsession with perfection plagued him as he struggled to understand the 'artistic mind', and occasionally pushed his boundaries from genius to religious fanatic. In later years Dürer's work became less symbolic, and he distanced himself from human emotion, becoming more engaged with scientific observation than painting emotive mythological or religious symbolism. There is no way of knowing if Dürer feared his own body's aging process, or becoming frail or ill, but it is noteworthy that his last self-portrait was as a young man at age 28, even though he lived another 30 years.

Munakara Planet and Sect Condition – how comfortable is the Moon?

Albrecht Dürer's Gemini Moon has no sect dignity, and in *Night & Day: Planetary Sect in Astrology*, Robert Hand says "If a planet's sect is not in accord with any one of these three factors, the planet is to that degree *out of sect* and is to that extent altered in its expression in the chart. The manner of alteration...seems to be a mixture of quantity and quality, that is, in some ways a planet out of sect seems to be merely inhibited in its expression, as if its power were lessened."[35] In specifically examining a Moon out of sect, Hand gives the following explanation, and it is relatable to Dürer's chart (*Fig. 12.3*) as his Moon has the same placement as Hand's example: "Even when it [the Moon] is strongly placed by house, those aspects of the native's chart that are connected to the Moon are a source of difficulty. For example, the Moon in the 10th house in a diurnal chart [Dürer's Moon is in the 10th], a diurnal placement in a diurnal chart, may indicate difficulty with female persons in the pursuit of one's career. It may also indicate some problems with the mother."[36]

Dürer's Moon is conjunct the South Node which is considered by traditional astrologers as a malefic point that diminishes a planet's power. The Moon is in a stellium in Gemini with Saturn, and whilst their degrees are wide, there is still a connection by sign, and this aspect to Saturn would be especially disturbing for an out-of-sect Moon in munakara. The Moon squares Jupiter in detriment (also disposited by Mercury), and this aspect would be challenging for Dürer's emotional and mental stability. Gemini Moon (and Venus) are both in trine aspect to modern Uranus, another indication of the Moon's unrest, nervous irritability, and an easily agitated emotional state of mind (and a need for emotional freedom and independence from another's emotional demands).

In notes transcribed from Hand's 2015 webinar on Sect he says that the absence of sect dignity "affects the Moon's tranquillity, its femininity, and its ability to care unconditionally.....out-of-sect Moon strains conditions for support, protection, nurturing and giving love."[37] We cannot know what Dürer's ability to give or receive love from another human being might have

Albrecht Durer — ☽'s Sect Dignity			
Planet	Sect 1 Status	Sect 2 Hemisphere	Sect 3 Sign
♊ ☽	Day	With the Sun	Air
N	D	D	D

Table 12.6: Albrecht Dürer: Munakara Moon Sect Dignity

been, as his work seems to have consumed much of his time and passion. We know that his wife was chosen by his father and that the marriage was an unhappy one, he wrote letters to friends full of abuse and insults about Agnes,[38] but we have no other proof of his intimate relationships apart from his correspondence with male friends and fellow artists.

Gemini Venus is the Moon's outcome planet, and is conjunct the Moon but is not in munakara state, as its dispositor, Mercury in Taurus, exchanges signs with Venus. When there is an aspect between planets exchanging signs the term used is 'mutual reception, but when no Ptolemaic aspect exists – Taurus to Gemini – the term for this exchange is 'generosity'; the two planets are 'generous' towards each other but cannot give true benefit as there is no aspect between the two signs. They are not connected, so therefore they can be of little use to one another. Munakara Moon's dispositor, Venus, shares the same fate as the Moon so far as sect dignity is concerned, as Venus is also out-of-sect, and Hand describes the effects of out-of-sect Venus on the individual's love-life as "someone who gives love on condition and is more self-centred. It is a self-indulgent Venus that is more concerned for its own needs than in caring for others."[39]

Munakara Moon's dispositor, diurnal Mercury, fares much better so far as sect is concerned as the chart is diurnal, and Mercury is travelling in the same hemisphere as the Sun, therefore diurnal Mercury would be described as being in 'halb.'

Munakara Moon: Albrecht Dürer

"Why has God given me such magnificent talent? It's a curse as well as a great blessing."[40] – Albrecht Dürer

Munakara Moon in Gemini in 10th House (Placidus and Whole Sign)

Most art historians will say that Albrecht Dürer was as much an entrepreneur as he was an artist. He holds a special place in history because he brought art to the ordinary person through his combined gifts of printmaker, painter and engraver. With his business acumen Dürer ensured that art was no longer for the privileged few, the royal court, the rich merchant, or the lord in his manor house. Availability and affordability placed his works in the hands of commoners, and for this alone we can be grateful for his munakara Moon in Gemini. Dürer had a head for business, and his skill in developing mass produced artworks at the turn of the 16th

Chapter Twelve • *Munakara Moon Delineations*

century, is a gift we totally take for granted in our times of multiple images across any medium. It was unknown in his time for an artist to sign his works but Dürer's distinctive AD initials – the letter A drawn as an Oriental-shaped shelter for the letter D snuggled beneath – was proudly displayed on every piece of his work and when others imitated his stamp he went to the Venetian government to prevent forgeries of his signature, and won the case thereby protecting it for posterity.

Dürer's chart (*Fig. 12.3*) shows Saturn and the Sun in Gemini, in the same sign as Moon and Venus, and all four planets are dispositied by Mercury. There are thirteen degrees separating Sun/Saturn and Venus/Moon and whilst this distance may seem a little too wide an orb, there is no doubt that Saturn affected his Moon, as Dürer's private letters talk about his depression and anxiety, and his exploration of melancholy has been the seed of his most famous works. Saturn's rulership of 5th and 6th house – 5th is his creative and artistic ability – but 6th house is a concern for his physical and mental health when in conjunction to a contentious Moon.

Saturn and munakara Moon in the same stellium highlights the animosity that exists between these two planets and accentuates the 5th- and 11th-house axis of Capricorn and Cancer, representing artistic and creative endeavours (5th) and group dynamics and mentorship (11th). From 1512 until his death in January 1519, Maximilian I, Holy Roman Emperor was Dürer's patron, but Maximilian was a very cash-strapped prince who sometimes failed to pay for him commissions. However, Dürer benefited in other ways as artists and learned men were highly esteemed in the emperor's court and success and reputation (10th-house Moon ruling 11th house) were measured by Maximilian's patronage and through membership in his elevated circle of talented and enlightened individuals. *Portrait of Emperor Maximilian I* was commissioned in 1518 and completed after Maximilian's death in 1519.

The years 1513 and 1514 were artistically productive years for Albrecht Dürer producing a trio of famous engravings collectively titled *Meisterstiche* (Master Engravings): *Knight, Death and the Devil* (1513), *Saint Jerome in his Study* (1514) and *Melencolia I* (1514). Together they have been cast to represent the three spheres of human activity: the active, contemplative and intellectual,[41] but there are other interpretations too. Art historian Erwin Panofsky wrote in *The Life and Art of Albrecht Dürer* that the three engravings form more of a spiritual unity based on the scholastic classifications of the virtues: *The Knight* shows 'the life of the Christian in the practical world of decision and action'; *St Jerome* shows 'the life of the saint in the spiritual world of sacred contemplation' and *Melencolia I* shows 'the life of the secular genius in the rational and imaginative worlds of science and art.'[42]

The years marked a sad and lonely period of grief and separation for Dürer as the deaths of several close friends were closely followed by the painful death of his mother. We might assume that his grief is the basis for his state of melancholy at that time, and munakara Moon's outlet once more became his art during these difficult two years. Dürer was close to his mother, and painted two portraits of her; one in 1490 that shows a strong dignified woman in her middle years (*Portrait of Dürer's Mother Barbara, nee Hopler*), and the second portrait in 1514, two months before her death (*Portrait of the Artist's Mother at the Age of 63*). The second portrait shows an old woman, her body stooped and her face ravaged by the effects of age, pain and disease. Between the strokes is a son's grief and concern at her obvious pain and a child's feeling of hopelessness at being unable to relieve their mother's suffering. Barbara Dürer's life was a hard one and her marriage as a 15-year-old teenager to a 40-year-old man produced eighteen children, with Albrecht surviving to adulthood with only two other siblings.

After her death Dürer wrote: "This, my pious Mother bore, and brought up eighteen children; she often had the plague and many other severe and strange illnesses, and she suffered great poverty, scorn, contempt, mocking words, terrors, and great adversities. Yet she bore no malice....I felt so grieved for her that I cannot express it. God be merciful to her."[43]

Munakara Moon can describe a mother's difficult life, as well as giving indications as to the emotional landscape and physical state of the individual. Dürer does not expand on his statement to explain why his mother 'suffered great poverty, scorn, contempt and mocking words.' Suffice to say, he was aware of his mother's suffering and the hardship experienced by his mother is further evidence of his Moon in contention.

Albrecht's painting of his mother is both personal and impersonal, the hardships of her life etched on her face combined with the clinical assessment of her illness' effect on her face. He was fascinated by the disintegration of the body and often forensically detailed the effects of aging on others, but to witness it in his beloved mother would have been heartbreaking for him. It is noteworthy that although Dürer lived and worked until his death at age 57, he did not record his own aging process for prosperity as his last self-portrait was at age 28, when he was at his physical peak.

Chapter Twelve • *Munakara Moon Delineations*

First Dispositor: Diurnal Mercury in Taurus in 9th House

"There is no man on earth who can give a final judgment on what the most beautiful shape may be. Only God knows."[44] – Albrecht Dürer

Mercury resides in Dürer's 9th house, and Dürer was a devout Christian throughout his life, becoming inclined towards the Lutheran faith through friendships with Philip Melanchthon and Erasmus of Rotterdam, and with an admiration for Dr. Martin Luther, the instigator of the Protestant Reformation. Dürer's questioning of Catholic doctrine is suppressed in his religious works and may have contributed to the disquiet or unease of his munakara Moon, particularly as his artwork displayed so many fundamental principles of Catholicism and the idolatry of saints.

By 1500 Dürer was already the leading artist of the German Renaissance and had earned himself a small fortune as an entrepreneur of a new media. The constant sale of his woodcuts and engravings, plus his printmaking business meant that he was on top of the world before his 30th birthday. Mercury, Gemini Moon's dispositor rules Dürer's Ascendant and sits five degrees from his Mid-Heaven. In Whole Sign, Mercury would also rule his tenth sign (Gemini) and this house of mutability would contain not only his munakara Moon, but also in numerical order, Saturn, Sun, Venus and South Node in Gemini.

Mercury rules Dürer's 2nd house in Placidus, and Venus is the second sign's ruler in the Whole Sign system, so either way, the two planets work together to make life comfortable for this Renaissance master. Dürer's reputation, wealth and success should have created a self-satisfied artist who fulfils all his dreams at a young age. However, Mercury and Venus tell a different story and may be what lies behind his Moon's dissatisfaction and his obsession with aging and the body's distortions.

Dürer's *Praying Hands* (1508) are perhaps his most recognisable image which is constantly visible today on bibles, t-shirts, and eulogy pamphlets at funerals, and even featured on the tombstone of Andy Warhol.[45] The hands are not just startlingly lifelike – a brilliant example of his physiological knowledge (munakara Moon in Gemini) – they also convey themes of emotion linked to spirituality such as piety, peace, faith, acceptance and hope. What makes *Praying Hands* – painted in 1508 – so significant, is that almost seven years later the comparison to the hands in *Melencolia I* – 1514 – is a telling testament to the artist's changed state of mind and perhaps his doubts about his spirituality. *Praying Hands* show a supplicant's hands, fingers lightly touching and held together in prayer. There is a simplicity and innocence to the hands as though the belief that a prayer will be answered by God is a given expectation. In contrast, *Melencolia I* depicts a winged figure's clenched fist clutched against a face in despair and a feeling that God has abandoned the figure in their hour of need.

Dürer's Mid-heaven is in Taurus with its ruler, Venus in Gemini. Venus is elevated in the 10th house, but there is aversion (no sight) between Taurus (MC) and Venus (its ruler). The Whole Sign house system will show mutable signs for the angular signs of Virgo, Sagittarius, Pisces and Gemini, and the Mid-heaven will slip back to the Whole Sign 9th house. Venus will remain as the ruler of the MC, however, Mercury becomes the ruler of the Whole Sign tenth sign, the place of reputation, ambition, success and public acclaim. Fixed signs are a weakness for aversion and Mercury in Taurus has a similar issue to Venus in Gemini, since being in the fixed sign (Taurus) it cannot see the mutable sign (Gemini) on the Whole Sign 10th-house cusp.

This means that *neither* of the planets in charge of Dürer's 10th-house principles can see its neighbouring sign. There is aversion between munakara Moon's first dispositor, Mercury, and the 10th house, or the Moon's outcome planet, Venus, and the Mid-heaven. Aversion between the 10th-house lord or the lord of the Mid-heaven tends to frustrate the individual who cannot seem to reach a point of satisfaction, a pinnacle is beyond their sight, and they are torn between choices that present themselves (or fail to present themselves) when accessing the 10th house. This feeling of 'not quite getting there' is regardless of outward trappings, others' envy or adoration, accolades or social and professional success. A sense of hollowness or fear of exposure or imposter's syndrome seems to dog the ruler of the 10th/MC who cannot see its sign or the chart's culmination point.

The outcome planet: Venus in Gemini in 10th House

In similarity to the chart example of photographer Diane Arbus (*Fig. 12.4*), Albrecht Dürer also has munakara Moon conjunct Venus and brings together the contentious planet with its outcome planet from the same sect category. The air element features in both conjunctions but Arbus's two nocturnal planets are in Aquarius (Saturn is in Libra) whereas Dürer has his conjunction in Gemini with Mercury in Taurus being the connector between Moon and Venus. For Dürer, the conjunction connects the planet

Chapter Twelve • *Munakara Moon Delineations*

in munakara with its outcome planet and ties them together beautifully to create sheer cunning, business acumen, a large dose of prudence and a creative genius with no equal in the Renaissance. Dürer honed his intellectual and physical skills to create drawings, woodcuts and engravings with an exceptional eye for detail, and a steady hand with incredibly fine-tuned motor skills.

Dürer mastered the burin, an engraving tool for metal or wood ground down to form a diamond-shaped tip and one only has to view his woodcuts in the sixteen designs of the *Apocalypse* series, particularly the 1498 *The Four Horsemen of the Apocalypse* featuring Death, Famine, War and Plague to appreciate his artistry. His later woodcuts *Small Passion*, a series of 36 woodcuts depicting the life of Christ, was produced in 1511 and printed for prayer books for the devout and circulated in their hundreds throughout Europe. Venus, the Moon's outcome planet, rules Dürer's 2nd house by Whole Sign, and Dürer was an expert on knowing what would appeal to the paying public or to the pious for their daily prayers. Banking on their popularity, Dürer also republished his earlier works including *Apocalypse*, keeping his name and works constantly in the public eye and creating further wealth for himself.

In Dürer's chart Jupiter in Virgo squares both the Moon and Venus, and Albrecht's marriage was arranged by his parents for two reasons; to elevate their son's social status as Agnes's family were prominent musicians, and to allow Albrecht to open his own workshop, as marriage was a prerequisite for any new business venture in Nuremburg. Unfortunately, Jupiter's detriment did little to provide a happy union witnessed by Dürer's letter to a friend describing Agnes as an 'old crow' and complaining she was a miserly shrew with a bitter tongue.[46] In other correspondence he says he 'hates her friends' and that they eat separately. This seems an unfair judgement and may be part of Moon's contention as Dürer abandoned her several times to travel across Europe – the first time two months after their marriage in 1494 when there was an outbreak of the plague in Nuremburg – and left her at home (where the disease was rife) to sell his prints at market stalls and fairs.

The artwork titled *My Agnes* was a pen-and-ink portrait created by Dürer in 1494 and it shows tenderness and intimacy between artist and subject so perhaps the marriage soured after Albrecht deserted her in August 1494. He painted Agnes's portrait several times, one from 1475 survives, and the last known portrait of her was in 1521 to commemorate their 27th wedding anniversary.[47]

Despite Dürer's unkind descriptions of his wife, Agnes was responsible for the marketing of her husband's prints, and they regularly visited fairs together to sell his engravings. During her husband's second trip to Italy Agnes faithfully ran the workshop in his absence and in the years 1520 and 1521 the couple travelled together in the Netherlands. For a wife that supposedly brought such misery (munakara Moon) Albrecht trusted her with his business (Mercury disposits to Venus) and the couple spent large amounts of time together selling prints at the weekly Nuremberg markets when Dürer was in his home city.

There has been speculation that Albrecht was bisexual, if not homosexual,[48] as several of his works such as *The Men's Bath House* (1496) are believed to contain themes of homosexual desire and his correspondence with close male friends was extremely intimate in nature.[49] A judgement on Dürer's sexuality based on his art may be presumptive as two works from the same year, *The Woman's Bath*, and *Four Witches (Four Naked Women)* show a similar appreciation and familiarity with the female form. In his later years Dürer was obsessed with scientific writings, mathematics and illustrations of the body's mathematical proportions producing his *Four Books on Measurement* and *Four Books on Human Proportion*, around the same period as Leonardo da Vinci's release of the Vitruvian Man, c. 1490. Dürer's *Four Books* were published months after his death in 1528 at age 57, and Agnes continued to sell his prints and copies of his books until her own demise in 1539.

Munakara Moon: Diane Arbus

A Brief Biography of Diane Arbus

American photographer Diane Arbus (nee Nemerov) was born 14th March, 1923 in New York. She is best known for her compelling, often disturbing, portraits of people from the edges of society. Arbus was the daughter of Gertrude and David Nemerov, proprietors of a New York department store. In 1937, at age 14, Arbus fell in love with Allan Arbus, a 19-year-old copy boy working in her family's store. Her parents disapproved of the match but they finally gave in to their daughter's wishes and allowed her to marry Arbus in 1941 just after he 18th birthday. The pair worked collaboratively, first taking photographs and creating advertisements for the store, and then branching out to commercial fashion photography for *Harper's Bazaar, Show, Esquire, Glamour, The New York Times*, and *Vogue*.

Chapter Twelve • *Munakara Moon Delineations*

Arbus gave up commercial work in 1956 to pursue her own work after her teacher, Lisette Model, an Austrian-born documentary photographer encouraged her to pursue her interest in fine-art photography. In 1959 Arbus separated from her husband and they were divorced in 1969. Arbus had two daughters with Allan Arbus, Doon born in 1945 and Amy born in 1954. Her eldest daughter, Doon Arbus, is a writer and journalist who contributed to five books on Diane Arbus's work. Doon was 26 at the time when her mother committed suicide and became responsible for the management of her mother's estate. Amy Arbus is an American photographer and has published several books on photography.

In 1960 *Esquire* published Arbus's first photo-essay, an image of contradiction between the squalor and privilege in New York City. In 1963 and 1966 Arbus received Guggenheim fellowships to be part of a project titled "American Rites, Manners, and Customs." She began at that time to explore the subjects that would occupy her for much of her career: individuals who lived on the outskirts of society or "normalcy," such as nudists, transvestites, dwarfs, and the mentally or physically handicapped.

In 1970 she was the recipient of the Robert Leavitt Award and her role as Instructor of Photography was reinstated until her death on 26th July 1971. She committed suicide while still definitively at the height of her career leaving no note, and the reasons for taking her own life are unknown. A year after her death, Arbus's work was selected for inclusion in the Venice Biennale, the first time any photographer has been so honoured. In 1972, the Museum of Modern Art (MoMA) held a retrospective of her work that travelled throughout the United States and Canada from 1972 to 1975.[50] At the same time, the Aperture Foundation published an accompanying catalogue: the Aperture monograph has sold more than 12 million copies to date.[51] In 2007 Arbus's estate gifted her complete archives – including photographic equipment, diary pages, and the negatives of some 7,500 rolls of film – to the Metropolitan Museum of Art in New York City.

"Her own evident intimacy with the extraordinary subjects of her photos resulted in images that engage the sympathy and collusion of the viewer and elicit a strong response. Some critics saw her work as remarkably empathetic to its subjects, while others were disturbed by what they saw as a harsh, voyeuristic look into the lives of the disadvantaged."[52]

Munakara in Practice

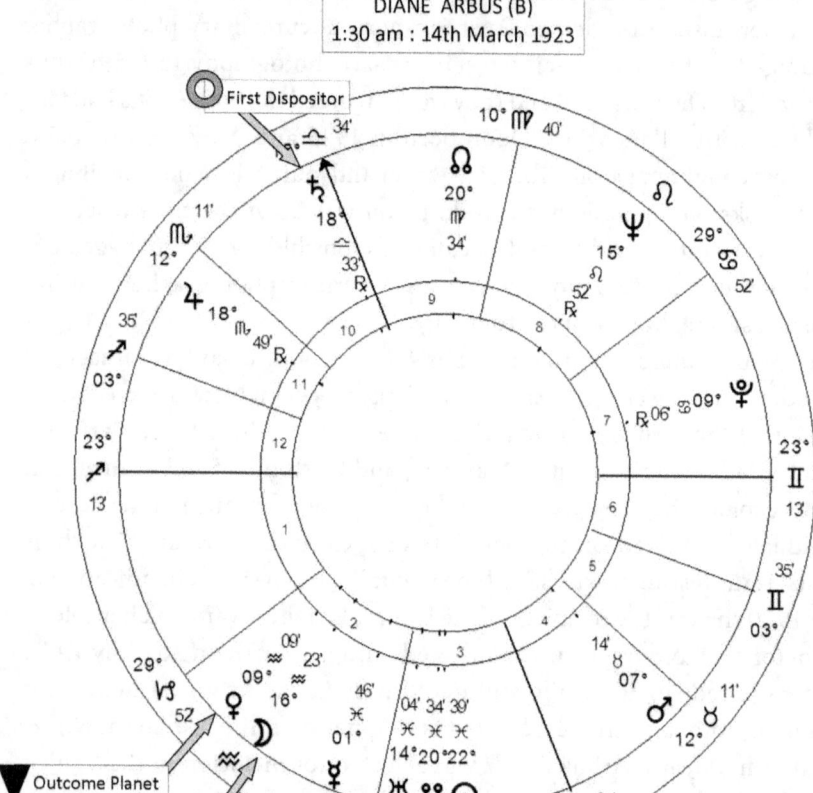

Fig. 12.4: Diane Arbus Natal Chart: Moon in Munakara

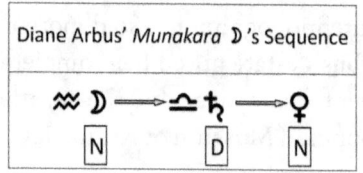

Table 12.7: Diane Arbus: Munakara Moon's Sect Dignity

Aquarius Moon in Munakara: Diane Arbus

- **Key Questions:**
- What does Diane Arbus's Moon contend with?
- What is its driving force?
- What is its trigger? What is its outcome?

Chapter Twelve • *Munakara Moon Delineations*

Arbus's munakara Moon is contentious because it uses confrontational images to force viewers to deal with their opinions on individuals who are shunned by society or do not conform to society's models of normality. Her images were produced in the late 1960s when society was keen to see photographs of the lucky few who were rich, famous and beautiful (Venus as Moon's outcome planet). It is no coincidence that Arbus's early career in photography was in the glittering world of fashion magazines, but her contentious Moon was not satisfied with staying in the safe and lucrative world of fashion. Arbus would roam the streets of New York looking for subjects to photograph and her pictures caught looks that seemed hostile or defiant due to her unique style of using a flash (to illuminate and startle), and holding the camera directly opposite the faces of her subjects.[53]

"For me the subject of the picture is always more important than the picture. And more complicated."[54] – Diane Arbus

The Moon's dispositor is Saturn, indicating a life of comfort and ease was never going to satisfy her munakara Moon. Both mother Gertrude and daughter Diane suffered from depression, and her identification with her subjects demonstrates the bleakness of her own emotions and her feelings of separation when she was not coping with life. Saturn accentuates munakara Moon's search for peace of mind and shows the drive behind Arbus's connection to individuals who were rejected by the community because of physical differences or personal choices that were different from the norm. Saturn is exalted in Libra and its sign ruler, Venus, is the outcome planet for Arbus's Moon. Through her artistry and her skills in photography Arbus's art is able to capture a moment or a look that in other circumstances, society would be questioning the moral decency of staring at something or someone different.

In her article *The Politics of Staring*,[55] Rosemarie Garland-Thomson writes on the history of disabled people in the Western world. In her article she remarks on the inconsistency between disabled people being placed on public display, at the same time as being socially and politically invisible, especially when it comes to society's responsibility to care for all its members with equity rather than equality.

Photography authorizes staring. People are made to be looked at.... Photos absolve viewers of responsibility to the objects of their stares at the same time that they permit a more intense form of staring than an actual social interchange might support. Disability photography thus offers the spectator the pleasure of unaccountable, uninhibited, insistent looking. This license to stare becomes a powerful rhetorical device that can be mobilized to manipulate viewers.[56]

Garland-Thomson states there are four primary expressions of, or intentions for, disability photography. The wondrous (elicits amazement and admiration); the sentimental (diminishes the disabled as it produces the helpless sufferer, invoking pity for the subject and superiority in the viewer); the exotic (presents disabled figures as alien, distant, often sensationalized or entertaining in their difference); and realistic (creates the illusion of reality but is just as constructed and convention-bound as the previous three).

Diane Arbus's work continues to enjoy great popularity in the 21st century (Venus is Moon's outcome planet), but there is always contention around her work and sometimes this contention is deliberately exploited. The 2022 Zwirner Exhibition held in New York deliberately invited controversy when it displayed these (and other similar) comments in the foyer at the entrance to her exhibition.

> "(Arbus) shows us people, so locked into their physical and mental limitations, that their movements are meaningless charades. They are losers almost to a man."
>
> "In photographing dwarfs you don't get majesty and beauty. You get dwarfs."[57]

Whether their presence at her exhibition were meant to bait the public, or excite the viewer, is a moot point, but there may come a time when her photographs become dated (Saturn's influence), and an equity-based society re-evaluates where her art fits within the realm of disability photography. The question remains whether Diane Arbus's munakara Moon was a tool for exploitation in the 1960s and 70s, or whether we applaud her visual honesty in 'befriending her subjects and capturing rare psychological intensity in her work.'[58]

Munakara Planet and Sect Condition – how comfortable is the Moon?

The munakara Moon is Diane's prime luminary and a nocturnal chart supports the Moon's sect dignity even though the Moon is travelling in the same hemisphere as the Sun and in a masculine diurnal sign (Aquarius). Robert Hand states that the Moon in a nocturnal chart "is a strong Moon" and that it achieves success through embodying the aspirations of others and serving their needs.[59] In his 2015 webinar Hand added to the Moon's state in sect dignity as he believed a nocturnal chart helped the Moon to achieve tranquillity through the values of compassion and understanding.[60] The Moon's sect dignity seems to support the belief that perhaps Diane Arbus did relate to her subjects with care and compassion, and rather than her pictures 'authorizing staring' for the curious spectator, it was her aim to give her subjects power and dignity in a world that chose to look past them, rather than acknowledge them as relevant and valuable members of society.

Diane Arbus— ☽'s Sect Dignity			
Planet	Sect 1 Status	Sect 2 Hemisphere	Sect 3 Sign
♒ ☽	Night	With the Sun	Air
N	N	D	D

Table 12.8: Diane Arbus: Munakara Moon's Sect Dignity

Moon in Aquarius suffers no debility but it is still disposited by its enemy Saturn, and Saturn has poor sect condition in Diane's chart. Saturn is separated from the Sun in a nocturnal chart (*Fig. 12.4*) and although it is highly elevated in position (on the MC) and in sign in Libra (exaltation) its nature tends to be colder and more severe in its expression. Robert Hand calls an out of sect Saturn "intrinsically unlucky and malevolent"[61] and for Diane Arbus Saturn may have represented not only her subjects' situations (Saturn on MC), but also the state of her own mental anguish, possibly inherited from her mother (munakara Moon, Saturn in 10th house of mother).

Diane's battle with depression and her photography's confrontational nature signal that Saturn lacks comfort in the chart, and for all her Moon's compassion, her subjects were still destined to be disconnected from society. Venus (outcome planet) is better suited to a nocturnal chart so this may explain her continued popularity as a female photographer whose portraiture focused on disenfranchised members of society (Venus in Aquarius).

"A photograph is a secret about a secret. The more it tells you the less you know."[62] – Diane Arbus

Munakara Moon in Aquarius in 2nd House (Placidus)

Diane Arbus' relationship with her subjects has been described as a delicate balance of communication and empathy and this description rings true for Aquarian Moon in munakara status. The Moon in contention is often a story of the person's struggle to fit into a specific community or section of society, as they constantly feel secluded, judged, or alienated from others. Arbus's identification with her subjects may have been motivated by her own sense of alienation, and not simply a way to gain their trust. In her eyes, her fine-art photography was not exploitation, but rather an opportunity to present her subject's story of living as an outcast on society's fringes. Her subjects obviously warmed to her as they chose to invite her into their lives, and often she would photograph the same person several times as she followed their progression through life.

Munakara Moon sits in Arbus' 2nd house, and what began as a source of income, later developed into a mode of communication using light, perspective and careful staging to capture the image she wanted to provide for public viewing. Aquarius Moon moves forward into the 3rd house in Whole Sign, and the conjunction between Moon in contention and its outcome planet, Venus, is obvious in the unique quality of her work. Her artistry is confronting and uncomfortable at times, but it starts conversations and forces the airing of opinions that may be awkward or confrontational, and perhaps this was Arbus's intention.

Aquarius is an air sign, and Diane would often be called to defend her work, saying it was neither false nor deliberately orchestrated to be something to shock or titillate the senses. With munakara Moon in Aquarius, Diane Arbus stressed that her images were about the viewer, not the subject matter, and the photos were not on display for the audience to judge her people, but rather to examine their own attitudes and responses to the image.

> "Most people go through life dreading they'll have a traumatic experience. Freaks (Arbus's term) were born with their trauma. They've already passed their test in life. They're aristocrats."[63] – Diane Arbus

Diane's Moon has a number of important aspects which contribute to the nature of her planet in contention. Venus, her outcome planet is the ruler of the MC and the conjunction to the Moon brings fame and success, regardless of Arbus' contentious material. The munakara Moon also squares Jupiter, her Ascendant lord and the ruler of her Pisces stellium (Mercury,

Chapter Twelve • *Munakara Moon Delineations*

Uranus, South Node and Sun), and this aspect may help to promote the idea that Arbus acted with compassion and understanding. Aquarius Moon trines Libran Saturn (its dispositor) on the Mid-heaven and a productive aspect (trine) between the two air signs shows her personal drive to be authentic to both in honouring her subject matter and to her professional integrity as an artist. Munakara Moon opposes Neptune and this planet has the potential to add physical challenges to the Moon by weakening the body and creating super-sensitivity to the Moon's environment. The opposition makes a T-square between Neptune, Moon and Jupiter (Ascendant's ruler) and adds to the physical and mental health issues experienced by Arbus, especially as Venus (conjunct Moon) is the ruler of the 6th house by Whole Sign. Neptune adds difficulty for the Moon to draw strong emotional boundaries between outside influences and the individual's true feelings, so whilst Arbus believed that she distanced herself by being the photographer, not the subject, the boundaries between herself and her 'freaks' was always going to be compromised.

Diane Arbus's struggle with the frailty of her mental health was a lifelong battle. In 1968 Arbus wrote to her friend: *"I go up and down a lot....I begin lots of things or think about what I want to do and get all breathless with excitement and then quite suddenly either through tiredness or a disappointment or something more mysterious the energy vanished, leaving me harassed, swamped, distraught, frightened by the very things I thought I was so eager for! I'm sure this is quite classic."*[64]

The relationship between a planet in munakara state and the house or houses it rules is an important feature of its story. Arbus's Aquarian Moon is in aversion to Cancer, the sign on Diane's 8th-house cusp, and part of her darkness may have come from feeling ill-equipped to reconcile her intellect and creative eye with her own fractured emotional landscape. The fact that she identified with her outsiders and formed strong emotional bonds with her subjects suggests that whilst her physical appearance as an attractive woman was embraced by society, she secretly felt her internal 'freakishness' made *her* the outsider.

The separation from her husband and former business partner Allan Arbus in 1959 was amicable but Allan attributed the breakdown of their marriage to Diane's depressive episodes – made worse by the debilitating effects of hepatitis – and the randomness of her violent mood changes, perhaps a genetic inheritance from a mother who suffered similar episodes during Diane's childhood years.

First Dispositor: Saturn in Libra conjunct MC

Arbus' munakara Moon is in the fixed air sign of Aquarius, disposited by Saturn in exaltation on the Mid-heaven. In her lifetime only a few museums exhibitions marked the specialness of her work, but in 1972, a year after her suicide, Arbus became the first photographer to be included in the international cultural exhibition, Venice Biennale. A retrospective exhibition in recognition of her work was held the same year at the Museum of Modern Art (MoMA) in New York City and was the highest attended exhibition in MoMA's history.

Saturn rules her 2nd house, and Arbus's struggle to support herself was evident in her correspondence to friends as she complained that lack of money was a persistent concern. Saturn's two consecutive signs tie the 2nd house of resources (Capricorn) with the 3rd house where Venus and Moon reside (Aquarius). Ironically, her magazine assignments decreased as her fame as an artist increased but this may be because of the genre she chose to portray in her photographs. Fashion magazines were reluctant to associate themselves with a woman who photographed 'freaks', and feared they would suffer a dive in their own popularity with women, if they published her evolving photography fetishes. Late in her career, The Metropolitan Museum of Art showed interest in three of Arbus's photographs but chose only two at $75 a piece citing a lack of funds to buy the third photograph. At the time Arbus wrote to her former husband: "So I guess being poor is no disgrace."[65]

As a child Arbus was no stranger to affluence and privilege. She had been raised in a wealthy family by parents who owned Russeks, a Fifth Avenue department store co-founded by her grandfather Frank Russek. Her family connections certainly opened doors for her early commercial photography business with clients such as *Glamour, Seventeen, Harper's Bazaar, Esquire* and *Vogue,* but there is no record to confirm that Diane inherited any of the family's wealth. The subjects of her later career alienated her from her former clients as these were magazines that focused on the beautiful and glamorous members of society and their readers wanted to emulate them, not the outsiders who became the focus of Arbus's later photographic work.

Saturn is the dispositor for her munakara Moon, and Diane had a distant relationship with her busy socialite mother, Gertrude Nemerov, as she was mainly raised by staff, maids and governesses. Diane's mother became further removed from her child when Gertrude suffered clinical depression for about a year, and silently withdrew from her family. Diane was the middle child and as such, she may have felt her siblings outshone her (Saturn rules Whole Sign 3rd house with Venus and munakara Moon in situ). Her younger sister enjoyed success early in life as a noted sculptor and designer, and her older brother Howard Nemerov, was a famous poet and winner of numerous awards, and a Pulitzer Prize recipient in 1978, as well as serving two terms as the United States Poet Laureate from 1988 to 1990.

The outcome planet: Venus in Aquarius

Diane Arbus was one of 80 women interviewed for *Viewpoints of Women* hosted by WNYC Program Director Richard Pyatt in January and February 1971. At the time, Arbus was struggling to pay her rent, recovering from two bouts of hepatitis, and living with depression. Four months after the WNYC program was broadcast in March, she would take her own life at the age of 48 in July 1971.

In the interview Richard Pyatt asks: *"What would you consider to be the greatest problem in being a woman today?"*

To which Arbus immediately replies: *Today*.[66]

As the article (written September 27, 2023) points out, this was 1971. A woman could not have a credit card in her own name and was not permitted to fight on the front lines in the military. A woman could be fired if she became pregnant. Spousal rape would not be outlawed until 1993. A woman could not sue for sexual harassment and if permitted to work, were paid, on average, 57 cents to every dollar that men earned.

Arbus's munakara Moon was not just one story of a woman taking black and white photographs in the park. Venus as munakara Moon's outcome is the story of women in Western societies during the middle years of the last century. Their struggles, their challenges and their roles as contentious women are a part of Arbus's photographic memories and she was a single woman who refused to be quiet and remain as the background decoration to men's stories.

Rattled by Diane's answer, Pyatt continues with the next question, asking: 'Or what would you consider to be the most enjoyable thing about being a woman?

Diane Arbus answers: *"I think sexual freedom is very enjoyable...The woman part of it is sort of terrific fun 'cause women have a lot more power now sexually in the first place, but that sort of spills over...it's important. Just the sense that women* can now experience the same variety as men have traditionally experienced... I think sex is very educational."[67]

This answer totally confounds the interviewer as he then attempts to counter her statement by telling Arbus that men and women are "chromosomally different" and cannot possibly enjoy the same sexual freedoms. She interrupts him mid-flight with: *"Oh, really?"*

Thirty two years after her death – a full Saturn Return – *Diane Arbus Revelations* was published in 2003 by her elder daughter Doon Arbus, who was experiencing her own Saturn Return at age twenty six at the time of her mother's suicide. Doon became responsible for the management of her mother's estate, and she has authored or contributed to five books on her mother's work, including *An Aperture Monograph* published in 1972 to accompany her first MoMA exhibition, a year after Diane's death.

Doon's *Revelations* revisits the origins, scope and aspirations of her artist mother, and a journalist for *New York Times Magazine*, Arthur Lubow wrote on the book's release: *"She was fascinated by people who were visibly creating their own identities – cross-dressers, nudists, sideshow performers, tattooed men, the nouveaux riches, the movie-star fans – and by those who were trapped in a uniform that no longer provided any security or comfort."*

With his words Lubow has unwittingly encapsulated the sequence of three planets crossing the boundaries of sect. Diane Arbus's munakara Moon was increasingly trapped in Saturn's 'uniform that no longer provided security or comfort' and Arbus's suicide in 1971 provided a premature exit from life's restrictions, from financial strain, from depression and debilitating illness.

Venus in Aquarius rules Diane's Mid-heaven, and the relationship between Saturn in Libra and Venus in Aquarius is one of mutual reception as both signs are in placed in the air element. The movement from exalted Saturn to Venus in Aquarius is one of ease, and although Diane Arbus was unable to find happiness by finding her own emotional peace, her uniqueness lies in not keeping her subjects at a safe impartial distance as is most photographers' technique, but instead offering them an accepting and non-judgemental relationship, which is immortalized in her photography. As Arbus repeatedly stated, if viewers were squeamish, then it was their problem, and this feeling, although fleeting, may give them a small insight into how the subject matter feels under the harsh scrutiny of a world that cannot tolerate or embrace the different or the unusual.

Australian feminist Germaine Greer was not one of Diane Arbus's fans. Perhaps Greer disliked the mirror Arbus held up for her to view a less flattering image of herself: after all, Greer's own Aquarian Sun and Ascendant conjunct Arbus's Moon in contention. Greer posed for Arbus in 1971 (the year of her death), and Greer wrote a retrospective piece on her experience of the meeting for The Guardian in 2005 titled *Wrestling with Diane Arbus*.[68] In the article Greer describes Arbus instructing her to lie on her back on the bed. The photographer straddled Greer and aggressively poked a lens in her face, obviously hoping to antagonise her subject and gain a negative reaction for the camera. Greer refused to give Arbus the satisfaction of photographing her discomfort, and the two women stayed in their relative positions for hour after hour, Greer pinned to the bed by her antagonist, Arbus inches from her face and intent on catching the feminist's worst expression in an image that would give insight into the famous writer and feminist.

This experience did not endear Greer to Arbus's somewhat ruthless technique to gain an image that may not be truthful, and she does not share everyone's enthusiasm for Diane Arbus's talents, or believe that she was driven by compassion to share her subjects' stories. Greer's analysis of Diane Arbus's character and her art is especially harsh:

> *The emotion that thrills through every Arbus icon making them haunting and unforgettable is a relentless, all-encompassing loathing (for her subjects).... To say that Arbus' creativity was driven by disgust is not to dismiss her as an artist. It is a curiously moralistic view of art that says it cannot be generated by negative emotion....Arbus is not an artist who makes us see the world anew; she embeds us in our own limitations, our lack of empathy, our kneejerk reactions, our incuriosity and lack of concern. Hers is a world without horizons where there is no escape from self.*[69]

Munakara Moon: Evel Knievel

A Brief Biography of Evel Knievel

Robert Craig Knievel (17 October 1938 – 30 November 2007) was born in Butte, Montana, USA. He used his professional name 'Evel' Knievel during his fifteen year career (1965–1980) as an American stunt performer and motorbike daredevil, attempting 168 jumps on his motorcycle soaring in the air over cars, fountains, canyons and sharks and only 19 of these jumps were failures that ended in crashes.

Most of his escapades he performed across the States of America, but with television transmissions beaming across the globe beginning in March 25, 1967,[70] the rest of the world knew his name and witnessed his escapades from their own living rooms. His most famous stunt was a thrilling jump over the fountains at Caesars Palace Hotel in Las Vegas on December 31, 1967. But it wasn't an extravaganza without incident. Knievel cleared the fountains but crashed on landing,[71] and it was his most serious accident with broken ribs, broken hip, fractures to a wrist and both ankles, a crushed pelvis and a stint in hospital for one month. For much of this time in hospital he was rumoured to be comatose, but this was denied by his family in the documentary film *Being Evel* (2015).

Evel performed twice to international audiences during his career; in 1974 he successfully jumped 13 Mac trucks in Toronto, Ontario, and nine months later in May 1975 he attempted to jump 13 single-decker buses at Wembley Stadium in London, England but failed to clear the thirteenth bus, and suffered a fractured pelvis, broken hand and concussion.

In 1975, five years before his official retirement, Knievel held the record for the most broken bones in a lifetime in the Guinness World Records when it was reported that in total, he had suffered 433 bone fractures. The following year in 1976 he was seriously injured during a televised attempt to jump a tank full of sharks at the International Amphitheatre in Chicago, Illinois. Compared to his earlier jumps, the Chicago jump was not his longest distance but Evel couldn't resist the extra danger of adding sharks to his potent mix of potential disaster, especially as *Jaws* had been released in the same year and Knievel was inspired by the film. Unfortunately he crashed during a practice jump and suffered a fractured collarbone, concussion and two broken arms.

One blood transfusion Knievel received prior to 1992 was contaminated and he contracted Hepatitis C as a result. By early 1999, the disease was shutting down his liver and he was sent home from the hospital to die in peace. En route to his home, the hospital recalled him saying that a young man had died in a motor cycle accident and his family had donated his organs for transplant purposes. Knievel received a liver transplant and lived a further eight years. However, he was not free from illness as he was diagnosed with pulmonary fibrosis, a terminal lung disease in 2005, suffered two strokes, had diabetes, and in 2006, had a surgically implanted morphine pain pump to relieve the pain in his lower back as a result of countless injuries from his heyday. Knievel died on November 30, 2007, at the age of 69 due to diabetes and pulmonary fibrosis.

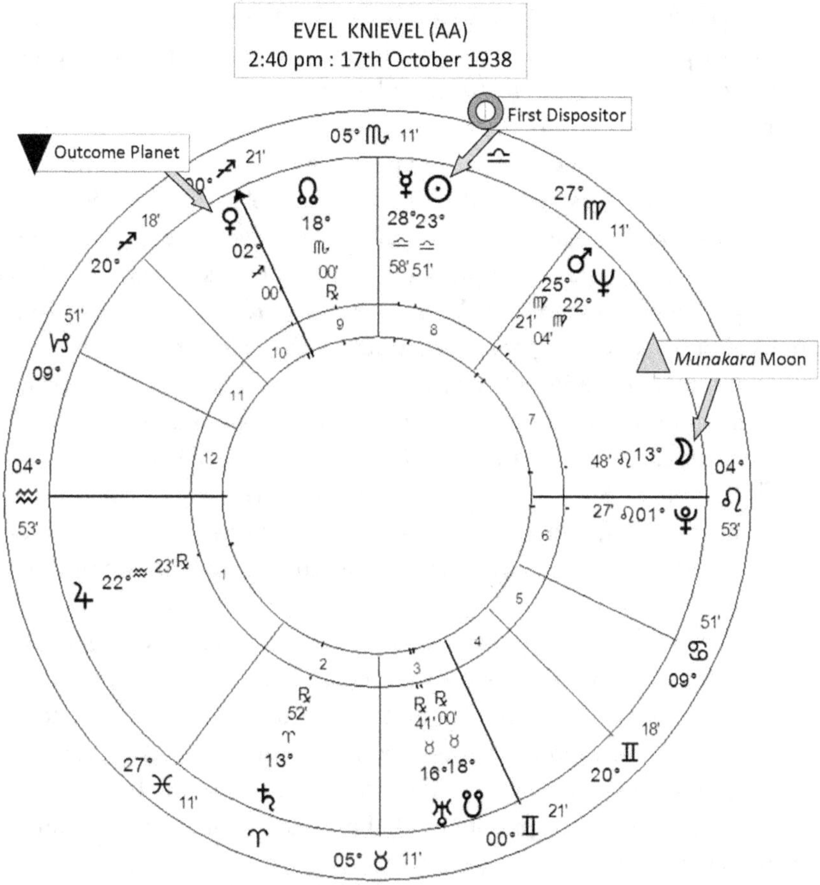

Chapter Twelve • *Munakara Moon Delineations*

Fig. 12.5: Evel Knievel Natal Chart: Moon in Munakara

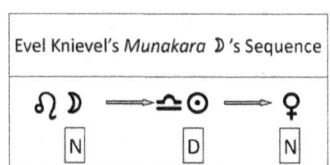

Table 12.9: Evel Knievel: Munakara Moon's Sequence

Leo Moon in Munakara: Evel Knievel

- **Key Questions:**
- What does Evel Knievel's Moon contend with?
- What is its driving force?
- What is its trigger? What is its outcome?

Evel Knievel's Leo Moon Leo expresses itself by the stuntman's burning desire to gather an audience together that would admire and praise his bravado, and his courage to complete tasks that were dangerous and somewhat pointless in their objective. Adding contention to the Leo Moon raised the risk that Knievel was prepared to take to gain this attention and munakara Moon was prepared to endure any level of pain, physical suffering and long-term damage to achieve that goal. Knievel's passion lay in beating the obstacles (and challenging fate) through his skill, speed and agility, pitting his own body against the obstacles, regardless of whether they were rows of buses, deep canyons, shark tanks, or huge fountains.

There is no tension between the three planets in the Moon's sequence but the Moon's dispositor is the Sun which is in fall in Libra, and the Sun is also in munakara status (*Table 12.11*), resulting in both Knievel's luminaries being in contention. The Sun's influence over the Moon becomes a little more challenging, and any stress the Sun is experiencing through its own state of contention will immediately flow through to the Moon in its sign of Leo.

The Sun and Moon in munakara paints a picture of someone who was desperate for attention, and who was prepared to forfeit his health and safety, in order to provide a spectacle and enjoy notoriety, even if it lasted just a few minutes. His munakara Moon was constantly placed in grave danger, and although he pushed his good fortune to the absolute limit, he became an individual with an appetite to challenge safe limits and constantly put himself at risk.

Venus, the Moon's outcome planet (and Sun's first dispositor) is high in the chart, two degrees from the chart's culminating point at zero Sagittarius, and its influence over the MC brings crowd popularity and an art form of some kind. Venus's own dispositor is retrograde Jupiter in the 1st house, so by his own bizarre actions (1st house), Knievel gained notoriety and a measure of popularity (including a doll-size action figure in his image) amongst those who watched his exploits, and wondered if he would survive the next great challenge.

The outcome is entertainment, love and admiration from his audience, and the personal exhilaration of surviving against all odds. Speed and danger can be another form of addiction, and the Moon's blind rulership over Evel Knievel's 6th house, suggests that the thought of injury and damage to his body was the furthest thought from his mind. Glory, recognition, popularity, and his name in record books – a form of immortality – were his goals and ambitions, and he was not going to let his body's weaknesses stand in his way. The attention Knievel sought was fleeting, and his munakara Moon paid the price for a hungry Sun in fall, but one that believed that if he knew what he was doing, he could control his environment, a sure sign that the Sun is in perfect sect condition (*hayz*) in his chart.

Munakara Planet and Sect Condition – how comfortable is the Moon?

Evel Knievel's munakara Moon is completely without sect dignity, and this is a warning to anyone who is operating in a hostile environment that has little ability to protect or nurture the physical body (Moon). Even with all his careful preparations, many of Knievel's accidents occurred in the 'dry runs' before the main event.

Evel Knievel — ☽'s Sect Dignity			
Planet	Sect 1 Status	Sect 2 Hemisphere	Sect 3 Sign
♌ ☽	Day	With the Sun	Fire
	N	D	D	D

Table 12.10: Evel Knievel: Munakara Moon Sect Dignity

His munakara Moon is situated above the horizon in the 7th house in a diurnal chart, and presumably Knievel had a reliable team at his side when he prepared for his jumps. Leo is a fire sign, and when the Moon is in this sign it can forget past hurts and get carried away by enthusiasm, often inquisitive as to what it can achieve, and how it can attract glory and bring focus to the individual's courage or skills. In Evel Knievel's case, the event was often advertised months in advance of him mobilising his team, setting up the obstacle course, and actually practising to see if the promised act was in fact possible. In some cases his venues were very public – Caesars Palace Hotel in Las Vegas – so preparation for the main event was impossible to carry out in privacy. Or they were places of difficult terrain, such as the Snake River Canyon in Idaho, and therefore too expensive or too remote to set up practice runs. Knievel had chosen Snake River Canyon because he saw it from an aeroplane window as he was flying over on his way home from another performance.

Robert Hand describes out-of-sect Moon as "either quite weak or a source of difficulty The Moon in a diurnal chart or diurnally placed in the chart (in this case, both of these) is at a severe disadvantage... The examples from the ancients...suggest that such a Moon is less able to withstand impediments from various sources."[72] In Knievel's case, he was constantly adding 'impediments' to his Moon by deliberately placing it in circumstances and situations that put it in danger. Perhaps it is a testament to contention that Evel Knievel challenged himself to such lengths that he did not die as a result of a terrible accident, but instead survived to the relatively old age of 68.

Munakara Moon: Robert "Evel" Knievel

During a 1968 interview discussing the Grand Canyon jump Knievel stated: "I don't care if they say, 'Look, kid, you're going to drive that thing off the edge of the Canyon and die,' I'm going to do it. I want to be the first. If they'd let me go to the moon, I'd crawl all the way to Cape Kennedy just to do it. I'd like to go to the moon, but I don't want to be the second man to go there."[73]

Munakara Moon in Leo in 7th House (Placidus and Whole Sign)

Seventh-house Leo Moon in munakara made everyone feel as though E.K. had performed his tricks as a personal treat for them, and the public devoured his homespun philosophies on manliness, family values, motor helmet safety promotions, and anti-drug messages aimed at the kiddies before each event. Leo Moon can crave love and attention, but in this case, with the addition of contention, it created a daredevil who constantly risked his body to gain a special kind of notoriety. Contention can mean the planet goes into battle, and Evel Knievel's choices involved pitting himself against obstacles that he flew over on a heavy Harley-Davidson XR-750 motorcycle that was never designed to leave the ground, let alone jump over a row of buses.

"Bones heal, pain is temporary, and chicks dig scars."[74] – Evel Knievel

His Moon in Leo is in aversion to its sign of Cancer on the 6th-house cusp, and whilst Knievel performed stunts year after tortuous year, he seemed incapable of believing or accepting the seriousness of his injuries, and the chronic damage he was doing to his body by constantly risking his health.

Robert Hand says of an out-of-sect Moon: "Even when the Moon is strongly placed by house (Knievel's is angular in 7th house), those aspects of the native's chart that are connected to the Moon are a source of difficulty."[75] Evel Knievel's Leo Moon in munakara has several aspects to planets that will add to its out-of-sect difficulty. His munakara Leo Moon trines Saturn in Aries and together the two planets rule the dark axis of the 6th and 12th houses, houses of injury, illness, withdrawal and incapacity. Saturn's rulership also extends to his Aquarian Ascendant, and the lack of caution is indicated by the fire trine, together with Saturn's poor condition, and the Moon's contention suggests the speed in which injury (Moon's 6th house) occurs to the body (1st house ruler Saturn). Trines are not always auspicious or favourable aspects, particularly when they denote speed in action, circumstances beyond one's control, and the somewhat naive concept that events will turn out in your favour.

The trine may also signify the family's ongoing legacy as Robbie Knievel became his father's successor, completing a 69 metre jump over the Grand Canyon in May 1999, but losing control of the bike and breaking his leg in the crash. Evel had wanted to jump the Grand Canyon thirty years earlier in 1968 but had failed to get permission from the park authorities and the US government. A publicity stunt to promote the Grand Canyon jump shows Knievel holding a gigantic $6 million check in supposed payment for the stunt, but the check proved to be a fake as the jump was never approved, and Knievel's credibility (Saturn) was compromised for the sake of showmanship (Leo Moon).

In Knievel's chart the munakara Moon squares Uranus (speed, danger, physical irregularities and sudden changes in physical health) and it has a wide opposition to retrograde Jupiter in the 1st house. Jupiter is connected to his second munakara planet, the Sun, and is its outcome planet. Through Knievel's escapades he gained a reputation and some wealth from Jupiter, but ultimately he was disgraced when details of his private life were disclosed in a biography on his life.

First Dispositor: Sun in Libra in 9th House

"A man can fall many times in life, but he's never a failure until he refuses to get back up."[76] – Evel Knievel

His Leo Moon is not helped by its first dispositor (the Sun) being in a debilitated state in fall, and also in the tricky position of joining ranks as another planet in munakara. Libran Sun rules the 7th house, and Knievel was a dealmaker and a dream whisperer long before he was a stuntman. In 1959 he started a semi-pro hockey team, the Butte Bombers and to raise money he convinced the Czechoslavakian Olympic ice hockey team to play his team in a warm-up game to the 1960 Winter Olympics. Knievel became agitated during the game and was ejected from the game minutes into the third period, whereby he promptly left the stadium. At the game's end the Czechoslovakian officials arrived at the box office to collect their share of the money to be told that the game's receipts had been stolen. In order to avoid an international incident the United States Olympic Committee covered the stolen money which was never recovered. There is no proof that Evel stole the game's earnings but a cloud of doubt hung over his head and perhaps drove him later to go to great lengths to prove his honesty and protect his credibility.

The same Saturn in Aries which trines Evel Knievel's munakara Moon in Leo also opposes his munakara Sun in Libra, and parental love and care were absent from his childhood. Two-year-old Robert (Evel's birth name), along with his baby brother Nic, were abandoned by their mother and father who left Butte independently after their divorce in 1940. Both boys were raised by their paternal grandparents, and perhaps this abandonment led to his burning need to feel the love of others, even if they were strangers (Moon in Leo), and to be admired, adored and honoured by the public (Libran Sun's dispositor conjuncts MC).

The Moon's outcome planet (and Sun's First Dispositor): Venus in Sagittarius conjunct MC

"I decided to fly through the air and live in the sunlight and enjoy life as much as I could."[77] – Evel Knievel

Knievel was as much a showman as he was a stuntman, and he was a master at working the crowd and grabbing the public's interest when it came to promoting his upcoming exhibitions. Like a modern-day snake oil salesman, Knievel would exaggerate his feats to the point of lying, which is ironic, given that one of his greatest claims was that he was an honest man to be trusted for keeping his word (Libran Mercury conjuncts the Sun). He had a thirst for seeing his name in the papers, and even as a boy he had decided that motorcycle stunts were his style. For his first stunt he rented a venue, wrote the press releases, sold the tickets and set up the show where he became his own master of ceremonies. He did a few wheelies to excite the small audience and then jumped a 20-foot-long box of rattlesnakes and a caged cougar. He landed short and broke the box of rattlesnakes releasing them into the crowd, but he was unhurt and show business was now in his blood.

Chapter Twelve • *Munakara Moon Delineations*

Evel Knievel was born three years after Elvis Presley and was doing stunts at the same time as Elvis was crooning his music, so we could say that one was entertaining the parents whilst the other was engaging the youth of America.

> "I guess I thought I was Elvis Presley but I'll tell ya something. All Elvis did was stand on a stage and play a guitar. He never fell off on that pavement at no 80 mph."[78] – Evel Knievel

No pictures exist of the two performers together but Evel claimed Elvis as a friend, as he did with Steve McQueen and Mohammad Ali, but this may be bragging on his part. According to a 2022 interview with Elvis' stepbrother and bodyguard David Stanley, Elvis was desperate to play London's Wembley Stadium in 1977 "after being inspired by motorbike daredevil pal Evel Knievel jumping across buses there live on TV in 1975."[79] Colonel Tom Parker's refusal to arrange the tour "was one of the key moments that tipped Elvis into depressive drug use, eventually culminating in his death in August 1977." Both men began wearing white jumpsuits around the same time so it is hard to gauge the style's originator, whether one was in homage to the other, or whether the duplicated imagery was deliberate or not. Elvis first wore his white bell-bottomed jumpsuit at a concert in Hawai'i, whilst Evel is first recorded for a jump dressed in a leather white jumpsuit in 1972. Elvis may have been born three years before Evel, but the stuntman outlived the musician by 30 years, Elvis dying in 1977, and Evel passing away in 2007.

Libra Sun in Munakara: Evel Knievel

- **Key Questions:**
- What does Evel Knievel's Sun contend with?
- What is its driving force?
- What is its trigger? What is its outcome?

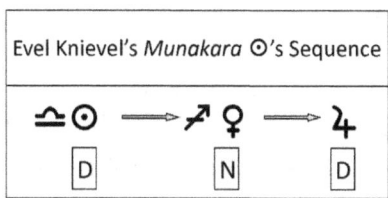

Table 12.11: Evel Knievel: Munakara Sun's Sequence

There is no doubt that Evel Knievel's munakara Sun craved attention and the adoration of the crowd. But one must wonder if the short-term breakages and long-term effects of countless broken bones, lacerations, bruising and internal injuries were really worth a few minutes of the audience being shocked and astounded by his feats. If attention was his munakara Sun's main aim, then it would no doubt love the fact that Evel Knievel merchandise and doll-size replicas of the stuntman were in great demand by children who adored his stunts. Nocturnal Mercury's conjunction to his Libran Sun shows proficiency in marketing, and the trine aspect to Jupiter in the 1st house – the Sun's outcome planet – would feed his conceit, as well as adding to his income (Jupiter rules 2nd house).

Jupiter's placement in the 1st house encourages Knievel's sense of freedom and adventure, providing him with a huge incentive to keep pushing for more dangerous stunts to keep him in the public eye (Jupiter rules his MC). His outcome planet, Jupiter, has an over-riding sense of optimism, and Knievel coupled this with the belief that he could achieve everything he promised to his audience. But there were also times when munakara Sun experienced a fall from grace, and Evel's carefully constructed 'good reputation' eventually became tarnished by his actions when the cameras were not focused on him.

Both Saturn (in fall) and munakara Sun (in fall) oppose one another in Knievel's chart and this aspect reflects the animosity that exists between through their signs of rulership and debility. Together the two planets rule his relationship axis (1st/7th houses) and perhaps the 1959 Butte Bombers fiasco is just one example of his reputation being besmirched by a series of coincidences. Years later, when Knievel's career was well established, he brokered a contract with the Ideal Toy Company, which supplemented his income with profits from lookalike action figures. Ideal claimed that in the five years between 1972 and 1977, the company had sold more than $125 million worth of Knievel merchandise.[80]

The commercial goldmine looked to continue beyond 1977 with Knievel's latest stunt with the sharks in Chicago hyping his popularity and accelerating the sale of his merchandise. However, his munakara Sun was about to take a tumble, and once more Saturn was involved in the destruction of his reputation. The book *Evel Knievel on Tour* was written by Shelly Saltman, the promoter from the earlier Snake River Canyon jump in 1975. Knievel and his lawyers had been given editorial access to the book, and had approved and signed off on its content before publication.

Chapter Twelve • *Munakara Moon Delineations*

However, when the book came out accusing Knievel of abusing his wife and children and revealed his long-term drug use, Knievel went ballistic and attacked Saltman with a baseball bat. Saltman protected his head from the blows raining down on it, but his arm and wrist were shattered in several places before he fell to the ground unconscious. Knievel received a sentence of six months in a county jail for battery and three years' probation. In a civil lawsuit that followed, the judge called Knievel's acts "cowardly" and awarded Saltman $12.75 million in damages. Knievel declared bankruptcy and none of the civil award was paid.[81]

The book was withdrawn from publication, but the incident left Knievel's public image in tatters. All marketing endorsements were withdrawn, upcoming deals were cancelled, including those with Harley-Davidson and Ideal Toys, and Evel was forced to declare bankruptcy. Aquarian Jupiter, the Sun's outcome planet, sits in the 1st house but is blind to the 2nd house with Pisces on the cusp. Likewise, Jupiter is the lord of the Mid-heaven and as it links Knievel's public disgrace with his financial security, the air trine between munakara Sun and its outcome planet Jupiter, strips wealth quickly and efficiently as rumours and negative media coverage destroy his reputation.

Munakara Planet and Sect Condition – how comfortable is the Sun

"You come to a point in your life when you really don't care what people think about you, you just care what you think about yourself."[82] – Evel Knievel

Evel Knievel's Sun has full sect dignity; chart, hemisphere and sign all align with the diurnal luminary at the top of Knievel's chart. Hand says that the Sun has maximum power in a daytime chart and that success is granted due to the native's own personal strength, ambition, drive and ego. A daytime chart improves the Sun's level of activity and strengthens its masculinity. Daytime creates an environment of clarity and definition, bringing clear limits and boundaries. From this analysis we can assume that it is not the sect dignity that brings

Evel Knievel — ☉'s Sect Dignity			
Planet	Sect 1 Status	Sect 2 Hemisphere	Sect 3 Sign
♎ ☉	Day	Sun Defines	Air
D	D	D	D

Table 12.12: Evel Knievel: Munakara Sun Sect Dignity

the Sun's downfall. Rather, it is the Sun in the sign of its fall opposing Saturn (also in the sign of its fall), that brings disgrace and pubic ruin.

In Knievel's chart the Sun conjuncts Mercury, but as Mercury is behind the luminary it is a nocturnal planet, completely out of sect (diurnal chart, diurnal hemisphere, masculine sign), and extremely uncomfortable in its surroundings. At the height of his popularity Knievel was publicly exposed in a biography he supposedly approved, and nocturnal Mercury out of sect exposed him as a fraud and a liar when everything he was publicly opposed to – drugs, domestic abuse, violence – was a significant factor in his private behaviour (Mercury rules his IC).

Munakara Moon: Christopher Reeve

A Brief Biography of Christopher Reeve

Christopher Reeve (25 September, 1952 – 10 October, 2004) was an American actor who was first known to the movie-going public as the title character in *Superman* (1978) and went on to star in three sequels as well as a number of other films.

After a fall from a horse during an equestrian competition in 1995 broke his neck and left him a quadriplegic, however, he took on a new, even more heroic role – that of activist for medical research, including the search for a cure for spinal-cord injuries.[83]

In 2000, five years after the injury, Reeve had involuntarily moved the index finger on his right hand. His wife Dana was with him and watched as he commanded his finger to move and it responded. Functional MRI tests proved that the finger command had come from the correct side of his brain, and doctors and therapists began to build on this action leading to his movements expanding to a much larger range with a change in exercises, and with the introduction of water therapy. Six months later Reeve's ability to move muscles had taken a tremendous leap forward and his ability to feel sensation in 70% of his body was recorded by his medical team.

The American Spinal Injury Association (ASIA) has five classifications for SCI ranging from Class A (no function below the level of injury) to Class E, normal function. For the first five years, from 1995 to 2000, Reeve had been Class A. In 2001 he was reclassified as a promotion to Class C. Before Reeve's reclassification no record existed of anyone having a delayed recovery after such a long period of time. Previous studies had shown that most recovery occurs in the first six months, or that any recovery possible

Chapter Twelve • *Munakara Moon Delineations*

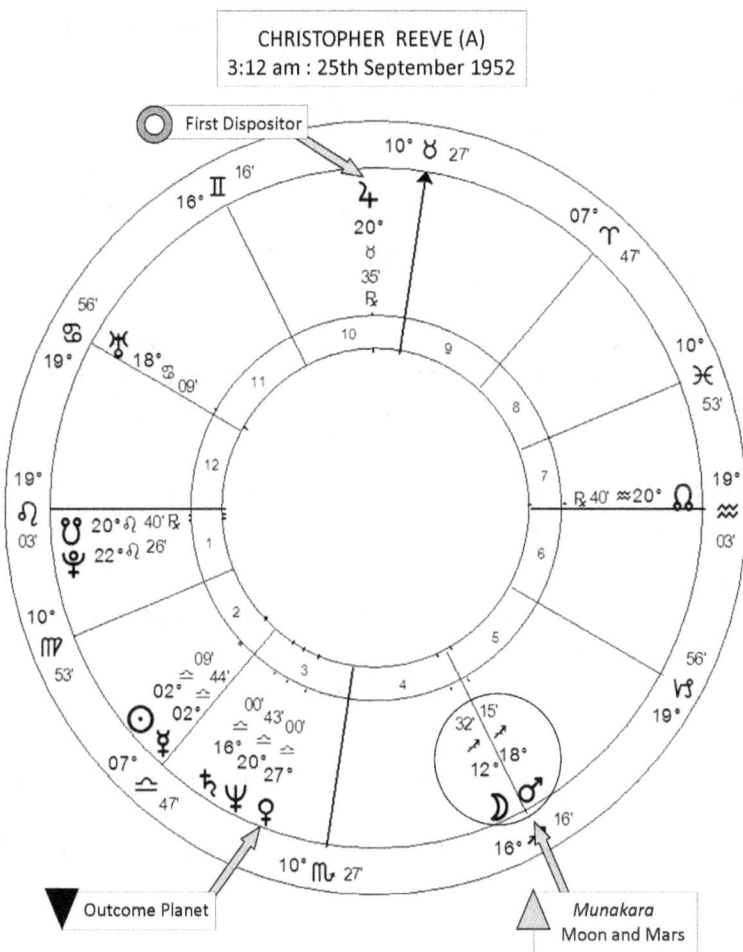

Fig. 12.6: Christopher Reeve Natal Chart: Moon in Munakara

will be made within two and half years of the injury. Christopher Reeve had made medical history by jumping two ASIA grades six years out from his injury.

Unfortunately, it took until five years after Reeve's death in 2004 for President Barack Obama to sign an executive order on 9th March 2009 reversing federal opposition to embryonic stem cell therapy. Reeve had spoken at the 2001 Senate Committee meeting discussing the possibility of legislation for therapeutic cloning for regenerative medicine stating: "Some people are willing to accept living with a severe disability – I am NOT one of them."[84]

Munakara in Practice

In 2020, medical journals reported the advancement of epidural stimulation as an experimental therapy for SPI,[85] whilst the Mayo Clinic announced the commencement of Phase Two in CELLTOP, the injection of adipose-derived stem cells for patients with severe spinal-cord injury.[86] Covid has grabbed much of the news on medical research since the CELLTOP announcement but review articles on SCI are keeping the public abreast of new developments and conversations are still happening over the use of stem cell therapy for intractable diseases.[87]

> "I thought I had to put a human face on a condition that the scientists were not really able to dramatize. You hve to move politically, but you also have to reach the people's hearts."[88] – Christopher Reeve, *Time*, August 26, 1996

Sagittarius Moon and Mars Duet in Munakara: Christopher Reeve

- **Key Questions:**
- What does Christopher Reeve's Moon and Mars contend with?
- What is its driving force?
- What is its trigger? What is its outcome?

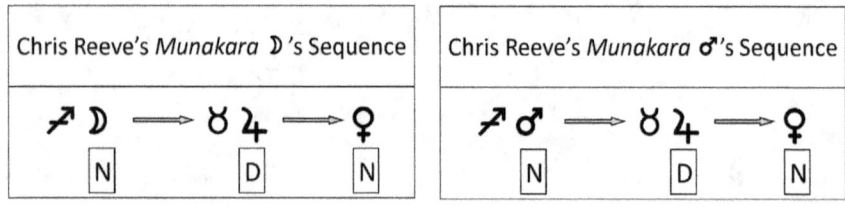

Table 12.13: Christopher Reeve: Munakara Moon and Mars Sequence

Christopher Reeve's munakara planets, Moon and Mars, are both in Sagittarius dispositing to Jupiter in Taurus, and with outcome planet, Venus so for ease of description I have called them 'duets' when two planets share an identical sequence. Sharing the same sequence creates a dual contention situation between Moon and Mars and the two planets must work together to overcome their independent issues with munakara.

In Christopher Reeve's chart the duet of munakara Moon and Mars are located in his Whole Sign 5th house, and many of Reeve's leisure activities, including showjumping, climbing, sailing, and flying his plane, were interests that carried a high level of risk. Whilst the two planets in contention

Chapter Twelve • *Munakara Moon Delineations*

tested his skills and added that extra charge of adrenaline to the things he loved, they also describe the riding accident which stole his mobility. The Moon and Mars in contention is one expression for Reeve's frustration with the restriction of physical freedom and lack of independence that was taken from him on that day. But the duet in munakara also describes his courage and tenacity, as well as his daily determination to pursue a rigorous exercise regime in the hope that one day a cure would be found, and he would be ready to walk again.

Jupiter is the dispositor of the duet in munakara, and in spite the doctors' prognosis, Jupiter's driving force kept the actor in fighting mode, regardless of the odds of ever regaining movement. His research, his political voice, his organization, and his legacy benefits society which causes the world to cherish his memory, and to provide hope and encouragement to those who are still struggling with their own on-going disabilities.

> *"In the morning I need 20 minutes to cry....To say this really sucks, to allow the feeling of loss to be acknowledged."* After his long cry every day, he wiped his tears and told himself, *"And now, forward!"*[89]

Most people are aware of Christopher Reeve's story and I spent a great deal of time considering whether to include his chart in my list of examples on munakara Moon. Ultimately I made the choice to use Reeve's chart because it is a story of triumph, not a story of defeat. It is the story of one man's monumental challenge and its on-going impact on society, and it is the story of others who continue to benefit from the Christopher and Dana Reeve Foundation.

Munakara Planet and Sect Condition – how comfortable is the Moon and Mars Duet?

Reeve's chart is a nocturnal chart and this suits the Moon as the luminary of the night. Robert Hand states in his booklet, *Night & Day: Planetary Sect in Astrology*, that the Moon in a nocturnal chart is a strong Moon. "Whatever the Moon signifies in a chart is a source of strength for the native assuming that the Moon is not severely impeded."[90] Reeve's munakara Mars is conjunct his Moon, and consideration is needed to decide if Mars being in a state of munakara, is enough to qualify it as a malefic planet severely impeding the Moon, in the same munakara condition.

Mars in sect dignity loses some of its jarring qualities and instead, gains the advantage of becoming more connecting, feeling, more sensitive and more inclined to nurture. "The moisture of the night cools Mars down and connects it. The nocturnal Mars...more often manifests as a defensive, sustaining energy"[91] that is more inclined towards being a protective force rather than vehicle for aggression.

Jupiter is the dispositor of Reeve's Sagittarian Moon and Mars' and Jupiter is out-of-sect in Reeve's chart – in a nocturnal chart, nocturnally placed and in a feminine sign – so Jupiter's good effects are somewhat compromised by its discomfort in the chart and its lack of connection to the Sun, its diurnal luminary. Robert Hand says "(Jupiter) loses the ability to withstand an affliction by a malefic. When out-of-sect Jupiter is afflicted, almost all of its virtue is lost, according to the ancients."[92] Twenty years later Hand said in a 2015 webinar on sect that Jupiter severely out of sect was "more selfish and entitled and less concerned about general welfare."[93] This may be true, but the fact is that when Jupiter is out of sect and everything in its environment is hugely hostile towards it, as in the case of Christopher Reeve, the individual's survival may be rather more important than concerns over others' welfare.

Christopher Reeve— ☾'s Sect Dignity			
Planet	Sect 1 Status	Sect 2 Hemisphere	Sect 3 Sign
♐ ☾	Night	With the Sun	Fire
	N	N	D	D

Christopher Reeve— ♂'s Sect Dignity			
Planet	Sect 1 Status	Sect 2 Hemisphere	Sect 3 Sign
♐ ♂	Night	With the Sun	Fire
	N	N	D	✓

Table 12.14: Christopher Reeve: Munakara Moon and Mars Sect Dignity

Munakara Moon and Mars Duet: Christopher Reeve

"Your body is not who you are. The mind and spirit transcend the body."[94]
– Christopher Reeve

Munakara Moon / Mars in Sagittarius in 4th House (Placidus)

Reeve's Sagittarian Moon, along with his Mars, are munakara and it would be an easy assumption to link the significator of his physical body, munakara

Chapter Twelve • *Munakara Moon Delineations*

Moon, with the sudden violence of his accident, munakara Mars, and to point to the combination as the signature for the resultant disability Reeve endured for the last nine years of his life. However, this would be a disservice both to the man, and to his daily courage and determination to live life to the best of his limited ability, so I choose not to link one event to the two planets in contention.

Over twenty years ago Matthew Exton Reeve produced a documentary on his famous father titled *Christopher Reeve: Hope in Motion*. The film recorded eighteen months in the life of Christopher Reeve, beginning on May 27th 2001 – the sixth anniversary of his accident – to Reeve's 50th birthday on 25th September 2002, just two years before he would pass away. The film documents Reeve's rigorous exercise regime, a daily five-hour labour that seems to produce little benefits at the beginning. In the documentary Chris Fantini, a medical expert on paralysis who had been working with Reeve for years, comments on his excitement at Reeve's advances. Fantini says, "We're starting to see things that we really didn't think were possible and maybe it's because nobody in his condition ever worked that hard, for this long, so there's no precedent to understand what's going on."

Christopher Reeve's munakara Moon and Mars are two nocturnal planets – in sect – working together to keep focused on his goal to walk again. Sadly, this dream never materialized as Reeve died from heart failure just after his 52nd birthday in October 2004. *Hope in Motion* is hard to watch with this knowledge in mind, but there can be no doubting Reeve's conviction that science, in the form of stem cell therapy, would one day provide the answer if he kept his muscles in condition for that event at some time in the future.

Reeve's munakara Moon shifts from 4th house to 5th house by Whole Sign and Matthew Reeve's documentary is a work showing the love and admiration he has for his father. Mars rules Reeve's 4th house with Scorpio on the cusp (family and legacies) and ties it to Aries, Mars' other sign, on the 9th house, the house of research, publication and possibly, non-profit organisations focused on scientific research.

At the time of Reeve's horse-riding accident in 1995 Matthew was 15, his sister Alexandra was 11, and his youngest son, Will, was two years old. Since 2020 all three children have served on the board of directors of the Christopher and Dana Reeve Foundation, a charitable organization dedicated to finding treatments and cures for paralysis caused by spinal cord injury (SCI). The Foundation also aims to improve the quality of life for people living with paralysis through grants, information and advocacy.[95]

First Dispositor: Jupiter in Taurus in 10th House

"It's very hard for me to be silly about Superman, because I've seen firsthand how he actually transforms people's lives. I have seen children dying of brain tumours who wanted as their last request to talk to me, and have gone to their graves with a peace brought on by knowing that their belief in this kind of character really matters. It's not Superman the tongue-in-cheek cartoon character they're connecting with; they're connecting with something very basic: the ability to overcome obstacles, the ability to persevere, the ability to understand difficulty and to turn your back on it."[96]
– Christopher Reeve, *Time*, March 14, 1988

Jupiter is the most elevated planet in Christopher Reeve's chart and is the dispositor for both Moon and Mars in Sagittarius. Jupiter rules Reeve's 5th house of children, creativity and entertainment and his 8th house of trauma and death. Reeve worked tirelessly on travelling and educating the public and speaking with governments across the globe regardless of his demanding exercise regime, his work schedules, and the physical restrictions of his munakara Moon, simply because he believed that improvements could be made for SCI sufferers. He believed that the key to the future for millions of people was the hope that science would succeed, but that politics, religion and economics had to be pushed aside in order for this to happen.

In Reeve's chart Jupiter is in a partile (same degree) square to the Moon's Nodes, and this position is referred to as the Bendings. In her work on the Nodal Cycle in *Classical Astrology for Modern Living* author Lee Lehman says "Planets at the bendings represent critical issues which can change the flow of life. Since most people are resistant to change, the usual response is to build up a rigidity around these planets, which makes the issues represented by them problematic. In extreme cases, this rigidity can have physical/ medical manifestation."[97]

In Reeve's case, Jupiter is challenged by its lack of freedom and Jupiter ruling munakara Moon and Mars in Sagittarius is best described in Reeve's own words, recorded in *Hope in Motion*:

One of the real losses is the loss of independence. I was always an incredibly independent person. I loved to spend time alone and that's been very hard because for six years now I've never once been able to be alone. To be a grown man that has to be washed and dressed and fed by other people. It's kind of a cruel irony that someone who loves to sail alone and fly my airplane across the Atlantic alone now can't even make it to the driveway by myself.

The outcome planet: Venus in Libra in 3rd House

Hope in Motion ends with Chris surrounded by his family at home celebrating his 50th birthday and talking of his plans for 2003 – working hard on diaphragm exercises so that he can go off his ventilator, directing a movie (*The Brooke Ellison Story*), and the continuation of fundraising for cutting-edge research for SCI.

Mars in contention rules his 4th and 9th houses and for Reeve, his family and his spiritual beliefs through Unitarian Universalism (UU) fortified and nourished him through the last nine years of his life. His munakara Moon rules the 12th house, the house of fears and imprisonment, but Reeve fought against self-pity. Rather than his misfortune causing him to retreat within himself, it galvanized him into creating practical help for those less visible members of society who were disabled, but lacked the attention his star status afforded him. Reeve's munakara Moon shone a light on people who didn't have his money and resources, or were discarded by society when their bodies were broken, and they were considered a drain on the country's social services.

Reeve's legacy is the Christopher and Dana Reeve Foundation and the co-founding of Reeve-Irvine Research Center. Venus is in rulership in Reeve's chart, and it shows the way in which he and Dana Reeve are loved and remembered by their family, their friends, Chris' carers, and the organization which bears their joint names and carries their dreams into the future. Venus is the outcome planet for Moon and Mars and whilst its conjunction with a health statement of the potential for the skeletal system's breakdown – Saturn with Neptune – Saturn's exaltation lifts Reeve's disability beyond his own misery, and makes it a process to overcome 3rd-house difficulties of communication, movement, and knowledge learned from life's experiences.

In *Hope in Motion* Reeve talks frankly about the time directly after his accident and his request to Dana to release him and let him die, but her declaration of love was powerful and positive (Pluto sextiles Venus), and together, they chose to fight his disability as a partnership. Saturn rules both Reeve's 6th house of illness and his 7th house of relationship, and Dana was his strength and his refuge with Saturn forming a sextile aspect to Reeve's munakara Moon and Mars.

The man who played an alien superhero on film became a man whose life is remembered as a personal triumph. Avatars of Christopher Reeve's quality are few and far between in this world. If munakara Moon and Mars played a role in this transformation, the personal cost was extraordinarily high for Christopher Reeve, but the dividends paid forward to others are priceless.

Munakara Moon: Michael Moore

A Brief Biography of Michael Moore

Michael Moore (born 23rd April 1954) is an American film director, producer, screenwriter and author whose work frequently addresses social, political, and economic topics. Moore is a filmmaker, author, social commentator and political activist whose views are always passionate, and often highly controversial. His targets have been large corporations, such as General Motors, who closed down an entire town by moving their business in order to exploit a cheaper workforce (*Roger & Me*, 1989), or Nike, who causes mass layoffs by outsourcing shoe production to Indonesia (*The Big One*, 1997).

Over twenty years has passed since Michael Moore released the documentary film *Bowling for Columbine* (2002). The movie tells the story of the 1999 Columbine High School massacre when two students killed twelve classmates and a teacher before shooting themselves. The title refers to the legend that the two boys were bowling at the local bowling alley on the morning of the massacre. Moore's comments included a call for the tightening of gun control laws so that children can attend school without fear, and his thoughts on changing an American psyche that combats fear with consumerism.

He has spoken out against governments which are run by warmongers (*Fahrenheit 9/11*, 2004) when Moore examined America in the aftermath of the September 11 attacks. *Fahrenheit 9/11* was awarded the *Palme d'Or*, the top honour at the 2004 Cannes Film Festival. It was the first documentary film to win the prize since 1956's *The Silent World*.

In his 2007 documentary titled *Sicko*, Moore highlighted the broken, profit-driven US health system that failed to care for those who had paid their fees and expected their health care to be covered in times of illness. He featured ordinary citizens like Donna Smith who testified to the US House Judiciary Committee in July 2007 on her family's medical debt and the fear of bankruptcy faced by insured Americans. Almost twenty years later, Donna was still fighting for justice.[98]

Capitalism: A Love Story, released in September 2009, focused on the financial crisis of 2007 – 2008 and the US economy during the transition between the outgoing Bush Administration and the incoming Obama Administration. Moore's *Where to Invade Next* (2015) examined the benefits of progressive social policies in various countries. In 2019 Moore was executive producer of the documentary *Planet of the Humans* which argued

Chapter Twelve • *Munakara Moon Delineations*

that since the first Earth Day (an annual event to demonstrate environmental protection) in April 1970, the condition of the planet has worsened, and raised questions over whether mainstream approaches adopted by industry were mitigating climate change.

Moore has written and co-written eight non-fiction books, mostly on similar subject matters to his documentaries and several of his books have made bestseller lists.[99]

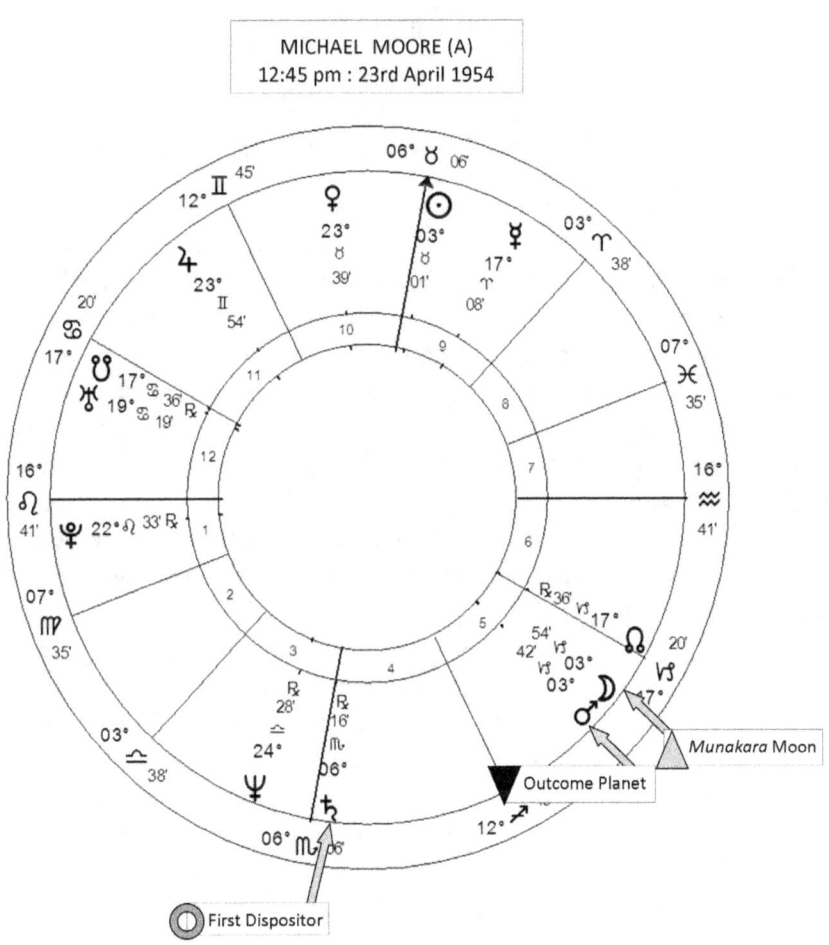

Fig. 12.7: Michael Moore Natal Chart: Moon in Munakara

Munakara in Practice

Capricorn Moon in Munakara: Michael Moore

- **Key Questions:**
- What does Michael Moore's Moon contend with?
- What is its driving force?
- What is its trigger? What is its outcome?

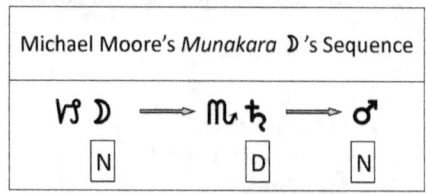

Table 12.15: *Michael Moore: Munakara Moon's Sequence*

Michael Moore's munakara Moon contends with his heartfelt ambition that we could do better as a human race. We could be more compassionate and less paranoid, more forgiving and less accusatory, more protective of our children, our elders, our loved ones, our society and our environment. With Saturn as the Moon's driving force Moore's efforts to interview, observe and make comparisons with history's past mistakes are his way of trying to attack the problem and gain a better result in the future. Mars is munakara Moon's outcome planet and Mars often presents Moore as aggressive and a left-wing vigilante. However, Mars is a trigger for munakara Moon as it makes him relentless in his hounding of those powerful individuals and corporations that should be caring for society, but are more concerned with their own ambitions and profit margins.

Moore's chart (*Fig. 12.7*) has a partile conjunction between munakara Moon, and its outcome planet Mars, and presumably this aspect constantly drives Moore forward to address injustice and ignorance. It gives him the energy and conviction to take on opponents that seem too large for anyone else. Moore's munakara Moon in detriment is uncomfortable with accepting things as they are and therefore, it is constantly on the lookout for trouble. Perhaps Mars' exaltation in Capricorn demonstrates that there are accolades and success to be had if the principles behind munakara Moon are honourable, and Moore attempts to serve others' interests rather than his own. Fortunately Mars is not in contention – it is in mutual reception with its dispositor Saturn – as Moore needs time to recuperate and heal from each battle and munakara Mars may not have allowed him the luxury of downtime to replenish his reserves. Saturn is a major player in Michael Moore's chart, as it is munakara

Chapter Twelve • *Munakara Moon Delineations*

Moon (and Mars's) dispositor and sextiles the two planets from its powerful position on the IC opposing the Sun on the MC.

Moore's munakara Moon sequence is not a friendly combination of planets which are designed to aid one another, or make the impact of contention an easy matter. The Moon is in detriment in Saturn's sign (Saturn is the Moon's enemy) and contention is likely to isolate the individual, as well as cause them to feel deeply when it comes to others' emotional pain. Mars as the Moon's outcome planet is naturally hostile towards the Moon (fall signs for both planets are in opposition) and often Mars creates disharmony, sudden heated separations, and health issues of an inflammatory nature for the individual with this munakara Moon sequence.

Munakara Planet and Sect Condition – how comfortable is the Moon?

Michael Moore's Capricorn Moon gains sect dignity, firstly by its position in the chart away from the Sun's hemisphere (*halb*), and secondly, in its placement in a feminine sign.

Robert Hand says of the Moon that is nocturnally placed (travelling in the opposite hemisphere to the Sun): "The Moon...nocturnally placed in a chart is a strong Moon. Whatever the Moon signifies in chart is a source of strength for the native assuming that the Moon is not severely impeded."[100]

Michael Moore— ☽'s Sect Dignity			
Planet	Sect 1 Status	Sect 2 Hemisphere	Sect 3 Sign
♑ ☽	Day	No Sun	Earth
N	D	N	N

Table 12.16: Michael Moore: Munakara Moon Sect Dignity

Unfortunately, Moore's munakara Moon is severely impeded by being in detriment in Capricorn and in partile conjunction to Mars (an enemy in its exaltation). The Moon is the representative of the body's physical state and shows the body's ability to resist or recover from illness or accident. When the Moon is compromised by aspects to the malefics, Saturn and Mars, then there are attacks on the individual's health and delays on its recovery. Occasionally reports crop up over incidents concerning Michael Moore's health. In 2016 Moore spent a week in intensive care at a New York hospital with pneumonia, and was forced to cancel all promotional stops for his movie *Where to Invade Next*.[101] For all his public pieces Moore is an intensely private man and very few reliable reports exist on the state of his health. However, he did admit in a

MSNBC interview in August 2017 promoting his one-man show *The Terms of My Surrender* that he has bad eating habits and that he rarely exercises.

Hand does mention that a strong Moon in sect indicates "an individual who succeeds by embodying the aspirations of others and serving their needs."[102] This statement on the Moon in sect dignity (in a nocturnally placed hemisphere) is particularly relevant for Michael Moore given his political activism and his passion for tackling major social issues. In 1972 at age 18, Moore ran for a seat on the Flint school board and became one of the youngest people in the US to win an election for public office.[103]

Munakara Moon: Michael Moore

"If I were just making a political statement, I'd run for office, and if I were giving a sermon, I'd be a preacher. I'm making a movie, an entertaining experience. And if a few people leave thinking about the issues, great. If one becomes active, great. I keep my expectations low. I know where I live."[104] – Michael Moore, Interview, 2002, on release of *Bowling for Columbine*

Munakara Moon in Capricorn in detriment in 5th House (Placidus)

Michael Moore has a strong social conscience and a burning desire to see his country's government right its wrongs, its citizens to move beyond their crippling fear, and for large corporations to take responsibility for their actions. Moon in contention conjuncts Mars and what often appears as a jovial unpretentious character is someone who often masks their anger and channels their outrage in order to force change.

Moore has two planets in munakara: his Capricorn Moon, which is in a wide applying square to his second planet in contention, Aries Mercury in 9th house. The Moon is fourteen degrees from Mercury and will not make a partile (same degree) aspect for at least another day. However, both planets' munakara sequence involves the same two malefic planets, Saturn and Mars – but in reverse order for diurnal Mercury – and the tension of a cardinal square is likely to galvanize this man into action.

Michael's munakara Moon in Capricorn is situated in the 5th house in the Placidus chart, and even though Moore's documentaries often have dark and distressing content, they use humour as much as factual information to hold the audience's attention. The documentarian understands that nothing reduces an audience's attention span like preaching when teaching, and sharing information is ultimately the main aim of a documentary film.

Chapter Twelve • *Munakara Moon Delineations*

The Moon in its sign of detriment can affect many things: weaken the state of an individual's body, suggest a hostile or unsafe environment, highlight a highly sensitive emotional or physical state, or isolate the individual from parents and loved ones. These are just a few of its manifestations, but it can also show sensitivity towards, or an intolerance of social inequalities. Moore's munakara Moon in detriment has given him compassion and sensitivity towards others' hardship and his judgements are not reserved for sufferers, but rather for the governments, financial groups or corporations that have created the suffering. His munakara Moon is focused on the underdog, a person who has little status or power in society, and Moore uses his intelligence and skills to side with them and fight for their cause.

The earth trine between Moore's elevated Taurus Sun on the Mid-heaven and Capricorn Moon and Mars in the 5th house highlights his desire to bring about real change that has long-term benefits, and this is done via the world of entertainment. His diurnal chart's main luminary (Sun) conjuncts the Mid-heaven and opposes Saturn, so there will always be issues that Moore feels he needs to bring to society's attention in the hope that change and improvement are an eventuality, rather than a vague possibility. For all his negative journalism, and his detractors' callouts on distorted news reportage, Moore must be an optimist at heart, and his hopes that the better side of human nature will prevail over negativity and fear could be a good indicator that his munakara Moon and munakara Mercury are working to this end.

It is hard not to wonder how he hasn't burnt out emotionally and physically with a munakara Moon in detriment wedded to Mars, the planet of agitation and aggression. Watching the randomness of violence of any kind whether it is social, racial, gender-based on a domestic or international plane must be exhausting for this Moon ruling the 12th house. However, if there is such a thing as a compulsion to speak out because it is too painful to be silent – munakara Mercury at the Nodal Bendings – then this man suffers from it, at the same time as being able to enjoy the freedom of a career that is financially viable.

First Dispositor: Saturn in Scorpio on the IC

Saturn lies at the base of Moore's chart opposing the Sun at the opposite point, and together the two planets accentuate his sense of social and political responsibility. Both planets have flowing aspects to Moore's Capricorn Moon/Mars: Saturn is in sextile and the Sun forms a trine in the earth element. Saturn in opposition to the Sun is somewhat of a conundrum for Moore, as the desire to rebel against authority is strong in this aspect, but at the same time, there is an almost compulsive need to be approved by the same institutions that one is attacking. Awards and accolades are necessary in the film industry to promote conversation and convert interest into money via the viewing public, but there is still discomfort in knowing that one is still 'playing by the rules' to gain success and exposure. A crushing fear of failure often accompanies an aspect between the Sun and Saturn and the need to gain credibility is a powerful motivator, but an underlying terror of others' judgement or criticism is part of gaining a high profile in public life. Moore's munakara Moon in Capricorn adds extra sensitivity to criticism along with the fear of displeasing others who you admire or want to hold a good opinion of you.

The aspect of Saturn's opposition to the Sun is also reflected in Moore's relationship axis with Leo (Sun's sign) on the Ascendant and Aquarius (Saturn's sign) on the Descendant. Moore's liberal views and his criticisms of Republican former president Donald Trump (2016–2020) have drawn many enemies on the conservative side of politics and right-wing websites are full of attacks on his professionalism, his integrity and his ethics. However, these attacks are unlikely to hit the mark provided that Moore has faith in the truth of his work (munakara Mercury in the 9th house) and he feels emotionally bound to those who cannot act in their own defence (munakara Moon in Capricorn).

Together munakara Moon and its dispositor Saturn rule the difficult 6th- and 12th-house axis, and perhaps the easier aspect between them (sextile) relieves the tension that usually exists between the enemy planets. Mars and Moon's movement into the 6th house by Whole Sign shows ambition, relentless drive and a determination that often ignores the body's need for rest or nourishment. Saturn's 'devil' drives both planets through aspect and sign ownership, and can create bad eating habits and poor sleeping patterns, ultimately punishing the body with exhaustion or chronic illnesses. Michael Moore does not look like a healthy man and Saturn dispositing the Moon and Mars will stress one (the Moon) and drive the other (Mars) relentlessly towards its goal. With issues such as inequality, unsupportive health systems, systemic racism, climate disintegration, and corporate or political corruption prominent in his vision, at age 70, Michael Moore may feel that time is running out on him.

Chapter Twelve • *Munakara Moon Delineations*

The outcome planet: Mars in Capricorn in exaltation

Mars in exaltation completes the Moon's munakara sequence and neatly ends back where the whole process began. Mars not only fuels the Moon's anguish, it also gives it courage to keep fighting, even though the battle seems hopeless at times. Capricorn Mars rules Michael Moore's IC, and the base foundation stone of his core beliefs can be seen from this rulership. It also provides Moore with the tenacity to call out what he sees as the foes of the 'little people' whose voices are rarely heard, and whose sporadic appearances on the nightly news are accompanied by tragedy and despair.

An exalted Mars does not accept defeat for two reasons. One, it believes it is in the right, and two, it is disposited by Saturn, and Saturn wears down the stone one steady drip at a time. Moore's Mars also rules his 9th house – where munakara Mercury in Aries resides – and journalism is in this man's blood.

When the subject of the 1992 LA riots came up in an interview with Moore in 2002 he answered: "[We] all knew that it could happen anytime, anywhere, because we have refused to deal with the problem [of racism]. I'm not going to refuse to deal with it. I'm going to talk about it and talk about it, and I want to see change in my lifetime."[105]

Aries Mercury in Munakara: Michael Moore

- **Key Questions:**
- What does Michael Moore's Mercury contend with?
- What is its driving force?
- What is its trigger? What is its outcome?

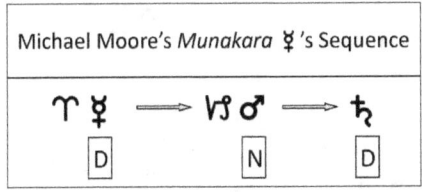

Table 12.17: Michael Moore: Munakara Mercury Sequence

For Michael Moore his munakara Mercury is largely occupied with chasing information or exploring a volatile situation, and finding a way in which he can combine fact-finding with entertainment. The gift of his munakara Mercury lies in granting him the ability to make documentaries that people *want* to see, rather than knowing they *should* see it because the topic is important to them. His Mercury in contention plays the role of devil's advocate, and perhaps because it sits exactly at the Northern Bendings, halfway between North and South Node, the world stops to listen to him, even though they may not agree, or like what he has to say.

People who have planets at the Bendings often have an impact on society, and when the same planet is in munakara, then it becomes truly confrontational, and often not very popular with the establishment or political power of the citizen's country. Although some of Michael Moore's documentaries are overwhelmingly bleak, Mercury's driving force is Mars exalted in Capricorn and perhaps he truly believes that whilst things are bad, they are not completely hopeless. It may be the eleventh hour for humanity, but Moore hopes there is still sixty minutes where we might do something useful to avert disaster. Saturn is diurnal Mercury's outcome planet in its munakara sequence and Saturn's placement on the IC is a statement of Moore's attachment to his country of birth (4th house) and how no matter what its problems, he is convinced that its nation's citizens can strengthen the principles of Saturn – honesty, integrity, fairness, and pride in its achievements.

Munakara Planet and Sect Condition – how comfortable is Mercury?

Diurnal Mercury in Aries has full sect dignity in Moore's chart. Munakara Mercury's excellent *hayz* condition lends a sense of self-righteousness especially when Moore is chasing an interviewee, or presenting some outrage, in a documentary fashioned to put across his views to the detriment of others' position on an issue. It does not help the balance of opinions when Mercury's dispositor is an exalted Mars, again adding to the belief of being vindicated in one's views.

Michael Moore— ☿'s Sect Dignity			
Planet	Sect 1 Status	Sect 2 Hemisphere	Sect 3 Sign
♈ ☿	Day	With the Sun	Fire
D	D	D	D

Table 12.18: Michael Moore: Munakara Mercury Sect Dignity

Diurnal Mercury's munakara sequence uses the same two planets, Mars and Saturn, as his Moon's sequence, and having the two malefic involved in contention can result in some dangerous situations where Moore risks his physical safety (Mars) or jeopardizes his reputation (Saturn) for the sake of telling a story or voicing his opinions (Mercury). Thankfully, Mars (in good sect dignity) is in mutual reception with Saturn, and in a sextile aspect, which should mean that Moore does indeed know his boundaries (for both planets), and that he errs on the side of caution, particularly if the situation is becoming too intense, or his viewpoint is inflaming a situation. If this happens, Moore calms the situation with his trademark humour, or curbs his enthusiasm in order to de-escalate the tension and reclaim control of the situation.

Munakara Mercury: Michael Moore

"I'm speaking in a very spiritual sense here: I am not allowed to not speak out. Whatever that judgment day is, I will not be granted any kind of eternity if I benefit as a result of others' hardships. Especially, when it's because of the colour of their skin. I'm not waiting for that day. I ask myself this every day: what is it that I'm doing?.....We will be judged by how we treat the least among us. And so, as my books or films become more successful, I'm challenged more."[106]

Munakara Mercury resides in Moore's 9th house, and his expression for this planet is a fine balance between his journalism and his spiritual beliefs. He failed to complete his college education, instead dropping out in his first year and founding an alternate weekly magazine which began small as *The Flint Voice* named after his hometown and morphing into *The Michigan Voice* as it expanded to cover the entire state. Even at age 22 Moore could sell an idea and his initial financial backing came from pop star Harry Chapin who Moore convinced to perform a concert and dedicate its earnings to the magazine.

Mercury in munakara often goes through its own trials and tribulations but with exalted Mars as its dispositor, and first dispositor in mutual reception to Mercury's outcome planet, Saturn, often pennies drop from heaven when least expected by the chart owner. Munakara Mercury in Aries is tenacious and sometimes reckless but contention can sometimes put these attributes to good use. Moore was able to finance his first film *Roger & Me*, a story on the General Motors plant closures in his hometown, from his out of court settlement for wrongful dismissal from the liberal political magazine *Mother Jones*. Moore was fired after an argument with his editor who refused to let him publish an article in the magazine which was the basis for his first film.

Not all of Moore's documentaries have hit their mark as the example of 2019's *Planet of the Humans* demonstrates. In the documentary Moore argued that electric cars and solar energy were unreliable and relied on fossil fuels to function whilst environmentalist Al Gore is accused of bolstering corporations that push flawed technologies over real solutions to the climate crisis. Climate change experts and activists angrily demanded the film be withdrawn from public viewing for its potential damage to the green movement.[107]

Moore was trying to make the point that environmentalists were targeting the wrong area. Rather than praising themselves for the advancement of technological fixes, they should instead be focusing on how to restrain economic excess (the explosion of consumerism), and the ongoing effects of population growth on climate change. Moore (through his munakara Mercury) was trying to make the point that we need to put our climate heroes under the same scrutiny as those who deny climate change. Rather than relying on technology to save humankind, we need to show some restraint (Saturn) and rein in our excesses as part of our overall solution. Right message, munakara Mercury, but the wrong delivery can mean the message goes unheard or unheeded.

CHAPTER THIRTEEN
Munakara Mercury Delineations

The charts in this chapter give examples for Mercury in contention; the following two charts, John Glenn and Mark Ruffalo, have diurnal Mercury in munakara, and nocturnal Mercury is featured in the charts of Kurt Cobain and Dave Grohl. These charts form the basis of the discussion on Mercury in its potential to belong to both sect divisions and in its ability to find itself in a state of munakara.

Diurnal Mercury in Munakara

John Glenn and Mark Ruffalo have diurnal Mercury in water signs ruled by two different nocturnal planets. Both examples also have a munakara duet involving diurnal Mercury and the Sun. John Glenn has Cancer Mercury/Sun disposited by Capricorn Moon ending in Saturn as its outcome planet, and Mark Ruffalo has Scorpio Mercury/Sun disposited by Capricorn Mars and the third planet, the outcome planet is Saturn. The first dispositor is in Capricorn, and for one planet (the Moon) it signals debility, whilst the other dispositor celebrates its exaltation (Mars). Either way, both diurnal Mercury/Sun sequences finish with Saturn as their outcome planet.

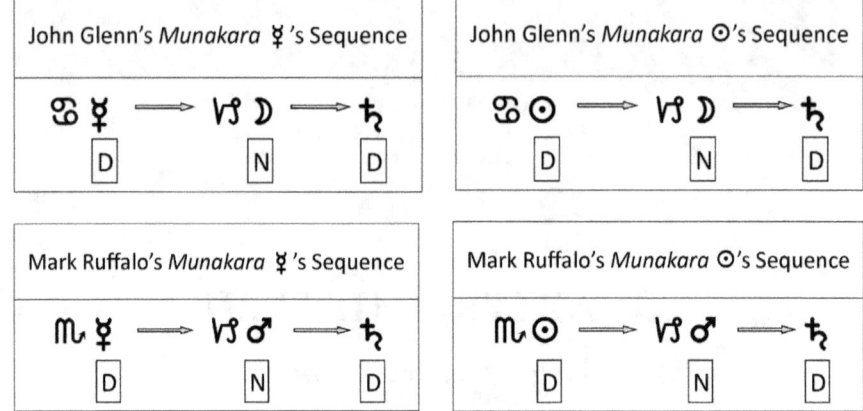

Table 13.1: Munakara Tables for Diurnal Mercury and the Sun

Munakara Diurnal Mercury: John Glenn

A Brief Biography of John Glenn

John Glenn Jr. (18th July 1921 – 8th December 2016) was an American aviator, engineer, astronaut, businessman and politician. He was a member of the Mercury 7 crew, and the spacecraft was named *Friendship 7* in honour of the number of astronauts and the group's reliance on each other for a safe return to Earth. Project Mercury was named after the Roman god of financial gain, commerce, eloquence, messages, communication, travellers, luck and trickery, and ran from 1958 to 1963. It promised to be America's first human spaceflight. Originally Russia was beating America in the Space Race as Soviet cosmonaut Yuri Gagarin was the first man to travel to space, and the first person to orbit the Earth on April 12, 1961. Project Mercury's goal was to catch up with Russia and to put their own man into Earth orbit and then return him safely, all the while gauging his reactions to his orbit through space.

On February 20, 1962, ten months after Gagarin's orbit, astronaut John Herschel Glenn Jr. became the first American to orbit the Earth during the three-orbit Mercury-Atlas 6 mission, aboard the *Friendship 7* spacecraft. Small signs of Mercury in contention were visible even for this great moment in history. Glenn was over 40 years of age at the time and there was speculation that he was too old for the mission and that a younger man's body could better resist the physical stress. In hindsight, this speculation seems ridiculous given that in 1998, thirty six years after his first orbit, Glenn took to space at age 77 for a nine-day ride aboard the space shuttle Discovery on its STS-95 mission.

Chapter Thirteen • *Munakara Mercury Delineations*

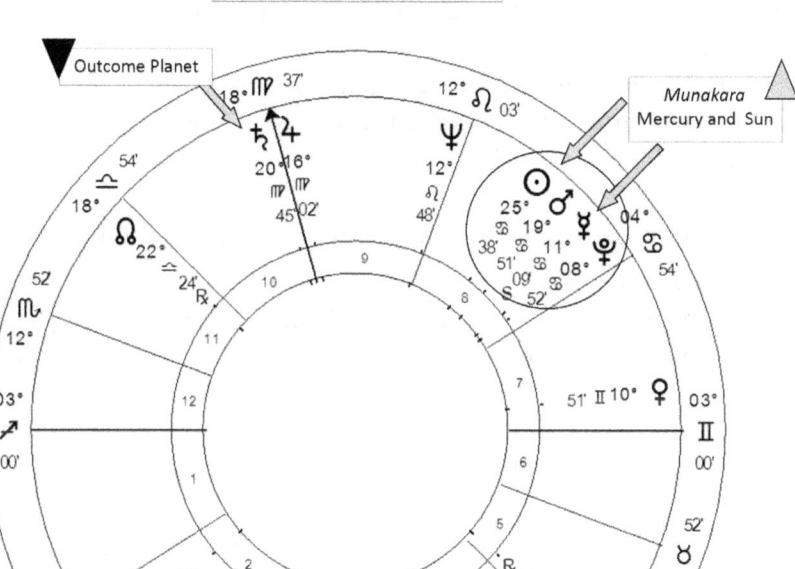

Fig. 13.1: John Glenn Natal Chart: Diurnal Mercury in Munakara

One journalist commented on Glenn's 1998 flight as a jolt to society's negative attitudes on ageism, his munakara Mercury/Sun reminding the nation that stereotypes, prejudices and discrimination abound when it comes to attitudes towards the older generation: *"In a coarsening culture littered with the shards of clay feet, an authentic untarnished hero like Glenn is suddenly perceived as a fragile, endangered species. In a kind of reverse Rip van Winkle effect, it is as if his astonishing return to space had reawakened a whole segment of society."*[1]

Glenn had retired from his political career by this time – he served from 1974 to 1999 as a US Senator from Ohio – and there was conjecture that it was a waste of NASA's resources (contentious Mercury/Sun in 8th house).

Munakara in Practice

However, Glenn's persistent requests for one last space flight were fruitful when, at the behest of President Clinton whom Glenn had supported in his 1992 Presidential Campaign, the mission was approved.

Glenn was inducted into the US Astronaut Hall of Fame in 1990, and received the Presidential Medal of Freedom in 2012. Glenn, both the oldest and the last surviving member of the Mercury 7, died at the age of 95 on December 8, 2016.

Cancer Mercury and Sun Duet in Munakara: John Glenn

- **Key Questions:**
- What does John Glenn's Mercury and Sun contend with?
- What is its driving force?
- What is its trigger? What is its outcome?

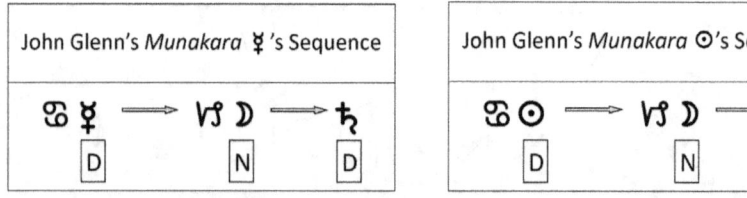

Table 13.2: John Glenn: Diurnal Mercury and Sun Sequence

Munakara Mercury and the Sun are featured in a stellium in Cancer with Pluto and Mars. The two diurnal planets (Mercury and Sun) share more than an aspect by conjunction, as the same munakara sequence links them in unison, creating a duet that deals with contention as a team, rather than as two individual planets. Mark Ruffalo (*Fig. 13.2*) and Kurt Cobain (*Fig. 13.3*) also have duets of Mercury with another planet in the same sign, and with an identical munakara sequence. Mark Ruffalo has Scorpio Mercury and Scorpio Sun with Mars in Capricorn, and Kurt Cobain has Pisces Mercury and Pisces Venus with Jupiter in Cancer. The planets differ in the two examples' munakara duet, but interestingly, they involve a first dispositor which is in its sign of exaltation (Mars for Ruffalo, and Jupiter for Cobain).

John Glenn's munakara Mercury and Sun provide the strength and dedication that drives this man to be an early pioneer in the US space mission program, and to be the first US citizen to orbit the Earth in 1962. The boundaries that both the Sun and Mercury were determined to cross took him to the extremes of space at a time when it was presumed to be a dream not

Chapter Thirteen • *Munakara Mercury Delineations*

a reality (Saturn is the duet's outcome planet). His Capricorn Moon opposes the stellium in Cancer, and is a telling signature for a man who is entirely alone in space (Moon) whilst the rest of Earth goes about its daily business (Cancer stellium).

Capricorn Moon is both Sun and Mercury's dispositor and the Moon's state of detriment describes the trauma Glenn allowed his body to be subjected to in the late 1950s. The preparatory work needed to condition the mind and body for the experience of space travel involved experimental drugs, extended periods of extreme physical discomfort, exposure to high levels of radiation, and hours of confinement in heavy bulky spacesuits or in gravity-free chambers. Once in space, the isolation from humanity has a psychological effect, and together Saturn and Jupiter on the Mid-heaven describe the ultimate separation from humanity that Glenn endured whilst orbiting in outer space.

Munakara Planet and Sect Condition – how comfortable is Mercury and the Sun?

Glenn's Mercury and Sun are in *halb* condition according to sect dignity, as they travel together in a diurnal chart and Mercury is in the same hemisphere as the Sun – which as the planet that sets the condition – will always in *halb*. The diurnal duet does not qualify for *hayz* (all three sect conditions met) as they are in the feminine sign of Cancer. Robert Hand states "diurnal planets all require, or create in the case of the Sun, an environment of clarity and definition with clear limits and boundaries.² The Sun creates this environment as it illuminates the hemisphere in which it finds itself, and diurnal Mercury is happy to take advantage of the Sun's direction. Success may be a little easier to achieve, especially if the individual with a diurnal chart is clear about their goals, and knows exactly how to

John Glenn — ☿'s Sect Dignity			
Planet	Sect 1 Status	Sect 2 Hemisphere	Sect 3 Sign
♋ ☿	Day	With the Sun	Water
D	D	D	N

John Glenn — ☉'s Sect Dignity			
Planet	Sect 1 Status	Sect 2 Hemisphere	Sect 3 Sign
♋ ☉	Day	Sun Defines	Water
D	D	D	N

Table 13.3: John Glenn: Diurnal Mercury and Sun Sect Dignity

harness their drive, organise their time, and use their ambitions to manifest these goals. With Sun and Mercury in good sect dignity, it seems totally apt that Glenn became a prominent member of Project Mercury 7, the name given by the US space program to tag their country's race to space.

Munakara Mercury and Sun Duet: John Herschel Glenn Jr.

"You can't get up there and then be screwing something up."[3] – John Glenn

Munakara Mercury and Sun in Cancer in 8th House

Like his father before him, John Herschel Glenn Jr., carried as his first and middle name, the name of famous composer, astronomer and photographer whose own father, Sir William Herschel, had discovered the planet Uranus in 1791. John Herschel Glenn Sr. ran a plumbing business and never fulfilled the promise of his name, so perhaps John Jr. with a munakara Sun in Cancer carried not only his father's aspirations, but also the memory and past hopes of his famous English namesake who was born long before the possibility of space travel.

The 8th house is a pretty intense place to find not one, but two planets in munakara given that it is the house that is blind to the Ascendant and signifies death, chaos and sudden endings. Munakara Mercury and Sun are in conjunction with two dangerous highly volatile and explosive planets in the form of Pluto and Mars. The stellium in Cancer is opposed by the sign's ruler, the Moon, in the sign of Capricorn. Sixty years ago death was a very real possibility if you were an astronaut in the initial stages of space exploration. Even before Glenn entered the space program he had 149 combat missions in World War II and Korea to his credit, earning the nickname 'Old Magnet Ass' because of his uncanny ability to keep his airplane under him even with huge holes blown through it.[4]

In February 1962, millions of viewers around the world were glued to their television sets as they held their breath and waited for Glenn's space capsule to splash down in the Atlantic Ocean. A collective sigh of relief rolled across the world as Glenn's space craft skittered into the ocean, totally unaware that the spacecraft's heatshield and compressed landing bag had become unattached and were only connected by straps rather than being locked into position.[5] Luckily the straps held, but had they not Glenn risked being incinerated on television at the time of his landing. Garbled communications were being hastily barked at him at each of the tracking stations as Glenn momentarily

Chapter Thirteen • *Munakara Mercury Delineations*

flew past, with the astronaut knowing something had happened, but had no clue as to what it could be, or how it would affect his safety or influence the success of his landing. This kind of uncertainty and 'seat of the pants' stuff could never happen in today's space technology but Glenn's first orbit around Earth took place over sixty years ago.

An article from 2019 titled *The Complex Relationship between Mental Health and Space Travel*[6] discusses the impact that the two years of intensive training required just to enter the program, to be chosen as an astronaut, and coming to terms with *not* being an astronaut after years of dedication, has on the tiny number of gifted individuals who are selected for space exploration. Recent psychiatry studies have found "high-risk individuals such as pilot astronauts have between 3% to 58% chance of developing Post-Traumatic Stress Disorder (PTSD), an alarming increase when compared to the general population's 1% to 14% chance."[7] The article provides current assessments by Diagnostic and Statistical Manual of Mental Disorders, 5th Edition (DSM-5) on the damage that PTSD can have on those who suffer from the disorder: 85% chance of alcoholism, 42% chance of drug abuse, 68% chance of depression, and 26% chance of antisocial personality disorder.[8] None of this research on the link between mental health and space exploration would have been conceived, let alone available, to Glenn or anyone else who volunteered for the 1960s space program. Even if Glenn had been aware of the potential harm, it is unlikely that his munakara Mercury would have given it a second thought. Sun in munakara, and Mercury's rulership over two of his angles (7th and 10th house) would have propelled him forwards, trusting in experts in the medical and psychological fields (7th), and anticipating the glory of writing his name in the history of space exploration (10th).

First Dispositor: Moon in Capricorn in 2nd House

Cancer is a fertile sign belonging to the Moon, so when munakara Mercury and Sun are in conjunction with Pluto and Mars, the individual focuses their intensity and passion on something they believe in, and fervently want to bring to fruition in some way. Contention is the perfect vehicle for dedication like this, as all things are possible with this kind of mindset, but loved ones may suffer or find themselves playing second fiddle to whatever form the obsession takes for the individual. John Glenn married Anna Castor in 1943 and the couple were married for 73 years and eight months until Glenn's death in 2016. Glenn's munakara Mercury rules his 7th house of relationships, and often contention can be as much a part of the partner's life as it is for the recipient of a contentious planet. Annie Glenn experienced a speech stutter – present in 85% of her verbal utterances[9] – throughout her life.[10] Annie was an advocate for people with disabilities and communication disorders and at age 53, she attended a three-week treatment course at Hollins Communications Research Institute in Virginia to help with her dysfluency. She later became an adjunct professor with Ohio State's Speech Pathology Department.[11]

The Moon opposing the Cancer stellium demonstrates John Glenn's determination and willpower, even when it isolates him or puts him at a physical or emotional disadvantage (Moon in detriment). The duet of munakara Sun and Mercury together rule the 9th (Leo) and 10th houses (Virgo) and Glenn's spiritual and philosophical quest involved his ambition to be the first American to orbit Earth. Glenn was a Freemason, and an ordained elder of the Presbyterian Church, and his religious faith was reinforced after he travelled in space in 1962. On his second and final space voyage in 1998 Glenn said, "To look out at this kind of creation and not believe in God is to me impossible."[12] On October 29, 1998, at the age of 77, John Glenn became the oldest person ever to venture into space. It is a record that still stands. Glenn's Moon in Capricorn is the dispositor for his munakara Mercury/Sun and the Moon in detriment shows that even at the advanced age of 77 his mind over-rides his body's reluctance to undertake rigorous physical and mental training, almost forty years after his initial space flight.

Some of his Glenn's colleagues, themselves retired, derided his 1998 re-flight as a publicity stunt. Eugene Cernan, the last man to walk on the moon, and 64 years old at the time, told *Vanity Fair* "I don't care if John just stares out the window for 10 days. He's earned it."[13] Cernan might have joked that Glenn would merely act as a passenger on the flight, but this is not strictly true. Glenn was expected to be an active participant – an accident or his death in flight would have been a media disaster for NASA. One can only wonder at the amount of stress his Mercury and Sun duet (disposited by Moon in detriment) endured, in order to complete the six gruelling months that preceded the October 29 flight.

The technological advancement during the four decades between Glenn's first and second space flight would be mind-boggling, and even the simplest tasks for a man nearing his eightieth year, regardless of their former training, would be mentally and emotionally challenging to say the least. Knowing the world was watching in judgement, and that an entire space program, plus the President of the United States, was relying on him to make this mission a success must have been a huge burden to carry into his second mission.

Chapter Thirteen • *Munakara Mercury Delineations*

The outcome planet: Saturn in Virgo conjunct Mid-heaven

Saturn is the outcome planet for Mercury and the Sun. Saturn sits with Jupiter (in detriment) atop the chart in Virgo. There is a neat conclusion for Glenn's Mercury in contention, as Mercury is Saturn's dispositor, and so the circle closes like an orbit around his chart. Jupiter may be in detriment in its conjunction with Saturn, but detriment does not mean an ineffective or useless planet. Rather it indicates difference, and unlikely, but not impossible success, particularly in a field which is not considered mainstream in public opinion. At the time of Project Mercury's creation, earlier models in American spacecraft were either crashing at lift-off, or burning up at re-entry, so the work was both extremely experimental and extremely dangerous, when Glenn put his body on the line to orbit the Earth. Jupiter rules Glenn's Ascendant and his 4th house, and as a veteran of 149 combat missions, the constant risk of death was a part of this man's life.

Munakara Mercury and Sun reside in the 8th house, and with the Sun ruling the 9th house, Glenn was a strange spiritual mixture of Freemason with Christian beliefs and a scientific background. During his first flight Glenn noticed tiny glowing particles that seemed to be dancing around the *Friendship 7* capsule. Glenn likened them to fireflies and told Mission Control "I'm in a big mass of some very small particles that are brilliantly lit up like they're luminescent. I never saw anything like it. They're coming by the capsule, and they look like little stars. A whole shower of them coming by."[14]

"As decades passed, Glenn never forgot about the "fireflies". As a man of devout faith, he could live with not knowing (the scientific reason behind them). He did wonder whether that beautiful sight was not guardian angels or divine entities guiding him through the darkness. After 35 years, when he embarked on space flight again at the age of 77, he remain convinced that such magnificence was proof of a higher power."[15]

Jupiter in Virgo is applying to Saturn and together the two planets hug Glenn's MC. The synodic conjunction between Jupiter and Saturn took place two months after Glenn's birth. Two cycles and forty years later, Jupiter and Saturn once more began another synodic cycle in an earth sign at 25 Capricorn (opposite Glenn's munakara Sun) on February 19, 1961, two months before Gagarin's orbit in space, and a year before Glenn's own orbit.

Ironically, Glenn was told that at age 43 he would be ruled out as a future candidate for lunar landings being developed as a result of his successful orbit, so when he resigned from NASA in 1964 he announced his Democratic Party candidacy for the US Senate. It would take a further ten years for success to arrive in 1974, and in the meantime Glenn passed the decade by entering the world of commerce. During his 1974 campaign, his opponent thought to take advantage of a perceived weakness by drawing attention to the fact that John Glenn had never drawn a wage, and therefore could not relate to the struggles of the average blue-collar worker. Glenn's munakara Mercury and Sun counter-attacked with gusto: creating an emotion-charged response which became known as the "Gold Star Mothers" speech telling his opponent to go to a veteran's hospital and "look those men with mangled bodies in the eyes and tell them they didn't hold a job. You go with me to any Gold Star mother and you look her in the eye and tell her that her son did not hold a job."[16] Glenn won the seat and would continue to serve in the US Senate for 24 years until he retired in January 1999.

Gemini Venus in Munakara: John Glenn

- **Key Questions:**
- What does John Glenn's Venus contend with?
- What is its driving force?
- What is its trigger? What is its outcome?

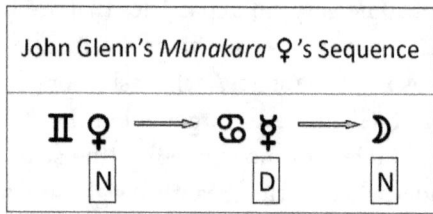

Table 13.4: John Glenn: Venus Munakara Sequence

Munakara Venus in Gemini resides in the 7th house, and his wife Annie's speech impediment has been mentioned earlier in Mercury's rulership of the relationship house. Glenn loved flying and was ecstatic at being chosen as the fifth man in space, but he was uncomfortable with the fame, exposure and public adoration that followed his flight.

Venus rules Glenn's 11th house and his new friend, President Kennedy, pinned a medal on him after which the hero astronaut addressed a joint session of Congress. Over four million people turned out to honour him in a ticker-tape parade through the canyons of Manhattan.[17] According to NASA officials Glenn was the only astronaut who required full-time staff just to cope

Chapter Thirteen • *Munakara Mercury Delineations*

with his mail. This level of popularity lasted until Neil Armstrong stepped on the moon in 1969 and the public turned their attention from Glenn to Armstrong.[18]

Munakara Venus rules Glenn's 6th house, and in an odd turn of fate Glenn was injured just after he retired from the space program in 1964 when he slipped on a rug in his bathroom and fell, hitting his head on the floor. For a man who had recently survived a death-defying re-entry to Earth, his concussion was so severe Glenn took almost a year to recover from brain injury. He was so concerned about permanent disability that he took himself back through all the old astronaut balance tests. He said later about the incident, "There I was, flat on my back, out of money and a job. Big hero astronaut. Big deal."[19]

Munakara Venus can speak of a whiff of scandal, especially when it is also out-of-sect (*Table 13.5, next page*). Glenn's Gemini Venus resides in his 7th house, and not all his associations were squeaky clean during the time when he was a politician serving in the US Senate. The announcement on October 12, 1989 that Senator John Glenn would be the grand marshal for the 101st Tournament of Roses parade praised Glenn as 'a hero with steely nerves and harmonious hometown values...' but controversy immediately flared over the committee's choice. In a case of poor timing, the day after the Rose Parade announcement, on October 13, 1989, the Common Cause citizens' lobby called for investigations of five senators, including Glenn, on charges they improperly interfered with a federal investigation of the now-bankrupt Lincoln Savings & Loan in Irvine. It was claimed that two years earlier, in 1987, Glenn had been bought by Lincoln owner Charles Keating with a $200,000 contribution to a political action committee overseen by Glenn.[20]

Glenn hardly needed the bribe to prop up his finances – he became a multimillionaire through investment in hotels, and his net worth at the time was over $7 million. Known as the "Keating 5" scandal, Glenn defended himself with an eight-page statement explaining his actions and galvanising his three munakara planets – Sun, Mercury and Venus – always ready to enter into a fight, "My life has been, and remains, an open book....It's been a life based on decency, honour, integrity and the highest ethical standards. I have not changed, and with every fibre of my being, I resent anyone implying otherwise."[21]

Munakara Planet and Sect Condition – how comfortable is Venus?

John Glenn's Venus is completely out of sect, and the discomfort Venus feels in its environment may be explained by Glenn loving his job but feeling awkward about the infamy and popularity that came with it. As an astronaut Glenn's strengths lay in "the disciplined mastery of complex systems" but as a politician "his attention to detail was seen by some as a flaw that sometimes left him awash in minutiae; his devotion to his convictions translated as uncompromising rigidity."[22] In March 1984 Glenn abandoned a run for the US presidency after running up a campaign debt of $3 million as his weakness for "punchless canned answers" to issue questions earned him The Washington Post's nickname "Mr. Checklist" for lacking flexibility and the suppleness of mind needed for the role of president.

John Glenn — ♀'s Sect Dignity			
Planet	Sect 1 Status	Sect 2 Hemisphere	Sect 3 Sign
♊ ♀	Day	With the Sun	Air
N	D	D	D

Table 13.5: John Glenn: Munakara Venus Sect Dignity

Robert Hand says out of sect Venus 'was a matter of the ancient writers thinking that the diurnal Venus behaved in a manner that was not appropriate to Venus'.[23] Venus out of sect and in munakara suggests a belief that there a some environments where a woman is not welcome, and in a woman's chart, she is likely to feel this strongly and fight for her place amongst those who spurn her, or discourage any active involvement on her part. In a man's chart, this can be his conviction of what is 'appropriate and inappropriate for women', and he will fight to keep women away from somewhere he believes they will disrupt or cause distraction within an environment.

The following story seems to support Glenn's traditional belief that, in his opinion there was no viable role for women in the field of space exploration. Unfortunately, his strong opposition thwarted women's ambitions to participate equally as astronauts for dozens of years thereafter. In 1962, the same year as Glenn's orbit, NASA was contemplating recruiting women to the astronaut corps from Mercury 13, an experimental group of thirteen highly skilled and gifted women participants being tested for spaceflight. The women were veteran pilots and had served in war alongside their male equals in the same way that Glenn had risen through the military ranks to become an astronaut a few years earlier. The women were due to join the Mercury Boys' space program on September 17, 1961, but it was abruptly halted and no reasons for cancellation were forthcoming.

A hearing before the House Space Committee was scheduled in the following July (1962), to discuss the possibility of resurrecting women's spaceflight options, and John Glenn was invited to present his opinion on women in the space program. His orbit five months earlier had solidified his role as a national hero, and any comments he made would be deemed crucial to the argument.

Glenn told the Committee, *"I think this gets back to the way our social order is organized, really. It is just a fact. The men go off and fight the wars and fly the airplanes and come back and help design and build and test them. The fact that women are not in this field is a fact of our social order."*[24]

His words carried so much weight that unfortunately, he singlehandedly killed the debate and omitted American female astronauts from the program for the next 20 years. In May 1965, after he left NASA, Glenn was quoted as saying NASA should "offer a serious chance to women as scientist astronauts"[25] meaning he thought they could participate on the ground, but not go into space as pilots.

Munakara Diurnal Mercury: Mark Ruffalo

A Brief Biography of Mark Ruffalo

Mark Ruffalo, born 22nd November 1967, is an American actor and an environmental, political and civil activist. At school he struggled with undiagnosed dyslexia and ADHD, and on completion of his high school, he moved with his parents and three siblings to San Diego where his father struggled to support his family. Ruffalo moved to Los Angeles to attend classes at the Stella Adler Conservatory and co-founded the Orpheus Theatre Company where he wrote, directed, and starred in a number of plays. He spent close to a decade supporting himself as a bartender whilst establishing his struggling career as an actor.[26]

His big break would come with a chance meeting and resulting collaboration with playwright/screenwriter Kenneth Lonergan. Ruffalo won success in Lonergan's 1996 off-Broadway play "This Is Our Youth," a story about troubled young adults. This led to his male lead in Lonergan's Oscar-winning film drama *You Can Count on Me* (2000). The performance drew rave reviews and invited comparisons to an early Marlon Brando.[27]

Notable roles followed including *The Last Castle* (2001), however, after completing work on *The Last Castle*, Ruffalo was diagnosed with an acoustic neuroma, a type of brain tumour located above his left ear. At the time he was due to start filming in *Signs* but had to drop out and the role was given to Joaquin Phoenix. The tumour was benign, but the surgery to remove the mass resulted in partial facial paralysis which took a year to subside, and has left the actor deaf in his left ear.[28]

Ruffalo was able to return to acting after his recovery and was offered major roles in *XX/XY* (2002) and *Windtalkers* (2002) *In the Cut* (2003), *View from the Top* (2003), *We Don't Live Here Anymore* (2004), *Eternal Sunshine of the Spotless Mind* (2004), *13 Going on 30* (2004), and *Collateral* (2004).

On December 1, 2008 Ruffalo's younger brother, Scott, was found outside his home in Beverley Hills with a bullet wound to the head. He was rushed to the hospital but when it became obvious he would not recover, his life support was switched off and his death remains unsolved.[29] Two other people were present at the scene and told investigators it was a self-inflicted wound that occurred as a result of Scott playing Russian roulette under the influence of cocaine and morphine.[30]

At the time, Ruffalo was scheduled to start work on Noah Baumbach's film *Greenberg*. but he dropped out to deal with his grief over the loss of his brother. It was a blessing in disguise because it allowed him to take other roles that wound up being better for him. He earned Oscar nominations for *The Kids Are All Right* (2010), *Foxcatcher* (2014) and *Spotlight* (2015). He also won an Emmy Award for his role as Ned Weeks in HBO's *The Normal Heart* in 2014. The actor has joked "My friends have a term, getting 'Ruffaloed,' It's when you have what seems to be bad luck that actually turns into good luck later."[31] Ruffalo's appearance as Dr. Bruce Banner, aka The Hulk, in Joss Whedon's movie blockbuster *The Avengers* (2012) cemented his role as the Marvel superhero and the Avenger films that followed have guaranteed The Hulk's position in May 2024 by Comic Book Resources (CBR) as the third highest ranked superheroes behind Wolverine and Spider Man.[32]

Accusations of terrorism dogged him in 2010, when it was reported by CBS News that Ruffalo had been placed on a terror advisory list by Pennsylvania's Office of Homeland Security, after helping to promote the documentary *Gasland*, and speaking out about his concerns over natural gas drilling.[33] He helped to organise screenings of the film in an effort to raise awareness of fracking's potentially disastrous effects on the environment, and on those living near the drill sites. The bureau denied everything saying "There is

Chapter Thirteen • Munakara Mercury Delineations

no list, we never even had a list", but as more news companies picked it up Ruffalo was forced to conduct interviews denying the story. "It wasn't until The Washington Times finally nailed the story that it went away."[34]

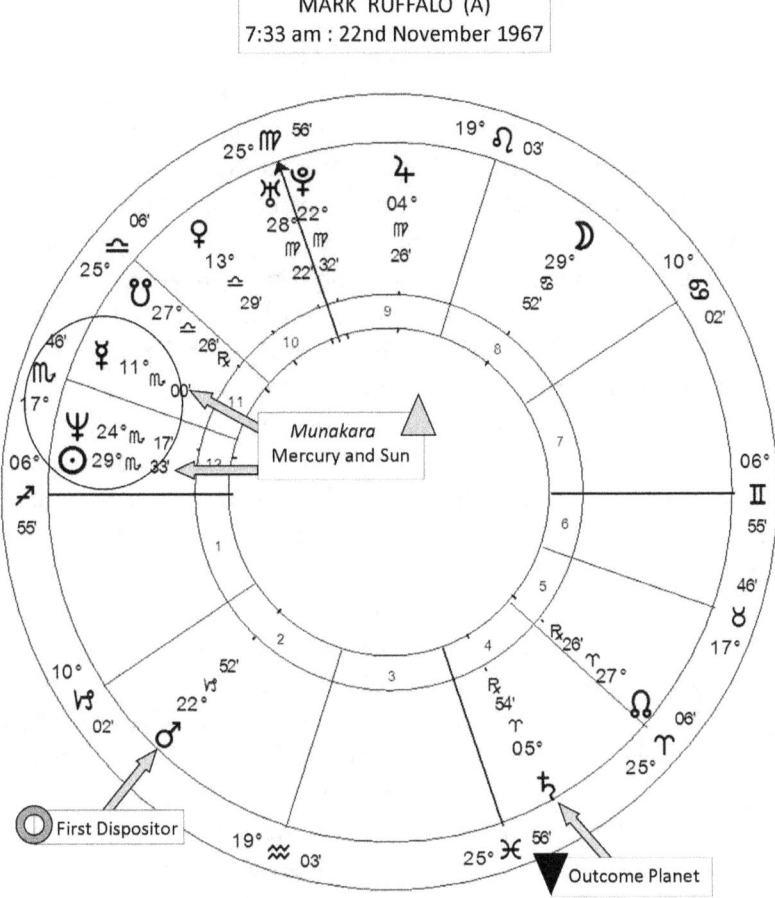

Fig. 13.2: Mark Ruffalo Natal Chart: Diurnal Mercury in Munakara

Scorpio Mercury and Sun Duet in Munakara: Mark Ruffalo

- **Key Questions:**
- What does Mark Ruffalo's Mercury and Sun contend with?
- What is its driving force?
- What is its trigger? What is its outcome?

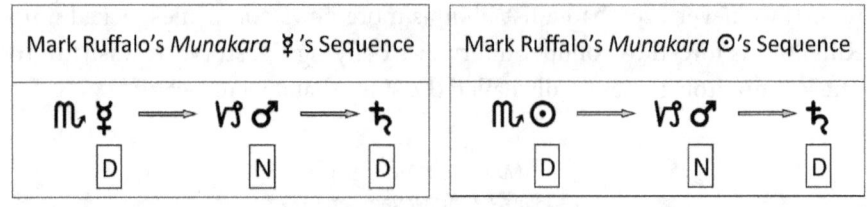

Table 13.6: Mark Ruffalo: Munakara Mercury and Sun Sequence

Mark Ruffalo is the second example for diurnal Mercury in munakara, and similar to John Glenn's chart, the Sun and Mercury share the same munakara sequence. The distance between these two planets in contention is slightly wider for Ruffalo. His Sun and Mercury are eighteen degrees apart, but a duet still exists as both planets share the same munakara sequence.

This situation of both planets in contention draws the Sun and Mercury together, and their sequence involves the two most difficult planets, Mars and Saturn. Contention can be confronting, and the inclusion of these two planets can result in a mindset (Mercury) that life has somehow robbed the individual of opportunities to shine (munakara Sun). Traditional astrologers considered Mars and Saturn to be malefic planets, and munakara sequences containing both malefic can indicate someone who sees life as a constant battle (Mars) over which they have very little control (Saturn).

Mark Ruffalo's duet of munakara Mercury and Sun are both disposited by Mars exalted in Capricorn and his successful career (Mercury rules MC) and strong relationship with his wife of 24 years (Mercury rules 7th house) show the benefits that munakara Mercury can produce when disposited by an exalted Mars. However, earlier in life Ruffalo's struggles were around undiagnosed dyslexia in his childhood years, rage issues in his early adult years, and on-going mental health issues throughout his life. He needed to find less destructive ways to deal with his frustrations, fears and anxieties, and the daily practiced of meditation (Saturn as outcome planet) has been his saviour. Munakara Mercury will signify different principles from the Sun but their mutual search for tranquillity, self-expression, and a positive and calm mind that finds balance in dark moments, will be through the same pathway – via Capricorn Mars and Aries Saturn.

Throughout his career Ruffalo has quested to become an actor of quality, honing his skills in order to express himself, and to bring a truthful interpretation to his characters on screen and stage. Mars' early frustrations and failures drove Ruffalo's duet in contention to excel and perfect his craft, and only through Saturn's perseverance, has Ruffalo been able to hold his position as a reputable actor. Even then, poor timing and serious health issues almost robbed him of his opportunities, but his determination and a belief in his own talents meant that he continued to pursue his passion for acting. Perhaps it is ironic that the role he has claimed as his own is as a superhero with a short temper and a destructive nature (Mars), who has lost emotional and physical self-control (Saturn), due to a scientific experiment.

Another much lighter side of munakara Mercury and Sun is shown in Ruffalo's reputation amongst his fellow Marvel actors, who affectionately tease him about being a 'blabbermouth', when it comes to gaffes he has made in interviews or film previews, prior to the launch of several Avenger movies. In October 2017 Ruffalo decided to do a live stream on Facebook as he sat in his seat in the theatre about to watch the premiere of *Thor: Ragnorok*. Unfortunately he did not end the stream before putting the phone back in his pocket to watch the movie, and almost 20 minutes of the film's auditory track went live on his stream. It would have been much longer except an executive from Marvel alerted him and asked him to turn the phone off. In another incident, Ruffalo gave away the ending of *Avengers: Infinity War* in July 2017 when quipping "Wait until you see the next one. Ha – everyone dies!" In his defence, Ruffalo didn't realise he had just dropped a spoiler as Marvel Studios had strategies in place that would stop these kinds of spoiler issues. For instance, they were famous for giving their actors different scripts and making them film different scenes that were meant to be cut, but the damage was done.[35]

Munakara Planet and Sect Condition – how comfortable is Mercury and Sun?

The placement of the two diurnal planets in munakara in a diurnal chart, and in '*halb*', is enough to bolster the confidence of Mercury and the Sun, and hopefully to shift any gloom produced by Mars or Saturn. The feminine water sign of Scorpio prevents the bestowing of full sect honours to the two masculine diurnal planets, but the fact that both planets disposit to an exalted Mars gives them a bolster to assist in Ruffalo's chosen career.

Robert Hand says that apart from defining Mercury's sect preference according to its relation to the Sun, we know very little about the effects of sect upon Mercury. Hand says: "However, we do not have any examples of delineations that distinguish between the diurnal or nocturnal placements of Mercury. Everything we say is somewhat conjectural and not derived from actual experience or ancient sources."[36] Hand had not changed this opinion in 2015 saying Mercury was "not strongly affected" by sect.

With this in mind, I suggest that it makes a huge difference to how we interpret Mercury depending on its sect dignity. Paulus Alexandrinus called Jupiter and Saturn "spear-bearers" of the Sun but nothing was mentioned about Mercury's place as a diurnal planet. "The Sun, then, was allotted the day and the morning rising and the masculine *zoidia* (signs), and it has the stars of Kronos (Saturn) and Zeus (Jupiter) as spear-bearers (Greek, *doruphoros*)."[37]

Mark Ruffalo — ☿'s Sect Dignity			
Planet	Sect 1 Status	Sect 2 Hemisphere	Sect 3 Sign
♏ ☿	Day	With the Sun	Water
D	D	D	N

Mark Ruffalo — ☉'s Sect Dignity			
Planet	Sect 1 Status	Sect 2 Hemisphere	Sect 3 Sign
♏ ☉	Day	Sun Defines	Water
D	D	D	N

Table 13.7: Mark Ruffalo: Diurnal Mercury and Sun in Munakara, Sect Dignity

Diurnal Mercury, however temporary its position, it is also a spear-bearer to the Sun. Its role is to promote solar principles such as honour, success, ambition, leverage and defence of a society's values. If diurnal Mercury is in good sect condition – and it usually is as its zodiacal position is always close to the Sun – then it will do everything in its power (and condition) to assist the Sun in achieving its aims. This is the case in Mark Ruffalo's chart, as even though there is 12th-house placement for Sun and Mercury (by Whole Sign), munakara Mercury will still use its skills in communication, memory, intelligence and opinion to assist the solar luminary.

Munakara Mercury and Sun Duet: Mark Ruffalo

"I'm a huge fan of the way you lose control and turn into an enormous green rage monster." – Tony Stark on meeting Bruce Banner for the first time

Munakara Diurnal Mercury and Sun in Scorpio in 11th House (Placidus)

Ruffalo's Mercury in munakara moves from 11th house to the 12th house in Whole Sign, as Scorpio is the sign directly before his Sagittarian Ascendant.

Chapter Thirteen • *Munakara Mercury Delineations*

Even without the added challenge of munakara, and all the things that transpire for Mercury in contention, Mercury in a feminine fixed sign has two features which require attention and care, especially when dealing with a healthy mental attitude. Scorpio, a water sign belonging to Mars, can get stuck in an emotional rut that keeps replaying past hurts, angry confrontations and hidden betrayals. Forgiving and forgetting sounds great in principle but this Mercury takes a long time to move into a forgiving state, and 'forgetting' requires control and compassion, which is often not Mars' forte.

The second challenge for fixed Mercury is its inability to see one of its signs, and in this case, the 7th house with Gemini on its cusp is in aversion to Mercury in Scorpio. Withdrawing from loved ones, and those who look to support Ruffalo through difficult times, is part of his Mercury's contention, as the less he communicates the harder it is to re-engage with the world. This was an obvious challenge, when Ruffalo's speech and hearing suffered for months as a result of surgery to remove a brain tumour. Munakara Mercury can see the Mid-heaven in Virgo, even though it is blind to Gemini, and Ruffalo's withdrawal to the 12th house in order to facilitate his full recovery was necessary for Munakara Mercury. Saturn, Mercury's outcome planet, can require time to pause and re-assess priorities, and time was essential for Ruffalo to fully recover from the after-effects of his surgery before re-entering the demanding world of acting

Mark Ruffalo is the third actor to step into the role of Bruce Banner, the scientist who changes into the Incredible Hulk, an enormous destructive green giant in the Marvel Comics. The Hulk was earlier played by actors Eric Bana (2003) and Edward Norton (2008), but it is Mark Ruffalo's portrayal which has won over audiences across the world, as he plays a believable role struggling between the mild-mannered scientist and his destructive alter-ego. In *Avengers*, Bruce Banner sums this up perfectly, when he tells Captain America that his secret in producing the Hulk on queue is 'because he is always angry,' meaning the Hulk is never far away.

The transformation from intelligent and reasonable scientist to a raging, incoherent monster is a painful journey for Bruce Banner, but one which achieves resolution in *Endgame* when he finds a way to amalgamate the two factions, and learns to appreciate both facets of his personality.

An articulate and relaxed 'Smart' Hulk explains: *"For years, I've been treating the Hulk like he's some kind of disease, something to get rid of. But then I start looking at him as the cure. Eighteen months in the gamma lab, I put the brains and the brawn together and now look at me. Best of both worlds."*

Munakara Sun conjunct Neptune draws attention to the relationship with father, and adds further weight to a Sun situated in the 12th house suggesting either a missing father, or a father who requires caution or watchfulness, in case they disappear or become frightening or dangerous in the child's eyes. Ruffalo had a good relationship with his father but his father's bankruptcy meant the family's move to San Diego to live "in a seedy community full of burnouts and meth"[38] where his father quit his painting business and tried selling a new invention, the Soda Butler, that turned water into soda water. Ruffalo says his father was "20 years ahead of his time. I always say he was an artist who never found his art form."[39] With his marriage splintered and no money his father moved back to Wisconsin alone and back into painting. "Within six months we went from normal to bankrupt and eliminated as a family."[40]

Neptune's conjunction to the Sun further supports feelings of invisibility, or lost chances for success, or acknowledgement, and does little to relieve the Sun's need to fight for energy, strength or success. Neptune's other release is spirituality and Ruffalo says that he was brought up in a household that had three religions in it: (born-again) Christianity, Catholicism and Bahai'ism (his father was a Bahai) and this fits perfectly with the Sun's rulership of the 9th house. Ruffalo has said "...there were different viewpoints and a lot of debate about that (religion), and I immediately began to understand that all these people that I loved very much had very strong feelings about faith, but all of them were valid to me. I felt that none of them, my grandmother, my father or my mother, was better or worse than the other."[41]

Munakara Sun's sextile to its dispositor, Mars, might alleviate the dips and dives of energy, or the Sun's loss of drive, ambition or clear direction in life created by the conjunction with Neptune. Success may come through the Sun's sextile to Uranus and Pluto on the Mid-heaven, but there can be a fear that it can be quickly snatched away as the two planets on the MC are highly unreliable, and designed to create chaos, especially when they begin a synodic cycle in a new sign (in this case, Mercury's sign of Virgo).

Given Munakara Sun's experience of three faiths in his childhood (Sun rules 9th house) Ruffalo has needed to find his own spiritual path that works for him, one that guides his Sun and gives it purpose, as well as giving his Mercury the opportunity to experience peace of mind. The Sun's journey has been disrupted by three big energies, Neptune, Uranus, and Pluto, but the trine to the Moon in rulership has hopefully steered him through some tough times.

Ruffalo says the discipline of meditation has completely changed his outlook: "It's pretty much a daily practice that quiets your brain and oddly enough, actually slows down time, so you're not so much trapped in your immediate reactions to things."[42] Soon after starting his meditation practice Ruffalo says "Everything changed. My work started to change, my luck started to change. The way the world looked at me changed."[43]

First Dispositor: Mars in Capricorn in 2nd House

The super chill man with the ready smile in interviews was actually a closer real-life version to the Hulk in his younger days, when odd jobs kept him afloat whilst spending a decade travelling between fruitless auditions for small acting roles. Years of financial strain (Saturn rules 2nd house where first dispositor Mars is situated) and rejection (munakara Mercury rules MC) cultivated an angry young man, prone to punching walls and destroying anything that wasn't nailed down in his apartment. "You should have seen me in my 20s, man, I was the poster definition of an angry young man with a persecution complex."[44] Meditation helped Mark to bring his anger under control, also minimising the symptoms of his dysthymia, a low-grade depression which has plagued him for most of his life.

The Greek word *dysthymia* means "bad state of mind" or "ill humour," and although it has less severe symptoms than major depression, it can last longer, and can have at least two of the following symptoms: poor appetite, insomnia, low energy or fatigue, low self-esteem, poor concentration or indecisiveness.

> "A lot of people are living with mental illness around them. Either you love one or you are one." – Mark Ruffalo

Scorpio Mercury rising ahead of the Sun is diurnal and disposits to Capricorn Mars which sees Saturn as the outcome planet in the sequence, which results in Mercury being in contention. Mars is a powerful player in Ruffalo's chart: it is the malefic at the Southern Bendings, it opposes the Moon (on the Northern Bendings), and trines the Pluto Uranus conjunction on the Mid-heaven.

Mars is the significator for knives, blood, cutting, and surgery, and Ruffalo's Capricorn Mars opposing Cancer Moon demonstrates two great powers at loggerheads in Ruffalo's chart, and this is not helped by the fact that both planets are at the Nodal Bendings. In 2002, the discovery of a brain tumour that needed immediate surgery put a halt to several big projects which would have secured Ruffalo's reputation as a talented actor. He was told by doctors that he had a mass behind his left ear the size of a golf ball, and his surgeon warned that as a result of surgery there was an 80% chance he would lose his hearing and 20% chance his facial nerves would be permanently damaged. It is munakara Mercury's movement into the 12th house by Whole Sign and ruling the Mid-heaven which shows the impact of his surgery. The tumour was benign, but the surgery created serious after-effects. Ruffalo was left with paralysis on the left side of his face, hearing loss, loss of balance, and conceptual confusion. All trademarks for Mercury in contention. Doctors were unsure of whether it was a temporary or permanent disability, and his publicists hid his condition for the next year (munakara Mercury), whilst Ruffalo retreated from the world and undertook a daily regime of acupuncture, herbal therapy, physiotherapy and physical exercise. Saturn, Mercury's outcome planet, may have brought about his withdrawal, but it also created the necessary discipline and commitment to ensure a full recovery.

The root of Mark Ruffalo's dysthymia may lie with the two diurnal planets in munakara, dispositing to two malefic planets, thereby affecting his thought processes and holding the key to his journey towards sound mental health, and a good dose of self-respect and self-love.

Second-house Mars in its exalted sign rules Ruffalo's 5th house of creativity and is the house of children and entertainment so this is a perfect place to find a superhero with human flaws and failings. Ruffalo's acting skills go far beyond making the Hulk's conversion from a mild-mannered man to a destructive monster a believable transformation for the audience. Rather, munakara Mercury and the Sun have created a version of the Hulk that captures universal empathy and understanding. We may not identify with a huge green giant who throws cars around like they were toys, but we can all connect with the regret, guilt and shame the Hulk feels when the rage subsides, and there is nothing but shattered lives, lost opportunities, damaged goods, and broken relationships in its aftermath.

The outcome planet: Saturn in Aries

Even at the best of times, Mercury in Scorpio is intense, repetitive in thought patterns with passionate ideals. Mercury is inclined to get stuck in a mental rut when clearly Mars as its dispositor, is not conducive to peace of mind. Contention takes Mercury to the next level when crossing back from nocturnal Mars (Scorpio's dispositor), to diurnal Saturn when Mars is in

Capricorn. In truth, Mars and Saturn are in mutual reception but this may not help Mercury's battle to overcome its demons. It has taken years for Ruffalo to channel his thoughts into a more positive frame of mind, and to calm his anxieties, as not only has he battled years of low-grade depression, he has also faced the trauma of sensitive brain surgery with long-term consequences to his career and private life (hearing loss – munakara Mercury).

Mars and Saturn have a complicated relationship in Ruffalo's chart. They reside in each other's sign, and are in mutual reception by sign as Aries squares Capricorn. However, Capricorn Mars is exalted whilst Aries Saturn is in fall, and the discrepancy between good essential dignity, and poor essential dignity, creates tension between the two malefics who technically, should be supporting one another by being mutual dispositors.

Ideally, this imbalance should give Mars the upper hand, but Saturn rails against its fallen state, and together they manifest some of the symptoms of dysthymia. If both Sun and Mercury in munakara are additional factors, then we have a cocktail for "ill humour" and a "bad state of mind". Mars' placement at the centre of Ruffalo's Mercury and Sun sequence makes it a pivotal planet when it comes to his peace of mind, and with time he has learned to control the destructive energy of rage, and to balance this emotion with alleviating his depression (Saturn as outcome planet). Ruffalo's management of these two difficult sectors of his personality are a credit to him, even more so than his fame as a Marvel superhero, as his genuine, engaging personality is a large part of his appeal, both to the public, and to his fellow actors.

Nocturnal Mercury in Munakara: Kurt Cobain and Dave Grohl

Kurt Cobain and David Grohl were both members of the supergroup, Nirvana, and together they created *Nevermind*, the 1991 album which became one of the most iconic albums in rock music history. Kurt Cobain's munakara Mercury sequence features three planets heavily influenced by the rules of Essential Dignity. Cobain's Mercury in Pisces is debilitated in this sign being both in detriment and in fall; Mercury's dispositor, Jupiter is exalted in Cancer, and the Moon, the second nocturnal planet in Mercury's sequence, is in rulership in Cancer and in a wide conjunction to Jupiter, the planet it disposits in Cobain's chart. Dave Grohl survived the breakup of Nirvana after Cobain's death, and avoided the same fate as his fellow band member, continuing his career in the music industry and creating another legend in his longstanding band, Foo Fighters.

Life is about choices, and as a teenager encountering the destructive side of rock music fame in the 1990s, Grohl was careful to take a hard look at the excess, craziness, and chaos surrounding him, and took stock of its lethal consequences. In many ways, Grohl used his munakara Mercury to choose the exact opposite of his daily environment during this period in his life. Grohl was a rebel within a world of rebels, choosing a temperate existence in a world of excess, steadiness over craziness, and solitary song-writing amidst the chaos. Grohl chose separation instead – Saturn is his first dispositor – nurturing his creativity, and focusing on composing lyrics and melodies that witnessed others' pain, rather than experiencing it for himself.

For Grohl, song writing has always been munakara Mercury's release, and music has been his saviour in keeping his mind steady, whilst at the same time, his words express the darkness of Mercury's sequence planets, Saturn in Aries, and Mars in Scorpio. Grohl's autobiographical book is titled *The Storyteller* (2021) – a fitting title for a man with munakara Mercury – and his book tells the story of someone who has not only survived for decades in a crazy and often destructive industry, but has influenced more than one generation through his talent and his love of music.

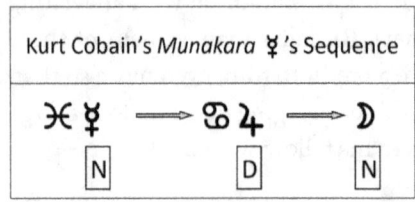
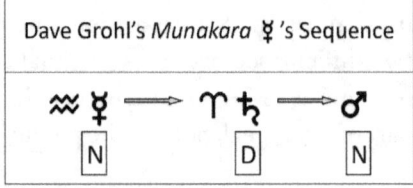

Table 13.8: *Munakara Tables for Kurt Cobain and Dave Grohl's Nocturnal Mercury*

Munakara Nocturnal Mercury: Kurt Cobain

A Brief Biography of Kurt Cobain

American rock musician Kurt Cobain (20th February 1967 – 5th April 1994) was born nine months after actor Mark Ruffalo, and two years before fellow Nirvana bandmate Dave Grohl. Cobain rose to fame as the lead vocalist, guitarist, primary songwriter, and founding member of the grunge band Nirvana.[45] He was heralded as a spokesman for Generation X, the wild children who followed the responsible Baby Boomers, and Cobain is widely recognised as one of the world's most influential alternative rock musicians.

Chapter Thirteen • *Munakara Mercury Delineations*

His parents divorced when Cobain was nine years old, and later he cites the divorce as having a profound effect on his life, turning him from a happy child into one who was angry, defiant and withdrawn.[46] In a 1993 interview, Cobain said he felt ashamed of his parents as a child and desperately wanted to have a "typical family...I wanted that security, so I resented my parents for quite a few years because of that."[47]

Cobain refused to live with his mother after the marriage breakup as she was in an abusive relationship with her new partner. Instead, he moved in with his father and his new wife and her two daughters by a previous relationship. When his stepmother gave birth to a baby boy in January 1979, Cobain's behaviour in their home became intolerable, and at high school it deteriorated into fighting and bullying other students. Cobain's mother, Wendy, granted full custody of her son to his father on June 28, 1979, but he could not cope with his wild son, and he placed him into the care of family and friends. Cobain moved between various relatives' houses, stayed with friends' parents, and occasionally slept under bridges, experimenting with drugs, and taking part in petty vandalism as his form of teenage rebellion.[48]

In one of his friend's family stays Cobain became a devout Christian and attended church services regularly. He later renounced Christianity, engaging in "anti-God" rants in his stage performances, but spirituality remained an important part of his personal life and beliefs.[49] Cobain loved to sketch and draw in his diaries, and he often used Christian imagery in his art work, along with developing an interest in Jainism and Buddhist philosophy.

Cobain founded Nirvana with Krist Novoselic and Aaron Burckhard in 1987. Burckhard was replaced by Chad Channing before the band released their debut album *Bleach* (1989), and Channing was replaced by Dave Grohl who was the drummer on their second album *Nevermind* (1991), an iconic album of 90s grunge music which became a worldwide hit. Although Cobain was hailed as the voice of his generation following Nirvana's sudden success, he was uncomfortable with this role.[50]

Cobain insisted that the music was more important than the lyrics in his songs, often changing the content and order of lyrics during his live performances.[51] He would describe his own lyrics as "a big pile of contradictions. They're split down the middle between very sincere opinions that I have, and sarcastic opinions and feelings that I have, and sarcastic and hopeful, humorous rebuttals towards cliché bohemian ideals that have been exhausted for years."[52]

During his years with Nirvana Cobain struggled with a heroin addiction, had chronic depression and suffered from crippling stomach pain which had begun in his childhood.[53] It is believed "the chronic pain exacerbated Kurt Cobain's mental health struggles, fuelling frustration, despair, and isolation. It strained his relationships and contributed to his sense of alienation. Even in his suicide note, Cobain hinted at the immense physical and emotional pain he suffered, referring to his "burning, nauseous stomach.""[54]

Diagnosed with ADHD in second grade, Cobain was prescribed Ritalin as a child, and in his teens, diagnosed with bipolar disorder. For Cobain, his mania manifested as high energy, rage, prolific creativity, and impulsive behaviour, evident in his art, performances, and personal life.[55] He had a lifelong struggle with bronchitis, made worse by his heavy tobacco and marijuana habit, and exacerbated by involuntary smoke from other band members, poorly ventilated pubs, and smoky music venues. He suffered from headaches, insomnia, weight and appetite loss, and fought constant exhaustion. There are theories that Cobain's use of heroin was not so much as a recreational drug than a desperate attempt to self-medicate his chronic pain and alleviate the physical torment he endured for almost two decades.[56]

He struggled with the pressure of fame, and was often in the spotlight for his tumultuous relationships, the final one ending in marriage in February 1992 to fellow musician Courtney Love, with whom he had a daughter named Frances.[57] In March 1994, Cobain overdosed on a combination of champagne and Rohypnol, subsequently undergoing an intervention and detox program. On April 8, 1994, he was found dead at his Seattle home at the age of 27, with police concluding that he had died around three days earlier from a self-inflicted shotgun wound to the head.

Pisces Mercury and Venus Duet in Munakara: Kurt Cobain

- **Key Questions:**
- What does Kurt Cobain's Mercury and Venus contend with?
- What is its driving force?
- What is its trigger? What is its outcome?

Essential dignity and debility is important to the planets in Cobain's duet, and Pisces is a critical sign for both Venus and Mercury, who do not necessarily make good bedfellows. Pisces works well for Venus as its exaltation sign, as a planet representing love, comfort, beauty, popularity

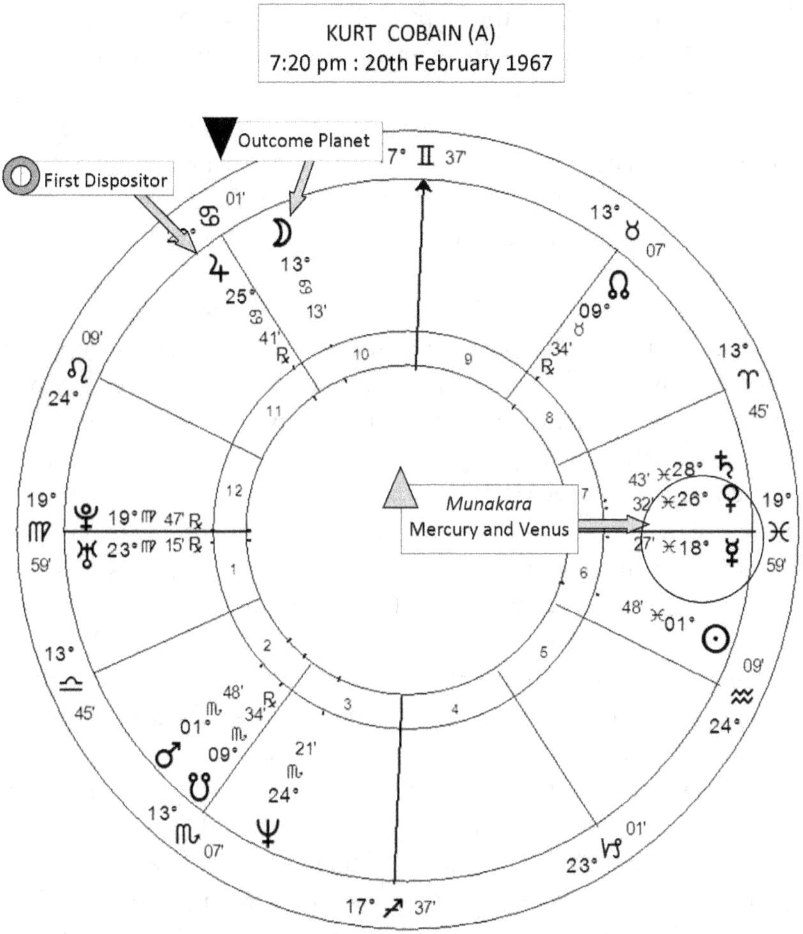

Chapter Thirteen • *Munakara Mercury Delineations*

Fig. 13.3: Kurt Cobain Natal Chart: Nocturnal Mercury in Munakara

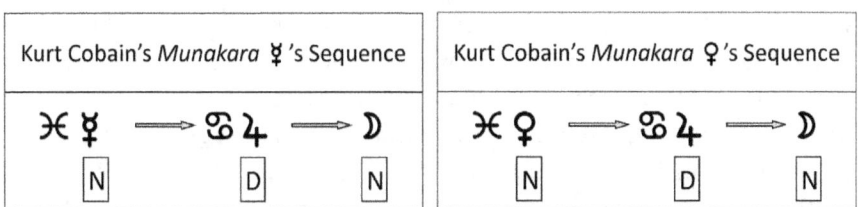

Table 13.9: Kurt Cobain: Nocturnal Mercury and Venus Munakara Sequence

and sexual pleasures gives the impression that these themes should be a constant source of happiness and contentment for the individual. However, munakara Venus dispositied by Jupiter shows attachments that can strangle and bind, and this was Cobain's experience of unrelenting admiration from strangers who loved a man that simply didn't exist in reality. Even in the halls of fame, Cobain was surrounded by sadness and loneliness, and it seems the more he was exalted as a rock star, the less he liked the man he became as a result of his success.

Munakara Mercury is in fall and detriment in Pisces, and Cobain's mind did not have clarity, self-expression or self-awareness, when the topic came to anything outside the realms of music. Music gave him the freedom to communicate his thoughts and feelings, but it frustrated him as well. He had no clear vision of what he wanted to accomplish, and his lyrics were more angry incoherent rants, than well thought out prose or insightful self-examination. Granted, this was the music of his era, and he was a clever showman who used shock tactics as his stage tricks, but off-stage, Kurt barely spoke a word to anyone, and never shared his thoughts with band members or those closest to him in his revolving round of relationships. Saturn conjunct Venus kept everyone at arm's length, and perhaps he was terrified that if they saw the real person behind the mask (munakara Mercury), they would desert him, in the same way as his parents had done in his childhood.

Kurt Cobain's life began to fall apart at the age of nine when his parents separated and divorced. From then into his early adult years munakara Mercury and Venus became escape mechanisms whenever he felt alone, neglected by his parents, or hopelessly lost in his misery. Although Cobain began daily drug use to alleviate chronic stomach pain, it also soothed his feelings of social isolation, and as his dreams of fame started to manifest, heroin gave him a sense of peace and solace from the world's encroaching demands on him. When fame beyond his wildest dreams did arrive, Cobain found hated the attention as suddenly he lost the things he truly cherished – a sacred space for his song-writing, and privacy to play his guitar – these were things that provided him with temporary peace, escape, and purpose. The nature of contention is that it should come with a warning label – 'be careful what you ask for, you just might get it' – and Cobain is an example of reaching your peak too early, and wondering where on Earth, to go from there.

The two nocturnal planets in Pisces are a duet as both Mercury and Venus will be disposited by Jupiter in exaltation in Cancer, and the third planet involved in their sequence will be the Moon, which is twelve degrees away from Jupiter in its own sign. Jupiter, first dispositor and the Moon, outcome planet, are in wide conjunction and this sequence describes the incredible rise to fame that Cobain experienced, along with his inability to deal with the intensity of his emotions. Jupiter Moon occupies both the 10th (Placidus) and 11th (Whole Sign) houses and Cobain's mental health (Mercury) and physical health (Moon) were fragile commodities throughout his life. Jupiter rules the 7th house, and its position at the top of the chart, along with the Moon, suggests that the world witnessed this talented and tragic musician spiralling out of control through constant self-abuse. Even if anyone had cared to help him – and his trips to rehabilitation showed that somebody did care – others were happy to capitalize on his misery (Jupiter ruling 7th house), too greedy, too dependent, or too in awe of his fame to want to stop the Kurt Cobain gravy train.

Munakara Planet and Sect Condition – how comfortable is Mercury and Venus Duet?

Munakara Venus is in better condition than its duet partner, Mercury. Venus in Pisces has exaltation in this sign, and its sect condition is excellent as it complies with all three sect rules: the chart (nocturnal), the hemisphere is opposite to the Sun's hemisphere (nocturnal) and Venus is in a feminine sign. Venus is in *hayz*, the term used when all three rules are successfully achieved. Robert Hand says Venus in a nocturnal chart or nocturnally placed would be "the more traditional Venus, soft, feminine, etc. A woman with such placement would be such a woman. A male with such a Venus would have a preference for such women."[58] Cobain described himself as being "feminine" in childhood, and often wore dresses and other stereotypically feminine clothing. When asked in 1992 if he was gay, Cobain replied, "If I wasn't

Kurt Cobain — ☿'s Sect Dignity			
Planet	Sect 1 Status	Sect 2 Hemisphere	Sect 3 Sign
♓ ☿	Night	With the Sun	Water
N	N	D	N

Kurt Cobain — ♀'s Sect Dignity			
Planet	Sect 1 Status	Sect 2 Hemisphere	Sect 3 Sign
♓ ♀	Night	No Sun	Water
N	N	N	N

Table 13.10: Kurt Cobain: Nocturnal Mercury and Venus in Munakara, Sect and Sequence

attracted to Courtney (Love), I'd be bisexual."⁵⁹ Normally Robert Hand's delineations on sect give an insight into how a planet whose environment is in perfect union with its nature might gain the advantage of manifesting its full potential. Our assumption that 'full potential' equates to 'positive expression' needs to be checked, and I am reminded of Robert Zoller's words in the mid 1990s, "a happy planet does not necessarily mean a happy person."

In the case of munakara Venus in excellent sect condition, I am inclined to believe that conditions were perfect for this otherwise unknown musician to take the world by storm, especially after the release of Nirvana's second album, *Nevermind*. Cobain encapsulated the lost innocence of Generation X, and he played a major role in its rebranding as a cynical, disaffected generation. In the 1990s Gen X were in their teens and their strong social-tribal identity found expression in music genres such as punk, post-punk, rave, grunge and heavy metal; music to describe their juvenile rage at society's norms and the complacent generation of Baby Boomers that preceded them.

Simply due to the environment at that time, Kurt Cobain's exalted Venus in *hayz* plucked him from obscurity, and elevated him to rock star status, with Venus's conjunction to Saturn and Mercury, in opposition to Gen X's synodic cycle of Pluto Uranus. Cobain's profanity, his insolence, his open drug use, his scruffiness, and his careless attitude that seemed to denigrate his fans, were a panacea to Gen X's passion for shocking their elders and rejecting old values.

Munakara Mercury in Pisces fares slightly worse than Venus in its condition (in detriment and fall), and although the nocturnal chart suits Mercury, the planet had just set after Cobain's birth Mercury was travelling with the Sun below the horizon, and therefore is denied both conditions of *halb* (Rule 2 of sect) and *hayz* (Rules 1, 2, and 3 of sect).

Munakara Mercury and Venus Duet: Kurt Cobain

Nirvana's co-founder, Krist Novaselic once wrote: "He (Kurt) talked about how ugly he thought he was all of the time. I remember the day he looked in a mirror and almost shed a tear because he was so uncomfortable in his own skin. He was really insecure..."⁶⁰

Munakara Mercury and Venus in Pisces in 7th House

Kurt Cobain's stellium in Pisces contains two diurnal planets, Sun and Saturn, and two nocturnal planets, Mercury and Venus, both with very different essential dignity statements. All four planets disposit to an exalted

Chapter Thirteen • *Munakara Mercury Delineations*

Jupiter, with Cancer belonging to the nocturnal Moon, but only two planets will follow through to a sequence that ends in munakara status.

Mercury is the Ascendant Lord and the ruler of Kurt's Mid-heaven, and according to Ptolemy from 1st century CE, a man makes his own destiny when Virgo rises, and Gemini culminates ten signs away, bringing fulfilment and success, through Mercury's efforts: "If Virgo of Pisces be on the ascendant, the native will create his own dignity,"[61] and "Those having Virgo or Pisces rising will be the cause of their own authority."[62]

Mercury on an angle, and ruling both critical points in the chart, has the potential to gain attention through fame or notoriety, but it can also be destructive, especially when Mercury opposes the Ascendant in its debilitated state. The two years prior to 1967 (Cobain's year of birth) saw the beginning of the synodic cycle between Uranus and Pluto in Virgo, an explosive combination at the best of times, but not good when the ruler of Virgo is in opposition, and witnessing this cold mess. Uranus and Pluto coming together in a cold dry sign (Virgo) adds a calculating purpose to its chaos, and whilst it looks as the potentially violent outbursts are random and unplanned, there is usually an agenda and a desired result, which is about taking control (Pluto), or breaking down order to instigate sudden change for the mere sake of it (Uranus). Cobain put this insane, unpredictable energy to good use in his musical performances, but unfortunately, Pisces Mercury in contention did not have the power, or the will, to turn it off when he had left the stage.

The tight degrees between Ascendant, Mid-heaven and their joint ruler Mercury are best described by the unravelling of Kurt's life at age nine, when his mother (10th house) began divorce proceedings against his father (4th house, Mercury's dispositor). Don and Wendy Cobain were teenage sweethearts at Aberdeen High, and Wendy fell pregnant soon after graduation, giving birth to Kurt when she was nineteen. After the divorce Kurt's mother gained custody of Kurt and his younger sister, and although Don had never been a model father, Kurt was still torn between his two parents. Kurt scrawled this poem on his bedroom wall: "I hate Mom. I hate Dad. Dad hates Mom, Mom hates Dad, it simply makes you want to be sad."[63]

Two years before his parents' divorce, Kurt's Mercury was fighting to find balance and a place of acceptance. Seven-year-old Kurt was diagnosed as a hyperactive child (ADHD), and administered with Ritalin, a synthetic drug that stimulates the central nervous system. Ritalin was much in use in the 1970s, with little awareness at that time of the drug's side effects, which included anxiety, agitation, mood changes, insomnia, and stomach issues – all symptoms experienced by the young child whose home life was disintegrating around him. By the time Cobain was a teenager he was convinced that he had bi-polar disorder, and was self-medicating with every drug he could lay his hands on.

Cobain disappeared from the Exodus Recovery Centre where he was undergoing a detox program on 30th March 1994. Nial Stimson, his final counsellor at the Centre said: "Addiction is part of mental illness, and he (Cobain) was definitely suffering some kind of mental illness."[64] One week later his body was discovered at his home by an electrician who had come to install a security system. A suicide note was found next to the body alongside a shotgun which Cobain used to shoot himself. The note was addressed to 'Boddah', his imaginary friend from his childhood and said: "This note should be pretty easy to understand....I haven't felt the excitement of listening to as well as creating music along with reading and writing for too many years now. I feel guilty beyond words about these things."[65]

The second nocturnal planet in munakara is exalted Venus in Pisces, and its conjunction to Saturn, and opposing the Pluto Uranus conjunction on the Ascendant, has the potential to feel alienated from others (Saturn Venus in 7th house). Instant fame and adoration may be munakara Venus's pipe dream when it is in a water Grand Trine with exalted Jupiter and Neptune in Scorpio. But for Kurt Cobain, the reality was cruel, jarring, and intrusive, particularly for a strange, shy boy who was isolated from his family, and who had few genuine friends.

> "When you're in the public eye you have no choice but to be raped over and over again – they'll take every ounce of blood out of you until you're exhausted. Well...it won't last. I'm looking forward to the future. It will only be another year and then everyone will forget about it."[66] – Kurt Cobain, *Flipside* 78 (1992 May–June)

Exalted Venus and Debilitated Mercury in 7th House

"Now he's gone and joined that stupid club. I told him not to...." – Kurt Cobain's mother, Wendy, after being told of his death (in reference to the 27 Club)

Three women now control the publicity rights to Cobain's name and image: his mother Wendy, his sister Kimberley, and his daughter Frances Bean Cobain. In 2018 the trio organised an exhibition of Kurt's childhood possessions in Ireland called *Growing Up Kurt Cobain*. In an interview to promote the exhibition Frances praises the normality her grandmother Wendy, and her Aunt Kimberley, gave to her early life.

"Nothing was consistent in my day to day life at all but when I would go to the farm in Olympia it was the most grounding experience."[67] Saturn, ruler of Kurt's 5th house, is conjunct Venus, so perhaps the trio of women show the control that Cobain could never access during his own lifetime.

Situated in the same sign as Mercury, munakara Venus also disposits to Jupiter which then passes to Moon through Cancer. Unlike Mercury, Venus is exalted, but the idea of powerful women who controlled him may have been irksome for Cobain when he was alive. Cobain's experience of munakara Venus is demonstrated by his shyness and his lack of social skills, his horror and fascination with being loved by strangers, the majority of whom had no clue of his insecurities, and by the women who played the role of enabler to his self-destructive tendencies.

Cobain resented the fact that he became an icon, believing that the public had misrepresented his artistic talents, and cheapened the messages which underpinned his music. When *Nevermind* was under production, Cobain tagged it with the working title *Sheep*, a sly dig directed at the people he expected to obediently line up to buy the album, simply because they were fans of Nirvana. In his journal he wrote a fake advertisement for *Sheep* with the slogan: "Because you want to not (buy it); because everyone else is."[68]

Women chose him, rather than the other way around. When they ended the relationship – possibly because the man was vastly different from the idol – it reinforced Cobain's self-loathing, and reminding him of his mother's abandonment when he was as child. He was fascinated with the feminist 'riot grrrl' scene, and when he first met Bikini Kills vocalist, Tobi Vail, his anxiety was so great that he vomited afterwards. He was devastated when she lost interest in him, when he wanted a more traditional relationship. Courtney Love (ironic stage name considering his munakara Venus) was the driving force behind their relationship, and soon after they went public, his family members spoke disparagingly about his new love interest, claiming cynically that she wanted to accelerate her own fame through association with Cobain. Courtney is still not finished with him, announcing in 2022 the completion of her memoirs, *The Girl with the Most Cake*, and featuring details of her and Cobain's marriage, but a release date for publication has yet to be decided.[69]

Kurt Cobain already had two loves in his life, and women were either appendages, or passing infatuations. The two *femme fatales* who demanded his time, his energy and his devotion were music and drugs. He lived and died for both passions, and whilst his relationship with Courtney Love cultivated a frenzy of media attention, and spawned countless interviews and articles, Kurt was never classified as 'a ladies' man.

His excesses were self-destructive, and with both Venus and Jupiter in exaltation, they led to extremes of hedonism that can only be understood by those who lived (and survived) the late 1990s rockstar life. Once more the Cancer Moon in rulership is the outcome planet for Venus, and even though his physical and emotional excesses were long-term habits, a Moon in rulership resists destruction even after years of drug use.

First Dispositor: Jupiter in Cancer in 11th House

Jupiter's exaltation in Cancer can bring good fortune, but in Cobain's chart Jupiter is out of sect, suggesting discomfort and embarrassment in equal measures of happiness at receiving Fortuna's benefits. Exalted Jupiter trines the two planets it disposits – Mercury and Venus – and also manages to pick up Saturn in the trine aspect. However, Neptune's presence in Scorpio completes a Grand Trine in water, and this is not particularly stable for either munakara Mercury or Venus. Neptune tends to give munakara Venus big dreams that result in disappointment or disillusionments, and Neptune, even in a so-called 'easy aspect' such as trine, confuses Mercury, particularly when it is in contention, as it struggles to create order in its thoughts, or to objectively find sound problem-solving techniques.

Jupiter's involvement in Cobain's water Grand Trine, is unlikely to clarify these thoughts, or aid in the discipline or regulation of any of the strategies mentioned earlier in munakara Mercury's personal challenges, any of which might help to gain mental clarity. Rather, Jupiter will amplify the problems, and its exaltation will involve Cancer Moon's powerful involvement in Cobain's mental and emotional landscape. The Moon is *hayz* in Cobain's chart, and it certainly relished the high-octane life of a rock star, but it also accentuated his pain, and its approaching conjunction to Jupiter did little to bring emotional balance or self-control.

When exalted Jupiter is a planet's dispositor, it can go in one of two ways: Jupiter may improve a situation and create opportunities for the planet in its sign, or it may exacerbate an everyday situation, and amplify it into an overwhelming problem, with an even worse solution. Kurt's Jupiter rules the two angles which oppose Mercury's 1st and 10th houses, that is, the 7th (relationships) and 4th house (father's house). Kurt's father was a bully who had little time for his sensitive artistic son. Don Cobain's solution was to 'toughen up' his son by enrolling him in the junior high school wrestling team, and then the baseball team when Kurt failed miserably at wrestling.

Exalted Jupiter in Cancer ruling father's house (4th) shows Kurt's desperation to be loved by his father and to be acknowledged as a complex and sensitive soul who needed gentle guidance and acceptance, not tough love. When Don remarried, he had another son in 1979 and Kurt felt replaced, 'something in the way': the title of a song written by him when he ran away from home, and performed years later by his super-group, Nirvana. Kurt's mother also remarried after her divorce, but her new husband was violent, cruel and sadistic, and Curt often witnessed his mother's fear and misery in her new relationship.

A family history of odd behaviour and violent death created a bloodline of mental issues that fed Cobain's fascination with death and suicide. Cancer Jupiter ruling 4th house, produced a great-grandfather on his mother's side whose life ended in a mental hospital from a self-inflicted wound. A great-grandfather on his father's side had been a county sheriff, who allegedly died when his pistol fell to the ground and dislodged a bullet killing him instantly. Two of the sheriff's sons chose suicide by gunshot and all his life Cobain believed there were 'suicide genes' in his family.

Introverted, shy, and often physically wasted from heroin addiction, Kurt came to life when he stepped onstage. Nirvana's performances are where Kurt Cobain shone, and where Mercury and Venus' dispositor came into its exaltation, as Jupiter's position in 11th house is the place where Jupiter finds its joy. For a short period in the right atmosphere, a different persona took over. Cobain became a wild, crazy man whose passion for grunge rocketed him to fame. Rather than ecstatic passion initiated by music, his audience was really witnessing munakara Mercury in the form of bipolar disorder – crazed body jerking and freakish behaviour borne of uncontrolled rage bordering on madness, and they loved it (munakara Venus) and couldn't get enough. After the shows Cobain would retreat into a semi-catatonic state fuelled by alcohol and heroin. Success gave him no respite from his self-loathing, writing in his journal in 1990: "I am obsessed with the fact that I am skinny and stupid."[70]

Exalted Jupiter also rules Kurt Cobain's 7th house of relationships where his Pisces stellium is situated. His most famous relationship with Courtney Love was his last, but she was more a convenient heroin supplier than a beloved muse. Before Courtney entered his life, Cobain was infatuated with Tobi Vail. Her rejection inspired the iconic songs on *Nevermind*

(1991), the album which was described in 2004 as "culturally, historically, and aesthetically important", and the album has lost none of its potency, frequently being ranked high on lists of the greatest albums of all time. The destructive pairing of Courtney and Kurt consumed the media, especially when *Vanity Fair* claimed that Courtney had continued her heroin habit when she was pregnant with their daughter Frances, born in August 1992, eighteen months before her father's death by suicide.[71]

The outcome planet: Moon in Cancer

Cobain's Cancer Moon trines munakara Mercury, and is in an applying conjunction to Jupiter, and his nine-year-old body reacted to the stress of his family' break-up even before he could understand its impact on his life, and his emotional disturbances transferred to physical ailments. He began complaining of stomach pains which continued into adulthood, and his initial use of heroin was to ease the pain. In 1989 Cobain consulted several gastroenterologists who could find nothing more than 'an inflamed irritation' in his gut to explain his persistent stomach pain. Cobain wrote in his journal: "I decided to use heroin on a daily basis because of an ongoing stomach ailment that I have been suffering from for the past five years that had literally taken me to the point of wanting to kill myself. For five years every single day of my life."[72]

Kurt's relationship with his mother, Wendy, was often strained, and for a number of years they did not communicate with each other. Cobain's Cancer Moon was in rulership but this fact rarely guarantees an easy access to love and acceptance from the planet representing mother. Rather, mother is a *big figure in the psyche*, and the individual with Cancer Moon can spend a lifetime reconciling the reality of mother's behaviour, with the planet's expectations of perfection from nurturing figures.

When Kurt had been an unmanageable teenager, newly re-married Wendy had thrown her son out of the family home, causing him to live on the streets until a school friend took him home to live with his own family for a year. The boy's father, Lamont Schillinger, was an English teacher at Aberdeen High, and he recalls: "We never heard one word from his mom, dad, grandpa, anything"[73] even though the two houses were a short walk apart.

Fame can change people's behaviour (Cancer Moon trine munakara Mercury), and when Nirvana was touring Europe in November 1991, his mother Wendy, wrote to her local newspaper, letting them know of her familial connection to the famous Kurt Cobain, and including this cringe-

Chapter Thirteen • *Munakara Mercury Delineations*

worthy advice to her 24-year-old son, via the paper: "Kurt, if you happen to read this, we are so proud of you and you are truly one of the nicest sons a mother could have. Please don't forget to eat your vegetables or brush your teeth and now you can have your maid make your bed."[74]

At the time Wendy was publicly giving mum's advice to her travelling son, he and Courtney were using heroin daily, after accelerating the habit in Amsterdam where drugs were easy to obtain whilst they were on the road. Returning from the tour in December, Kurt overdosed, and would continue to do so several times during the remaining two and a half years of his life.

Nirvana's second studio album *Nevermind* was released in September 1991, two months before the European tour and became one of the most acclaimed and influential albums of all time. The album is quintessential Cobain, given that he wrote the lyrics to all songs on the album, and suggesting *Nevermind*'s legendary cover, a naked baby boy swimming towards a US dollar bill. Cobain gave the album its title because it was a metaphor for his attitude to life, and because it was deliberately grammatically incorrect (munakara Mercury), and was his gesture of defiance to the Establishment. For all intents and purposes, *Nevermind* was Kurt Cobain's emotional baby, created after a relationship break-up and with lyrics described as 'dark, humorous and disturbing.'[75] Its success was his undoing.

Twelve degrees separate Cancer Moon from Jupiter, but the connection between first dispositor and outcome planet is strong, and emotive themes such as sexism, frustration, loneliness, sickness, and troubled love abound,[76] often with lyrics finished moments before recording. Cobain told Dave Grohl that when he wrote, "Music comes first and lyrics come second" and critics complained that Cobain's singing made the lyrics indistinct and difficult to understand. The album's producer Butch Vig admitted the truth of this after its release "Even though you couldn't quite tell what he was singing about, you knew it was intense as hell."[77] During the recording of *Nevermind*, there was a frailty to Cobain's mental health, and Vig noted that Kurt would be engaged and focused for an hour, and then he would withdraw physically and mentally, sitting in a corner of the studio, and saying nothing for the following hour.

The sequence of munakara duet, Mercury and Venus, goes through the process of incredible fame (Jupiter), but contention often involves heartbreak, struggle and metaphorical resurrection and sadly, Kurt Cobain's Moon (as the outcome planet) was not strong enough to cope with his sadness, his string of illnesses, his self-inflicted abuse, or his fascination with his family's so-called 'suicide gene' to live long enough to overcome his contentious issues.

Munakara Nocturnal Mercury: Dave Grohl

A Brief Biography of Dave Grohl[78]

David Grohl, born 14th January 1969, Is an American musician best known as the founder and lead singer of the alternative rock band Foo Fighters and the former drummer of the influential 1990s grunge rock band Nirvana. Grohl is known for his energy and musical proficiency, despite never having learned to read music. Groh is also a film director, initially directing music videos for Foo Fighters, and later moving to an interest in directing documentaries. He is considered one of the most influential rock musicians of his era. During his career, Grohl has won 17 Grammy Awards.

Grohl's mother was an English teacher and his father was a journalist. His parents divorced when he was age 6 and he lived with his mother and sister. At age 10 Grohl formed his first band with a friend and soon after he started to learn to play the guitar. At age 13, Grohl attended his first live punk concert in Chicago where he became fascinated by punk music, and endeavoured to teach himself to play the drums. After dropping out of high school in his junior year, he went on to become the drummer for Scream, an independent punk group based in Washington, DC.

In October 1990, Grohl was invited by rock musician Kurt Cobain to audition for the drums for a then unknown Seattle band named Nirvana. Grohl spent eight months living with Cobain, who was the band's front man and main songwriter. About the same time that Nirvana's fame was skyrocketing, Grohl was writing, recording, and playing all the instruments for his own demo project, resulting in the release of a cassette album in 1992.

After the death of Kurt Cobain in 1994, and the subsequent breakup of Nirvana, Grohl started a new project as the sole member of Foo Fighters. He played every instrument, and wrote and provided vocals on every song on the debut album, *Foo Fighters*, released in 1995. By 1997 he had recruited other musicians to complete the heavy punk rock sound he was seeking. The group's first studio album, *The Colour and the Shape* (1997) as an international success. The second album *There Is Nothing Left to Lose* (1999) won a Grammy Award for best rock album in 2000.

In 2009 Grohl launched his supergroup Them Crooked Vultures, which along with himself, featured band members from Queens of the Stone Age and Led Zeppelin. In 2012, the Foo Fighters announced they were taking a hiatus and Grohl returned to his second band Queens of the Stone Age as drummer for their 2013 album *Like Clockwork*. In the same year Grohl

Chapter Thirteen • *Munakara Mercury Delineations*

directed a documentary about the legendary Los Angeles recording studio Sound City. Foo Fighters continues to produce albums with their eleventh album *But Here We Are* (released in 2023) dedicated to Taylor Hawkins and Grohl's mother, Virginia, both of whom died in 2022. Dave Grohl's autobiography *The Storyteller: Tales of Life and Music* was released in 2021.

Introduction to *The Storyteller* (2021): "A collection of memories of a life lived loud. From my early days growing up in the suburbs of Washington, DC, to hitting the road at the age of 18, and all the music that followed, I can now share these adventures with the world, as seen and heard from behind the microphone. Turn it up!"

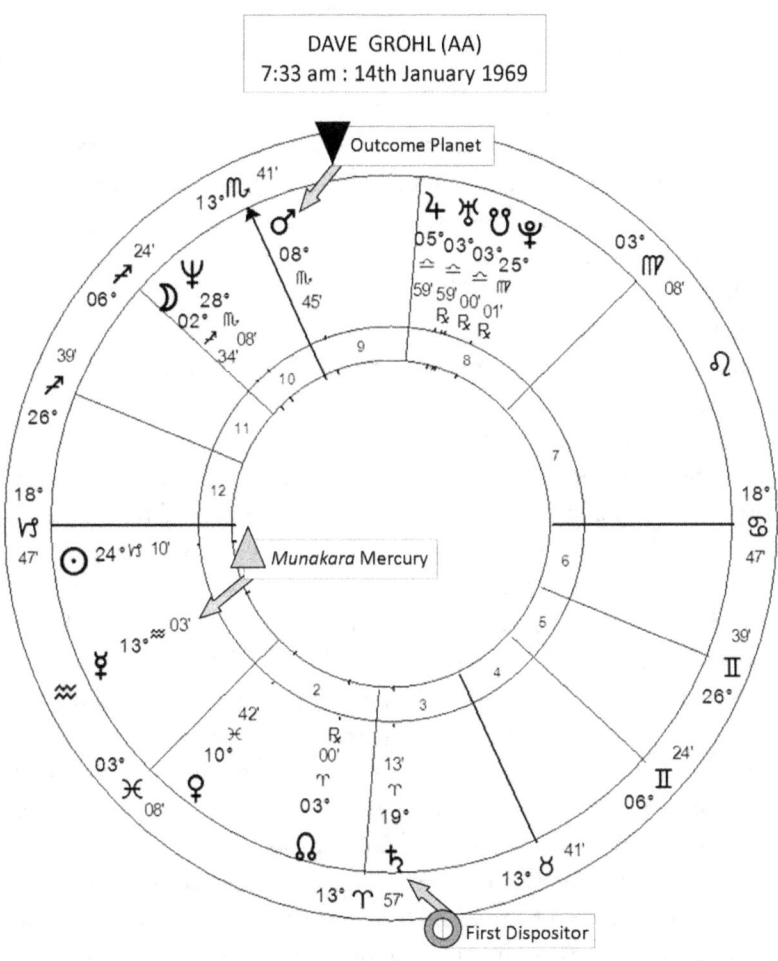

Fig. 13.4: Dave Grohl Natal Chart: Nocturnal Mercury in Munakara

Aquarius Mercury in Munakara: Dave Grohl

- **Key Questions:**
- What does Tee Corinne's Sun contend with?
- What is its driving force?
- What is its trigger? What is its outcome?

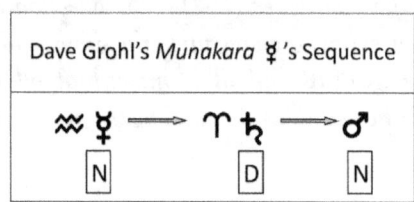

Table 13.11: Dave Grohl: Nocturnal Mercury in Munakara, Sect and Sequence

In *The Storyteller*, Grohl describes the moment early in puberty when the desire to become a musician became an obsession for him: "When your heart, mind, and soul cannot control or refuse the desire to create a sound, or lyric, or rhythm, and you are helpless against the burning impulse to purge these inner demons, you are forever committed to a lifetime of chasing the next song."[79]

A planet in contention often shows a disadvantage that the planet in munakara is called to overcome, or to find a different way to move through the impasse. In Dave Grohl's case munakara Mercury in Aquarius found a vision that he was desperate to bring into reality. His Mercury moves from 1st house (body and actions) in the Placidus system to 2nd house (finances) in the Whole Sign system. With no ability to read music, and no excess money from a struggling household to buy musical instruments, a young Grohl's mind developed a neurological condition known as synesthesia. Synesthesia occurs when one sense (hearing) is activated in synchronicity with another unrelated sense (vision), enabling the ability for Grohl to 'see' the music. Like Lego building blocks placed one row atop of the one below, Grohl's synesthesia (munakara Mercury in Aquarius) allowed him to focus on what he heard in his mind, and then to move to the mental process of constructing a visual image, one that would then crystallize his compositions and give him an invisible structure to his musical arrangements.

Grohl says that from an early age he played the drums with his teeth, sliding his jaw back and forth as he beat out a rhythm in his mouth without opening his lips. He also says that the only other person he had met in his life who did a similar thing was fellow musician, Kurt Cobain, who used an

Chapter Thirteen • *Munakara Mercury Delineations*

internal metronome to constantly play his guitar in his mind, through moving his jaw to the imaginary beat playing in his head.

In Grohl's opinion each musician feels the music differently, 'It is something divine that only the universe can create, like a heartbeat or a star'[80] but for both Nirvana members, the music needed no instrument, but was as natural to their bodies as it was to their mind and soul.

Saturn is munakara Mercury's dispositor, and Grohl watched firsthand the disintegration and death of his friend, idol, and fellow band member Kurt Cobain. Grohl's song *Friend of a friend* was performed after Cobain's death by his new band the Foo Fighters, but it was written much earlier in 1990 when he was new to Nirvana and staying in Kurt's Olympia apartment after he left Seattle to join the band. The track is about his first impressions of Nirvana's frontman, Kurt Cobain, and bassist Krist Novoselic, who was devoted to Cobain and was deeply concerned about his friend's unravelling sanity.

Whilst still reeling from Cobain's death, Grohl withdrew and travelled through Europe in the months following Nirvana's disbandment. Whilst in Ireland he picked up a young hitchhiker who happened to be wearing a Kurt Cobain T-shirt, and Grohl realised there was nowhere on Earth he could go to avoid his past.[81] After he returned home, Grohl's munakara Mercury moved quickly, and Foo Fighters was created within months as a one-man project, named by Grohl after the nickname given to unexplained flying objects (UFOs) by fighter pilots when spotting something unusual during their flights (Mars, outcome planet).

Friend of a friend revived Grohl's career after Cobain's death and Nirvana's disbandment. Saturn's dispositor, Mars, is in rulership and on the Midheaven, and Mars fought to establish Grohl as a musician, independent from Cobain, and to take him out of the shadows of his former bandmate to cement his own reputation in the music industry.

In a 2010 interview Grohl admitted Foo Fighters was never intended to stay as a permanent band name: 'Around the time that I recorded the first Foo Fighters tape, I was reading a lot of books on UFO's. Not only is it a fascinating subject, but there's a treasure trove of band names in those UFO books!' Then adding ruefully, 'Had I considered this to be a career, I probably would have called it something else, because it's the stupidest **** band name in the world.'[82] Grohl recorded fifteen of his own songs, and the first Foo Fighters album was released in 1995, with a full band needing to be hastily assembled to accommodate the demand to tour and to record future albums under the same name.

Munakara Planet and Sect Condition – how comfortable is Mercury?

Dave Grohl's Mercury in Aquarius sits beneath the horizon with his Capricorn Sun in a nocturnal chart. Both planets are disposited by Saturn, but only one of them is nocturnal (Mercury), and therefore capable of being in munakara state. Aquarius does not sit well for nocturnal Mercury, which would prefer feminine signs, either water or earth, for sect compatibility.

Dave Grohl — ☿ 's Sect Dignity			
Planet	Sect 1 Status	Sect 2 Hemisphere	Sect 3 Sign
♒ ☿	Night	With the Sun	Air
N	N	D	D

Table 13.12: Dave Grohl: Nocturnal Mercury in Munakara, Sect Dignity

Mercury connects with its dispositor (Saturn) through a sextile aspect, but Saturn's condition in Aries (fall), may cause some issues for Mercury, and these issues may be concerning feelings of inadequacy, when it comes to hearing, communicating, or understanding the nature of one's environment. Saturn's harsh qualities are alleviated by its own situation in the chart – in *halb* and in correct masculine sign – and Robert Hand is inclined to believe that Saturn with some sect dignity 'increases its energy levels, improves its masculinity to be steady and constant, and gives Saturn the ability to define and set goals that are worthy, capable and reachable.'[83]

The third planet in Mercury's sequence is Mars, strengthened by being in its own sign by essential dignity, in a nocturnal chart and in *halb*, and positioned as the most elevated planet, conjunct the Mid-heaven, and ruling it. Mars' situation will surely improve Saturn's plight, as even though Saturn is in fall in Aries, it is disposted by a powerful Mars, and this should help Saturn to rise again (like the Phoenix), even after it has suffered a fall of some note. Falls are spectacular with Mars like this, but so too are the resurrections.

Munakara Mercury: Dave Grohl

"Miraculously, my memory has remained relatively intact ....My mind faithfully relies on songs, albums, and bands to remember a particular time and place. From seventies AM radio to every microphone I've stood before, I could tell you who, what, where, and when from the first few notes of any song that has crept from a speaker to my soul. Or from my soul to your speakers." – Dave Grohl, Introduction to *The Storyteller*

Chapter Thirteen • *Munakara Mercury Delineations*

Munakara Mercury Nocturnal in Aquarius in 1st House (Placidus)

Dave Grohl is a survivor in the tumultuous world of rock and roll music. He began his career as a seventeen-year-old drummer, touring the US and Europe with Scream, and became the third member of Nirvana when Scream disbanded in 1990. Grohl was not the original drummer, as Nirvana had recorded their debut album *Bleach* with drummer Chad Channing, but Grohl was the final Nirvana member who created a magical trio, a trio of musicians responsible for *Nevermind*, one of the most significant albums in modern music history. Krist Novoselic, the third member of Nirvana, has both his diurnal Sun, and nocturnal Mars in a state of munakara, but it is the comparison of nocturnal Mercury, in the two nocturnal charts of Kurt Cobain, and Dave Grohl, which I felt would best demonstrate the diversity of expression for the same planet in contention.

Dave Grohl's Mercury is a perfect example that not all munakara planets need to be draped in sacrifice or tragedy. Both Kurt and Dave came from the experience of divorced parents – Kurt at age nine and Dave at age six – but the impact was different for both boys. Both musicians experienced loneliness, and felt at odds with other children, using their passion for music to banish their insecurities and give them a feeling of belonging. Both boys had little academic interest, and left school to pursue their dreams to become a rock star, and together they achieved that aim when Nirvana's *Nevermind* was released in 1991. But here the similarities end, as Mercury's sign and dispositor differ, as does its house placement, and the houses it rules through its signs of Gemini and Virgo.

A mid-January birth finds Grohl's Mercury in Aquarius, and with his time of birth, places Mercury in the 1st house by Placidus, but moving to the 2nd house by Whole Sign. Unlike Kurt's Mercury opposition to the Uranus Pluto conjunction, Dave's Mercury has no aspectual relationship with the separating synodic cycle, but it does square his outcome planet, Mars, in its munakara sequence.

Nocturnal Mercury in munakara rules Grohl's 5th and 6th houses (Placidus) and 6th house (Whole Sign), and one of the serious effects of being an entertainer in the vicinity of constant and excessive music over decades, has meant that Dave Grohl suffers from deafness. For years he has relied on lip-reading as a necessary skill to compensate for his loss of hearing. He says that his ears are "still tuned in to certain frequencies, meaning he is still able to pick up on minute sonic details – even down to the slightest differences between cymbal crashes."[84]

Munakara Mercury also rules Grohl's Whole Sign 9th house, and Grohl has spent years touring every continent across the globe. "I was 17 and extremely anxious to see the world, so I did."[85] His Sagittarian Moon is also in munakara and Grohl frequently speaks about how much he feels the separation from his wife and children in the months when he is touring. The pull between the lifestyle he has to pursue his passion for music and the emotional angst he feels when he misses precious time away from his loved ones.

First Dispositor: Saturn in Aries in fall

Munakara Mercury moves to the 2nd house of finances in the Whole Sign system, and Saturn ruling this house shows the tough financial circumstances under which his mother, Virginia, laboured as a single mother raising two children in the 1970s. Grohl maintained a close loving relationship with his mother until her death in 2022, and his appreciation for her sacrifices are a strong theme running throughout *The Storyteller*. Fiduciary hardship is shown by Saturn, Mercury's dispositor, in fall in Whole Sign's 4th house (a missing figure in father's house). However, the sextile aspect between Mercury and Saturn eases his early memories, as his book focuses more on his treasured experiences of childhood friendships and joyous summers of freedom, than on his family's adversity, or his difficult relationship with his father.

Nor was joining Nirvana an instant ticket to wealth and fame, as he and Kurt shared a one-bedroom unit at the back of a dilapidated old house, Kurt claiming the bedroom, and Dave ensconced in a sleeping bag on an old brown couch. Saturn in fall in 4th house (Whole Sign) is the experience of cramped and squalid living conditions, but munakara Mercury describes how Grohl spent the first check as a paid member of Nirvana. Forget spending his $400 on food and basic necessities to relieve his poverty. Like any crazy 22-year-old who suddenly comes into the first payday of their professional life, Grohl blew the check on a BB gun, a Nintendo console, and the first of his many tattoos. "Our squalid den of filth was now transformed into an adolescent center from hell. To me, this was Versailles."[86]

Grohl touches upon a strained relationship with a distant and judgmental father in his book. Part of his determination to succeed as a musician is driven by his father's prophetic words "This will never last."[87] James Grohl, an award-winning journalist, had dreams of his son becoming an upstanding Republican businessman. Father and son were estranged for years as a result of James' disappointment. He feared that Dave's career in music would falter, once his moment faded and the public focused on a new rockstar.

Chapter Thirteen • *Munakara Mercury Delineations*

The outcome planet: Mars in Scorpio conjunct MC

Saturn may be in fall in Dave Grohl's chart, but Mars is elevated on the Mid-heaven, and is situated in its rulership sign of Scorpio. Both munakara Mercury and Mars (its outcome planet) celebrate the fact that Grohl's chart is nocturnal, and an accommodating environment that has served both planets well, as it has also served the Moon, which is the second planet that is munakara in Grohl's chart.

Grohl's frenetic drumming is a perfect outlet for Mars in Scorpio, and his chosen career has more in common with a battlefield born of fierce competition, sheer guts, enormous self-belief in one's talents, and an instinctive cunning that makes the right music to appeal to the right people at the right time. Nirvana's albums gave birth to the term 'grunge', and the trio not only hated the label, but also the fact that ironically, instant fame was tantamount to 'fitting in' with society, thereby robbing them of their rebellion, and replacing it with mainstream popularity.

However, it was Dave Grohl who would adapt the most comfortably to their success, and grow beyond it, putting his mark on his own music after Kurt's death and the disintegration of Nirvana. Kurt Cobain wasn't as lucky as Grohl: he did not have a strong planet, in good dignity, ruling his own MC as debilitated munakara Mercury ruled Cobain's Mid-heaven and Mercury was besieged by difficult planets, Saturn, Uranus and Pluto. Sadly, Cobain floundered rather than thrived under the intense media attention, retreating further into drug addiction and depression, and finally fulfilling his obsession with death by committing suicide on April 5, 1994.

Sagittarius Moon in Munakara: Dave Grohl

- **Key Questions:**
- What does Tee Corinne's Sun contend with?
- What is its driving force?
- What is its trigger? What is its outcome?

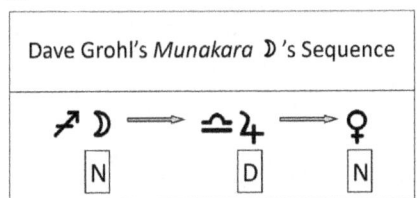

Table 13.13: Dave Grohl: Munakara Moon's Sequence

Dave Grohl was born two years after Kurt Cobain, and in this time, Uranus had moved away from Pluto in Virgo, and Jupiter had caught up with Uranus in early degrees of Libra. With two years dividing their births, the boys were both members of Generation X, but Grohl's signature synodic cycle – Jupiter / Uranus – is still rebellious, but it differs from Cobain's heavier, and potentially more destructive, Uranus / Pluto conjunction.

Grohl's munakara Moon is disposited by Jupiter, and the synodic cycle between Jupiter and Uranus may explain why Dave Grohl's Moon has been more resilient in adapting to his family's breakdown. Kurt Cobain's inability to accept the change and move on from similar circumstances may be one of the signatures of his Uranus / Pluto opposition to his munakara Mercury.

The first person described by Dave Grohl's munakara Moon is his mother, whose challenge lay in being a single, divorced woman in the 1970s, raising a family on her own on a modest teacher's wage. His mother had no desire to remarry and relieve her financial situation by adding another income to the home – at the same time forfeiting her independence and freedom – and this may be due to the fact that the Moon's dispositor, Jupiter, is conjunct Uranus in the Whole Sign 10th house, the house of mother.

Grohl would have watched his mother's constant struggle, and perhaps compared it to his father's easier (and more lucrative) road as an award-winning journalist who served as the special assistant to Republican Senator Robert Taft Jr. Grohl's later success as a highly paid musician finally provided his mother with financial security, and a home of comfort and beauty, a fact of which Grohl is extremely proud.

Grohl's Moon rules 7th house, and his driving force has been to pursue the career he loves, at the same time as providing love and security for his wife and partner. Grohl is the proud father of three young girls, and his family is his pride and joy. The sextile aspect between the Moon and its dispositor, Jupiter, is a gift that keeps on giving, provided the Moon has the freedom to express itself, and Grohl is encouraged to keep touring, rather than feel guilty about missing his parental and partnership responsibilities. Keeping him as a free-roaming musician is a wise decision on his partner's part, as this is when he is at his emotional peak, even though contention for his Moon means he is torn between his two loves: music and his five girls – mother, wife and three daughters.

Grohl has been happily married to his wife Jordyn for over two decades and his eldest daughter, Violet, has performed with her father on several occasions. Her first professional appearance as a musician occurred in 2018 when Violet was 12 years old. In 2022 she participated in tribute shows to Foo Fighter's late drummer Taylor Hawkins that took place in Wembley – singing Jeff Buckley's "Last Goodbye" – and in Inglewood, California – singing a cover of "Hallelujah."[88]

The Moon's sequence incorporates Jupiter and Venus, and the Moon has no issue with either its first dispositor (Jupiter), or its outcome planet (Venus). Jupiter is just separating from Uranus which began in the previous December as a synodic cycle in Libra. Jupiter Uranus does not have the same dark centre as Uranus Pluto, but it still carries its own frenetic energy, and the world of rock music is a perfect foil for its erratic nature, provided the person carrying it is able to put their own restraints on its accelerated energy. In this case, the munakara Moon which is disposited by Jupiter, must find its own leveller, and Grohl has been extremely lucky (or well-balanced) to choose a partner in life who has supported his music career, and given him the stability at home, so that he might tour for months on end. Pisces Venus is exalted in Dave Grohl's nocturnal chart, but unlike Cobain's Venus, this is not in munakara state, as Jupiter and Venus are in each other's signs in generosity (rather than mutual reception), meaning there is no third planet involved in Venus' sequence.

Munakara Planet and Sect Condition – how comfortable is the Moon?

Dave Grohl's Moon is situated in a nocturnal chart and has the benefit of being in *halb* – travelling in the opposite hemisphere to the Sun. It does not receive full sect honours as it is not in *hayz* being in a masculine sign, Sagittarius, rather than its preferred feminine sign. The Moon in sect dignity is a source of strength, has strong mother connections, has more opportunity to find tranquillity in its environment, and success is achieved through embodying the aspirations of others and serving their needs.[89] The Moon's outcome planet, Venus, is also in sect and this dignity gives Venus the ability to draw people together in pleasure and harmony, supporting the unity principle of bringing Venus' products – music, rhythm, and enjoyment – to diverse groups of people.[90]

Dave Grohl — ☽'s Sect Dignity			
Planet	Sect 1 Status	Sect 2 Hemisphere	Sect 3 Sign
♐ ☽	Night	No Sun	Fire
N	N	N	D

Table 13.14: Dave Grohl: Munakara Moon, Sect Dignity

Munakara Moon: Dave Grohl

"There were certain things in my life that I relied on unconditionally and in which I had unwavering faith – the love of my mother, my love for her, and the love that filled my heart when I played music."[91]

Grohl's munakara Moon has several good omens in the chart, and this fact suggests the Moon has a stabilizing effect in his otherwise outrageously crazy life as a rock star icon. The chart is nocturnal and as such, the Moon is the prime luminary, plus the strengthening factor that the Moon is in the opposite hemisphere to the Sun (in *halb*). Two powerful sect conditions are met and the Moon's dialogue is set, 'So long as you follow your heart, nourish your dreams and fulfil your passions you will find your way in life.' The Moon rules the 7th house of relationships and although at first glance there seems to be aversion between the two signs of Sagittarius and Cancer, the gift of contra-antiscia – equal rising times – allows for the Moon to govern its house. After a few initial heartbreaks and a failed first marriage, Dave Grohl's Moon found the person he was seeking in Jordyn Blum, his wife of almost twenty years.

In Jordyn, the mother of his three daughters, he was able to find someone who could nurture his Sagittarian Moon's love of music, whilst not feeling resentful of his long periods of time away from home touring with Foo Fighters. Even though Dave Grohl's history is unique to him, the theme of being caught between two passions seems to be a common thread in the stories of munakara Moon. In Grohl's case, the two benefic planets in Moon's sequence are not difficult planets for the lunar luminary, and both Jupiter (Moon's dispositor) and nocturnal Venus (outcome planet) are favourably placed in his chart, thereby avoiding a great deal of angst for this munakara Moon. His Moon certainly shows his mother's struggles when her children were young, and the physical exhaustion of working three jobs to keep afloat, but her frustrations did not infringe on her relationship with her son. Grohl says that his mother is, and always has been, his best friend.

"I like to say now that she [his mother] disciplined me with freedom by allowing me to wander, to find my path, and ultimately find myself."[92]

Perhaps one of the most conclusive indicators for the combination of both nocturnal Mercury, and the Moon in munakara, is the effect they have had on Grohl's hearing. Moon, the significator for the body, plus Mercury ruling his

Chapter Thirteen • *Munakara Mercury Delineations*

6th house, means decades of performing excessively loud music on stage, plus the long-term condition of tinnitus, has meant that Grohl's hearing has been damaged which puts a barrier between himself and other people when he is engaged in conversation. He has learnt to lipread over the past twenty years, but deafness is an isolating condition in social situations, and his deafness has affected his daily life and his profession as a musician. His stubborn refusal to wear protective earpiece monitors (as he says they interfere with his connection to the music) has not helped his condition, and the only time he has been forced to resort to them, was at the 2016 Academy Awards when he sang Paul McCartney's 'Blackbird' for the 'In Memoriam' segment honouring those artists who had passed away in the previous year.[93]

The Storyteller was released in October 2021, six months before the sudden death of Foo Fighters drummer, Taylor Hawkins, in Bogota, Columbia on 25th March 2022 at the age of 50. Hawkins had been with the band since 1997 and Dave Grohl describes him as 'my brother from another mother'. Grohl carries with him the grief he has felt since losing two other 'brothers' – Kurt Cobain, and his childhood friend Jimmy Swanson – so we can only surmise the shock and sadness that envelopes him since writing this passage on Taylor in the Conclusion chapter of his book:

> *Upon first meeting (Taylor), our bond was immediate, and we grew closer with every day, every song, every note that we ever played together. I am not afraid to say that our chance meeting was a kind of love at first sight, igniting a musical "twin flame" that still burns today. Together, we have become an unstoppable duo, onstage and off, in pursuit of any and all adventure we can find. We are absolutely meant to be, and I am grateful that we found each other in this lifetime.*

There is no confirmed birth time for Taylor Hawkins, but his birth took place on 17th February 1972, three years after Dave Grohl was born, and it produces a nocturnal Aquarian Mercury disposited by Saturn in Taurus – another munakara Mercury – so perhaps this is the universal attraction which brought these two musicians together. At Taylor Hawkins' Tribute Concert, held at Wembley Stadium in London on September 3, 2022 to a crowd of 90,000, a visibly emotional Dave Grohl broke down singing the second verse of *Times Like These*, remembering that four years earlier, Taylor had helped him sing the same verse, when Grohl's voice failed and he could not complete the song.[94]

Munakara in Practice

At that moment the world was witnessing Grohl's Moon and Mercury in munakara state; a man torn between the need to publicly honour his friend, but at the same time, the pain of bearing the weight of his own private grief.

CHAPTER FOURTEEN
Munakara Venus Delineations

Lord Alfred Tennyson

A Brief Biography of Alfred Tennyson[1]

Alfred Tennyson was born in Lincolnshire, England, on August 6, 1809, the fourth of 12 children. His grandfather was a member of Parliament and his father, the Reverend George Clayton Tennyson, was the rector of a Somersby parish. In 1824 the health of his father began to break down, and he took refuge in drink. Alfred, though depressed by unhappiness at home, continued to write, collaborating with his brothers, fellow poets, Frederick and Charles, in *Poems, by Two Brothers* (1827). The three brothers were born in consecutive years; Frederick in June 1807, Charles in July 1808, and Alfred in August 1809. Frederick contributed four poems to his brothers' book, but it was Charles who describes his friendship and "heart union" with Alfred in his writings in *Poems, by Two Brothers*.

The same year Alfred and Charles joined Frederick at Trinity College in Cambridge where Alfred became a close friend of fellow poet, Arthur Hallam. This was the deepest friendship of Tennyson's life[2] and the friends became members of the Apostles, an exclusive undergraduate club of earnest intellectual interests. In 1829 he won the chancellor's gold medal for his poem *Timbuctoo*. Tennyson's father died in 1831, and Alfred's misery was increased by his grandfather's discovery of his father's debts. He was forced to leave Cambridge without taking a degree and return home.

In 1833 he published a volume of poems that included the first version of his famous *The Lotus-Eaters* and *The Lady of Shalott*. That same year Hallam died suddenly and the shock to Tennyson was severe. It came at a depressing time in his life; three of his brothers, Edward, Charles, and Septimus, were suffering from mental illness, and the bad reception of his own work added to the gloom.[3] Grief-stricken, Tennyson turned to questions of death, suicide, religious faith, and immortality in a series of short poems. These were eventually linked together in the great elegy *In Memoriam A.H.H. (Arthur Henry Hallam)* composed in honour of his deceased friend and published years later in 1850.

By 1837 Tennyson's financial affairs were in such poor shape that he had to put aside his plans to marry his fiancée Emily Sellwood – the sister of his brother's wife – whom he had fallen in love with at his brother Charles's wedding, in 1836. Emily's father disapproved of Alfred because of his bohemianism, addiction to port and tobacco, and his liberal religious views; and in 1840 he forbade any correspondence between the lovers.[4]

The best of his earlier poems and some new ones – *Ulysses* and *Locksley Hall* – were published in a two-volume edition in 1842. He was now regarded as the chief young poet of the day but his income was still too small to permit the extravagance of marriage. It did little to help his finances when he risked his small inheritance in an investment and lost everything he owned.

His poem *The Princess* (1847) supported women's rights and was better received by the public once the ending had been altered to finish with a royal wedding. *In Memoriam* was published three years later in 1850 and became an immediate success. Royalties began to flow in, and he was finally able to marry Sellwood on June 13 1850 after a thirteen year courtship. They bought a home and farm on the Isle of Wight and had two sons, Hallam and Lionel. The same year Tennyson was named poet laureate to Queen Victoria and with royal patronage, wrote memorable poems for special occasions: *Ode on the Death of the Duke of Wellington* and *The Charge of the Light Brigade*.

Tennyson spent the later years of his life creating a series of 12 Arthurian poems called *Idylls of the King*. He also wrote several verse dramas dealing with events in English history. In 1883 Tennyson reluctantly accepted a barony offered by Prime Minister William Gladstone, and he assumed the title lord – the first English writer to win so high a title for his work alone. Tennyson remained alert and vigorous up to the end of his life. He was past 80 when he published *Demeter and Other Poems* in 1889. Tennyson died on October 6, 1892. He is buried in the Poets' Corner of Westminster Abbey.

Chapter Fourteen • *Munakara Venus Delineations*

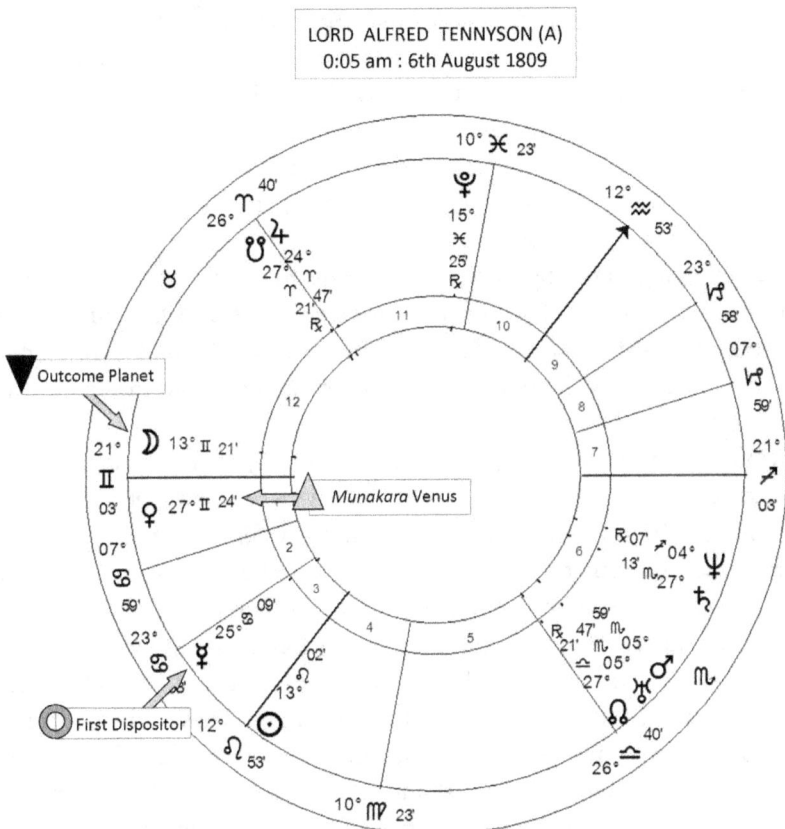

Fig. 14.1: Alfred, Lord Tennyson Natal Chart – Venus in Munakara

Gemini Venus in Munakara: Lord Alfred Tennyson

- **Key Questions:**
- What does Alfred Tennyson's Venus contend with?
- What is its driving force?
- What is its trigger? What is its outcome?

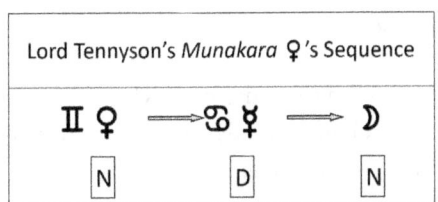

Table 14.1: Alfred, Lord Tennyson: Munakara Venus Sequence

Venus in Gemini will always be disposited by Mercury, but when this planet is diurnal and sits in Cancer, Venus's munakara sequence becomes completed by the Moon as its outcome planet. When Gemini Venus is in munakara it often finds itself caught in a dilemma between two opposing opinions, and in Tennyson's case, it was in conflict over a woman's role in society, as well as the dilemma of social equality (particularly regarding education) between the rich and the poor classes.

The following quote by Tennyson displays his opinions which relate to munakara Venus's sensitivity on both topics. In the 1840s Tennyson was reported as saying that, "the two great social questions impending in England were the education of the poor man before making him our master, and the higher education of women."[5]

Two of Tennyson's pieces stand out as testimony to his munakara Venus (disposited by Mercury) which is conflicted between two attitudes towards women in the Victorian era. *The Lady of Shalott* (1833) was perhaps the first of Tennyson's movement towards his beloved Arthurian poems written late in life. *The Lady of Shalott* is the story of unrequited love on the part of the delicate and doomed Lady Elaine of Astolat, cursed to live in a tower removed from the world, but fascinated by ordinary people she observes through a magical mirror. Every day she weaves beautiful tapestries of the people and events she witnesses in her mirror, but she remains aloof until the day she spies the English knight, Sir Lancelot and falls madly in love with him. Lady Elaine impulsively takes three steps across the room to look at Lancelot more closely, thereby breaking the mirror, and therefore the curse, which has held her prisoner in the tower.

Part III last verse tells of the broken mirror and her release from a life where "She lives with little joy or fear."[6]

> Out flew the web and floated wide;
> *The mirror crack'd from side to side;*
> *"The curse has come upon me" cried*
> *The Lady of Shalott.*[7]

Elaine finds a boat by the river and carves her name into its side, boarding it to travel downriver to Camelot, only to freeze to death in the cold night air as she searches for her one true love.

Tennyson's *Lady of Shalott* is tragic and romantic, but its underlying message is also clear: women, especially those of high rank, are frail creatures

Chapter Fourteen • *Munakara Venus Delineations*

inclined to be irrational and emotional beings who are best safeguarded and removed from ordinary life, as similar to Elaine, they cannot survive life's trials without a man's love or protection.

Most scholars believe Tennyson was speaking of his personal dilemma of artistic isolation when he wrote Lady of Shalott. "The poem is often interpreted as a metaphor for the solitary nature of the artist's creative life, suggesting that the artist must be distanced, and inevitably isolated, from the surrounding world."[8]

Munakara Venus in Gemini would support this theory as Venus expresses itself through writing (Mercury) and often taking the artist's own emotions, and translating them through their art. The modern interpretation is that Tennyson yearns for engagement but it distracts him, and he is torn between the realities of a harsh world, and a safe world of idyllic love and detachment, especially given the trauma of his own difficult childhood. In the poem, connection with the physical world shatters Lady Elaine's reflective mirror and dooms her to heartache, loss and death. Perhaps Tennyson's identification with his heroine is his need to block his own painful emotions (Moon as outcome planet) and create a place of fantasy where romantic love is idealistic and fanciful (munakara Gemini Venus) but not attainable.

On a more practical level, Tennyson may have feared that the world would not understand his poetry, and in fact, he released two versions of *The Lady of Shalott*, the first of which was published in his *Poems* (1832) and the second in 1842, also called *Poems*. The first version was so savaged by the critics that he withdrew his work for a decade, refusing to expose it to a world that might destroy it. The allegory of Lady Elaine destroyed by a heartless knight who lacked compassion for her love is not wasted on Tennyson who felt any public rejection of his early work very deeply (Venus in munakara).

Tennyson's other poem specifically based on women's issues was a tale titled *The Princess*, which tells the story of the heroic Princess Ida who turns her back on the world of men, marriage, and a life of ease with her betrothed prince, choosing instead to found a women's university where men are forbidden to enter. The story's premise is to promote the education of women, in order that they might be financially and socially independent, and have the choice of an alternative lifestyle over the safety of marriage (munakara Venus in 1st house with dispositor, Mercury, in 2nd house in Whole Sign.

The Princess (1847) was published fourteen years after *The Lady of Shalott*, but it was written in the late 1830s as a response to criticism that Tennyson was not writing about serious social issues. The publication of *The Princess* coincided with the 1847 opening of Queen's College, London, Britain's first college for women. The public's cool reception to *The Princess* caused Tennyson to revise it considerably to make it more palatable to a conservative society unsure of whether education for women was a good idea. Privately, Tennyson wrote to a friend, "I hate it, and so will you."[9]

In the revised edition of *The Princess*, the prince defies the university's ban on men and he and his two friends disguise themselves as women in an attempt to enrol in the university. The new 'students' debate the merits of women's equality with Princess Ida, but when they are exposed as men, a battle ensues between Ida's father and the prince. The prince is injured and Ida abandons her university to tend to him, whereupon she falls in love with him and marries the prince. Love (Venus) has won over education (Mercury) and society need not be unsettled by the idea of a woman choosing knowledge, over affairs of the heart.

The Princess has divided opinion about where Tennyson's sympathies lie. The poet's son Hallam wrote that his father held that "the sooner woman finds out, before the great educational movement begins, that 'woman is not underdeveloped man, but diverse,' the better it will be for the progress of the world."[10] The early critics considered Tennyson to be sympathetic to a progressive view of women's education, but feared that his views would be unpopular within the dictates of Victoria society.[11] Tennyson tried to rebalance the issues in his 1850 revision, writing "I thought that the poem would explain itself, but the public did not see the drift."[12] Modern critics believe that the final message of *The Princess* – where Ida abandons her education to marry the prince – is obvious on where her priorities should lie, and is anti-feminist in its message.[13]

Munakara Planet and Sect Condition – how comfortable is Venus?

Lord Tennyson was born just after midnight on 6th August 1809, and the nocturnal chart suits Gemini Venus which sits beneath the horizon, six degrees later than the Ascendant degree, and in 1st house in Lord Tennyson's chart. Venus in a nocturnal chart is likely to conform to the more conservative ideas of women and their place in society, and it seems we have not moved far from Tennyson's version of women where its sect condition is concerned. Robert Hand writes that Venus in sect is "the more traditional Venus, soft, feminine, etc."[14]

Chapter Fourteen • *Munakara Venus Delineations*

As Alfred Tennyson is male, his munakara Venus describes not only his art, but also the women in his life. Similar to Prince Albert who had Venus in contention (Part One, *Fig. 5.1*), an influential partner played a significant role in his life. Emily Sarah Tennyson (nee Sellwood) was born four years after Tennyson in 1813. The two met as children through her father – a prosperous solicitor who acted for the larger Tennyson family on many occasions. Alfred is said to have fallen in love with Emily at the marriage of his brother Charles to her younger sister, Louisa (Gemini Venus), in May 1836,[15] just before Emily's 23rd birthday.

Lord Tennyson — ♀'s Sect Dignity			
Planet	Sect 1 Status	Sect 2 Hemisphere	Sect 3 Sign
♊ ♀	Night [N]	With the Sun [D]	Air [D]

Table 14.2: Alfred, Lord Tennyson: Munakara Venus Sect Dignity

Whilst there is no recorded time for Emily Tennyson's birth on July 9, 1813, nocturnal Mercury in Leo was munakara throughout the day, and her Cancer Sun was possibly a second planet in contention, given that the Moon entered Sagittarius at midday. Emily would wait thirteen years for her father to approve of her choice in husband (Cancer Sun in munakara), and for Alfred to be financially viable to marry, and for many years she was forbidden to correspond with Alfred (munakara Mercury). Emily was 37 by the time she married, and perhaps her patience bears witness to Hand's statement that Venus in sect is "the more traditional Venus" which conforms to Victorian society's expectation that women wait silently and politely, like Lady Elaine, for marriage to provide status and meaning to their lives.

Emily was the eldest of three girls, and her mother died when she was three years old. Her father made sure that all three daughters were well educated, and Emily was an author and a composer in her own right. Alfred relied heavily on Emily after their marriage in 1850 as she performed the role of a business manager and secretary, and as his popularity soared, Emily became his promoter, the entertainer to guests who would often stay for weeks, and his protector, when Alfred could not cope with the commotion and attention he was now attracting in his new role as poet laureate.[16]

Victorian photographer Julia Margaret Cameron described Emily as a "living stream of love whose font is never dry."[17] Fellow poet, Coventry Patmore, described Emily as cultivated, charming "but her mind seems always deeper than her cultivation, and her heart always deeper than her mind – or rather constituting the main element of her mind."[18]

Munakara Venus: Lord Alfred Tennyson
Munakara Venus in Gemini in 1st House (Placidus and Whole Sign)

Tennyson's munakara Venus conjuncts his Ascendant and in the Whole Sign system Venus rules the 5th house of friends, entertainment, and creativity, and the 12th house of isolation, withdrawal, hidden enemies, and personal 'imprisonment' through fears, health issues and insecurities.

Lord Tennyson's early poetry was scattered with powerful visual imagery (5th house), its effect so strong that it was a major influence on the Pre-Raphaelite Brotherhood, a group of English painters, poets and art critics founded in 1848 by William Holden Hunt. Tennyson's Gemini Venus was drawn to 'brotherhoods', beginning with his escape from a miserable childhood home to Trinity College, Cambridge. There he joined other young boys with the same passion as his own for knowledge, arts, and classical mythology. His first book of poems was written at Trinity with his older brother Charles, titled *Poems by Two Brothers* (1827), and it was at Trinity that he first met his closest friend, Arthur Hallam, where 'The friendship of Hallam and Tennyson was swift and deep.'[19] Both boys entered the Chancellor's Prize Poem Competition which Tennyson won, and then together they were invited to join a private debating society known as the Cambridge Apostles, who met once a week to discuss serious questions of religion, literature, and society.

Hallam visited Tennyson in the holidays and fell madly in love with Alfred's younger sister Emilia (Gemini Venus), asking for her hand in marriage in December 1830, but his wealthy parents disapproved of the match, and Hallam was banned from visiting the Tennyson family until he came of age at twenty-one. Sadly, the marriage did not take place, and the two 'brothers' never became brothers-in-law as Arthur Hallam died suddenly of a stroke at the age of 22. Tennyson was inconsolable, and wrote one of his major works *In Memoriam* for his friend. When asked to write an introduction to Hallam's poems published posthumously by his father, Tennyson replied: 'I attempted to draw a memoir of his (Hallam's) life and character, but I failed to do him justice. I failed even to please myself. I could scarcely have pleased you.'[20]

The astrological technique known as 'deriving the houses' is often applied to gain further information on someone critical to the individual through identifying their 'house', and counting forward through the houses that follow on. For instance, counting from the 7th house gives information pertinent to the partner, counting from 10th house (mother), shows insight Into her life, counting from the fifth becomes the first-born's house and provides details on

Chapter Fourteen • *Munakara Venus Delineations*

their life, etc. In Tennyson's chart munakara Venus rules both the 5th and 12th houses; the fifth (my friend Hallam) counts forward to find the 12th house is my friend's death (8 houses from the 5th house). When Venus in contention brings these two houses together through rulership, there is little doubt that Tennyson was devastated by the death of his friend (12th house) and that it triggered his creative mind to honour Hallam (5th house).

Tennyson wrote *In Memoriam A.H.H. (Arthur Henry Hallam)* in honour of his friend, and the following is an excerpt from his poem. The poem was instrumental to cementing Tennyson's appointment as poet laureate, as Queen Victoria recorded in her journal after the death of her husband, Prince Albert in 1861, "Much soothed & pleased with Tennyson's "In Memoriam." Only those who have suffered, as I do, can understand these beautiful poems" 5 Jan 1862).[21]

The last two lines are very familiar in English language and it is worth noting that Tennyson is the ninth most frequently quoted writer in *The Oxford Dictionary of Quotations*.[22]

> *I hold it true, whate'er befall;*
> *I feel it, when I sorrow most;*
> *'Tis better to have loved and lost*
> *Than never to have loved at all.*
>   Alfred, Lord Tennyson, *In Memoriam A.H.H.*

The 12th house can also be seen to describe my partner's illnesses and accidents (moving forward six houses from the 7th house), and for Emily Tennyson munakara Venus's rulership of this house, would help to describe the debilitating illnesses she suffered after the birth of their second child, Lionel. One biographer writes "over time, the degree of responsibility was so stressful that it weakened her health,"[23] and that she wrote in her journal that she longed for periods "for reading and thinking, to restore the elasticity of one's mind, now too like a bow spoilt by long bending."[24] Emily became an invalid and was no longer able to entertain or perform managerial or secretarial duties (Gemini Venus disposited by Mercury), as she had in the past.[25] Alfred died in 1892 and Emily passed away four years later in 1896, but her dedication to her late husband was such that despite her failing health, Emily spent her final years working with their eldest son Hallam (named after his friend) collating and organising Tennyson's life's work for his biography.

First Dispositor: Diurnal Mercury in Cancer

Tennyson was the son of a vicar, George Clayton Tennyson (Jr), the eldest son of attorney and MP George Tennyson (Snr), who had been pushed into a career in the church and passed over as heir in favour of his younger brother, Charles. Mercury in Cancer is in Tennyson's Whole Sign 2nd house (outcome planet, the Moon, rules 2nd house), and his father accumulated debts after being bypassed in favour of his younger brother who inherited the title, the money, and the family estate.

Tennyson's father was severely epileptic, a condition made worse by alcoholism, and fuelled by petulance and rage over his own father's betrayal. Mercury in Cancer rules father's house (4th house) by Whole Sign, and his father's illness and his lack of responsibility may have been some of the reasons behind his disinheritance. His father, George Clayton Tennyson, is described by both the Leo Sun on the IC, and by the rulership of the fourth sign, Virgo, by Mercury in the Whole Sign system. Tennyson's father is said to have carefully attended to the education and training of his children, and passed on his literary skills to his sons, but George's own mental instability and his alcoholism, created a miserable childhood for his family.

George Tennyson passed away in 1831 at age 73, when 22-year-old Alfred was enjoying freedom from his family's woes, and blossoming in the academic life at Trinity College. His father's death left the family bankrupt, and Alfred was forced to leave his beloved College before taking his degree, returning to his father's parish to care for his mother and younger siblings for six years, until the Church forced the family to vacate the rectory.

Tennyson had a lifelong fear and fascination with mental illness, and was prone to periods of depression and lethargy. Throughout his life Tennyson struggled with long debilitating bouts of depression and unstable mood swings, with some experts diagnosing Tennyson's condition as a bi-polar disorder. The Lady of Shalott's imprisonment in "four gray walls, and four gray towers,"[26] may be a reference to Tennyson's own depressive state, and after seeing two young lovers wed, she sighs: "I am half sick of shadows."[27]

The male side of Alfred Tennyson's family were not unfamiliar with issues of mental illness. His father, grandfather, two of his great-grandfathers, as well as five of his seven brothers, were at one time or another medically diagnosed with insanity, melancholia, fits of uncontrollable rage, or what we might today describe as a manic-depressive illness. His brother Edward was confined to an asylum for nearly 60 years before dying from 'manic exhaustion.' Creativity and bi-polar disorder can run parallel paths in certain families (Venus to

Chapter Fourteen • *Munakara Venus Delineations*

Mercury to Moon). Tennyson often expressed the fear that he might inherit the madness or "taint of blood", as it was referred to in Victorian times.[28]

Two of Alfred's gifted siblings, Edward and Arthur, developed long-term mental health problems, further compounding the issue by becoming substance abusers. His brother Charles had bouts of depression, but seemed to recover by the time of his marriage to Emily's sister, Louisa. Charles became an ordained priest of the Church of England, but sadly Louisa later suffered from mental illness and became an opium addict.

For Tennyson, Gemini Venus in contention may describe his difficulties in maintaining an even emotional base. Today's awareness of bi-polar signatures such as abnormal changes in mood, energy, activity levels, and the ability to carry out repetitive daily tasks might have helped Tennyson to understand and mange his condition. Bi-polar disorder often affects relationships (Venus) as unpredictable behaviour – animation, irritability, and impulsiveness – makes it difficult to relate in a steady and rational manner. In the depressive state anxiety, lethargy and a sense of hopelessness affects the ability to engage in, or enjoy, activities the rest of the world is experiencing, and these are all things experienced and described by Tennyson in *The Lady of Shalott*.

The outcome planet: Moon in Gemini

In 1830, a year before his father's death, Tennyson checked himself into a sanatorium for observation when his worry about being mentally unstable became almost unbearable. With a family history such as his own, Moon in Gemini became the terror of 'bad blood', feeding his fear that he may not escape the hereditary taint of madness and suicide, especially amongst the male members of his family.

Mercury and the Moon reside in signs which belong to each other, and whilst there is no aspect possible between Gemini and Cancer, there is no mutual reception as the two signs are in aversion.

Tennyson's Gemini Moon is applying to his Venus in munakara, and the thirteen degree gap may seem wide, but this aspect of conjunction will join together the planet at the beginning of the sequence (Venus), and the nocturnal planet (Moon), that completes the munakara sequence. This situation might describe a circle that uses creativity as a safe place to resolve something, or on a less positive note, a place where you find yourself going in ever decreasing circles. Both possibilities are samples in Tennyson's experiences and expressions for his Venus and its outcome planet. The two planets have the potential to produce beautiful prose with great emotional depth, and an understanding of love, loss and yearning. But they also create the shadow and the fear (Venus on the Ascendant ruling 12th house) that Tennyson will follow in the footprints of a family plagued by misery and mental illness (Gemini Moon conjunct munakara Venus).

Munakara Venus: Tee Corinne

A Brief Biography of Tee Corinne[29]

Prolific artist, writer and lesbian activist Tee A. Corinne was born November 3, 1943 in St. Petersburg, Florida. Corinne had a turbulent childhood as her mother and stepfather were alcoholics. At age three-and-a-half, she was diagnosed with tuberculosis. She spent three months recovering in a nursing home, and nineteen months with her grandparents in Yankeetown, Florida, where she grew to love country living. She was not permitted to resume normal activity until age eight.

Early in 1965 Corinne became involved with Robert Kamen, a folk musician from Queens. In December she moved to New York City with him and they married ten months later. In 1968 she received an MFA (Master of Fine Arts) in drawing and sculpture from Pratt Institute. She was interested in the sexual imagery of the "great masters" of art history, and in 1968 Corinne began locating and collecting books containing these images. Such books had previously been banned by the US government, but the new era of 1970s sexual freedom was on its way.

In 1969, having finished a year of postgraduate work in sculpture, Corinne and Kamen moved to Connecticut where he attended graduate school, and she taught college art, made life-size sculptures, and became increasingly depressed. Corinne stopped making art when the couple moved to San Francisco in 1972, and then separated in 1973. She began making art again, this time boldly committed to using explicit sexual imagery. Recognizing that her sexual art could not be exhibited in traditional art galleries, Corinne sought out alternative venues such as women's coffeehouses, bookstores, and lesbian bars. Her images were frequently published in the emerging feminist press.

In San Francisco, Corinne began to work in sex education, whilst still continuing her interest in photography. Out of her work in sex education, she became aware of the need for accessible images of female genitalia. In November 1975 she self-published *The ..... Colouring Book* (later rebranded as *Labiaflowers*), a collection of line drawings of vulvas that is still in print.

Chapter Fourteen • *Munakara Venus Delineations*

In the same year, Corinne entered her first long term relationship with a woman, photographer Honey Lee Cottrell, with whom she often collaborated on imagery and shows. They remained together until 1977. The same year Corinne visited Mountaingroves at Golden, where she fell in love with the idea of living in a gay owned, communal property in Southern Oregon. In 1989 Corinne began a relationship with author and rural activist Beverly A. Brown, founding editor of *Maize* magazine, a relationship which would continue until Brown's death in 2005. Corinne died the following year on August 27, 2006 after a struggle with liver cancer. She was 62 years old.

"I'm interested in loving, beautiful, sexy images...I also want the images to be a turn on, create an adrenaline high, a rush of desire so intense that the act of looking is sexual."[30] – Tee Corinne

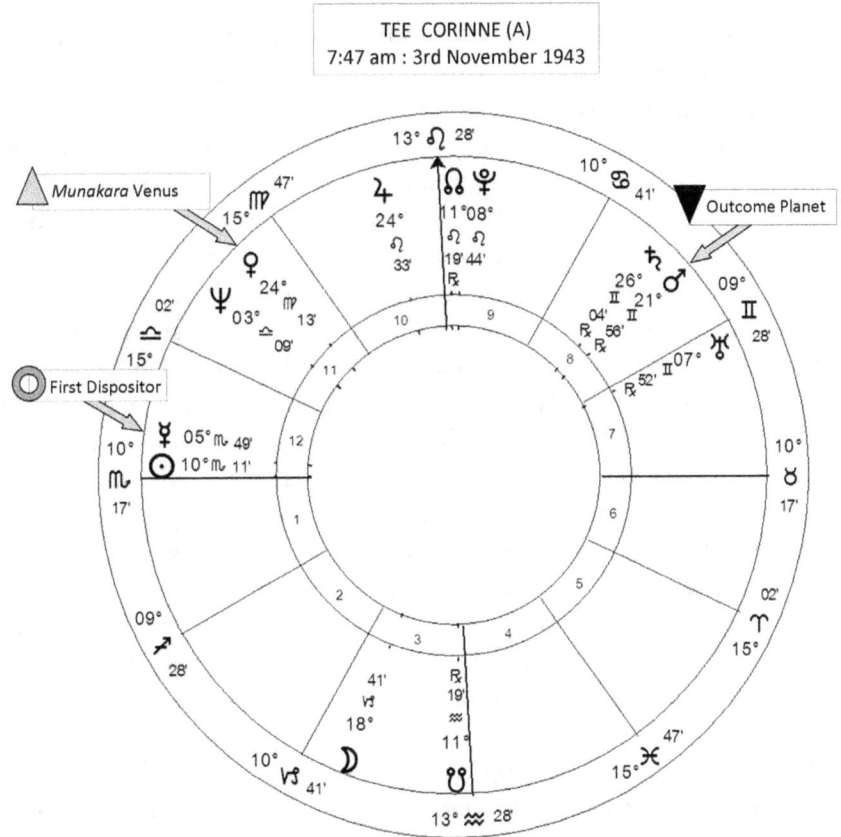

Fig. 14.2: Tee Corinne Natal Chart: Munakara Venus

Virgo Venus in Munakara: Tee Corinne

- **Key Questions:**
- What does Tee Corinne's Venus contend with?
- What is its driving force?
- What is its trigger? What is its outcome?

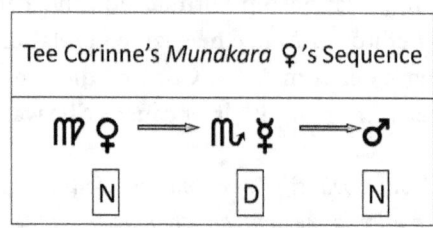

Table 14.3: Tee Corinne: Munakara Venus Sequence

Virgo Venus in munakara presents itself as Tee Corinne's talent as an artist, a photographer, an author, a sex educator, a lecturer, and as an art historian specializing in lesbianism. She worked tirelessly to promote sex positivity, and increase lesbian visibility, realizing at age 27, that although her art education had enabled her to depict male genitals, she had not observed her own genitalia since she was a child. "I knew that the things we don't have names for, or images of, are the ones we label crazy or bad. I believed that reclaiming labial imagery was a route to claiming personal power for women."[31]

Tee Corinne's Virgo Venus in munakara is a planet in fall, and its condition shows Corinne's fight to educate women on the beauty of their bodies, in spite of society's strict conformity to what it judged as beauty and attractiveness in a woman. Munakara Venus in fall depicts Corinne's battle to be recognised as an artist of unusual perspective, who fought narrow-minded authorities, conventional art galleries, censorship boards, and the general public's impression of what was 'nice' or 'ladylike' behaviour and imagery.

Diurnal Mercury in Scorpio is Venus's dispositor, and Corinne was not only a voice for women to stop feeling embarrassed or ashamed of their bodies, but also an educated guide to physically exploring their sexuality, and to re-assess the concept of femininity beyond the realms of society's limited classifications of beauty.

Mars in Gemini is munakara Venus's outcome planet, and whilst Corinne admitted she 'didn't like confrontation', Mars is a planet geared for battle and is ready to fight when it sees something it cannot accept as the 'norm'. Mars can be an uncomfortable outcome planet for munakara Venus; the two

Chapter Fourteen • *Munakara Venus Delineations*

planets are enemies, and Venus will look for compromise whilst Mars looks for confrontation. However, Mars also takes Venus out of its comfort zone and ignites a complacent Venus, sending it into battle when Venus would prefer to remain safe and neutral on the sidelines. Mars is the ruler of Corinne's Ascendant, and the dispositor for Scorpio Sun (also munakara) and Mercury in Scorpio, so it was always going to have an impact on her munakara Venus (ruling the 7th and 12th houses).

Corinne was articulate, passionate, and driven to change society's images and perception of women, and she happily played the role of modern-day warrior to achieve her aim. Venus in Virgo will not be silenced, especially when it is munakara, and its last bastion is Mars in Gemini: I may make you uncomfortable, but you will hear me, you will see me, you will be forced to think about me....And you will change.

Munakara Venus squares its outcome planet, Mars, in mutable signs, both planets are disposited by Mercury, and both planets are in aspect to Saturn, by either a square (Venus) or a conjunction (Mars). Saturn suggests defiance of authority, government, or father figures, and whilst Saturn itself in not a munakara planet in Corinne's chart, it will help manifest munakara Venus's actualization, particularly through its aspect to both nocturnal planets in Venus's sequence.

As much as squares bring tension and disruption – Venus squares Mars/Saturn – they also have the potential to bring change, freedom, new opinion, and honest conversation to a subject that is feared or is taboo. Corinne was not just about promoting her own work, as she was tireless in supporting other lesbian artists. She wrote about art for a variety of publications, and she was a co-founder and co-chair of the Gay & Lesbian Caucus for Art. In 1991 she was chosen by *Lambda Book Report* as one of the fifty most influential lesbians and gay men of the decade.[32]

Sun on the Ascendant: Diurnal or Nocturnal Chart?

Tee Corinne was reportedly born at 7:47am (Rodden A-rating), and her Sun is within minutes of the Ascendant's position in the chart. Some astrologers might argue that the Sun's rays would be showing above the horizon at the time of her birth, and therefore the chart is diurnal. However, the Sun's position makes it difficult to determine whether the chart is truly diurnal, or if the birth time is slightly out, and this will affect the accuracy of the Ascendant's degree. If Corinne's birth took place five minutes earlier, the chart would be nocturnal. For this reason, there is little point in discussing the sect dignity of Tee Corinne's Venus as it will vary according to the Sun's position above or below the horizon.

Having said that, the circumstances of Corinne's life and the focus of her art suggests the likelihood that it *is* a diurnal chart, and that by placing Venus in an out-of-sect position (in a diurnal chart, diurnally placed) might, according to Robert Hand, "indicate a rather strong kind of feminine sexuality which in a traditional patriarchal society would incline a female native toward immorality and lascivious behaviour,"[33] This opinion would confirm the attitudes of a conservative society from the last century which frowns on Corinne's subject matter, and condemns it to be 'inappropriate' to be displayed publicly as serious art work.

Munakara Venus: Tee Corinne

"Sometimes I think I have the wrong kind of personality to be making art out of sexual imagery. I don't like confrontation, don't like negative public commotion. Nonetheless, since 1974 I have been actively involved with labia imagery and with images of women making love with other women or with themselves." – Tee Corinne, Artist's Statement: On Sexual Art, *Art Essay, Feminist Studies*, 19, (1993)[34]

Munakara Venus in Virgo in 11th House (Placidus and Whole Sign)

Venus, the planet associated with pleasure, women, and relationship may seem to prefer conformity, and be resistant to turbulence or radical change, but when it is in contention Venus will rouse itself from apathy, and fight when there is no longer any pleasure in life. Mercury rules Virgo, and whilst its exaltation sign opposes Venus across the Thema Mundi chart (meaning the two planets are enemies), nonetheless, Mercury will apply reason, logic, and offer practical solutions to help release Venus from its despair.

At her coming of age in the late 1950s, Corinne chose the conventional life of a middle-class woman: a college degree in printmaking and painting, graduation in 1965 and marriage to the man she loved in the following year. She then undertook more study with a Masters in Fine Arts in drawing and sculpture, followed by a few years in teaching and backpacking across Europe. However, what seemed to be a perfect life was destroying Tee who, in her own words, was 'sliding into suicidal depression.' Munakara Venus had lost its way, and she no longer practised art, or felt passionate about anything.

At this point of desperation, Corinne examined her life, and made radical changes through therapy, parting from her husband, joining the Women's

Movement, and choosing female lovers over male partners. Her artwork took a dramatic turn when she came out as lesbian in 1975, and true to Venus in contention, Corrine found herself irritated by the genitalia imbalance in art, and decided to produce a book of artistic images of vulvas, with her controversial title, *The .... Colouring Book*, later renamed by her publisher, as the less offensive, *Labiaflowers*. In conversation with Corrine twenty years later, she talks about her choice to publish drawings of female genitalia, and that as a 27-year-old, she had experimented with the drawings, but had hidden them from her husband because she thought he would not approve, later shredding them into small pieces.

Like the true quiet warrior that Venus in contention becomes (often later in life), Corrine did soft pencil drawings of every woman who gave their permission, converting them into ink drawings, and making copies on card stock to distribute and sell through local women's bookstores. Sadly, at the time, society did not approve, and her artwork was totally misunderstood by government censorship agencies who banned her work, and sent it underground, to be distributed amongst women's groups who were sympathetic to her designs and ideas (munakara Venus in Gemini in 11th house).

Corinne's munakara Venus is nourished and encouraged by women through its placement in the 11th house of groups and like-minded individuals. However, Venus rules the 12th house where the unknown or the 'minority' creates oppression, and fear becomes the end product when Venus squares Saturn and Mars in the 8th house. Corinne's work remained controversial throughout the final years of the last century. As late as 1998, when her artwork was used as an example of pornography by the Traditional Values Coalition in a presentation to the Senate.[35] Libra (Venus's sign) is symbolized by the scales of balance, however, there is little balance in art for both males and females, when fair representation seems to be missing on the topic of female genitalia. It is true that female nudes abound in art, but the focus is on breasts and buttocks, and again, tends to favour a male's point of view of what is judged to be beautiful about a woman's body.

Munakara Venus is not always an easy journey for women who chose non-conformity, and Tee Corinne's exotic images, which should be appreciated for their form and beauty, may be rejected by some members of society who do not share her views on sexuality. In an interview conducted in 2000, when Corinne was asked why she chose photography as her medium she answered:

"I wanted to do something where content and politics could be satisfied. Fine art has problems with accessibility. I was a southerner active in the civil rights movement in the south. Printmaking was one way I could integrate art with politics. Photography is another."[36]

Corinne's final work, and the most painful in terms of her Venus, is titled *Scars, Stoma, Ostomy Bag, Portacath: Picturing Cancer In Our Lives*, and is a photographic study of the decline in her partner, Beverley Brown's, health as a result of cancer. In Corinne's chart, Venus rules the combination of 7th house (partners), and the 12th house (six houses away by derivation is my partner's ill health), and her record of her partner's final journey is both heart-breaking, and a visual testimony to her love for Brown.

Even in this sad situation, munakara Venus was present, and added more pain to the experience than it needed to be. Corinne's partner of sixteen years, Beverley announced that she had fallen in love with someone else, and that their relationship was over. Beverley moved out, and instead of cherishing Beverley's last year and spending it together as a couple, the pair was estranged for seven months. Finally, Corinne felt compelled to risk rejection, and unbidden, journeyed to Beverley's new home in order to spend time with her ex-lover. The weekend was a loving reunion and past wounds were healed in some measure, but Beverley passed away five days after the visit.

Munakara Venus still held challenges for Tee Corinne, and its final act was a crushing blow. Four months after Beverley's death, when the intimate photography of her lover's terminal illness, and the accompanying journal of her decline were being compiled by Corrine, she was diagnosed with a tumour in the liver caused by cancer of the bile ducts. She recorded at the time: "I had less chance of living than a coin toss would give me. Triage. What could be discarded, what was most important? I have chosen to complete this collaborative project and share it via a CD with text. It is a passionate work, a final act of love."[37]

Beverley died on October 27, 2005 and Tee Corinne followed ten months later on August 27, 2006 – Beverley's photos a precursor to what she herself would suffer at the hands of the same cruel disease.

First Dispositor: Diurnal Mercury in Scorpio on the Ascendant

"The images we see, as a culture, help define and expand our dreams, our perceptions of what is possible. Pictures of who we are help us visualize who we can be."[38] – Tee Corinne

Chapter Fourteen • *Munakara Venus Delineations*

Munakara Venus in Mercury's earth sign (Virgo) identifies Tee Corrine's three passions – women, art, and her love of nature. Once Corrine had identified her first two loves and moved towards incorporating them into her life, it became possible for her to fulfil her third love.

She had recuperated after her tuberculosis at her grandparents' home in the countryside, and she yearned to find a home that would give her the same sense of belonging. In 1976 she met Ruth Mountaingrove, the publisher and editor of *WomanSpirit* magazine, and together they visited Ruth's commune, named in her honour, Mountaingroves, a gay owned, communal, rural land in Golden, Southern Oregon. Immediately loving the lifestyle, Corrine saw that it was possible to live close to the land without sacrificing contact with a vibrant artistic community. She fell in love with the area around southern Oregon, and in the 1980s lived in women's communities, often situated in wilder areas away from towns and cities. Later, she bought her own land and lived near the woods for twenty years until her death in 2006. In one of her manuscripts, she wrote of her early discovery of the country's beauty, "Slowly, in Oregon, I reconnected with the deep levels of creativity that run in me and began producing work which pleased me."[39]

Mercury conjunct the Sun (in contention) is situated on the Ascendant, and Corrine's writing career, as well as her art and printmaking, provided her with the flexibility to live independently, in an environment that supported her artistic nature. She was an author of many novels with lesbian themes, four books of poetry, and numerous artists' books and small edition publications. She also received several awards for her photography as well as her writing.

Mercury in its fixed water sign plays a dual role in Corrine's two munakara sequences. It is the first dispositor for Venus in Virgo, and the final outcome planet for the Sun in Scorpio, as it rises before the Sun and is a diurnal planet. The artist was posthumously honoured in 2006 by Moonforce Media with the creation of the *Tee A. Corrine Prize for Lesbian Media Artists*, an annual thousand dollar unrestricted grant for an artist working in photography, film, digital media or any new media form, to promote and encourage the preservation of lesbian art. Mercury in Scorpio is intense and focused, especially when pursuing its passions and bringing them to a concrete form. Corinne's efforts to overcome prejudice and censorship was a lifelong battle, but the combination of her eloquence with her eye for startling and provocative beauty, especially where the female form was concerned, has well-earned the right to be remembered in the words of the *Gay and Lesbian Encyclopedia* as "one of the most visible and accessible lesbian artists in the world."

The outcome planet: Mars in Gemini

Mars is also involved in both Venus, and the Sun's munakara sequence, as it is the outcome planet for nocturnal Venus, and the Scorpio Sun's first dispositor. Situated in Gemini, Mars has the energy and motivation to keep pace with Mercury's passion, particularly given the diversity of projects that Corinne kept afloat at the same time. Mars is conjunct Saturn, and the combination may give some indication as to her tough childhood experiences (Mars rules 6th house of poor health, and Saturn rules the 4th house of father or step-father). Themes which were explored in Corinne's mixed media show *Family: Growing Up in an Alcoholic Family* (1990).

Both Saturn and Mars form a square to Corinne's Venus in contention, and her observations on her childhood are themes which repeat themselves in her planets' sequencing. Munakara Venus squares Gemini Mars, and the tension between the first and last planet in Venus' sequence is accentuated by the signs on the horizon: Mars as the Ascendant Lord, and Venus rules the Descendant. When Saturn – the ruler of the IC – is pulled into the equation, by its conjunction to the Ascendant Lord, and a tight square to munakara Venus in Virgo, we now have three rulers of Tee Corinne's fixed Cross of Matter. The past (Saturn) and the relating axis (Mars and Venus) give some clues as to why Corinne not only felt it necessary to cut ties with her family, but to also delve into her family's past history, in order to move forward as a functioning adult who wanted to engage in healthy relationships with other women.

Scorpio Sun in Munakara: Tee Corinne

- **Key Questions:**
- What does Tee Corinne's Sun contend with?
- What is its driving force?
- What is its trigger? What is its outcome?

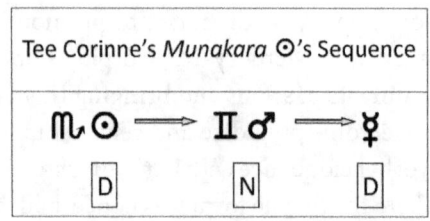

Table 14.4: Tee Corinne: Munakara Sun Sect and Sequence

Corinne's munakara Sun rules her 10th house, the house of mother, and squares its house with Leo on the cusp. The Nodal axis is within two degrees of her MC/IC axis, with Pluto conjunct North Node at the culminating point, and Scorpio Mercury conjunct munakara Sun at the Moon's Northern Bendings. Lee Lehman's work on the Nodal Cycle states, "[A planet] approaching, or at the Northern Bending, the individual becomes the embodiment or personification for a theme which permeates the era. However, prominence does not necessarily equate to popularity or 'success' as we might be tempted to define it."[40]

Perhaps the best way to describe Tee Corinne's munakara Scorpio Sun dispositing to Gemini Mars, is to let her words speak for themselves. After all, Scorpio Mercury is a player in the sequences of both planets in contention. The following extract is from promotional information for Tee Corrine's 1990 visual exhibition titled, *Family: Growing Up in an Alcoholic Family.*

> *"There is a brooding, Baudelairian side to my family which sometimes surfaces as dogmatic opinion, sarcasm, verbal and physical abuse. As a child I didn't know other families were different. Slowly I learned to 'un-tolerate' abusive behaviour in myself and others. This is an ongoing process.*
>
> *Something was always going on in my family of origin: someone's picture in the paper, public events, awards, parties, fights. Life was seldom uneventful, never dull. From that family I learned to care for plants, arrange flowers.... paint, crochet, meet people, move into a strange house or a new city. They taught me to love the water, open spaces, storms and clouds and blooming things."*

Munakara Sun: Tee Corinne

Corinne's Scorpio Sun is on her Ascendant and rules the Mid-Heaven. It is halfway between the North and South Nodes, at the Bendings and Pluto squares both the Sun and Mercury. Corinne's battle to be acknowledged as an artist, a spokesperson, an activist, and a woman in her own right, is as much about her identity as a woman as it is about her sexuality, as a woman who loved herself and other women. Again, from Corinne's 1990 exhibition,

> *They (my family) were a tremendous energy force, sometimes exploding, sometimes fuelling a positive forward motion. It's been my job to separate the useful from the destructive. Perhaps this is what we each need to learn in order to go our own way as adults. As a child I developed inappropriate caretaking patterns, often confusing these with love. I have now learned new ways to care*

for myself, ways to stop focusing my attention on others, to understand first my own needs and goals."[41]

When planets sit on the Ascendant there are two choices open to the individual: either the planet describes the immediate environment and you adapt to that environment, or *you become the environment* and others' adapt to your behaviour and your personality, as described by the nature of the planet on the Ascendant. But when the two planets are Mercury (involved in both sequences) and the Sun (in contention) then life tends to thrust you forward into the limelight.

Generally speaking, munakara Sun does not crave the spotlight. Attention equals judgment, and this Sun is sensitive to others' criticisms and fears retribution, even when it is unfairly earned. Instead Sun in contention sits patiently waiting for someone else to step forward and take control. Some signs wait more patiently than others, but tradition, or precedence, or events take control and your Sun has no other choice but to take up the mantle of responsibility, or face the consequences.

Corinne completes her *Family* exhibition with these words: *"As I learn not to run to the rescue of others, I find myself freed from old, recurrent cycles of anger, resentment and depression, cycles which had not made sense to me before. In the process of becoming conscious of and changing my behaviours, I have had to locate and listen carefully to the child within me."*[42]

Amongst Corrine's many photographs of herself and her lovers is an old photo of her grandmother Mabel taken around 1910 when she was a young widow with a small child. In the picture Mabel is sitting on the floor leaning back against the legs of a woman, identified as Gertie, who is seated in a chair behind Mabel. Corinne says 'they were holding hands, facing the camera with looks of such complicity that they took my breath away. I am sure they were lovers."[43] The search for history had uncovered a link between her life, and the life of her grandmother, whose love for Gertie would not be so openly acknowledged at the beginning of a previous century. This photo personalizes Corinne's journey towards finding self-identification, and doing so through art which would previously been seen as vulgar, unfit for viewing, or identified under the damning label of 'pornographic.'

Scorpio Sun in contention disposited by Mars in Gemini is the desire to broadcast one's own individuality, and to take the battle to those who are ignorant or narrow-minded in their attitude towards women of difference. With Leo on the Mid-heaven, there is no retreat and no succour, especially

Chapter Fourteen • *Munakara Venus Delineations*

if censorship is demonstrative of petty prejudices, or the individual is robbed of the Solar right to self-identity, and the civil rights to be different from society's 'norms'. Sometimes shock is the only strategy that will generate change – a shock of images, or, the use of a word that makes society recoil – but Tee Corinne's images are not brutal, violent, or titillating for the sake of controversy of sexual arousal. They are merely images of munakara Venus and munakara Sun: personal and loving images, with a longevity born of someone with something important to say, and through their planet in munakara, found the right medium in which to say it, long before society was ready to hear her message.

Munakara Venus: Malala Yousafzai

A Brief Biography of Malala Yousafzai[44]

Malala Yousafzai was born on July 12, 1997 in Pakistan to outspoken social activist and educator, Ziauddin Yousafzai, and Toor Pekai Yousafzai. Her family is Sunni Muslim and she was the first born of three children and the only girl in the family. Her father established and administered the Khushal Girls High School and College. Malala was a student at her father's school when the Tehrik-e-Taliban (TTP) invaded the Swat valley in 2007. The TTP began imposing strict Islamic law, destroying or shutting down girls' schools, banning women from any active role in society, and carrying out suicide bombings. Yousafzai and her family fled the region for their safety, but they returned when tensions and violence eased.

On September 1, 2008, when Yousafzai was 11 years old, her father took her to a local press club in Peshawar to protest the school closings, and she gave her first speech "How Dare the Taliban Take Away My Basic Right to Education?" Her speech was publicized throughout Pakistan. Toward the end of 2008, the TTP announced that all girls' schools in Swat would be shut down on January 15, 2009. The British Broadcasting Corporation (BBC) approached Yousafzai's father in search of someone who might blog for them about what it was like to live under TTP rule. Under the pseudonym *Gul Makai* (Urdu for '*cornflower*') Yousafzai began writing regular entries for BBC Urdu about her daily life.

In late February 2009 the TTP, responding to an increasing backlash throughout Pakistan, agreed to a cease-fire, lifted the restriction against girls, and allowed them to attend school on the condition that they wear burkas. In early 2009 *The New York Times* reporter Adam Ellick worked with

Yousafzai to make a documentary, *Class Dismissed*, a 13-minute piece about the school shutdown. Ellick made a second film with her, titled *A Schoolgirl's Odyssey*.

By December 2009 it had become apparent that Yousafzai was the BBC's young blogger and in October 2011 she was nominated by human rights activist Desmond Tutu for the International Children's Peace Prize. One year later, on October 9, 2012, while riding the bus home from school Yousafzai was shot in the head by a TTP gunman in an assassination attempt targeting her for her activism. She survived the attack and was flown from Peshawar to Birmingham, England, for surgery. The incident elicited protests, and her cause was taken up around the world, including by the UN special envoy for global education, Gordon Brown, who introduced a petition that called for all children around the world to be back in school by 2015. That petition led to the ratification of Pakistan's first Right to Education bill. In December 2012 Pakistani President Asif Ali Zardari announced the launch of a $10 million education fund in Yousafzai's honour. About the same time, the Malala Fund was established by the Vital Voices Global Partnership to support education for all girls around the world.

For the first time since being shot, Yousafzai appeared in public, addressing an audience of 500 at the United Nations in New York in 2013 on her 16th birthday. Among her many awards, in 2013 she won the United Nations Human Rights Prize, awarded every five years. She was named one of *TIME* magazine's most influential people in 2013, and with Christina Lamb, co-authored a memoir *I Am Malala: The Girl Who Stood Up for Education and Was Shot by the Taliban* (2013). Four years later she wrote the picture book for children titled *Malala's Magic Pencil* (2017) which was based on her childhood.

In 2014 Yousafzai was the co-recipient of the 2014 Nobel Peace Prize along with Indian social reformer Kailash Satyarthi. Malala Yousafzai was 17 years old at the time, and was the youngest-ever Nobel Prize laureate. Satyarthi shared the Nobel Peace Prize with Yousafzai "for their struggle against the suppression of children and young people and for the right of all children to education."[45] Satyarthi (born January 11, 1954) has munakara Venus in his birth chart (Capricorn Venus to Scorpio Saturn to Mars).

> *"One child, one teacher, one book, one pen can change the world. When the whole world is silent, even one voice becomes powerful."*[20] – Malala Yousafzai

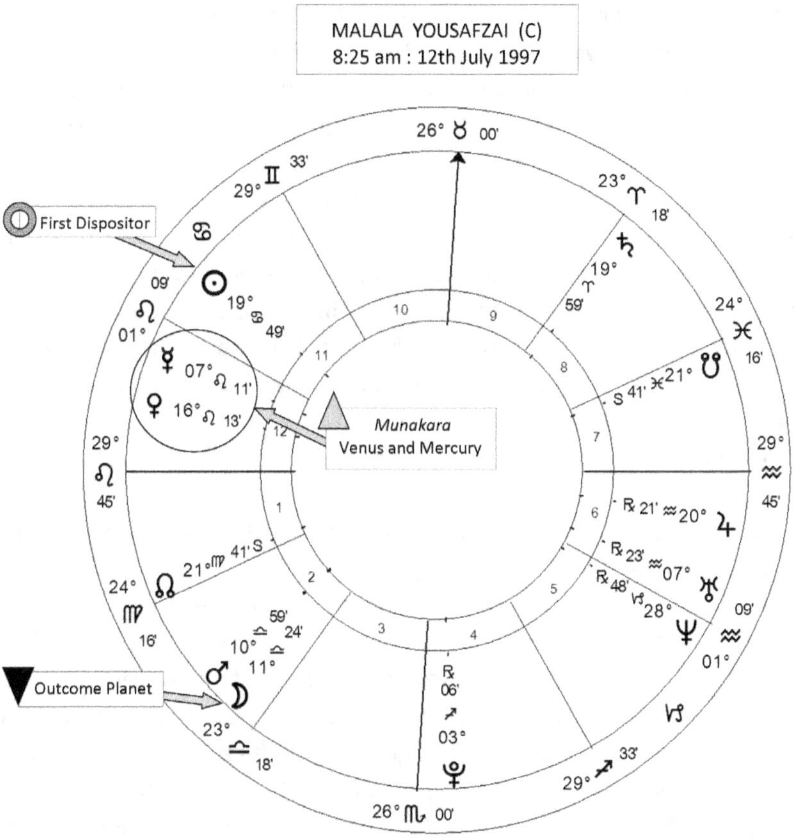

Chapter Fourteen • *Munakara Venus Delineations*

Fig. 14.3: Malala Yousafzai Natal Chart: Munakara Venus and Mercury Duet

Leo Venus and Mercury Duet in Munakara: Malala Yousafzai

- **Key Questions:**
- What does Malala Yousafzai's Venus and Mercury duet contend with?
- What is its driving force?
- What is its trigger? What is its outcome?

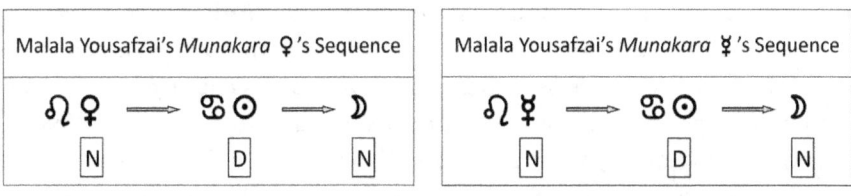

Table 14.5: Malala Yousafzai: Munakara Venus and Mercury Sequence

Malala means "grief-stricken" in the Pashto language and she was named after Malalai of Maiwand, a famous Pashtun poet and warrior woman from southern Afghanistan.[47] Her namesake was a folk hero who was said to have fought and died in the Second Anglo-Afghan War (1878–1880). With two planets in contention, Malala Yousafzai is well named and her Venus and Mercury in munakara are perfect planets to reflect her role model, a famous poet and rebel, who refused to stand aside and silently be defeated by her enemies. In Malala's chart, the two nocturnal planets in contention are a duet, as their sequences are identical and nine degrees separates them in a conjunction in Leo. The nature of this duet is no surprise given what we know of Malala's history and her drive to speak the truth – regardless of her own safety – especially on the subject of equality in basic education for young girls, and higher education opportunities, for female teens and women of any age.

Malala's parents have been a constant support for her, but her father in particular, has led by example (Cancer Sun disposits both nocturnal planets), running a series of schools for girls in Pakistan before the Taliban invasion in 2007. Ziauddin Yousafzai is now as an integral part of her Malala Fund, raising money around the world to support the education of girls in poorer countries, and highlighting the lack of opportunity in countries where women's education is discouraged, or forbidden for religious or social reasons. Ziauddin was born on April 20, 1969, and although no time of birth is available, both Sagittarian Mars and Aries Saturn were in a state of munakara on the day of his birth. Mars in Sagittarius disposits to Jupiter in Virgo, and Mercury was nocturnal during the days around his birth. Saturn in Aries disposits to Mars in Sagittarius with Jupiter as the outcome planet in Saturn's sequence.

In Malala's chart the Moon is the outcome planet for munakara Venus and nocturnal Mercury, and Malala's Moon is in tight conjunction with her Mars in Libra. Both Moon and Mars are disposited by Venus, so there seems to be a cyclic nature to Malala's munakara Venus, and perhaps it is one which keeps feeding her passion, and keeps her fighting spirit alive, even under the most difficult and threatening situations. Mars rules the 9th house of foreign countries and foreign ideals, and the story of Malala's courage to speak out on a blog when her homeland was under siege, and to risk personal harm, is both the beginning of her story, and the outcome of her transportation (whilst unconscious and in mortal danger), to a new life and a new country.

Munakara Planet and Sect Condition – how comfortable is Venus and Mercury Duet?

There is some debate over Malala's birth time which affects the ability to know whether her correct rising sign is Leo or Virgo. Malala's chart in *Astro-databank*[48] is based on the middle range of the time given by her parents, between 8:00am to 9:00am, and therefore has a less reliable 'C' Rating. The time of 8:30am produces an Ascendant of zero Virgo, but Malala says she feels as though she relates better to a Leo rising chart. If the time is reduced by five minutes we find an Ascendant of 29 degrees Leo, and this is the chart which I have used for her munakara Venus and Mercury. This late degree of Leo places her two planets in the Placidus 12th house, but by moving to the Whole Sign system, both will take a new position in the 1st house. First-house Venus in contention ruling the Mid-heaven, and the 3rd house of communication, is a planet honour-bound to speak out, even though the cost is high, and in Malala's case, almost takes her life.

Malala Yousafzai — ♀'s Sect Dignity			
Planet	Sect 1 Status	Sect 2 Hemisphere	Sect 3 Sign
♌ ♀	Day	With the Sun	Fire
N	D	D	D

Malala Yousafzai — ☿'s Sect Dignity			
Planet	Sect 1 Status	Sect 2 Hemisphere	Sect 3 Sign
♌ ☿	Day	With the Sun	Fire
N	D	D	D

Table 14.6: Malala Yousafzai: Munakara Venus and Mercury Sect Dignity

Regardless of whether Malala's Ascendant is in Leo or Virgo, her Cancer Sun has already risen by the time of her birth (8:00am at the earliest) and this will give her a diurnal chart. Knowing what we do of her history so far, it would be an easy assumption to believe that both nocturnal planets are severely out of sect – in a diurnal chart, diurnally placed in the Sun's hemisphere and in the masculine sign of Leo – planets that are in an uncomfortable or unsafe environment.

Robert Hand's assessment of diurnal Venus as "a warrior type goddess" and his expectation that "diurnal Venus in a woman's chart indicates a woman who would have difficulty accepting the traditional female role in society"[49] seems to concur with Malala Yousafzai's need for independence and self expression for herself and her 'sisters' in her country of birth.

Munakara Venus and Mercury Duet: Malala Yousafzai

"Our men think earning money and ordering others around is where power lies. They don't think power is in the hands of the woman, who takes care of everyone all day long, and gives birth to their children."[50] – Malala Yousafzai

Munakara Venus and Mercury Duet in Leo in 12th House (Placidus)

Venus and Mercury are situated in the sign of Leo in the chart belonging to Malala Yousafzai. Both planets are nocturnal, dispositied by the Cancer Sun, which in its turn, is disposited by the Moon. Either one of these two planets can be examined for their impact on what we know so far about Malala's life, but as a duet they work together in their battle to contend with a disadvantage, or a situation which needs courage or fortitude to address, when others ignore the issue or are too afraid for their safety to speak up. Malala is a fighter who believes that girls deserve the same right to education as their male peers, and how better to celebrate munakara Venus Mercury duet in Leo than to establish an international, non-profit organization – bearing your name – that advocates for girls' education worldwide?

The UNESCO Malala Fund for Girls' Right to Education was established in 2012 to expand girls' access to quality, and gender-responsive education, and to ensure safe learning environments, especially in countries affected by conflict and disaster. On her own webpage for Malala's Fund she says of her birth on 2th July 1997: "Welcoming a baby girl is not always cause for celebration in Pakistan – but my father, Ziauddin Yousafzai, was determined to give me every opportunity a boy would have."[51]

The birth time for Malala Yousafzai is a little wobbly but it is likely that either her Munakara Venus rules her Mid-heaven (Taurus), or that munakara Mercury will be the ruler of her MC if the following sign of Gemini moved onto the Mid-heaven with a later birth time. In either scenario, one of the planets from her munakara duet is the driving force behind this young woman's exposure to the world as a teenager under dangerous and trying circumstances. A contentious duet between Venus and Mercury (especially in Leo) will battle to speak out against social injustice, particularly where women are the recipients of bullying or inequality based on their gender.

In 2012, a masked gunman boarded Malala's bus when it was en route to school, and the gunman, a member of the Pakistani Taliban, demanded that she reveal her identity to him. When she stood, he shot one bullet into her left temple, grazing her left eye, skull and brain, and lacerating her facial

Chapter Fourteen • *Munakara Venus Delineations*

nerve. The bullet had hit her left brow and instead of penetrating her skull, it travelled underneath the skin, the length of the side of her head and into her shoulder. Emergency surgeons removed her left temporal skull bone to create space for her brain to swell in response to the injury, and placed her into an induced coma. They relocated the skull bone into her stomach, so that in the future, another surgery would be able to place it back in her head. The titanium plate replaced the skull bone, and UK surgeons removed the skull from her stomach. 'Today it sits on my bookshelf'[52] says Malala.

Miraculously Malala suffered no major brain or nerve damage, and she was flown from Peshawar to Birmingham, England where she underwent surgery to have a titanium plate fitted, as well as a cochlear implant in her skull, to restore her hearing. Months of surgeries and rehabilitation followed, but Malala was not about to abandon her goal, even when the Taliban threatened a second attempt on her life.

Instead, she writes in true munakara Venus and Mercury fashion, recording her decision in 2014, on her Malala Fund website: "It was then I knew I had a choice: I could live a quiet life, or I could make the most of this new life I have been given. I determined to continue my fight until every girl could go to school."[53]

First Dispositor: Sun in Cancer

Malala's Sun in Cancer is in aversion to Leo, if Leo is indeed the correct sign on her Ascendant. To be honest, whether Leo is rising, or Virgo is rising at the time of Malala's birth, both rulers are incapable of seeing – or managing – the affairs represented by the Ascendant. Affairs such as the ability to understand threats to the immediate environment, or to know when there is danger to one's physical safety. Aversion between the planet ruling the Ascendant and its sign often carries with it the mistaken belief that invisibility is your mask and your strength, and brings with it the misconception that you are capable of avoiding danger, and can stay out of harm's way. All of these factors are at risk when the Lord of the Ascendant is blind, as in the case of Leo Mercury ruling Virgo Ascendant, or Cancer Sun ruling Leo Ascendant.

The Sun disposits munakara Venus and Mercury, and Malala's television appearances and interviews in February 2009, and two documentaries released by *The New York Times* in the same year made it impossible to hide her identity from the Taliban. It was perhaps naive of her father (Cancer Sun) to believe there would be no repercussions for her actions, and given her coverage in the local and international media (Venus and Mercury in munakara), her anonymity as a blogger was totally destroyed by December 2009. Her lack of protection, and her exposure to danger were genuine concerns that were not being addressed (munakara Mercury), but even if Malala was aware of them, the damage had already been done and it was only a matter of time before she was marked for execution by the Taliban.

Malala wrote notes in a journal under the pseudonym Gul Makai, the name borrowed from a fictional character in a Pashtun folk story of a girl in a kind of Romeo and Juliet tale. The Sun often represents the father figure and Malala has always been close to her father. In Gul Makai's journal Yousafzai writes that as a child her father, Ziauddin, had an ironic curse: although he loved poetry and words, he had a horrible stutter that made it difficult for him to communicate. His stutter was worsened by the fact that his own father (Malala's grandfather), Rohul Amin, had a beautiful, clear voice.[54] Rohul was a popular theology teacher, widely praised for his electrifying speeches and sermons. Rohul took his son to get various treatments for his stutter, but none of them worked.

In Chapter Two of her book *I Am Malala*, she draws a sharp contrast between her own relationship with her father who she describes as loving and, supportive, and her father's relationship with his own aggressive, intimidating father. Munakara Mercury in Leo describes her father's speech impediment and Ziauddin worked hard to overcome his stutter to become a good speaker and communicator. Malala writes that he passed on his father's wisdom to his daughter, and that he treasured communication because of his own efforts to overcome a stumbling block in his own speech.[55] Yousafzai writes that despite her father's stutter he attended the best schools in the valley, 'a luxury that didn't extend to his sisters' and her father remembers that he was better fed than his sisters, and (unlike his sisters) was permitted to listen to Rohul discuss politics and current events with many of Pakistan's greatest political leaders, including Mohammad Ali Jinnah, the founder of the country.[56] Noticing the divide between his education and his sisters' education, Ziauddin was determined that when he had a daughter, she would receive the same educational and philosophical training as his sons.[57]

The partile square between Cancer Sun and Saturn in Aries (a difficult fall sign) links the Ascendant ruler (Sun) with the ruler of the 6th and 7th houses (Saturn). In August 2021, Malala wrote in a blog published on Podium: "Two weeks ago, while US troops withdrew from Afghanistan and the Taliban gained control, I lay in a hospital bed in Boston, undergoing my sixth surgery, as doctors continued to repair the Taliban's damage to my body."

Chapter Fourteen • *Munakara Venus Delineations*

We may see the courage and the passion of her munakara planets, but the cost is high when her suffering is an ongoing reality. In a blog post titled 'Healing from one Taliban bullet', Malala says she recently called her friend who had witnessed the shooting on the bus to ask what happened on that day. Her friend replied that she had stood still and silent when her name was called out, staring into the face of her would-be assassin, her only reaction the clutching of her friend's hand, "You held my hand so tightly that I felt the pain for days. He recognised you and started firing. You covered your face with your hands and tried to bend down. A second later, you fell into my lap."[58]

Malala consistently received her parents' support and encouragement for her activism, and this support is shown by her Sun and Moon's involvement with her two planets in contention. Malala calls her father her ally and inspiration, as Ziauddin Yousafzai has been an educator and activist involved in humanitarian work throughout his life. It was her father's idea she start the BBC blog, and together, father and daughter established the Malala Fund, a charity dedicated to giving girls an opportunity to achieve a future of their own choosing. Munakara Venus and Mercury's dispositor is her Cancer Sun, and in recognition for her work Malala received the Nobel Peace Prize in December 2014, and became the youngest-ever Nobel laureate.

The outcome planet: Moon in Libra

My mother always told me, 'Hide your face. People are looking at you.' I would reply, 'It does not matter; I am also looking at them.'"[59]

Malala Yousafzai's chart (*Fig. 14.3*) has a nine degree gap in the conjunction between Venus and Mercury, and the Mars/Moon conjunction in Libra forms a sextile aspect to the two nocturnal planets in munakara status. The Moon is the third planet in the duet's munakara sequence, and with Venus as dispositor for Libra Mars / Moon, there is a circular effect to the three-step process that starts with Venus and circles back to complete with Venus. The sextile aspect also ties the four nocturnal planets together in a non-threatening aspect that can have enormous energy and drive when two of these planets are a duet in munakara.

The Moon is the outcome planet for munakara Venus / Mercury duet, and its close conjunction to Mars gives some clue as to the physical struggles which will be an ongoing part of her life. They are the result of a singular act of violence designed to silence her voice, but contention is often a double-edged sword, and the desired outcome of her name disappearing forever did not happen. Instead, her whisper became a roar that was heard around the world, and still has positive long-term effects through her Foundation.

Saturn (in fall) o opposes her Libra Mars /Moon, and with its rulership of 6th and 7th houses, there are always going to be battles ahead, whether they are Malala's personal battles, or those she fights for silenced girls across the globe, desperately hoping for the chance to gain access to a decent education.

In her youth Malala vowed that if she did marry at all, it would not be until she was at least 35, perhaps due to the fact that Saturn opposes her Moon and squares her Venus in contention. However, in November 2021, at age 24, Malala exchanged vows with 27-year-old Asser Malik, whom she had met at Oxford in 2018 when he was visiting friends there. Malala says, "I wasn't against marriage, but I was cautious about its practice. I feared losing my humanity, my independence, my womanhood – my solution was to avoid getting married at all. I couldn't call myself a feminist if I didn't have reservations."[60]

The pair share a love of cricket, with Malala recounting how she played backyard cricket with her younger brothers and their friends but was frustrated with gently thrown balls. She would shout to them to bowl to her 'like they would if she were a boy.' In reflection of Mars and Saturn's impact on the Moon Malala says, "Playing sports helped give me the boldness to be competitive and resilient in my fight for girls' education and equality."[61]

Asser Malik has been the High Performance General Manager for the Pakistan Cricket Board since 2020, and previous to this appointment, was a managing director at a player-management agency for the sport. He is also co-founder of the amateur cricket league "Last Man Stands", which helps to give amateur and recreational players the opportunity to hone their skills, and increase their experience in case they wish to move into professional cricket. His passion for supporting others' dreams is perhaps the reason why he understands Malala's drive and enthusiasm for her own cause, and why she feels she can maintain her independence, freedom and integrity within the bounds of her marriage. Uranus opposes her munakara Mercury, so only time will tell if she can continue to grow her cause, and still feel she has support from her husband.

The Moon represents mother in the chart, and Malala's Moon aspects two difficult planets, the malefic pair, Mars (in detriment) and Saturn (in fall). Not only do these aspects describe Malala's ongoing struggles to repair her body, but they are also a reflection of the adjustment her mother has needed to make to her own life after Malala's shooting. Toor Pekai Yousafzai spoke

Chapter Fourteen • *Munakara Venus Delineations*

with BBC Radio 4 Woman's Hour in April 2017, and candidly talked about the sudden change in her family's life, and her sadness in knowing that she will probably never live in her homeland again. "It was very hard when I left everyone behind. We didn't expect to live in a foreign country...we couldn't prepare (for it). We had to suddenly leave Pakistan. The attack changed everything. We had to focus on Malala's life."[62]

Whilst Malala was recovering from surgery in Birmingham, England, her parents and two brothers were scrambling to pack up their belongings because their lives were in danger too, and they needed to flee the country after so much worldwide publicity. If Leo is indeed Malala's rising sign, then Cancer sits on her 12th-house cusp by Whole Sign, and the fear of hidden enemies still intent on revenge, is as much a problem for her family, as it is for the young woman who refuses to be silenced.

Malala's father is unusually liberal in his views on equality for women, and he often accompanies his daughter to high-profile functions to promote her cause. But her mother stays in the background and rarely grants an interview (the title of the BBC is *Malala Yousafzai's mother: Out of the shadows*). Her daughter's comments on the power of women who undertake the daily care of their families, and her concerns on the sacrifice of a woman's identity to marriage, is perhaps an interesting reflection on witnessing her own mother's experiences.

Whilst Malala has flourished in England, gaining her BA in Philosophy, Politics and Economics (PPE) in 2020 at Oxford University, her mother has struggled with a new language, and a foreign culture, as well as experiencing isolation from her friends and family in Pakistan. Malala's focus on the plight of young girls is understandable as she relates to women within her own age bracket, but perhaps munakara Venus and Mercury needs to be reminded sometimes that women of all ages can suffer from inequality, isolation and powerlessness. Circumstances can shift so quickly, and a woman will adapt not only for her own survival, but according to her family's needs, and often, like her mother, they make choices of invisibility in order for the next generation to shine. The old saying 'A mother is only as happy as her most miserable child' is too often true, and if Malala becomes a parent herself, the sequence of munakara Venus, to Cancer Sun, to Moon, will challenge her planet in contention, regardless of whether she births a daughter – who she will teach to fight for equality – or a son, who will learn to value and respect women, without compromising his masculinity, or his heritage.

CHAPTER FIFTEEN
Munakara Sun Delineations

Friedrich Nietzsche

A Brief Biography of Friedrich Nietzsche[1]

Friedrich Nietzsche was born on 15th October 1844 in Saxony, Prussia (Germany). He was a German classical scholar, philosopher, composer, and critic of culture, who became one of the most influential of all modern thinkers. He is famous for uncompromising criticisms of traditional European morality and religion.

Nietzsche was the son of a Lutheran pastor who died in 1849, just before Nietzsche's fifth birthday. His mother, Franziska, took him and his younger sister, Elizabeth, to live with her mother and her two sisters. Nietzsche had a brilliant school and university career, culminating in May 1869 when he was called to a chair in classical philology (the study of language) at Basel University in Switzerland. At age 24, he was the youngest person ever appointed to that post. During his years at school, Nietzsche discovered the philosophy of Arthur Schopenhauer and met the great operatic composer Richard Wagner whose music he greatly admired. Nietzsche's friendship with Wagner initially flourished and he seized every opportunity to visit the composer and his wife, Cosima. Wagner appreciated Nietzsche as a brilliant professional apostle, but Wagner's chauvinism and anti-Semitism proved to be more than Nietzsche could tolerate and the relationship soured. By 1878 the breach between the two became final, turning them into open enemies.

Chapter Fifteen • *Munakara Sun Delineations*

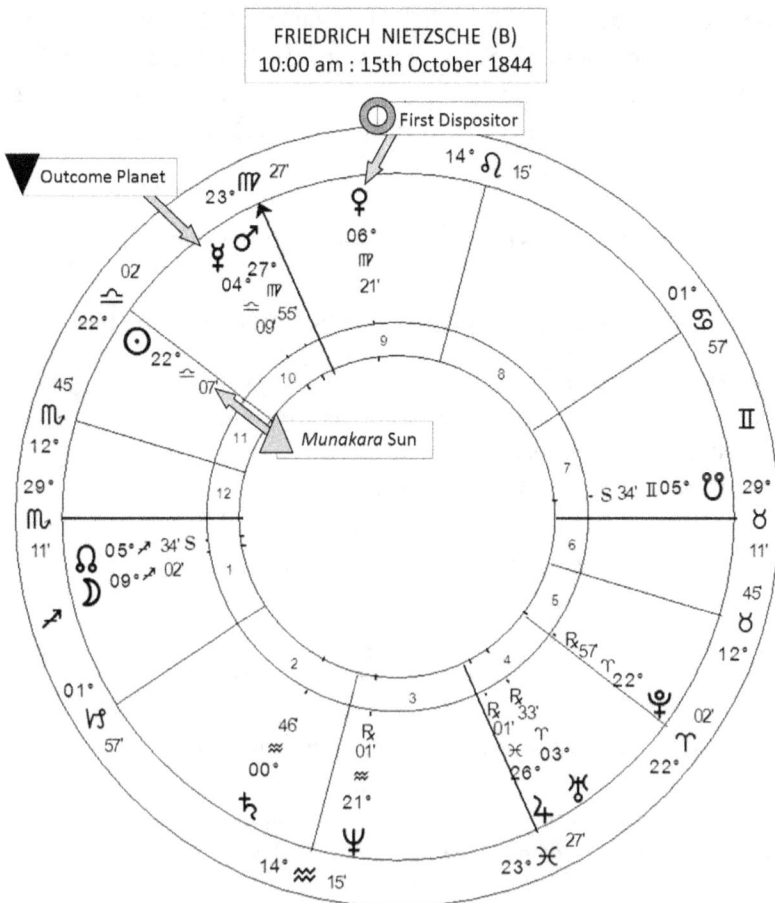

Fig. 15.1: *Friedrich Nietzsche: Munakara Sun in Libra*

Nietzsche obtained leave from his teaching post to serve as a volunteer medical orderly in August 1870, after the outbreak of the Franco-German War. Within a month, he contracted dysentery and diphtheria, which ruined his health permanently. He resigned his professional chair in June 1879 due to his deteriorating health and was granted a pension of 3,000 Swiss francs per year for six years. Nietzsche's acknowledged literary and philosophical masterpiece in biblical-narrative form, *Thus Spoke Zarathustra*, was published between 1883 and 1885 in four parts, the last of which was a private printing at his own expense. As with most of his works, it received little attention. In 1886 he published *Beyond Good and Evil* and the following year, 1887, *On the Genealogy of Morals* but these too failed to win a proper audience.

Nietzsche collapsed in Turin, Italy, in January 1889, having lost control of his mental faculties completely. He spent the last 11 years of his life in total mental darkness, first in a Basel asylum, then in Naumburg under his mother's care and, after her death in 1897, in Weimer in his sister's care. Nietzsche died in 1900 at age 55.

"One must still have chaos in oneself to be able to give birth to a dancing star."[2]

Libra Sun in Munakara: Friedrich Nietzsche

- **Key Questions:**
- What does Friedrich Nietzsche's Sun contend with?
- What is its driving force?
- What is its trigger? What is its outcome?

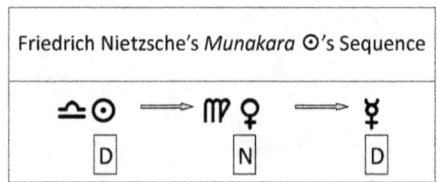

Table 15.1: Friedrich Nietzsche: Munakara Sun's Sequence

"I have a terrible fear that one day I shall be pronounced 'holy'. I do not want to be saint, rather a buffoon ... perhaps I am a buffoon."[3]

Friedrich Nietzsche's munakara Sun shows his battle with his ego and his spirit, his rejection of God, but also his need to find the divine within himself, posing the question "Is man merely a mistake of God's? Or God merely a mistake of man?"[4] Nietzsche's munakara Sun demonstrates his desperate need for social order – describing himself as 'a philosopher of perhaps' – in contrast with his need to destroy the things that created social order, namely 'ideas and fictions like god, science, and belief in progress.'[5] Nietzsche hugely admired Christ the man, even identifying Christ-like behaviour within himself (munakara Sun), but at the same time, he rebelled against the constraints and the hypocrisy of the Christian Church.

As a self-appointed philosopher, Nietzsche observed society, but with a Libran Sun disposited by Venus in fall, his anti-social nature and his poor health produced long periods of isolation where he rarely engaged in

Chapter Fifteen • *Munakara Sun Delineations*

social situations. His pleasures were music and art, and whilst he talked enthusiastically about Dionysian abandonment to the senses, it was all theory (Mercury is Sun's outcome planet), and Nietzsche was incapable of releasing his own inhibitions, preferring to abstain from any intimacy or sexual union with either gender.

His attempts at finding love were pitiful failures, and rejection by various love interests' hurt his pride, striking back by producing misogynistic statements such as, 'God created women. And boredom did indeed cease from that moment – but many other things ceased as well!' 'Woman was God's second mistake.'[6] Or 'You go to women? Do not forget the whip!'[7]

Venus in Virgo – the second planet in fall – is the Sun's dispositor, and rather than pouring his heart into emotional attachments with others, instead Nietzsche was a lover of language, but even this passion brought him heartache and mental despair. As a child brought up in a strict Lutheran atmosphere, he had been encouraged to believe that the main function of words was to express reverence for God. Any other communication was wasteful and irrelevant, so that when his university studies took him to philology – the study of language in oral and written historical sources – he discovered the world of Plato and the Greek classical myths. The pull between silence (or religious reflection) and the ideas presented by the Greek philosophers was just one more dichotomy that Nietzsche tried to reconcile in his tortured mind.

Nietzsche has been described as 'a deeply religious unbeliever',[8] and he had the same complex relationship with language, as he did with religion and God (Mercury is munakara Sun's outcome planet). When Nietzsche wrote, it was like taking dictation from an inner voice, and he liked to jot down phrases for their verbal appeal, rather than for their actual meaning. Yet at other times, he compared language to a prison-house, and to a net, saying language was like an umbrella, 'we hold it up to shield ourselves from awareness that the universe is at best indifferent and at worst hostile.'[9]

He despised the women in his family who treated him as a demigod – his mother, Franziska, and his sister Elisabeth – who tended to his every whim both in childhood, and in his final eleven years of insanity, confiding to a friend in March 1883,

I do not like my mother and it is painful to me to hear my sister's voice. I always became ill when I was with them. We have hardly ever quarrelled....I know how to get on with them, though it does not suit me.[10]

Any record of a close loving bond between brother and sister was a carefully constructed fantasy on the part of his sister, Elisabeth, who had her own reasons for creating a utopian vision of the siblings' relationship. Mercury is the Sun's outcome planet, and Mercury often represents a sibling. Mercury in Libra (along with his Libran Sun) moves to Nietzsche's Whole Sign 12th house of hidden enemies and trines Nietzsche's Aquarian Saturn ruling his 3rd house. Unbeknownst to Friedrich, Elizabeth was his hidden enemy, the destroyer of his ideals and visions for *Übermensch*, his superman, and her evil machinations have twisted his words (outcome planet, Mercury) and ruined his reputation (munakara Sun) for over a hundred years.

Munakara Planet and Sect Condition – how comfortable is the Sun?

Nietzsche's morning birth places his Libran Sun above the horizon in a diurnal chart, but in different houses according to the choice of house system. The Placidus quadrant-based system finds the Sun in Nietzsche's 11th house, whilst the Whole Sign system of one sign per house, sees Libran Sun slip to the 12th sign position, directly ahead of his late-degree Scorpio Ascendant. Either way, the Sun has risen over the horizon, and receives all three sect dignities (*hayz*). Nietzsche resented the fact that, during his cognitive years, he did not gain true recognition for the genius he believed himself to be, but the combination of 12th-house Sun, with munakara status, would support these feelings of being ignored, invisible, under-valued or unappreciated by the society of his time.

Friedrich Nietzsche — ☉'s Sect Dignity			
Planet	Sect 1 Status	Sect 2 Hemisphere	Sect 3 Sign
♎☉	Day	Sun Defines	Air
D	D	D	D

Table 15.2: Friedrich Nietzsche: Munakara Sun's Sect Dignity

Munakara Sun can accentuate the fear of being an imposter who, with time, will be exposed. The Sun in contention can give the individual an uncomfortable feeling of impersonating something which is disingenuous to their nature, social position, or belief system. Circumstances beyond their control can lead to these situations, or simple mistakes, or misinterpretation, but it does little to help their self-confidence or reputation if they are accused of insincerity, dishonesty, or duplicity.

Chapter Fifteen • *Munakara Sun Delineations*

As an unqualified student taking up a professorship at Basel University, Nietzsche was aware of this feeling of being 'fake' in some way: *"The most irksome thing of all is that I am always having to impersonate someone – the teacher, the philologist, the human being."*[11]

Sue Prideaux, author of one biography on Nietzsche, titled *I Am Dynamite! A Life of Friedrich Nietzsche*, comments on his discomfort with the roles he was expected to play in society 'given that he was a young man dressing like an old man to impersonate wisdom, an undergraduate impersonating a professor, an exasperated son impersonating a good son to his irritating mother, and a loving and dutiful son to the memory of his dead Christian father while in the process of losing his Christian faith.'[12]

Virgo Mars in Munakara: Friedrich Nietzsche

- **Key Questions:**
- What does Friedrich Nietzsche's Mars contend with?
- What is its driving force?
- What is its trigger? What is its outcome?

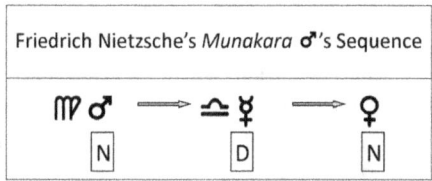

Table 15.3: Friedrich Nietzsche: Munakara Mars' Sequence

Virgo Mars is the second planet in a state of munakara in Friedrich Nietzsche's chart, and the nocturnal Mars' sequence sees both Mercury and Venus involved, but in the reverse order of diurnal Sun's munakara sequence. Virgo Mars (disposited by Mercury) is munakara in Nietzsche's chart, and its role is to fight battles through language, communication, heated discussion and dissent with others. Mars is a planet of hot separations and being munakara can accelerate its desire to challenge or compete with others. Strong opinions or passionate rhetoric become reinforced by a contentious Mars, becoming easily accessible tools at its disposal, especially when Mercury is its dispositor.

Mercury drives Virgo Mars to engage the mind, but without balance (or in munakara status), Libran Mercury can become focused on the negative, or feel hopelessly inadequate to deal with a crisis. This may have been one of the reasons for Nietzsche's conviction that society was sliding into decadence and moral decay. Venus in Virgo (in fall) is Mars's outcome planet, and may have helped create the fictional madman in his 1882 book *The Joyful Wisdom*, who, in his ranting, declared 'God is dead!...We have killed him – you and I!'[13]

With the hindsight of history it appears that Nietzsche's munakara Mars fought two major battles, but tragically, these battles were unwinnable for a man who was emotionally, physically and spiritually conflicted throughout his lifetime. The first conflict lies is the fact that Nietzsche craved recognition and fame during his sane years, and was deeply hurt and disillusioned when only a handful of his books were sold on their release. His fame increased dramatically in the last ten years of the nineteenth century, but by then, Nietzsche had lost his mind and was totally unaware of his latent popularity.

The second deep wounding for Nietzsche's reputation occurred after his death, through the deliberate misinterpretation of his work to promote the Nazi cause as it rose to power. Nietzsche died in August 1900, but he would have been appalled at seeing his works manipulated to serve German nationalism (which he hated in his lifetime), or to substantiate the anti-Semitic ranting and ravings of an aspiring dictator (whom he would have hated even more, had he known Hitler).

Virgo Mars in contention follows the philosopher beyond the grave, as the twisting of his words to create division, hatred, and war would have been heartbreaking for Nietzsche, had he survived into the early years of the twentieth century. As it is, Nietzsche's work still carries the stain of racism, and Nietzsche's rise and fall in popularity has mimicked his two planets – one diurnal (Libran Sun) and one nocturnal (Virgo Mars) in munakara. Nietzsche's philosophical writings were twisted and turned by his sister, Elizabeth (Venus in fall), and yet, his munakara Mars' affirmation of resilience has become one of his most famous quotes:

"From the military school of life: That which does not kill me makes me stronger"[14] – Aphorism #8 from *Twilight of the Idols* (1888)

Munakara Planet and Sect Condition – how comfortable is Mars?

Nietzsche's 'military school of life' must have been a real battlefield for him given that his munakara Mars is in poor sect quality in his chart, and is therefore agitated by being in a diurnal chart, travelling with the Sun in the same hemisphere, and placed in a feminine sign (Virgo).

Chapter Fifteen • *Munakara Sun Delineations*

In his 1995 book on Planetary Sect Robert Hand calls a planet with no access to sect dignity, *ex conditione,* and in his opinion Mars is particularly affected when it is devoid of sect dignity according to the three classifications for sect. Mars' hot dry nature intensifies in the presence of the Sun making it 'the perfectly diurnal Mars...that is, ferociously active, but has its feelings completely in check so that it can with perfect discipline and order create mayhem. It is therefore unlucky and unfortunate.'[15]

Twenty years later Hand says in his 2015 webinar on Sect, that when the lesser malefic (Mars) is without sect dignity, it is 'more belligerent, competitive and selfish in its effects; it wants to win at all costs; it likes to fight but there is no clear objective set......out-of-sect Mars has no understanding of the effects of fighting on others, and the damage it inflicts on others.'[16]

There is some debate over Friedrich Nietzsche's birth time (Rodden: B Rating), but the two possibilities of either 9:11 am or 10:00 am will retain his Scorpio Ascendant, and by Whole Sign, Mars rules the worrisome combination of Ascendant (physical vitality) and the 6th house (the destruction of health) with Aries on its cusp. Mars in munakara produced a lifetime of extremely poor health for Nietzsche, both in his childhood, and during the twenty three years of his adult sanity (he was 44 years old when he was institutionalized). He suffered from headaches that lasted for days (Mars rules *'pains in the head'*),[17] terrible pain in and around his eyes which led to partial blindness (Sun, Moon and Mars rule blindness and *'eye trouble'*),[18] excruciating stomach cramps (*'muscles of the stomach ruled by Mars'*),[19] all of which were physical disabilities he experienced from his childhood years, and into adulthood.

Nietzsche served a short stint in the Prussian Army in 1866 at age 23 as an artilleryman on horseback but was badly injured when he misjudged mounting his moving horse (through his partial blindness), and crashed into the saddle's pommel. The wound took months to heal and he was left with deep scars on his chest. Two years later, in 1870, Nietzsche enlisted as a medical orderly in the Franco-Prussian War, but was granted a medical discharge for the second time, when he became infected by diphtheria and dysentery.

Nietzsche's father passed away at age thirty five, and his son was terrified that he would die at a similar age, from a similar condition. This was not an unreasonable fear given that Karl Ludwig Nietzsche had suffered from 'softening of the brain'. This state began as nervous disorders, but his condition deteriorated into a year of agonising headaches, fits of vomiting, semi-blindness, and total invalidism, Karl finally losing the power to speak in his final months. His father's condition might see a modern diagnosis of a variety of degenerative brain diseases, a brain tumour, or slow bleeding into the brain, but the judgement at the time of Karl's death was insanity and blindness.[20] There was a history of mental problems on both sides of the family: one uncle committed suicide to avoid commitment to a lunatic asylum, and his paternal grandmother had three siblings, all of whom were described as 'mentally abnormal'.[21]

Nietzsche's Voices:
Apollo (Munakara Sun) and Dionysus (Munakara Mars)

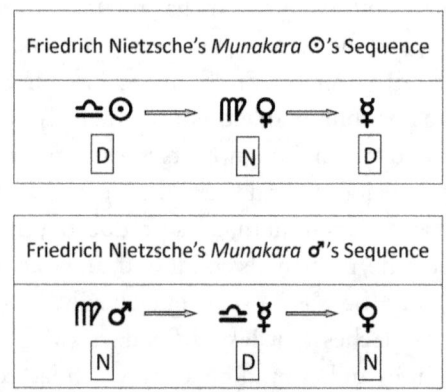

Table 15.4: Friedrich Nietzsche: Munakara Sun in Libra, Munakara Mars in Virgo

"He who fights with monsters should look to it that he does not become a monster himself. And if you gaze long into the abyss, the abyss gazes back into you." – Nietzsche, *Beyond Good and Evil*, 'Epigrams and Entr'actes', 146

Friedrich Nietzsche's two planets in contention are not a duet, as they are neither in the same sign, nor are they from the same sect division. His diurnal Sun and nocturnal Mars' sequences contain the same two planets – Venus and Mercury – but their order differs, as Venus is the Sun's dispositor and Mars' outcome planet, and diurnal Mercury is the Sun's outcome planet, and Mars' first dispositor. This emphasis on two munakara planets from different sect divisions (diurnal and nocturnal), tends to create tension between the two planets, and although there is no aspect from the Sun to Mars, they seem to wage a constant war against one another within Nietzsche's mind and psyche.

Chapter Fifteen • *Munakara Sun Delineations*

Nietzsche's expertise in philology exposed him to the Greek classics, and initially, he was an inspired lecturer who spoke with 'astounding precocity and confident self-assurance.'[22] Unfortunately, he could not maintain his high level of lecturing as his sight suddenly deteriorated, and he was unable to read his notes, or comprehensively follow his chaotic scribbling. Enrolment in his classes dropped so dramatically that eventually there were no students in his classes, and the University was forced to rescind his tenure, and offered him a small pension until he could re-establish himself in a new profession.

Before his professorship when Nietzsche was a student, he wrote an award-winning essay based on a line from Pindar's *Pythiam Odes* – a line he would treasure all his life: "Become what you are, having learned what that is."[23]

'Becoming what he was' emerged as a constant theme in his life, and Nietzsche's work is littered with 'solar' words such 'self-conquest', 'self-division', 'self-analysis', and 'secret self-ravishing' – 'Behold, I am that which must always conquer itself'. At the same time, Nietzsche's belief in his own power was unshakeable as his dialogues with his fictional characters shows: 'And you too, truth-seeker, are only a path and a footprint of my will. Truly, my will to power walks on the heels of your will to truth...'[24]

Nietzsche's munakara Sun (22 Libra) is in partile opposition to Pluto (22 Aries), and he mirrored his own need and desire for power, with the stories of the Greeks gods who used power to create, and then just as easily, to destroy their creations. His Libran Sun trines Neptune (fantasy), and is in quincunx aspect to Jupiter in rulership, so it is no surprise that his worldview became increasingly populated by monsters, demons, and gods.

The voices in Nietzsche's head were loud, constant and contradictory, so much so that he described them as belonging to a singular primal mythological monster with a hundred independent heads, each of which had a different opinion, and each head was happy to argue and debate at length on their own perspective of life. The clamour in his head was incessant, but Nietzsche could not abandon his 100-headed monster, or to make any attempts to quieten the noise as he believed the creature to be the fountainhead of his genius.

Nietzsche had a particular attachment to two of the Greek gods who shared a common father in Zeus, the dominant god in Greek mythology. Apollo, son of Leto, was a sun god, a god loved by the Greeks who valued rational thinking and order, raising logic, prudence and truth, above all virtues. Zeus had many sons, but Apollo was said to be his favourite son, Zeus crowning him in gold, and honouring Apollo as the god of youth and culture, to complement Zeus' own rule over age and law.

One of Apollo's divine step-brothers was Dionysus, who was also fathered by Zeus to Semele, but Dionysus' experience of childhood was very different from Apollo's upbringing. Zeus' wife, Hera, was particularly incensed by the child's creation, especially when Zeus predicted that this new son would be the father of the next generation of gods. Hera's own son, Ares, had been rejected by Zeus, and in her rage, Hera destroyed Semele by tricking Zeus into incinerating his pregnant lover. However, the foetus was saved and sown into Zeus' thigh, and the babe, known as Dionysus ('twice-born'), was spirited away when the pregnancy came to full-term and the child emerged from Zeus' leg.

In Orphic legend, Dionysus was originally the son born to Persephone and Zeus, but jealous Hera ordered the child to be killed and its body to be dissected, cooked and eaten, and when Athena snatched the beating heart, she gave it back to Zeus to implant in Semele as a new life (Dionysus, 'twice-born'). Whatever the origin, Dionysus' mind was deeply affected by the trauma of his double-birth experience, and his myth reflects his instability.

Virtually raised as an orphan, and brought back from the brink of death and madness, Dionysus had some major parental issues, so it seems relevant that he became the god of excess, revelling in wine, dance, and sexual abandonment, encouraging his devotees to lose themselves in ecstasy, and actively promoting chaos, passion, emotions, and unfettered instincts. The ancient Greeks did not see the half-brothers as rivals, and originally, neither did Nietzsche, writing in his first book *The Birth of Tragedy from the Spirit of Music*, "They (Apollo and Dionysus) walk side by side...inciting each other to increasingly powerful births."[25]

Apollo was the principle of individuation, and as such, Nietzsche sought to honour, and perhaps worship, the sun god as an intellectual god of wisdom, prophecy, order, and truth. With Libra Sun in munakara, the German philosopher sought to create his own version of Apollo in his four books, using the teachings of his pagan prophet in *Thus Spoke Zarathustra*. Nietzsche's fictitious figure was based on the Persian prophet, Zoroaster, the founder of the 6th-century BCE, pre-Islamic religion which preached eternal punishment, metered out according to the individual's good and evil deeds on Earth.

In the holy prophet's four books, Nietzsche could see himself as "The Champion of Knowledge", preaching to his disciples, but never actually interacting with them on a personal or emotional level (sun god, Apollo, and munakara Sun). As Zarathustra, he could let loose the voices in his head, becoming wise and omnipotent, the fatherly divinity (munakara Sun) who

Chapter Fifteen • *Munakara Sun Delineations*

guided his mortal children to enlightenment: '(A man) must not only love his enemies, he must also be able to hate his friends', and 'You are rewarding a teacher poorly if you always remain a pupil.'[26]

However, it was Dionysus (his Virgo Mars in munakara) who would eventually control Nietzsche, destroying his sanity in the same way as Dionysus descended into madness after being cut to pieces, and then re-assembled by the gods. In his *Will to Power*, quote #1050, Nietzsche defines Dionysus as 'a drive towards unity, reaching beyond personality, the quotidian (daily routine), society, reality, across the chasm of transitoriness: an impassioned and painful overflowing into darker, fuller, more buoyant states; an ecstatic affirmation of the totality of life...the awareness that creation and destruction are inseparable.'

When Nietzsche broke down in January 1889, he closest friends feared that he had taken his Dionysian dream of disintegration too far. At first, they believed he was faking his madness, endeavouring to simulate the Greek god's ultimate experience through a deliberately induced dissolution of imagined or real boundaries. Eventually, his behaviour convinced them that his breakdown was genuine, and likely to be permanent for the remainder of his years. Nietzsche's mental disorder was believed to be the result of syphilis, but the length of his survival in this state (11 years) was far longer than the disease's usual prognosis, and there is evidence to support the idea that Nietzsche's sexual experiences were non-existent, and that syphilis was unlikely to be the cause of his insanity.

Throughout his life Nietzsche searched for father figures to replace the father who was infirmed during his infancy, who died before he was five years old, and who was missing throughout his lifetime (munakara Sun). His search for a father – a mortal Apollo – was as tragic as any Greek myth. He desperately wanted an older male figure who would give him structure, stability, wisdom and self-identification, but ultimately, each one he chose failed him, and he became disillusioned by each new idol's human foibles.

The sign of Libra belongs to Venus, but Saturn is its second ruler through the Essential Dignity known as exaltation. Nietzsche's Saturn is in Aquarius, in rulership, and although there is no aspect by degree between Libra's two ruling planets, the element of air links them, and there is still some quality of Saturn's idolization of father through the munakara Sun in Libra. The Sun's three-step sequence finishes with its outcome planet, diurnal Mercury, also in Libra, and Mercury's early degrees means it does indeed, form a trine aspect with Saturn in Aquarius, linking air to air sign.

Nietzsche's relationships with his adoptive father figures created a pattern of instant connection and adoration, shortly followed by disillusionment and separation. It became one of the main themes of his life, and it is safe to say that his relationship with older men reflected the sometimes strained relationship between the Greek gods Zeus (father) and Apollo (son). The two gods had very little interaction in the mythological world, but many versions recount that Apollo was given the gift of prophecy by Zeus. However, in tales of the Trojan War, Apollo constantly challenged Zeus and tried to overthrow him to take control of the war. Zeus was never going to let this happen, and as punishment, Apollo and Poseidon (Zeus's son and brother, but natural enemies) were forced by Zeus to cooperate in order to build the walls of Troy. Zeus killed Apollo's son Asclepius for having the audacity to raise the dead, and Apollo retaliated by killing the favoured Cyclops who forged Zeus' thunderbolt. Apollo was banished from the heavens and lost his immortality in one story, but in another, Zeus sided with Apollo when Hermes stole his brother's oxen. In other words, another complicated father-son relationship.

Whenever and wherever Nietzsche travelled in life, he kept a shrine to his dead father: a photograph of Karl Ludwig which sat beneath a small oil painting of Christ's deposition from the Cross.[27] In his mind Nietzsche may have fused the two images together – a missing father and the Son of God – to create the idea that 'God is dead!' Nietzsche's anguish at being physically separated from his father at such a young age, was compounded by his spiritual separation from two generations of Lutheran ministers, the religious vocation chosen by his father and his grandfather. Munakara Sun rules the Placidus 9th house and the Whole Sign 10th house, and as the sole male heir, Friedrich had been expected to follow the family tradition of studying theology, in preparation to become the family's next generation of Church representatives.

In order to deal with these two separations, Nietzsche needed a male figure to adore and idolise, and to provide him with both an Apollonian sense of structure and discipline, as well as a Dionysian model to act as an artistic, spiritual guide and mentor. Nietzsche gravitated to a number of older men, scholars, philosophers and men of intellect and deep thought: men such as his distinguished professor and mentor Friedrich Ritschl, who recognised his brilliance as a philologist, and recommended him for the post at Basel University, and Jacob Burckhardt, the Swiss historian who shared Nietzsche's passion for the ancient Greek world, and the modern philosophy of Arthur Schopenhauer (1788–1860).

Chapter Fifteen • *Munakara Sun Delineations*

However, it was his adoration for the composer, Richard Wagner – 31 years his senior – which would combine Nietzsche's love of music, and provide him with his spiritual and philosophical equal, as well as satisfying his need for a beloved replacement father-figure.

> *"You need hashish to get rid of unbearable pressure. Well then, I need Wagner. He is the antidote to all things German."* – Nietzsche, in *Ecco Homo*, 'Why am I So Clever', Section 6

In the end, Nietzsche's adoration of Wagner waned, and the two men parted ways for several reasons. Wagner's ego grew with his sizable reputation, and Nietzsche felt that Wagner sacrificed their friendship (munakara Libran Sun dispositod by Venus). Wagner lost Nietzsche's respect when Wagner swapped integrity for wealth, and began compromising the quality of his later compositions to cater for wealthy clients with little artistic appreciation. Nietzsche became increasingly uncomfortable with Wagner's growing circle of anti-Semitic friends, and the two men's common views, which had originally drawn them together, began to take separate pathways, especially when Nietzsche lost interest in the philosopher Schopenhauer, a definite favourite with Wagner.

In 1876, whilst writing a book on the individual genius' effect on the culture of an age, and using a less than flattering version of Wagner as his subject, Nietzsche began to understand that his quest for self-individualisation was being swallowed up by his obsession with Wagner and his music. Libran Sun in contention, and opposing Pluto caused him to recognise Wagner's power over him, and he wrote, 'Nietzsche's 'becoming' required the 'overcoming' of Wagner'.[28]

In Wagner, Nietzsche saw the father figure who began as the benevolent Apollo, but who over time, transformed into another morally-corrupt human who revelled in the destructive forces of Dionysian ecstasy. In Nietzsche's mind – munakara Libra Sun, to Venus, to Mercury – Wagner became a terrible danger who had captured his emotions and swept away his freewill, creating 'the delirious, befogging metaphysical seduction that had once seemed like the highest redemption of life.' His growing realization of Wagner's metamorphosis from the god of order (Apollo) into the god of chaos (Dionysus), caused Nietzsche to lash out in print, criticising Wagner for being 'a romantic histrionic, a spurious tyrant, a sensual manipulator' who had shattered his nerves and ruined his health.[29]

Then came one last blow from which the relationship could never recover (Virgo Mars in munakara). Nietzsche had visited Wagner in Italy, and concerned for his friend's deteriorating sight, Wagner had written to a doctor friend in Frankfurt, Otto Eiser, asking that he grant his ailing friend a thorough consultation to determine the cause of Nietzsche's blindness. Unwisely, Wagner added his own insensitive thoughts (and the general belief at the time), voicing his suspicions that Nietzsche's severe eye problems and poor health originated from excessive masturbation. Wagner went on to say: 'Ever since I observed N. (Nietzsche) closely, guided by such experiences, all his traits of temperament and characteristic habits have transformed my fear into a conviction.'[30]

Dr Eiser replied to Wagner's letter, saying that after examination, he agreed with Wagner, but whilst there had been cases of recovery by neurotic, hysterical patients who had been debilitated by masturbation, but that in his professional opinion, a cure for Nietzsche was not possible, as his eyesight was past restoring, due to the extensive damage and deterioration to his eyes. A highly private man, and one with huge sexual inhibitions, Nietzsche would have been horrified had he been aware of their private correspondence on his health and its origins. But worse was to come, and the letter was circulated (Wagner being blamed for its exposure) amongst his friends and colleagues and could not have come at a worse time for the shy philosopher, who was consequently branded as a sexual deviant.

Platonic *'menage a trois'*: A Beauty, a Writer, and a Genius
Munakara Sun and Munakara Mars

*"Almost all my human relationships have resulted from attacks of a feeling of isolation....My mind is burdened with a thousand shaming memories of such weak moments, in which I absolutely could not endure solitude any more... **there is about me something very remote and alien so that my words have other colours than the same words from other people**."* (my bold italics on the quote) – Correspondence from Friedrich to Elisabeth (sister), on the eve of her wedding, May 1885

Paul Ree was a philosopher and writer, a few years younger than Nietzsche, and the two men formed a friendship that lasted around six years, between October 1876 and 1882. Together they collaborated to produce

Chapter Fifteen • *Munakara Sun Delineations*

literary works which influenced each other's style and thought. In March 1882, Ree met Lou Salome, 'an elegant and cosmopolitan twenty-one-year-old half-Russian girl of great magnetism, originality and intelligence'.[31] Ree was smitten by her, and in conversation Ree passionately shared the work he was engaged in with his friend, Nietzsche. Salome was so impressed by his description of Nietzsche that she had a dream in which she saw the three of them – Ree, herself and Nietzsche – living in Paris as a platonic *ménage a trois*, a Holy Trinity of philosophising free spirits 'filled almost to bursting with spirituality and keenness of mind'.[32]

The idea was doomed from the start, as naturally, both men fell madly in love with the beautiful Lou, and both tried to independently woo her without the other's knowledge, and gain her consent to their independent proposals of marriage. On May 5 1882, Nietzsche shook off his persistent rival suitor, and he and Salome climbed to the peak of Monte Sacro in the northern Italian Alps, sharing an intellectual and spiritual communion that deeply affected both of them. Even after the events that followed, Nietzsche's appreciation of the sacred moment could not be tarnished, and he would describe the ascent with Lou, as 'the most exquisite dream of my life'.[33]

Nietzsche unwisely put the two young women in his life together, his possessive sister, Elisabeth, and his new love, Lou Salome, but sparks flew as Elisabeth became insanely jealous of Lou's beauty. Elizabeth was no match for Lou's sparkle and she resented the attention she drew when the women were out together socially. Elisabeth was terrified that the prospective bride (in Nietzsche's eyes only), would usurp her power over her brother, and destroy his affection for her, transferring his fraternal love, and replacing it with passion for his new wife. Determined to break the lovers' affections, Elisabeth wrote to their mother, telling her of Lou's flirtations, and Friedrich's intentions to marry 'a brazen hussy'. Nietzsche returned home to be berated by Franziska as a liar and a coward for not revealing his intentions to his mother. Striking the greatest blow to her son, she continued by telling him he was a disgrace to his father's name and that he had dishonoured his father's grave.

The Holy Trinity – Paul Ree, Lou, and Friedrich – reunited in Leipzig in October 1882, but Nietzsche's hopes to win Lou were in tatters. Wagner's letter to his doctor, written five years earlier, expressing his opinion on the reason behind Nietzsche's poor health, had been maliciously circulated by Wagner's publisher, and Nietzsche was mortified by the letter's content and the public ridicule that followed. On November 5, 1882, Lou and Ree stole away together in the middle of the night, abandoning Nietzsche who was distraught and heartbroken by their joint betrayal.

Huge doses of opium did little to relieve Nietzsche's emotional and mental anguish, but the first book of *Thus Spoke Zarathustra* (*TSZ*) was born from this experience. *TSZ* is the teachings of a prophet who has risen above human interaction to preach to his loyal devotees, and whilst the book contains no direct reference to Lou Salome and Paul Ree, a general disgust for women flavours Zarathustra's warnings to his male audience:

> *Is it not better to fall into the hands of a murderer than into the fantasies of a lecherous woman?...Do I recommend chastity? With some, chastity is a virtue, but with most, nearly a vice. It is true that they abstain, but the bitch sensuality looks enviously out of everything they do... And how gracefully the bitch sensuality knows how to beg for a piece of spirit when denied a piece of flesh!* – Zarathustra, Part One, 'On Chastity'

'I Am Dynamite'
Munakara Sun and Munakara Mars

> "I know my fate.
> *One day there will be associated with my name the recollection of something frightful – of a crisis like no other before on earth, of the profoundest collision of conscience, of a decision evoked against everything that until then had been believed in, demanded, sanctified. I am not a man, I am dynamite.*"
> – Ecco Homo, 'Why I am a Destiny', Section 1

Nietzsche's mental breakdown took place in January 1889, but the previous year had seen a slow descent into madness and megalomania, evidenced by his choice to begin another book on 15th October 1888, on the eve of his forty fourth birthday. The book was to be titled *Ecco Homo*, intended to be an autobiography, a summary of his books, his views, his life stories, and his psychology, and it would be completed on 4th November, 1888, eighteen days after it was begun. Referring to himself in the third-person, Nietzsche wrote to a friend, on 13th November, 1888, nine days after completing his manuscript, 'Mankind, who had paid him no attention, would at last see its luck as he revealed the light and fright of himself'.[34]

Chapter headings in the book such as 'Why I am so Wise', 'Why I am so Clever', 'Why I write such Good Books', and 'Why I am a Destiny' were alarming, but they contained a hidden irony for Nietzsche – if he was going to write his own story for prosperity – then he might as well exaggerate, and present himself in the best possible light. In hindsight, his irony was lost on his readers, given that his mind deteriorated into madness less than three months after writing *Ecco Homo*.

This private joke may have been an edgy observation on human vanity, had it not been for the letters that Nietzsche was writing to his friends, with a new aggressive and combative tone emerging in his correspondence (munakara Mars in Virgo). He began making claims of his own divinity (munakara Sun) and referring to himself in the letters as Christ (signing as 'The Crucified') or as Dionysus, God, or King Ludwig I Bavaria, or Ferdinand de Lesseps (the French diplomat who helped in building the Panama Canal), or Count Robilant (Italian Ambassador to London), to name just a few.

After his release from the asylum, Nietzsche was given into the care of his mother Franziska, who passed away in April 1887, three years before her son's death in 1900. Elizabeth, his younger sister, took over his care and moved him to Weimar, the seat of 'German Athens'. She persuaded her brother's former friends to finance the purchase of Villa Silberblick, a manor house which Elizabeth refurbished with their donations, creating the Nietzsche archive which would include notes, letters, drafts of his book, and any memorabilia that she has been slowly collecting since 1890.

In the last decade before the turn of the twentieth century, Nietzsche's work had become popular in Europe due to the efforts of four distinguished individuals: Danish literary critic Georg Brandes, Swedish playwright, August Strindberg, Norwegian painter, Edvard Munch (his 1893 painting *The Scream* depicts his character's reaction to the proclamation, 'God is dead!'), and former love interest, Lou Salome, who had become a writer, analyst, and biographer of Nietzsche's life.

Elizabeth wrote her own version of Nietzsche's life, with herself as the central figure – munakara Mars in Virgo, to Libra Mercury, to Venus – and republished many of his books but with her own agenda, twisting his philosophy to suit her own political leanings. Unlike Nietzsche, who hated anti-Semitic sympathies, Elisabeth worshipped Adolf Hitler, and dedicated her brother's work to win support for the new Chancellor of Germany. Elisabeth had a long life, and she had exclusive copyright to manipulate his work to her ends, including the eleven years of his insanity, and with the gift of longevity, a further thirty five years following Nietzsche's death in 1900.

Munakara in Practice

Nietzsche's *Übermensch*, roughly translated as 'superman' (munakara Sun opposing Pluto: munakara Mars opposes Jupiter in rulership) was first introduced in *Zarathustra* after the prophet declares that all gods are dead, and that this superior version of man is not held back by superstitions, dead religions, or 'eternal reason-spiders (gods) who send punishment from above to punish the sinner.'[35]

The superman needed to reject all systems and all philosophies that reduced the world to a single system. He had the intellect and insight (munakara Sun) to understand that truth had no single definition, and instead *Übermensch* needed to question everything, and to embrace everything as a question of perspectives (Virgo Mars in munakara). The *Übermensch* understood that no eternal Being pulled the strings, that experiences were 'merely accidents on the dance floor of life',[36] but that existence was no less meaningful for the lack of a supreme Being.

The Third Reich took Neitzsche's superman, twisting it and warping it to indoctrinate Hitler Youth, an organization started in 1922 to train teenagers in Nazi principles. This was the absolute antithesis of Nietzsche's *Übermensch* who is best described in his final book *Ecco Homo*. Here Nietzsche describes his ideal man as being cut from wood that is simultaneously hard, gentle and fragrant. 'He works out how to repair damage, he uses mishaps to advantage and he knows how to forget. He is strong enough that everything turns out for the best for him, and whatever doesn't kill him only makes him stronger.'[37]

For Nietzsche *Übermensch* was not the Aryan 'super-race' promoted by Hitler as the ideal soldier of war and destruction. Rather, the superman was the perfect foil for his munakara Sun – "a man at peace with himself, finding joy in his earthly purpose, rejoicing in the sheer magnificence of existence and content with the finitude of his mortality."[38]

In Nietzsche's chart his munakara Mars forms an out of sign trine to Saturn in Aquarius. In Whole Sign, Virgo Mars sits in the 9th house of philosophy, and trines Saturn in rulership, in his 3rd house of siblings. Elisabeth both adored and resented her brilliant and fragile brother, who would demand that she drop everything to attend to him when his health brought episodes of acute pain that left him bedridden (munakara Mars rules both 1st and 6th house). By all accounts, Elizabeth was an intelligent woman, but she refused to be educated when Nietzsche offered to pay her tuition, and instead she hid her ignorance and prejudice behind the less demanding role of a domesticated female.

Throughout their lives Nietzsche called Elisabeth by his pet name for her, 'Llama'. He used the name because the description he had read in his childhood animal book was one that he believed best described his sister. The text read, 'The llama is a remarkable animal; it willingly carries the heaviest burdens, but when a llama does not want to go on, it turns its head round and discharges its saliva, which has an unpleasant odour, into the rider's face. If coerced or treated badly, it refuses to take any nourishment and lies down in the dust to die.'[39]

He could not have known as a child when he saw the resemblance between a llama and his sister's nature, that his 'Llama' would turn on him and spit in his philosopher's face, and that for half a century the type of society he most hated, would applaud her actions in distorting his beliefs for their political gain.

In 1885 Elisabeth married a leading chauvinist and anti-Semite, Bernhard Forster, and the pair emigrated with a handful of 'pioneers' to Paraguay to establish a settlement as a new 'Fatherland' where an Aryan race could prosper. Forster suicided in 1889 when the settlement failed, and Elizabeth returned to Germany to a shattered brother on the brink of insanity. Elisabeth worked diligently to refashion Nietzsche in Forster's image, and to recreate a hero for the Aryan cause. She maintained ruthless control over Nietzsche's literary estate and dominated by greed, produced collections of his "works" consisting of discarded notes, such as *The Will to Power*, published in 1901, a year after her brother's death. She also committed petty forgeries. Generations of commentators were misled by what they believed to be Nietzsche's words which had been twisted by Elizabeth to support her Nazi sympathies. Nietzsche was an ardent foe of nationalism, anti-Semitism, and power politics, but his name was later invoked by fascists to advance the very things he loathed.[40]

Munakara Sun: Vincent van Gogh

Brief Biography of Vincent van Gogh[41]

Vincent van Gogh was born nine years after Friedrich Nietzsche on 30th March 1853 in the Netherlands. He was a Dutch Post-Impressionist artist who is among the most famous and influential figures in the history of Western art. He was a prolific painter given that in just over a decade, he created approximately 2100 artworks, including around 860 oil paintings, most of them in the last two years of his life. Van Gogh's work was beginning to gain critical attention before he died from a self-inflicted gunshot wound in 1890 at age 37.⁴² Only one of van Gogh's paintings, *The Red Vineyard*, was sold during his lifetime (6 March 1890 for 400 francs).⁴³

Van Gogh was the eldest of six children, born to a Protestant pastor from an upper-middle-class background. As a young man, he worked as an art dealer, but became depressed after he was transferred to London, where he fell in love and was rejected in 1874. He turned to religion, and impelled by a longing to serve humanity, he planned to enter the ministry. However, he abandoned this project in 1878 swapping to short-term training as an evangelist in Brussels. A conflict with the church's authority ensued, and he left to do missionary work among the impoverished population of the Borinage, a coal-mining region in south-western Belgium. There, in the winter of 1879–80, he experienced the first great spiritual crisis of his life. Living among the poor, he gave away all his worldly goods in an impassioned moment; he was thereupon dismissed by church authorities for a too-literal interpretation of Christian teaching.⁴⁴

Penniless and feeling his faith destroyed, van Gogh sank into despair and withdrew from everyone. It was then that he began to draw seriously, thereby discovering his true vocation as an artist. Van Gogh decided that his mission from then on would be to bring consolation to humanity through art. In 1886, he moved to Paris where he stayed for two years developing his own style after meeting with artists from the Impressionist group. He left Paris in February 1888 and moved to Arles, in south-eastern France.

The time in Arles was one of his most prolific periods: he completed 200 paintings and more than 100 drawings and watercolours.⁴⁵ French painter Paul Gauguin joined him in Arles in October 1888, but the visit did not end well. In May 1889, van Gogh began to falter and fearing for his sanity, he was admitted by his own volition to the asylum in Saint-Remy-de-Provence in order to be under medical supervision.⁴⁶ He stayed there for 12 months, alternating between moods of calm and despair, and working intermittently. He returned to Paris in May 1890 and two months later took his own life.

*"I am seeking, I am striving, I am in it with all my heart."*⁴⁷
– Vincent van Gogh

Chapter Fifteen • *Munakara Sun Delineations*

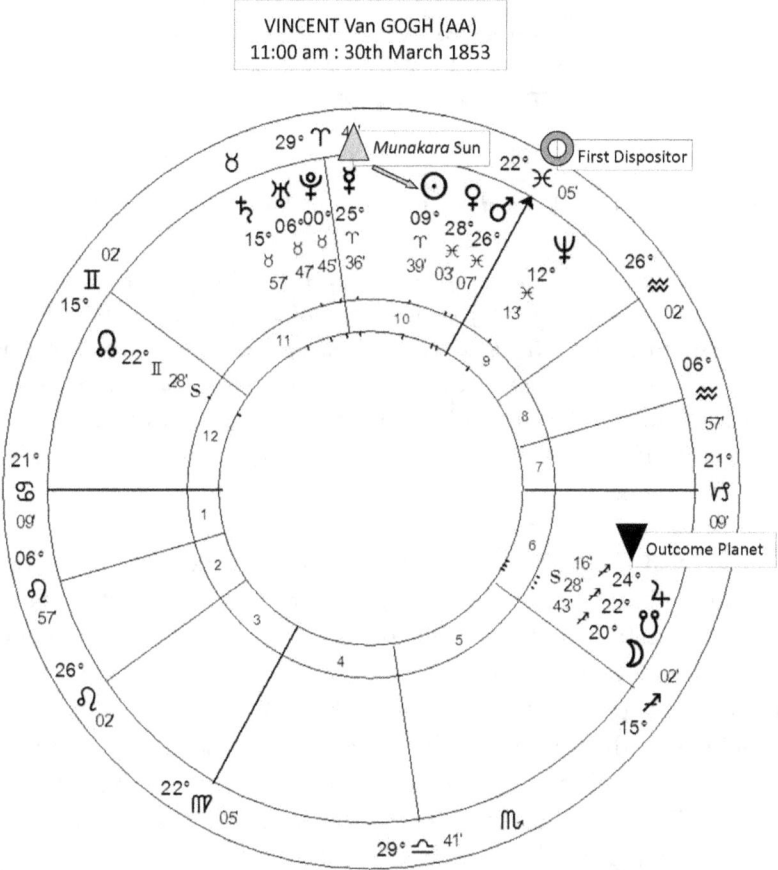

Fig. 15.2: Vincent van Gogh: Munakara Sun in Aries

Aries Sun in Munakara: Vincent van Gogh

"A great fire burns within me, but no one stops to warm themselves at it, and passers-by only see a wisp of smoke."[48] – Vincent van Gogh

- **Key Questions:**
- What does Vincent van Gogh's Sun contend with?
- What is its driving force?
- What is its trigger? What is its outcome?

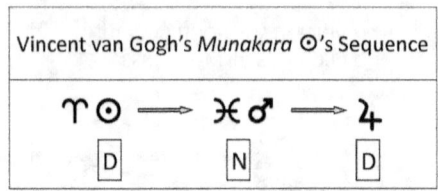

Table 15.5: Vincent van Gogh: Munakara Sun Sequence

What am I in the eyes of most people – a nonentity, an eccentric, or an unpleasant person – somebody who has no position in society and will never have; in short, the lowest of the low. All right, then – even if that were absolutely true, then I should one day like to show my work – what such an eccentric, such a nobody, has in his heart. That is my ambition, based less on resentment than on love in spite of everything, based more on a feeling of serenity than on passion.[49]

Vincent van Gogh's Sun is in is exalted sign of Aries and yet his letters to his brother Leo are a painful display of the artist's lack of self-confidence, his enormous self-doubt in the value of his work, and his estimation of how poorly he was viewed by society.

His munakara Sun in Aries disposits to Mars in Pisces and perhaps part of self-doubt lies with Mars on the Mid-heaven. Pisces Mars on the Mid-heaven demonstrates van Gogh's desperation to be noticed, valued and lauded by his peers – "I want to touch people with my art. I want them to say 'he feels deeply, he feels tenderly'."[50]

Van Gogh's despair and disappointment at his art's lack of popularity, became an even greater burden when Mars conjuncts Venus (in exaltation), and both planets disposit to Jupiter in rulership on the South Node. The two planets on the MC – Mars and Venus – are both important players for van Gogh's two planets in munakara. Munakara Sun in Aries disposits to Mars and munakara Saturn in Taurus disposits to Venus. Together, the nocturnal planets show great creativity (Venus in exaltation) and self-sacrifice (Mars in Pisces), and many of van Gogh's letters to his brother Theo are detailed descriptions given with great vigour on whichever painting or drawing Vincent was working on at the time of his correspondence. Van Gogh simply could not believe that his work would go 'undiscovered', particularly when both nocturnal planets were disposited by Jupiter in rulership.

However, the outcome planet (Jupiter) is poorly situated, both by house position (6th house), and by aspect (conjunct the South Node). Sagittarius

Chapter Fifteen • *Munakara Sun Delineations*

Moon sits on the other side of the South Node, and it too, is affected by the malefic Node, which is inclined to diminish the power and strength of any planet in its vicinity. Jupiter, Moon and South Node are in the 6th house of illness, accident, self-imposed hardships, and constant toil. There has been much conjecture over the root cause of van Gogh's mental and physical illnesses, but the list is long, and includes epilepsy, bipolar disorder, schizophrenia, lead poisoning, gonorrhoea, Meniere's disease (vertigo, hearing loss and tinnitus), sunstroke, and substance abuse disorder. Whatever the diagnosis, his condition was likely worsened by malnutrition, overwork, insomnia, and alcohol.[51]

When Jupiter in Sagittarius is the outcome planet for both of his munakara planets – Sun and Saturn – there are extremes of over-work (6th house), illness, and mental and physical exhaustion. Van Gogh was obviously a brilliant artist, but he had little self-control or discipline (munakara Saturn) and his need for external validation (munakara Sun) gave him no inner peace and eventually, drove him to the point of madness.

Jupiter's rulership over the Moon is a hint as to van Gogh's extreme behaviour (Moon rules Cancer Ascendant), and his high-strung nature exhausted him and gave him little perception of the effects of his behaviour on other people. With Sagittarius Moon disposited by Jupiter in rulership, van Gogh felt every emotion with great intensity, and he was constantly wavering between the extremes of great joy and great despair.

Outcome planets in munakara sequences are likely to act as triggers (in this case, Jupiter's manic work ethic) and van Gogh was known to complete a work in 36 hours before moving on the his next project. His plethora of Jupiterian output strained his limited resources (munakara Sun rules 2nd house), and he was constantly writing to Theo asking to be provided with more money to restock his paints, brushes and canvasses. At the same time, van Gogh reinvented his style several times in the hope that he would catch the eye of the public (Jupiter ruling MC), and that finally, he would receive acknowledgement and wealth as a result of his efforts (Jupiter as outcome planet).

Munakara Planet and Sect Condition – how comfortable is the Sun?

Van Gogh's Sun conforms to all three sect rules and would therefore be classified as being in *hayz*. Robert Hand says that the Sun is much more powerful above the horizon and that the Sun has 'a tendency toward show, the desire to achieve dominance in the outer world.'[52] Hand's 2015 summation of the Sun in a diurnal chart is that good sect dignity improves the Sun's level of activity, sharpens and gives it the ability to create and maintain clear definitions and boundaries.[53]

Vincent van Gogh — ☉'s Sect Dignity			
Planet	Sect 1 Status	Sect 2 Hemisphere	Sect 3 Sign
♈ ☉	Day	Sun Defines	Fire
	D	D	D	D

Table 15.6: Vincent van Gogh: Munakara Sun's Sect Dignity

The extra gift of exaltation to the Aries Sun makes the Sun's creative output prolific, and van Gogh's works number over 2000 in paintings and drawings, as good planetary sect gives the Sun the opportunity to fulfil its passion and its need for self-expression. Often an artist's work is judged by its popularity (Aries Sun in Whole Sign 10th house), or by its ability to gain monetary value (munakara Sun ruling 2nd house,) but van Gogh received neither benefit to feed his hungry Sun that craved attention and prestige. Instead, his munakara Sun left him feeling ignored, under-valued, and unappreciated for his artistic genius.

In other words, good sect dignity may provide opportunity through connections, friendships, teachers and mentors in the sphere that interests you: van Gogh's grandfather and three of his uncles were wealthy art dealers, his brother Theo financially supported him, and his first teacher and admirer, artist Anton Mauve, was a second cousin.

However, good sect positioning does not guarantee success, especially when the planet in question is in a state of munakara. Struggle, obstacles, setbacks regularly occur to challenge and test the individual's resilience, and constant reassessment of values and beliefs centre around the planet in contention and what it signifies in the chart. There are often frustrations and delays when contention is a part of the astrological picture, and learning to manoeuvre through the difficulties presented by planets in munakara is a major growth experience for anyone with these planets.

Taurus Saturn in Munakara: Vincent van Gogh

- **Key Questions:**
- What does Vincent van Gogh's Saturn contend with?
- What is its driving force?
- What is its trigger? What is its outcome?

Chapter Fifteen • *Munakara Sun Delineations*

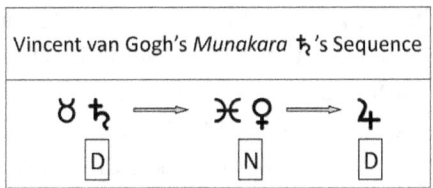

Table 15.7: Vincent van Gogh: Munakara Saturn Sequence

"Art is to console those who are broken by life."[54] – Vincent van Gogh

Munakara Saturn often struggles with authority figures, and there were several notable instances when van Gogh disagreed with his theologian instructors, and when he changed his career, to argue with respected teachers and highly qualified experts whom he challenged as an inexperienced art student. For all van Gogh's insecurities, he felt he knew better than they did, and he lost several positions and opportunities due to his arrogance and his high-handed manner (Jupiter is Saturn and the Sun's outcome planet).

Van Gogh argued with his instructors at the seminary when he confronted them on their orthodox doctrinal approach.[55] He challenged the church authorities, who objected when he gave away all his worldly goods to the poor, writing to his brother Theo, "They think I'm a madman because I wanted to be a true Christian. They turned me out like a dog, saying that I was causing a scandal."[56] His too-liberal interpretation of Christian teaching was uncomfortable for the church, and having one of their missionaries discarding their belongings was confrontational, especially for any church elders who lived a religious life in comfort and privilege.

His enrolment at Antwerp Academy in Belgium was abruptly terminated when van Gogh refused to follow the academy's dictates. He stated the drawing classes were far too traditional for him and he wrote to Theo on 20 January 1886 from Antwerp, criticising the Academy and voicing his concerns over the quality of their teaching skills. "I actually find all the drawings I see there are hopelessly bad – and fundamentally wrong. And I know that mine are totally different – time will just have to tell who's right. Damn it, not one of them has any feeling for what a classical statue is."[57]

Munakara Saturn rules 7th house of relationships, and after three months of disagreements that turned to unpleasant heated disputes with tutors and other students, van Gogh left the Academy and returned to Paris to live with Theo, and explore the Parisian art scene. Two years later, van Gogh moved to Arles in the country, and his famous dispute with fellow artist Paul Gauguin became a pivotal point in his life (Venus is Saturn's dispositor).

When he returned to Paris in May 1890 after his year-long stint in the asylum he went to stay at the home of a homeopathic doctor-artist named Paul-Ferdinand Gachet. For a while he worked diligently painting nature and regaining some spiritual relief. But once again, arguments arose and quarrels with Gachet forced him to seek other accommodation. Depression set in once more, this time involving feelings of guilt over his financial dependence on Theo, and frustrations over his failure to succeed as an artist (munakara Saturn ruling 8th house). In total despair, van Gogh shot himself and when found wounded in his bed he said, "I shot myself…I only hope I haven't botched it." When the authorities arrived the same evening to interrogate him as suicide was a matter for the police, van Gogh refused to answer questions, saying, "What I have done is nobody else's business. I am free to do what I like with my own body."[58]

In each one of these examples, munakara Saturn in Taurus will not bend to another's authority, nor will it compromise in order to keep the peace or find a place of compromise (Venus is Saturn's dispositor). Van Gogh's inflexibility was part of the reason for his isolation and loneliness, and friendships rarely lasted long, or ended well for him (munakara Saturn rules 7th house). Even in affairs of the heart – in his pursuit of the widow, Kee Vos, or the protection he gave Sien Hoornik – he refused to see the reality of the situation, preferring to take a romantic or idealistic stand (Jupiter as Saturn's outcome planet), rather than acknowledge if these two women truly had feelings for him.

Munakara Planet and Sect Condition – how comfortable is Saturn?

Van Gogh's munakara Saturn is in good sect dignity, and Robert Hand writes in 1995 that Saturn in a diurnal chart and diurnally placed (above the horizon with the Sun) "produces the best qualities of Saturn, discipline, order, and respect. It is even capable of indicating great success and social standing."[59] In his 2015 webinar on sect, Hand says good sect condition

Vincent van Gogh — ♄'s Sect Dignity			
Planet	Sect 1 Status	Sect 2 Hemisphere	Sect 3 Sign
♉ ♄	Day	With the Sun	Earth
D	D	D	N

Table 15.8: Vincent van Gogh: Munakara Saturn's Sect Dignity

"raises Saturn's energy level, increases its masculinity (improves hot/dry qualities in keeping with the Sun), and gives Saturn the ability to define and set goals that are worthy, capable, and reachable."[60]

Saturn in good sect condition provided van Gogh with the opportunities to learn from others more skilled and with more experienced than himself. Anton Mauve, his cousin by marriage, was a talented artist who took the young man under his wing, and guided him for many years, until the two men became estranged after one of van Gogh's episodes. His grandfather (after whom he was named) was a prominent art dealer, and three of his uncles followed their father into business, becoming reputable art dealers themselves. A young van Gogh was given employment in London, and later in Belgium, in one of his uncle's art salons, but he left to join the seminary when he wanted to become a cleric. Even his brother Theo followed in the family's tradition, becoming a successful art dealer in Paris, and providing him with constant financial and emotional support in his career as an artist.

Van Gogh's mother, Anna, also came from a prosperous family in The Hague (Saturn's dispositor is Venus in exaltation), and she instilled in all her children a duty to uphold the family's high social position.[61]

Saturn in good sect dignity had opportunity, wealth and good prospects, but its state of munakara indicates that van Gogh's erratic behaviour, his extreme opinions, and his impulsive and often unwise choices spoiled much of the benefits that Saturn's good sect could have provided, had he chosen an easier and more successful lifestyle.

Van Gogh's Father Issues
Munakara Sun and Munakara Saturn

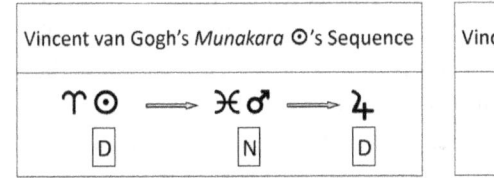
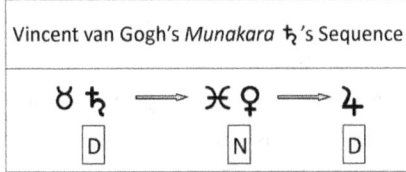

Table 15.9: Vincent van Gogh: Munakara Sun in Aries, Munakara Saturn in Taurus

Van Gogh's munakara Sun is situated in his 10th house in both the Placidus chart and in the Whole Sign system. Aries Sun rules the 2nd house (finances) in both house systems, and also rules the 3rd house (siblings) in the Placidus chart.

Munakara Saturn in Taurus remains in the 11th house in both house systems – the house of hopes and dreams – and often where like-minded people gather to support our ideas and interests. Taurus Saturn rules the 7th and 8th houses in the Whole Sign system and adds the 9th house to make three houses ruled by Saturn in the Placidus chart.

Both the Sun and Saturn represent father. The Sun represents one image of father as a warm, benevolent and supportive male figure who protects the child, nourishes the spirit, and gently and lovingly guiding the child into adulthood. Saturn, on the other hand, is the parent of boundaries and restrictions, both for the sake of physical safety, and for spiritual and temporal matters that dominate a family's expectations of their offspring.

Vincent van Gogh wanted to make his father Theodorus van Gogh proud of him. But he felt he had disappointed his father, a pastor, by giving up his ambition to be a preacher. Van Gogh hoped to become a respected artist instead, but his father died in 1885 from a stroke and never saw his son's paintings exhibited at major expositions.[62]

The Letters of Vincent van Gogh is a collection of 903 surviving letters written by van Gogh (820), or received by the artist (83). Within van Gogh's correspondence, more that 650 of these were letters written from Vincent to his brother Theo, who died six months after his older brother.[63] Theo van Gogh, born 1 May 1857 at 3:30am in Zundert, Netherlands, had the Moon in munakara (Leo Moon to Taurus Sun to Venus) and, like Vincent, Saturn in munakara (Cancer Saturn to Leo Moon to Sun).

The letters were translated into English and published by Theo's widow, Johanna van Gogh-Bonger, who had inherited Theo's collection of art and the letters after her husband's death, and it was her dedication and determination that saw her brother-in-law's art finally recognised. Johanna, born 4 October 1862 at 2:00am in Amsterdam, Netherlands) had the Moon in munakara (Aquarius Moon to Virgo Saturn to nocturnal Mercury).

By deriving the houses, it can be seen that my brother's wife (7 houses from 3rd house of siblings) is the 9th house. In the Placidus chart,munakara Saturn rules Johanna van Gogh-Bonger's house with Aquarius on the cusp. In the Whole Sign chart, the sign of Pisces (ruled by outcome planet, Jupiter) will move to the 9th house, and will include van Gogh's Mid-heaven, and his Venus (Joanna) and Mars in Pisces, conjunct the MC.

Leo is on the cusp of the 3rd house of siblings in van Gogh's Placidus chart,

Chapter Fifteen • *Munakara Sun Delineations*

and munakara Sun ruling the 3rd house would describe his relationship with younger brothers, Theo and Cor, and his three sisters, Elisabeth, Anna and Willemina (known as 'Wil"). Munakara Sun ruling the 3rd house might also draw attention to the fact that Vincent had a stillborn brother born exactly one year, to the day, before him, and that both sons were called Vincent, in honour of their grandfather. The time of birth for Vincent van Gogh's elder (stillborn) brother is unknown, but the chart has no planets in munakara – neither the Aries Sun (disposits to Mars in Cancer), nor Saturn in Taurus (disposits to Venus in Taurus). Perhaps if the first-born Vincent had lived, he would not have caused his parents' heartache in the way that second-born Vincent did, but the world may not have seen an artist with exceptional talents, without the two planets in munakara.

In 1877 his father, Theodorus van Gogh senior wrote to Theo about his concerns over Vincent's religious zeal when he was studying theology:

> *Oh, if only he (Vincent) would learn to be simple like a child, and not to bandy biblical texts about in such an exaggerated and overwrought manner – it is the cause of increasing worry to us and I fear that one day he will become unfit for practical life. It is such a great pity. What are his letters to you like? If he wants to be an evangelist, he must be willing to undertake the **preparation** and necessary **study** [his father's emphasis]. Then I would have more faith in it. We are tired and not very cheerful, if only things would brighten up.*[64]

Van Gogh's correspondence with his brother Theo has been well-documented but there are few letters saved that he wrote to his parents, Theodorus and Anna. One letter he signs as 'Most loving and affectionate Vincent' on 17 November 1876 (#098), and 'Your loving Vincent 'on 16 February 1881 (#163). However, frustrations between himself and his father were building by late 1881, and when he returned from The Hague in mid-December he wrote to Theo on 23 December 1881 (#193) about his embarrassment at being financial dependent on his father (munakara Sun rules 2nd house).

> *Admittedly, Pa said that I needn't be afraid of the inevitable expense (of leasing a studio), and Pa is pleased with what Alton Mauve (his teacher) himself said to him, and also with the studied and drawings I brought back. But I do find it utterly, utterly wretched that Pa should suffer by it. Because since I've been here Pa really hasn't profited from me, ...And, as I've told you before, I find it absolutely terrible not to be free at all. Because even though Pa doesn't ask me*

to account for literally every penny, still, he always knows exactly how much I spend and what I spend it on. And now, although I don't necessarily have any secrets, I don't really like people being able to look at my cards. Even my secrets aren't necessarily secrets to those for who I feel sympathy.[65]

Van Gogh continues the letter as he discusses his affection for his family, and his frustrations with their religious beliefs:

> But Pa isn't the kind of man for whom I can feel what I feel for you (Theo), for example, or for Mauve (his cousin and art teacher). I really do love Pa and Ma, …but Pa cannot empathize or sympathize with me, and I cannot settle in to Pa and Ma's routine, it's too constricting for me – it would suffocate me.
>
> Whenever I tell Pa anything, it's just idle talk to him, and certainly no less so to Ma, and I find Pa and Ma's sermons and ideas about God, people, morality, virtue, almost complete nonsense… I see completely different things in the Bible than Pa sees, and I can't agree at all with what Pa makes of it in his petty, academic way.[66]

Six days later, on 29th December 1881, van Gogh wrote to his brother (#194 – van Gogh's emphasis in bold):

> At Christmas I had a rather violent argument with Pa, and feelings ran so high that Pa said it would be better if I left home. Well, it was said so decidedly that I actually left the same day.
>
> Things came to a head because I didn't go to church, and also said that if going to church was something forced and I **had** to go to church, I'd most certainly never go again, not even out of politeness, as I've been doing fairly regularly the whole time I've been in Etten. But oh, there's actually much more to it, including the whole story of what happened this summer between me and K.V [his cousin Kee Vos].
>
> I was angrier than I ever remember being in my whole life, and I told Pa plainly that I found the whole system of that religion loathsome, and precisely because I dwelled on those things too much during a miserable time in my life [his religious studies and missionary work from early 1877 to August 1880]. I don't want anything more to do with it, and have to guard against it as against something fatal.
>
> Was I **too** angry, **too** violent? – so be it, but even supposing that to be the case, then at least now it's over and done with.….Pa told me that if I needed money he would lend it to me if necessary, but now that's impossible, I must

Chapter Fifteen • *Munakara Sun Delineations*

remain completely independent of Pa. How? I don't know yet,... So far as the relations between Pa and Ma and me are concerned, they can't be put to rights so very quickly. The difference in our mentality and outlook on life is simply too great.

And although I spoke in anger, I said things that I also think when I'm in a calmer mood. So I don't take back what I said, and anyway Pa has now heard it plainly. If I'd been calmer, I'd have said it in other, less extreme colours, but basically I'd have thought the same... **I don't want to consider it a misfortune** *that it's turned out this way, on the contrary, despite all the emotion I feel a certain calm.* **There is safety in the midst of danger.** *What would life be if we didn't dare to take things in hand?*[67]

Necessity caused van Gogh to reconcile with his parents and he was back living with his family and painting when his father died suddenly on 26 March 1885 from a stroke. He sent a telegram to Theo on the following day: "our father fatal stroke, come, but it is over, van gogh." (#487)

His sister Willemina (Wil) was also living with her parents at the time, and she witnessed her father's death. Of his three sisters, Wil was the closest to Vincent: they both had difficulties at school, both "rejected society's prevailing norms" and both siblings "struggled with their mental health, which they discussed openly with each other."[68]

Wil wrote to her friend on 26 August, 1886, eighteen months after their father's funeral, defending her brother's behaviour at the difficult family gathering:

(Vincent's) disappointments often embittered him and made him not a normal person. That was a difficult thing for my parents, who could not always follow him and often misunderstood him. My father was a stickler for the proper form, and he (Vincent) never concerned himself with all that; naturally that often caused clashes, and neither of the parties readily forgot words that were spoken in anger. So for the last eight years Vincent had been a problem to many people, and because of the outward appearances they all too often forget the great deal of good that was in him. The last few years he worked at home with us; after my father's death Anna (their sister) thought it would be more peaceful to Ma if he were not to live at home any longer and contrived that he left us. He took that so badly that we have heard nothing from him since then and we only know about him through Theo. I do so hope that he will gradually forget his grievances, for it is such a sad relationship, and something like this so easily leads to discord.[69]

Sisters Elizabeth (known as 'Lies') and Anna had far less patience with their older brother's behaviour. Anna wrote in 1923: "The summer that Pa died I spent several weeks at the parsonage with the two children and the nursemaid, and I saw and noticed a great deal that was bad. He (Vincent) gave in to all his desires, and spared nothing and no one. How Pa must have suffered (living with Vincent). Although I, too, admire his art, I despise his person. Theo must also have suffered so much."[70]

In reference to the incident with Anna, Vincent wrote to Theo on 6 April 1885 in letter #490 (van Gogh's emphasis in bold):

*As to Anna – you mustn't think that I'll continue to take something like that amiss or hold a grudge about it – but only, it's a shame that they think to do Ma a service with something like that – and that's stupid and unwise. As long as Ma and Wil (Willemein) are here, nothing unpleasant will happen between them and me; I don't think so. Only it's certain that Ma simply cannot comprehend that painting **is a faith** and that it brings with it **the duty** to pay no heed to public opinion – and that in it one conquers by **perseverance** and not by **giving in.***[71]

Van Gogh's Relationships

Munakara Sun and Munakara Saturn

"I try more and more to be myself, caring relatively little whether people approve or disapprove."

The two planets that come together at the culmination of his chart – Mars and Venus – are dispositors for the Sun (Mars) and Saturn (Venus), and therefore bind the two munakara planets in such a way that any passion van Gogh expresses is likely to come through the two nocturnal planets in Pisces, disposited by Jupiter in rulership. His munakara Sun in 10th house rules the 2nd house of finances, and his munakara Saturn, in the 11th house rules the 7th house of relationships and the 8th house of 'other people's money'.

Love interest: Kee Vos, 1881

On his Saturn return, at age 28, in November 1881, van Gogh fell in love with his cousin, Kee Vos, who was seven years his senior, and a widow with an eight-year-old son. Vos would have nothing to do with him but van Gogh convinced himself that his love for her would be reciprocated if he was persistent. He could not believe he had overstepped the bounds of decency and good manners, by pursuing her when she clearly was not romantically interested in a younger man who was unemployed, and had no real prospects as a suitable second husband.

Letter 180 to Theo states:

> And then I began – at first clumsily, awkwardly and yet resolutely, and it ended with the words 'Kee, I feel exactly as though you were the closest person to me and I the closest person to you in the fullest sense of the word, I love you as I love myself' – and then she said, no, nay, never. No, nay, never, what's the opposite of that? Love on!*[72]*

Van Gogh continues in the letter, "Love is indeed something positive, something strong, something so real that it's just as impossible for someone who loves to take back that feeling as it is to take one's own life. If you reply to this by saying 'but there are in fact people who take their own life', then I simply answer: I don't really think that I am a man with such inclinations."[73] Interestingly, in this early stage of his life, he disregards the possibility of suicide and believed himself to not possess the temperament to take his own life.

His uncle, Johannes Paulus Stricker Sr and Kee's father, wrote to his parents that "his persistence is *disgusting*."[74] In despair (and in shades of later self-harm), the lovestruck suitor held his left hand in the flame of a lamp, dramatically pleading: "Let me see her for as long as I can keep my hand in the flame."[75] He did not recall the event well, but later assumed his uncle had blown out the lamp's flame and sent him on his way.

Finally, in letter #222 written to Theo on 1 May 1882, van Gogh admitted Kee Vos was beyond his reach as a viable marriage partner:

> Last year I wrote you a great many letters telling you what I thought about love. I'm not doing so now, because I'm busy putting those same things into practice. The person for whom I felt what I wrote to you is not on my path, is beyond my reach, despite all my longing for her. Would I have done better to go on thinking of her and to overlook what came my way? I cannot decide whether I am acting consistently or inconsistently.[76]

Love interest: Sien Hoornik, 1882

Months later, still reeling from Kee's rejection, Van Gogh met Sien Hoornik in early 1882. She became both his model and his lover. Vincent's friends and family were shocked with the arrangement as Sien was a former prostitute, and at the time, pregnant with her second child.

Letter #225 on 10 May 1882 to Theo on the topic of Sien:

If I were to speak of it (the relationship), Pa would most likely think he had to play the part of policeman, which would be completely inappropriate and of little use. So you'll excuse me if I don't breathe a word of this to Pa and Ma, and have no desire for them to interfere. If Pa refused to give his consent, there are legal provisions that guarantee me, as an adult, my independence, but I don't think that Pa will go so far as to oppose it.

He then talks about his rejection by Kee Vos and returns to the subject of Sien:

I was perhaps more able than others to understand her, because she has a couple of peculiar habits that many would find repellent. First of all, her speech, which is ugly and which is the result of her illness, then her temper, which stems from a nervous disposition, causing her to have moods that many would find unbearable.[77]

Van Gogh wrote to Theo from The Hague about Sien Hoornik:

I feel more compassion for the woman than ever before because I see that she's very unsettled. I believe that at the moment she has no better friend than me, who would sincerely help her more if she allowed me to. But she doesn't seek my trust, and makes me absolutely powerless by giving her trust to those who are in fact her enemies. I truly believe that she doesn't understand that there is evil in what she does – or doesn't want to understand it, I sometimes think.[78]

The relationship lasted approximately eighteen months; in a letter to Theo on 14 September 1883: "I knew from the outset that her character is a ruined character, but I had hopes of her finding her feet and now, precisely when I don't see her anymore and think about the things I saw in her, I increasingly come to realize that she was already too far gone to find her feet."[79]

Chapter Fifteen • *Munakara Sun Delineations*

Fallout with artist and teacher Anton Mauve, 1882

In the same letter to Leo (#224, dated 7 May 1882) where van Gogh introduces his relationship with Sien Hoornik, he adds the disturbing news that he and Anton Maeve, his cousin by marriage and his first art tutor, have fallen out. The letter begins:

> Today I met Mauve and had a very regrettable conversation with him which made I clear to me that Mauve and I have parted ways forever. Maeve has gone so far that he can't retract it, or at least certainly wouldn't want to. I asked him to come and see my work and talk things over afterwards. Mauve refused outright, "I certainly won't come to see you, it's over and done with'. In the end he said, 'you have a vicious character'. At that point I turned around – it was in the dunes – and walked home alone.[80]

Fallout with fellow artist Paul Gauguin, 1888

Van Gogh's munakara Saturn resides in his 11th house and rules his 7th house. Perhaps van Gogh's most famous conflict occurred when his friend and fellow artist, Paul Gauguin, joined him in Arles in August 1888. Both men had fiery temperaments, were highly sensitive to any criticism of their work, and shared a taste for huge amounts of alcohol so they were bound to clash when they spent an large amount of time together.

Neither artist had much money, and van Gogh had paid for Gauguin's ticket to Arles because he admired Gauguin's approach to painting, and wanted to try a collaboration because he knew that 'some tasks were beyond the power of isolated individuals to accomplish.'[81] But hopes of the joint project went horribly wrong, and on Christmas Eve, 1888, the arguments became physical, and van Gogh allegedly attacked Gauguin with a razor. Legend has it that Gauguin was unhurt, but that in deep remorse, van Gogh sliced off his own ear and delivered the bloodied ear to a nearby brothel telling one of the girls, "Guard this object carefully."[82]

Art historians, Hans Kaufmann and Rita Wildegans, examined contemporary police records of the incident, and reviewed both artists' correspondence independently. They concluded that it was actually Gauguin who mutilated van Gogh's ear[83] and that he did so with a sword, as he often bragged about his skills as an accomplished swordsman.[84] Whatever transpired, van Gogh took responsibility and was hospitalized, and Gauguin fled to Paris. Van Gogh returned home a fortnight later and resumed painting, producing a mirror-image *Self-Portrait with Bandaged Ear and Pipe*.

Gauguin left on 25 December, but two weeks before the famous incident, he had already made up his mind to leave Arles and return to Paris. On 11 December 1888, Gauguin, who often corresponded with Theo in his capacity as an owner of an art gallery in Paris, wrote to him: "Taking everything into account I am obliged to return to Paris; Vincent and I can absolutely not live side by side without trouble, as a result of incompatibility of temperament, and both he and I need tranquillity for our work. He is a man of remarkable intelligence, whom I greatly respect and whom I leave with regret, but I repeat, it is necessary."[85]

On the same day (11 December 1888) van Gogh also wrote to his brother:

My dear Theo,... I myself think that Gauguin had become a little disheartened by the good town of Arles, by the little yellow house where we work, and above all by me. Indeed, there are bound to be grave difficulties still to overcome here, for him as well as for me. But these difficulties are rather within ourselves than elsewhere...Gauguin is very strong, very creative, but precisely because of that he must have peace. Will he find it elsewhere if he doesn't find it here? I'm waiting with absolute serenity for him to make a decision.[86]

Fallout with art dealer Hermanus Giijsbertus Tersteeg (H.G.T.)

Hermanus Gijsbertus Tersteeg (H.G.T.) was an art dealer and manager at the Goupil gallery in The Hague. He had employed Vincent as an art dealer in London, and later van Gogh worked for Tersteeg as a clerk from August 1869 to May 1873. Van Gogh constantly badgered Tersteeg for commissions from Goupil's clientele, but one letter to Theo on 11 March 1882 reveals their mutual animosity:

Tersteeg is someone who is extremely hard of hearing, though I don't consider him deaf. He must be told things very decidedly, otherwise it doesn't penetrate his armour. For years he's thought me a kind of blockhead and dreamer, he still views me as such, and even says about my drawings: that's a kid of opium daze you administer to yourself so as not to feel the pain you suffer at not being able to make watercolours. Mr T's 'practical talks' on art couldn't be more impracticable. It doesn't help him even if he uses as arguments some things that could be called conversation killers, because it's difficult to find an answer to them. Enough – I don't deserve his reproaches, ... he condemns drawings of mine which contain much that is good, ... If I make serious studies from a model it's a lot more practical than his practical talks about saleability or unsaleability. I'd prefer to lose his friendship than agree with him about this.[87]

Fear of fallout with his brother, Theo

Van Gogh feared that Theo would abandon him too, and whilst Theo's place in the chart would generally be considered as a 3rd house matter (siblings), their relationship was also a partnership. Theo's constant financial support on which Vincent relied each month becomes a matter for the 7th and 8th houses, both of which are ruled by munakara Saturn (Capricorn and Aquarius on the house cusps). Letter #226, written 13 May 1882:

> *Now I hope you won't blame me for being a little worried because you haven't given me answers to various things. I don't believe you'll think ill of me for being with Christien (Sien). I don't believe that you'll abandon me altogether for that or any other reason of etiquette or whatever. But is it any wonder that after what happened with Mauve and H.G.T. (Tersteeg) I sometimes think with a certain melancholy, perhaps it's happening with him (Theo) as well?*
>
> *If I could rent the house next door, if I could have a weekly allowance, it would be wonderful. If not, I won't give up hope and shall wait a while longer. But if the first is possible, it would be so fortunate for me, and would give me more strength for my work that is otherwise absorbed by cares.*
>
> *I wish that those who wish me well understood that what I'm doing is prompted by a deep feeling of and need for love, that frivolity and arrogance and indifference are not the springs that drive the machine, and that if I take this step it's proof that I'm taking root close to the ground.*
>
> *And that's why I say: Theo, I intend to marry this woman, to whom I am attached and she to me. If this should unhappily result in a change of attitude towards me on your part, I hope that you won't withdraw your help without warning me in advance, and that you will continue to tell me clearly and plainly what you think.*[88]

By early February 1886, van Gogh's romance with Sien was well and truly over, but his financial woes continued to haunt him. He wrote to Theo from Antwerp: "My dear Theo, It's at the moment when my money has entirely gone – entirely – that I write to you again. If you can send anything, even if it were five francs, don't neglect to do it; there are still 10 days in the month and how am I to get through them? For I have absolutely nothing left."

By the end of the month van Gogh had left Antwerp for Paris without paying his bills (he confessed this in letter 623, written two years later in June 1888). On 28 February 1886, he wrote to Theo: "My dear Theo, Don't be cross with me that I've come all of a sudden. I've thought about it so much and I think we'll save time this way. Will be at the Louvre from midday, or earlier if you like. As for expenses, I repeat, it comes to the same thing. I have some money left, that goes without saying, and I want to talk to you before spending anything. We'll sort things out, you'll see. So get there as soon as possible."[89]

He wrote to Theo from Arles on 20 August 1888, asking Theo to finance his project with Gauguin: "My dear Theo, Many thanks for your kind letter and for the 100-franc note that was included with it. And you're very kind to promise Gauguin and me to put us in a position to carry out the partnership project."[90] Van Gogh then continues by asking Theo for a sizeable amount to pay for lodgings for the two artists for a year. "Look here: The day when you could, would you – not give me, but lend me 300 francs for a year, all at one go? ...Then I'd buy two good beds, complete, at 100 francs each, and other furniture for 100 francs. That would put me in a position to sleep at home, and to be able to put up Gauguin or another person there as well."[91]

Van Gogh's Symbolism: Sunflowers and Cypresses
Munakara Sun and Munakara Saturn

"If I am worth anything later, I am worth something now. For wheat is wheat, even if people think it is grass in the beginning."[92]

When van Gogh voluntarily admitted himself to the asylum of Saint-Paul-de-Mausole, in Saint-Remy, it was for the reason of immersing himself deeper into his art in an atmosphere where others were responsible for his well-being (munakara Saturn, outcome Jupiter). For a year his diet improved, his sleep patterns became more normal, his medication was monitored by a team of doctors, and alcohol was at last, out of his reach.

"It's beautiful as regards lines and proportions, like an Egyptian obelisk. And the green has such a distinguished quality."[93] – Van Gogh's comment on cypresses

In van Gogh's paintings and drawings, sunflowers were symbols of joy and devotion, and his stars were glimmers of heaven. In his final years van

Chapter Fifteen • *Munakara Sun Delineations*

Gogh became obsessed with cypress trees, and they became his symbol of fortitude.

Van Gogh had perceived a similarity between the form of the cypress tree and obelisks, after reading about Egyptian architecture displayed at the Paris World's Fair of 1889. Obelisks were structures initially symbolizing rebirth, and were characterised by a four-sided square base that tapered into an isosceles pyramidion at the top. The obelisk was designed and constructed in honour of the Egyptian kings of the fifth dynasty (2465–2323 BCE), and in reverence to the sun god, Re/Ra. They were used as funerary monuments, and were believed to attract the reviving rays of the sun, thereby allowing the resurrection of the deceased. They often had kingly connotations, representing a connection between the spirit (*ka*) of the king, and the sun god (Re/Ra).[94] Van Gogh saw the resemblance between the man-made monument and its natural equivalent and he used the cypress in several paintings in 1889 and 1890, most notably in his famous work, *The Starry Night*.[95]

Van Gogh's Cypresses was the first exhibition to focus on the use of the tree as symbolism in of the artist's work during the twelve months he was painting and living within the walls of the asylum in Saint-Remy, France. Opened in July 2023 at the Metropolitan Museum of Art in New York, its curator Susan Alyson Stein told BBC Culture: "He appreciated that these were century-old trees, and certainly knew their associations with rebirth, immortality and death. From the get-go he associated them with stars and wheat, which were his tried-and-true metaphors for eternity and the eternal cycles of life. They stood for millennia as protectors and guardians of the countryside from the fierce northerly mistral winds.[96]

Egyptian obelisks were symbols of Ra, the Sun God and, like cypresses stretched vertically into the empyrean, linking the cold ground to the fire of the heavens, expressing hope and immortality.[97] By painting cypresses like obelisks, van Gogh's aim was to express grandeur, timelessness, and monumentality of nature, something he could draw solace from at his moment of despair."[98]

Vincent wrote to Theo on his fascination for the cypress trees: "It's the dark patch in a sun-drenched landscape. But it's one of the most interesting dark notes, the most difficult to hit off exactly that I can imagine." The darkness that van Gogh saw and tried to capture in his paintings echoes traditional associations of cypresses with death and immortality. Cypresses were often planted in cemeteries and their wood was used for coffins. In the writings of classical authors like Ovid and Horace, they appeared in the context of bereavement. These associations persisted through the centuries, reappearing in the plays of Shakespeare and the novels of Victor Hugo, authors that van Gogh knew and admired.[99]

Van Gogh shot himself in July 1890, two months after he left the asylum. At his funeral, the artist's coffin was strewn with sunflowers (munakara Sun) and cypress branches (munakara Saturn), the artist's two signature motifs. Nowadays van Gogh is mainly associated with sunflowers: a symbol of temporal devotion and transient joy as the blooms follow the sun's light. Van Gogh called his sunflowers "the complimentary and yet the equivalent" to his cypresses, which stood for the steadfast and the eternal.

Legend has it that van Gogh's last words to Theo were "This sadness will last forever."[100] It is a tragic thing to say at the end of life, especially considering it was said by a man whose art has brought wonder and beauty to millions through his symbols of light and dark. I truly hope he was wrong, and that his spirit found peace and happiness, somewhere, somehow.

CHAPTER SIXTEEN
Munakara Mars Delineations

Dennis Rodman

A Brief Biography of Dennis Rodman[1]

Dennis Rodman (born 13 May 1961) is a retired American professional basketball player who was one of the most skilled rebounders, best defenders, and most outrageous characters in the history of the professional game. He was a key part of two National Basketball Association (NBA) championship teams with the Detroit Pistons (1989–90) and three with the Chicago Bulls (1996–98) and was inducted into the Naismith Memorial Basketball Hall of Fame in 2011.

Rodman was 5 feet 9 inches (1.7 metres) tall when he graduated from high school in Dallas, and tried and failed to make the school basketball team four times. He shot up more than another 9 inches (20 cm), and in 1981, he earned a spot on the Cooke County Junior College team in Dallas. A scholarship to play at Southeastern Oklahoma State University followed. Proving himself to a be a prodigious collegiate rebounder, he was drafted in 1986 by the Pistons and was pivotal to the success of Detroit's "Bad Boys".

In addition to being a tenacious defensive player (he was the NBA's Defensive Player of the Year in 1989–90 and 1990–91 and was names seven times to the league's All-Defensive team), Rodman became a ferocious rebounder. Although he was not an exceptional leaper, his timing, tenacity, and desire, combined with his ability to enrage opponents by holding, grabbing, and shoving, made Rodman one of the league's top rebounders. He led the league in rebounds per game seven straight seasons (1991–92 to 1997–98), finishing with an astounding total of 11,954 in 14 seasons in the NBA.

Following his tenure with the Pistons, Rodman played briefly with the San Antonio Spurs (1993–95), before moving on to play for the Bulls. It was during this period that Rodman – having already established a reputation for on-court temper tantrums and erratic off-court behaviour – became known for outlandish antics that made him a national celebrity. In addition to repeatedly defying the authority of coaches and league officials, Rodman turned his body into a gallery of tattoos, piercings, and ever-shifting day-glo hair colour; he also engaged in a wild partying lifestyle, famously dating popular music diva Madonna. He was later briefly married to *Baywatch* television actress Carmen Electra (his second marriage), and at one point, clad in a bride's gown, he staged a wedding with himself. At times, when Rodman's mood swings made his behaviour seem uncontrollable, even his admirers suspected a breakdown was near. The image most fans preferred for Rodman was as a Bad Boy, living on the edge.

At the end of a 20-year career on the court, Rodman tried his hand at acting in motion pictures, and at professional wrestling, but was not particularly successful in either of these fields. Rodman was author and co-author of three works of autobiography – *As Bad as I Wanna Be* (1996), *Walk on the Wild Side* (1997), and *I Should Be Dead by Now* (2005) and he appeared in a number of reality television programs. In 2013, he courted publicity by travelling with a documentary crew to North Korea, where he became the first American to meet the country's new leader, Kim Jong-Un. The two men struck up a friendship when they attended an exhibition basketball game in North Korea featuring members of the Harlem Globetrotters. The trip – bankrolled by an American media company – drew a negative response from the US government, and public reactions ranged from amusement to criticism of Rodman, as someone who naively allowed himself to be used by Jong-Un in a bid for international attention.

Rodman played in 14 NBA seasons and played a further six years with minor leagues when he retired in 2006. Despite a 20-year career as a professional basketballer Rodman's net worth in 2024 was only US$500,000 in spite of his multi-million dollar legacy. A lifelong struggle with a gambling addiction has contributed to this loss of great wealth, plus three extremely costly divorces, but it is mostly due to a number of shady business deals that saw his long-term financial advisor embezzling millions from his personal fortune.[2]

Chapter Sixteen • *Munakara Mars Delineations*

For all Rodman's charisma, controversy, bizarre behaviour, and off-court trips in and out of reality, two facts will stand out clearly amid the confusion surrounding Rodman's NBA career. He was a great rebounder and an even more spectacular entertainer. When the final verdict on the Rodman enigma arrives, his strange, powerful personality will likely take precedence over mere basketball statistics.[3]

"They didn't have a problem with me being wild and crazy when it came time to fill the arenas."[4] – Dennis Rodman

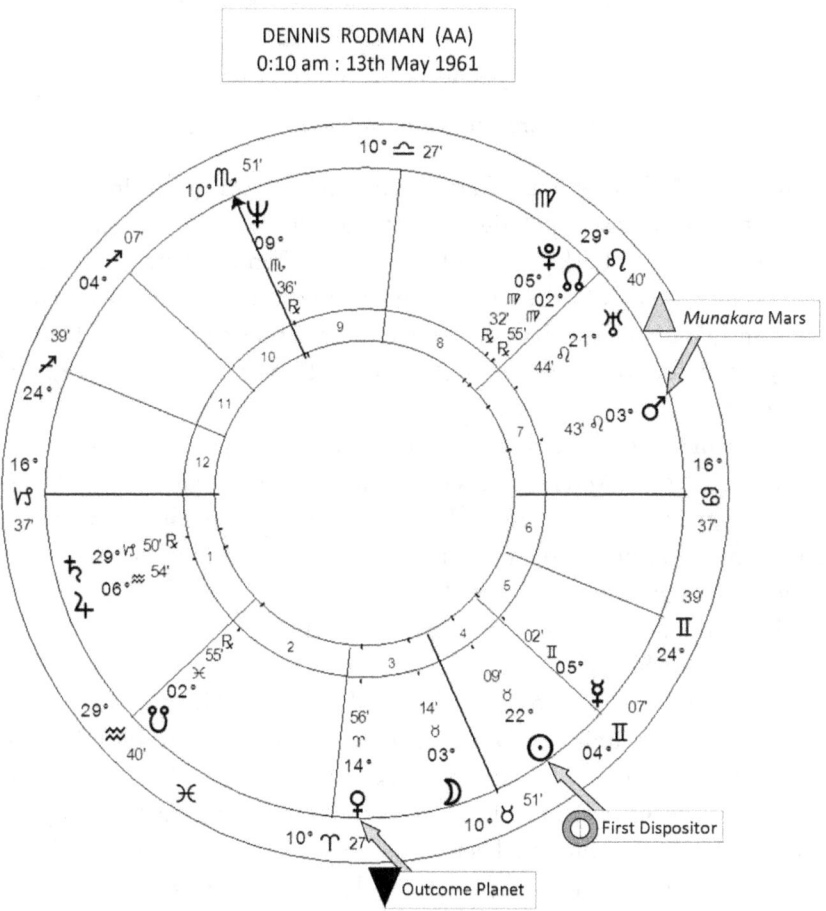

Fig. 16.1: Dennis Rodman: Munakara Mars in Leo

Leo Mars in Munakara: Dennis Rodman

- **Key Questions:**
- What does Dennis Rodman's Mars contend with?
- What is its driving force?
- What is its trigger? What is its outcome?

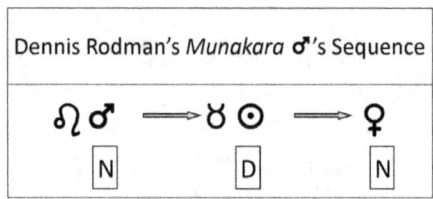

Table 16.1: Dennis Rodman: Munakara Mars' Sequence

Dennis Rodman's munakara Mars served him well in the world of professional basketball during his younger years. He was always a contentious figure both on and off the court, often challenging the roles of sports' superstars and their huge influence over the public. Rodman was constantly blurring the lines on expectations of how a male should look and act, years before the world of NBA basketball was ready to deal with issues of gender identity.

Rodman's Leo Mars disposits to the Sun in Taurus and Venus is the outcome planet for Mars' sequence. The two nocturnal planets are not friends as their signs oppose another and their principles – separation for Mars and cohesion for Venus – are at odds, which creates tension between the two planets that signify opposing genders.

Rodman's desire for self-identity was the driving force behind his Mars, and even at the height of his career with the Detroit Pistons, Rodman was on the road to self-destruction – that is, until he realized he needed to express himself in his own unique way. Mars and the Sun have a natural affinity – Mars lends its sign, Aries, to the Sun for its exaltation – and whilst Mars becomes extreme in the Sun's vicinity, it also has similar traits to the Sun. Both planets understand the need for goal-setting, both planets use energy and focus to achieve these goals, and both planets revel in the victory of winning the goal, before moving quickly on to the next challenge.

For Rodman, Mars and the Sun's goal was to find a balance between the masculine and the feminine qualities of his psyche, to learn to express his two genders, and to feel comfortable and safe within himself, regardless of how other people reacted to his goal. Munakara Mars does not lack courage, it is drawn to taking risks, or liking to shock a little, and Rodman's experimentation with his gender balance was openly defiant. He risked ridicule from within the NBA world, with his team-mates who could have rejected him, his opposition teams who weaponized his new look to taunt him on the court, and his fans who may have abandoned him as his outfits and behaviour became more outlandish with the exploration of his duality (Venus, outcome planet).

Venus is the other nocturnal planet in Mars's munakara sequence, and Venus returns to the source by being in Aries, a sign belonging to Mars. Venus in Aries is a perfect assignment to describe a more robust Venus that fights for self-love and acceptance, and even its degrees in the middle of Aries makes it hard to connect through aspect to other planets in Rodman's chart, which are mainly in very early degrees, or very late degrees of their signs.

Even without comfort or assurance from other planets, Venus in Aries squares his Capricorn Ascendant and supports the idea of Venus in detriment, especially during his NBA career: Rodman is remembered as the man in women's clothing that everyone from the opposing side loved to hate, and everyone supporting his home team hated to love.

Munakara Planet and Sect Condition – how comfortable is Mars?

Dennis Rodman's munakara Mars is in a condition known as *hayz* – all three sect conditions have been met – and Mars has the great fortune to be in its most comfortable position according to the classification of this particular accidental dignity. Robert Hand described Mars with a good sect rating as, 'slows down its frenetic energy, tempers its masculinity, makes it more capable of doing whatever is necessary to protect and defend, and can be self-sacrificing.'[5]

Dennis Rodman — ♂'s Sect Dignity			
Planet	Sect 1 Status	Sect 2 Hemisphere	Sect 3 Sign
♌ ♂	Night	No Sun	Fire
	N	N	N	✓

Table 16.2: Dennis Rodman: Munakara Mars' Sect Dignity

Rodman's munakara Mars in *hayz* demonstrates that once he had worked out a solution for his inner demons, he was able to moderate his energy both on the court, and in his personal life. When Rodman no longer cared about what people thought of him, he was able to gain the advantage of pleasing himself rather than pleasing others, and in this way munakara Mars, in sect, was able to protect and defend its space. In this perfect sect condition, munakara Mars had the potential to work its surroundings to Rodman's advantage, often unsettling the media and creating outrageous headlines. It didn't matter whether it was a basketball court, a wrestling arena, a diplomatic mission to befriend a dictator (Kim Jong-Un), or a comfort in expressing his male and female selves, Rodman's munakara Mars was able to relax, and to find strength and resilience within its environment.

Munakara Mars: Dennis Rodman

When Dennis was asked one day if his antics had brought him close to death he answered, "At least 50 times. I've jumped off a building, jumped off a cliff in a car. I've been in bedrooms when women came in with knives and guns."[6]

Munakara Mars in Leo in 7th House (Placidus)

Dennis "the Worm" Rodman is a man whose words and behaviour still invite strong reactions, even though he has now entered his 60s. In a 2019 interview for *The Jump*, with Rodman, Scottie Pippen (his Bulls teammate), and presenter, Rachel Nichols, the trio discussed the often brutal tactics employed by the Detroit Pistons' 'Bad Boys' in the late 1990s. Another former teammate, reminiscing on the good old days, makes this statement in a voice-over comment "The Bad Boys was a monika (nickname) to a lot of the guys on the Pistons. (But) to Dennis Rodman it was real. He loved everything about that very insulated 'us-against-the-world' mentality that the Pistons had."[7]

Dennis was born with a fixed Grand Cross involving the Moon (Taurus), Mars (Leo), Jupiter (Aquarius), and Neptune (Scorpio), but it is the Leo Mars which draws our focus, given that it is the planet in munakara. Jupiter's opposition to a Mars in contention helped to create a virtual warrior on the basketball court, and Dennis earned NBA All-Defensive Team honours seven times, and won NBA Defensive Player of the Year Award twice.

Dennis has said "I'm hungrier than those other guys out there. Every rebound is a personal challenge"[8] and perhaps this is true, given that Mars in Leo rules his Mid-heaven and opposes Jupiter, one of its natural enemies. Neptune squaring Mars adds bouts of super-human strength, but there is often a price to pay for these physical exertions – and the adrenaline rush it

Chapter Sixteen • *Munakara Mars Delineations*

creates – so perhaps this is where the Neptune opposing the Moon has the potential to take his body beyond its limits.

"I go out there and get my eyes gouged, my nose busted, my body slammed. I love the pain of the game."[9] Munakara Mars squares an exalted Moon in the same degree, displaying not only the physical threat he poses when it comes to opponents (angular Mars in Placidus 7th house), it also indicates more self-destructive tendencies, given that we are aware of Dennis' battle with alcoholism over the years. Dennis starred in a number of reality shows in 2009 involving his struggle to rehabilitate himself, and his reunion on *Sober House* with his mother, Shirley, after years of estrangement, is yet another reminder of the tension existing between Mars in contention, and the Moon ruled by Venus in Aries.

Rodman's release of his second autobiography *Bad as I Wanna Be* in 1996 disclosed how close Mars in contention brought Dennis to self-destruction. The cover of *Bad as I Wanna Be* has playful Mars and Venus overtones as a naked Rodman lies draped suggestively across the seat of a motorcycle with only a basketball to cover his genitalia. However, the book itself contained a painful revelation that Dennis had contemplated suicide during the final year he played with the Pistons. Mars moves from the 7th house in Placidus to the 8th sign/house in the Whole Sign system, and this movement shows the desperation Rodman must have felt at a time when he was at the top of his game, but felt trapped by the violent role he was expected to play on court.

In February 1993 (when the Uranus Neptune conjunction at 19 Capricorn had just made a transit over his Ascendant), Dennis drove his truck to a gay bar with the intention of shooting himself with a gun he carried in the cabin of his truck. When asked why he didn't fire the loaded rifle, Rodman answered "I decided that (instead of killing myself) I was going to kill the imposter that was leading Dennis Rodman to a place he didn't want to go. So I just said "I'm going to live my life the way I want to live it and be happy doing it." At that moment I turned my whole life around. I killed the person I didn't want to be."[10]

Professionally, Dennis was in the most productive and popular period of his life, but his self-loathing, and his one-sided personality was destroying him. Any planet in the 4th house, especially in Whole Sign, is not solely concerned with describing just bricks and mortar. Figuratively speaking, the 4th house is the foundation stone of our chart – we trace our roots and heritage from this point – but as we live our lives as adults, it becomes the basic and essential element of ourselves that holds us firm, especially in times when we feel lost or abandoned. Mars rules the fourth sign by Whole Sign, and Venus is blind to the Taurus IC, so this should give us some indication as to how desperate Dennis became on this dark night in February 1993. Metaphorically, he says he *'killed the imposter'*, and from this point on he allowed Venus to guide him. However, this can be a dangerous thing for a male who depends on his brute force to provide success in his professional life (munakara Mars squares the MC and is its ruler).

The Pistons would have renewed the contract of their most powerful rebounder, but Dennis pleaded to be released, and he was traded to the San Antonio Spurs in July 1993. Dennis' rebounding skills took second place in the media, who insisted on reported on the constantly changing colours of his hair, the tattoos – at a time before tattoos were socially acceptable – and strange outfits that bewildered and baffled any clear boundary of what male or female attire should look like. When asked 'Why?' by the media, the born-again version of Dennis answered with statements such as "If I want to wear a dress, I'll wear a dress"[11] or "I'll be the judge of my own manliness."[12]

The basketball world thought Dennis had clearly lost his mind when he turned up in a blonde wig and white wedding dress to promote his book, stating that he was 'marrying himself' (literally, Mars/Venus). This new version of Dennis was clearly exploring fresh options to tame his destructive qualities, and trying to live his life in his most authentic way. This freedom that Dennis allowed himself to make these explorations in a male-based testosterone-heavy environment, shows munakara Mars in *hayz*, totally at ease and unaffected by others' reactions. Costume changes, cheeky outfits and coloured hair was a far more positive way to express munakara Mars, than by being a Bad Boy who used bullying tactics and rough play to intimidate the opposition.

During Dennis' NBA career, the press were totally perplexed by the dramatic and constant changes in his physical appearance, and believed that he was reinforcing, and perhaps emerging deeper, into the Bad Boy character he had developed during his time with the Pistons. But they were wrong. He had finally found the courage to become Dennis Rodman, and to love and respect himself in the process. "Here's the thing everyone should understand. I like my character"[13] is a statement Dennis Rodman made back in the late 1990s when he was busy discovering himself.

His munakara Mars took a more sinister note as with time Rodman aged, retired from the NBA, and lost the attention of his fans, the public and the media. Without the drive and focus and the physical outlet of basketball, Rodman's munakara Mars faltered and fell into self-destructive habits, possibly fuelled by rage and frustration over the loss of his former glory (Leo Mars disposits to the Sun). Munakara Mars's involvement in the Grand Square with Neptune, Jupiter and the Moon has not helped: taking Rodman from the highs of wild parties, joyrides and exhilarating celebrity jaunts, to deterioration into alcohol abuse, arrests for domestic violence and several lawsuits for alleged sexual abuse (settled out of court).

Mars in contention moves from the 7th house in Placidus (relationship issues) to the Whole Sign 8th house (money issues) and even here, Rodman has not escaped the negative influences of munakara Mars. Rodman's lucrative NBA earnings – his playing career spanned 20 years from 1986 to 2006 – has whittled away through bad investments (8th house) and his gullibility in trusting his fortune to professional scam artist/fraudster Peggy Ann Fulford, giving her permission to extract funds for retirement investments, and to make child-support payments on his behalf.[14] Fulford was convicted and sentenced to 10 years in prison in February 2018 and ordered by the court to pay full financial restitution for her victims, but this will be unlikely given the fact that the money she stole had already been spent.[15]

First Dispositor: Sun in Taurus

Basketball has definitely been a positive outlet for Dennis Rodman, but one that came surprisingly late compared with other professional players' experience. Unlike other stars in the NBA, Rodman showed no physical prowess in his early years, or even when he finished high school. When talent scouts were roaming school gyms looking for the next big thing for recruitment into the NBA, they wouldn't have given him a second glance. He was a boy of short stature, he couldn't do a lay-up, and he fumbled the ball so much that he spent more time on the bench, than on the court during his high school years. Then, at the age of 19 when most boys had stopped growing, Rodman had a growth spurt and his height blossomed from 5'9" to 6'8" (exalted Moon in Whole Sign 5th house). He says for a long time he refused to leave the house because he felt so odd (Sun's placement in Placidus' 4th house). But his basketball skills improved with his gained height, and with the existing friendship between munakara Mars and its dispositor, the Sun, Rodman landed a two-year scholarship in Gainesville, Texas.[16]

His Taurus Sun in the 4th house could not supply Dennis with a consistent supportive father – he tells people that he is the eldest of 28 siblings on his father's side – particularly given that its own dispositor (Venus) is in detriment and is in aversion to Taurus on the 4th-house cusp – but the Sun's movement from 4th to 5th house in Whole Sign opened up the world of sport and entertainment via the NBA.

In al-Biruni's *Table of Friendships and Enmities*, the Sun and Mars are friendly towards one another, as the Sun asks to borrow Aries for its exaltation. No doubt the adoration Dennis received from his basketball fans (Taurus Sun), pushed his munakara Mars to win at all costs under the basket, and added greatly to his professional success. The Sun provided well financially during his playing career, as the Sun squaring Saturn links his 8th-house ruler (the Sun), money from contracts, endorsements, TV appearances, with his 2nd-house ruler (Saturn), and the place of his income and wealth. Unfortunately, it did not guard against his excesses, or provide him with a sound financial plan for his retirement.

Rodman's Grand Cross is a combination of Jupiter, an exalted Moon, munakara Mars and Neptune on the Mid-heaven, and perhaps Rodman believed his good fortune would follow him throughout life (Jupiter opposing munakara Mars and squaring Neptune/MC). To some extent it did, blessing him with fame a second time when he reappeared in the news after his trip to North Korea. But munakara Mars (square exalted Moon) was still in destructive mode with his agent, Darren Prince, reporting that Rodman had been heavily drinking "to an extent that none of us had seen before."[17]

Rodman's Taurus Sun is his first dispositor in Mars' munakara sequence, and his powerful need to understand the true nature of his spirit, was a journey with too many eyes and too many snide remarks in an industry that thrives on macho behaviour. The media could not reconcile Rodman's urge to express his femininity, with the ferocious man who annihilated his opponents on the basketball court.

Rodman's Whole Sign 5th house plays a large role in his munakara Mars story, given that Mars's dispositor, the Sun is in the 5th house, and Venus, its outcome planet, rules the 5th house of sport, entertainment, leisure pursuits, and children.

Two of Rodman's children have pursued careers in sports. His son, Dennis Thayne "DJ" Rodman, followed in his father's footsteps and is a professional basketball player for the Capital City Go-Go of the NBA G League. His second daughter, Trinity Rain Moyer-Rodman, is a professional soccer player for the

Chapter Sixteen • *Munakara Mars Delineations*

Washington Spirit, and played for her country at the 2024 Paris Olympics, where the United States won a gold medal. Trinity scored three goals at the Olympics to assist her team to win gold.

Rodman's contact with his daughter is sporadic, and interviews with Trinity often touch on the subject of her relationship with her famous father. She and her brother, DJ, were raised primarily by their mother in southern California after their parents separated and her mother, Michelle Moyer, filed for divorce in 2004 when Trinity was two years old. Trinity has said she went through long stretched without speaking to her father, and financial support was as scarce as parental support in her childhood memories of Rodman. In 2012 the marriage was officially dissolved, and Rodman allegedly owed $860, 376 in child and spousal support.[18] Rodman was also in a desperate predicament at that time in his life. In March 2012, it was reported that Rodman's mounting debts could see him facing time in jail, his financial advisor defending him at the time, said "In all honesty, Dennis although a very sweet person, is an alcoholic. His sickness impacts his ability to get work."[19]

In an interview with Alex Cooper, host of the podcast Call Her Daddy in December 2024, Trinity admitted that at one point her mother, brother and she, were living in a car for a short period of time because they had very little money. She said, "We tried to live with him (Dennis), but he's having parties 24/7, he is bringing random b*itches in. He loves the spotlight. He loves the cameras....I think he's an extremely selfish human being. I think everything has always been about him."[20]

Rodman showed up unannounced at a Spirit playoff game in 2021 after having no contact with Trinity for months before the match. She was emotional during the game and angry at his sudden appearance, but when a photo of them hugging after the match went viral, she thought that her father might have re-entered her life. However, Rodman made no further attempt to contact her in the months after their tearful reunion, and they did not speak again until 2023,[21] possibly after Trinity was named to the US squad for the 2023 FIFA Women's World Cup in Australia and New Zealand. On 9 July 2023, Trinity scored a brace (a hat-trick) and was named Woman of the Match after being the youngest player in the national team's history to score a brace.[22] Trinity said in the 2024 interview, "I think after that was when I lost hope of ever getting him back. It's just like, he's popping in whenever he's going to be on camera. Even at that game, I don't think it's for me, I think he wanted to have a good conscience and then be like, 'Headline, Dennis Rodman showed up to his daughter's game."[23]

The outcome planet: Venus in Aries

Dennis has always had a love-hate relationship with his mother: adoring and exalting her as a child (Taurus Moon), but at the same time feeling ignored when his mother favoured his more athletically-inclined sisters. In his recollections of childhood Rodman says, "I felt shut out not having a father, always having to look out for myself. And my mother just didn't have time for me. She was always more interested in my sisters."[24]

Dennis' early jealousy of his sisters' basketball prowess (Mars rules Placidus 3rd house), and what he perceived as the battle with his siblings for his mother's attention, is expressed by Venus situated in the Placidus 3rd house. Venus in Aries (in detriment) moves to the angular 4th house in the Whole Sign system, where Mars become the ruler of the 4th house and Venus' dispositor. This movement may not improve or ease Dennis' early resentment of his younger sisters. His mother Shirley said in 1988, "It was a female family and I think we just overwhelmed Dennis."[25]

Dennis Rodman's munakara planet is a trail which leads from the nocturnal Mars in Leo to his Taurus Sun, and returns back to a nocturnal planet in Venus in Aries. This situation leaves Mars in contention, sending it constantly running back to the battlefield, battered, bruised and in terrible pain, but Rodman is terrified that his courage or motivation will be questioned, or he will be found wanting at a critical moment. For instance, when his daughter needs him to be a consistent presence in her life (Venus in Aries), but he's not there for her (munakara Mars).

Venus is the final planet in the three-step process, so perhaps we can see why women both frighten and enchant this man. In Rodman's life, Venus has been a contradiction of extremes in what represents 'female' in his chart. Is it his wardrobe and his penchant for female clothing? Is it his early relationship with his mother and sisters? Is it his partying with a string of different women for entertainment? Is it his dominance over female partners? Is it his negligence of his daughters?

I doubt even Rodman understands where he sits on reconciling his 'feminine side' with his history of the women in his life. However, when Venus is the outcome planet for munakara Mars, these are important questions he needs to answer if he wishes to find peace within himself. Mars in contention can be a powerful force of aggression, anger, and potential violence. Whilst it has served Rodman well in his 'warrior' years on the basketball court, it's not a pleasant energy for him to live with, particularly if there is no reconciliation between the planet in contention and the two planets in its sequence.

Chapter Sixteen • *Munakara Mars Delineations*

For Rodman, Aries Venus – the outcome planet – is the key to containing munakara Mars's rage. His munakara sequence is a reminder of the snake swallowing its own tail, the mythic ouroboros that symbolises mbol of cosmic harmony. In Rodman's chart, Venus in Aries constantly returns to Mars, its dispositor, and the whole cycle repeats itself. Each time he activates his munakara Mars, the sequence planets will follow, and each time, he ends back at Leo Mars in contention – the snake swallowing its own tail.

Munakara Mars: Michael J. Fox

A Brief Biography of Michael J. Fox[26]

Michael J. Fox (born 9 June 1961) is a Canadian American actor and activist who rose to fame in the 1980s for his comedic roles, and who later became involved in Parkinson disease research after being diagnosed with the disorder.

Fox grew up on Canadian military bases and moved to Los Angeles at age 18. He won three Emmy Awards (1986–88) for his role as Alex P. Keaton on the popular television series *Family Ties* (1982–89), where he worked with Tracy Pollan, his future wife. He later starred in the series *Spin City* (1996–2002), winning an Emmy in 2000, his last year on the show. Fox also appeared in feature films, notably portraying Marty McFly in the hit comedy *Back to the Future* (1985) and its sequels (1989 and 1990).

In 1991, at the age of 30, Fox was diagnosed with Parkinson disease. Nine years later he founded the Michael J. Fox Foundation for Parkinson's Research in 2000, a non-profit organization that has raised over $2 billion to fund research programs into a cure for the disease.[27] Fox limited his acting to focus on the illness but made guest appearances on several TV series, including *Boston Legal* as the slippery lawyer Louis Canning who exploits his disability to win his cases; *Rescue Me*, for which he received an Emmy in 2009 for his portrayal of pill-popping paraplegic Dwight; *The Good Wife*; and *Designated Survivor*. He briefly starred in *The Michael J. Fox Show* (2013–14), a comedy in which he played a news anchor with Parkinson disease.

Fox wrote the memoirs *Lucky Man* (2002), *Always Looking Up: The Adventures of an Incurable Optimist* (2009), and *No Time Like the Future: An Optimist Considers Mortality* (2020).

Still: A Michael J. Fox Movie (2023) is a documentary about his life and career. The movie won the award for Best Documentary Film from the National Board of Review and received seven nominations at the 75th

Primetime Emmy Awards. American film critic Stephanie Zacharek wrote (on behalf of *TIME*), "*Still: A Michael J. Fox Movie* reminds us that a person stricken with a disease doesn't *become* that disease...What stikes about *Still* is how celebratory it is. This isn't the story of a wonderful actor felled by an illness; it's the story of a wonderful actor."[28]

The trailer for *Still* begins with the interviewer asking Fox "What does it mean to be 'Still'? to which Fox replies, "I don't know. I was never 'still'." The three minute trailer ends with Fox stating "To deny that part of me that wants to continue and go on and do things is to quit. ...(but) I'm a tough son of a bitch."[29]

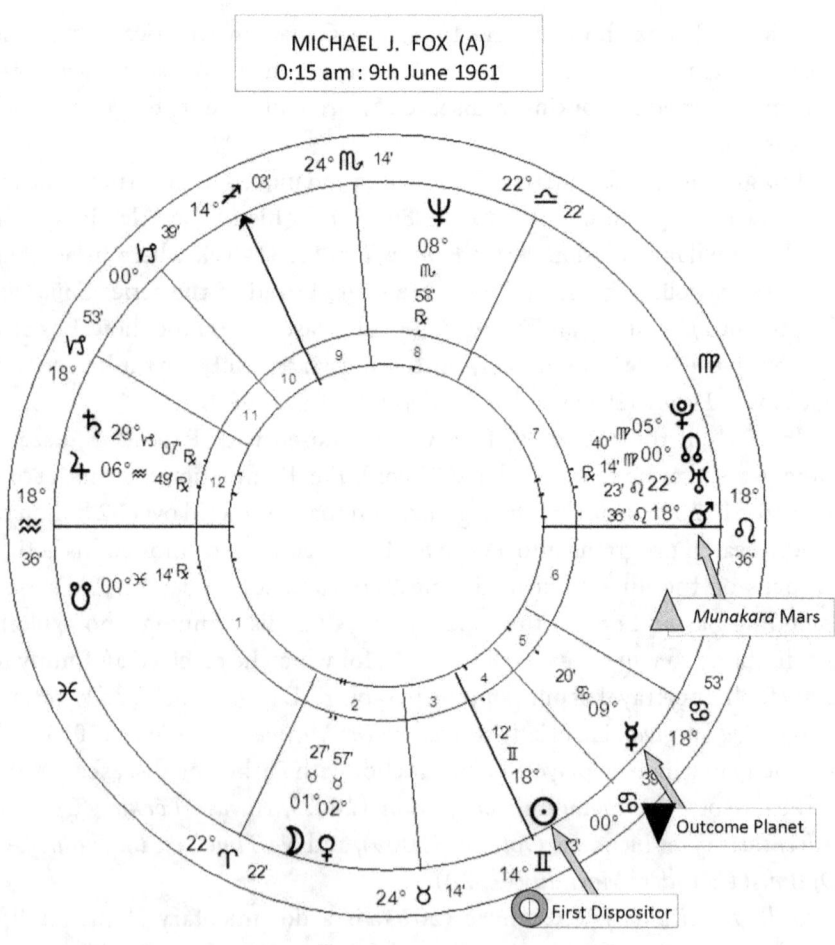

Fig. 16.2: Michael J. Fox: Munakara Mars in Leo

Chapter Sixteen • *Munakara Mars Delineations*

"Life delivered me a catastrophe, but I found a richness of soul. The more I expect, the more unhappy I am going to be. The more I accept, the more serene I am."[30] – Michael J. Fox

Similarities between the charts of Dennis Rodman and Michael J. Fox

Twenty six days separate the births of NBA superstar, Dennis Rodman, and actor, Michael J. Fox. During this interval, Mars has left its early degrees of Leo, moving away from Rodman's fixed square, and joining Uranus in late degrees of Leo.

The slower-moving planets, including Jupiter and Saturn, are in similar degrees in both charts (*Figs. 16.1; 16.2*), but the faster-moving planets – Venus, Sun and Mercury – have moved on to the next sign from their positions in Rodman's chart with a birth date of 13 May, 1961. Venus has moved from Aries to Taurus (from detriment to dignity), the Sun has moved from Taurus to Gemini, and Mercury has moved from Gemini to Cancer.

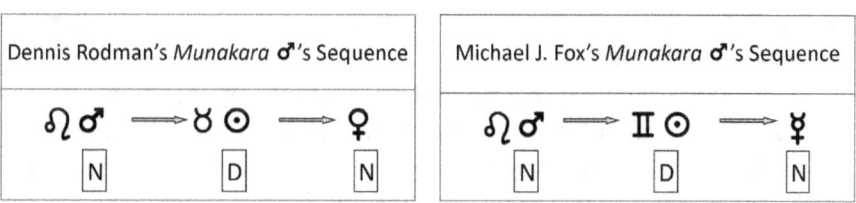

Table 16.3: Dennis Rodman and Michael J. Fox: Munakara Mars' Sequence

In munakara sequence, Leo Mars still disposits to the Sun, but the Sun's new position in Gemini, means the outcome planet has now changed, and Rodman's Venus, has been replaced by Fox's nocturnal Mercury.

Mars no longer squares the Moon, or opposes Jupiter, or squares Neptune for that matter (Rodman's chart), as Mars has moved far enough away from the T-square to prevent a reoccurrence of Rodman's Grand Cross in the four fixed signs. Instead, Fox's munakara Mars in Leo sextiles the Sun in Gemini, and whilst this seems to be Mars' only aspect, the separating square to Neptune is still a concern, even though ten degrees separate the two planets.

The month between the two births places Fox's Moon in a similar degree in Taurus, and in an echo of Rodman's chart, Fox's Taurus Moon opposes Neptune. Fox's Moon conjuncts its dispositor, Venus, and the three planets

– Moon, Venus and Neptune – are in a square aspect, from opposing sides, to Jupiter in Aquarius. Fox's fixed T-square (*Fig. 16.2*) moves into angular houses in the Whole Sign system; Jupiter moves to the Ascendant's sign of Aquarius, the Moon and Venus in Taurus move to the fourth sign, and Neptune moves to the tenth sign of Scorpio. These are statements on the physical health of Michael J. Fox, and his thirty year struggle with Parkinson's disease (PD) is well documented in the media, and through the Foundation which bears his name.

Both men's Ascendants are ruled by Saturn in Capricorn – Rodman's in Capricorn and Fox's in Aquarius – and in the Whole Sign chart, Rodman's Saturn will move into the 1st house of Capricorn, but for Fox, Capricorn Saturn will remain in his 12th house. In another odd coincidence, the 5th house in their Whole Sign charts will contain Mars' dispositor (the Sun), and will be ruled by Mars' outcome planet (either Venus or Mercury).

For instance, in Rodman's munakara sequence, Mars' dispositor, the Sun in Taurus, is located in his Whole Sign 5th house, which is ruled by Venus, his outcome planet. In Fox's munakara sequence, Mars' dispositor, the Sun in Gemini, is located in his Whole Sign 5th house, which is ruled by Mercury, his outcome planet.

This is not as startling as it first sounds when it becomes apparent that the first dispositor, and the outcome planet, have both moved to the next sign in the twenty six day interval between the two births. What makes it a coincidence is the fact that the Ascendant sign for Rodman has moved one sign from Capricorn to Aquarius, and this movement has accommodated the similarity of 5th-house involvement in munakara Mars' sequencing planets. The truly interesting factor is the difference in the house placement of the two outcome planets: Rodman's Venus is angular in his Whole Sign 4th house, and Fox's Mercury is cadent in his Whole Sign 6th house.

This factor seems to accentuate Fox's health problems (outcome planet, Mercury in 6th house), but Rodman fares little better, when Venus in Aries highlights the anguish of a missing father, which then has repercussions for his inability, or his unwillingness, to be a father to his own children (outcome planet, Venus in detriment in 4th house).

The relationship each father has with their children is very different, as is their history of health problems, and this may be in some way the responsibility of their munakara Mars and the planets involved in its sequence.

Chapter Sixteen • *Munakara Mars Delineations*

Leo Mars in Munakara: Michael J. Fox

- **Key Questions:**
- What does Michael J. Fox's Mars contend with?
- What is its driving force?
- What is its trigger? What is its outcome?

Table 16.4: Michael J. Fox: Munakara Mars' Sequence

Michael J. Fox's munakara Mars is engaged in a constant battle to cope with the strain under which his body operates on a daily basis. He fights to maintain his optimistic outlook on life, despite living a life that is both physically exhausting, and mentally frustrating (Mercury, outcome planet). His munakara Mars shows his gutsy determination to continue his career as an actor, despite the drawbacks of his physical complications. Fox retired for the second time in 2020, mainly due to the deterioration of his speech and what he felt to be its unreliability, and the fact that he was now experiencing memory loss due to the advancement of the disease[31] (Mercury, outcome planet).

Mars in Leo is dispositied by his Gemini Sun, and since his diagnosis of early onset Parkinson's disease in 1991, Fox has refused to be defined by his condition. In a career spanning over 40 years (1978–2020) – working 29 of these years under the cloak of his illness – Fox's Gemini Sun has constantly adapted so that the actor could further his artistic and personal development.

Mercury is the outcome planet for Fox's munakara Mars, and whilst it sits in the Placidus 5th house of entertainment and self-expression, it will move into the 6th house by Whole Sign with Cancer on its cusp. In Fox's chart, Mercury sextiles the conjunction of Moon and Venus, both in good condition in Taurus, and this indicates Fox's popularity within his profession. Mercury sextiles Pluto and trines Neptune so whilst Pluto adds determination, stubbornness and resilience to Mercury (munakara Mars' outcome planet), Neptune's aspect to Mercury plays the long game and ultimately, his mind will deteriorate in the final stages of this cruel degenerative disease. For Michael J. Fox, his munakara Mars has led him to live an exemplary life of courage, determination, optimism and generosity of spirit. In the face of almost three decades of living under the shadow of Parkinson's disease, Fox's munakara Mars sequence – Leo Mars to Gemini Sun to Mercury in Cancer – has created an inspirational story, not only for others on a similar life journey, but for anyone who has faced, and fought, a seemingly insurmountable difficulty.

Munakara Planet and Sect Condition – how comfortable is Mars?

Michael J. Fox's birth data (9 June, 1961 at 0:15 am) has a Rodden 'A' rating,[32] with the time based on a quote directly from him. This places its accuracy under question, and with munakara Mars perched *exactly* on the Descendant, it is difficult to determine if Fox's Mars is above or below the horizon at the time of his birth. If the birth time is correct, Mars would be in *hayz* – separated from the Sun by the horizon, and placed in a nocturnal chart, in a masculine sign. However, if the birth had occurred a little later, Mars would be beneath the horizon by the time Fox was born, and although it is still situated close to the Ascendant horizon, it would present in the same hemisphere as the Sun (below the horizon) rather than above it, and Mars would no longer be in *hayz*.

Michael J. Fox — ♂'s Sect Dignity			
Planet	Sect 1 Status	Sect 2 Hemisphere	Sect 3 Sign
♌♂	Night	With/No Sun	Fire
N	N	?	✓

Table 16.5: Michael J. Fox: Munakara Mars' Sect Dignity

Mars still has sect dignity as the chart remains nocturnal, as does Mars' position in a fire sign, but the subtle drop from angularity and *hayz*, to a more challenging position in the 6th house (in Placidus), says something about the battles munakara Mars has had to wage over the years. His munakara Mars describes the attack on Fox's physical strength (Mars opposes the Ascendant), and Saturn's proximity to a square aspect to the Moon, would be a second indicator of chronic health issues, indicated by the Ascendant Lord (Saturn) squaring the 6th-house ruler (the Moon).

So far as sect is concerned, Mars in a nocturnal chart plays the role of protector rather than agitator, and its Whole Sign rulership of the 3rd house (Aries) and the 10th house (Scorpio) combines the house of communication, with career and professional standing. There may be an inclination to believe that munakara Mars has destroyed Fox's career, but I believe that its sect dignity – in a nocturnal chart, and potentially, nocturnally-placed in a masculine sign – has protected his career, more than it has harmed it. The challenge to both houses ruled by munakara Mars (3rd and 10th house) has seen the accumulation of Fox's credentials as a first-rate actor over his 40 year career. The world has watched him evolve from a young, frenetic, visual entertainer with comedic talent, to mature into an astute, deep thinking actor, who has chosen complicated characters with physical limitations to hone his craft. Some of his later portrayals have earned awards in his industry (10th house), whilst in tandem with his personal journey, Fox has brilliantly incorporated his illness into the roles he has played on screen (3rd house).

Munakara Mars: Michael J. Fox

Munakara Mars in Leo opposing Ascendant

The 7th house is considered by traditional astrologers to be a place where the Ascendant meets obstacles, threats and dangers, and munakara Mars on this point – opposing the Ascendant degree – is a planet that can block, challenge, or destroy good health. His munakara Mars in this position challenges Fox's ability for him to enjoy a safe and hazard-free environment, and brings conflict for his body, and tests his will-power by constantly presenting him with frustration and delay. If his 0:15am birth time is correct, then munakara Mars and his horizon's degree are identical, and conditions have been set in play for Fox to experience struggle, animosity, or friction with his surroundings when Mars opposes his Ascendant. Leo Mars can disrupt and endanger the harmony of any Aquarian Ascendant, but when contention is also present in a difficult planet in this space, then Fox will be forced to make a stand early in life, asserting his personality on a hostile environment, and adapting quickly to any situation which physically challenges him.

> "I can't always control my body the way I want to, and I can't control when I feel good or when I don't. I can control how clear my mind is. And I can control how willing I am to step up if somebody needs me."[33]

One of the symptoms of Parkinson's disease is known as festination (Latin: '*festinare*' meaning 'to hasten'), and is the term given to the familiar Parkinsonian gait. Festination is defined as an involuntary hurried walk, brought about by the disconnection between the body's natural balance in moving the feet at the correct speed, in coordination with the rest of the body. The footfall increases at a faster rate than the body can maintain, and as the stride shortens, the feet come together on tiptoe, and the body starts to tumble forwards. The result of festination is the body is in conflict with its surroundings, and what should be the simple act of walking morphs into a dangerous threat of constant falls, through the inability to control one's own speed. Fox describes this dilemma in words that echo the effects of a contentious Mars.

He says: "Over 30 years of PD, I've progressed into something dangerous. I've been weaponized. I've become a tornado of terror....I simply can't feel how fast I'm going. I cannot determine my position and my velocity at the same time. The world is a pinball game and I am the steel ball fired from the spring plunger."[34]

Michael J. Fox's fourth book, and the latest autobiography on his journey through life, is titled *No Time Like the Future: An Optimist Considers Mortality* (2020), and in it he describes his own version of *'annus horribilis'* (Latin: 'horrible year'), a twelve month period beginning with the death of his father-in-law in January 2018, coupled with an on-going battle with neurofibromyalgia, a chronic disorder affecting the way the brain processes pain signals. This condition materialized in the months leading up to 2018, coupled with crippling pain in his back and leg from a pinched sciatic nerve. When a noticeable increase in his deteriorating balance became evident, and weakness in his upper limbs and legs was detected, specialists realized a growth they had been monitoring on Michael's spine, had now developed into a tumour. Immediate major surgery was recommended, and Michael had little choice but to risk going under the knife in order to remove the invasive tumour.

Months of intensive physiotherapy followed the operation to help Fox to regain his mobility, but three months after surgery, and the first time he was home alone, Michael had a horrendous fall which shattered his arm, and once more put him back into hospital to repair the arm with a stainless-steel plate and nineteen screws to hold it back in place. For Fox, 2018 was a year of no mobility, no freewill and no control, and it sorely tested his usually positive attitude towards the trials his body endures, as a sufferer of Parkinson's disease.

After surviving his *annus horribilis* Fox decided in 2019, at the age of fifty eight, that he needed a tattoo to mark his progress through life. He chose a black-and-gray sea turtle gliding along the inside of his right forearm and facing his right hand. The tattooed turtle swims through five rings, the ripples of water representing the five decades of his life. Fox says in *No Time Like the Future* that the rings also signify emergence, of coming through difficult periods, but feeling that he now swims through calmer waters. He knows he bears battle scars, but like the turtle he met whilst swimming in the Virgin Islands in 1999, these scars are a mark of his will to survive, the power of resilience, and the earned right to feel proud of his own struggle and determination to keep swimming forwards, no matter what obstacles he faced in the past, or what obstacles lay ahead for him in the future.

In the Whole Sign system, Fox's Leo Mars in munakara rules the third and tenth signs, and Fox's fight has been very public as he managed to communicate as an actor (3rd house) for several decades after his diagnosis (10th house). In any Whole Sign chart there is a sextile aspect between the first and third signs, and the aspect is a reminder that the 3rd house represents much more than siblings and short journeys. The sextile from first sign to third sign demonstrates a flowing connection between the physical body's strength and vitality (1st house), and a house that describes the type of movements we make that are often without our awareness, but usually, with our consent. The 3rd house describes skills which come naturally to us, and it is the quick transmission of information from brain to muscle movement. Everyone's skills are different – some with more grace, talent or physical acumen – in the same way, that everyone's 3rd-house ruler (and planets in the house) is vastly different.

The skills we take for granted, that allow us to safely manoeuvre through our surroundings, are learned very early in life as we watch and copy the actions of those with more ability than ourselves. From our older siblings, parents, teachers, etc, we learned to walk, talk, perform, act, and any other habits we might have picked up from them along the way.

The 3rd house is a cadent house and the square to the cadent houses either side of it, the 6th and the 12th house, show the damage that can occur to 3rd house skills through illness, accident (6th house), or long stints of physical inactivity, such as hospital, invalid state, or imprisonment of the body (12th house). In Fox's case, his Mars ruling the 3rd house, shows munakara Mars' constant battle to maintain his motor skills as the disease rages through his nervous system. Freezing and festinating are the two primary symptoms of Parkinson's disease, and both are extremes that demonstrate the squares between Fox's 3rd house (ruled by munakara Mars), and the houses in quartile aspect either side of it (6th house ruled by the Moon, and 12th house ruled by Saturn).

First Dispositor: Sun in Gemini opposing MC

The same-degree (partile) sextile between Leo Mars and Gemini Sun is an asset to Mars, as the Sun rules the 7th house of relationships and partnerships. At the same time as gaining a lifelong partner who has lovingly supported him through difficult years, Gemini Sun has also assisted his positive attitude, even as munakara Mars continues its attack on his body. Fox is an individual whose daily practice of acceptance, gratitude, and optimism has led to a full and happy life, regardless of his situation.

Fox's Gemini Sun sits on his IC opposing his Mid-heaven, and in the light of Gemini's dual capacity to reinvent oneself, Michael J. Fox has experienced two distinct periods in his career, which can be described as pre-Parkinson's and post-Parkinson's. As a young actor Fox found success as Alex P. Keaton in the sitcom *Family Ties* (1982–1989), and the *Back to the Future* trilogy (1985–1990), with a string of successful movies to his name plus the lead role in the sitcom *Spin City* (1996–2000). Fox retired from acting in 2000, believing that Parkinson's disease would mean the end of his career, particularly as his earlier roles were highly physical, often involving fast-paced wild energy, and dozens of close-up shots that utilized his mastery of vivid facial expressions designed to convey more of his thoughts, than the actual dialogue.

Taking a break from the demanding schedule of rehearsals, and the stress of live taping in a regular sitcom series, Fox found a movement disorder specialist who changed his medication and his lifestyle, incorporating an emphasis on physical therapy, diet and fitness. The Sun rules Leo on Fox's 7th house cusp, and munakara Mars situated in 7th house has the ability to call on specialists (professional expertise particularly in the medical field), when contention becomes problematic. With Mars ruling the Whole Sign 10th house, these changes in managing the disease brought back his audience in a totally different way from his previous roles as a young actor where he relied on dexterity and comedic timing.

Fox returned to the small screen in 2004 in *Scrubs* playing Dr. Kevin Casey, an eccentric neurosurgeon with obsessive-compulsive disorder, and followed up this role as Daniel Post in *Boston Legal* (2006), Dwight in *Rescue Me* (2009), and the manipulative and loathsome litigator Louis Canning in six seasons in *The Good Wife* (2010–2016), returning to the character in 2020 for two episodes of the spin-off series *The Good Fight*.

Fox says he learnt a great deal during the first fortnight on *Scrubs*: "I realized that we all have our burdens. Every character has a bear inside that they're wrestling with, no matter where they are and what they're doing. As an

Chapter Sixteen • *Munakara Mars Delineations*

actor, I suddenly wanted more opportunities to take on that bear.... I can play anyone. And as I was discovering, everyone has Parkinson's."[35]

The Michael J. Fox Foundation for Parkinson's Research was established by Fox in 2000, and has since become the world's largest non-profit funder of Parkinson's disease research. The Fox Foundation which carries his name (Gemini Sun opposing Mid-heaven) has raised over $2bn for research into the disease. PD is undetectable until the symptoms have begun to show, and by then, much of the damage has already occurred.

Fox says, "The only X-ray we have for Parkinson's disease is the patient, and by extension, the PD community. We found that when patients meet, our conversation becomes a dialogue about symptoms and challenges, trying to triangulate what we learn from each other."[36] These conversations have led to an online program called "Fox Insight" where people share their lived experience, and this information becomes valuable data for scientists studying the disease.

Fox's Gemini Sun rules his 7th house, and there is no doubt that the love and support he has received from his wife of 34 years has been a constant strength for him, and a key reason for the optimism which has sustained Fox throughout his 30 year journey with PD.

"So what I say about Tracy is this: Tracy's big challenge is not having a Parkinson's patient for a husband. It's having me for a husband. I happen to be a Parkinson's patient."[37]

Fox first met Tracy Pollen on the set of *Family Ties* where she played the girlfriend of his character, Alex Keaton. The couple married in 1988 and the marriage – along with their firstborn, Sam – was only three years old when Fox was diagnosed with Parkinson's disease. Michael credits Tracy with pulling him out of his depressive slump during his *annus horribilis* in 2018, and getting him back on track, but some of his previous unstoppable optimism has been dented as Fox admits, "My optimism is suddenly finite."[38]

Fox acknowledges that his wife Tracy has seen the best and worst of his debilitation under the constraints of PD, and its wearing effect on their marriage and family life (Sun on IC), but that she cares about him deeply, and that whilst she is devoted to him, she does not pander to him or treat him like an invalid. Taurus is the sign for the Moon's exaltation, and Venus is in rulership in Taurus, so the conjunction between the two planets and their movement into the Whole Sign 4th house, is an indicator of how important

Tracy has been to Fox over the past three decades. Her strength of character, as much as her love, has supported him throughout his journey, and he returns her love with the same dedication and appreciation for the years they have shared together as man and wife.

The outcome planet: Nocturnal Mercury in Cancer

"I often say now I don't have any choice whether or not I have Parkinson's, but surrounding that non-choice is a million other choices that I can make."[39]

The four-week period between Dennis Rodman's birth (May 13, 1961) and Michael J. Fox's birth (June 9, 1961) sees the Sun move from Taurus to Gemini producing a different outcome planet for the two men: Venus in Aries for Rodman and nocturnal Mercury in Cancer for Fox.

Mercury sits in Fox's Whole Sign 6th house and rules the 8th house. Mercury by placement and sign (disposited by the Moon) indicates health issues for the body and Fox has undertaken two potentially life-threatening operations in his lifetime. The first in 1998, (the same year as Fox went public with his condition) when specialists recommended he undergo a thalamotomy, that is, brain surgery which is deliberately designed to destroy specific cells in the part of the brain called the thalamus which controls involuntary movement. And secondly in 2018 when delicate surgery was required to remove the tumour that was strangling Fox's spinal cord. Fortunately, Fox's nervous system did not deteriorate as a result of either procedure.

Fox tells us in his latest book, *No Time Like the Future*, that Parkinson's disease is a movement disorder. It is not a mental disorder or an emotional one, although these issues can develop depending on the personality. It is neurological, and manifests in a corruption of movement. Parkinson's disease is a constant battle, exhausting for both mind and body. Fox says part of the battle for him is an on-going process whereby he teaches his mind to perform one exercise, while his body performs another: "I need to create new pathways in my brain, new ways of compartmentalizing actions and words."[40]

The ticks and tremors characterized by Parkinson's are just one side of the disease, but the other effect is one which Fox says is much more difficult to accept, and this is the diminishment of movement. Bradykinesia is the term for sudden, unexpected moments when the sufferer is frozen, immobile, stone-faced and mute, leaving the person feeling embarrassed, and entirely at the mercy of their environment.

Chapter Sixteen • *Munakara Mars Delineations*

"As much as Parkinson's is about movement, the end stage is being frozen. So the more I let that happen, the more I'm gonna be stuck within that and unable to reverse it."[41]

Both munakara Mars' position on the Descendant – opposing the Ascendant – plus Mercury's 6th-house placement by Whole Sign, shows the frustration of the first planet (Mars) and the third planet (Mercury) in Fox's munakara sequence. When the body wants to be still, it moves erratically – hence the title, *Still*, for the 2023 documentary on his life – and when it desperately needs to express itself through movement, especially facial expression, it lacks the ability to relay the message from the brain, through the nervous system, to activate the muscles of the face and body. Mercury knows what it wants to do, but cannot convey its desire for stillness, or to show expression, and munakara Mars either over-reacts, or does not react at all.

Gemini is the sign on the IC (where the Sun sits), but it is also the sign that moves to the 5th house by Whole Sign. Mercury's rulership over this point has brought Fox some joy through his love of the game of golf, something he discovered after his diagnosis. He says he can see similarities between golf, and his life under the restrictions of the illness, that they intersect and overlap by representing examples for hubris and humility, delusion and desire, futility and resilience. His golf game and Parkinson's test these principles, and any minor victory in either field is exhilarating, regardless of how anyone else is managing the handicaps of either the game of golf, or life in general.

In May 2024 Fox accepted the second annual TIME100 Impact Award – an award that recognizes a global trailblazer who is pushing boundaries in their industry – and in his acceptance speech Fox paid tribute to his father, who he described as a 'funny, smart guy who never finished high school', but who loved words and puzzles, and who could recite poems "off the top of his head". One of his father's favourite poems has a vague familiarity, but most people are unaware of its title, *Antigonish*, or its author, 19th-century poet, Hughes Mearns. The poem is named after a small town in Canada, and is inspired by reports of a ghost of a man roaming the stairs of a haunted house in Antigonish, Nova Scotia. The first verse reads:

> *Yesterday, upon the stair,*
> *I met a man who wasn't there*
> *He wasn't there again today*
> *wish, I wish he'd go away*

In his acceptance speech, Fox recites the first verse and then continues to say,

> *How is this relevant? It turns out it's a perfect metaphor for young onset's Parkinson's. I was climbing a golden staircase, minding my own business, when suddenly I was blocked by someone neither I, nor anyone else, could see. Time passed, and no change, no-one could see it, but I knew it was there. It was blocking me from moving forward and (it was) pushing me backward. And I was doing a lot of hiding. And the one thing that wasn't going to work was wishing it away.*
>
> *As time passed I was lucky enough to gain the support of hundreds of thousands and eventually, millions, of others who wanted to climb those stairs to their own futures as badly as I did mine.... (together) we threw a $2 billion bag around the little monster on the stairs, and we now have a better sense of what we are dealing with.*[42]

Fox's munakara Mars on his Descendant describes more than one single person's battle in the face of illness. Helping others is a motivating force for his 7th house Leo Mars in contention and Gemini Sun on the IC, with Cancer Mercury's help in the 6th house, makes a huge difference in people's lives through advocacy and education on Parkinson's disease. Fox's Mars being motivated to lend his name (Gemini Sun), to create a place for global networking for PD sufferers, and to accelerate knowledge on the disease (Cancer Mercury), will be Michael J. Fox's legacy, and his greatest gift to future generations of PD sufferers who may have an easier road to walk because of his munakara Mars. And when they meet 'the man who wasn't there', they know he won't hold them back, or stop them from climbing their own staircase.

CHAPTER SEVENTEEN
Munakara Jupiter Delineations

Wolfgang Amadeus Mozart

A Brief Biography of Wolfgang Amadeus Mozart:

Johannes Chrysostomus Wolfgangus Theophilus Mozart (27 January 1756 – 5 December 1791) was a prolific and influential composer of the Classical period, composing more than 600 works within his short lifetime. Wolfgang's middle name, Theophilus, means "loved by God" in Greek. However, Mozart preferred to use the Latin translation, "Amadeus". Mozart's father, Leopold, described Mozart's birth as a "miracle from God" because he seemed too small and weak to survive. He was the youngest of seven children, five of whom died in infancy.

By the age of 3, Mozart had learned to play a clavier, which was an old-fashioned stringed instrument that had a keyboard. By the age of 5, he was playing the harpsichord and violin as well as a professional musician. He could write music before he could write words, and in fact, he could listen to music once, and then write it down from memory without any mistakes. Mozart began as a child prodigy, playing in front of royalty when he was just six, and composing his first musical composition at five years of age. By the time he reached puberty, Mozart had toured and performed before most of Europe's nobility. Mozart, his father, and his sister, Maria Anna (1751–1829) travelled around the noble courts of Europe to perform music. Travel was perilous and money was scarce for the family, and all three Mozarts suffered serious illnesses on the road. Wolfgang never grew to be a strong man, and researchers believe his many illnesses as a child left him small, pale, and delicate.

Count Hieronymus von Colloredo (1732–1812), archbishop of Salzburg, is famous for being one of Mozart's patrons and employers. He eventually became annoyed with Mozart's frequent absences and dismissed him with a kick from his secretary's boot administered to Mozart's behind, and the famous words "He may leave, I don't need him!"[1]

Mozart fell ill while in Prague whilst attending the September 6, 1791, premier of his opera *La clemenza di Tito*. He died in his home on December 5, 1791. Even while ill, he was occupied with the task of finishing his *Requiem*. Count Franz von Walsegg had commissioned Mozart to write his famous requiem under the terms that Mozart would do so anonymously so that von Walsegg could claim it as his own work. Years later, Mozart's wife, Constanze, would claim that Mozart had believed he was being poisoned and that he was composing his *Requiem* for himself. Researchers have hypothesized at least 118 causes of death for Mozart, including rheumatic fever, influenza, trichinosis (parasitic disease caused by roundworms), mercury poisoning, kidney ailment, and streptococcal infection.

> "I cannot write poetically, for I am no poet. I cannot make fine artistic phrases that cast light and shadow, for I am no Painter. I can neither by signs nor by pantomime express my thoughts and feelings, for I am no dancer; but I can by tones, for I am a musician." – Wolfgang Amadeus Mozart

Libra Jupiter in Munakara: Wolfgang Amadeus Mozart

- **Key Questions:**
- What does Wolfgang Mozart's Jupiter contend with?
- What is its driving force?
- What is its trigger? What is its outcome?

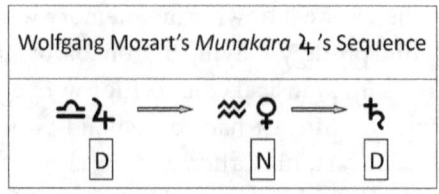

Table 17.1: Wolfgang Amadeus Mozart: Jupiter in munakara

Chapter Seventeen • *Munakara Jupiter Delineations*

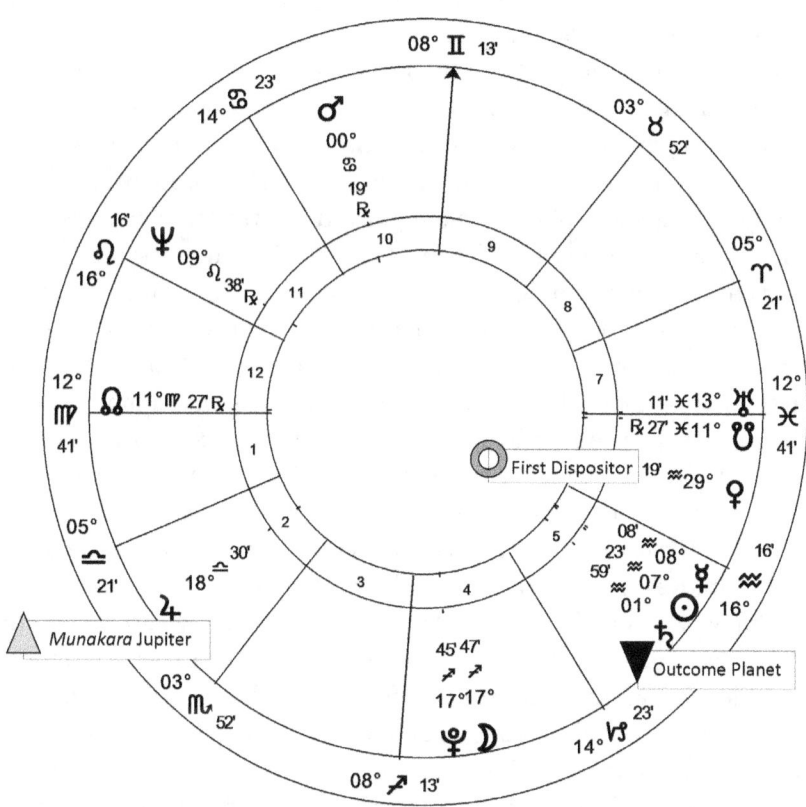

Fig. 17.1: *Wolfgang Amadeus Mozart: Jupiter in munakara*

It seems fitting that Mozart's last symphony (no. 41), composed in 1788, is nicknamed "Jupiter" after the Roman sky god. The nickname was given to the symphony by Johann Peter Salomon, a German impresario, after Mozart's death. The name was likely first used in print in a London concert program in 1821. The symphony's grandeur and qualities are said to mirror those of the Roman god Jupiter. The symphony is known for its good humour, energy, and scale, which are unusual for a Classical period symphony.

Jupiter is one of two planets in munakara in Mozart's chart, Sagittarius Moon is his other, and there is more than odd coincidence in an identification of his final symphony in 1821 with one of his planets in contention, simply because the qualities of his symphony were simpatico with Jupiter's qualities. It may be that there are echoes of Mozart's childhood style in no. 41, as the music Mozart played as a child was called Rococo, the "gallant style," which was part of a larger artistic movement. Rococo was noted for its more jocular, florid, and playful style. Mozart would later move away from the gallant style to become an archetype of the classical style.[2]

Munakara Jupiter can play out as a person who is often trying to prove themselves to be better than anyone else; more skilled, more intelligent, more successful, more pious or more powerful. If the individual feels they are not receiving the praise or admiration they believe they deserve, they can carry a chip on their shoulder, or they can search for reasons why 'somebody else' is achieving more than them. They may want to belong to an elevated class with more wealth and better connections, even though they may secretly despise those they emulate in public. Inferiority complexes often accompany such feelings, and even the world's greatest composer, I suspect, was guilty of constantly made to feel shunned, humiliated, and simply "not good enough" by those who claimed a more noble lineage.

Venus is Jupiter's dispositor, and 6th house can be a bleak house for the planet that loves the distractions of pleasure, entertainment and frivolity. Venus in Mozart's 6th house is in Aquarius, disposited by Saturn, and this may be a truer picture of Mozart, turning his back on pleasures and toiling to complete commissioned works with tight deadlines. Even the fact that he was robbed of a childhood, play and innocence sacrificed for his artistic genius as he was dragged about Europe performing for royalty, whilst at the same time suffering from malnutrition, and picking up diseases that would ruin his health, weaken his body, and diminish his stature as an adult (Saturn as outcome planet).

A recently published book by retired British surgeon, Jonathan Noble, titled *That Jealous Demon, My Wretched Health* (2018) disputes the unfairly tarnished reputations of 70 composers, all of whom were rumoured to have died from either alcoholism or syphilis. Noble uses Mozart's death as one of his examples of a serious musician being maligned by rumour and innuendo. The final portrait of Mozart, painted in 1790 a year before his death, portrays his face as puffy and bloated, and some biographers used this portrait as confirmation of Mozart's excessive drinking habits. However, Noble maintains Mozart was not, in fact, an alcoholic. The author states that alcoholism was rare amongst composers – including Mozart – as

Chapter Seventeen • *Munakara Jupiter Delineations*

he would have been unable to write such complicated compositions with a befuddled brain under the influence of alcohol. Noble states: "Alcoholism is inconsistent with serious, sustained musical composition...If you're a true alcoholic, there's no way you can go around composing operas, symphonies or string quartets....Maybe alcoholism inspires great poetry, but with music you come to very different conclusion."³

Saturn, as the second diurnal planet in Jupiter's sequence, is an extremely tricky situation for Jupiter, and generally adds to its stress levels as a planet in contention. Saturn is particularly harsh on the greater benefic as al-Biruni's *Table of Friendship and Enmities* tells us that Saturn does harm to Jupiter, because it is the owner of Jupiter's fall sign, Capricorn. When Saturn is munakara Jupiter's outcome planet, there is bound to be hardship, restrictions, separation and rejection in the story of Jupiter's munakara state.

Mozart's example is very clear – munakara Jupiter in 2nd house has an outcome of Aquarius Saturn in a stellium in Whole Sign 6th house – no matter how much money is coming in (2nd house), daily expenses will always outnumber incoming funds, and the person will have to increase their workload to meet their expenses (Saturn, outcome planet). But when money comes in, Venus ruling 2nd house and munakara Jupiter's placement in 2nd house, the person stretches the budget once more (usually buying Venusian pleasures), and Saturn has to double its workload once more. If sickness intervenes, or work is scarce (Saturn in, and ruling 6th house), munakara Jupiter may encourage the person to console themselves by going on spending sprees to cheer themselves up, rather than pulling in the belt and putting in some restrictions to get through the hard times (Saturn, outcome planet).

At the time of his death, Mozart's young family should have been comfortably provided for, as Mozart had been paid for his new opera, *The Magic Flute*, and had received some payment for the mysterious *Requiem*. He also had several wealthy patrons lined up to pay him annuities in exchange for the occasional composition. However, the couple's lavish lifestyle habits had gotten out of hand, and his wife Constanze is recorded as appealing to the Emperor for money, just five days after Mozart's death, claiming poverty and crippling debt. Constanze was also desperate to find a substitute composer to complete the requiem begun by Mozart but now unfinished, in order that she might receive a final payment for the commission, so she too is represented by Libra Jupiter in munakara as it rules the 7th house of 'spouse'.

Munakara Planet and Sect Condition – how comfortable is Jupiter?

Jupiter is a diurnal planet and as such, it prefers to travel in the same hemisphere as the Sun, even if the chart itself is nocturnal and the birth occurs during the night-time hours.

Both the Sun and Jupiter are in air signs, and whilst the gap between them creates a wide trine, Jupiter in Libra is still able to assist Mozart's Sun in Aquarius in the Placidus chart's 5th house of creativity. Robert Hand tells us that Jupiter in sect produces the best manifestations of Jupiter; success, power, wealth, knowledge and awareness. Good sect dignity gives Jupiter resilience to overcome harm.[4]

Wolfgang Mozart — ♃'s Sect Dignity			
Planet	Sect 1 Status	Sect 2 Hemisphere	Sect 3 Sign
♎♃	Night	With the Sun	Air
D	N	D	D

Table 17.2: Wolfgang Mozart: Munakara Jupiter's Sect Dignity

However, being in the state of munakara is inclined to add conflict, difficulty, hardship or an unforeseen challenge to any situation, especially when Saturn is the outcome planet. Whilst these statements ring true for Wolfgang Mozart, there is still frustration and bitterness when Jupiter's gifts are not long-term, and success feels like a fleeting moment. Jupiter in sect, and in trine aspect to the Sun brought Mozart great benefits that perhaps he didn't utilize to the best of his ability. He was born a virtuoso to a father who is himself, intelligent, gifted, and self-sacrificing in putting his son's career ambitions in front of his own aspirations. And yet, Mozart was often unemployed, chasing short-term appointments, or trying to separate his wealthy, but stingy clients, from the money they owed him for his compositions.

Munakara Jupiter (ruling the 4th house of father) is as much the story of the father as it is the record of his famous son's life. Leopold Mozart (14 November 1719–28 May 1787) was born with three planets in munakara – Sun, Saturn and diurnal Mercury in Scorpio, all disposit to Mars in Pisces, with Jupiter as their outcome planet – and history's judgement of Opinion is divided over whether Leopold was dogmatic and controlling – he has been described by some biographers as a pedagogue (a strict, critical master) – or he was an inspirational teacher to his two talented progeny. The discovery of his children's talent is considered to have been a life-transforming event for Leopold Mozart. The *Grove Dictionary of Music And Musicians* references the correspondence between father and his son and daughter Maria (nickname

Nannerl) stating: "The recognition of this 'miracle' struck Leopold with the force of a divine revelation and he felt his responsibility to be not merely a father's and teacher's but a missionary's as well."[5] By "missionary", the *Grove Dictionary* refers to the family's constant tours through royal courts in need of 'enlightenment'.

In his youth Leopold Mozart studied philosophy and jurisprudence (the theory of law) and at one time, his study in theology might have led him into a career as a Catholic priest. Instead, Leopold began a career as a professional musician and in 1758 he was promoted to second violinist, and in 1763, to elevated to deputy Kapellmeister (the leader of an ensemble of musicians) in the musical establishment of the ruling Prince-Archbishop of Salzburg.[6] He rose no further, while others less skilled were repeatedly promoted over him to the head position of Kapellmeister. *Grove Dictionary* states that Leopold's failure to advance to the top position was not dictated by his lack of skill, but rather he was disadvantaged by the great amount of time the family's tours consumed and he was forced to temporarily abandon his post at Salzburg. His daughter Nannerl wrote years later that her father "entirely gave up both violin instruction and composition in order to direct that time not claimed in service to the prince (Prince-Archbishop of Salzburg) to the education of his two children."[7]

Munakara Jupiter: Wolfgang Amadeus Mozart

"The music is not in the notes, but in the silence between. Neither a lofty degree of intelligence nor imagination nor both together go to the making of genius. Love, love, love, that is the soul of genius."[8] – Wolfgang Amadeus Mozart

Munakara Jupiter in Libra in the 2nd House

Throughout his lifetime Mozart travelled extensively. He spent 14 of his 36 years away from home, and munakara Jupiter would describe Mozart's wanderlust for exploring new countries, the challenge of performing for royal courts, and the experience of new music and exotic languages.

In many instances, Jupiter in the 2nd house tends to fortify the finances, but Mozart's money management was erratic, and his extravagant lifestyle meant accumulating debt so that financial security was always a hit-and-miss affair. Perhaps he learnt early from Leopold (Jupiter rules 4th house of father), that an appearance of wealth was everything, as the family's expenses when they were touring were used to purchase beautiful costumes for Nannerl and Wolfgang, expensive instruments, and useless paraphernalia for the children when they entertained the court. Monarchs and emperors may have lavished praise and attention on the child prodigies, but they were not involved in the lowly act of payment for services, and Leopold may have been nervous of offending his wealthy patrons.

"The miracle which God let be born in Salzburg"[9] was part of Leopold's patter when he introduced his son, and he was consciously aware that it was his duty to God to draw The Miracle to the notice of the world (and to profit from it). Amadeus means *'loved by God,'* and Leopold fostered a type of affected snobbery in Wolfgang which bordered on a God-complex, leading the boy, and then the man, to believe that he was entitled to the same lavish lifestyle as his benefactors – even though he was often having to survive on the wages of a lowly musician. This is the statement of Jupiter in munakara – a lack of humility, a touch of the divine, too much hubris – can be a misplaced sense of privilege that may not be supported by reality.

Mozart certainly had a vast range of incredible talents, but there were contributing factors beyond his control that constantly tested his Jupiter in the 2nd house, especially when it also ruled his 7th house of allies and open enemies. The Mozarts were of German Austrian extraction, pedalling their compositions at a time when Italian opera was in higher popular demand. In truth, the rivalry between Mozart and Antonio Salieri was more an issue of race (heavy German melodies and language verses the lighter operas written in Italian) than personal rancour, but it began when Mozart, a travelling musician at age eleven, visiting Vienna for the first time, where the seventeen-year-old Salieri was already established as the favourite in the Roman Emperor court of Joseph II. Joseph was a passionate supporter of Italian opera, so the young composer from Venice was naturally going to be more appealing than the novelty of an inexperienced child from Salzburg.

Jupiter in contention (ruling father's house) came into play again, when in Mozart's youth, it was Leopold who was responsible for choosing his son's wealthy benefactors. Unfortunately Leopold was a poor business man, and his choice of his son's mentors were often erroneous or misguided, as he would target benefactors who were either out of pocket themselves, or were too miserly to pay a decent wage for a young musician.

First Dispositor: Venus in Aquarius in 6th House

Munakara Jupiter rules Mozart's 7th house, and Venus is its dispositor, so relationships – both good and bad – are going to play a major role in the story of Wolfgang Mozart's life. Mozart fell in love with, and courted two sisters: the elder, Aloysia Weber, whom Mozart met in 1777 when he became her singing teacher when Aloysia was 17 years old. Mozart was trained in childhood as a (former) soprano until his voice broke at puberty so it was natural for him to seek employment to further Aloysia's education. He expressed his desire to marry her, but the romance progressed no further as Mozart left to pursue work in Paris. He tried to rekindle her affections when he passed through Munich where she was increasingly successful as a professional singer. According to the draft biography written by Georg Nikolaus von Nissen (later to become Constanze's second husband), the reunion did not go well: "When he entered, she appeared no longer to know him, for whom she previously wept. Accordingly, he sat down at the piano and sang in a loud voice, "The one who doesn't want me can kiss my..."[10]

Four years later, Mozart moved to Vienna where the Weber family were now living. Aloysia had married and brought her sisters and widowed mother to Vienna where she was employed as a soprano singer. Their home took in boarders to financially help the family, and Mozart took a room at the lodgings. Before long he was courting the third sister, 19-year-old Constanze, and her mother asking him to leave her house.

Leopold refused to grant his permission for the wedding (Saturn is Venus's dispositor), and scandal broke out when Constanze moved in with Mozart who was now in different lodgings. Letters record Constanze's sister, Sophie, tearfully declaring that her mother would send the police (Saturn, outcome planet) after Constanze if she did not return home.[11] Mozart wrote to Leopold begging for permission to marry, writing to him on 31 July 1782, "All the good and well-intentioned advice you have sent fails to address the case of a man who has already gone so far with a maiden. Further postponement is out of the question."[12]

The marriage took place on 4 August, 1782, and one day later, Leopold's letter of consent arrived in the post. Their marriage was happy but short, Mozart passing away nine years later. They had six children, but only two sons survived to adulthood. Eighteen years after Mozart's death Constanze married Nissen and wrote in December 1929,"I have had two most excellent husbands by whom I was loved and honoured – even I have to say, adored; they, too were both equally loved by me with the utmost tenderness, thus I was twice completely happy."[13]

In the latter years, when Mozart's operas were much in demand in Vienna, he and his wife Constanze spent any money that came into the household on servants, furnishings for their expensive home, all manner of luxuries including exquisite costumes, beautiful adornments, jewellery, and opulent social gatherings. When a benefactor disappeared or the money dried up, they would sell everything to pay the debt, and hope for better times to come.

The outcome planet: Saturn in Aquarius in 5th House (Placidus) and 6th House (Whole Sign)

Twelve years after his childhood experience performing for Joseph II at age 14, in the early 1780s, Mozart was summoned to Vienna by his employer, Archbishop Colloredo. Leopold remained in Salzburg, but his influence was always paramount to Mozart's decisions. Saturn is munakara Jupiter's outcome planet and Jupiter rules the 4th house of father, so Leopold was always going to play an important and influential role in Mozart's life.

Debate surrounds the temperament of Mozart's father, Johann Georg Leopold Mozart (1719–1787). Some scholars cast him as tyrannical, mendacious, and possessive, while others argue Leopold was a sensible guide for an irresponsible Wolfgang.[14]

Even after Mozart had moved away from his father, Leopold continued to influence his son's opinions, his behaviour and his career choices (Aquarius Mercury rules his Ascendant and MC; Saturn is dispositor for Mozart's Sun, Mercury, and Venus in Aquarius). Father and son exchanged letters accusing "Italians led by Salieri" of actively putting obstacles in the way of Mozart obtain certain posts or staging his operas. Mozart's jealousy of his rival was fanned by Leopold's correspondence (munakara Jupiter ruling 4th house) and in December 1781 Mozart wrote to his father that "the only one who counts in the Emperor's eyes is Salieri."[15]

Eighteen months later, in May 1783, Mozart wrote to Leopold complaining again of his treatment at court, and his frustration at being excluded from privileges bestowed on his rival. The letter mentions Salieri and Lorenzo Da Ponte, the court poet: "You know those Italian gentlemen; they are very nice to your face! Enough, we all know about them. And if Da Ponte is in league with Salieri, I'll never get to show him (the emperor) what I can really do with an Italian opera."[16]

The rivalry between Mozart and Salieri became publicly visible (Saturn disposits and conjuncts Mercury, ruler of MC) in 1786 when Emperor Joseph II held an opera composition competition and Mozart was considered to be the loser of the competition.[17]

Unfortunately for Mozart, Jupiter in munakara is inclined to exaggerate its own capabilities – although in Mozart's case perhaps this belief in his

Chapter Seventeen • *Munakara Jupiter Delineations*

superiority was justified – and if Salieri's services were in greater demand, or his wages were higher, or a privileged child's tutoring was taken by the Italian. It rankled Mozart, and he returned letters to his father complaining of his unfair treatment at court. Truthfully Salieri's income was as much based on his popularity as was Mozart's, but Salieri managed his finances better by being able to maintain his household in lean times, and raise his eight children in modest accommodations.

Decades later, Salieri would be accused of poisoning Mozart, and although the only thing that supports this rumour, is Salieri's supposed self-confession, after he attempted suicide in November 1823 – thirty-two years after Mozart's death – the scandal had started, and fictional stories turned rumour into 'fact.'. Salieri was committed to medical care and suffered dementia for the last eighteen months of his life, passing away at age 74.

Salieri's natal Saturn is in munakara – Scorpio Saturn to Leo Mars to the Sun – and the fate of both composers are inexplicably linked. Whilst Mozart's music grew in fame and popularity, Salieri's compositions became outmoded, but ironically, Peter Shaffer's play *Amadeus* (1979) and its 1984 film version, directed by Milos Forman, revived interest in Salieri's music and there has been a resurgence in his music (and his life story) since the start of this century.

Sagittarius Moon in Munakara: Wolfgang Amadeus Mozart

- **Key Questions:**
- What does Mozart's Moon contend with?
- What is its driving force?
- What is its trigger? What is its outcome?

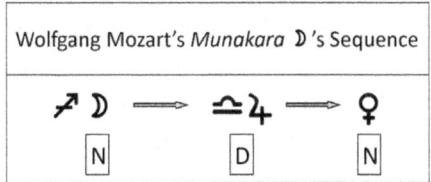

Table 17.3: Wolfgang Amadeus Mozart: Moon in munakara

Mozart's Moon in Sagittarius is one of his two planets which are in a state of munakara. From its state of contention, I would expect to see a history of indications that the Moon, and all that it signifies, has been under duress due to the double-change in dispositors from one sect to the other and back again: in this case, from nocturnal Moon, to diurnal Jupiter, to nocturnal Venus.

The Moon signifies the mother, the family situation, the state of the physical body, and the fluidity for their emotional landscape to flourish, and to nourish the individual. When the Moon is munakara, I would anticipate one or more of the following scenarios: a struggling mother caught in poor circumstances, tense family relations, or health issues for the individual. There may be challenges in maintaining physical strength or mobility, suffering a broken heart somewhere along the line, or experience emotional upheavals brought on by sensitivity to rejection, isolation, betrayal, or jealousy. At the other end of the spectrum, munakara Moo can produce quite opposite reactions, such as a lack of awareness or complete disinterest in others' feeling states.

Mozart's Sagittarian Moon is disposited by his Jupiter, which in turn is disposited by Venus. This indicates a tendency towards self-indulgence, and joins the Moon (already a highly subjective planet), with two planets that can show excessive behaviour with little restraint. Records of Mozart's life suggest that he was prone to unbridled appetites, and was likely to have very little self-control when it came to hedonistic pleasures, irresponsible spending (Jupiter in 2nd house), or restraint or self-discipline when it comes to denying himself pleasures (Venus as outcome planet). Even his odd sense of humour shows signs of munakara Moon, as the Mozart family, mostly female members including his mother, sister and cousins, were known for scatological humour, that is, 'a type of off-colour humour dealing with defecation (including diarrhea and constipation), urination and flatulence, and to a lesser extent vomiting and other bodily functions.'

As for munakara Moon's connection to his finances (Moon sextiles Jupiter in 2nd house), in 1788, Mozart saw a 66% decline in his income compared to his best years in 1781.[18] Mozart began to borrow money, most often from his friend and fellow Mason and wealthy merchant, Johann von Puchberg (Mozart's Moon rules 11th house)., and "a pitiful sequence of letters pleading for loans" survives.[19] Some biographers have suggested that Mozart was suffering from depression (Saturn's involvement with Jupiter's sequence), and it seems his musical output slowed.[20]

Mozart joined the Freemasons in 1784 (munakara Moon rules 11th house), seven years before his death, and the Masonic order played an important role in his life and work. There was secrecy and power attached to the Freemasons that satisfied his Pluto Moon, and even the name of the Viennese Masonic lodge to which he was admitted as an Apprentice on 14 December 1784 carried the flavour of his Sagittarian Moon and its dispositor. The English translation of the lodge's name was "Benificence," and according to the

Austrian musicologist Otto Erich Duetsch, this lodge was "the largest and most aristocratic in Vienna...Mozart, as the best of the musical 'Brothers,' was welcome in all the lodges."[21]

Venus is the outcome planet for the Moon, and apart from his stints of professional jealously and his financial woes, it appears that Mozart was happy in his marriage to Constanze (Venus, outcome planet), was travelling constantly with his music in huge in demand across Europe, and was busily composing up until his final illness and death. In fact, in the final years of his life, Mozart seemed to rally from depression and wrote many of his best-known works, including his last three symphonies, culminating in the no. 41 *'Jupiter'* Symphony, as well as four operas, and his unfinished work on *Requiem*.

The combination of the three planets – Moon, Jupiter, and Venus – produced great genius and creativity, feeding Mozart's passion to explore music in a brilliant and innovative way. However, the three planets, placed in sequence, may also have shattered his reason – he believed he had been poisoned by an enemy – and plagued those things which are signified by his Moon: the grief over losing his beloved mother, his poor health, and his somewhat precarious peace of mind. Jupiter's placement in the house of money is anxiety for the comforts which the dispirited Moon seeks, and Venus' 6th-house placement is a warning of toil, poverty, or the potential for a weakened constitution, if this man cannot bring his excesses, or his paranoia, under control.

Munakara Planet and Sect Condition – how comfortable is the Moon?

Mozart's munakara Moon is greatly helped by his night birth, thereby, creating a nocturnal chart. The Moon becomes the main luminary in his chart, and Mozart's close and loving relationship with his mother is one expression for a Moon in sect. Moon with good sect dignity (a nocturnal chart) is a source of emotional strength, and can bring success through embodying the aspirations of others and serving their needs.[22]

Wolfgang Mozart — ☽'s Sect Dignity			
Planet	Sect 1 Status	Sect 2 Hemisphere	Sect 3 Sign
♐ ☽	Night	With the Sun	Fire
D	N	D	D

Table 17.4: *Wolfgang Mozart: Munakara Moon's Sect Dignity*

Unfortunately, Mozart's in sect Moon was not able to protect his physical health, as the conjunction to Pluto shows the danger and stress the body experiences when Pluto/Moon is in square aspect to the Ascendant degree. Saturn's strong influence in the Whole Sign 6th house, along with Mercury, the ruler of his Ascendant, indicates the battles munakara Moon must undertake to help Mozart's body to survive his childhood illnesses, but ultimately, Mozart's lifestyle choices were not good, and possibly contributed to his early death.

Munakara Moon: Wolfgang Mozart
Munakara Moon in Sagittarius in the 4th House

Wolfgang's mother, Anna Maria Mozart (*nee*, Pertl), was one of three daughters born in Salzburg in 1720 to a local administrator who fell deeply into debt, before his death when Anna was four years old. When all their possessions were sold to pay his debts, her mother and older sisters (one of whom died in 1728, when Anna was eight years old) lived on a charity pension of eight florins a month. We know that Anna Maria was a frail child, as legal documents describe her as "constantly ill" (1733) and as "the constantly ill bedridden daughter" (1739). Anna married Leopold Mozart in 1747, presumably on her Saturn Return, with one writer recording "the two were regarded at the time as the handsomest couple in Salzburg." Leopold was estranged from his own family of good standing, mainly architects and bookbinders, and scraped a living as a music teacher. His one claim to fame was the publication of a violin manual in the year of his famous son's birth.

Anna gave birth to seven live children over a period of eight years, but only two were destined to survive infancy; their fourth child, Maria Anna "Nannerl" (born 1751), and their last child, Johann Chrysostomus Wolfgang Amadeus (born 1756).

Mozart's chart shows a tight conjunction between his Moon and Pluto, so it is not surprising to learn of his mother's grief at having to bury five babies, some of whom lived only days, but most that did not survive to their first birthday.[23] Anna Maria almost died giving birth to her last child, Wolfgang, as her womb retained the placenta and its forced removal posed an extreme risk of fatal infection for her.

Mozart's Moon Pluto is in the 4th house, and his parents' marriage does not seem to be a particularly happy one. Leopold was controlling, his nature was described as "phlegmatic and painfully conscientious," and he relentlessly

Chapter Seventeen • *Munakara Jupiter Delineations*

drove his two talented children to achieve perfection at all cost. Leopold was sensitive to others' criticisms and perceived slights, was mistrustful (bordering on paranoia), he was frustrated in his own ambitions, explosive, possibly violent, and extremely difficult to live with. Mozart inherited many of these characteristics from his father, and these unsettling traits were fanned by the letters he later received from Leopold, when he was an adult living in Vienna.

Surviving letters describe how Mozart's mother "will have drawn a veil over many an unpleasant incident not merely out of prudence, but also from fear. She was utterly devoted to him [Leopold] and willingly submitted to the strict regime to which he inevitably and unquestioningly subjected her."[24]

We are told from these letters that Anna Maria was a caring mother, and a refuge for her children when Leopold's hand fell heavily upon them, and that Wolfgang loved and admired her to distraction. Anna Maria accompanied her young family on a series of tours (1762–1768), living in squalid dwellings and travelling in primitive conditions, whilst exhibiting her two children before nobility and the royal courts of Europe. Mozart's munakara Moon rules his 11th house, and not all receptions were warm, with many courtiers whispering their suspicions that it was Leopold, not Wolfgang, who was the true author of many of the compositions attributed to the child. Both mother and children succumbed to illness on their travels, and Wolfgang contracted smallpox during this period. When Nannerl became too old at age eighteen, to be classified as a 'child prodigy', Leopold left mother and daughter in Salzburg to fend for themselves, whilst he took Wolfgang on the road again for the next four years.

By 1777, Leopold had secured a position for Wolfgang back in Salzburg, but father and son were ambitious for more, and Leopold ordered Wolfgang back to touring to find a more lucrative benefactor. At this time Leopold was in jeopardy of losing his own benefactor so Anna Maria was forced to accompany her son on the trip to Paris to find better employment for Wolfgang. His mother had objected that she was too old for this lifestyle, but Leopold didn't trust his wayward son, and regardless of her protests, Anna Maria was sent on the arduous journey. Whilst Wolfgang made regular, and often humiliating, visits to Parisian nobles to ply his trade as court musician, his mother waited for his return in cold, dank lodgings. Food in Paris was expensive and often bad, and Anna Maria's health deteriorated to the point that she became too weak to leave her bed. Wolfgang was already in debt and selling valuables to survive, and there was no money for medical attention for his mother. Anna Maria died in Paris with her 21-year-old son by her side on 3ʳᵈ July 1778, and was buried the next day in a foreign city, far from home. Her death was the first that he had witnessed, and and the trauma of losing his mother may have been a contributing factor to the transient fits of melancholy Mozart suffered through the remainder of his life,.

Munakara Moon often indicates health afflictions, and Mozart's constitution was never strong. A full medical analysis of Mozart's health is available from the September 1983 JRSM (Journal of Royal Society of Medicine).[25] And it shows Mozart suffered from frequent attacks of tonsillitis, constant upper respiratory tract infections, the long-term effects of rheumatic fever which he contracted in 1763, at age seven, and experienced re-occurring bouts throughout his life. He also contracted small pox and typhoid fever as a child, whilst travelling on the road from one infected city to the next. The Journal states that Mozart suffered chronic ill health during the last six months of his life. Recurring violent headaches and blackouts suggest epilepsy, worsening depression, paranoid delusions that someone was poisoning him, and a maddening belief that an anonymous patron has commissioned him to write his own Requiem.

Given the summary of his various medical conditions, it seems unfair that biographers have accused Mozart of hypochondria, but if this is true, then it may have been a contributing factor in his death. Mozart had great faith in the benefits of blood-letting as a health restorative, and was prone to its overuse whenever he fell ill. He also took regular doses of the purgative metal, antimony, and an excessive quantity induces intense vomiting, fever, swollen abdomen and swollen limbs – all symptoms which Mozart displayed during his final two weeks. He was convinced that he was slowly and systematically being poisoned, but he had no idea it was by his own hand, and not by the nefarious actions of his rival, Antonio Salieri.

Munakara Jupiter: Cindy Sherman

A Brief Biography of Cindy Sherman

Cindy Sherman (born 19 January 1954) is an American photographer known for her images – particularly her elaborately "disguised" self-portraits – that comment on social role-playing and sexual stereotypes.[26] Sherman has been called one of the best-known and most important artists working today. Her decades-long performative practice of photographing herself under different guises has produced many of contemporary art's

Chapter Seventeen • *Munakara Jupiter Delineations*

most iconic and influential images. At the heart of Sherman's work is the multitude of identity stereotypes that have arisen throughout both the history of art, and the history of advertising, cinema, and media.[27]

Sherman first found fame in 1977 with her *Untitled Film Stills* (1977–80), and they are still one of her best-known series. The series of black-and-white photographs featuring Sherman in a variety of roles is reminiscent of 'film noir' and presents viewers with an ambiguous portrayal of women as sex objects. Sherman stated that the series was "about the fakeness of role-playing was well as contempt for the domineering 'male' audience who would mistakenly read the images as sexy."[28]

She continued to be the model in her photographs, donning wigs and costumes that evoke images from the realms of advertising, television, film, and fashion and that, in turn, challenge the cultural stereotypes supported by these media.

Sherman's images took a different turn in the 1980s when she swapped to colour film and moved into the realm of the grotesque and the sinister with photographs that featured mutilated bodies and reflected such concerns as eating disorders, insanity, and death.[29]

In the 1990s Sherman's style changed once more, and she returned to a photographic commentary on clichéd female identities using mannequins in some of her work. In 1999 she exhibited disturbing images of savaged dolls and doll parts that explored her interest in juxtaposing violence and artificiality. In the 2000 series of photographs Sherman posed as Hollywood women with overblown makeup and silicone breast implants, aiming for results of enigmatic pathos.[30]

In 2016 Sherman was awarded the *Praemium Imperiale* prize in painting, a category that also encompasses photography. Also in 2016 she debuted a series of new photographs in the exhibition "Imitation of Life" at the Broad Museum, Los Angeles, and Metro Pictures, New York. In 2017 Sherman caused a sensation when she made her private Instagram account public. The social media platform, where users can exhibit vignettes of their daily lives and manipulate their appearance through filters, has caused Sherman to be celebrated for her deft use of the application (Instagram) to make art.[31]

"Everyone thinks these are self-portraits but they aren't meant to be. I just use myself as a model because I know I can push myself to extremes, make each shot as ugly or goofy or silly as possible."[32] – Cindy Sherman

Munakara in Practice

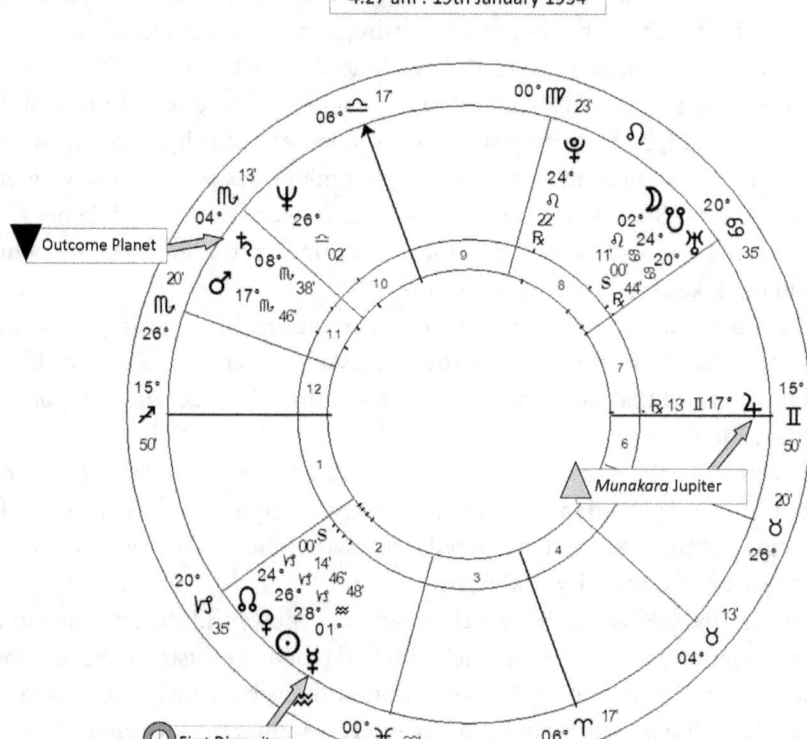

Fig. 17.2: Cindy Sherman Natal Chart: Munakara Jupiter's Sequence

Gemini Jupiter in Munakara: Cindy Sherman

- **Key Questions:**
- What does Cindy Sherman's Jupiter contend with?
- What is its driving force?
- What is its trigger? What is its outcome?

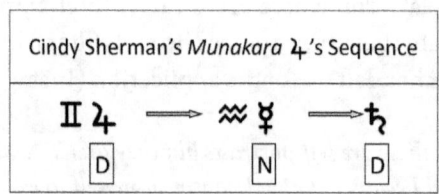

Table 17.5: Cindy Sherman: Munakara Jupiter's Sequence

Chapter Seventeen • *Munakara Jupiter Delineations*

Sherman's munakara Jupiter rules her Sagittarian Ascendant, and with its placement two degrees from the Descendant, and in detriment, there is little doubt that relationships have been challenging for Cindy Sherman. Jupiter's placement on Sherman's relating axis can be a constant reminder that intimate relationships are not easy, and that partners may mistake her self-portraiture artwork for the private person behind the art. Munakara Jupiter has provided Sherman with a number of high profile partners; a 17 year marriage to video artist Michel Auder who was addicted to heroin for much of the time, a painful relationship with a film-maker called Paul H-O who secretly taped, and then released, a documentary on her private life titled *Guest of Cindy Sherman*, and a long time affair with Talking Heads frontman David Byrne, which ended around the same time as her 2010 *Untitled* series was released. In a 2016 interview with *The Guardian*, Sherman says she now prefers to live alone with her 25-year-old macaw saying that being single has liberated her.[33]

Nocturnal Mercury is the second planet in Jupiter's munakara sequence, and its position in Aquarius, an air sign, gives Sherman a special insight into how she wishes to portray big ideas behind images, that seem so ordinary at first glance. Sherman's outcome planet is Saturn, as nocturnal Mercury resides in Aquarius, and Saturn's position in Scorpio creates a square aspect between Mercury (first dispositor) and Saturn (second dispositor).

Mercury too is in munakara status, and Saturn is out of sect, but Sherman's photography does well to encapsulate the three planets in Jupiter's munakara sequence, as her imagery is often awkward, staged, and uncomfortable to feel at ease with (Saturn as outcome planet). Sherman's pointed message which she communicates through her photography (Aquarius Mercury) is designed to highlight how society makes women feel unsafe, or peculiar, particularly if they don't fit the 'normal' mould (Jupiter in detriment).

Munakara Planet and Sect Condition – how comfortable is Jupiter?

Jupiter is a diurnal planet and therefore would prefer a daytime chart, or, if this is not possible, to travel in the same hemisphere as its luminary, the Sun. However, Sherman's birth data has a Rodden 'AA' rating, and munakara Jupiter's placement two degrees above the horizon removes it from the light and warmth of the Sun. Jupiter's one saving grace is its placement in a masculine air sign, but unfortunately, it is also a sign belonging to its enemy Mercury.

Robert Hand notes that Jupiter in a nocturnal chart, and nocturnally placed (away from the Sun), is likely to 'increase its compassion and sensitivity, but it may operate without forethought.'³⁴ Hand's later observations in 2015 on sect, states that Jupiter severely out of sect is 'more selfish and entitled, less concerned about general welfare,' and somehow 'indicates being spoiled as children'.³⁵

Cindy Sherman — ♃'s Sect Dignity			
Planet	Sect 1 Status	Sect 2 Hemisphere	Sect 3 Sign
♊ ♃	Night	No Sun	Air
D	N	N	D

Table 17.6: Cindy Sherman: Munakara Jupiter Sect Dignity

Cindy Sherman would emphatically disagree with the last statement, given that she describes her childhood as miserable and lonely.³⁶ Munakara Jupiter in detriment, with poor sect dignity, can find the greater benefic struggling to appreciate its good fortune, whilst fearing that success or honours may disappear without warning. Cindy Sherman seems to relate to this aspect of her munakara Jupiter as she has said in an interview, "She can still feel overawed by the sudden attention she gets at a gallery opening, and that when she gets a response from people about new work she feels she has "dodged another bullet and it's OK."³⁷

Munakara Jupiter: Cindy Sherman

"We're all products of what we want to project to the world. Even people who don't spend any time, or think they don't, on preparing themselves for the world out there – I think that ultimately they have for their whole lives groomed themselves to be a certain way, to present a face to the world."³⁸
– Cindy Sherman

Munakara Jupiter in Gemini conjunct Descendant (Placidus and Whole Sign)

Photographic artist Cindy Sherman has been described as one of contemporary art's brightest and most influential voices, making her point through dressing up and photographing herself as a wide range of female archetypes. Sherman made a reputation for herself as a witty commentator of female stereotypes in cinema, advertising, and the media, and whilst her images were often playful, they also gave rise to the viewer experiencing feelings of unease, truthfulness, or painful self-recognition.

Chapter Seventeen • *Munakara Jupiter Delineations*

Munakara Jupiter in Gemini rules Sherman's Ascendant, and its position two degrees from the Descendant, in detriment, is confrontational for both the artist, and for those who view her artworks. Jupiter in contention is making its point by creating images that expose cultural stereotypes, and if discomfort for viewers, creates new thought and generates vigorous discussion, then munakara Jupiter has done its job.

Sherman's growing success and confidence as an appreciated artist has coincided with the explosion in society's obsession with mass media – represented by Gemini Jupiter in munakara – and Sherman's latest characters have evolved into more colourful, exaggerated and grotesque reflections of the media's exploitation of women. The advent of online cyber-bullying has made females feel even more vulnerable, unattractive and susceptible to ridicule. Sherman's evolving caricatures of women mirror their inner distress and burgeoning mental health issues, as today's modern woman struggles to cope with what feminist film theorist Laura Mulvey calls 'to-be-looked-at-ness'.

Mulvey's famous essay "Visual Pleasure and Narrative Cinema" was written almost fifty years ago, but many of its points ring true in society's attitude to women. Mulvey says, "In their traditional exhibitionist role (in cinema) women are simultaneously looked at and displayed, with their appearance coded for strong visual and erotic impact so that they can be said to connote 'to-be-looked-at-ness'."[39]

Munakara Jupiter's partile quincunx to Mars (Gemini to Scorpio) is a modern aspect, but it should not be ignored as it represents Sherman's attitude to the power of men and their control over women, both in works of art, and in society. Sherman's Mars is in rulership in Scorpio, and moves into 12th house by Whole Sign, so the unseen danger and hidden enemy becomes men, and their ability to be violent or threatening towards women. Saturn is the outcome planet in Jupiter's sequence – also the first dispositor for munakara Venus and Mercury – and the eleven degree separation is not insignificant when Saturn joins Mars in its feminine sign.

> *"The still must tease with the promise of a story the viewer of it itches to be told."*[40]
> Cindy Sherman

Untitled Film Stills (1977–1980) is a series of 70 black-and-white photographs which achieved international recognition for Sherman, and possibly the artist was familiar with Mulvey's essay on women in cinema.

Sherman mimics the characters of the 1930s to 1950s film era as she dresses her subjects up with costumes, wigs and makeup to copy different roles portrayed by famous actresses during this period. *Untitled Film Still #48*, (also known as *The Hitchhiker*) was shot in 1979 by Sherman's father, and shows a lone woman with her back to the camera, standing on the side of a road in the darkening light at dusk, with a suitcase by her side.[41] The figure looks fragile, alone, and vulnerable, and the backlit figure is oblivious to her audience, making the viewer feel as though they are in the role of either voyeur or predator.

Sherman's munakara Jupiter is using images that create conversations, by showing the void that exists between what is acceptable for each gender, and asks the viewer to think about how gender classification affects their perspective of the image. For instance, Sherman implies that if the same figure from the image in *The Hitchhiker* had been male, rather than female, there would be a different feel about the image; a male might be seen as courageous, adventurous or independently striking out on their own in the same pose. The artist is making a point, namely that this earlier era in cinema reinforces the concept of the powerlessness of women, who are limited to play constricting roles as mother, seductress (the fallen woman), or a victim of crime, or abuse. The woman is either suitably punished, or mercilessly preyed upon, but she is never the protagonist in control of her own destiny.

Cindy Sherman's munakara Jupiter rules her 4th house in the Whole Sign system, and she grew up as the youngest of five children with an age gap of nine years between herself and the next sibling. She described herself as a "total latecomer", who stood apart from a family that had existed for a decade before she joined them as their youngest member. Her original impulse to dress up and create her own fantasy world was born of isolation and anxiety (Saturn is Jupiter's outcome planet), and her strong impulse to be noticed by the rest of her family, constantly wondering, "If you don't like me this way, how about you like me this way? Or maybe you like this version of me?"[42] Munakara Jupiter rules Sherman's Ascendant and her early dress-ups are Jupiter's need to be noticed and valued, when Saturn (Jupiter's outcome planet) made Sherman feel lonely, ignored, and unimportant in her family unit.

Sherman remembers her mother as good to a fault, but her father she has described as stern, mean, bigoted and "a horrible self-centered person."[43] Mars in rulership rules her IC, and its quincunx to munakara Jupiter (her 4th-house Whole Sign ruler) may trigger her unhappy memories of her childhood relationship with her father. She recalls that his selfishness prevented him from appreciating his family, and the love freely given to him by his wife. After his death, his children found the thing they missed most about him was the fact that they no longer had the opportunity to swap tales about which child had received the cruellest attention from him during the week: "..like what did he do to you? I would be like, 'He wrote me this horrible letter.' It was ridiculous, the things he would do."[44]

Nowadays, Sherman's home is both her refuge and her work space, as most of Sherman's photographs were taken in her apartment in a room designed as her studio. She fossicks in thrift stores and yard sales for furs and costume jewellery, and works into the early hours of the morning, moving from kitchen to living area, until she finds an idea that inspires her, and then she retreats to her studio in the next room to work her magic with the camera. In her home studio Sherman undertakes her multiple roles as author, director, make-up artist, hairstylist, wardrobe mistress, and model.

First Dispositor: Nocturnal Mercury in Aquarius in 2nd House (Placidus)

"I didn't want to make 'high art', I had no interest in using paint, I wanted to find something that anyone could relate to without knowing about contemporary art. I wasn't thinking in terms of precious prints or archival quality; I didn't want the work to seem like a commodity."[45] – Cindy Sherman

Aquarian Mercury is three degrees behind Sherman's Capricorn Sun, and opposes her Moon in early degrees of Leo. She describes her process as intuitive, and that she responds to elements of a setting such as light, mood, location, and costume. She constantly experiments with her surroundings, and will continue to change external elements until she finds what she instinctively wants for her image, which will become permanent once it is captured as a photograph.

Nocturnal Mercury is the first dispositor for munakara Jupiter, but it too is a planet in munakara, and the struggles that Sherman has experienced in her personal relationship (Mercury rules 7th house), she believes stem back to the suicide of her older brother at age 27, around the time of his first Saturn return. The age gap between the siblings places Cindy at age 15 at the time of her brother's death, and is about the time she was experiencing her own first Saturn opposition. She is asked by one interviewer if it was her brother's death that prompted her decision to go to art school. Sherman admits it was a factor even though at the time she did not tie the two events together. She says,

"I never really thought of art as being therapeutic, but I guess it definitely was."[46]

Mercury is the general significator for siblings, and although it resides in the Placidus 2nd house of money, and provides Sherman with her financial resources, it shifts to the 3rd house of siblings by Whole Sign. "I found myself in long-term relationships about which I now think: why was I with that person for so long? It seems ridiculous, almost shameful that you let yourself be hoodwinked in that way. I suppose – going back to the therapy session – that all goes back to my brother's suicide. The fact that I couldn't help him, maybe I can help this guy who can't get his life together. So I made some very bad choices there. If only I had gone to a therapist earlier."[47]

It took years for Sherman to realize that therapy could alleviate some of her childhood trauma, and that she need not carry her family's past into her own future. "My family was always dead against therapy, it was like, we don't need any help! We are strong, we can get through things! And, boy, could they have used it..."[48]

The outcome planet: Saturn in Scorpio

Saturn's involvement with all three of Sherman's munakara sequences – outcome planet for Jupiter, and first dispositor for nocturnal Mercury and Venus – has peppered Cindy Sherman's career with achievements and awards, and given her stability within the often financially-fickle world of art. She has received just about every award available to an American artist, including a MacArthur fellowship "genius grant". She has twice represented her country at the Venice Biennale, and her original 1980s *Untitled Film Stills* photographs have sold for more than four million dollars (Saturn rules Sherman's 2nd house, and is dispositor for her North Node, Venus, Sun and Mercury in her Placidus 2nd house).

> *"I wanted pretty pictures of older women – women who are trying too hard but succeeding – pulling off an extreme look. What I didn't know would creep into the portraits was a vulnerability behind the strong façade that most of them wear."*[49]

Cindy Sherman has always played with the idea of aging, and is fascinated by society's rejection of women who have passed menopause. Unless fame has held society's attention, most post-menopausal women are generally judged by society as having lost their two most beneficial features – their fertility, and their 'to-be-looked-at-ness' – so the challenge for Sherman is to decide how she will portray a woman whose physical form changes to reflect the latter years of her life.

In Sherman's chart (*Fig. 17.2*), Saturn is involved in a T-square with Mercury (Jupiter's dispositor) and the Moon, and the three planets – Mercury opposing the Moon, both planets squaring Saturn – will move to cadent houses in the Whole Sign chart. Sherman admits that since her last series she has come through a few rough years. She says some of these issues – health and just getting older – took her by surprise, "A few years of not shooting, and then switching over to a higher resolution camera, really brought it home to me. Now it is not like adding wrinkles to look older; it is using the wrinkles to say something else. What is disturbing is not seeing more lines on my face, but seeing that the range of possibilities of what I can do is much more limited."[50]

Sherman's latest exhibition took place in January 2024 at Hauser & Wirth's Wooster Street location in New York City goes out of its way to draw a connection to the artist's past. Each picture is an amalgam of the artist's facial features collaged into a single image. An article in *Artnet.News* states: "the parts of Sherman we see in snippets are tender, vulnerable. On view – plainly, and in rich digital detail – is the 70-year-old artist's aging skin, her pores, her creases."[51] In an interview with *The New York Times* profiling the artist, Sherman said: "I'm not going to go into this aging process silently or happily. I feel like I'm preparing myself for it…This is what you're going to get, so get used to it. It's coming. It's hanging over all of our heads."[52]

Artnet.News summarizes the 2024 exhibition – whilst unwittingly also summarizing Sherman's three planets in munakara – stating: "The get-ups and collages turn the subjects of Sherman's new portraits into caricatures, but she knows that time has a way of doing that too, turning us all into distorted, fractured reflections of our past selves."[53]

Munakara Venus and Mercury Duet in Saturn's Signs

"Inconsiderate, rude behaviour drives me nuts. And I guess the inconsiderate rudeness of social ineptitude definitely fuels my work."[54]

Capricorn and Aquarius are the two signs belonging to Saturn, and the fact that they lie next to each other on the zodiac belt means that it is possible for two planets to be in Saturn's adjoining signs, and still be a duet, under the conditions of munakara.

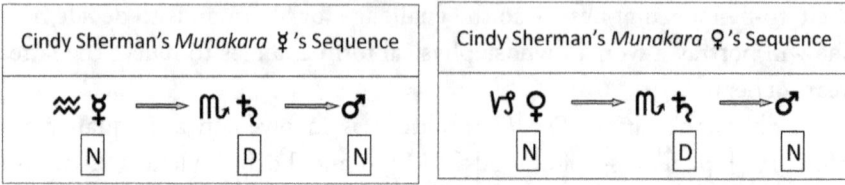

Table 17.7: Cindy Sherman: Munakara Mercury and Venus' Sequence

In Sherman's case, the two nocturnal planets are five degrees apart – Venus is in late degrees of Capricorn whilst Mercury has moved ahead to the second degree of Aquarius. The planets have an identical munakara sequence, Saturn in Scorpio will be the first dispositor, and Mars will be the outcome planet. Both planets also have a rulership connection to Sherman's career axis, as munakara Venus rules her Libran MC, and munakara Mercury rules Virgo, her tenth Whole Sign cusp, as Sagittarius is the mutable sign on her Ascendant. This MC/10th-house connection means that the rulers of these two places (Venus and Mercury) share a state of munakara, and this fact is likely to bring themes such as outrage, consternation, misinterpretation, or controversy to accompany Sherman's 'socially critical photography.'[55]

Sherman's Sun in Capricorn sits between Venus and Mercury in her chart, so whilst the Sun is not munakara as it disposits to another diurnal planet, Saturn, its activity and interpretation will be influenced by the two munakara planets situated either side of it. All three planets reside in the 2nd house, and Sherman's work has been financially rewarded through the art world acknowledging the value of her artistry and paying her handsomely for it.

> "I want there to be hints of narrative everywhere in the image so that people can make up their own stories about them. But I don't want to have my own narrative and force it on them."[56]

Saturn, dispositor for munakara Venus and Mercury duet, is situated in Sherman's 11th house in the Placidus system, but slips into 12th house in the Whole Sign chart. This movement could be advantageous if Saturn gives visibility, benefactors, and good fortune to Sherman who becomes a leader in her chosen field (Saturn in 11th house). At the same time, a planet in the 12th house can have an uncanny knack of finding a niche market within society that appreciates, and even yearns for, a statement to encapsulate a weakness with its ranks. Twelfth house is not confined to private misgivings, it also represents the undercurrents of fear and discomfort lurking within the

Chapter Seventeen • *Munakara Jupiter Delineations*

collective unconscious. Saturn in the 12th house is in its house of joy, and it is very astute at seeking out the collective fear, and capitalizing on it through a physical medium, such as a minority group, or a complicated social issue that is hidden from view.

Saturn is the lord of Time, and often the right timing can make an enormous difference to whether something is 'popular' or 'valuable' in the eyes of society, if it is perfectly synchronised with the exact time an artist is peddling their wares. Wolfgang Mozart is a perfect example of this – he was a musical genius – yet he was often unemployed and constantly searched for wealthy benefactors to pay for his symphonies, or teach piano lessons to his clients' indulged children. Dutch painter Vincent van Gogh relied on a stipend from his brother Theo to survive from one month to the next, and it took a century after his death for the world to appreciate his paintings, and raise their value to ridiculously high prices.

Mars, the outcome planet for both Venus and Mercury's munakara sequence, also moves from 11th to 12th house by a change in house systems. Sherman's memories of her father are not pleasant ones – Mars rules the IC, and Saturn is representative of father – and this may have a lot to do with these two planets moving from a social house (11th) to a house of fear (12th). However, it may be that Mars in its powerful position in Scorpio has been a great aid to Saturn, and that together, the two malefic planets have enabled Sherman's work to be appreciated and rewarded within her lifetime. They are separated by eleven-degrees, and Mars is moving away from Saturn, but it may be enough to strengthen the Venus/Mercury duet in munakara.

> *"The more horrific works came out of a feeling that everyone accepted my stuff too easily. I was deliberately trying to be antagonistic towards collectors and critics."*[57]

Even Sherman's more confronting works have been lauded, and she has found a 'voice' to express herself through the longevity of her 40-year career in photography (munakara Mercury). Sherman presents a unique perspective of society's attitude towards women in art, cinema, and lately, through social media platforms such as Instagram, where she invites the public to mimic her artistic style, by adding their own images, and mimicking her style in a way that pays homage to her work (munakara Venus).

From 1985 to 1989, Sherman shot her second series, *Disasters and Fairy Tales*, a series of confrontational images, targeted at challenging viewers to find beauty in ugly and grotesque images of fake vomit and rotting food. In 1992, Sherman produced her most disturbing work in *Sex Pictures* which removed her as the subject matter, and replaced it with life-size mannequins arranged in various positions of coitus. The images were so grotesque that they could not be confused as pornographic, but were intended to be a comment on how women are dehumanized when their bodies are purely objectified as sexual objects (munakara Venus).

The artist admits that being single is a good thing for her, but munakara Venus and Mercury (her 7th-house ruler), are disposited by Saturn, and this has meant that Sherman needed to reach a more mature age before she realized this fact.

> *"I think my whole adult life I have been so afraid to be alone that if someone acted as if they liked me a bit, I would be like, OK, you're my new boyfriend. I am a very loyal person. I found it hard to break up with people who I should have broken up with way earlier on in the relationship."*[58]

Sherman's preference is to work alone in her home studio, as she found out early in her art studies that working in collaboration with other artists was not for her (munakara Venus and Mercury deposited by Saturn),

> *I did two live performances my first year out of college, both collaborations. I hated doing it. I was a hopeless collaborator because of course I always acquiesced to the other person's usually bad ideas. Hence I always work alone. I never felt lonely. There is an aloneness to it. I have tons of friends; there is always someone to call.*[59]

Munakara Planet and Sect Condition – how comfortable are Venus and Mercury?

Both nocturnal Mercury and Venus have an advantage over diurnal Jupiter, in that Cindy Sherman was born with a nocturnal chart, during the hours when the Sun was beneath the horizon. Munakara Mercury's challenges have been described earlier in the text by the history of her brother's suicide, and her isolation as a child, but Mercury's opposition to the Moon, the main luminary in her chart, has meant that Sherman is as much a survivor, as the female characters she portrays in her photographs.

The Moon is the nocturnal chart's main luminary, and even its difficult square to Saturn – a big player in Sherman's three munakara sequences – has not made the Moon submissive or obedient to other's wishes, possibly because it has good sect dignity in the chart (nocturnal chart, nocturnally placed).

Sherman's mother (her Leo Moon) was 44 years of age when she was born in 1954, and even in those days she would be classified as a 'geriatric mother' (Saturn squares the Moon). By the time her last-born was a rebellious teenager, Sherman's mother seemed like an old lady, given that she was the same age as most of her friends' grandparents. Sherman recalls that her mother was like a martyr, a good person, and that she would always try to make her daughter be a good girl. But this ingrained training worked against Sherman's ability to speak out, or defend herself from criticism as an adult for fear that she would break her mother's mantra of 'always being nice to people' (munakara duet of Mercury and Venus).

Cindy Sherman			
Planet	Sect 1 Status	Sect 2 Hemisphere	Sect 3 Sign
♑ ♀	Night	With the Sun	Earth
N	N	D	N

Cindy Sherman			
Planet	Sect 1 Status	Sect 2 Hemisphere	Sect 3 Sign
♒ ☿	Night	With the Sun	Air
N	N	D	D

Table 17.8: Cindy Sherman: Munakara Mercury and Venus Sect Dignity

Nocturnal Mercury may have missed the second rule of sect, but it is not easy for Mercury to be separated from the Sun through the line of the horizon (Ascendant/Descendant axis), and the night chart is the very best option for this type of Mercury. Nocturnality allows for thoughts to flow easily without restriction, and bypasses the moral limitations of 'right or wrong' thinking, unfortunately, a logical process that often abruptly halts creative thought. Nocturnal Mercury, particularly in sect dignity, gifts the mind with poeticism, imagination, and fantasy, and allows images to be as present as language or mathematical equations. Nocturnal Mercury in Aquarius (disposited by Saturn) gives fluidity to time, and grants the mind permission to forage into the past for ideas, images, perceptions – even if they are not your own – and to bring those images into the present in a creative or unusual form.

"I think of becoming a different person. I look into a mirror next to the camera....it's trance-like. By staring into it I try to become that character through the lens...When I see what I want, my intuition takes over – both in the 'acting' and in the editing. Seeing that other person that's up there, that's what I want. It's like magic."⁶⁰

Sherman recalls that when she was a child she would play the same movies repeatedly, especially the ones from the horror genre, because she was fascinated by the actors' makeup, and the sequence of circumstances behind what culminated in the most gory scenes. Other children were terrified, but she remembers her fascination, and her early epiphany that everything she saw was fake, and merely a theatrical interpretation, rather than reality.

> "The work is what it is and hopefully it's seen as feminist work, or feminist-advised work, but I'm not going to go around espousing theoretical bullshit about feminist stuff."⁶¹

Munakara Venus is in sect in a nocturnal chart, and the artist in Sherman empathises with women who have battled through life. Her images are of women who are 'different', who have battled their environments and their situations to become survivors, rather than beauty queens, online influencers, and reality TV stars. The timeline of her most important work records her journey with munakara Venus, beginning in 1978 with a series of *Untitled Film Stills* which poked fun at the "coming of age" romances pumped out by Hollywood in the 1950s and 1960s. In the same series, Sherman changed her appearance repeatedly playing roles as girly pin-up, seductress, housewife, prostitute and damsel in distress, exploring everything that society classified as "feminine."

> "People assume that a self-portrait is narcissistic and you're trying to reveal something about yourself: fantasies or autobiographical information. In fact, none of my work is about me or my private life."⁶²

Munakara Jupiter: Oprah Winfrey

A Brief Biography of Oprah Winfrey⁶³

Oprah Winfrey (born 29 January 1954), often known simply as Oprah, is an American talk show host, television producer, actress, author, and philanthropist. Winfrey was born in Mississippi to a single teenage mother. After Winfrey's birth, her mother travelled north, and Winfrey spent her

Chapter Seventeen • *Munakara Jupiter Delineations*

first six years living in rural poverty with her maternal grandmother, Hattie Mae Lee. Her grandmother was so poor that Winfrey often wore dresses made from potato sacks, for which other children made fun of her. Her grandmother taught her to read before the age of three and took her to the local church, where she was nicknamed "The Preacher" for her ability to recite Bible verses.

At age six, Winfrey moved to an inner-city neighbourhood in Milwaukee, Wisconsin, with her mother, who was less supportive and encouraging than her grandmother had been, largely as a result of the long hours she worked as a maid. At 13, after suffering what she described as years of abuse, Winfrey ran away from home. When she was 14, she became pregnant, but her son was born prematurely and died shortly after birth. Her mother sent her to live with her father, Vernon in Nashville, and she began to flourish when he made her education a priority. In 1986, Winfrey said, "When my father took me, it changed the course of my life. He saved me. He simply knew what he wanted and expected. He would take nothing else."[64] She secured a full scholarship to Tennessee State University where she studied communication and worked in local media as a news anchor before moving to Baltimore to co-anchor the six o'clock news. In 1984 Winfrey relocated to Chicago to host a low-ranking morning chat show, which in time overtook the ratings for the *Donahue* show.

Over the course of her 25 years hosting The Oprah Winfrey Show (1986–2011) she never once missed a day through absenteeism. She taped 217 episodes dedicated to sexual abuse, having been a survivor of such abuse as a young girl. She was instrumental in the passage of the Oprah Bill, in the early 1990s. The bill was signed into law by President Bill Clinton and is aimed at stopping child abuse.[65] Winfrey transitioned her hit talk show into a media and business empire. Reinvested, the profits from her show, plus profits from films like *The Color Purple, Beloved* and *Selma* (which her Harpo Productions coproduced) add up to more than US$2.5 billion.

In 2011, she launched cable channel OWN (Oprah Winfrey Network) and sold most of her stake in the network to owner, Warner Bros. Discovery in 2020, in exchange for shares in the company. In 2015, Winfrey bought a 10% stake in WeightWatchers and donated her shares in February 2024 to the Smithsonian's National Museum of African American History and Culture. Her sprawling real estate portfolio includes homes in California and over a dozen properties including 2,100 acres of land in Hawaii.

Munakara in Practice

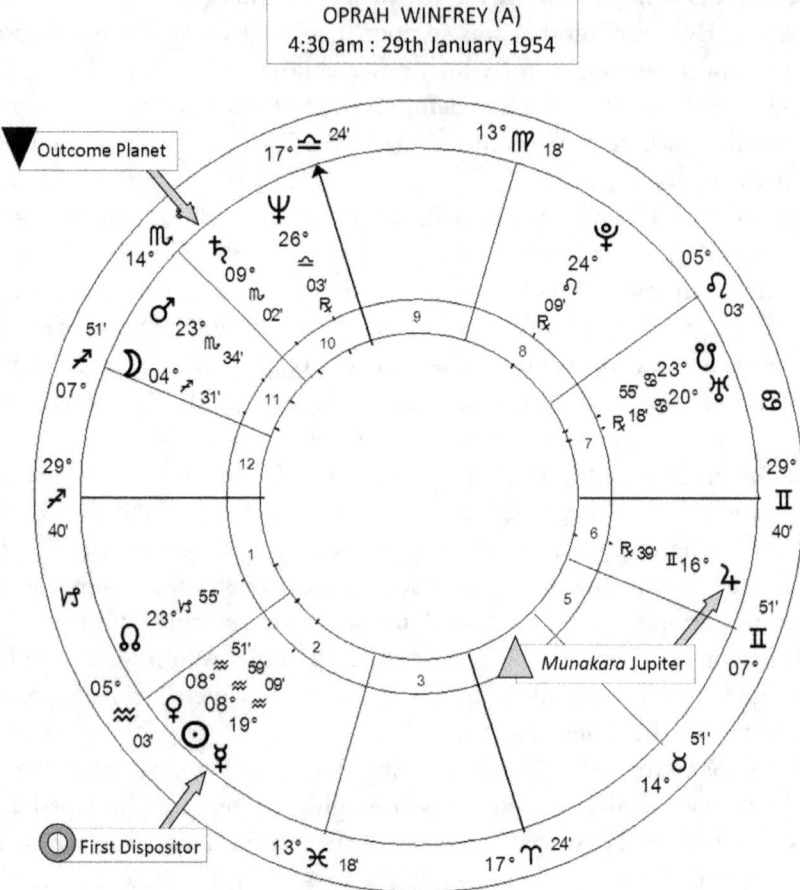

Fig. 17.3: Oprah Winfrey Natal Chart: Munakara Jupiter's Sequence

"Your life is your greatest teacher. Every single thing that's happening to you every day: your joys, your sadness, your challenges, your worries .....Everything is trying to take you home to yourself. And when you're at home with yourself... you are your best."[66] – Oprah Winfrey

Similarities between the charts of Cindy Sherman and Oprah Winfrey

Ten days separate the births of Cindy Sherman, born 19 January 1954 (*Fig. 17.2*), and Oprah Winfrey, born 29 January 1954 (*Fig. 17.3*). Both Sherman and Winfrey's births took place around 4:30 in the morning, and

Chapter Seventeen • *Munakara Jupiter Delineations*

although they were born in different time zones, the birth-time reflects the Sun's position in local time. Winfrey's rising sign is Sagittarius in its last degree, whilst Sherman's Ascendant is in mid-degrees of Sagittarius. Similar to Cindy Sherman's chart, Oprah Winfrey's munakara Jupiter will be the ruler of the Ascendant, munakara Mercury is the ruler of her Descendant (and her Whole Sign 10th house), and munakara Venus will be the Mid-heaven's ruling planet.

Munakara Jupiter, and its outcome planet Saturn, have barely moved in the ten-day interval between births, but Jupiter's first dispositor Mercury, has advanced a further eighteen degrees into the sign of Aquarius. This movement by Mercury, still in nocturnal position to the Sun, has created a trine aspect between munakara Jupiter in Gemini, and its dispositor, Mercury in Aquarius.

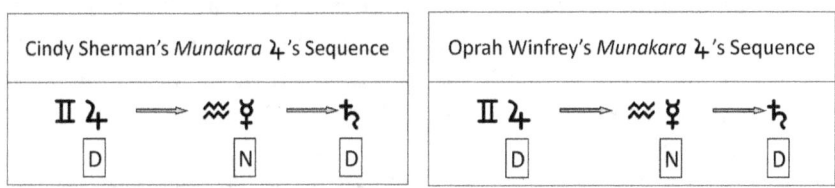

Table 17.9: Cindy Sherman and Oprah Winfrey: Munakara Jupiter's Sequence

Munakara Jupiter's sequence is the same for both charts – Gemini Jupiter disposits to nocturnal Mercury in Aquarius, which disposits to Saturn. However, as Mercury is the fastest-moving planet in the two munakara sequences – Oprah Winfrey's Mercury has moved away from Saturn – Mercury's square aspect is now separating, rather than applying to Saturn, its dispositor. During the ten days that separate the two births, Mercury has moved from 2° Aquarius to late degrees and formed an exact trine aspect with Jupiter two days before Oprah Winfrey's birth on 29 January, 1954.

Once more, Saturn is munakara Jupiter's outcome planet, and both women experienced strict male authoritarian figures in their childhood, and had fathers who felt the need to control their wayward daughters. Both women ignored the cynics and naysayers who told them they could not succeed, that the cards were stacked against them, and that invisible glass ceilings would stop disempowered women from rising to the top of their chosen profession. In spite of all this negativity thrown in their pathway – or maybe, because of it – instead, they found fame, wealth, and phenomenal success in their own right.

Munakara in Practice

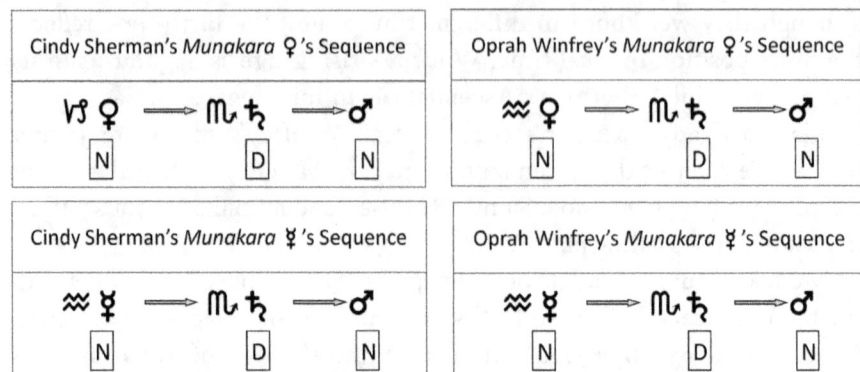

Table 17.10: Cindy Sherman and Oprah Winfrey:
Munakara Venus and Mercury's Sequence

The Sun has moved from the last two degrees of Capricorn in Sherman's chart (*Fig. 17.2*) to 8 Aquarius in Winfrey's chart (*Fig. 17.3*), whilst Mercury has moved quite quickly from 1 Aquarius to 19 Aquarius, it is still in higher degree than the Sun at 8 Aquarius and is behind the Sun, and therefore nocturnal in nature.

Mercury is still munakara, and it will present the same sequence in both women's charts. Winfrey's Venus has advanced from Capricorn to Aquarius, but as diurnal Saturn disposits both signs, the Venus sequence will stay the same, with Saturn as first dispositor for both nocturnal planets, and Mars as their outcome planet, as Saturn is in its sign of Scorpio.

As the Moon is the speediest of all the planets, it will show the greatest movement over in the ten day interval. Cindy Sherman's Moon is recorded as 2° Leo, and is disposited by her Capricorn Sun. Her Moon is not munakara as the Sun and Saturn are both diurnal planets. The Moon has moved into early degrees of Sagittarius by the time Oprah Winfrey was born (trining Sherman's Moon in Leo), and her Moon's dispositor is Jupiter in Gemini. Jupiter is disposited by nocturnal Mercury, completing the Moon's sequence – Moon to Jupiter to Mercury – thereby making Winfrey's Moon her fourth planet in munakara.

Gemini Jupiter in Munakara: Oprah Winfrey

- **Key Questions:**
- What does Oprah Winfrey's Jupiter contend with?
- What is its driving force?
- What is its trigger? What is its outcome?

Chapter Seventeen • *Munakara Jupiter Delineations*

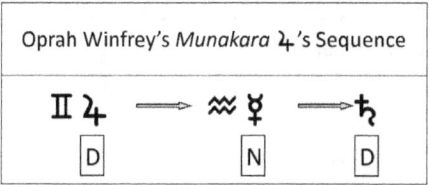

Table 17.11: Oprah Winfrey: Munakara Jupiter's Sequence

"All my life I have always known I was born to greatness."[67]

Oprah Winfrey's Jupiter in contention reflects the fighting spirit of a small town girl who was born without the protection of a father's name, to a mother who was barely past childhood herself. Her birth time has been given a Rodden 'A' Rating, supposedly confirmed by the media personality herself,[68] and this time places her Ascendant in the final degree of Sagittarius, making munakara Jupiter the lord of the Ascendant. Whilst some attribute Oprah's see-saw weight gains and losses to the mutable fire sign, Jupiter's rulership goes far beyond changes in the physique. In an interview with *People* magazine in 2019, titled "The 5 Moments That Changed My Life," Oprah said that if she had stayed trapped in a life in Milwaukee she would have been dead at 56, "I believe I would have been 437 lbs. I believe I would have had diabetes. I would have had high blood pressure. I would have suffocated knowing that things could have been different."[69]

Jupiter is in detriment in Gemini, and Jupiter's dispositor, Mercury, is another planet in munakara. Mercury in Aquarius can get very fixed in its views and opinions, but it can also be relentless in pushing a person towards their ideal self, especially when it is conjunct the Sun in the same sign. Oprah Winfrey does not have a mutable Cross of Matter, and the first two planets in Jupiter's sequence are not the joint rulers of the four critical points in her chart. With Libra on her Mid-heaven, Venus is its ruler, but Venus is in munakara too, and like Cindy Sherman, the two nocturnal planets in contention share honours for the highest place in the chart where honour and glory can be found. Venus may be the MC ruler, but Mercury rules the Whole Sign 10th house, and matters of communication, marketing, and social media messages, focus around women and where they feel valued (or ignored) by society.

In both women's charts, Saturn (only a degree apart) is the outcome planet for munakara Jupiter, and Saturn's position in Winfrey's natal chart will differ according to whether the chart is cast in the Placidus house system, or in the Whole Sign system. In Winfrey's Placidus chart, Saturn is in her 10th house, and the signs it rules are Capricorn, intercepted in the 1st house, and Aquarius, on the 2nd-house cusp. In her Whole Sign chart, Saturn has fallen to the 12th house because it is in the sign which precedes her Sagittarian Ascendant. This is a hazardous position for Saturn, especially as it joins Mars in the same house, suggesting father figures are missing, males have the potential to bring danger, authorities could be problematic, and isolation or depression may be possibilities with Saturn (and Mars) in this difficult house. In Winfrey's Whole Sign chart, Saturn rules the 2nd house, with Capricorn on the cusp, and the 3rd house, with Aquarius on the cusp.

Munakara Planet and Sect Condition – how comfortable is Jupiter?

Oprah Winfrey's munakara Jupiter has a better position, sect-wise, than Cindy Sherman's Jupiter which sits in the opposite hemisphere to her Sun. The two charts are still nocturnal with 4:30am births (*Figs. 17.2; 17.3*), but Winfrey's Jupiter is travelling with the Sun (in *halb*), and the Sun provides Jupiter with a purpose and a direction, so that *both* diurnal planets will benefit from Jupiter's improved sect condition. In his 2015 webinar on Sect, Robert Hand stated that Jupiter in a diurnal placement – that is, travelling with the Sun in the same hemisphere – gave Jupiter more 'masculine' qualities, presumably referring to Jupiter with sect dignity as a more direct, dynamic and goal-orientated Jupiter. The accidentally dignified Jupiter is capable of maintaining a higher level of activity, and sect dignity improves Jupiter's ability to see and work with the larger picture, meaning it can set a long-term goal, and work realistically towards achieving it. Hand also says that in-sect Jupiter uses good luck to the best advantage to achieve goals, and set boundaries that aid and maintain its success.[70]

Oprah Winfrey — ♃'s Sect Dignity			
Planet	Sect 1 Status	Sect 2 Hemisphere	Sect 3 Sign
♊ ♃	Night	With the Sun	Air
D	N	D	D

Table 17.12: Oprah Winfrey: Munakara Jupiter Sect Dignity

In his book *Night & Day: Planetary Sect in Astrology* published in 1995, Hand says: "Jupiter in a diurnal chart or diurnally placed within a chart (which Winfrey's Jupiter is) with all other things being equal produces the best manifestations of Jupiter, success, power, wealth, etc. But if a malefic (Saturn or Mars) aspects a diurnal Jupiter, its benefits are reduced somewhat but not eliminated."[71] Neither Saturn nor Mars is in aspect to Winfrey's diurnally-placed Jupiter, so we might expect sound results from this sect-advantaged Jupiter. However, the fact that Jupiter is in detriment, and Saturn is munakara Jupiter's outcome planet, is a reminder that there are other ways to spoil Jupiter's good fortune besides hard aspects, and contention requires serious consideration when deciding if a planet's benefits are reduced or eliminated through another avenue.

Munakara Jupiter: Oprah Winfrey

"Playing small doesn't serve me. The truth is, I want millions of people. I'm not one of those people who says, "Oh, if I change just one person's life..." Nope, not satisfied with just a few. I want millions of people!"[72]

Munakara Jupiter in Gemini in 6th House (Placidus)

In her 2019 interview with *People* magazine, Winfrey cites her decision in 1989, to go against the popular trend of producing inflammatory TV talk shows to guarantee high ratings, but also, generated negativity, misery, and vitriolic reactions from both guests and the live audience. Jupiter ruling the Ascendant tends to produce teachers and preachers, and even when contention is part of Jupiter's baggage, it is ultimately the individual's choice to imbue their personality with positivity, and to encourage others to adopt a kinder, and more forgiving attitude.

"Become the change you want to see – those are words I live by. Instead of belittling, uplift. Instead of demolishing, rebuild. Instead of misleading, light the way so that all of us can stand on higher ground."[73]

For all Oprah's good intentions, there have been times in her career where controversy has dogged her footsteps, and munakara Jupiter has placed her squarely in contentious positions with authorities, or groups, who have attacked her because of her ability to sway public opinion. When Oprah interviewed a cattle rancher at the height of the mad-cow scare in 1996, she declared his revelations about the beef industry would stop her eating another hamburger. Beef prices in the US plummeted after the show was aired, and a group of Texan cattle ranchers filed a $10.3 million lawsuit against Oprah, claiming she had defamed the entire industry. The case was dismissed two years later, but it should have been a valuable lesson to Oprah, that even off-hand, or thoughtless comments (munakara Jupiter in detriment) could be damaging to her reputation, and that the public's adoration can turn very quickly, when large amounts of revenue are at stake.

In November 2002, munakara Jupiter sailed Oprah perilously close to the wind, and public opinion could have turned against Oprah, when she risked alienating her post–9/11 audience, by vocalizing her concerns over the building tension of a US military forces' invasion of Iraq. Anti-war advocates sang her praises, but it might have turned ugly if Oprah hadn't stayed on the side of the government by scheduling a two-day special, "The World Speaks Out on Iraq," the day after Secretary of State, Colin Powell's, crucial speech before the UN in February 2003, a month before the invasion took place on March 20, 2003 (Saturn is munakara Jupiter's outcome planet).

First Dispositor: Nocturnal Mercury in Aquarius in 2nd House (Placidus)

Al-Biruni may cite Mercury as Jupiter's enemy as they rule opposing signs, but in Oprah Winfrey's chart, Jupiter is in an air trine aspect to Mercury, and this aspect fortifies the Whole Sign perspective of four mutable angles ruled by the two planets. Winfrey's role as an interviewer has used this trine admirably, and her early career decision as a twenty-year-old, to walk away from a stable news anchor role in Baltimore, in order to retrain as a TV chat show host in Chicago, was a brilliant move that worked to her strengths. That decision was the first of many munakara Jupiter moments (disposited by Mercury), which showed not only confidence and wisdom way beyond her years, but also her love of a challenge, especially when pitted against great odds.

Aquarius Mercury is a fixed air sign – belonging to Saturn – and in munakara state too, is the planet needed to provide the sheer willpower, energy and focus to drive Jupiter to pursue a successful 25-year career in daily broadcasting. "I would ask (my producers on the show) that my voice, the words that I choose, come from a place that is centred, and centred in the desire to be a force for good and connect in a way that would be meaningful to people."[74]

The opposition between munakara Mercury and Pluto gives Oprah's voice the power to be heard, and even as a young child she was known as The Preacher, as she made her rounds of local churches to spread the Gospel. Her grandmother Hattie Mae was a strict disciplinarian for the first six years of Oprah's life, but Oprah admits it was Hattie Mae who had encouraged her to speak in public and "gave me a positive sense of myself."[75]

This ability to influence others through her compassion, her firm convictions, and her intelligence translated to her many successful ventures beginning with the rebranding of *A.M. Chicago*, which Oprah had been hosting since 1984, to become the syndicated *Oprah Winfrey Show* two years later. In the same year, 1986, Harpo Productions was founded using the clever reversal of the letters of her first name (Harpo is Oprah spelled backwards).

Oprah's Mercury has a voracious appetite for new ways to manifest good fortune for herself and others, and her idea to raise funds for scholarships, housing, women's shelters and schools became Oprah's Angel Network in 1998, raising $3.5 million in the first twelve months of creation. Other enterprises followed in 2000 with *O, The Oprah Magazine* and the founding of the OWN (Oprah Winfrey Network) channel in 2011, after she retired her daily show.

The outcome planet: Saturn in Scorpio

"Your life's work is to find your life's work – and then to exercise the discipline, tenacity, and hard work it takes to pursue it." O, The Oprah Magazine, September 2001

In Oprah's Placidus chart, Saturn appears in the 10th house, and this would describe someone who has authority over their lives and considerable influence in the public arena. Her 25-year reputation was built on her commitment to the daily grind of producing and maintaining a successful five-day-a-week show. In an interview with Barbara Walters in her final 2010–2011 season Oprah's Saturn (Jupiter's outcome planet) speaks for itself.

> *"You can't call in sick: you can't ever give less than 100 percent. And if you are sick, which I have been a couple of times, that's when you've got to pull up to 110, 120. Because people have come from all over the country and this is their moment. They've saved their money, they've bought their airline tickets, they've got new outfits, they've called (their relatives), and that's why they're there, to see me. So I feel a sense of responsibility, a sense of obligation, a sense of respect, reverence, and honour for those people."*[76]

However, in the same manner as Cindy Sherman's Saturn falls into her cadent 12th house by Whole Sign, so too does Oprah Winfrey's Saturn find itself moved to the house of hidden enemies, and the place where irrational fears hold reason and logic a prisoner. Saturn is said to be in accidental dignity in the 12th house, in its joy, but this position does not necessarily augment well for the chart's owner.

Fourteenth-century astrologer Guido Bonatti said of Saturn in its house of 'joy': "Saturn rejoices in the 12th house because it is the house of sorrow, sadness, labor, lamentation, and weeping; and Saturn rejoices in these things and the like."[77] Saturn's sect condition is also poor in Sherman's and Winfrey's charts – in a nocturnal chart in the opposite hemisphere to the Sun, and placed in a feminine sign. There is no light or warmth transmitted by the Sun to Saturn in this condition, so whilst we might imagine a trouble-free life with few obstructions might have accompanied munakara Jupiter's phenomenal success, there are dark shadows here too. Firstly, munakara planets very rarely – if ever – experience a life of ease and comfort, and secondly, when Saturn or Mars are outcome planets for the munakara sequence, you know there will be obstacles that feel insurmountable at times, but when looking back in hindsight, munakara planets were there at watershed moments in life.

In 1991, Oprah relived her childhood experiences when she testified in front of the US Senate Judiciary Committee, in support of a national database of convicted child abusers. Two years later, President Clinton signed what became unofficially known as "Oprah's Bill" into law, and the data base was established. Exposing and reliving her own demons, in order to protect children of the future through law, is an unselfish act of Jupiter in contention, but one that would have cost her 12th-house Saturn deeply, as she was forced to relive the horrors of her past.

In an act of pure Jupiterian philanthropy, Oprah travelled to South Africain 2002 to give toys, books, school supplies, and clothes to fifty thousand children, and for most of these children it was the first time they had ever received a gift.[78] But munakara Jupiter's generosity did not end there. Oprah saw and reacted to the neglect in girls' schooling, and the disadvantage they suffered through being the 'wrong' gender to receive a decent education – munakara Jupiter in Gemini disposited by Mercury. On that trip Oprah announced her plan to build the Oprah Winfrey Leadership Academy for Girls. She would finance the project with $40 million (Saturn, Jupiter's outcome planet, rules her 2nd house), and not only was she financially invested, but she was heavily involved in every step of the planning, including the decoration of the dorm rooms. Saturn's influence in the program can be seen as Oprah helped to select the students who would live and study at the school. She chose girls for their ability and leadership qualities, as her Jupiter dream was for them to become major influencers in their own country.

Chapter Seventeen • *Munakara Jupiter Delineations*

The school opened in 2007, but planets in contention have 'teeth' which can come back to bite their owner, even those with the most altruist intentions. It is always a good idea to keep an eye on the outcome planet in a munakara sequence, as this can be the planet with the 'bullwhip effect' – you think you have a handle on something (Jupiter) but it is the sharp end of the whip gone out of control (Saturn) that inflicts pain or causes damage.

Less than a year after its very public opening, the Leadership Academy for Girls was back in the news, but this time for all the wrong reasons. Nine of the girls, aged between 13 and 15, accused the dorm matron of physical and sexual abuse, and the trial to prosecute the school's matron began in 2008. Two years later, the matron was acquitted when the magistrate ruled in her favour because there were too many contradictions in the alleged victims' statements, accurate dates of incidents were not provided, and witnesses were deemed to be unreliable.

Oprah's comment on the verdict "We began this child molestation trial in July 2008. More than two years later, I am profoundly disappointed at the outcome of the trial. I will forever be proud of the nine girls who testified with the courage and conviction to be heard."[79]

The school has survived, and Oprah's reputation has survived with it, in a situation where she carries no blame. One Johannesburg newspaper wrote, "it does not reflect badly on the famous talk-show host – it reflects badly on this nation"[80] – nonetheless, it hurt Oprah deeply, and propelled her back into her childhood past, to once again confront what if felt like to be a victim of abuse.

Sagittarius Moon in Munakara: Oprah Winfrey

- **Key Questions:**
- What does Oprah Winfrey's Moon contend with?
- What is its driving force?
- What is its trigger? What is its outcome?

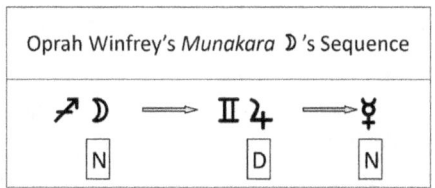

Table 17.13: Oprah Winfrey: Munakara Moon's Sequence

In the ten days that separate Cindy Sherman's birth on 19 January 1954, from Oprah Winfrey's birth on 29 January 1954, the Moon has moved away from its square to Saturn in Sherman's chart (*Fig. 17.2*), has passed across Saturn, and moved to a safe space where there is no aspectual relationship between the two planets that share enemy status (their rulership signs oppose one another). Her munakara Moon is approaching a sextile aspect to (munakara) Venus and the Sun, and the Moon in contention, is in an approaching opposition to its dispositor, (munakara) Jupiter. All three planets in Winfrey's Moon sequence are munakara planets, and this phenomenon has been discussed in detail in Part One, Chapter Ten, on Munakara Multiples.

Oprah's Moon is three degrees from her 12th-house cusp in the Placidus chart, and Winfrey's childhood has borne witness to periods of emotional stress and physical abuse at the hands of male family members. The Moon and Jupiter become angular planets when Winfrey's chart is converted to a Whole Sign house system, and although the degrees between them are wide, the signs of Sagittarius on the Ascendant, and Gemini on the Descendant, tie the Moon and its dispositor in a wide opposition. Over the years, Oprah's physical appearance has been the subject of much discussion, and any changes in weight particularly, have drawn harsh scrutiny from a critical public,

The type of unkind remarks and judgements on the topic of Oprah's weight, are a perfect example of nocturnal Mercury as the outcome planet for munakara Moon. Both Mercury and Jupiter are featured in Oprah's Moon sequence, and Jupiter (her Ascendant lord) being both in detriment, and in contention, cannot help but find itself constantly in the combat zone, and the focus of unflattering photos, and cruel headlines, in global newspapers and on social media. Oprah has now reached the age of 70, but she still has 23 million followers on Instagram, and this type of popularity and social relevance is one demonstration of the Whole Sign angularity of two of her munakara planets – Sagittarius Moon in the 1st house, and its dispositor, Jupiter, opposing it in the 7th house in Gemini. It would seem that the public still care what Oprah thinks, even though she is 'retired', and there will be reactions and re-tweets anytime she comments on her social media pages. Oprah's appearances during the 2024 US election campaign to elect Democrat nominee, Kamala Harris, demonstrated her continuing power, and even though the campaign was unsuccessful, Oprah Winfrey's addresses were a highlight of the campaign.

Oprah's munakara Moon is also the story of her mother, Vernita Lee, a struggling single mother who gave birth to four children, but was unable to fulfil the role of a stable mothering figure in their lives. It has been well

Chapter Seventeen • *Munakara Jupiter Delineations*

documented that Vernita and Oprah were estranged for a number of years, and it was only late in her mother's life that both women came to a peaceful resolution to a difficult mother/ daughter relationship. Munakara Moon can indicate a sensitive wound which has been inflicted by the nurturing figure as they struggle with her own demons. Generations of abandonment or rejection can be the experience of one person's munakara Moon, and healing or forgiveness is part of the story of a conflicted Moon, when there is a long history of abuse, neglect, or violence within a family.

Co-dependency can be another sign of a contentious Moon's desire to relieve emotional distress, and the female figure on whom one relies, may be a woman who is not a relative, but who has carried similar life experiences to them.

Oprah's friendship with broadcast journalist, Gayle King, has been a close one since they met in 1976 at a Baltimore, Maryland television station where they were both presenters. King is the editor-at-large for *O, The Oprah Magazine*, and has long been a confidante for the media tycoon. King was born eleven months after Winfrey on 28 December 1954,[81] and interestingly, she too has a munakara Moon – Aquarius Moon disposited by Saturn in Scorpio – so, although her upbringing was more stable than Winfrey's, there are still echoes of emotional instability and possible trust issues.

Winfrey has talked about her close friendship with King, saying, "Something about this relationship feels otherworldly to me, like it was designed by a power and a hand greater than my own. Whatever this friendship is, it's been a very fun ride."[82]

It is interesting to note that Gayle King has five of her seven planets in munakara.[83] One, her Moon in Aquarius is munakara (outcome planet, Mars). Two, her nocturnal Mercury in Capricorn is munakara (outcome planet, Mars). Three, her Mars in Pisces is munakara (outcome planet, the Moon). Four, her Jupiter in Cancer is munakara (outcome planet, Saturn). Five, her Saturn in Scorpio is munakara (outcome planet, Jupiter).

All five of Gayle King's munakara sequences contain other planets which are also in the state of munakara. Her Capricorn Sun, and Venus in Scorpio, are her two planets which are not in contention, nor do they play a part as first dispositor or outcome planet, in any of King's five munakara sequences.[84]

Media speculation has been rife over the women's close relationship as they often seem inseparable, but rather than it being a romantic connection, perhaps their bonding has occurred because they are 'munakara buddies' who understand and support the complexity of each other's lives.

In an interview with Barbara Walters in 2010 Winfrey said of King: "She is the mother I never had; she is the sister everybody would want; she is the friend everyone deserves; I don't know a better person."[85]

Munakara Planet and Sect Condition – how comfortable is the Moon?

Winfrey's Moon has good sect condition as she was born during the night-time hours, and the Moon is travelling in the hemisphere above the Sun. Moon's placement in a fire sign stops full sect dignity, but that is a minor setback, compared to the first and second rule of sect. Good sect dignity tends to give the Moon a stronger impulse to bounce back after adversity, and given that Winfrey has know plenty of heartbreak and hardship in her early years, the Moon's resilience has been a huge benefit to guide her throughout her life. Sect dignity strengthens the Moon, can bring tranquillity in times of stress, and has the ability to bring success through the person embodying the aspirations of others and serving their needs. In Winfrey's 25 years of her show, she projected a caring, empathetic, thoughtful, non-judgemental, and compassionate persona, so that many of her audience felt she spoke directly to them, and for one hour a day they felt safe, loved and understood by someone hundreds of miles away, but reaching out to them personally, through their television set.

Oprah Winfrey — ☽'s Sect Dignity			
Planet	Sect 1 Status	Sect 2 Hemisphere	Sect 3 Sign
♐ ☽	Night	Without the Sun	Fire
	N	N	N	D

Table 17.14: Oprah Winfrey: Munakara Moon Sect Dignity

In the years that her show ran on air, Oprah Winfrey was known for her incredible generosity (munakara Moon rules the 8th house) towards her in-house audience, giving away lavish gifts, such as diamond earrings, luxury handbags, and even brand new Volkswagen Beetles in 2010 to audience members for Christmas. One lucky recipient posted later that when the November 2010 show had ended, and the cameras were turned off, "She kicked off her gold high heel shoes, sat down on the edge of the stage and talked to all of us. And she said, 'I know you don't feel like you deserve any of this stuff, and you don't. None of you deserve it. But you are worthy of it, and I want you to remember that."[86]

Oprah has earned a lot of money – in 2024, Forbes valued her worth at US$3 billion – but her munakara Moon in sect dignity, has also given back, and I'm not sure every billionaire could make the same boast. Her foundation, the Oprah Winfrey Charitable Foundation, has donated $400 million in grants, and in addition, she donates at least 10% of her annual income to charity. She has also donated millions of dollars to support education for underprivileged children, for housing and services for homeless and low-income women, and donations to the Time's Up campaign, which aims to create a society free of gender-based discrimination.[87]

Aquarius Mercury and Venus Duet in Munakara: Oprah Winfrey

"Bravery shows up in everyday life when people have the courage to live their truth, their vision, and their dreams." – O, The Oprah Magazine, January 2015

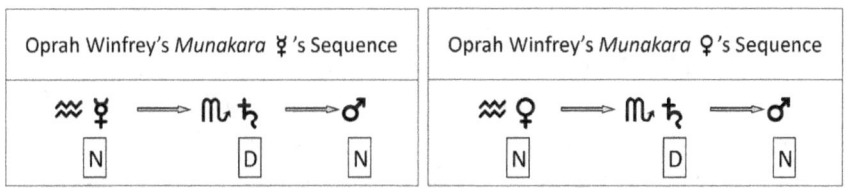

Table 17.15: Oprah Winfrey: Munakara Mercury and Venus Sequence

Eleven degrees separate munakara Venus and Mercury in Oprah Winfrey's chart, and the repetition of their munakara sequences would suggest that the two planets are in conjunction. They are located in her 2nd house of finances in her Placidus chart, but move to her 3rd house in the Whole Sign system. The combination of house systems suggests that Winfrey makes her money from communication and media outlets. Either one planet or the other planet in contention is the ruler of her house of career and public status: Venus rules her Libran Mid-heaven, and Mercury rules her Whole Sign 10th house, with Virgo on its cusp.

Oprah's Book Club was a brilliant idea based on the idea of a group of people, usually women, gathering together in someone's home to discuss a pre-arranged book of their choice. The Book Club was a great marketing ploy on Oprah's behalf, and authors were desperate to gain her attention as most of the books Oprah picked sold more than a million copies. This segment ran from 1996 to 2011 when Oprah's show wrapped up, Oprah would recommend a book on her show, wait one month for her viewers to read it, and then either dedicate an entire Book Club show to run a discussion on the book, or even better, invite the book's author to appear on her show for an interview.

> *"I'm now understanding that your energy, your essence, your juice cannot be instilled unless you're actually there. You have to be in it first, then you have to empower everybody else to at least know what the vision is in such a way that they can execute it."*[88] – Oprah Winfrey

But there were times when her munakara duet's involvement with the two malefic planets, Saturn and Mars, located in the 10th (Saturn) or 11th house of groups (Mars), brought controversy and trouble rather than a good outcome. Both Saturn and Mars in Scorpio slip to the Whole Sign 12th house, and sometimes, Oprah's endorsement of a particular book ended in strife or disapproval of Oprah's choices in the author or the book's subject matter (munakara Venus /Mercury in Aquarius).

In 2005, author James Frey was ejected from the Book Club, after it was disclosed that his autobiography, *A Million Little Pieces*, contained a large number of falsehoods, and embarrassed by her endorsement, Oprah insisted he revisit her show to explain his false claims to her disgruntled audience.

In another example of munakara Venus's misplaced belief in human goodness, combined with munakara Mercury's penchant for marketing gone wrong, Oprah created a phenomenal success in advertising when she promoted the 2006 book, *The Secret*, by Rhonda Byrne. *The Secret* was really an old idea revamped, and had originated in 1855 with the term "Law of Attraction" in *The Great Harmonia* written by American spiritualist, Andrew Jackson Davis. Oprah's audience went wild for *The Secret*, but bad publicity followed when one viewer declared her intent to cease chemotherapy treatment, and instead practice the principles promoted in the book. Her death from cancer in December 2010 drew worldwide attention to Oprah's recommendations of the book, and dampened some of the fervour created by the idea of positive thinking. Oprah stood her ground, insisting that the Law of Attraction had merit and could have a positive effect. However, Scorpio Saturn and Mars' movement to the worst of places in the 12th house (by Whole Sign), meant Oprah's munakara Venus and Mercury were at the mercy of hostile opposition from hidden enemies.

Chapter Seventeen • *Munakara Jupiter Delineations*

Munakara Mercury in 3rd house rules her seventh and tenth signs by Whole Sign, and Oprah suffered harm to her reputation, with medical experts quick to criticise the negative effects of her substantial influence over her more gullible viewers. Sometimes in her enthusiasm and optimistic viewpoint, Oprah was inclined to forget that a cosy chat in comfortable chairs quickly broadcasts to a world-wide audience where avid listeners take her recommendations as sacrosanct.

Oprah's promotion of health tips and positive living practices were often adopted by many of her daily 7 million viewers, but when in 2009, actress Suzanne Somers recommended hormone treatments with questionable success, the medical profession reacted strongly, and once more, Oprah was in trouble and held accountable for her guest's comments. Oprah's enthusiasm for novel cosmetic surgery did not go unnoticed by the media, and they were quick to report any unwelcome complications and trace responsibility back to Oprah's comments on said surgery.

A 2012 article written by journalist Jordan Weissmann titled "Stranger Than Fiction: Oprah Was Bad for Book Sales," claims that sales of fiction books fell because Oprah encouraged her readers to tackle longer, more sophisticated novels, than they would normally read.

"Oprah made her viewers a little more high brow, and publishers a little bit poorer."[89]

Research of book sales from 2001 to 2010 showed that sales from Oprah's recommended book shot up an average of 420% within a week of her show and were still up 160% six months later. However, there was an accompanying 5.1% decline in adult fiction sales after Oprah's recommendation, and that these books were well below the number count and quality content of Oprah's choices. Oprah's intention was to educate her audience but the publishing world preferred their readers to consume short, easy to read books with simple themes, so that they can quickly move on to the next 'best seller'.

Munakara Planets and Sect Condition – how comfortable is Mercury Venus Duet?

Contention brings a new perspective to a conjunction, especially when both planets are from the same sect, and they follow the same sequence to munakara. Together, they fight to overcome an obstacle that seems insurmountable, or raise their voices in unison to make an opinion known, to battle an authority, or change something that others insist is unchangeable.

Oprah's Mercury and Venus are comfortable and nourished within the bounds of her nocturnal chart, and gaining the prize of sect compatibility between the nature of the planet and the chart itself, is not dimmed by the noncompliance with the second (hemisphere) and third (sign) rule of sect. An air sign still helps Mercury even when it is disposited by Saturn, as intelligence, logic and common sense are vital attributes when one knows their aims in life. Saturn as dispositor, works tirelessly towards achieving these aims, and is a good resource for

Oprah Winfrey — ☿'s Sect Dignity			
Planet	Sect 1 Status	Sect 2 Hemisphere	Sect 3 Sign
♒ ☿	Night	With the Sun	Air
	N	D	D
N			

Oprah Winfrey — ♀'s Sect Dignity			
Planet	Sect 1 Status	Sect 2 Hemisphere	Sect 3 Sign
♒ ♀	Night	With the Sun	Air
	N	D	D
N			

Table 17.16: Oprah Winfrey: Munakara Mercury and Venus Sect Dignity

nocturnal Mercury in a state of munakara. The nocturnal chart complements Mercury when it follows the Sun, as this gives nocturnal Mercury the ability to rest and recuperate the mind, and to work on new ideas and concepts without becoming too frazzled or distracted by a diurnal chart.

Venus is in partile (in the same degree) conjunction to Oprah's Aquarian Sun, but as she has a nocturnal chart, this gives Venus the benefit of an environment that best suits its own temperament. A few hours after Oprah's birth, Venus and the Sun will have risen together, and perhaps the fact that Oprah Winfrey has remained one of the wealthiest and most influential women in the world throughout her adult life, owes something to her munakara Venus in sect dignity.

Robert Hand calls in-sect Venus a 'more traditional version of women, soft, feminine, charm and beauty'.[90] I am not convinced that Oprah's Venus conforms with this description, but what I do believe is that Oprah's Venus with sect dignity gives her excellent rapport with other women, and that when she is talking about harrowing experiences or disadvantages that are unique to women, then they relate to her language (in-sect Mercury), her compassion, and the veracity of her feelings (in-sect Venus).

Chapter Seventeen • *Munakara Jupiter Delineations*

Earlier relationships were hard work for Oprah, as Venus and Mercury in contention meant she often chose abusive men who would belittle her, or who refused to give her the approval she so desperately sought from them. The dual pairing of munakara Venus with Mercury, the ruler of Oprah's 7th house, directed her towards relationships which were destructive to her self-esteem, and her ability to see herself as a woman capable and worthy of being loved. Overcoming these negative opinions were the seeds of Oprah's passion to preach self-empowerment to her female audience, as she sums up in her interview with Michelle Obama on June 14, 2016: "Over the years I've interviewed thousands of people – most of them women – and I would say that the root or every dysfunction I've ever encountered, every problem, has been from some sense of a lacking of self-value or self-worth."[91]

CHAPTER EIGHTEEN
Munakara Saturn Delineations

Canadian-American animal rights activist, Paul Watson, was born three months before Scottish politician, Gordon Brown. Watson's birth took place on 2 December 1950 (*Fig. 18.2*), and Brown was born in the New Year on 20 February, 1951 (*Fig. 18.3*).

The three months that separate their births show Saturn in a very similar degree in the first and second degrees of Libra, and the two men share an identical sequence of planets for munakara Saturn. However, Watson's Saturn in its exalted sign is direct, and Saturn in Brown's chart is retrograde. Jupiter in rulership in Pisces, and it is Saturn's outcome planet. Jupiter plays a major role in both charts, as it is the dispositor for Venus (in both signs, Sagittarius and Pisces), plus it is the ruler of several important planets (Suns in Sagittarius and Pisces, Sagittarius Mercury in Watson's, and Pisces Mars in Brown's chart). Watson's munakara Saturn is in quincunx (150 degree non-aspect) to Jupiter, whilst there is no contact between the two diurnal planets in Brown's chart.

Prince Harry, Duke of Sussex, was born three months before NBA basketball player, LeBron James, and they too share the same pattern of planets in their munakara Saturn's sequence. Prince Harry was born on 15 September 1984 (*Part One, Fig. 9.2*), and LeBron James was born on 30 December 1984 (*Fig. 18.4*).

During the interval between their births, Saturn moved a further 12 degrees through the sign of Scorpio, so both men's Saturn is disposited by the nocturnal planet, Mars. First dispositor, Mars, travelled from Sagittarius

Chapter Eighteen • *Munakara Saturn Delineations*

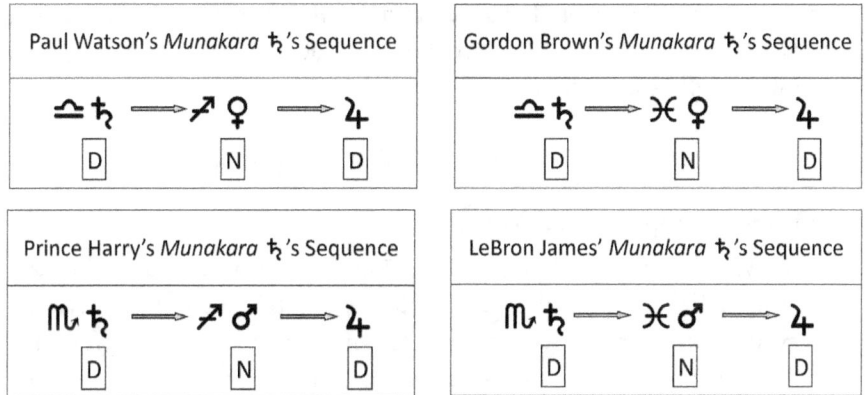

Fig. 18.1: Munakara Sequences for Saturn: Watson, Brown, Harry, and James

to Pisces, and both of these signs belong to Jupiter, another diurnal planet. For this reason, Jupiter is the outcome planet for Harry's Saturn sequence, and Jupiter is also the outcome planet for James's Saturn sequence. Jupiter is still in Capricorn, its sign of fall, by the time James was born three months after Prince Harry. The two charts have a planet which is conjunct their Mid-heavens, and they are Saturn (munakara planet) in Harry's chart, and Mars (first dispositor) in James' chart. James has a Capricorn Sun within two degrees of Harry's Capricorn Ascendant.

The comparisons between these two sets of birth data in close proximity may seem like a startling coincidence, and certainly, finding the first dispositor – Venus for the older set of charts, and Mars for the younger set – to have moved to another sign belonging to the same planet (Jupiter) is an odd happenstance. However, it should be remembered that the repetition in Saturn sequences is a reminder that, unlike the fast planets that move through their signs in short periods of time, for Saturn, it is *the first dispositor* that will determine Saturn's result as a planet in contention. Even Jupiter, with its twelve year cycle, changes dispositor every year, so over a twelve year period, Jupiter has the potential to be munakara for at least five years, and possibly seven, if Mercury is a nocturnal planet at the time Jupiter is in Gemini or Virgo.

But Saturn moves too slowly to constantly change its dispositor, spending over two years in each sign. Saturn becomes munakara because the nocturnal planets move quickly through the signs: the Moon in one month, Venus and nocturnal Mercury in one year, and Mars takes two and a half years to travel through the zodiac. The first consideration for Saturn to be munakara, is whether Saturn is even in a sign (for two and a half years) that belongs to a nocturnal planet, and secondly, to ascertain if *that* planet is in a sign belonging to a diurnal dispositor (NOT Saturn). If both of these conditions are met, then Saturn will be munakara.

Munakara Saturn: Paul Watson

A Brief Biography of Paul Watson[1]

Paul Watson (born 2 December 1950) is a Canadian-American environmental activist and founder of the Sea Shepherd Conservation Society. Watson was an early member of Greenpeace International (founded in 1971). During his years with the organization, he often employed daring and innovative tactics to defend wildlife from hunters, such as positioning his inflatable Zodiac boat between a pod of sperm whales and the harpoon of a large Soviet whaling vessel, or forcing sealing ships to a halt by standing on the ice in their path. In one campaign, he handcuffed himself to a pile of seal pelts being hoisted up onto a sealing vessel. Watson left Greenpeace because of conflicts over his direct and sometimes antagonistic, protection methods, and in 1977, he established the Sea Shepherd Conservation Society, an organization with an agenda that was more pro-active and confrontational than Greenpeace.

Sea Shepherd's battle with a Japanese whaling fleet in 2006–07 was recorded in a documentary film *At the Edge of the World* (2008). In 2010 one of the society's boats, the Ady Gil, sunk after colliding with a Japanese whaling boat. Patrolling the seas under a modified Jolly Roger pirate flag, Watson and his crew of volunteers endured aggressive attempts by whalers to thwart their interference with whaling operations, which included whalers assaulting them with water cannons, flash grenades, and LRADS (long-range acoustic devices).

Watson was arrested on several occasions, and in 2012 he was detained by German officials as Costa Rica sought to extradite him over a 2002 incident involving a Costa Rican boat that Watson claimed was shark finning (removing a shark's fins and discarding the rest of the shark at sea). In 2012 Watson stepped down as head of Sea Shepherd Conservation Society following a US court injunction that barred him and the organization from being near certain Japanese whaling vessels. In July 2024, Paul Watson was arrested on an international warrant in Greenland whilst refuelling his ship, MV John DeJoria, in nearby Nuuk, the capital of the autonomous Danish territory. He has spent the past four months in Anstalten, a high-

Chapter Eighteen • *Munakara Saturn Delineations*

security jail in south-east Greenland.[2] According to the Japan Coast Guard, Watson is facing charges including accomplice to assault and ship trespass. The charges stem from the anti-whaling group's alleged boarding of the Japanese whaling ship Shonan Maru 2 in February 2010. If extradited and convicted, Watson could face up to 15 years in prison in Japan.[3]

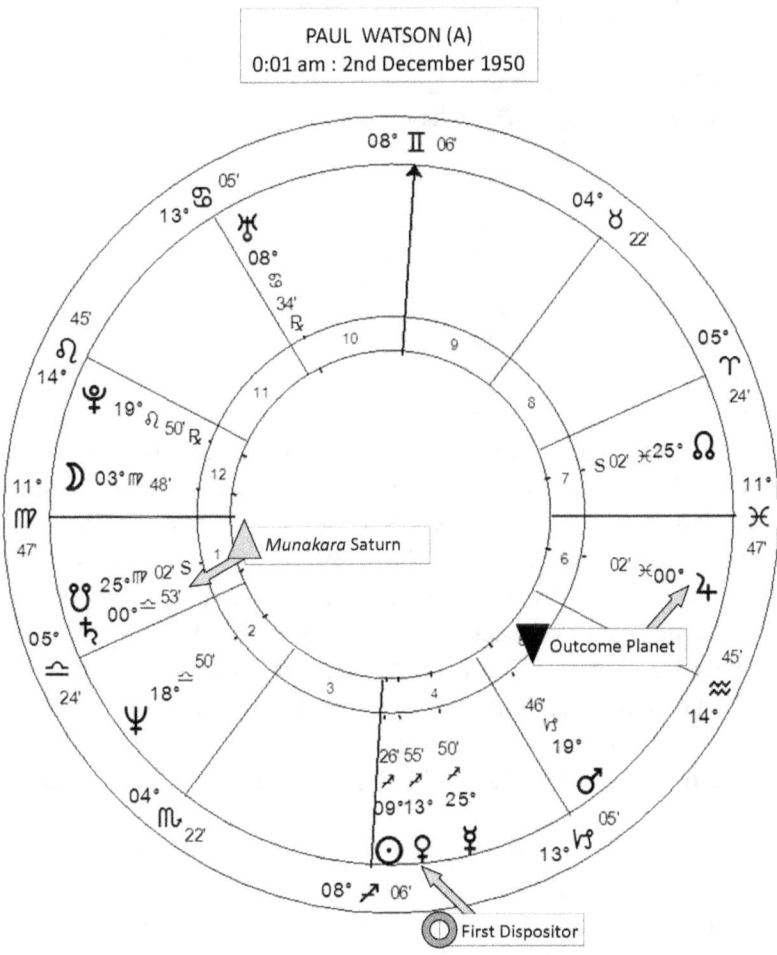

Fig. 18.2: Paul Watson Natal Chart: Munakara Saturn's Sequence

"I have been honoured to serve the whales, dolphins, seals – and all the other creatures on this Earth. Their beauty, intelligence, strength, and spirit have inspired me. These beings have spoken to me, touched me, and I have been rewarded by friendship with many members of different species.

Munakara in Practice

"If the whales survive and flourish, if the seals continue to live and give birth, and if I can contribute to ensuring their future prosperity, I will be forever happy."[4] – Paul Watson, Sea Shepherd Conservation Society

Libra Saturn in Munakara: Paul Watson

- **Key Questions:**
- What does Paul Watson's Saturn contend with?
- What is its driving force?
- What is its trigger? What is its outcome?

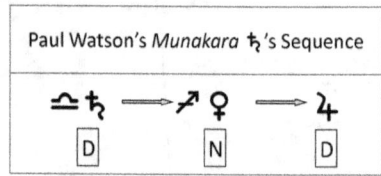

Table 18.1: Paul Watson: Munakara Saturn's Sequence

Paul Watson's munakara Saturn in 1st house (Placidus) carries a heavy burden of responsibility simply because he believes those who are in exalted positions of authority (Saturn in Libra), are the same people – companies, governments, and institutions – who are not doing their job properly.

Saturn is the lord of the sea and the patron god of sailors, and Watson feels the need to protect the wildlife that inhabits the ocean from their deadliest enemy, humankind. Munakara Saturn moves into Watson's 2nd house by Whole Sign and as a young man Watson's initial concern was earning a living by being at sea, joining the Canadian Coast Guard first in 1968, and then again, in early 70s, and later becoming a merchant seaman with the Norwegian Consulate in Vancouver (1969), and then shipping out of San Francisco with a Swedish bulk carrier (1972).

Saturn rules Watson's 6th house, the house of work, daily grind, and manual labour, but it also rules the 5th house of passion, good luck, and the things one loves, and when Saturn is involved, taking the time to appreciate the things that matter in life. The 5th house is a house of good fortune, simply because it contains the things that make life worth living, especially when miles from shore with only the ocean as the horizon, sea creatures bounding around the ship, and the birds wheeling overhead. These are the images Watson's Venus in Sagittarius carries with him wherever he goes, it is his love for the natural world which is the driving force behind his munakara Saturn in exaltation (Venus is Saturn's dispositor).

Chapter Eighteen • *Munakara Saturn Delineations*

Munakara Saturn's outcome planet is Jupiter, which has only just ingressed into its water sign of Pisces by the time Paul Watson was born on 2 December, 1950. Jupiter is in a partile (same degree) quincunx with Saturn, and this 'non-aspect' often describes a relationship that 'just can't be', so there is an agitation between the two planets unlike any of the Ptolemaic aspects which rely on sight, connection, and similarity, to link the two signs that supports their interaction.

The quincunx between the planet in contention (Saturn), and its outcome planet (Jupiter), indicates that in Watson's latest drama, his 2024 arrest in Greenland, even Watson has no idea where he is going with this, or even the process by which he got here. He was not at the scene of the alleged crime in 2010 when a Japanese whaling ship rammed and destroyed a hi-tech Sea Shepherd speedboat.[5] He denies playing any commanding role in it, yet Saturn in exaltation drives his passion to protect and defend, and denial will do very little to convince the Japanese authorities that he is innocent of this crime. Jupiter in rulership has meant that up until 2024, he has always managed to escape imprisonment or legal repercussions for his actions. Perhaps this time his luck has run out, and his enemies (Jupiter in Whole Sign 7th house) will finally have their day in court.

Japan has a 99% conviction rate in this type of case, and human rights groups often accuse the judiciary of being a little more than a rubber stamp for prosecutors.[6] The director of the Captain Paul Wilson Foundation, Haans Siver, said "It's definitely been a really harrowing last few months. They downsized his visitation rights and his phone rights, so it really has been hard on his mental health, for sure."[7] Ms Siver said Mr Watson believed the red notice had been lifted but accused Japan of reimposing it secretly. She also criticised the Greenland judicial process for prolonging the extradition process. *"I think this delay, delay, delay ... it's almost a Julian Assange tactic, isn't it?"*[8]

Munakara Planet and Sect Condition – how comfortable is Saturn?

Paul Watson's chart is nocturnal as his Sagittarian Sun is below the horizon. However, Saturn's sect dignity is assured because it travels beneath the horizon with the Sun (in *halb*), despite the chart being nocturnal. Saturn gains further sect dignity in a masculine sign, and is exalted in Libra. Robert Hand's comments in his 2015 webinar on Sect, that Saturn's good sect dignity "raises Saturn's energy levels, increases its masculinity, and gives Saturn the ability to define and set goals that are worthy, capable and reachable."[9] Watson's Saturn is *halb* – "*a diurnal planet above the ground by day and **beneath it at night**"*[10] and this is enough to give it the benefits of an in-sect Saturn. Hand's original text on sect, written in 1995, notes that Saturn "*... diurnally placed in the chart will, with all other things being equal, produce the best qualities of Saturn, discipline, order, and respect. It is even capable of indicating great success and social standing.*"[11]

Paul Watson — ♄'s Sect Dignity			
Planet	Sect 1 Status	Sect 2 Hemisphere	Sect 3 Sign
♎ ♄	Night	With the Sun	Air
D	N	D	D

Table 18.2: Paul Watson: Munakara Saturn's Sect Dignity

Venus, Saturn's dispositor, is well suited to a nocturnal chart as it matches its nature, and Venus is unfazed by its close proximity to the Sun at night, or its placement in a masculine sign. Jupiter is also *halb* in Watson's chart, *i.e.*, beneath the ground at night, but gains no further sect dignity as it has just entered its feminine sign of rulership.

Munakara Saturn: Paul Watson

"If we wipe out the fish, the oceans are going to die. If the oceans die, we die. We can't live on this planet with a dead ocean."[12] – Paul Watson

Munakara Saturn in Libra in 1st House (Placidus)

Paul Watson is a pioneering, polarizing figure in the conservation movement, and is primarily known for his high-profile campaigns to protect marine life. Saturn rules the 5th and 6th houses, and part of Watson's mystique is his passion – something that leads him into potential harm and physical injury – and has fascinated and entertained those who cannot leave their own commitments, but who support his cause through purchasing his videos, films, books, websites and podcasts.

Paul is a rogue and a non-for-profit pirate on the open seas, and many countries have tried unsuccessfully to prosecute him. However, until 2024, the only time Watson has been incarcerated is ten days in 1980 for assaulting a fisheries official at a Canadian seal protest. In 2012 Watson was forced to retire as head of Sea Shepherd after charges in Costa Rica, Japan, and

Chapter Eighteen • *Munakara Saturn Delineations*

Germany made it impossible for him to sail with the fleet without causing an international incident. All charges were dropped in 2019, and Watson continued his activities with Sea Shepherd until his resignation on 27th July 2022, when he created his own foundation under his name, Captain Paul Watson Foundation, stating in true munakara Saturn-style:

> *I was removed from the Board of Directors, my advice ignored, my close associates terminated and directors that supported me were removed. I was reduced to being a paid figurehead, denied the freedom to organize campaigns and the freedom to express the strong opinions that I have held for decades, opinions and campaigns that have shaped what Sea Shepherd has become and continues to be outside the borders of the United States.*[13]

Watson's munakara Saturn moves from his 1st house in Placidus, to his Whole Sign 2nd house, and the final insult (from Sea Shepherd, which he founded in 1977), was an offered bribe to be a puppet for an organisation he now calls 'an Uber for bureaucrats': "They wanted to pay me a lot of money – about $300,000 a year – to shut up and be like an impotent figurehead for the organisation."[14]

Munakara Saturn rules Watson's 6th house and his escapades have not been without incident, or potential harm to his health. In the year before leaving the Greenpeace banner, Watson was brought before the Greenpeace Board to explain his actions during an in-situ Greenpeace protest at the annual slaughter of seal cubs. Whilst being threatened by the sealers Watson grabbed a hunter's club and threw it into the sea, resulting in charges, later dropped, of theft and vandalism. This is the same campaign where Watson had handcuffed himself to the cable from the winch which holds the pelts. Watson lost consciousness when sealers repeatedly raised his body on the winch, dragged it across the ship's hull and dropped it at maximum speed back to the ground. He was eventually cut free and pulled on to the sealer's ship, where the crew covered his face in viscous seal blubber, and dragged him across the deck through seal fat and blood, kicking and spitting on him as he lay prone on his back.

Paul Watson's Saturn has seen him serve several roles as a gatekeeper for the environment. He was a field correspondent for Defenders of Wildlife from 1976 to 1980 and a field representative for the Fund for Animals from 1978 to 1981. He co-founded Friends of the Wolf and Earthforce Environmental Society. As a rogue environmentalist, and Saturn-rebel extraordinaire,

Watson published *Earthforce! An Earth Warrior's Guide to Strategy* in 1993 as a guide to environmental activists in tactics of sabotage, covert activity and direct action.

First Dispositor: Venus in Sagittarius in 4th House

"Sometimes going to jail is just the price you have to pay for social reform or social change."[15] – Paul Watson

Watson's memories of his father were not good ones, and even though Saturn is exalted in his chart, a contentious Saturn can produce a father who does not understand their chid or one who expects far too much from them. In an article written in December 2024 on his arrest in Greenland, Watson has expressed his concerns at being away from his two young sons, aged three and eight, who live with their mother in France. He is permitted to speak to them from prison on a video call for 10 minutes each week on a Sunday evening. On his son Tiger's birth in 2016[16] Watson elected to resign from long trips away from home, and he says that things were different when he was younger and often away from home on anti-whaling campaigns. He admits that his 44-year-old daughter from the first of his four marriages did not see him much during her childhood. He says now when he speaks to his sons "I don't feel upset, so they don't feel upset. I mean, I know what it's like (being separated from a parent). My mother died when I was 13. My father was extremely abusive. So I really didn't have that kind of, you know, happy childhood in that way. But that made me committed to making sure that my children are taken care of in every sense."[17]

Watson, a joint US-Canadian citizen, was born in Toronto but grew up in St Andrews, New Brunswick. His response to physical abuse from his father was to throw himself into the Kindness Club (Venus in 4th house), an animal welfare organisation founded by Aida Flemming, the wife of New Brunswick's premier Hugh John Flemming. It was a temporary fix (Mercury in detriment in 4th house). "I ran away from home when I was 14, 15, 16, and finally, permanently, I ran off to sea. I joined the Norwegian Merchant Marine," Watson says in the article.[18]

To truly acknowledge the impact of Paul's Saturn in contention, is to understand his passion, and the lengths to which he has gone, to protect the sea animals he adores, respects, and values, probably as much as human life.

Chapter Eighteen • *Munakara Saturn Delineations*

"I take a biocentric point of view. I look at things from the point of view of the Earth and the laws of ecology. As opposed to the anthropocentric point of view, where everything revolves around humanity."[19]

Venus conjuncts Watson's Sun and Mercury in Sagittarius, and he is very clear on the fact that his affinity lies with nature. Mercury in detriment ruling his MC demonstrates an unusual or unpopular view regarding his beliefs and principles. Biocentrism is the view that the rights and needs of humans are not more important than those of other living things. Venus, Saturn's dispositor, is the ruler of Watson's 9th house and the following quote encompasses his spiritual and philosophical beliefs.

"As for myself.....I do not believe in pie in the sky spirituality, I believe in rainbows, rivers, mountains, and moss. I do not believe in environmentalists, I believe in the environment. I am a proud traitor to my species in alliance with my mother Earth in opposition to those who would destroy her, those parasites who believe the Earth is here to serve human interests."[20]

The outcome planet: Jupiter in Pisces

Jupiter is the final diurnal planet in Saturn's munakara sequence, and it is the outcome planet for his exalted Saturn in contention. Jupiter has just entered Pisces, and the two diurnals form a quincunx in the zero degrees of their respective signs. Paul's Saturn may yearn for solitude and separation from the human race, but Jupiter in rulership shows he is adored and venerated by his supporters. However, his enemies are here too, and Paul Watson has challenged some powerful and wealthy people who control governments, and have incredible influence over law enforcement and industry.

In spite of their power and their animosity towards Paul Watson and Sea Shepherd over the years, Watson's dedication to his cause has not waivered, and perhaps Jupiter's opposition to the Moon – his primary luminary in a nocturnal chart – has helped keep him from physical harm throughout the years of his dangerous campaigns.

Watson writes his environmental curriculum vitae in *Earthforce*:

Since 1977 I have headed the Sea Shepherd Conservation Society and continue to do so. In that time, I have led three sea-going expeditions to oppose the Canadian seal slaughter, four sea-going expeditions to protect whales, two high seas expeditions to protect dolphins, five expeditions to oppose drift-netters, and one land-based expedition to protect wolves in British Columbia and the Yukon.

At the time of writing the book (1993) Watson's 20-year legacy with Sea Shepherd was mostly unblemished, and he has a right to be proud of in his achievements, as much as from avoiding criminal convictions, as part of his list of substantial Jupiterian successes. During his double decade as Captain Paul Watson, he was responsible for the sinking of eight illegal whaling ships, the sinking of one sealing ship, and the blockading of a Canadian sealing fleet. Sinking ships aside, Watson oversaw the destruction of a whale processing plant, the paint-bombing of a Soviet trawler, the ramming of two Japanese drift-net vessels, the ramming of a Mexican tuna seiner, and the ramming of a Taiwanese drift netter.

Under his captaincy, the activity of Neptune's Army (as Sea Shepherd volunteers were known) had received enough press coverage to bring sufficient heat and public outrage, to close down a Japanese dolphin hunt, as well as the closing down of seal hunts in Britain and Ireland. Over the thirty five years as head of Sea Shepherd (1977–2012), Watson has been involved in the interference in killing operations against marine mammals in thirteen countries. He is also proud of the fact that he invented the tactic of tree-spiking to protect old-growth forests. Finally, he makes the point that these things were accomplished without causing or sustaining a single injury, to his opposition, or to his crew. Additionally these missions did not result in a single criminal or civil conviction against himself, his society or his crew."[21]

The UN Charter for Nature was adopted on 28th October 1982; the vote was carried by 111 countries in favour of the Charter, one vote against (United States), and 18 abstentions. The Charter proclaimed five principles of conservation by which all human conduct affecting nature is to be guided and judged. Sea Shepherd's activity over its now 45-year lifespan has led to legal action from authorities in countries including the United States, Canada, Norway, Costa Rica and Japan, yet charges brought against Sea Shepherd have not resulted in criminal records or jail sentences for any of its members. Its founder Paul Watson has evaded imprisonment because of the existence of this Charter, specifically 37/7/3: Implementation, Notation 21, (my bold font) which reads: "*States and, to the extent they are able, other public authorities,* **international organizations, individuals, groups** *and corporations shall: …. (3) Implement the applicable international legal provisions for the conservation of nature and the protection of the environment.*"[22]

Sea Shepherd Global, and its infamous leader, has been able to walk a fine line over the years simply because it does target illegal operations, and although its methods often involve seditious or provocative behaviour, it has caused no physical harm to those breaking international conservation laws, regardless of the violence their own members have incurred during the movement's various campaigns.

Capricorn Mars in Munakara: Paul Watson

- **Key Questions:**
- What does Paul Watson's Mars contend with?
- What is its driving force?
- What is its trigger? What is its outcome?

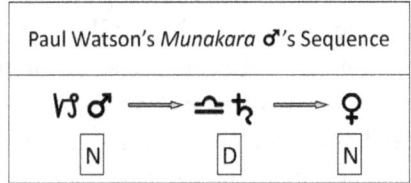

Table 18.3: Paul Watson: Munakara Mars' Sequence

Paul Watson's munakara Mars sequence involves two planets in exaltation – the nocturnal Mars in Capricorn and its dispositor, Saturn in Libra. The condition of exaltation may look at first glance, as if it is 'a gift from heaven' (literally), but there are always strings attached to its elevated dignity and in this case, double exaltation has led Mars down the road to become a planet in the state of munakara.

"I always say, 'I'm not a pirate, I just play one on TV.'"[23]

In Paul Watson's case, his exalted Mars has painted him in the role as a New Age pirate, sailing the seas, and if not exactly raiding ships, and making sailors walk the plank, then at least causing havoc, and drawing international attention to his enemies' more nefarious deeds at sea.

In wild and remote oceans where no cameras, television crews, or documentary hounds exist to record the illegal slaughter of whales, or the clubbing of baby seals, it is an easy task to be a pirate yourself, to ransack the ocean of its largest mammals, to pollute the ocean with waste products, and to visit isolated rocky outcrops to club its defenceless inhabitants to death.

> "Killing a baby seal is about the easiest thing you can do if you're inclined to be sadistic; you certainly can't say there's any sport in it – the animal is totally defenceless."[24]

Two munakara planets in their exalted signs are Paul Watson's greatest defence, and perhaps also, his greatest weakness. His munakara Saturn is quincunx its outcome planet, Jupiter, in rulership. This non-aspect suggests a lack of fear, or even responsibility, for his actions, or that his various rebellious acts against authority are justified, simply because Watson answers to 'a higher power.' Watson's munakara Mars is involved in a second quincunx to Pluto, and perhaps Pluto (in the 12th house) represents the powerful, wealthy countries or companies that Watson is prepared to fight (munakara Mars), but the quincunx suggests that it will be a losing battle he cannot win. It may be, his Mars in quincunx to Pluto, is symbolic of how tiny vessels, hovercrafts and speedboats are completely out of their league (munakara Mars), when new technology is making the whaling industry more lucrative, more deadly towards its enemies, and more efficient at killing, than ever before (Pluto).

Watson is enormously proud of the fact that his record shows he presents no threat to human life – the opposition cannot make the same claim against Sea Shepherd warriors – and perhaps that is partly due to Venus' involvement in both Watson's munakara sequences, as first dispositor to Saturn, and as nocturnal outcome planet for Mars.

Venus is not excited by bloodshed, it takes no glory in hurting or causing damage for the sake of it, but Venus in Sagittarius loves a good principle, and relishes the feeling of possessing a good moral compass (Venus trines Pluto), when the rest of the world sees nothing wrong with the carnage these activities cause at sea – a long, long way from civilization, and most people's comfort zone.

Watson does not describe himself as a protester. He regards himself as an enforcer of international treaties on whaling and animal welfare. He states that his work has never hurt anyone – despite the seriousness of Japan's current allegations, the only one harmed was a lightly injured Japanese crew member via a mild acidic burn from a stink bomb. Watson was not at the scene of the crime on February 2010 and he denies playing any commanding role in it, yet on the eve of his 74th birthday (2 December 2024), he was told by a judge that his detention in Greenland will be extended by at least another month.

With munakara Mars dispositing to Saturn, Watson has spent over fifty of his seventy four years putting himself in the way of harm, and he expects no

Chapter Eighteen • *Munakara Saturn Delineations*

less a sacrifice from his volunteers and his crew members. Before embarking on a new campaign, Watson would ask his crew members whether they were willing to lose their life to save that of a whale. "And if they said no, he would reply, 'Well, then we don't need you.'"[25]

Watson's total lack of compromise – munakara Mars disposited by munakara Saturn – saw him leave Greenpeace where he was one of the pioneers, and later to clash again with colleagues at the Sea Shepherd organisation he founded, when others wanted him to take a less controversial path. On 3 September, 2022, Watson announced that he was leaving Sea Shepherd and setting up a new organisation, the Captain Paul Watson Foundation. Munakara Mars's outcome planet, Venus, is conjunct his Sagittarian Sun, and his Sun is perched on the IC, just one degree from an opposition to the MC. Watson's third attempt at bringing his mission into concrete form has seen him create an organisation that bears his name, as he said at the time, "the reason I called it that is because it's pretty hard for anyone to infiltrate and take over an organisation that included my name."[26]

Munakara Planet and Sect Condition – how comfortable is Mars?

A nocturnal chart will suit Mars perfectly, even when there is no further sect dignity to be had from the second and third rule of sect. Hand says of Mars in a nocturnal chart, that it "slows down its frenetic energy, tempers its masculinity, and has the ability to create clear definition."[27] Twenty years earlier Hand wrote in 1995, "the moisture of the night cools Mars down and connects it. The nocturnal Mars is not a wholly benevolent energy, but it more often manifests, according to the ancients, as a defensive, sustaining energy....In general we see that the nocturnal planets are those whose virtue relies on feelings of connectedness, relatedness, support, and nurture, in other words, moisture."[28]

Paul Watson — ♂'s Sect Dignity

Planet	Sect 1 Status	Sect 2 Hemisphere	Sect 3 Sign
♑ ♂	Night	With the Sun	Earth
N	N	D	X

Table 18.4: Paul Watson: Munakara Mars' Sect Dignity

Mars' position in exaltation is helped by its dispositor Saturn also being in its sign of exaltation. As stated earlier, Saturn is in *halb* in Watson, chart, and Saturn's dispositor, Venus, like Mars, is happy in a nocturnal chart.

675

Munakara Mars: Paul Watson

"I do what I do because it is the right thing to do. I am a warrior, and it is the way of the warrior to fight superior odds."[29] – Captain Paul Watson

Munakara Mars in Capricorn in 5th House (Placidus)

Many of Sea Shepherd's crew are volunteers who give their spare time, or sacrifice their annual leave, to man the ships roaming the oceans to stop what is known as 'Illegal, Unreported and Unregulated' (IUU) fishing. Watson has defended his deliberate choice in using volunteer crew members over the years, saying, "It is true that many of the Sea Shepherd crew members are inexperienced, but the fact is that these volunteers bring a passion to the project that cannot be found in a hired crew."[30]

Sea Shepherd's website dedicates a page to recruiting 'Volunteers at Sea' to crew for 'Neptune's Navy', and advertises that volunteers come from over two dozen countries and five continents. These volunteer crew members are a key to the success of Sea Shepherd's direct-action campaigns, so when the call goes out for "passionate ocean defenders who aren't afraid of hard work no pay, long hours, dangerous conditions and extreme weather", they are searching for individuals who enjoy a challenge at the same time as wanting to "defend, conserve and protect marine wildlife."[31]

It is highly unlikely that Paul Watson wrote the spiel on the Sea Shepherd website, but his original concept may have been the fountainhead for the following quote. One can imagine Watson gathering together his motley crew of volunteers/pirates on the first day of a campaign at sea, and delivering a rallying speech to his excited devotees:

> *"Remember, always, that it is the nature of a warrior to act. Do not be daunted by the formidable strength of the opposition. Do not be depressed by doom and gloom predictions. A true warrior must welcome challenge and transform the impossible into the possible. Because you are living in these trying times, it is your task to confront situations created by human ignorance and apathy, and focus your actions through love for the future and all the children of all the children of all species."*[32]

Presumably Saturn, the patron of sailors and ships, would approve of Paul Watson as a gatekeeper of the seas. Marine species that are listed as 'extinct' are gone forever, and hopefully the death of the ocean is many generations away, but hopefully there will always be lone individuals with munakara planets that fight corporations and countries, when everyone is too busy, too complacent, or too frightened, to take the risks themselves.

> "This is not just a movement to defend whales and sharks, seals and fish, it is a movement to defend humanity and all other species on this planet ocean."[33]
> – Captain Paul Watson, 2023 Environmental Media Association (EMA) IMPACT Summit

Munakara Saturn: Gordon Brown

A Brief Biography of Gordon Brown

Gordon Brown (born 20 February, 1951) is a Scottish-born British Labour Party politician, who served as chancellor of the Exchequer for ten years (1997–2007) under Tony Blair, and became prime minister of the United Kingdom (2007–10).

Brown was the son of John Brown, a Labour Party–supporting Church of Scotland minister. At age 16 he won a scholarship to the University of Edinburgh – the youngest student to enter the university since World War II – where he studied history and immersed himself in student politics. It was at university that he began to have problems with his sight and doctors diagnosed him with a detached retina, which was caused by an injury he received in his final game for his school rugby team.[34]

Gordon Brown became MP for Dunfermline East in the 1983 General Election, and shared his first office in the House of Commons with Tony Blair, where they became friends. Later he became Shadow Chancellor and backed Blair for the leadership of the Labour Party. Working together they won a landslide majority in 1997.

He was Chancellor of the Exchequer during the longest ever period of economic growth in the UK. He also made the Bank of England independent, and announced, at the Gleneagles Summit in 2005, an agreement to support the world's poorest countries and to deal with climate change. His passion for global justice was shown in his negotiation to cancel the debts of the world's poorest nations and the tripling of the development budget.

At the time of his elevation to prime minister, he had been the longest continuously serving Chancellor of the Exchequer since the 1820s.[35] Gordon Brown became England's Prime Minister on 27 June 2007 after Tony Blair left office. During his time as Prime Minister he oversaw changes such as the introduction of neighbourhood policing in every area, a legally-enforceable right to early cancer screening and treatment, and the world's first ever Climate Change Act, which was implemented in autumn 2008.

The greatest challenge he faced in office was the worldwide financial crisis and the following recession. In April 2009, he hosted the G20 Summit in London where world leaders pledged to make an additional $1.1 trillion available to help the world economy through the crisis and restore credit, growth and jobs. They also pledged to improve financial supervision and regulation.[36] UK combat operations in Iraq, which began during his predecessor's time in office, came to an end under Gordon Brown. British forces withdrew from the country at the end of April 2009. During his time in office, Brown worked with his Irish counterpart Brian Cowen to negotiate the devolution of policing and justice powers in Northern Ireland. An agreement was finally reached in February 2010 and the powers were passed to Northern Ireland's government in the following April 2011, after Brown had been defeated and had tendered his resignation as prime minister. Brown retired from politics in May 2015.[37]

> "I hate prejudice, discrimination, and snobbishness of any kind – it always reflects on the person judging and not the person being judged. Everyone should be treated equally."[38] – Gordon Brown

Libra Saturn in Munakara: Gordon Brown

- **Key Questions:**
- What does Gordon Brown's Saturn contend with?
- What is its driving force?
- What is its trigger? What is its outcome?

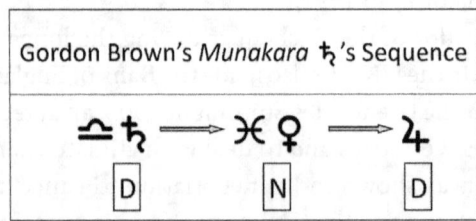

Table 18.5: Gordon Brown: Munakara Saturn's Sequence

Gordon Brown was born two months after Paul Watson, and Saturn in Libra had moved less than a degree in this time. Paul Watson's Saturn is

Chapter Eighteen • *Munakara Saturn Delineations*

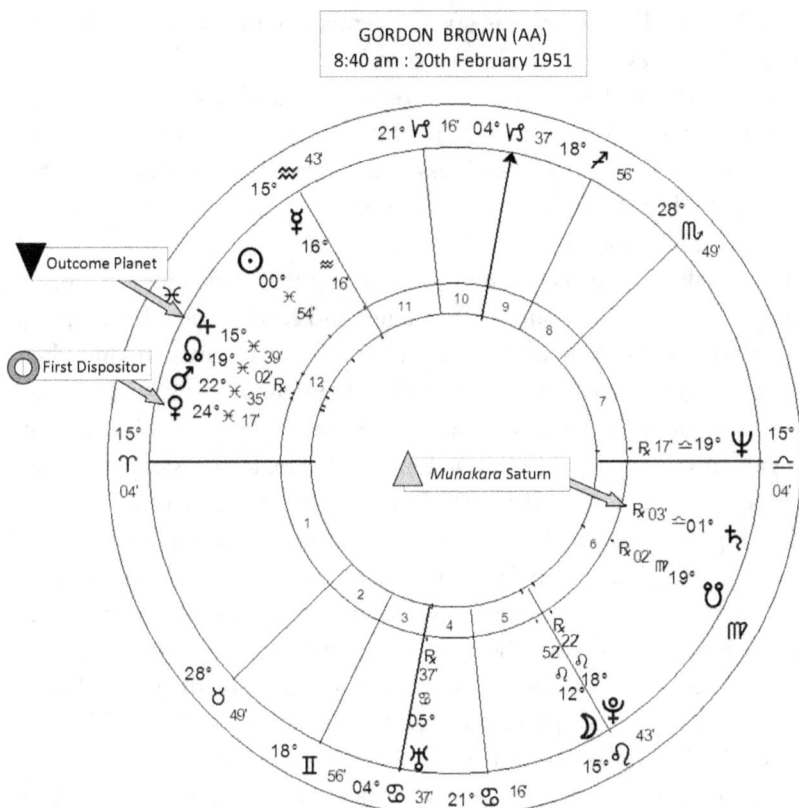

Fig. 18.3: Gordon Brown Natal Chart: Munakara Saturn's Sequence

direct, whilst Gordon Brown's Saturn is retrograde, and perhaps this small difference demonstrates someone who fights outside of the system (direct Saturn in contention), as opposed to someone who joins the government and fights the system from within its hallowed walls (retrograde Saturn in contention).

Twelfth-century astrologer, Ibn-Ezra wrote, "*A retrograde planet is like a rebellious and defiant person*"[39] and this is what Gordon Brown needed to be, whether he was fighting for social reform (Venus), or trying to rebalance a nation's wealth (Jupiter). Ibn-Ezra also said, "*You should know that when planets are retrograde, they are like a man who is weak, stunned and worried.*"[40] Ibn-Ezra's second comment on retrogradation describes exactly how Brown must have felt at the end of his term as prime minister, as he no longer had the fight to renew his position and serve a British public who abused and ridiculed him. His energy was spent (Venus conjuncts Mars, ruler of his Ascendant), and even though he was deeply hurt by the lack of support from his party at the end of his term (Pisces Venus is Saturn's dispositor), his Jupiter in Pisces must have felt relief when his workload lightened. Munakara Saturn was finally relieved of long, thankless hours spent on a job that was difficult and often highly unpopular with the public (munakara Saturn in 6th/7th house, ruling MC and the 11th).

His munakara Saturn's outcome planet is Jupiter in rulership, and Jupiter is the dispositor of Brown's Sun, Mars, Venus, and North Node. Jupiter allowed Brown the opportunity to move freely to the next adventure in his life when he accepted an unpaid advisory role at the World Economic Forum. In July 2012 Brown was named as a United Nations Special Envoy on Global Education and again, it was an unpaid position but one that he felt passionately invested in (Jupiter, outcome planet in 12th house). Brown is the author of several books (Jupiter rules the 9th house of publishing), including his memoir *My Life, Our Times* (2017), and *Seven Ways to Change the World: How to Fix The Most Pressing Problems We Face* (2021). The book features Brown's forensic examination of seven areas where global reform and action are essential.[41]

Two planets in exaltation – Saturn in Libra, and its dispositor Venus in Pisces – are a part of munakara Saturn's sequence, and the third planet involved, Jupiter, the outcome planet, is in rulership in Pisces. This munakara sequence may appear to be one of the fortunate combinations, given that it is Saturn, the great malefic, which is in the state of munakara. Gordon Brown's father was a passionate Labour Party member, and his son inherited his father's belief in the party. He has been quoted as saying, "I joined this party as a teenager…Its values are my moral compass."[42] But not everyone in his party possessed the same 'moral compass,' and munakara Saturn in 7th house (Whole Sign) would find out – to his detriment – that integrity, truth, and honour amongst colleagues can be sacrificed for the sake of power and ambition.

Munakara Planet and Sect Condition – how comfortable is Saturn?

Saturn works in a more beneficial manner if it gains some level of light and warmth from the Sun so a diurnal chart is perfect to exercise Saturn's better qualities. Saturn's exalted sign may belong to the nocturnal Venus, but the sign itself is masculine and again, Libra's combined qualities of hot and wet are soothing for Saturn, and act as a counter-balance for its own cold, dry qualities. Libra, and a diurnal chart, tends to make Saturn more compliant, more manageable, and more sociable, but only up to a certain point. The drawback for exaltation is that a planet believes in its own 'rightness', but in Saturn's case, this can easily turn into 'righteousness'. The individual with a munakara planet in a self-righteous state tends to put aside common sense and caution, in favour of a cause or a wrong that needs to be 'righted'. When the munakara planet is either Saturn or Mars, the actions a person takes are likely to be extreme and to end in separations, either a cold withdrawal or passive aggressive behaviour (Saturn), or a hot 'burn it down' and destroy everything in its path (Mars).

Gordon Brown — ♄'s Sect Dignity			
Planet	Sect 1 Status	Sect 2 Hemisphere	Sect 3 Sign
♎ ♄	Day	No Sun	Air
D	D	N	D

Table 18.6: Gordon Brown: Munakara Saturn's Sect Dignity

The benefit to Saturn being in a diurnal chart is that the environment created by the Sun (light and warmth) are a great boon to Saturn. It will be geared towards discipline and order, rather than stumbling around in the dark creating chaos and mayhem. The Sun gives Saturn direction and purpose in a diurnal chart, and boundaries are much easier to see and honour in the daylight hours.

Munakara Saturn: Gordon Brown

Munakara Saturn in Libra in 6th House (Placidus), and 7th House (Whole Sign)

Saturn moves to the angular 7th house in Whole Sign, and this describes Brown's partnership with Tony Blair, and his relationship with opponent, David Cameron. If he had been a little more ruthless towards both men, he may have succeeded, but munakara Saturn rarely plays dirty by betraying friendships, or spreading gossip to gain a personal advantage.

Brown had been widely regarded as the senior half of the Blair-Brown partnership and the one more likely to take his place. However, when former leader of the Labour Party, John Smith, died suddenly in May 1994, Blair had overtaken Brown as the preferred candidate for party activists and the wider public. Brown reluctantly stepped aside – munakara Saturn in Whole Sign 7th house – reportedly after Blair agreed to support Brown as his eventual successor. Speculation that a deal had been reached was confirmed by Brown in a 2010 interview, though he stated that the decision had not been made at a meeting in Granita, a London restaurant, as previously thought.[43]

Saturn in Libra is quincunx the Sun in Pisces and the axis of 5th house (Leo on the cusp) and 11th house (Aquarius on the cusp) indicated the friendship was never going to survive the individuals' political aspirations (a 'non' aspect). Brown was convinced that Blair had agreed to stand down as prime minister after two terms – that is, before the election in 2005 – and that Blair would give Brown free rein over economic policy at the Treasury. Blair had claimed that neither were firm promises. But importantly, Brown believed it was an honourable agreement between gentlemen, and he acted accordingly (munakara Saturn in 7th house).[44]

As it became clear that Blair had no intention of stepping aside after a second term, Brown became even more resentful at being duped by the smooth-tongued Blair. Even worse, the 'pact' became public knowledge (Brown's munakara Saturn in 7th house rules his MC) and was endlessly discussed; even becoming a television drama called *The Deal* in 2003. The deputy prime minister managed to broker a peace deal in 2003, in which Blair committed to stand down in 2004, and Brown promised he would cooperate with Blair's premiership. But neither side kept their bargain. Blair, most wickedly, by leading the Labour Party into their third election victory in 2005.[45]

The relationship between the two men became increasingly strained with many loyal to Blair (Venus, Saturn's dispositor in 12th house), claiming that Brown's supporters (munakara Saturn in 7th house) had been undermining Blair's leadership for several years. A document leaked in 2007 proved that Blair was so nervous of a challenge from Brown to his leadership, that he had even considered stripping Brown's chancellor role from him after the 2005 election. Munakara Saturn's dispositor, Venus, and outcome planet, Jupiter, are in signs of their essential dignity in Brown's chart. Venus is exalted in Pisces, and Jupiter is in rulership in Pisces. Both are powerful, but for whom? Venus and Jupiter are in Brown's 12th house, the house of hidden enemies. Do you really want enemies to be this powerful and this efficient at destroying you?[46] Benefics – Venus and Jupiter – count for very little when they are situated in the 12th house, and when they have dignity, they can indicate ruthless or ambitious friends who wish you harm.

Brown finally commenced his term as prime minister in 2007, and the media were promoting him as a potentially great PM: calling him masterly, energetic, and focused in his new role. Given his incredible success as Chancellor, many political analysts predicted that Brown would bring in wide-sweeping social reform, the likes of which had not been seen since Clement Attlee's Prime Ministership in the late 1940s. Praise and excitement surrounded him, and it looked as though the opposition in the form of leader, David Cameron, would be bested by Brown, and that Cameron's political career would suffer at the hand of Brown's first term as prime minister.

Brown acted decisively to introduce the first ever Climate Change Act (2008), and created the Counter-Terrorism Act (2008). He ordered the withdrawal of British troops from Iraq, and negotiated the devolution of policing and justice powers in Northern Ireland. All admirable Saturn achievements, given that exalted Saturn rules his Mid-heaven and the highly-political 11th house, and Saturn is angular (Whole Sign 7th house).

Two years later, munakara Saturn had taken its toll, but not on Cameron, as the transfer from steady Chancellor to isolated Prime Minister was punishing Brown for rising too high and paying the price. Journalist, Andy Beckett, wrote in June 2009 for *The Guardian*, a traditionally left-leaning paper, under the title, 'Where did it all go wrong for Gordon Brown?'[47] The article is a detailed analysis of the mistakes which began to accumulate towards the end of Brown's tenure. According to Beckett, "Brown is a prime minister so beleaguered, so unpopular and seemingly exhausted, so apparently luckless and unsuited to the job, that he attracts ridicule and even pity."[48] Political bloggers were describing Brown as a 'baited bear, a human car crash, painful to watch', and even former fans and well-connected members from his own party called Brown a "catastrophic leader". Claims of incompetency, poor judgment, indecisiveness, and a bitter failure, plagued Brown in the Murdoch dailies, and the Labour leader's unpopularity produced polls as low as between 22% and 16% when readers were quizzed on re-election preferences.

> "When something really matters, you should never give up or give in."[49]
> – Gordon Brown

Brown's munakara Saturn is situated in his Placidus 6th house, and there is little doubt that he took his duty seriously, and that he was committed to working tirelessly on a daily basis. But the strain of being prime minister also took a huge toll on his physical strength, and his poor sight, and Saturn in contention could not carry the weight of the countless hours dedicated to such a demanding job as the UK's Prime Minister. "On TV today, Brown looks tired and grey. Sometimes he has eye bags under his eye bags," commented Beckett in his 2009 article.[50]

Some of Brown's bad luck is tinged by local and global events which were entirely out of munakara Saturn's jurisdiction, and over which even exaltation would have been of very little benefit to Saturn. Brown took office in 2007 when his Party had already been in power for a decade, a long time in British politics. He followed in the footsteps of Tony Blair, a charismatic speaker and originally, a friend, whom Brown should have challenged earlier for leadership in the four years leading up to the election, but Brown kept missing the timing. Whether his hesitancy was out of fear of being outmanoeuvred, or through misplaced loyalty is hard to say, but by the time Blair stood down, it was too late for Brown to save himself or his Party. In 2007, the clouds of the global economic crisis were gathering and the bubble was about to burst on unsustainable property and personal debt.

Munakara Saturn rules Gordon Brown's Mid-heaven and his 11th house (Whole Sign), but it creeps into the rulership of his 12th house as well through the Placidus system where Aquarius is on the cusp of the house. One of the biggest scandals for Brown's tenure which was a factor in his loss for re-election, occurred in March 2010 when a number of ex-members from his government were caught in a cash-for-influence sting, secretly filmed offering access to senior ministers for up to five thousand pounds a day (Saturn's dispositor, Venus and outcome planet, Jupiter, are in his 12th house). Brown was not directly involved in the scandal, but as Leader of his party, he was held responsible for their corruption.[51] Cameron's colleagues were caught too, but his attack on Brown was so ferocious, and in perfect harmony with the public's poor opinion of Brown, that no amount of protestation or salvaged integrity could save Brown's beleaguered Saturn.

First Dispositor: Venus in Pisces in 12th House

"Getting married has certainly made a massive difference to my own life. So I am committed to giving support for family finances and having the right policies for work-life balance that make it easier for couples to have a rich family life."[52]

Exalted Venus is Saturn's dispositor, and the ruler of his 7th house. Throughout his past career and its recovery into his current successes and international titles, Gordon Brown has been supported by his wife Sarah Macaulay, whom he married in 2000 when he was 49 years of age. Sarah Brown rarely made official appearances (Venus in 12th house) but he has credited her love, strength, and support as major factors in his success.

The 7th house also represents the second-born child (3 houses from the 5th,

Chapter Eighteen • *Munakara Saturn Delineations*

the first-born) and Venus, its ruler in 12th house, has the potential to show the child's illness. In November 2006, four-month-old Fraser Brown was diagnosed with cystic fibrosis. Whilst the family was reeling from the terrible news, UK newspaper, *The Sun*, learned of the situation and published the story without gaining permission from either parent. In 2011, Brown publicly attacked *News International* accusing them of using disgusting methods to gain access to personal information, and that he and his wife were "in tears" when they had broken the news on the health status of their infant son.[53]

The outcome planet: Jupiter in Pisces

"I believe there is a moral sense and a global ethic that commands attention from people of every religion and every faith, and people of no faith. But I think what's new is that we now have the capacity to communicate instantaneously across frontiers right across the world."[54]

As an advocate for social change and a huge supporter for Britain's National Health System – Brown credited the saving of his eye from a detached retina to the NHS – his Jupiter in rulership is a more deserving legacy than his contentious Saturn. Even after his disastrous political defeat, the world stage was a part of his destiny and Brown has risen to prominence and power in his later roles. He began his post-political journey in education as he has always had a passion to educate, regardless of a person's social status, wealth, race, or religion. He currently serves as the UN Special Envoy for Global Education. To date his most challenging role – and munakara Saturn's ultimate victory over its past detractors – may be his current position, post-pandemic in 2022, in the World Health Organisation (WHO) as Ambassador for Global Health Financing.

An article written in May 2024 by *POLITICO* titled "Is Gordon Brown coming back? Sort of."[55] has fanned speculation that the two former friends and later rivals, Tony Blair and Gordon Brown, are watching the current political situation in the UK very closely and both men are thinking about a comeback to politics. Current prime minister since July 2024, Keir Starmer is struggling and says that he talks to Blair "a lot" about how he prepared for power in 1997. At the same time, the article states that Brown "recently set out arguing for constitutional reform" and several of his supporters say he will have a higher profile now that the Labour Party is in power. One of Brown's former aides, Stewart Wood told *POLITICO*, "He (Brown) is Labour through and through. He is passionate about core Labour values, equality, combating poverty, social cohesion – and angry about what the Tories have done to Britain and to public life. He has technical mastery of policy so, even 14 years after leaving power, he knows the fiscal and policy tricks needed to pull off change. And he is a master of the craft of political combat."[56] One ally of Starmer predicts there will be "jostling – not for influence on Keir but for control of the narrative."[57] It seems that even after two decades, the rivalry between Blair and Brown is still alive, and Brown's munakara Saturn has not finished its battle with his antagonist.

Munakara Saturn: LeBron James

A Brief Biography of LeBron James[58]

American professional basketball player LeBron James (born 30 December 1984) is widely considered one of the greatest all-round players of all time. James has won four National Basketball Association (NBA) championships with three teams (Miami Heat, Cleveland Cavaliers, and the Los Angeles Lakers). In 2023 LeBron James became the NBA's all-time leading scorer, breaking the record (38,387) previously held by Kareem Abdul-Jabbar. His dominance continued in 2024, when he recorded his 40,000 point scored.

A locally known basketball prodigy since elementary school, James was named Ohio's Mr. Basketball (high-school player of the year) three times, while leading Akron's St. Vincent–St. Mary High School to three Ohio state championships in his four years on the team. He became a national media sensation in his junior year, after appearing on the cover of *Sports Illustrated*, where he was billed by the magazine as "The Chosen One." He was selected by the Cleveland Cavaliers with the first overall selection of the 2003 NBA draft. He signed an unprecedented $90 million endorsement contract with the Nike shoe company before he ever played a professional game. Named the 2004 NBA Rookie of the Year,[59] James soon established himself as one of the league's premier players, leading the Cavaliers to their first NBA Finals appearance in 2007 and winning the NBA MVP (Most Valuable Player) award in 2009 and 2010.[60] James left the Cavaliers in 2010 as a free agent to join the Miami Heat;[61] this was announced in a nationally televised special titled *The Decision* and is amongst the most controversial free agency moves in sports history.

James joined the Heat and won his first two NBA Championships (2012 and 2013) whilst playing for them. He played four seasons with them (2010–2014) and then opted out of his contract, returning to the Cavaliers for four

Chapter Eighteen • *Munakara Saturn Delineations*

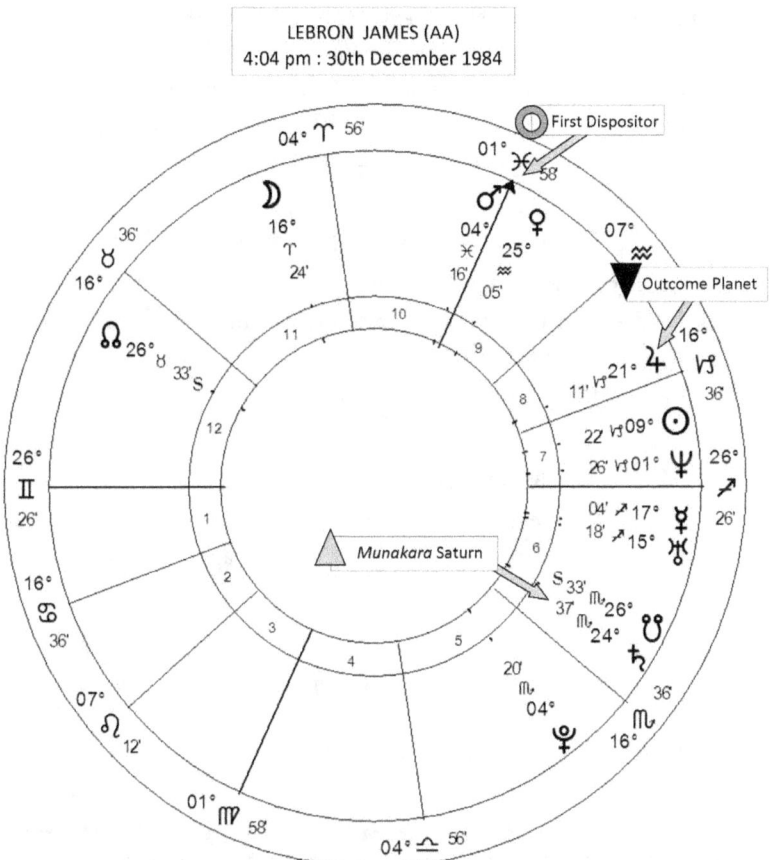

Fig. 18.4: LeBron James Natal Chart: Munakara Saturn's Sequence

more seasons (2014–2018). In 2016, he led the Cavaliers to victory at the NBA championships, ending the Cleveland 'sports curse' which had seen their failure to win a championship in 52 years. In 2018, James exercised his contract option to leave the Cavaliers and signed with the Lakers, where they won the 2020 NBA championship and his fourth MVP.[62] In 2024 he became part of the first father-son teammate duo in NBA history, playing alongside his son Bronny with the Lakers.

He leads the LeBron James Family Foundation, which has opened an elementary school in 2018, adding a housing complex, retail plaza, community hub in 2020,[63] and a medical centre in 2022 in Akron, Ohio.[64]

"All your life you are told the things you cannot do. All your life they will say *you're not good enough or strong enough or talented enough. They will say you're the wrong height or the wrong weight or the wrong type to play this or be this or achieve this. They will tell you no. A thousand times no. Until all the no's become meaningless. All your life they will tell you no. Quite firmly and very quickly. And you will tell them yes."*[65] – LeBron James

Scorpio Saturn in Munakara: LeBron James

- **Key Questions:**
- What does LeBron James's Saturn contend with?
- What is its driving force?
- What is its trigger? What is its outcome?

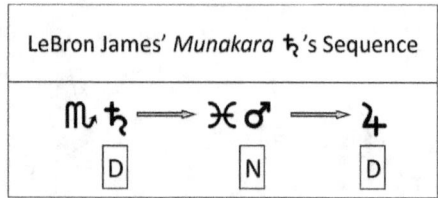

Table 18.7: LeBron James: Munakara Saturn's Sequence

"You have to be able to accept failure to get better."[66] – LeBron James

In everyone's life there are experiences that trigger feelings of isolation, fears of rejection, that instigate an inexplicable rage against injustice, or corruption, or abusive authority figures, experiences that make us feel powerless and angry at the unfairness of it all. These are common denominators that cause frustration and unhappiness, and in extreme circumstances, or under the right conditions, disrupt mental health with periods of stress, anxiety, lethargy, or depression. Saturn is not an easy planet to live with, but when it is munakara, these feelings become amplified, especially when Saturn in contention sets such a high bar for the world around it, and especially for the individual who has Saturn in this condition.

NBA superstar LeBron James has lived with his munakara Saturn for forty years (as has Harry, Duke of Sussex), and although they have had vastly different upbringings and social backgrounds, both men would agree they share feelings of being duty-bound, and of carrying others' huge expectations on their shoulders. And while they are carrying these burdens, both real and imaginary, they crave to be free of the responsibilities that bring little room

Chapter Eighteen • *Munakara Saturn Delineations*

for failure, and invite constant criticism from the media, the public, and sometimes, as in the case of Harry, from within their own family.

Mars is the nocturnal dispositor for both men's Scorpio Saturn in contention, and they have used Mars through its stereotype nature of engaging in battle, to release enormous amounts of energy, and to challenge themselves to achieve greater heights of success. For Harry, it was the military, and his comments on the pleasures of his military term are well documented. His father Charles' actions seem extraordinarily harsh (and a little vindictive) in stripping Harry of his honorary military titles and Harry has suffered humiliation through being ostracized from his beloved British Army.

For LeBron James, Saturn's dispositor, Mars, has given him the pleasure of continuing to compete in his twentieth year as a professional basketball player. Mars on the MC has brought James a swath of honours and awards through Saturn's hard work and commitment to perfection. Records such as the number of points scored by Kareem Abdul-Jabbar, a record he had held from 1984 to 2023, continue to fall and be claimed in victory by LeBron James. His Mars rules the 11th house, a lucky place if honours are bestowed on a person, and also the 6th house, not such a happy place if illness or injury causes distress or hardship. James has had some calf, foot, and ankle injuries in the 2024 season with the Lakers, but these are minor issues given that he will be a 40-year-old player at the end of 2024, and is pitted against young men half his age (like his son Bronny) on the basketball court.

Jupiter is LeBron James' outcome planet for his munakara Saturn, and Jupiter rules his Mid-heaven, where Mars proudly stands. Jupiter is in Saturn's sign, so technically, this is a Jupiter in fall, but I believe it is more a record of James' harsh beginnings, rather than a prediction of hardship for the future. In traditional texts, the 10th house is the house of mother (situated seven houses from the 4th house), and the story of his childhood and his mother's struggles are described by Jupiter in fall, ruling her house (the 10th house).

The outcome planet in a munakara sequence acts as both a trigger to prompt the munakara planet into action, and also as an indication of the end result of the challenges faced by a planet in contention. James's humanitarian interests, his passion for the education of underprivileged children, and his involvement in civil rights, is the statement of his Jupiter in fall, but it is not his fall from hubris, arrogance, or a belief that he is better than his peers. Rather, Jupiter in Capricorn is James' recognition that his physical ability is god-given, and that he has a religious duty to distribute benefits through education, healthcare, and community support, to those who did not experience his good fortune

Munakara Planet and Sect Condition – how comfortable is Saturn?

Saturn is a diurnal planet and a daytime chart – such as LeBron James' – will warm Saturn's nature and provides light to counter its natural propensity for darkness. Saturn would prefer to travel in the same hemisphere as its luminary, the Sun, but this is not necessary when the chart itself is diurnal, and the Sun is placed above the horizon. Scorpio is a feminine sign and not to Saturn's liking so far as sect is concerned. Again, a diurnal chart will compensate for both hemisphere and incorrect gender sign placement.

LeBron James — ♄'s Sect Dignity			
Planet	Sect 1 Status	Sect 2 Hemisphere	Sect 3 Sign
♏ ♄	Day	No Sun	Water
D	D	N	N

Table 18.8: LeBron James: Munakara Saturn's Sect Dignity

Robert Hand describes in-sect Saturn as a diurnal planet with an increase in energy levels and masculinity, able to define and set goals that are worthy, capable and reachable when the planet seeks respect, credibility and acknowledgement from its environment. Being in sect grants Saturn the ability to set realistic and achievable goals, thereby giving the individual pleasurable feelings of self-worth, success, value and good productivity.[67]

Mars, Saturn's dispositor, is in far more discomfort in James's chart, given that all three conditions of sect dignity are denied to this nocturnal planet – in a diurnal chart, travelling with the Sun, and in a feminine water sign. This may seem a strange occurrence given that this is the chart of a top professional athlete with a 20-year career, but in order to step onto a basketball court and succeed, LeBron James must be able to see this space as a hostile place, a field of combat, otherwise he becomes too comfortable, too complacent, too compassionate towards its enemy or opponent, and Mars cannot keep its edge or perform at its best, if it is distracted by these traits.

Jupiter, the outcome planet, is in good sect condition, being *halb*, but not *hayz*, as it is in a diurnal chart in the same hemisphere as the Sun, but not placed in a masculine sign. Jupiter may be in its fall sign, but good sect dignity has the potential to produce the best manifestations of Jupiter: success, power, wealth, knowledge, and awareness.

> *"Where I grew up – I grew up on the north side of Akron, lived in the projects. So those scared and lonely nights – that's every night. You hear a lot of police*

Chapter Eighteen • *Munakara Saturn Delineations*

sirens, you hear a lot of gunfire. Things that you don't want your kids to hear growing up."⁶⁸

Good sect dignity gives Jupiter the resilience to overcome harm, and when James' childhood is compared to his adulthood, it seems that sect has been a great benefit to his Jupiter in fall, ruler of the MC and his 7th house.

Munakara Saturn: LeBron James

*"My game is really played above time. I don't say that like I'm saying I'm ahead of my time. I'm saying, like, if I'm on the court and I throw a pass, the ball that I've thrown will lead my teammate right where he needs to go, before he even knows that that's the right place to go to."*⁶⁹ – LeBron James

Munakara Saturn in Scorpio conjunct South Node

Life started harshly for LeBron James. He learnt early about the scarcity of safety and security, being the child of a 16-year-old teenager, Gloria 'Glo' James, who lived with her grandmother, mother, and two brothers in a tough part of Akron, Ohio. Gloria's casual boyfriend was the baby's father, a boy with an extensive criminal record, and a man whom James has never met.

*"My father wasn't around when I was a kid, and I used to always say, 'Why me? Why don't I have a father? Why isn't he around? Why did he leave my mother?' But as I got older I looked deeper and thought, 'I don't know what my father was going through, but if he was around all the time, would I be who I am today?'"*⁷⁰ – LeBron James

This is one expression for munakara Saturn – a potentially wearying relationship with a father, or a father who cannot (or will not) protect the native from harm, especially when young. Within a year of the baby's birth Gloria's grandmother passed away, and six months later, shattering the family completely, her own mother died before Gloria's eighteenth birthday. Not much more than a child herself, Gloria was homeless with a young baby in her care. Somehow the mother and child survived the next seven years, and then their luck turned for the better.

Saturn rules James's 8th house and can signify the contracts, sponsorships, and the amount of money negotiated on his behalf through a network of his various agents. Aries Moon ruling the 2nd house may show how he loves to spend his money on philanthropic causes (education, youth, etc.) and creative pursuits (movies, productions, etc.) but munakara Saturn shows restraint rather than greed. True, for the ordinary person who could never imagine such wealth in one lifetime, James receives an inordinately large income for playing a game he loves (munakara Venus ruling 5th house). In December 2020 James signed a two-year $85 million extension with the LA Lakers that will cement his 2022–2023 season with the team.[71]

Faith is important to LeBron James. Raised as a Christian-Catholic, he credits God for his great talent and skill on the basketball court. Once, when losing an important game, he stated, "the Greater Man upstairs knows when it's my time. Right now, isn't my time."[72] It was quite a controversial statement when James made it in 2018, but not if you know your astrology. Saturn is the lord of Time and rules his 9th house so it makes sense when he considers divinity and timing to be inextricably linked together.

Saturn in munakara feels the need to be free of chains that bind it to established rules, or when it no longer respects or trusts an authority, to reject it for the sake of the individual's principles. Munakara Saturn strives to be authentic by following its own moral code, and it prides itself in being trustworthy or genuine when dealing with others. Sometimes this is an unusually high set of values which are hard to maintain, and Saturn, the planet of separation, can instigate situations which leave the person feeling vulnerable, rejected, isolated, and the subject of loathing or distrust.

Three times LeBron James has become an unrestricted free agent: on 1st July of 2010, 2014, and lastly 2018. His first release from the Cleveland Cavaliers in 2010 was a painful experience given that he underestimated the impact his change in clubs would have on his team and on his fans.

First Dispositor: Mars in Pisces on Mid-heaven

Mars is Saturn's friend (Saturn rules Capricorn, the sign of Mars's exaltation) and finally, after the first Saturn square, the dispositor shows up to provide a good male role model for James when Frank Walker, a local youth football coach took the boy into his home and introduced him to basketball (Mars rules 11th house – groups, and 6th house – daily life). James said "My life changed. I had shelter and food. I'll never forget what the Walkers did for me, especially Frank. He doesn't get the recognition he deserves because he's real quiet but he was the first one to give me a basketball and the first one to show a real interest (in me)."[73]

Fast forward a few years and LeBron James was a confident teenager with a passion for both football and basketball, and a loyal band of friends who dubbed themselves as the 'Fab Four', who played basketball together, and had

Chapter Eighteen • *Munakara Saturn Delineations*

made a vow to attend high school together. Already gaining local attention as young stars, the Fab Four chose to attend St. Vincent-St. Mary High School, a private Catholic school with predominantly white students.[74] Their decision upset the local community as rather than bring their talents to the local high school team, whose students were mainly poor and black, the four chose an alternate pathway. Saturn rules 9th house, and perhaps if James had realised the level of exposure – and income – his high school would receive due to his fame, he may have made a different choice.

James has been quoted as saying "The best ability is availability" and when he signed with the Lakers in 2018, his statistics showed that he had played in 95.1% of the combined 1,453 games across his 15-year career. Mars, the highly visible mark of an athlete, sits at the culminating point in James' chart and rules the 11th and 6th houses. An easy rulership flows from its position on the MC – his career status – to the 11th house of group activity where his Aries Moon sits, so perhaps we can understand why LeBron James has played a lot of basketball in his (now) twenty-year career with various NBA teams. His staggering record is a testament to his good fortune regarding health and minimal injury, and he is considered to be one of the most durable players ever. In his first 15 seasons from 2003 to 2018, James missed just 71 games due to injury and rest.

But as a recent article pointed out (3rd February 2022), "The complete LeBron James injury history: How Father Time is finally catching Lakers' superstar,"[75] in the last four seasons with the Lakers (2018–2024) James has been missing for the same amount (71 games) due to injury and rest. Father Time – Saturn in the 6th house – has been very lenient with James, but even he is slowing down as he approaches his 40th birthday.

There are some indicators in his natal chart that foresee health issues, and yet James has enjoyed a remarkably free run so far as injuries are concerned. Three areas in the chart are particularly important when making judgements about an individual's health status: the Moon, the Ascendant, and the 6th house are foci that draw our attention and help us evaluate physical strength and vitality. James's Moon in Aries trines Mercury, the Ascendant ruler, a good indicator for robust health. The Moon is disposited by Mars on the Midheaven – a great signature for an athlete, but his Ascendant ruler Mercury, is in detriment conjunct Uranus, and in the Placidus system, resides in the 6th house. In Whole sign Mercury in Sagittarius will become an angular planet, but the 7th house can indicate illness, because it opposes the Ascendant sign, and can 'attack' the person's vitality and well-being.

Mars rules his 6th house, where Saturn and the South Node reside and normally this can be a warning of Saturnian health issues – bone and skeletal breaks, malformations or weaknesses – particularly brought about by fire, cutting, operations, or violent experiences given that Mars is the ruler of the 6th house. James-led teams have advanced to the NBA Playoffs 16 times, and then advanced further to the NBA finals 10 times, and James has never missed a playoff game. He has chosen a highly physical career in professional basketball, so perhaps the friendship and support that Mars brings to munakara Saturn, has been the saving grace in enabling his outstanding record of longevity.

The outcome planet: Jupiter in Capricorn

The feelings of not belonging, of poverty, insecurity and fear that James experienced in the first few years of his life, may have been experiences exacerbated by Jupiter, the third planet in the three-step sequence. Saturn and Jupiter are not friends: Saturn injures Jupiter (owns Jupiter's fall sign) and this animosity is clearly demonstrated in James' own chart where Jupiter is in fall in Capricorn, and placed in the 8th house. As an eight-year-old James attended only 62 out of 162 days of school and says of this time "I saw drugs, guns, killings; it was crazy."[76] Gloria was having her own troubles with the law, and it looked as though this boy would be yet another wild child fending for themselves on the streets, until a miracle happened in the form of Frank Walker. Perhaps James is right to believe in a God that protects him not just spiritually, but physically as well, given the good fortune munakara Saturn has bestowed on this sports superstar.

Aquarius Venus in Munakara: LeBron James

- **Key Questions:**
- What does LeBron James's Venus contend with?
- What is its driving force?
- What is its trigger? What is its outcome?

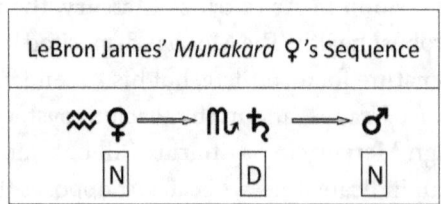

Table 18.9: LeBron James: Munakara Venus' Sequence

Chapter Eighteen • *Munakara Saturn Delineations*

In LeBron James' chart, Venus in Aquarius disposits to Saturn in Scorpio, belonging to Mars, and this sequence will create a situation of munakara for Venus. James's Venus forms a trine to his Gemini Ascendant, and his easy smile, natural good manners, and friendly nature, makes it hard to wonder what Venus could possibly have to get agitated about in this man's life.

LeBron James is a deeply religious man, and perhaps with his munakara Venus in 9th house, he is uncomfortable talking about his faith in an entertainment industry that can be a little cynical about spiritual matters. It may be that James's shyness is an issue for him, or the lack of privacy he is denied as a superstar is something that makes him uncomfortable. As a superstar James is constantly in the public eye, and playing a role which is exhausting, or impossible to maintain 24/7, and probably frustrating when dealing with annoying fans. This may explain Venus's distress when battling its demons in public, given that munakara Venus is the ruler of his reclusive 12th house. While public commitments, motivational speeches, endless interviews, and social media posts are good business tactics to promote the basketball industry (munakara Venus in Aquarius rules 5th house), they leave little room for Venus to relax or find down-time. It may be that Venus' on-and-off switch (public and private) becomes a little worn at times, and this describes a dilemma for munakara Venus – the desire to please and be loved, verses the need to revitalize energy, and find a place of peace and tranquillity.

Munakara Venus ruling the 5th house found another outlet for love when Bronny was born in 2004, with James commenting on his new role as a father, "But now, being a parent, I go home and see my son and I forget about any mistake I ever made or the reason I'm upset. I get home and my son is smiling or he comes running to me. It has just made me grow as an individual and grow as a man."[77]

However, even this love can have some contentious moments as James faced one of the scariest moments a parent can experience. On 24 July 2023 Bronny James collapsed during a practice session for his Ohio State, Oregon (USC) college. It was later revealed that the 20-year-old had suffered cardiac arrest caused by a congenital heart defect.[78] Less than five months later, he was fully recovered and made his collegiate debut. In early May 2024, Bronny James was medically cleared to be eligible for the NBA draft, and on 27 June 2024, he was selected by the Los Angeles Lakers.

James admits it has been hard for Bronny to enter the same profession and have to deal with negative reviews on his performance, "Just imagine if you were a kid, you were born into a situation where your dad was super famous, super wealthy and you the kid still had the drive to want to be able to accomplish things for yourself. I personally don't know if I would've been able to do that if the roles were reversed."[79]

Saturn is Venus' first dispositor, and it also is a planet in munakara, so the issues which affect Saturn are likely to cause agitation for Venus, and the square between the two planets shows that this is not always an easy relationship between the first and second planets in the nocturnal sequence. Saturn is Venus' driving force, but Saturn can be distracted by a demanding career, a club that expects to get its money's worth, and fans that want to critique his game every time James steps on to the basketball court. For more than twenty years, from the age of thirteen when roaming talent scouts first spotted LeBron James, he has been in the media spotlight. His Venus in contention is always on display, and even the slightest frown, curt reply, or perceived slight, will result in headlines, comments, and irate broadcasts across national and international media outlets within 24 hours of the alleged misdemeanour.

Venus' nocturnal outcome planet is Mars, also highly elevated in the chart, and as he approaches the milestone of his fortieth birthday, LeBron James must be wondering how he can occupy his Mars in a new career when he retires from basketball, given that it is Saturn's dispositor, and munakara Venus' outcome planet.

Munakara Planet and Sect Condition – how comfortable is Venus?

Venus has no sect dignity in LeBron James' chart as all three factors work against Venus finding comfort and support within its chart environment. Similar to Mars, Venus finds itself moving through hostile land, and nothing could exhibit this better than his decision to broadcast his new contract with Miami Heat in 2010. He failed to fully comprehend how his fans would react when he

LeBron James — ♀'s Sect Dignity			
Planet	Sect 1 Status	Sect 2 Hemisphere	Sect 3 Sign
♒ ♀	Day	With the Sun	Air
N	D	D	D

Table 18.10: LeBron James: Munakara Venus' Sequence

chose not to renew his contract with the Cleveland Cavaliers, without first taking them to a premiership. Robert Hand describes out-of-sect Venus as "a warrior-type Venus"[80] and this description certainly suits 9th-house Venus ruling the 5th house (sport and entertainment) and the 12th house ('hidden enemies, deceivers, persons who hate.')[81]

Munakara Venus: LeBron James

"I hate letting my teammates down. I know I'm not going to make every shot. Sometimes I try to make the right play, and if it results in a loss, I feel awful. I don't feel awful because I have to answer questions about it. I feel awful in that locker room because I could have done something more to help my teammates win." – LeBron James

Munakara Venus in Aquarius in 9th House (Placidus and Whole Sign)

James's Aquarian Venus is nocturnal, and is disposited by the same Saturn which is munakara, and is disposited by Mars. Munakara Venus has taught the eight-year-old boy, at the start of his second Venus cycle, the kindness of strangers (Venus rules 12th house) and the true meaning of friendship, teamwork, loyalty, and camaraderie through the aspect to its dispositor, Saturn. James has payed Walker's kindness forward in his own life as an adult funding the "I PROMISE" School in Akron aimed at educating at-risk children and the "I PROMISE" Village which provides accommodation for its students. Again, the connection between Venus' 5th house rulership (children) and its 12th house rulership (institutional protection) has brought out the best in James' munakara.

Dual munakara planets have also taught the man commitment and responsibility through the same square which has played out via Venus' rulership of the 5th house (sport and recreation). Given James' 62,000 minutes of playing time, counted in regular seasons and playoffs,[82] it has also imbued him with a strong work ethic as Saturn, Venus' dispositor, is placed in the 6th house.

Another curious aspect of munakara Venus ruling the 5th and 12th house, may have contributed to James's double-decade career, is the amount of time in which Venus needs to withdraw in order to keep competing in professional basketball. In one post-game press conference (Dec 15, 2021) James confirmed that he believes one of the reasons for his career's longevity is his dedication to getting 12 hours of sleep a night. "A multiple of his teammates over the years having joked that James is basically either sleeping or playing basketball."[83] Perhaps an odd bi-product of contention is that an aspect between two planets in munakara can create extreme behaviour, and not all munakara behaviour is necessarily bad.

First Dispositor: Saturn in Scorpio (First Dispositor also Munakara)

Venus is the planet of relationship and the astrological representative for women in general. Venus in Aquarius, disposited by Saturn and square Saturn in Scorpio, could have gone in many different directions relationship-wise for a man who has received so much adoration from fans, both male and female, since his boyhood and into adulthood.

Media attention could have focused on a tumultuous love-life over the past two decades, after all, magazines are full of the sexual exploits of many famous athletes and superstars. Instead, we find a man who meets his life partner at high school and remains married and faithful to the junior cheerleader he asked out as a teenager. His wife Savannah says "I just thought he would be a hometown hero for his era and it would be over."[84] Fidelity is obviously a big thing for LeBron James: fidelity to his wife and family, fidelity to his friends and to the management machine that works around him, fidelity to his NBA contracts, and fidelity to his teammates, in pushing for greater benefits for retired players and changing the league's salary cap in 2016. Pure Saturn/Venus energy talks when James says of his wife, "Savannah was down when I was at my high school, no cameras, no lights. And she was there with me," he told *People* magazine in 2018. "You wouldn't be talking to me right now if it weren't for her."[85]

The outcome planet: Mars in Pisces on MC

"Once you get on the playing field it's not about whether you're liked or not liked. All that matters is to play at a high level and do whatever it takes to help your team win. That's what it's about."[86] – LeBron James

The same Venus in munakara also has Mars as its final outcome planet, and this too has played out strongly in James' professional and personal life. In an unnerving echo of the three-step process for munakara, LeBron James fulfilled his contractual obligations and opted to become an unrestricted free agent not once, but three times in his basketball career. This bold move has been a signature of the past twenty years of his career, and as painful as it has been for him, it has revolutionized the contractual obligations of fellow basketball players. The elevated Mars rules the 11th house, and James served as the first vice president of the NBA's labour union, the National Basketball

Chapter Eighteen • *Munakara Saturn Delineations*

Players Association from 2015–2019. Mars is conjunct his Mid-heaven and can be seen as his mark as a professional athlete, but it also demonstrates the struggles he has endured along the way to fight his battles publicly, and to take the heat when he judges something to be unbalanced or unfair.

Much has been written about *'The Decision'*, a live interview held on 8th July 2010 with James, who had become an unrestricted free agent from Cleveland Cavaliers seven days before the interview. ESPN's Jim Gray grilled an uncomfortable James for 30 minutes, until his guest announced that he was leaving the Cavaliers and had signed with Miami Heat. The fall-out for James was cruel as his Cavalier fans turned on him, burning his shirts and destroying billboards with his image.

In 20/20 hindsight *The Decision* led to a new age in NBA history, which increased player empowerment, and made way for the first player-created NBA super-team in the 2010 Miami Heat, but James' Venus in contention paid a heavy price. Returning to his hometown stadium for the first time on 2nd December 2010 in an enemy's colours meant facing a barrage of hate and abuse, and James tried his best to ignore them, but he was clearly upset.

It wasn't until James re-signed with Cavaliers four years later in 2014, and won them the Championship in 2016 to break a 52-year drought, that his fans began to forgive him. One can only imagine the courage it would take to walk back into a hostile city, and to try to reclaim the hearts of those who had sworn that he would never earn their respect and trust after his public betrayal. Munakara is going into a foreign territory with no resources and no-one to trust, and this is exactly what LeBron James chose to do by returning to the Cavaliers. Ernest Hemingway once said "Courage is grace under pressure" and this feels like a perfect summary for LeBron James' Venus in munakara.

In LeBron James' first interview since joining the Los Angeles Lakers in 2018 he spoke to ESPN's Rachel Nichols in the library of his foundation's I Promise School in Akron, Ohio.

James tells Rachel, "We want to create an environment of family, where you want to always be around your family no matter the good and the bad, you always want to be around that support system."[87]

'I Promise' is a co-production between James' Foundation and the Akron Public School District, and is an ambitious project that began as a 5-mile bike race to raise funds for tutoring, and support all kinds of shoulder programming. The day of the interview was James' first visit to the school ready to begin with a student body of 240 at-risk kids who would participate in a program that has a longer school year, and longer school days. The school opens early in the morning to provide breakfast for its students, and the school day runs to 5 o'clock. The idea of a longer school day is designed to keep the students in a supported system that protects them from a dangerous world on the streets, to feed them breakfast, lunch and a snack, and to give them a safe environment in which they can grow and learn. The objective of 'I Promise' is to nurture, support, care for, and build a decent structure to educate those children who would normally slip through the cracks of the education establishment – all the best qualities of Saturn and Venus in munakara.

The taped interview begins with a quick tour of the school's main hallway and the camera captures just a sneak peak of James' face in rapture as he views the murals on the walls for the first time. Painted on the walls is an image of Martin Luther King Jr. alongside his words "There is no gain without struggle", but even more telling for Saturn and Venus in contention is The Promise, inscribed in huge lettering on the foyer walls:[88]

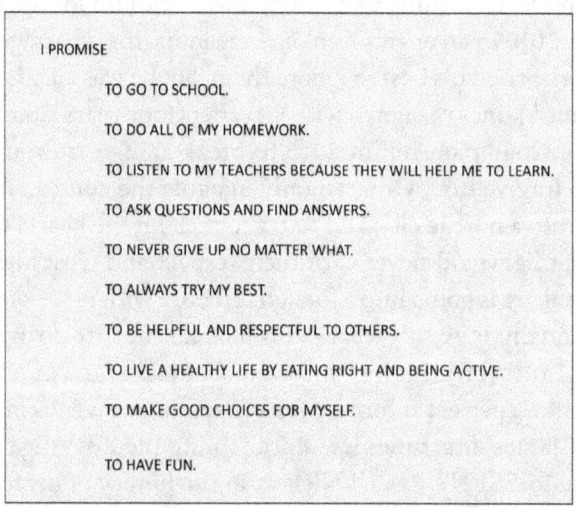

Table 18.11: LeBron James's: The 'I Promise' School Pledge

Munakara planets are planets that are familiar with criticism, naysayers, and outsiders who fault-find but offer few constructive solutions to a problem. Even good or unselfish acts can bring controversy and dispute or disapproval. The I Promise school is not without its detractors, and global news in July 2023 reported that year 8 students from James's school were failing to meet the required standards of education as no student had passed the state math test for the past three years.[89] Whilst the school board president feels

Chapter Eighteen • *Munakara Saturn Delineations*

despondent, he is also baffled by the poor results, saying "I just think about all the resources that we're providing, and I'm just disappointed that I don't think, it doesn't appear like we're seeing the kind of change that we would expect to see."[90]

But planets in contention are fighting planets and munakara Saturn and munakara Venus both involve James' Mars on his MC – as first dispositor for Saturn and outcome planet for Venus. You don't maintain a successful 20 year career in an elite sport without Mars being a particularly sharp and competitive battler. So it is no surprise when James' Family Foundation responded to the article with the following statement:

> "When we started this work to wraparound students through education, we entered this partnership with Akron Public School for the long haul because this work requires a long-term commitment, hard work, and a lot of love and care.
>
> And that's what we bring each and every day because the I Promise School is more than a school. We're here for the ups and downs, and will continue to wraparound our students and their entire families so they can be successful in school and in life, no matter the challenges and obstacles that come their way.
>
> Signed: LeBron James"[91]

A FINAL WORD ON MUNAKARA

Traditional astrologers can sometimes be accused of being rigid in adhering to the rules of judgement, or bleak in their assessment of a planet's pitfalls and potential effects on a chart. I was cautious to introduce yet another 'negative' ruling from an ancient source for fear of adding to the notion that traditionalists were perpetually pessimistic when it came to reading a chart.

Moreover, the topic of munakara is largely unchartered territory, and its unknown quality in chart delineation has made it, at times, a solitary journey. It has constantly tested my abilities and my resolve to publish the findings of my work on it. When I first discussed al-Biruni's text on munakara, I found the technique was unknown to the astrologers around me and I was frequently called to explain the sequencing process, thereby helping to cement it in my own mind. I often witnessed a resistance to the idea and sometimes found myself defending its application, or worse, justifying the merits of this process written down in the 12th century by an Iranian astrologer.

However, it is with deep gratitude to Jenn Zahrt of Revelore Press, whose enthusiasm for the subject material matched my own, that this book has taken life. Her encouragement and gentle guidance allowed me to meander through my own understanding of munakara on a practical level and gave rise to the book you hold now. The love and support of my partner, family, and friends have also nourished me over the past two years, and I thank them for their constant patience and understanding.

The principle of munakara is surprisingly simple, as long as the astrologer takes the time to develop their understanding of how to move planets back and forth between diurnal and nocturnal territories. A short, concise chapter on each planet could have been sufficient to explain munakara in its possible sequences. But the richness and depth of munakara is not found in its theoretical foundations, but in the practical application of them.

For that reason, I chose to dive into some example charts to demonstrate practical applications of munakara. My research unveiled a parade of fascinating discoveries – that Christopher Reeve's Moon was in munakara, that Elon Musk and Julian Assange share both Jupiter and Mars in contention, and that Harry and Meghan, Duke and Duchess of Sussex, are drawn together by their distrust of authority through Saturn in their charts being in contention. The fact that a number of brilliant, tortured artists – Janis Joplin, Elvis Presley, Kurt Cobain, Robin Williams, to name just a few – have a planet, or planets, that cross the sect divide, is noteworthy and knowing they all possess planets with munakara status may give some insight into the demons that plagued them.

Does this mean that all brilliant, tortured artists have munakara planets in conflict lurking somewhere in their chart? Of course not. But in my view, munakara is important. It has reaffirmed my belief in astrology's power to heal and convinced me that finding a planet or planets in munakara is not a cosmic curse, or even a divine blessing for that matter. Rather, contention is something that is outside our control, and it can provide an extra tool for better understanding the complexities of an individual's life.

My choice in example charts was measured, namely because their clarity demonstrated the possible difficulty when dealing with the energy of contentious planets. For example, Christopher Reeve's munakara Moon is not just the story of the extreme physical restrictions caused by his horse-riding accident. The paralysis certainly plays a large part in his later life, but his Sagittarian Moon in contention is not solely concentrated on his disability. Rather, the munakara Moon describes the mental strength Reeve displayed whilst enduring his gruelling daily rehabilitation schedule. It describes his courageous determination to challenge US laws outlawing embryonic stem cell therapy, fighting for justice in changing the laws so that he, and hundreds like him, could regain self-control over their lives.

Fifteenth-century artist Albrecht Dürer's Gemini Moon in contention is not restricted to his obsession with capturing the proportions of the human body and cataloguing its physical decline through the ravages of illness and old age. His luminary in munakara speaks of his need to capture the history of his mother's hard life through her early aging process and the wasting disease, possibly cancer, which took her life. His Moon disposited by Mercury gave him his steady hand for engraving and minute detail in his artwork. However, it also gave him the mindset to believe that through reproducing art in printing, he could gift ordinary people with the ability to view and purchase his work. His passion, his wisdom, and his sense of justice meant that original works of art were no longer solely in the hands of a privileged few, gathering dust in the halls of European noblemen, or held in the cloistered confines of the Church or the University. Generations of artists have Albrecht Dürer to thank for the broadening of their work, achieving success, popularity, and the ability to make a living from their artwork through sales in large numbers, rather than depending on sporadic commissions from a few wealthy aristocrats.

Whilst some individuals with planets in contention have overcome insurmountable odds, history shows that others made mistakes which have been severely judged by future generations. The tortured philosopher Friedrich Nietzsche had two planets in munakara, his Sun and Mars. Mercury's involvement with both planets' sequence – outcome planet for the Sun, and first dispositor for Mars – drove him to insanity through his relentless search for wisdom.

The charismatic creator of Nirvana, Kurt Cobain, lived his short life surrounded by a history of family violence and self-harm, and while temperance and self-control may have lengthened his life, it may also have destroyed his creative genius. The combination of debilitated Mercury and exalted Venus in Pisces produced two planets in munakara, and Cobain's angst over his lover's rejection was fertile ground for the musical poet, who encapsulated his generation's pain in *Nevermind*, Nirvana's timeless album.

It may be those charts which feature multiple munakara planets are the individuals who are pulled in a multitude of directions, so much so, that it seems their virtues are either stretched to the limit, or somehow become contorted to suit their personality.

Six out of seven planets in John Dee's chart (1527–1608) were munakara planets, with the exception being Mars in Scorpio. Dee was a 16th-century mathematician, astrologer, alchemist, and court astronomer to Queen Elizabeth I. However, his reputation diminished when Elizabeth I died and her successor, James I of England, banished Dee from the English Court. In his later years Dee's reputation was further ruined by his obsession to communicate with angels, who he believed would help him solve the mysteries of the universe through mathematics, optics, astrology, science, and navigation.

Christopher McCandless' search for an almost monastic lifestyle resulted in his death, captured in the story of *Into the Wild*. McCandless' journey into the wilderness may not have intentionally been his atonement for society's sins, but his rejection of physical comfort, security, wealth, and human contact became a symbol for the youth of the day. McCandless had five planets in a state of munakara – his luminaries, Aquarius Sun and Leo Moon, were free of contention – but his Saturn in Aries seems to be particularly prominent, given that it features in four of his five munakara sequences.

Munakara is not unique to the charts of the rich and famous; these burning bright stars with embattled luminaries pushing their limits to greatness. It exists in charts all around us, and my hope is that as it has for me, for you too, it may provide an extra lens through which to view the chart of an individual striving to understand their own complexities and battles. Contention has the potential to be an instrument for the client to lay foundations as to who they are, adding to the depths of their chart, and nourishing their soul's journey. My hope is that astrologers can take contention as another lens through which to view the world and guide themselves and their clients to a deeper understanding through an ancient and nearly lost pearl of wisdom.

My final thoughts on al-Biruni? First-century philosopher, Lucius Annaeus Seneca, believed that the great founders of philosophical schools gave human beings a way of life to follow, and even though they have long passed, we still have access to the gifts of knowledge they left behind. Similarly, the ancient astrologers added their own wisdom and they too have passed on many valuable treasures. I would like to think that by immersing ourselves in the works of al-Biruni, and all great astrologers from past times, we can learn from them in a time which is "boundless, ever-lasting, and which we share with better minds" (*Shortness of Life*, 14.1–2).

I sincerely hope that al-Biruni's words on munakara, and this, my humble attempt at a practical reference book on its application, will be useful additions to your own astrological practice and in your own boundless, ever-lasting search for knowledge.

ENDNOTES

All URLs last accessed April 2025.

Notes to Introduction

1. The Islamic Golden Age refers to a period in the history of Islam, traditionally dated from the 8th century to the 13th century, during which much of the historically Islamic world was ruled by various caliphates and science, economic development, and cultural works flourished." The Islamic Golden Age, World Civilization: lumenlearning.com.
2. Mohammad Ardi, Fatimah Abdullah, and Shihab Tamimi, "Al-Biruni: A Muslim Critical Thinker," *International Journal of Nusantara Islam* 4.1 (2016): 10.15575/ijni.v4i1.490.
3. Ardi et al., "Al-Biruni, A Muslim Critical Thinker." Zakaria Virk, "Al-Biruni: The Scholar and Saint (973–1048)," pp. 1–12 in https://www.academia.edu/6593351/Al_Biruni_a_distinguished_scientist_from_Afghanistan; Regarding al-Biruni's birth date of 15th September 973, enquiry to Z. Virk. Email from Z. Virk, dated 13th July 2022: "I got his date of birth from a book, link is given below https://catalogue.nla.gov.au/Record/136499 and https://catalogue.nla.gov.au/Record/1364990 Al-Biruni commemorative volume proceedings of international congress held in Karachi on the occasion of abu raihan Muhammad Ibn Ahmad al-Biruni 973–1051, Nov. 6, 1973 to Dec. 12, 1973."
4. Ardi *et al.*, "Al-Biruni, A Muslim Critical Thinker," p. 3.
5. Virk, "Al-Biruni: The Scholar and Saint."
6. *Ibid.*, p. 10.
7. Al-Biruni, *The Book of Instruction in the Elements of the Art of Astrology*, originally written in Ghaznah in 1029 CE, reproduced from British Museum MS Or. 8349, translation by R. Ramsay Wright, MA (LUZAC, 1934).
8. Virk, "Al-Biruni: The Scholar and Saint."
9. Bruce Lawrence, "Al-Biruni, Against the Grain," *Critical Muslim* 12.2 "Dangerous Freethinkers," (Oct–Dec 2014): https://www.criticalmuslim.io/al-baruni-against-the-grain/
10. Amelia Carolina Sparavigna, "The Science of Al-Biruni," *International Journal of Sciences* 2.12 (December 2013): 52–60, Available at SSRN: https://ssrn.com/abstract=2862369

Notes to Chapter One

1. Al-Biruni, *The Book of Instruction*, p. 308. Please note that al-Biruni uses the Arabic spelling of 'hayyiz', which is now more commonly latinised as 'hayz'.
2. *Ibid.*, p. 308.
3. https://www.shabdkosh.com/dictionary/punjabi-english/munakara/munakara-meaning-in-english

Notes to Chapter Two

1. Al-Biruni, *The Book of Instruction*, Notation 447 Friendship and Enmity of Planets, pp. 260–61.
2. *Ibid.*, p. 308.

Notes to Chapter Three

1. Last verse from *Society* from the album *Into the Wild* (2007) by Eddie Vedder and the soundtrack to the film of the same name, lyrics by Jerry Hannan. Book and film based on the true story of Christopher McCandless.
2. Peter Guralnick, *Careless Love: The Unmaking of Elvis Presley* (Back Bay Books, 1999), pp. 106, 108–11.
3. *Ibid.*, p. 110.
4. *Ibid.*, p. 119.
5. Greil Marcus, "Elvis Presley: The Ed Sullivan Shows" (2006): https://web.archive.org/web/20111219163909/http://www.msopr.com/n/past-campaigns/elvis-presley-the-ed-sullivan-shows/
6. https://lithub.com/when-young-elvis-met-the-legendary-b-b-king/
7. *Ibid.*
8. Peter Whitmer, *The Inner Elvis* (Hyperion, 1997).
9. Guralnick, *Careless Love*, p. 248.
10. Adam Victor, *The Elvis Encyclopedia* (Overlook, 2008), p. 419.
11. https://www.news.com.au/entertainment/celebrity-life/10-weird-things-you-might-not-know-about-elvis/news-story/2ddf3ff632d9103e54ccad3ef3fa824e
12. Guralnick, *Careless Love*, pp. 474–80.
13. https://www.thesun.co.uk/tvandshowbiz/18966268/gladys-presley-elvis-mum/
14. Guralnick, *Careless Love*, p. 13.
15. Peter Harry Brown and Pat H. Broeske, *Down at the End of Lonely Street: The Life and Death of Elvis Presley* (Signet, 1997), p. 55.
16. Victor, *The Elvis Encyclopedia*, p. 27.
17. Dave Rogers, *Rock 'n' Roll* (Routledge & Kegan Paul, 1982).
18. John Frayn Turner, *Frank Sinatra* (Taylor Trade, 2004), p. 104.
19. Earl Greenwood, *The Boy Who Would Be King* (Dutton, 1990), p.192.
20. Victor, *The Elvis Encyclopedia*, p. 527.
21. *Ibid.*, pp. 142–46.
22. Gilbert B. Rodman, *Elvis After Elvis: The Posthumous Career of a Living Legend* (Routledge, 1996), p. 193.

Notes

Notes to Chapter Four

1. James Herschel Holden, *Five Medieval Astrologers* (AFA, 2008), *The Centiloquy of Hermes Trismegistus*, p. 94.
2. https://www.hrp.org.uk/hampton-court-palace/history-and-stories/henry-viii/#gs.83s18h.
3. *Letters and Papers, Foreign and Domestic, of the Reign of Henry VIII: Jan.-Aug. 1540* (H.M. Stationery Office, 1896), p. 391.
4. *Ibid.*

Notes to Chapter Five

1. Robert Hand, *Night & Day: Planetary Sect in Astrology* (ARHAT, 1995), p. 8.
2. *Ibid.*, p. 25.
3. *Ibid.*
4. Robert Hand, Webinar, *Night & Day: The effects of daytime & night time on birth charts*, (27 July 2015), www.arhatmedia.com, [Accessed 3 August 2015]: Scoring Venus well in Points 24–28, Out of sect Venus, Point 30.
5. Notes from Hand, *Night & Day* (webinar).
6. Quote by Krist Novoselic, friend and bandmate of Kurt Cobain, and co-founder of Nirvana.
7. Hector Bolitho, *Albert, Prince Consort* (Bobbs-Merrill, 1964; repr. 2014, Endeavor Press, Kindle Ed.)
8. Amy Winehouse quote, https://www.imdb.com/name/nm1561881/quotes/
9. *Ibid.*
10. https://www.astro.com/astro-databank/Brando,_Cheyenne
11. https://pasajealaciencia.es/darwin-and-his-time-the-victorian-age/
12. *Ibid.*
13. Theodore Martin, *The Life of His Royal Highness the Prince Consort, Vol. 2*, (D. Appleton, 1877), p. 201–8, esp. 204–5.
14. Roger Fulford, *The Prince Consort* (Macmillan, 1949), pp. 57–58, 276; Hermione Hobhouse, *Prince Albert: His Life and Work* (Hamish Hamilton, 1983), pp. viii, 39.
15. https://kids.britannica.com/students/article/Albert-prince-consort-of-Great-Britain-and-Ireland/315979

Notes to Chapter Six

1. Vettius Valens, *The Anthologies, Book One,* trans. Mark Riley, (2010): http://www.csus.edu/indiv/r/rileymt/
2. Ami Sweetman, "Books: *Out of Chaos Comes a Dancing Star: Notes on Professional Burnout*: Stress Resilience." British Journal of General Practice 65.633 (2015): pp. 202–3.
3. Tee Corinne, "Artist's statement: On Sexual Art," *Feminist Studies* 19.2 (1993): pp. 369–76.
4. Pat Jordan, "Evel Never Dies" *Maxim* Magazine (Nov. 16, 2007).
5. https://www.cosmopolitan.com/uk/body/a33838303/katy-perry-depression-suicidal-thoughts/
6. *Ibid.*
7. Hannah Wootton, "'A tale of two teenage dreams': Katie Perry beats Katy Perry in court," *Financial Review* (April 27, 2023), https://www.afr.com/life-and-luxury/fashion-and-style/a-tale-of-two-teenage-dreams-katie-perry-beats-katy-perry-in-court-20230427-p5d3qr
8. Claire Hoffman, "Katy Conquers All," *Marie Claire* (Dec. 9, 2013): https://www.marieclaire.com/celebrity/a8596/katy-perry-interview-january-cover/

9. Amy Wallace, "Katy Perry's *GQ* Profile Outtakes: Going Back to School, Dating Musicians, and Plastic Surgery," *GQ* (January 19, 2014). https://www.gq.com/blogs/the-feed/2014/02/cover-katy-perry-interview-outtakes.html
10. Lynn Hirschberg, "Katy Perry," *W* (Oct. 22, 2013).
11. Hand, *Night & Day* (webinar).
12. Hoffman, "Katy Conquers All." *Op. cit.*
13. Nardine Saad, "Katy Perry's First *Vogue* Cover," *Los Angeles Times* (Jun. 18, 2013).
14. "Katy Perry: Part of Me," *Box Office Mojo*: https://www.boxofficemojo.com/release/rl3277686273/
15. Eric Frankenberg, "25 Biggest Concert Residencies of All Time" *Billboard* (Apr. 5, 2024).
16. Katy Perry, "I wrote the title track from the album when I was coming through one of the darkest periods of my life and had lost my smile. This whole album is my journey towards the light – with stories of resilience, hope, and love." (Jul. 9, 2020): https://x.com/katyperry/status/1281228120905793538
17. Janet Krajcsik, "Katy Perry reveals she felt suicidal during 2017 split from Orlando Bloom," *The Patriot News* (Jun. 29, 2020).
18. Gary Graff, "Interview: Katy Perry – Hot N Bold," *The Scotsman* (Feb. 21, 2009).
19. Katy Perry, *E! News* Interview, (Sept. 21, 2022): https://www.etonline.com/why-katy-perry-says-shell-never-have-a-full-time-nanny-for-daughter-daisy-191302
20. https://www.dailymail.co.uk/tvshowbiz/article-13168607/Kelly-Osbourne-Aimee-frosty-relationship.html
21. *Ibid.*
22. Kelly Osbourne, *There is no f*cking secret: Letters from a bad ass bitch* (Putnam & Sons, 2017), p. 191.
23. *Ibid.*, p. 209.
24. *Ibid.*, p. 211.
25. https://people.com/parents/kelly-osbourne-speaks-out-after-mom-sharon-reveals-baby-name/

Notes to Chapter Seven

1. Hand, *Night & Day, op. cit.*, pp. 23, 25.
2. https://www.astro.com/astro-databank/Bailey,_Alice_A.
3. https://blavatskytheosophy.com/14-good-reasons-to-reject-the-alice-bailey-teachings/
4. Ryan Holiday, *The Daily Stoic: 366 Meditations on Wisdom, Perseverance, and the Art of Living* (Portfolio, 2016), July 18: Each the Master of their Own Domain.
5. Friedrich Nietzsche, *Zarathustra's Prologue 3, Book 1*, https://www.age-of-the-sage.org/philosophy/nietzsche_philosophy.html#:~:text=%22Man%20is%20a%20rope%2C%20tied,overture%20and%20a%20going%20under.
6. Claudius Ptolemy, *Ptolemy's Tetrabiblos or Quadripartite*, Ashmand Translation, 1822, Appendix No. III, *The Centiloquy, or, Hundred Aphorisms of Claudius Ptolemy*, otherwise called *The Fruit of his Four Books*, p. 105.
7. https://www.independent.co.uk/life-style/royal-family/princess-diana-queen-elizabeth-relationship-b2170476.html
8. Gyles Brandreth, *Charles and Camilla: Portrait of a Love Affair* (Random House, 2007), p. 183–96; Carolly Erickson, *Lilibet: An Intimate Portrait of Elizabeth II*, (St. Martin's Griffin, 2005), p. 350.
9. https://www.history.com/news/princess-diana-bbc-interview-martin-bashir

Notes

10. Ptolemy's *Tetrabiblos or Quadripartite*, Ashmand Trans., p. 154.
11. https://www.fivecentsound.com/blog/progression-of-women-in-rock
12. Hand, *Night & Day, op. cit.*, p. 23.
13. Myra Friedman, *Buried Alive: The Biography of Janis Joplin*, 4th ed., (Harmony, 1992), Introduction.
14. John Byrne Cooke, *On the Road with Janis* Joplin (Berkley Books, 2014); John B. Cooke *Janis Joplin: A Performance Diary 1966–1970* (Acid Test, 1997), p. 126.
15. https://theconversation.com/on-the-50th-anniversary-of-her-death-janis-joplin-still-ignites-147097
16. "What Happened to Janis Joplin," (Dark Crimes, 2021): https://www.youtube.com/watch?v=EZ7VquVrDNc
17. "Janis: Little Girl Blue": https://www.youtube.com/watch?v=dnYfJTGTGk4
18. https://www.theguardian.com/music/article/2024/jun/13/she-knew-where-she-wanted-to-go-and-just-kept-going-the-real-janis-joplin-by-those-closest-to-her
19. "Dick Cavett TV Interview (1970)," *The Dick Cavett Show*. (Aug. 3, 1970).
20. https://www.theguardian.com/music/article/2024/jun/13/she-knew-where-she-wanted-to-go-and-just-kept-going-the-real-janis-joplin-by-those-closest-to-her
21. Murieln Dimen, "In the Zone of Ambivalence: A Journal of Competition," p. 363, in Susan Ostrov Weisser and Jennifer Fleischner, eds., *Feminist Nightmares: Women at Odds: Feminism and the Problem of Sisterhood* (NYU Press, 1994).
22. Janis Joplin interviewed on the *Pop Chronicles* (1969)
23. "The Tortured Life of Janis Joplin": https://www.youtube.com/watch?v=WknDN0X3CdQ
24. https://www.theguardian.com/music/article/2024/jun/13/she-knew-where-she-wanted-to-go-and-just-kept-going-the-real-janis-joplin-by-those-closest-to-her
25. "Janis: Little Girl Blue" *Op. cit.*
26. *Ibid.*, 1:16:46.
27. Paul Hendrickson, "Janis Joplin: A Cry Cutting through Time," *The Washington Post* (May 5, 1998).
28. Jesse Jarnow, "Woodstock Music and Arts Fair," *Oxford Music Online* – Oxford University Press. https://doi.org/10.1093/gmo/9781561592630.article.A2258729
29. Chris Albertson, *Bessie Smith: Empress of the Blues* (Macmillan, 1975). p. 277.
30. https://www.fugues.com/2020/10/01/the-redemption-of-peggy-caserta/
31. Hand, *Night & Day, op. cit.*, p. 25.

Notes to Chapter Eight

1. Ptolemy's *Tetrabiblos or Quadripartite*, Ashmand Trans., pp. 58, 59.
2. https://www.rollingstone.com/culture/culture-features/elon-musk-the-architect-of-tomorrow-120850/, Accessed August 2024
3. Holden, *The Centiloquy of Hermes Trismegistus, op. cit.*, p. 94.
4. https://www.britannica.com/money/Elon-Musk
5. https://www.investopedia.com/articles/investing/012715/5-richest-people-world.asp
6. https://www.britannica.com/money/Elon-Musk
7. https://www.britannica.com/biography/Julian-Assange
8. https://www.canberratimes.com.au/story/8694445/musk-donates-to-group-working-to-elect-trump-report/ ; https://www.bloomberg.com/news/articles/2024-07-12/elon-musk-donates-to-trump-tapping-vast-fortune-to-swing-2024-race
9. https://time.com/7021537/musk-x-post-trump-assassination-attempt/

10. https://newrepublic.com/post/185541/x-elon-musk-failure-platform-value
11. *Ibid.*
12. *Ibid.*
13. Hand, *Night & Day, op. cit.,* p. 22.
14. https://www.abc.net.au/news/2023-11-02/twitter-elon-musk-one-year-world-human-rights-x-social-media/103044304
15. *Ibid.*
16. https://www.theguardian.com/technology/2023/oct/10/eu-warns-elon-musk-over-disinformation-about-hamas-attack-on-x
17. https://www.goodreads.com/quotes/10991047-my-children-didn-t-choose-to-be-born-i-chose-to
18. https://www.businessinsider.com/elon-musk-children
19. https://futurism.com/neoscope/elon-musk-responds-to-health-concerns
20. https://www.indiatoday.in/technology/news/story/elon-musk-shares-his-secret-work-method-for-being-productive-120-hours-a-week-2519639-2024-03-26
21. https://www.cnbc.com/2023/05/18/elon-musk-sacrificing-sleep-for-productivity-gave-me-brain-pain.html#:~:text=Musk%20often%20works%20seven%20days,year%2C%20he%20said%20on%20Tuesday.
22. https://edition.cnn.com/2024/03/18/tech/elon-musk-ketamine-use-don-lemon-interview/index.html
23. https://www.healthline.com/health-news/elon-musk-ketamine-depression-treatment#What-is-ketamine?
24. https://www.youtube.com/watch?v=R2meHtrO1n8
25. https://www.theguardian.com/technology/2023/nov/02/top-tech-firms-to-let-governments-vet-ai-tools-sunak-says-at-safety-summit
26. https://www.theguardian.com/technology/2023/nov/01/elon-musk-calls-ai-one-of-the-biggest-threats-to-humanity-at-summit
27. https://www.britannica.com/biography/Elon-Musk
28. https://www.abc.net.au/news/2023-01-08/twitter-moderation-staff-cuts/101835434
29. https://futurism.com/neoscope/elon-musk-responds-to-health-concerns
30. https://www.abc.net.au/news/2023-11-02/twitter-elon-musk-one-year-world-human-rights-x-social-media/103044304
31. https://www.theguardian.com/technology/2022/nov/26/elon-musk-says-he-will-back-trump-rival-ron-desantis-in-2024-if-he-runs-for-president
32. https://www.bloomberg.com/news/articles/2024-07-16/elon-musk-becomes-donald-trump-s-kingmaker
33. https://edition.cnn.com/2024/07/12/tech/x-breaching-eu-rules-musk/index.html
34. https://www.theguardian.com/commentisfree/2023/oct/23/why-is-elon-musk-attacking-wikipedia-because-its-very-existence-offends-him
35. Hand, *Night & Day* (webinar), *op. cit.,* p. 6.
36. Hand, *Night & Day, op. cit.,* p. 23.
37. http://edition.cnn.com/2010/US/12/16/assange.dating.profile/index.html
38. *Julian Assange in His Own Words,* Compiled and Edited by Karen Sharpe, (O/R Books, 2021), p. 105.
39. Kim Zetter, "Video: The Time Julian Assange Hacked the Pentagon," *Wired*: https://www.wired.com/2010/12/wikirebels-documentary/
40. Andy Greenberg, *This Machine Kills Secrets: Julian Assange, the Cypherpunks, and their Fight to Empower Whistleblowers* (Plume, 2013).

Notes

41. David Leigh, and Luke Harding, "Julian Assange: the teen hacker who became insurgent in information war," *The Guardian*. (Jan. 30, 2011).
42. Andrew Fowler, *The Most Dangerous Man in the World: Julian Assange and WikiLeaks' Fight for Freedom*, 2nd ed., (Melbourne UP, 2020).
43. *Julian Assange in His Own Words*, p. 19.
44. *Ibid.*, p. 33.
45. Fowler, *The Most Dangerous Man in the World*.
46. *Ibid.*, p. 40.
47. *Ibid.*, p. 40.
48. *Ibid.*, p. 41.
49. *Julian Assange: The Unauthorised Autobiography* (Text, 2011), p. 32.
50. https://www.astro.com/astro-databank/Assange,_Julian
51. John F. Burns, Ravi Somaiya, "WikiLeaks Founder on the Run, Trailed by Notoriety," *The New York Times* (Oct. 23, 2010).
52. *Ibid.*
53. *Julian Assange in His Own Words*, p. 20.
54. *Ibid.*, p. 33.
55. Fowler, *The Most Dangerous Man in the World*, p. xxx.
56. *Ibid.*
57. https://www.youtube.com/watch?v=P6bVl47kdNk
58. https://www.wsws.org/en/articles/2023/11/02/bkke-n02.html Albanese's comments expose charade that Australian government is trying to free Julian Assange.
59. https://www.thesaturdaypaper.com.au/comment/topic/2023/11/04/assange-test-us-friendship#mtr
60. *Julian Assange in His Own Words*, p. 163.
61. *Ibid.*, p. 158.
62. Fowler, *The Most Dangerous Man in the World*, Introduction.
63. *Ibid.*, p. 39.

Notes to Chapter Nine

1. https://web.archive.org/web/20061204162542/http://www.ala.org/ala/ppo/currentprograms/frankenstein/exhibittext.pdf
2. https://www.aruma.com.au/about-us/blog/8-incredible-facts-about-helen-keller/
3. https://www.brainyquote.com/quotes/epictetus_106298
4. https://www.standard.co.uk/news/royals/prince-harry-best-quotes-meghan-markle-a4005271.html
5. Amber Raiken, "Prince Harry recalls fight with Meghan Markle that led him to seek therapy," *The Independent* (Jan. 6, 2023).
6. Andrea Michelson, "Prince Harry says 'pain and suffering' is in the royal family's DNA. Here's how genetic trauma works," *Insider* (May 19, 2021).
7. Karen Mizoguchi, Simon Perry, "Prince Harry Says Requests for Help to His Family Were 'Met with Total Silence, Total Neglect,'" *People* (May 20, 2021).
8. https://www.bbc.com/news/uk-64185317
9. https://nypost.com/2024/07/29/entertainment/why-prince-harrys-huge-inheritance-was-saved-until-his-40th-birthday/
10. https://people.com/royals/prince-harry-on-history-repeating-itself-its-incredibly-triggering-to-potentially-lose-another-woman-in-my-life/#:~:text=You%20want%20

11. https://theconversation.com/prince-harry-says-his-military-kills-were-like-chess-pieces-the-problem-of-seeing-war-as-a-game-197835#:~:text=Harry%20revealed%20that%20he%20killed,to%20call%20for%20his%20prosecution.
12. https://www.standard.co.uk/news/royals/prince-harry-best-quotes-meghan-markle-a4005271.html
13. https://www.abc.net.au/news/2024-07-25/prince-harry-speaks-for-first-time-since-mirror-group-court-case/104139454
14. https://www.abc.net.au/news/2024-07-25/
15. https://people.com/royals/prince-harry-on-history-repeating-itself-its-incredibly-triggering-to-potentially-lose-another-woman-in-my-life/#:~:text=You%20want%20to%20talk%20about,business%20model%2C%20the%20same%20industry.
16. https://www.standard.co.uk/news/royals/prince-harry-best-quotes-meghan-markle-a4005271.html
17. https://people.com/royals/prince-harry-on-history-repeating-itself-its-incredibly-triggering-to-potentially-lose-another-woman-in-my-life/#:~:text=You%20want%20to%20talk%20about,business%20model%2C%20the%20same%20industry.
18. https://www.theguardian.com/uk-news/2024/apr/15/prince-harry-duke-of-sussex-loses-initial-attempt-to-appeal-against-security-ruling
19. https://www.dailymail.co.uk/news/article-13322811/Prince-Harrys-decision-use-date-Meghan-evicted-Frogmore-Cottage-start-residency-reveals-irritation-King-Charles-confirmation-couple-no-intention-living-UK-near-future-royal-experts-say.html
20. https://www.heritage.org/immigration/commentary/my-mission-unlock-the-truth-about-harrys-visa-isnt-personal-its-americas
21. https://www.royal.uk/invictus-games#:~:text=Launching%20the%20Games%2C%20Prince%20Harry,in%20their%20journey%20of%20recovery.%22
22. https://www.news.com.au/sport/more-sports/controversy-erupts-as-prince-harry-awarded-pat-tillman-award-at-the-espys/news-story/b7c9338d0d863cd31fca4b776956b2f4
23. independent.co.uk/news/uk/home-news/prince-harry-invictus-games-award-b2582298.html
24. https://www.livemint.com/news/trends/too-royal-issues-with-meghan-markle-why-2-000-veterans-left-prince-harrys-invictus-games-11714746521507.html
25. https://www.news.com.au/entertainment/celebrity-life/royals/never-see-the-kids-again-prince-harry-accused-of-blackmailing-king-charles/news-story/6db08d2ac156c34333bf35eee31efe94
26. https://uk.style.yahoo.com/inside-prince-charles-harry-difficult-relationship-151659872.html
27. https://www.nowtolove.com.au/royals/king-charles-archie-lilibet/
28. Australian streaming service Stan features a documentary *Meghan and Harry: The New Revelations* (2021) in the usual manner of footage of the couple interspersed with comments from Royal Editors from various publications, two Royal Biographers, and two ladies from the English peerage, and a lawyer and equal rights activist. The documentary discusses claims made in a recent book titled *Finding Freedom and the Making of a Modern Royal Family* by Omid Scobie and Carolyn Durand. Quote by Dylon Howard, author of *Royals at War* (2020).
29. *Meghan and Harry: The New Revelations.*
30. https://people.com/royals/meghan-markle-empowering-quotes/

Notes

31. Kate Shaw, "Oprah with Prince Harry and Meghan Markle — Interview Transcript," (Apr. 4, 2021).
32. https://www.brainyquote.com/authors/meghan-markle-quotes#:~:text=Make%20a%20choice%3A%20continue%20living,your%20parents%20happen%20to%20be.
33. *Ibid.*
34. Andrew Morton, *Meghan: A Hollywood Princess* (Grand Central, 2018).
35. *Ibid.*, Introduction.
36. Shaw, "Oprah with Prince Harry and Meghan Markle."
37. https://edition.cnn.com/2018/02/28/europe/meghan-markle-royal-foundation-forum-intl/index.html
38. *Ibid.*
39. https://todifordaily.com/2020/11/andrew-morton-predicts-a-california-christmas-for-prince-harry-and-meghan-markle/
40. Andrew Morton, *Meghan and the Unmasking of the Monarchy: A Hollywood Princess*, Updated version, (Grand Central, 2021).
41. https://www.businessinsider.com/prince-harry-meghan-markle-king-edward-viii-wallis-simpson-2020-1#markle-revealed-to-winfrey-that-she-began-having-suicidal-thoughts-after-joining-the-royal-family-20
42. https://todifordaily.com/2021/10/talking-to-andrew-morton-about-meghan-and-the-unmasking-of-the-monarchy-meghan-markle-book-video/
43. https://www.washingtonpost.com/world/2022/01/06/meghan-markle-court-case-privacy-daily-mail/
44. https://www.mercurynews.com/2022/04/08/does-meghan-markle-think-she-can-own-the-word-archetypes/
45. Judy Kurtz, "Harry and Meghan's Archewell Audio parts ways with Spotify," *The Hill* (Jun. 16, 2023).
46. Caroline Frost, "Meghan Markle Gives Up On Archetypes Podcast After One Series; Trademark Application Abandoned," *Deadline* (Sept. 23, 2023).
47. https://www.elle.com/uk/life-and-culture/culture/news/a41993/meghan-markle-women-times-up-me-too/
48. *Meghan and Harry: The New Revelations*, op cit. https://www.imdb.com/title/tt14534410/plotsummary/?ref_=tt_ov_pl
49. Birth data obtained directly from Paul Watson via email correspondence on Sept. 25, 2018. From Paul Watson via Caroline Castro, Sea Shepherd Global, Campaigns Media Coordinator: "December 02, 1950. 1 minute after midnight. Born at Women's College Hospital Toronto, York County, Ontario, Canada."

Notes to Chapter Ten

1. https://www.brainyquote.com/authors/amy-winehouse-quotes
2. https://www.nbcnews.com/think/opinion/queen-elizabeth-loved-horses-not-just-corgis-need-celebrate-rcna47762
3. https://www.royal.uk/christmas-broadcast-1966#:~:text=Yet%2C%20in%20spite%20of%20these,determination%20and%20tenacity%20of%20women.
4. https://www.tatler.com/article/the-queens-best-quotes-duty-marriage-motherhood#:~:text=and%20the%20Commonwealth.-,',
5. https://www.bbc.co.uk/newsround/57596969
6. *Ibid.*

7. https://www.rd.com/article/queen-elizabeth-princess-diana-truth-relationship/
8. https://www.royal.uk/christmas-broadcast-2008
9. https://www.abc.net.au/news/2022-11-08/the-crown-season-5-netflix-where-to-watch/101585762
10. https://www.linkedin.com/pulse/work-rent-you-pay-room-occupy-earth-queen-elizabeth-faltot-rittman-1e/
11. Deborah Houlding, *The Houses: Temples of the Sky* (Wessex Astrologer, 2006), p. 11.
12. Pamela Stephenson, *Billy* (HarperCollins, 2001).
13. "Billy Connolly 'most influential comedian of all time'," *BBC News* (Jan. 30, 2012); "Billy Connolly retains top spot in C4 poll" *Comedy.co.uk* (Apr. 11, 2010).
14. Peter Stanford, "Billy Connolly: 'My art is about revealing myself – like being a flasher in a park'," *The Telegraph* (Mar. 11, 2020).
15. https://en.wikipedia.org/wiki/Shrink_Rap_(TV_series)
16. Billy Connolly, *Windswept and Interesting: My Autobiography* (Two Roads, 2021), Unabridged audiobook written and narrated by him.
17. *Ibid.*
18. https://www.britannica.com/biography/Cher
19. *Ibid.*
20. https://www.brainyquote.com/quotes/cher_163347
21. https://www.independent.co.uk/life-style/fashion/cher-balmain-paris-surprise-appearance-b2177848.html
22. Grant McCracken, *Transformations: Identity Construction in Contemporary Culture* (Indiana UP, 2008), p. 27.
23. Caroline Ramazanoglu, *Up Against Foucault: Explorations of Some Tensions Between Foucault and Feminism* (Routledge, 1993), p. 197.
24. https://time.com/4336945/cher-quotes-birthday/
25. James R. Paris and Michael R. Pitts, *Hollywood Songsters: Allyson to Funicello* (Routledge, 2003).
26. https://www.britannica.com/biography/Caitlyn-Jenner
27. *Ibid.*
28. https://www.vanityfair.com/hollywood/2015/06/caitlyn-jenner-bruce-cover-annie-leibovitz
29. David Crary, "LGBTQ activists not excited by Caitlyn Jenner's campaign for governor" *The Associated Press* (Apr. 24, 2021).
30. Katelyn Burns, "Trans people are dreading Caitlyn Jenner's run for governor," *Vox* (Apr. 30, 2021).
31. https://www.britannica.com/biography/Diana-princess-of-Wales
32. *Ibid.*
33. https://en.wikiquote.org/wiki/Diana,_Princess_of_Wales#:~:text=I%20do%20things%20differently%2C%20because,my%20work%2C%20I%20understand%20that.
34. https://www.vanityfair.com/style/2022/04/how-dianas-dance-with-the-media-impacted-william-and-harry
35. https://people.com/royals/all-about-john-spencer-frances-shand-kydd-princess-diana-parents/#:~:text=Diana%20had%20a%20difficult%20relationship,down%20terribly%20with%20the%20wedding
36. https://people.com/royals/charles-spencer-childhood-trauma-sister-princess-diana-new-interview/
37. https://www.goalcast.com/princess-diana-mother-relationship/#:~:text=Princess%20

Notes

Diana%20had%20a%20rocky,spiteful%20towards%20her%20own%20daughter
38. https://www.britannica.com/biography/Catherine-the-Great
39. https://www.alexanderpalace.org/palace/catherine.php
40. https://www.forbes.com/quotes/author/catherine-the-great/
41. https://www.azquotes.com/author/5836-Catherine_the_Great
42. Isabel De Madariaga, "The Foundation of the Russian Educational System by Catherine II," *Slavonic and East European Review* 57.3 (July 1979): pp. 369–95.
43. https://www.azquotes.com/author/5836-Catherine_the_Great
44. Robert K. Massie, *Nagy Katalin: Egy asszony potréja* [*Catherine the Great: Portrait of a Woman*] (in Hungarian) (I.K.C. Könyvek Kft., 2013), p. 22.
45. https://www.alexanderpalace.org/palace/Paul.php
46. Robert Coughlan, and Jay Gold, ed., *Elizabeth and Catherine: Empresses of All the Russias* (Millington, 1974), p. 12.
47. https://www.alexanderpalace.org/palace/Paul.php
48. Susan Jaques, *The Empress of Art* (Simon and Schuster, 2016), Chapter 3.
49. https://www.alexanderpalace.org/palace/Paul.php
50. Ibid.
51. https://www.azquotes.com/quote/1160122
52. https://www.history.com/news/catherine-the-great-enemies-sex-myths
53. Ibid.
54. Ibid.
55. https://commons.wikimedia.org/wiki/File:An_Imperial_stride!_(BM_1868,0808.6035).jpg
56. https://www.oxfordreference.com/display/10.1093/acref/9780191843730.001.0001/q-oro-ed5-00002750#:~:text=Catherine%20the%20Great%201729%E2%80%9396, will%20forgive%20me%3A%20that's%20his.
57. Robert K. Massie, *Catherine the Great: Portrait of a Woman* (Random House, 2011). pp. 274–75.
58. https://www.britannica.com/biography/Catherine-the-Great
59. https://www.britannica.com/event/Instruction-of-Catherine-the-Great
60. https://www.britannica.com/biography/Catherine-the-Great
61. https://www.brainyquote.com/quotes/catherine_the_great_388523#:~:text=Catherine%20the%20Great%20Quotes&text=A%20great%20wind%20is%20blowing%2C%20and%20that%20gives,either%20imagination%20or%20a%20headache.
62. https://www.britannica.com/biography/Edgar-Degas
63. https://www.denverartmuseum.org/en/blog/20-quotes-edgar-degas
64. Ambroise Vollard, *Dega: An Intimate Portrait* (Dover, 1986), p. 64.
65. Marilyn Brown, *Degas and the Business of Art: a Cotton Office in New Orleans* (PSU Press, 1994), p. 11.
66. https://www.sothebys.com/en/articles/21-facts-about-edgar-degas#:~:text=The%20famously%20misanthropic%2C%20cantankerous%20and,was%20one%20of%20the%20last
67. Ibid.
68. Ibid.
69. Ibid.
70. Ibid., p. 32.
71. https://www.denverartmuseum.org/en/blog/20-quotes-edgar-degas
72. Ibid.
73. Vollard, *Dega: An Intimate Portrait*, p. 67.

74. *Ibid.*, p. 42.
75. https://www.denverartmuseum.org/en/blog/20-quotes-edgar-degas
76. https://archive.org/details/degaspor00voll/page/n1/mode/2up
77. https://www.denverartmuseum.org/en/blog/20-quotes-edgar-degas
78. "Neil Diamond retires from touring after Parkinson's diagnosis," *BBC News* (Jan. 22, 2018).
79. Laura Jackson, *Neil Diamond: His Life, His Music, His Passion* (ECW Press, 2005), p. 95.
80. https://www.neildiamond.com/neil-diamond-announces-retirement-concert-touring-australian-new-zealand-tour-dates-cancelled/#/
81. Greg Evans, "Neil Diamond Musical 'A Beautiful Noise' Scores $1M For Opening Week – Broadway Box Office," *Deadline* (Dec. 6, 2022).
82. Eliot Tiegel, "Neil Diamond's Emergence on All Fronts Will Make Him Recognizable Once and for All," *Billboard* (Feb. 19, 1977), pp. 32–33.
83. Chrissie Iley, Interview with Neil Diamond, "Neil Diamond at 71 – in Fashion and in Love," *The Telegraph* (Dec. 2012): https://web.archive.org/web/20121203115817/http://www.telegraph.co.uk/culture/music/9714553/Neil-Diamond-at-71-in-fashion-and-in-love.html
84. *Ibid.*
85. *Ibid.*
86. Rachel Cooke, Interview with Neil Diamond, "Another Sad Lament," *The Guardian* (Apr. 2006): https://www.theguardian.com/music/2006/apr/09/popandrock2
87. *Ibid.*
88. *Ibid.*
89. https://web.archive.org/web/20121203115817/http://www.telegraph.co.uk/culture/music/9714553/Neil-Diamond-at-71-in-fashion-and-in-love.html
90. Interview with Neil Diamond by Anna Pukas in *Express*, (May 2008), after an announcement that Diamond would play at Glastonbury Festival in June 2008. https://www.express.co.uk/expressyourself/43907/NEIL-DIAMOND-I-m-too-much-of-a-loner
91. *Ibid.*
92. *Ibid.*
93. Interview with Barry Egan, "Neil Diamond in the Rough," *Independent* (Oct. 2014): https://www.independent.ie/entertainment/music/neil-diamond-in-the-rough-30690967.html
94. https://www.britannica.com/biography/Robin-Williams
95. *Robin Williams: Come Inside My Mind* (HBO Documentary Films, 2018), Directed by Marina Zenovich: https://www.youtube.com/watch?v=FBg0d63ZHbk
96. https://www.reddit.com/r/MadeMeSmile/comments/13mf36u/robin_williams/
97. https://www.nytimes.com/2013/04/16/arts/television/robin-williams-recalls-the-lessons-of-jonathan-winters.html
98. https://www.imdb.com/name/nm0000245/bio/?ref_=nm_ov_bio_sm
99. *Ibid.*
100. *Ibid.*
101. *Ibid.*
102. *Robin's Wish*, 2020, a film by Tylor Norwood: https://www.robinswishfilm.com/
103. *Ibid.*
104. *Factual America Podcast*: "Robin Williams: Who Robin Williams Really Was" (Nov. 10, 2020): https://www.youtube.com/watch?v=0pECxalROFI&t=3012s
105. Susan Schneider Williams, "The terrorist inside my husband's brain," *Neurology* 87.13 (Sept. 27, 2016), https://n.neurology.org/content/87/13/1308
106. https://www.imdb.com/name/nm0000245/bio/?ref_=nm_ov_bio_sm
107. https://www.britannica.com/biography/Amy-Winehouse

Notes

108. https://ew.com/article/2007/03/09/back-black/
109. https://americansongwriter.com/the-25-best-amy-winehouse-quotes/
110. *Ibid.*
111. https://www.standard.co.uk/lifestyle/amy-winehouse-ex-husband-blake-fielder-civil-b1055469.html
112. https://people.com/celebrity/divorce-drama-for-amy-winehouse/
113. https://www.standard.co.uk/lifestyle/amy-winehouse-ex-husband-blake-fielder-civil-b1055469.html
114. https://www.theguardian.com/music/2015/may/01/mitch-winehouse-interview-amy-documentary-film
115. *Ibid.*
116. https://www.theguardian.com/music/2013/jun/23/amy-winehouse-growing-up-sister
117. https://www.brainyquote.com/authors/amy-winehouse-quotes
118. https://www.britannica.com/biography/Christopher-McCandless
119. Craig Medred, "The fiction that is Jon Krakauer's 'Into the Wild'," *Alaska Dispatch News* (Jan. 10, 2015).
120. Jon Krakauer, *Into the Wild*, p. 169.
121. Jon Krakauer, "Death of an Innocent: How Christopher McCandless Lost His Way in the Wilds," *Outside* (Jan. 1993).
122. "Scan of Chris McCandless' note": https://web.archive.org/web/20121113204007/http://www.christophermccandless.info/images/chris-mccandless_sos_lancastria.jpg
123. Krakauer, *Into the Wild*, p. 23.
124. *Ibid.*, p. 34.
125. *Ibid.*, p. 65.
126. https://www.dispatch.com/story/entertainment/books/2014/11/08/the-wild-truth-sister-sheds/23791334007/
127. https://www.goodreads.com/quotes/720820-chastity-is-the-flowering-of-man-and-what-are-called
128. *Ibid.*, p. 67.
129. https://www.goodreads.com/author/quotes/7902.Boris_Pasternak?page=2#:~:text=And%20so%20it%20turned%20out,unshared%20happiness%20is%20not%20happiness.
130. *Ibid.*, p. 188.
131. https://www.britannica.com/biography/Christopher-McCandless
132. Eddie Vedder, "Water on the Road – Full Concert," 17:30–18:40: https://www.youtube.com/watch?v=bAzFiZok_hw
133. Katie Nicholl, *The New Royals: Queen Elizabeth's Legacy and the Future of the Crown* (Little Brown, 2022).
134. https://nypost.com/2022/09/27/prince-george-warned-pals-my-dad-will-be-king-so-you-better-watch-out-book-says/
135. Andre Rhoden-Paul and Sean Coughlan, "Catherine, Princess of Wales, in hospital after abdominal surgery," *BBC News* (Jan. 17, 2024).
136. Sean Coughlin, "Princess of Wales says she is undergoing cancer treatment," *BBC News*. (Mar. 22, 2024).
137. Hannah Furness, "Princess of Wales: My chemotherapy is over, now I'm focused on staying cancer-free," *The Daily Telegraph* (Sept. 9, 2024).
138. Jadie Troy-Pryde, "Prince George will never be King, according to history writer," *Marie Claire* (Nov.11, 2022).
139. *Ibid.*

140. https://www.britannica.com/biography/John-Dee
141. R. Julian Roberts, ed., "A John Dee Chronology, 1509–1609," *Renaissance Man: The Reconstructed Libraries of European Scholars: 1450–1700 Series One: The Books and Manuscripts of John Dee, 1527–1608* (Adam Matthew, 2005).
142. https://www.historyextra.com/period/tudor/john-dee-elizabeth-i-tudor-scientist-magician-spy-007-james-bond
143. Ibid.
144. Charlotte Fell Smith, *The Life of Dr. John Dee (1527–1608)* (Constable, 1909).
145. "Books owned by John Dee," St. John's College, Cambridge: https://www.joh.cam.ac.uk/library/special_collections/early_books/dee.htm
146. Gwyn A. Williams, *When was Wales?: A History of the Welsh* (Black Raven Press, 1985), p. 124.
147. György E. Szönyi, (2015), "Layers of Meaning in Alchemy in John Dee's Monas hieroglyphica and its Relevance in a Central European Context," pp. 100–30, in Tomáš Nejeschleba; Jiří Michalík, eds., *Latin Alchemical Literature of Czech Provenance* (Centre for Renaissance Texts, 2015).
148. John Keay and Julia Keay, *Collins Encyclopaedia of Scotland* (HarperCollins, 1994), p. 556.
149. https://www.historyextra.com/period/tudor/john-dee-elizabeth-i-tudor-scientist-magician-spy-007-james-bond/
150. Ibid.
151. Fell Smith, *The Life of Dr. John Dee*, op. cit.
152. Lorenzo DiTommaso, (2018). "Echoes of Enoch in Early Modern England: 'Enoch Prayer' (London, British Library MS Sloane 3821)," pp. 45–71, here p. 60. In, J. Harold Ellens *et al.* eds., *Wisdom Poured Out Like Water: Studies on Jewish and Christian Antiquity in Honor of Gabriele Boccaccini*. Deuterocanonical and Cognate Literature Series. Vol. 38 (De Gruyter, 2018).
153. Katherine Neal, "The Rhetoric of Utility: Avoiding Occult Associations for Mathematics through Profitability and Pleasure," *History of Science* 37.2 (1999): pp. 151–78.
154. I. R. F. Calder, *John Dee studied as an English neoplatonist* (PhD Thesis, University of London, 1952): http://www.johndee.org/calder/html/TOC.html
155. Hugh, Chisholm, ed., "Dee, John," *Encyclopædia Britannica*, Vol. 7, 11th ed., (Cambridge UP, 1911).
156. John Dee, Edward Kelly, and Meric Casaubon, Meric, *A True & Faithful Relation of what Passed for Many Yeers Between Dr. John Dee and Some Spirits* (T Garthwait, 1659).
157. Ibid.
158. Walter I. Trattner, "God and Expansion in Elizabethan England: John Dee, 1527–1583," *Journal of the History of Ideas* 25.1 (Jan. 1964): pp. 17–34.
159. Frances A. Yates, *Theatre of the World* (University of Chicago Press, 1969).
160. Fell Smith, *The Life of Dr. John Dee*, op. cit.
161. "Deaf, Blind Woman to Get College Degree," *The New York Times* (Jun. 6, 1983).
162. https://time.com/3923213/helen-keller-radicalism/
163. Arpita Aneja and Olivia B. Waxman, "The Helen Keller You Didn't Learn About in School," *TIME* (Dec. 15, 2020).
164. https://time.com/3923213/helen-keller-radicalism/
165. https://grasshopperfilm.com/film/her-socialist-smile/
166. https://afb.org/about-afb/history/helen-keller/helen-keller-quotes/helen-keller-quotes-about-herself
167. Kim E. Nielsen, *The Radical Lives of Helen Keller* (NYU Press, 2004), p. 134.

168. https://www.belllegacy.org/articles/what-was-bells-relationship-to-helen-keller/
169. https://www.cbc.ca/radio/ideas/unsound-the-legacy-of-alexander-graham-bell-1.6020596/alexander-graham-bell-s-oralist-mission-still-harms-deaf-and-hard-of-hearing-people-say-critics-1.6025659
170. The Frost King incident, reference to Keller's *The Story of My Life*, p 64–65, 74: https://www.perkins.org/the-frost-king-incident/
171. *Ibid.*
172. Helen Keller, *The Story of My Life* (1903): https://www.afb.org/about-afb/history/online-library/story-my-life
173. *Ibid.*, p. 134, Reference #21, p. 164.
174. *Ibid.*, p. 125.
175. *Ibid.*, p. 33.
176. *Ibid.*, p. 21.
177. Nielson, *The Radical Lives of Helen Keller*, p. 118.
178. *Ibid.*, p. 8.
179. https://www.amazon.com.au/Radical-Lives-Helen-Keller/dp/0814758142#detailBullets_feature_div
180. Nielson, *The Radical Lives of Helen Keller*, p. 11.
181. https://afb.org/about-afb/history/helen-keller/helen-keller-quotes/helen-keller-quotes-about-herself

Notes to Chapter Eleven

1. Al-Biruni, *The Book of Instruction*, p. 239.
2. Joy Usher, *A Tiny Universe's Companion* (Xlibris, 2018), pp. 463–660.
3. Al-Biruni, *The Book of Instruction*, pp. 255, 239.
4. *Ibid.*, p. 255.
5. Robert Hand, "Firdar, Alfridaria, or Alfridaries," (Arhat 1998–2010, revised June 2012): https://www.arhatmedia.com/firdar2.htm
6. https://basketnews.com/news-212768-lebron-and-bronny-james-to-play-together-on-opening-night.htm
7. Lawrence Donegan, "America's Most Wanted." *The Observer* (Mar. 2, 2003).
8. https://www.espn.com/nba/story/_/id/24194051/lebron-james-discusses-opening-public-school-akron-move-los-angeles-lakers-nba
9. Donegan, "America's Most Wanted."
10. *Ibid.*
11. LeBron James and Buzz Bissinger, "LeBron's Band of Brothers," *Vanity Fair* (October 2009).
12. *Ibid.*
13. *Ibid.*
14. *Ibid.*
15. *Ibid.*
16. https://www.britannica.com/biography/Frida-Kahlo/
17. Paula M. Cooey, *Religious Imagination and the Body: A Feminist Analysis* (Oxford UP, 1994), p. 99.
18. Alyce Mahon, "The Lost Secret: Frida Kahlo and The Surrealist Imaginary," *Journal of Surrealism and the Americas* 5.1–2 (2011): pp. 33–54.
19. *Ibid.*, fn. 13; Nancy Newhall, ed., *The Day Books of Edward Weston: I, Mexico, II California* (Aperture, 1990).

20. Martha Zamora, *Frida Kahlo: The Brush of Anguish* (Chronicle Books, 1990), p. 42–43.
21. https://lisawallerrogers.com/2009/05/26/frida-kahlos-first-bad-accident/
22. https://lisawallerrogers.com/2009/05/27/frida-kahlos-other-accident/
23. *Ibid.*
24. Zamora, *Frida Kahlo: The Brush of Anguish*, p. 16.
25. https://en.wikipedia.org/wiki/Frida_Kahlo#cite_note-195
26. Evelyn Torton Beck, "Kahlo's World Split Open," *Feminist Studies* 32.1 (Spring 2006). Based on chapter 5 of Beck's second PhD dissertation, see "Speaking in Pictures," Beck's *Physical Illness, Psychological Woundedness, and the Healing Power of Art in the Life and Work of Franz Kafka and Frida Kahlo* (The Fielding Graduate Institute, 2004).
27. Hayden Herrera, *Frida, a Biography of Frida Kahlo* (Harper & Row, 1983; repr. Perennial, 2002), p. 230–32.
28. *Ibid.*
29. Amy Fine Collins, "Diary of a Mad Artist," *Vanity Fair* (Sept. 3, 2013).
30. https://www.carredartistes.com/en-fr/blog/frida-kahlo-artistic-current-and-painting-style#:~:text=While%20some%20art%20specialists%20see,are%20irrational%2C%20strange%20and%20magical
31. Rebecca Block and Lynda Hoffman-Jeep, "Fashioning National Identity: Frida Kahlo in 'Gringoland'," *Woman's Art Journal* 19.2 (Autumn, 1998 – Winter, 1999): pp. 8–12.
32. Herrera, *Frida*, op. cit., pp. 425–33.
33. Frida Kahlo, *The Diary of Friday Kahlo: An Intimate Self-portrait* (Harry N. Abrams, 1995).
34. Peter Wollen, *Writings on Art* (Verso, 2004), p. 236.
35. Kahlo, *The Diary of Friday Kahlo*, p. 21.
36. "Diana Tells of Camilla Encounter," *BBC News* (Mar. 12, 2004).
37. https://www.rferl.org/a/1079558.html#:~:text=Prince%20Harry%20has%20said%20he,Taliban%20and%20Al%2DQaeda%20fighters.
38. Official Letter to the Press (Nov. 8, 2016): https://www.royal.uk/statement-communications-secretary-prince-harry
39. Hilary Weaver, "Prince Harry Reveals He Went to Therapy to Deal with Princess Diana's Death," *Vanity Fair* (Apr. 17, 2017).
40. Kevin Mitchell, "The mental health benefits of boxing," *The Guardian* (Apr. 17, 2017).
41. Amber Raiken, "Prince Harry opens up about 'healing' from PTSI after Diana's death: What is Post Traumatic Stress Injury?" *The Independent* (Jan. 9, 2023).
42. Erin Hill, "Meghan Markle and Prince Harry Have Split Royal Households from Kate Middleton and Prince William," *People* (Mar. 14, 2019).
43. *Julian Assange in His Own Words*, op. cit., p. 32.
44. *Ibid.*, p. 11.
45. Fowler, *The Most Dangerous Man in the World*, op. cit., p. 5.
46. *Ibid.*, p. 16.
47. *Ibid.*, p. 11.
48. *Ibid.*
49. *Ibid.*, p. 13.
50. *Ibid.*, p. 23.
51. Greenberg, *This Machine Kills Secrets*, op. cit.
52. *Ibid.*, p. 32.
53. *Ibid.*, p. 37.
54. https://www.industryweek.com/leadership/change-management/article/22009725/dont-build-a-ship-create-a-yearning-for-the-seas

Notes

55. *Ibid.*, p. 41
56. *Julian Assange in His Own Words, op. cit.*, p. 156.
57. "Chronology. Events concerning Julian Assange in chronological order". Swedish Prosecution Authority.
58. https://www.theguardian.com/media/2018/feb/11/sweden-tried-to-drop-assange-extradition-in-2013-cps-emails-show
59. "Julian Assange: Wikileaks founder refused extradition to US, judge rules," *BBC News* (Jan. 4, 2021).
60. Becky Morton, "Julian Assange can be extradited to the US, court rules," *BBC News* (Dec. 10, 2021).
61. Jamie Grierson and Ben Quinn, "Julian Assange's extradition from UK to US approved by home secretary," *The Guardian* (Jun. 17, 2022).
62. Michael Holden, "Julian Assange appeals to European court over US extradition," *Reuters* (Dec. 3, 2022).
63. Nils Melzer, *The Trial of Julian Assange: A Story of Persecution* (Verso, 2022).
64. Riley Stuart, "Julian Assange too ill to attend as court hears claim of 'breathtaking' plot to poison him," *ABC* (Feb. 20, 2024).
65. Ben Quinn, "Julian Assange wins right to appeal against extradition to US," *The Guardian* (May 20, 2024).
66. Renju Jose, "Australia PM backs parliament motion calling for Julian Assange's release," Reuters (Feb. 15, 2024).
67. Salvador Rizzo, Rachel Weiner, and Ellen Nakashima, "Assange Plea Came after Warning that US would Lose Extradition Fight," *Washington Post* (Jun. 28, 2024).
68. "Julian Assange live news: WikiLeaks founder pleads guilty and awaits sentencing in Saipan district courtroom," *The Guardian* (Jun. 26, 2024).
69. Tilman Blasshofer and Tassilo Hummel, "I chose freedom over justice, Julian Assange says in first comments after detention," *Reuters* (Oct. 1, 2024): https://www.youtube.com/watch?v=Ai34Uxnv_4s

Notes to Chapter Twelve

1. Christopher Hibbert, *Queen Victoria: A Personal History* (HarperCollins, 2000), p. 27–28.
2. Giles St. Aubyn, (1991), *Queen Victoria: A Portrait* (Sinclair-Stevenson, 1991), p. 340.
3. Lucy Worsley, "Queen Victoria's unhappy childhood: life under the 'Kensington System'," *HistoryExtra* (Dec. 27, 2023).
4. Kate Williams, "Queen Victoria: The woman who redefined Britain's monarchy," *BBC i-Wonder.* (Apr. 12, 2015).
5. Cecil, Woodham-Smith, *Queen Victoria: Her Life and Times 1819–1861* (Hamish Hamilton, 1972), p. 175.
6. https://www.royal.uk/timeline-queen-victoria-and-prince-albert
7. Woodham-Smith, *Queen Victoria: Her Life and Times 1819–1861*, p. 220.
8. Hibbert, *Queen Victoria*, p. 149
9. St. Aubyn, *Queen Victoria: A Portrait*, p. 159.
10. *Ibid.*, p. 318.
11. https://www.theguardian.com/commentisfree/2013/jan/09/queen-victoria-tyrant-honest-children-sex
12. D. M. Potts, W. T. W. Potts, (1995), *Queen Victoria's Gene: Haemophilia and the Royal Family*, (Alan Sutton, 1995), pp. 55–65, quoted in Hibbert, *Queen Victoria*, p. 217.

13. Hibbert, *Queen Victoria*, pp. 32, 33.
14. Victor A. McKusick, (1965), "The Royal Hemophilia," *Scientific American* 213.2 (1965): p. 91, doi:10.1038/scientificamerican0865-88, PMID 14319025; Steve Jones, *The Language of the Genes* (HarperCollins, 1993), p. 69; Steve Jones, *In the Blood: God, Genes and Destiny* (HarperCollins, 1993), p. 270; Alan R. Rushton, Royal Maladies: Inherited Diseases in the Royal Houses of Europe (Trafford, 2008), pp. 31–32.
15. *Hemophilia B*, National Hemophilia Foundation, 5 March 2014
16. Christopher Dobson, ed., *Chronicle of England*, Chronique ed. (French transl.), (1998), p. 405.
17. Wilhelm Ober, "Obstetrical Events That Shaped Western European History," *Yale Journal of Biology and Medicine* 65 (1992): pp. 208–9.
18. Andrew Sinclair, *Victoria – Kaiserin für 99 Tage* (Gustav Lübbe Verlag, Bergisch Gladbach, 1987), p. 307.
19. Franz Herre, *Kaiserin Friedrich – Victoria, eine Engländerin in Deutschland* (Hohenheim Verlag, 2006), p. 302.
20. Matthew Dennison, *The Last Princess: The Devoted Life of Queen Victoria's Youngest Daughter* (Weidenfeld and Nicolson, 2007), p. 3.
21. *Ibid.*, p. 11.
22. *Ibid.*, p. 13.
23. David Duff, *The Shy Princess* (Evans Brothers, 1958), p. 10.
24. Dennison, *The Last Princess*, p. 130.
25. *Ibid.*, 213.
26. https://en.wikipedia.org/wiki/Princess_Beatrice_of_the_United_Kingdom#cite_note-Royal1-56
27. "Collections in the Royal Archives," Official website of the British Monarchy. 2008–2009.
28. Nicholas Crane, *Mercator: The Man who Mapped the Planet* (Orion, 2010), p. 74.
29. Marc Lachièze-Rey and Jean-Pierre Luminet, Bibliothèque nationale de France, *Celestial Treasury: From the Music of the Spheres to the Conquest of Space* (Cambridge UP, 2001), p. 86.
30. https://www.metmuseum.org/art/collection/search/336229
31. https://www.metmuseum.org/perspectives/melencolia-i
32. Albrecht Dürer, *Dürer in Dublin: Engravings and woodcuts of Albrecht Dürer from the Chester Beatty Library* (Verlag Hans Carl, 1983).
33. https://www.metmuseum.org/perspectives/melencolia-i
34. Iván Fenyő, *Albrecht Dürer* (Corvina, 1956), p. 51.
35. Hand, *Night & Day* (webinar), *op. cit.*, p. 6.
36. Hand, *Night & Day*, p. 27.
37. Hand, *Night & Day* (webinar), *op. cit.*, p. 5.
38. https://homework.study.com/explanation/how-many-children-did-albrecht-durer-have.html#:~:text=Answer%20and%20Explanation%3A,a%20loveless%20and%20childless%20marriage
39. Hand, *Night & Day* (webinar), *op. cit.*, p. 5.
40. https://www.brainyquote.com/quotes/albrecht_durer_297549
41. Summary of Albrecht Dürer: https://www.theartstory.org/artist/durer-albrecht/
42. Erwin Panofsky, *The Life and Art of Albrecht Dürer* (1943; 3rd Ed. Princeton UP, 1955), p. 151.
43. Thomas Sturge Moore, *Albert Dürer* (Kessinger, 2004), p. 71.
44. https://en.wikiquote.org/wiki/Albrecht_Durer#: https://quotefancy.com/quote/1170208/Albrecht-D-rer-
45. Jane D. Dillenberger, *The Religious Art of Andy Warhol* (Continuum, 2001), p. 20.

Notes

46. Harry John Wilmot-Buxton and Edward John Poynter, *German, Flemish and Dutch Painting*. Scribner and Welford, 1881), p. 24.
47. Hans Rupprich, ed., *Dürer Written papers. Volume 1, autobiographical writings, correspondence, seals, inscriptions, notes and reports, certificates for personal life* (German Association for the Arts, 1956).
48. Robert Mills, *Seeing Sodomy in the Middle Ages* (University of Chicago Press, 2015), p. 332, n. 93.
49. George Haggerty, *Encyclopedia of Gay Histories and Cultures* (Taylor & Francis, 2013), p. 262.
50. https://fraenkelgallery.com/artists/diane-arbus
51. https://www.artnet.com/artists/diane-arbus/
52. https://www.britannica.com/biography/Diane-Arbus
53. https://www.icp.org/browse/archive/constituents/diane-arbus?all/all/all/all/0
54. https://fraenkelgallery.com/artists/diane-arbus
55. Rosemarie Garland-Thomson, "The Politics of Staring: Visual Rhetorics of Disability in Popular Photography," *Disability Studies: Enabling the Humanities* (MLA, 2002), Bibliography; Nielsen *Radical Lives of Helen Keller*, op. cit., p. 173; Kim E. Nielsen, "Helen Keller and the Politics of Civic Fitness," pp. 268–90 in Paul K. Longmore and Lauri Umansky, eds, *The New Disability History: American Perspectives* (NYU Press, 2001).
56. Garland-Thomson, "The Politics of Staring," p. 335–74.
57. Comments on Diane Arbus' work at the 2022 Zwirner Exhibition at the West 20 Street gallery in New York, see Sebastian Smee, "Diane Arbus was accused of exploiting 'freaks.' We misunderstood her art," *Washington Post*, Sept. 26, 2022): https://www.washingtonpost.com/arts-entertainment/2022/09/26/diane-arbus-exhibit-zwirner/
58. Lynne M. Somers-Davis, *Encyclopedia of Twentieth-Century Photography* (Routledge, 2006), pp. 51–56.
59. Hand, *Night & Day*, op. cit., p. 21.
60. Notes on Hand, *Night & Day* (webinar), op. cit.
61. Hand, *Night & Day*, op. cit., p. 21.
62. https://www.forbes.com/quotes/2167/ ; quote from *Artform* magazine, 1971
63. https://www.brainyquote.com/quotes/diane_arbus_146260
64. Arthur Lubow, "Arbus Reconsidered," *The New York Times* (Sept. 14, 2003).
65. Diane Arbus, *Diane Arbus: Revelations* (Random House, 2003).
66. https://www.wnyc.org/story/diane-arbus-rare-interview/
67. *Ibid.*
68. https://www.theguardian.com/artanddesign/2005/oct/08/photography
69. *Ibid.*
70. https://www.youtube.com/watch?v=9SGNFEwuxKQ
71. https://www.youtube.com/watch?v=kYGGCVE2lKY
72. Hand, *Night & Day*, op. cit., p.26.
73. https://vault.si.com/vault/1968/02/05/hes-not-a-bird-hes-not-a-plane#
74. https://www.goodreads.com/quotes/44727
75. Hand, *Night & Day*, op. cit., p. 27.
76. https://quotefancy.com/quote/1277296/
77. https://www.brainyquote.com/lists/authors/top-10-evel-knievel-quotes#
78. https://www.brainyquote.com/quotes/evel_knievel_326218
79. https://www.mirror.co.uk/3am/celebrity-news/elvis-dreamed-playing-wembley-manager-27351001

80. Associated Press, "Christmas Is Year-Round Business for Toymakers," *The Times-News* (Feb. 14, 1977).
81. "Knievel attack victim wants cash," *BBC News* (Dec. 4, 2007).
82. https://www.brainyquote.com/authors/evel-knievel-quotes#
83. https://www.britannica.com/biography/Christopher-Reeve
84. https://www.capedwonder.com/christopher-reeve-quotes/
85. https://www.medicaldevice-network.com/comment/epidural-stimulation/#:~:text=patients%2C%20until%20recently.-,Epidural%20stimulation%20is%20an%20experimental%20therapy%20that%20has%20the%20potential,coating%20of%20the%20spinal%20cord.
86. https://www.mayoclinic.org/medical-professionals/neurology-neurosurgery/news/stem-cell-treatment-after-spinal-cord-injury-the-next-steps/mac-20488605
87. https://sci.amegroups.com/article/view/102197/html
88. https://www.capedwonder.com/christopher-reeve-quotes/
89. https://www.youtube.com/watch?v=i43OVrwhW_E
90. Hand, *Night & Day, op. cit.*, p. 27.
91. *Ibid.*, p. 24.
92. *Ibid.*, p. 23.
93. Hand, *Night & Day* (webinar), *op. cit.*, p. 5.
94. https://www.capedwonder.com/christopher-reeve-quotes/
95. "Christopher and Dana Reeve Foundation Press Kit": https://web.archive.org/web/20070403030234/http://www.christopherreeve.org/site/c.geIMLPOpGjF/b.1231837/k.FB68/Press_Kit.htm
96. https://www.capedwonder.com/christopher-reeve-quotes/
97. J. Lee Lehman, *Classical Astrology for Modern Living: From Ptolemy to Psychology & Back Again* (Whitford Press, 1996), p. 207.
98. https://healthcareuncovered.substack.com/p/16-years-ago-my-story-was-told-in
99. Dwight Garner, "Inside the List," *The New York Times* (Sept. 12, 2008).
100. Hand, *Night & Day, op. cit.*, p. 26.
101. https://respiratory-therapy.com/disorders-diseases/infectious-diseases/other-infections/michael-moore-hospitalized-pneumonia-ahead-film-release/
102. Hand, *Night & Day, op. cit.*, p. 27.
103. http://movies.nytimes.com/person/103383/Michael-Moore/biography
104. https://www.popmatters.com/moore-michael-2496101383.html
105. *Ibid.*
106. *Ibid.*
107. Oliver Milman, "Climate experts call for 'dangerous' Michael Moore film to be taken down," *The Guardian* (Apr. 28, 2020).

Notes to Chapter Thirteen

1. https://www.washingtonpost.com/wp-srv/national/longterm/glenn/stories/profile.htm#:~:text=Back%20when%20Glenn%20was%20struggling,ago%2C%20if%20he%20could%20have.
2. Hand, *Night & Day* (webinar), *op. cit.*, p. 6.
3. https://www.washingtonpost.com/wp-srv/national/longterm/glenn/stories/profile.htm
4. *Ibid.*
5. https://ameshistory.org/tribunearchives/watching-john-glenns-splashdown

Notes

6. https://www.supercluster.com/editorial/the-complex-relationship-between-mental-health-and-space-travel
7. *Ibid.*
8. *Ibid.*
9. "Annie Glenn: 'When I called John, he cried. People just couldn't believe that I could really talk.'". *The Washington Post* (Dec. 9, 2016).
10. "Annie Glenn". *johnglennhome.org*.
11. "Annie Glenn An Amazing Life": https://www.youtube.com/watch?v=1Aw4_bsU-_U
12. Julie Zauzmer, "In space, John Glenn saw the face of God: "It just strengthens my faith"". *The Washington Post* (Dec. 8, 2016).
13. https://www.washingtonpost.com/wp-srv/national/longterm/glenn/stories/profile.htm
14. https://explorersweb.com/exploration-mysteries-john-glenn-and-the-fireflies-in-space/
15. *Ibid.*
16. Eugene Kennedy, "John Glenn's Presidential Countdown". *The New York Times* (Oct. 11, 1981).
17. https://www.washingtonpost.com/wp-srv/national/longterm/glenn/stories/profile.htm
18. *Ibid.*
19. *Ibid.*
20. Associated Press, ""Crackdown's delay laid to five," *St. Louis Post Dispatch* (Dec. 6, 1990), p. 8.
21. https://www.latimes.com/archives/la-xpm-1990-01-01-vw-147-story.html
22. https://www.washingtonpost.com/wp-srv/national/longterm/glenn/stories/profile.htm
23. Hand, *Night & Day, op. cit.*, p. 25.
24. *One giant leap - backward: Part 2*: http://www.theglobeandmail.com/series/astronauts/astronauts02.html
25. John Glenn's fan mail shows many girls dreamed of the stars – but sexism in the early space program thwarted their ambitions
26. Simon Dumenco, "The Kid Stays In the Pictures," *New York* (Mar. 31, 2003).
27. https://www.imdb.com/name/nm0749263/bio/
28. Zoe Williams, "Out of the Traps," *The Guardian* (Jun. 10, 2005).
29. https://www.imdb.com/news/ni53345332/
30. https://www.youtube.com/watch?v=pE1Qk90pxE4
31. *Ibid.*
32. https://www.cbr.com/popular-marvel-characters/#:~:text=Spider%2DMan%20has%20long%20been,merchandise%20like%20no%20one%20else.
33. https://www.theguardian.com/film/2010/nov/29/mark-ruffalo-terrorism-watchlist-gasland
34. *Ibid.*
35. https://www.cultureslate.com/lists/all-of-the-times-mark-ruffalo-accidentally-leaked-mcu-plot-points
36. Hand, *Night & Day, op. cit.*, p. 25.
37. Paulus Alexandrinus, *Introductory Matters*, Translated by Robert Schmidt, Edited by Robert Hand, Project Hindsight: Greek Track, Volume I (Golden Hind Press, 1993), p. 15.
38. https://www.youtube.com/watch?v=pE1Qk90pxE4
39. *Ibid.*
40. *Ibid.*
41. Elisa Leonelli, "Oral History: Mark Ruffalo on Religion," *Golden Globe Awards* (Mar. 22, 2021).

42. https://www.youtube.com/watch?v=pE1Qk90pxE4
43. *Ibid.*
44. *Ibid.*
45. https://www.britannica.com/biography/Kurt-Cobain
46. Michael Azerrad, *Come as You Are: The Story of Nirvana* (Knopf Doubleday, 1993), p. 17.
47. John Savage, "Kurt Cobain: The Lost Interview," *NirvanaFreak.net*. (July 1993).
48. Charles R. Cross, *Heavier Than Heaven* (Hyperion Books, 2001), p. 27.
49. *Ibid.*, p. 69, p. 196.
50. Robert Hilburn, "From the Archives: Nirvana's Kurt Cobain was a reluctant hero who spoke to his generation," *The Los Angeles Times* (Apr. 5, 2019).
51. Cross, *Heavier Than Heaven*, p. 177.
52. *Sliver: The Best of the Box* album booklet.
53. Mark Mazullo, "The Man Whom the World Sold: Kurt Cobain, Rock's Progressive Aesthetic, and the Challenges of Authenticity," *The Musical Quarterly* 84.4 (2000): pp. 713–49.
54. https://www.musiclipse.com/2024/03/20/10-facts-about-kurt-cobain-health-you-need-to-know/#:~:text=9.,Cobain's%20Bronchitis%20and%20Respiratory%20Issues&text=Kurt%20Cobain's%20biographies%20reveal%20a,childhood%20and%20worsened%20over%20time.
55. *Ibid.*
56. *Ibid.*
57. Lynn Hirschberg, "Strange Love: The Story of Kurt Cobain and Courtney Love," *Vanity Fair Hollywood Daily* (Sept. 1, 1992).
58. Hand, *Night & Day, op. cit.*, p. 25.
59. James Crotty, "Go for the Grunge," *Monk Magazine* (Oct. 30, 1992).
60. https://www.daringcoco.com/2011/11/kurt-cobain.html
61. Ptolemy's *Tetrabiblos or Quadripartite*, Ashmand Trans., p. 156.
62. Holden, *Five Medieval Astrologers* (AFA, 2008), Ptolemy's *Centiloquy*, No. 37, p. 75.
63. https://startmediation.co.uk/dad-hates-mom-mom-hates-dad-it-just-makes-you-want-to-be-so-sad/
64. Howard Sounes, *Amy, 27: Amy Winehouse and the 27 Club* (Hodder & Stoughton, 2013), p. 239
65. *Ibid.*
66. https://archive.org/details/flipsideissue78/page/n35/mode/2up
67. https://www.independent.ie/entertainment/music/who-courtney-knew-was-a-very-different-person-to-who-they-intimately-knew-frances-bean-on-kurt-cobain-exhibition-curated-by-his-mother-and-sister-37132951.html
68. Cross, *Heavier Than Heaven*, p. 154.
69. Tom Murray, "Courtney Love announces she's finished her memoir after 'decade' of writing: 'F*** an untrue narrative'," *Independent* (Aug. 5 2022).
70. *Ibid.*, p. 102
71. Hirschberg, "Strange Love."
72. *Ibid.*, p. 102
73. *Ibid.*, p. 40.
74. *Ibid.*, p. 132.
75. Josh Sheppherd, ""Nevermind"—Nirvana (1991)" (Library of Congress, 2004): https://www.loc.gov/static/programs/national-recording-preservation-board/documents/Nevermind.pdf

Notes

76. Stevie Chick, "Nirvana: The stories behind every song on Nevermind," *Kerrang!* (Sept. 23, 2021).
77. *Classic Albums—Nirvana: Nevermind* [DVD] (Isis Productions, 2004).
78. https://www.britannica.com/biography/Dave-Grohl
79. Dave Grohl, *The Storyteller: Tales of Life and Music* (Simon & Schuster, 2021), pp. 64–65.
80. *Ibid.*, p. 67.
81. Bob Alexa, "How Dave Grohl Dealt with Kurt Cobain's Death," (Oct. 16, 2022).
82. https://www.clashmusic.com/news/foo-fighters-on-their-band-name
83. Hand, *Night & Day* (webinar), *op. cit.*
84. "Dave Grohl Details His Hearing Loss," *The Howard Stern Show* (Feb. 15, 2022).
85. Azzerrad, *Come as You Are*, p. 150.
86. Grohl, *The Storyteller*, p. 137.
87. *Ibid.*, p. 369.
88. Terry Zeller, "Violet Grohl: 5 Things About Dave Grohl's Daughter, 16, Who Performed At Taylor Hawkins Tribute," *Hollywood Life* (Sept. 29, 2022).
89. Hand, *Night & Day, op. cit.*, p.26
90. Hand, *Night & Day* (webinar), *op. cit.*
91. Grohl, *The Storyteller*, p. 69.
92. *Ibid.*, p. 84
93. *Ibid.*, p. 356
94. Dave Grohl at Taylor Hawkins' Memorial Concert, September 2022: https://www.youtube.com/watch?v=ta5h6IwpVbg

Notes to Chapter Fourteen

1. https://kids.britannica.com/students/article/Alfred-Lord-Tennyson/277302#:~:text=He%20was%20the%20first%20English,and%20Other%20Poems%20in%201889.
2. https://www.britannica.com/biography/Alfred-Lord-Tennyson
3. *Ibid.*
4. *Ibid.*
5. Hallam Tennyson, ed., *Alfred Lord Tennyson: A Memoir by His Son* (1897; repr. Kessinger, 2005).
6. https://www.poetryfoundation.org/poems/45359/the-lady-of-shalott-1832
7. *Ibid.*
8. https://www.litcharts.com/poetry/alfred-lord-tennyson/the-lady-of-shalott#:~:text=The%20poem%20is%20often%20interpreted,of%20E2%80%9CThe%20Lady%20of%20Shalott%E2%80%9D
9. Tennyson, *Alfred Lord Tennyson, op. cit.*
10. *Ibid.*, p. 249, quoted on p. 230 in Alisa Clapp-Itnyre, "Marginalized Musical Interludes: Tennyson's Critique of Conventionality in *The Princess*," *Victorian Poetry* 38.2 (Summer 2000): pp. 227–48.
11. Clapp-Itnyre, "Marginalized Musical Interludes."
12. Tennyson, *Alfred Lord Tennyson, op. cit.*, p. 254, quoted in Clapp-Itnyre, "Marginalized Musical Interludes," p. 230.
13. Marion Shaw, *Alfred Lord Tennyson (Feminist Readings)* (Humanities Press, 1988), p. 47, quoted in Clapp-Itnyre, "Marginalized Musical Interludes," p. 227.
14. Hand, *Night & Day, op. cit.*, p. 25.
15. Joanna Richardson, "Emily, Lady Tennyson," *History Today* 29.3 (Mar. 1979).

16. Ethna Viney, "Wife story," *The Irish Times* (Oct. 12, 1986).
17. "Emily Tennyson". *Tennyson's Celebrity Circle - Poet Laureate Alfred Lord Tennyson: University of Portsmouth* (Nov. 8, 2011).
18. "Lady Tennyson," *Royal Academy of Arts*: https://www.royalacademy.org.uk/art-artists/work-of-art/lady-tennyson
19. C. Ricks, *Tennyson* (Macmillan, 1972).
20. Tennyson, *Alfred Lord Tennyson.*
21. Royal Collection Trust, https://www.rct.uk/collection/1005991-a/tis-better-to-have-loved-amp-lost-than-never-to-have-loved-at-all (RA VIC/MAIN/QVJ (W) Jan. 5, 1862).
22. *The Oxford Dictionary of Quotations*, 5th ed., (Oxford UP, 1999).
23. Viney, "Wife Story."
24. *Ibid.*
25. "Obituary for Lady Emily Tennyson," *The Boston Globe* (Aug. 11, 1896), p. 7.
26. https://www.poetryfoundation.org/poems/45360/the-lady-of-shalott-1842
27. *Ibid.*
28. https://www.writework.com/essay/alfred-lord-tennyson-art-fueled-madness-and-battle-manic-d
29. https://scua.uoregon.edu/repositories/2/resources/2179
30. https://www.photoquotations.com/a/161/Tee+Corinne
31. Corinne, "Artist's statement," *op. cit.*
32. http://www.glbtqarchive.com/arts/corinne_ta_A.pdf
33. Hand, *Night & Day, op. cit.*, p. 25.
34. https://www.jstor.org/stable/3178374?origin=crossref
35. https://epgn.com/2021/10/20/tee-a-corinne-photographer-of-lesbian-sexuality/
36. *Ibid.*
37. https://queerculturalcenter.org/picturing-cancer/
38. https://www.photoquotations.com/a/161/Tee+Corinne
39. Elisa Rolle, "queerplaces - Tee Corinne," *www.elisarolle.com*.
40. Lehman, *Classical Astrology for Modern Living, op. cit.*, p. 210.
41. https://lesbianartandartists.tumblr.com/post/130224089706/tee-corinne-my-mother-lost-to-her-dreams-mixed
42. *Ibid.*
43. https://queerculturalcenter.org/picturing-cancer/
44. https://www.britannica.com/biography/Malala-Yousafzai
45. "The Nobel Peace Prize for 2014" (Press release), Nobel Media AB (Oct. 10, 2014).
46. https://www.goodreads.com/author/quotes/7064545.Malala_Yousafzai#
47. "Bacha Khan's philosophy of non-violence and Benazir Bhutto's charisma inspires Malala," *The Express Tribune* (Jan. 16, 2012).
48. https://www.astro.com/astro-databank/Yousafzai,_Malala
49. Hand, *Night & Day, op. cit.*, p. 25.
50. https://thegrowthfaculty.com/articles/favouritequotesfrommalala
51. https://malala.org/malalas-story
52. https://www.indiatoday.in/trending-news/story/when-taliban-shot-malala-in-the-head-this-is-what-she-did-her-story-1845128-2021-08-25
53. https://www.glamourmagazine.co.uk/article/malala-yousafzai-quotes#
54. https://www.litcharts.com/lit/i-am-malala/chapter-2-my-father-the-falcon#:~
55. *Ibid.*
56. *Ibid.*

57. *Ibid.*
58. *Ibid.*
59. https://www.goodreads.com/author/quotes/7064545.Malala_Yousafzai#:~
60. https://people.com/human-interest/malala-yousafzai-says-relationship-with-husband-asser-malik-changed-stance-on-marriage/
61. https://people.com/human-interest/who-is-asser-malik-malala-yousafzai-husband/
62. https://www.bbc.com/news/world-39550681

Notes to Chapter Fifteen

1. https://www.britannica.com/biography/Friedrich-Nietzsche
2. https://parade.com/living/friedrich-nietzsche-quotes#:
3. https://richardswsmith.wordpress.com/2019/07/04/nietzsche-neither-nazi-saint-nor-buffoon-but-the-philosopher-of-perhaps/#:~:text=A%20%E2%80%9Cphilosopher%20of%20perhaps%2C%E2%80%9D,science%2C%20and%20belief%20in%20progress.
4. https://www.goodreads.com/quotes/63480-is-man-merely-a-mistake-of-god-s-or-god-merely
5. https://richardswsmith.wordpress.com/2019/07/04/nietzsche-neither-nazi-saint-nor-buffoon-but-the-philosopher-of-perhaps/#:~:text=A%20%E2%80%9Cphilosopher%20of%20perhaps%2C%E2%80%9D,science%2C%20and%20belief%20in%20progress.
6. Aphorism from *Thus Spoke Zarathustra*, Part One, 'On Little Women Old and Young' p. 391.
7. Aphorism on Women from *The Anti-Christ*, Section 48.
8. *Ibid.*, p. 12.
9. *Ibid.*, p. 24.
10. Ronald Hayman, *Nietzsche: Nietzsche's Voices, Series: The Great Philosophers* (1997; repr. Weidenfeld & Nicolson, 2021), p. 9.
11. Private letter from Nietzsche to Erwin Rohde, February, 1870.
12. Sue Prideaux, *I Am Dynamite! A Life of Friedrich Nietzsche* (Faber & Faber, 2018), p. 50.
13. Hayman, *Nietzsche's Voices*, p. 4
14. https://www.thecollector.com/what-are-nietzsche-most-famous-quotes/
15. Hand, *Night & Day*, op. cit., p. 23.
16. Hand, *Night & Day* (webinar), *op. cit.*
17. H.L. Cornell, *Encyclopaedia of Medical Astrology*, (1972; repr. Samuel Weiser, 1992), p. 324.
18. *Ibid.*, p. 52, p. 224.
19. *Ibid.*, p. 8.
20. *I Am Dynamite!*, p. 12.
21. *Ibid.*, p. 12.
22. *I Am Dynamite!*, p. 44.
23. *Ibid.*, p. 44.
24. *Ibid.*, p. 41.
25. *Ibid.*, p. 22.
26. Friedrich Nietzsche, *Thus Spoke Zarathustra*, Part One, 'On the Virtue of Giving', (1881).
27. *I Am Dynamite!*, p. 42.
28. *Ibid.*, p. 143.
29. *Ibid.*
30. *Ibid.*, p. 168, Reference, Notes, #18 for Chapter 9, p. 406.
31. *Ibid.*, p. 193.
32. *Ibid.*, p. 197.

33. *Ibid.*, p. 206.
34. *Ibid.*, Notes, # 8, p. 414, letter written by Nietzsche to Franz Overbeck, describing *Ecco Homo*, Nov. 13, 1888, nine days after the book was completed.
35. *Ibid.*, p. 229.
36. *Ibid.*, p. 367.
37. *Ibid.*, p. 257; Notes, p. 411, ref. #4 *Ecco Homo*, 'Why am I so Wise, Section 2.
38. https://richardswsmith.wordpress.com/2019/07/04/nietzsche-neither-nazi-saint-nor-buffoon-but-the-philosopher-of-perhaps/#:~:text=A%20%E2%80%9Cphilosopher%20of%20perhaps%2C%E2%80%9D,science%2C%20and%20belief%20in%20progress.
39. Notes, p. 411, reference from #4 *Ecco Homo*, 'Why am I so Wise, Section 2, p. 20.
40. https://www.britannica.com/biography/Friedrich-Nietzsche/Decade-of-isolation-and-creativity-1879-89
41. https://www.britannica.com/biography/Vincent-van-Gogh
42. Department of European Paintings, "Vincent van Gogh (1853–1890)," *The Met's Heilbrunn Timeline of Art History*: https://www.metmuseum.org/essays/vincent-van-gogh-1853-1890
43. https://vangoghletters.org/vg/letters/let855/letter.html
44. https://www.britannica.com/biography/Vincent-van-Gogh
45. Ronald Pickvance, "English Influences on Vincent van Gogh," catalog from an exhibition organised by the Fine Art Department, University of Nottingham and the Arts Council of Great Britain, 1974–75.
46. https://www.britannica.com/biography/Vincent-van-Gogh/The-productive-decade
47. https://www.goodreads.com/author/quotes/34583.Vincent_van_Gogh#:~:text=I%20don't%20know%20anything%20with%20certainty%2C%20but,Tags:%20stars%2Ddreams%20%C2%B7%20Like%20%C2%B7%20likes:%202008.
48. *Ibid.*
49. *Ibid.*
50. *Ibid.*
51. Dietrich Blumer, "The Illness of Vincent van Gogh," American Journal of Psychiatry 159.4 (2002): pp. 519–26.
52. Hand, *Night & Day, op. cit.*, p. 24.
53. Hand, *Night & Day* (webinar), *op. cit.*
54. https://www.goodreads.com/author/quotes/34583.Vincent_van_Gogh#
55. https://www.britannica.com/biography/Vincent-van-Gogh#ref2761
56. *Ibid.*
57. https://www.vangoghmuseum.nl/en/art-and-stories/vincents-life-1853-1890/peasant-painter
58. https://www.britannica.com/biography/Vincent-van-Gogh/The-productive-decade
59. Hand, *Night & Day, op. cit.*, p. 21.
60. Hand, *Night & Day* (webinar), *op. cit.*
61. Steven W. Naifeh and Gregory White Smith, *Van Gogh: The Life* (Random House, 2011), p. 31–32.
62. https://www.vangoghstudio.com/how-was-van-goghs-relationship-with-his-father/
63. https://vangoghletters.org/vg/overview.html
64. https://www.dbnl.org/tekst/_van012200301_01/_van012200301_01_0009.php
65. https://vangoghletters.org/vg/letters/let193/letter.html
66. *Ibid.*
67. https://vangoghletters.org/vg/letters/let194/letter.html
68. Willem-Jan Verlinden, *The Van Gogh Sisters* (Thames & Hudson, 2021), p. 11.

69. https://vangoghletters.org/vg/letters/let490/letter.html (FR b4536. Breda, 26 August 1886)
70. https://vangoghletters.org/vg/letters/let490/letter.html (Van Gogh Museum Doc., bd57).
71. https://vangoghletters.org/vg/letters/let490/letter.html
72. https://vangoghletters.org/vg/letters/let180/letter.html
73. *Ibid.*, p. 74; https://vangoghletters.org/vg/letters/let228/letter.html (Vincent to Theo van Gogh, The Hague, on or about Tues., May 16, 1882).
75. *Ibid.*
76. https://vangoghletters.org/vg/letters/let222/letter.html
77. *Ibid.*
78. https://www.vangoghstudio.com/your-daily-dose-van-gogh-ebook-for-free/
79. https://www.vangoghmuseum.nl/en/art-and-stories/vincents-life-1853-1890/first-steps-as-an-artist
80. https://vangoghletters.org/vg/letters/let224/letter.html
81. https://www.britannica.com/biography/Vincent-van-Gogh/The-productive-decade
82. https://www.britannica.com/biography/Vincent-van-Gogh/The-productive-decade
83. Hans Kaufmann and Rita Wildegans, *Van Gogh's Ear: Paul Gauguin and the Pact of Silence* (Osburg, 2008).
84. https://vangoghsear.com/
85. *https://www.vangoghstudio.com/your-daily-dose-van-gogh-ebook-for-free/*
86. https://vangoghletters.org/vg/letters/let724/letter.html
87. https://vangoghletters.org/vg/letters/let210/letter.html
88. https://vangoghletters.org/vg/letters/let226/letter.html
89. https://vangoghletters.org/vg/letters/let567/letter.html
90. https://vangoghletters.org/vg/letters/let664/letter.html
91. *Ibid.*
92. https://www.goodreads.com/author/quotes/34583.Vincent_van_Gogh#
93. https://www.bbc.com/culture/article/20230612-from-the-starry-night-to-a-wheatfield-van-goghs-darkest-symbol
94. http://omeka.wellesley.edu/piranesi-rome/exhibits/show/romanobelisks/obelisks-in-egypt#:
95. https://www.bbc.com/culture/article/20230612-from-the-starry-night-to-a-wheatfield-van-goghs-darkest-symbol
96. *Ibid.*
97. *Ibid.*
98. *Ibid.*
99. *Ibid.*
100. https://www.goodreads.com/quotes/12025308-van-gogh

Notes to Chapter Sixteen

1. https://www.britannica.com/biography/Dennis-Rodman
2. https://sports.yahoo.com/dennis-rodman-net-worth-doesn-215832609.html#:~:text=Unfortunately%2C%20Dennis%20Rodman%20wasn't,casinos%20and%20backroom%20card%20games; https://www.theguardian.com/us-news/2023/nov/14/woman-scammed-dennis-rodman-prison-early-release
3. https://www.britannica.com/biography/Dennis-Rodman
4. https://www.brainyquote.com/authors/dennis-rodman-quotes

5. Hand, *Night & Day* (webinar), *op. cit.*
6. https://www.allgreatquotes.com/authors/dennis-rodman/
7. https://www.youtube.com/watch?v=cSL7KTAhytk
8. https://www.brainyquote.com/citation/quotes/dennis_rodman_393725
9. *Ibid.*
10. https://web.archive.org/web/20080428120325/http://findarticles.com/p/articles/mi_m1285/is_n2_v27/ai_19192189
11. https://www.brainyquote.com/citation/quotes/dennis_rodman_393725
12. *Ibid.*
13. https://jokermag.com/dennis-rodman-quotes/
14. Alex Prewitt, "The Peggy Show: Every athlete's worst nightmare," *Sports Illustrated* (Sept. 19, 2019).
15. https://www.theguardian.com/us-news/2023/nov/14/woman-scammed-dennis-rodman-prison-early-release
16. https://web.archive.org/web/20080617184025/http://vault.sportsillustrated.cnn.com/vault/article/magazine/MAG1067269/index.htm
17. Steve Forrest, "Dennis Rodman checks into alcohol rehab after N. Korea trip," *CNN* (Jan. 19, 2014).
18. "Dennis Rodman could face jail over child and spousal support," *Los Angeles Times* (Mar. 28, 2012).
19. "Dennis Rodman in debt, faces possible jail time," *CBS News* (Mar. 28, 2012).
20. https://edition.cnn.com/2024/12/18/sport/trinity-rodman-criticizes-dennis-rodman-spt-intl/index.html
21. Jack Baer and Liz Roscher, "Trinity Rodman opens up about relationship with father Dennis: 'He's not a dad. Maybe by blood, but nothing else'". *Yahoo! Sports* (Dec. 18, 2024).
22. Meg Linehan, "Trinity Rodman's late brace shows depth, versatility of USWNT's forwards," *The Athletic* (Jul. 9, 2023).
23. https://www.espn.com.au/football/story/_/id/43062107/usa-star-trinity-rodman-relationship-dennis-strained
24. https://web.archive.org/web/20080617184025/http://vault.sportsillustrated.cnn.com/vault/article/magazine/MAG1067269/index.htm
25. *Ibid.*
26. https://www.britannica.com/biography/Michael-J-Fox
27. https://www.michaeljfox.org/
28. Stephanie Zacharek, "'Still: A Michael J. Fox Movie' Is Unsparing and Darkly Funny, " *TIME* (May 12, 2023).
29. https://www.imdb.com/video/vi3993158681/?playlistId=tt19853258&ref_=tt_ov_vi
30. https://www.brainyquote.com/authors/michael-j-fox-quotes#:~:text=Life%20delivered%20me%20a%20catastrophe,found%20a%20richness%20of%20soul.&text=The%20more%20I%20expect%2C%20the,the%20more%20serene%20I%20am.
31. Andrew Corsello, "Michael J. Fox Is Ready to Tackle Whatever Comes Next". *AARP: The Magazine* (Nov. 30, 2021): pp. 36–41.
32. https://www.astro.com/astro-databank/Fox,_Michael_J.
33. https://www.brainyquote.com/authors/michael-j-fox-quotes
34. Michael J. Fox, *No Time Like the Future: An Optimist Considers Mortality* (Headline, 2020), pp.75, 76.
35. *Ibid.*, p. 25.
36. *Ibid.*, p. 156.

37. https://www.brainyquote.com/authors/michael-j-fox-quotes
38. https://www.theguardian.com/culture/2020/nov/21/michael-j-fox-every-step-now-is-a-frigging-math-problem-so-i-take-it-slow
39. https://www.brainyquote.com/authors/michael-j-fox-quotes#:~:text=Life%20delivered%20me%20a%20catastrophe,found%20a%20richness%20of%20soul.&text=The%20more%20I%20expect%2C%20the,the%20more%20serene%20I%20am.
40. Fox, *No Time Like the Future*, p. 71.
41. https://www.brainyquote.com/authors/michael-j-fox-quotes_2
42. https://www.youtube.com/watch?v=B7dYWkwNE7g

Notes to Chapter Seventeen

1. https://www.factretriever.com/mozart-facts
2. Ibid.
3. https://timesofindia.indiatimes.com/life-style/books/features/mozart-was-not-an-alcoholic-suggests-a-new-book/articleshow/64218218.cms
4. Hand, *Night & Day, op. cit.*, p. 22.
5. Cliff Eisen, "(Johann Georg) Leopold Mozart", (part of the major article "Mozart"), *Grove Dictionary of Music and Musicians*, (Oxford UP, 1878–*present*).
6. Ibid.
7. Ibid.
8. https://www.goodreads.com/author/quotes/22051.Wolfgang_Amadeus_Mozart#
9. Eisen, "(Johann Georg) Leopold Mozart," *op. cit.*
10. Quoted from Maynard Solomon, *Mozart: A Life* (HarperCollins, 1995), p. 169.
11. Daniel Heartz, *Mozart, Haydn and early Beethoven, 1781–1802* (W. W. Norton, 2009), p. 47.
12. Ibid.
13. https://mozarteum.at/en/wolfgang-amade-mozart
14. Ruth Halliwell, *The Mozart Family: Four Lives in a Social Context* (Oxford UP, 1998), p. 649.
15. Robert Spaethling, *Mozart's Letters, Mozart's Life* (W. W. Norton, 2000), p. 294.
16. *Mozart's Letters*, trans. by Emily Anderson, (Little, Brown, 1990), pp. 184–85.
17. Paolo Budroni, *Mozart und Salieri: Partner oder Rivalen?: Das Fest in der Orangerie zu Schönbrunn vom 7. February 1786* (Vandenhoeck & Ruprecht Unipress, 2008), pp. 49–66.
18. Solomon, *Mozart: A Life*, pp. 427, 432.
19. Stanley Sadie, ed., *The New Grove Dictionary of Music and Musicians*, 6th ed., (Oxford UP, 1980). Vol. 12, p. 710.
20. Andrew Steptoe, *The Mozart–Da Ponte Operas: The Cultural and Musical Background to Le nozze di Figaro, Don Giovanni, and Così fan tutte* (Clarendon, 1990), p. 208.
21. Otto E. Deutsch, *Mozart: A Documentary Biography* (Stanford UP, 1965), p. 231.
22. Hand, *Night & Day, op. cit.*, p. 23.
23. "Mozart Day by Day: 1750". Mozarteum.
24. Hermann Abert, *W. A. Mozart*, Trans. by Stewart Spencer. Annotated by Cliff Eisen. (1920; Yale UP, 2007), p. 18.
25. https://www.ncbi.nlm.nih.gov/pmc/articles/PMC1439384/?page=1
26. https://www.britannica.com/biography/Cindy-Sherman
27. https://www.thebroad.org/art/cindy-sherman
28. https://www.britannica.com/biography/Cindy-Sherman
29. Ibid.

30. *Ibid.*
31. *Ibid.*
32. https://www.brainyquote.com/authors/cindy-sherman-quotes
33. Tim Adams, "Cindy Sherman: 'Why am I in these photos?'" *The Guardian* (Jul. 3, 2016).
34. Hand, *Night & Day*, op. cit., p. 23.
35. Hand, *Night & Day* (webinar), *op. cit.*
36. Adams, "Cindy Sherman: 'Why am I in these photos?'"
37. *Ibid.*
38. https://www.brainyquote.com/topics/project-quotes#
39. Laura Mulvey, "Visual Pleasure and Narrative Cinema," *Screen* (1975): pp. 803–16.
40. https://www.brainyquote.com/authors/cindy-sherman-quotes
41. Cindy Sherman, *Untitled Film Stills #48:* https://www.thecollector.com/cindy-sherman-iconic-representation-of-women/
42. https://www.theartstory.org/artist/sherman-cindy/
43. https://www.brainyquote.com/authors/cindy-sherman-quotes
44. Adams, "Cindy Sherman: 'Why am I in these photos?'"
45. https://libquotes.com/cindy-sherman/quote/lbw6e5t#:~:text=interest%20in...-,I%20didn't%20want%20to%20make%20'high'%20art%2C,to%20seem%20like%20a%20commodity.
46. Adams, "Cindy Sherman: 'Why am I in these photos?'"
47. *Ibid.*
48. *Ibid.*
49. https://www.brainyquote.com/authors/cindy-sherman-quotes
50. Adams, "Cindy Sherman: 'Why am I in these photos?'"
51. https://news.artnet.com/art-world/cindy-sherman-new-portraits-hauser-wirth-2423424
52. *Ibid.*
53. *Ibid.*
54. https://www.brainyquote.com/authors/cindy-sherman-quotes
55. https://www.theartstory.org/artist/sherman-cindy/
56. https://www.brainyquote.com/authors/cindy-sherman-quotes
57. *Ibid.*
58. Adams, "Cindy Sherman: 'Why am I in these photos?'"
59. *Ibid.*
60. https://photoquotes.com/author/cindy-sherman-#google_vignette
61. https://artrkl.com/blogs/news/cindy-sherman-and-feminist-art#:
62. https://www.brainyquote.com/authors/cindy-sherman-quotes
63. https://www.forbes.com/profile/oprah-winfrey/
64. Jill Nelson, "The Man Who Saved Oprah Winfrey," *The Washington Post* (Dec. 14, 1986).
65. https://www.imdb.com/name/nm0001856/bio/?ref_=nm_ov_bio_sm
66. Oprah Winfrey, interview at Stanford Graduate School of Business (Apr. 16, 2014), in Oprah Winfrey, Anjali Becker, ed., *Own It: Oprah Winfrey in her Own Words* (Agate B2, 2016).
67. https://quotefancy.com/quote/879489/Oprah-Winfrey
68. https://www.astro.com/astro-databank/Winfrey,_Oprah
69. Oprah Winfrey, "The 5 Moments that Changed my Life," *People* (Oct. 9, 2019).
70. Hand, *Night & Day* (webinar), *op. cit.*
71. Hand, *Night & Day*, op. cit., p. 22.
72. Winfrey, *Own It*, p. 61, quote from *Fortune* (Sept. 30, 2010).
73. Oprah Winfrey, *What I Know For Sure* (Flatiron, 2014), p. 200.

Notes

74. Oprah Winfrey in an interview with LinkedIn CEO Jeff Weiner, Oct. 15, 2015.
75. Mel Novit, "Oprah: Talk Show Dynamo Treats the Audience Like a Friend", *Syracuse Post-Standard* (Sept. 14, 1986), p. A9.
76. Oprah Winfrey, interview with Barbara Walters (Dec. 9, 2010), in *Own It*, p. 52.
77. Guido Bonatti, *Liber Astronomiae, Books One, Two and Three,* trans. by Robert Zoller, (Spica, 1998), Second Tractate – Part 3, Chapter 60, In What Houses the Planets Rejoice, p. 95.
78. Barbara Kramer, *Who is Oprah Winfrey?* (Penguin Workshop Series by Penguin Random House, 2019), p. 86.
79. https://www.theguardian.com/world/2010/oct/12/oprah-winfrey-school-south-africa-matron
80. http://content.time.com/time/specials/packages/article/0,28804,1939460_1939452_1939416,00.html
81. https://www.astro.com/astro-databank/King,_Gayle
82. http://www.people.com/people/article/0%2C26334%2C1215402%2C00.html
83. https://www.astro.com/astro-databank/King,_Gayle
84. Ibid.
85. Barbara Walters, "Oprah on Oprah: Talk show host sits down with Barbara Walters for a soul-searching interview," *ABC News* (Dec. 10, 2010).
86. https://www.news.com.au/entertainment/tv/morning-shows/i-got-a-free-car-from-oprah-heres-what-she-really-said-offcamera-in-2010/news-story/c138d8a227acecc525965d0e9d6b8e6e
87. https://march8.com/articles/the-philanthropic-ventures-of-oprah-winfrey
88. *Oprah Builds a Network,* Jul. 8, 2012, referenced in *Own It,* p. 10.
89. Jordan Weissmann, "Stranger Than Fiction: Oprah Was Bad for Book Sales," *The Atlantic* (Mar. 19, 2012).
90. Hand, *Night & Day, op. cit.,* p. 25.
91. https://obamawhitehouse.archives.gov/the-press-office/2016/06/14/remarks-first-lady-and-oprah-winfrey-conversation-united-state-women

Notes to Chapter Eighteen

1. https://explore.britannica.com/explore/savingearth/paul-watson
2. Daniel Boffey, "'If I'm sent to Japan, I'm not coming home': jailed anti-whaler defiant in face of extradition threat," *The Guardian* (Dec. 1, 2024).
3. https://www.theguardian.com/world/article/2024/jul/31/sea-shepherd-founder-anti-whaling-activist-paul-watson-arrest-japan-ntwnfb
4. http://www.seashepherd.org/who-we-are/captain-watsons-biography.html
5. Boffey, "'If I'm sent to Japan, I'm not coming home'."
6. https://www.abc.net.au/news/2024-11-14/sea-shepherd-paul-watson-detention-extended-in-greenland/104509814
7. Ibid.
8. Ibid.
9. Notes from Hand, *Night & Day* (webinar), *op. cit.*
10. Al-Biruni, *The Book of Instruction, op. cit.,* p. 308.
11. Hand, *Night & Day, op. cit.,* p. 21.
12. https://www.brainyquote.com/authors/paul-watson-quotes
13. https://www.onegreenplanet.org/animals/captain-paul-watson-cuts-ties-with-sea-shepherd-usa-after-disagreement-of-organizations-path/

14. Mike Seccombe, "The last pirate: Paul Watson splits with Sea Shepherd," The Saturday Paper (Oct. 15, 2022).
15. https://www.brainyquote.com/authors/paul-watson-quotes
16. https://web.archive.org/web/20180119175542/http://celebritybabies.people.com/2016/10/05/whale-wars-captain-paul-watson-welcomes-son/
17. Boffey, "'If I'm sent to Japan, I'm not coming home'."
18. *Ibid.*
19. https://www.brainyquote.com/authors/paul-watson-quotes
20. https://bonobo.tv/ebooks/sailors/files/basic-html/page103.html
21. http://www.rainforestinfo.org.au/wrr36/seashep.htm
22. UN World Charter for Nature, www.un.org/documents/ga/res/37/a37r007.htm
23. https://www.brainyquote.com/authors/paul-watson-quotes
24. *Ibid.*
25. Boffey, "'If I'm sent to Japan, I'm not coming home'."
26. Seccombe, "The last pirate: Paul Watson splits with Sea Shepherd."
27. Hand, *Night & Day* (webinar), *op. cit.*
28. Hand, *Night & Day, op. cit.*, p. 24.
29. https://www.brainyquote.com/quotes/paul_watson_641862
30. https://www.seashepherd.org.au/get-involved/volunteer-sea/
31. *Ibid.*
32. *Ibid.*
33. Environmental Media Association, 2023 EMA IMPACT Summit: https://www.youtube.com/watch?v=zwsw-0_sVAY
34. https://www.gov.uk/government/history/past-prime-ministers/gordon-brown
35. https://www.britannica.com/biography/Gordon-Brown
36. https://www.gov.uk/government/history/past-prime-ministers/gordon-brown
37. *Ibid.*
38. https://www.brainyquote.com/authors/gordon-brown-quotes
39. Holden, *Five Medieval Astrologers*, Note 2, p. 111.
40. Abraham Ibn-Ezra, *The Beginning of Wisdom*, trans. by Meira Epstein, and Robert Hand, ed., (Arhat, 1998), Note 92, p. 137.
41. "Book review: Seven Ways To Change The World, by Gordon Brown," *www.scotsman.com* (Jun. 11, 2021).
42. "Gordon Brown: 'I joined this party as a teenager ... Its values are my moral compass'," *The Independent* (Jun. 25, 2007).
43. https://www.britannica.com/biography/Gordon-Brown
44. https://www.institutmontaigne.org/en/expressions/kinship-daggers-drawn-tony-blair-and-gordon-brown
45. *Ibid.*
46. https://www.britannica.com/biography/Gordon-Brown
47. https://www.theguardian.com/politics/2009/jun/03/gordon-brown-scandal-unpopularity-election
48. *Ibid.*
49. https://www.brainyquote.com/quotes/gordon_brown_758447
50. https://www.theguardian.com/politics/2009/jun/03/gordon-brown-scandal-unpopularity-election
51. https://www.irishtimes.com/news/gordon-brown-faced-with-cash-for-influence-scandal-1.641089

Notes

52. https://www.brainyquote.com/quotes/gordon_brown_758413
53. https://www.bbc.com/news/uk-politics-14119225
54. https://www.brainyquote.com/authors/gordon-brown-quotes
55. https://www.politico.eu/article/labour-party-victory-gordon-brown-tony-blair-uk-politics-conservative-policy/
56. Ibid.
57. Ibid.
58. https://www.britannica.com/biography/LeBron-James
59. Roger Gordon, *Tales from the Cleveland Cavaliers Locker Room: The Rookie Season of LeBron James* (Simon and Schuster, 2021), p. 173.
60. "LeBron James Stats" from *Basketball Reference. Sports Reference* (Jun. 12, 2004): https://www.basketball-reference.com/players/j/jamesle01.html
61. Tom Withers, "AP Was There: LeBron James dumps Cleveland for Miami," *AP News* (Apr. 6, 2022).
62. Sam Quinn, "LeBron James wins fourth NBA Finals MVP award, becomes first player to earn honor with three different teams," *CBS Sports* (Oct. 12, 2020).
63. Sean Gregory, "Exclusive: LeBron James to Open New Community Hub in Akron," *TIME* (December 15, 2020).
64. "LeBron James foundation to open new medical center". *Fox 8.com (WJW-TV)* (Jun. 7, 2022).
65. https://www.inc.com/marcel-schwantes/10-lebron-james-quotes-from-his-legendary-career-that-will-inspire-you.html
66. https://www.brainyquote.com/authors/lebron-james-quotes
67. Notes from Hand, *Night & Day* (webinar), *op. cit.*
68. https://www.brainyquote.com/authors/lebron-james-quotes
69. https://www.brainyquote.com/quotes/lebron_james_433532
70. https://www.brainyquote.com/authors/lebron-james-quotes
71. https://www.si.com/nba/2020/12/02/lebron-james-lakers-two-year-contract-extension#:~:text=LeBron%20James%20has%20agreed%20to,enter%20the%20NBA%2C%20per%20Charania.
72. https://www.beliefnet.com/celebrity-faith-database/j/lebron-james.aspx
73. https://www.theguardian.com/sport/2003/mar/02/ussport
74. https://web.archive.org/web/20131224102803/http://www.startribune.com/entertainment/movies/64387712.html?elr=KArksD:aDyaEP:kD:aUnc5PDiUiD3aPc:_Yyc:aULPQL7PQLanchO7DiUr
75. https://www.sportingnews.com/au/nba/news/lebron-james-lakers-complete-injury-history/lb5uoovslhhc1ppum59w340hf
76. https://www.theguardian.com/sport/2003/mar/02/ussport
77. https://www.brainyquote.com/authors/lebron-james-quotes
78. Tania Ganguli, Billy Witz, Gina Kolata, "Bronny James, Son of LeBron James, Is Stable After Cardiac Arrest," *The New York Times* (July 25, 2023).
79. https://www.sportingnews.com/au/nba/news/lebron-james-bronny-criticism-lakers/634c8c0cece276803e96faaf#:~:text
80. Hand, *Night & Day, op. cit.*, p. 25.
81. Bonatti, *Liber Astronomiae, op. cit.*, p. 75.
82. https://www.sportingnews.com/au/nba/news/lebron-james-lakers-complete-injury-history/lb5uoovslhhc1ppum59w340hf
83. https://www.silverscreenandroll.com/2021/12/15/22833551/lebron-james-longevity-

key-rem-sleep-goat-lakers-video-medical-analysis
84. https://www.mentalfloss.com/article/577784/lebron-james-facts
85. https://people.com/sports/lebron-james-praises-wife-savannah-enduring-relationship/#:~:text=%E2%80%9C%5BSavannah%5D%20was%20down%20when,she%20was%20there%20with%20me.
86. https://www.brainyquote.com/authors/lebron-james-quotes
87. https://www.espn.com/nba/story/_/id/24194051/lebron-james-discusses-opening-public-school-akron-move-los-angeles-lakers-nba
88. *Ibid.*
89. https://www.dailymail.co.uk/sport/nba/article-12353973/LeBron-James-backed-Promise-School-delivers-discouraging-results-despite-8m-public-funding-revealed-NO-eighth-grade-student-passed-state-math-test-five-years.html
90. *Ibid.*
91. *Ibid.*

ABOUT THE AUTHOR

Joy Usher is an Australian astrologer who has been teaching, consulting and lecturing in astrology for the past 30 years. She has studied traditional techniques since the early 1990s and incorporated these methods in the consulting room and the classroom since 2002. She is co-principle of the astrological school AstroMundi and co-wrote 'Scala Coeli: The Ladder to Heaven', a series of essays on astrology with co-principle Mari Garcia. In 2018 she published two books – *A Tiny Universe* and *A Tiny Universe's Companion* – with Xlibris Publishing. Her book *Munakara: Planets in Contention* is her first book with Revelore Press.